W9-BKE-465

CALIFORNIA NATURAL HISTORY GUIDES

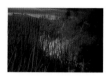

CALIFORNIA INDIANS
AND THEIR ENVIRONMENT

California Natural History Guides

Phyllis M. Faber and Bruce M. Pavlik, General Editors

CALIFORNIA INDIANS
and THEIR
ENVIRONMENT
An Introduction

Kent G. Lightfoot
and Otis Parrish

Contributions by Lee M. Panich, Tsim D. Schneider,
and K. Elizabeth Soluri

UNIVERSITY OF CALIFORNIA PRESS
Berkeley   Los Angeles   London

For Roberta Jewett: This book would never have been written without her loving encouragement, excellent advice, and unbounded support.

———————

University of California Press, one of the most distinguished university presses in the United States, enriches lives around the world by advancing scholarship in the humanities, social sciences, and natural sciences. Its activities are supported by the UC Press Foundation and by philanthropic contributions from individuals and institutions. For more information, visit www.ucpress.edu.

California Natural History Guide Series, No. 96

University of California Press
Berkeley and Los Angeles, California

University of California Press, Ltd.
London, England

Library of Congress Cataloging-in-Publication Data

Lightfoot, Kent G., 1953-
   California Indians and their environment : an introduction / Kent G. Lightfoot, Otis Parrish.
      p.   cm. — (California natural history guides ; 96)
   Includes bibliographical references and index.
   ISBN 978-0-520-24471-9 (cloth : alk. paper) — ISBN 978-0-520-25690-3 (pbk. : alk. paper)
   1. Indians of North America—California—Social life and customs. 2. Indians of North America—California—Hunting. 3. Hunting and gathering societies—California. 4. Human ecology—California—History. 5. Indigenous peoples—Ecology—California. 6. California—Environmental conditions—History.
I. Parrish, Otis. II. Title.

   E78.C15L54 2009
   979.4′01—dc22
                                                                        2008027795

Manufactured in China
17   16   15   14   13   12   11   10   09
10   9   8   7   6   5   4   3   2   1

The paper used in this publication meets the minimum requirements of ANSI/NISO Z 39.48–1992 (R 1997)(*Permanence of Paper*).

Cover: Teresa Castro (Paipai) processing yucca (*Yucca* spp.) into fiber for making nets and sandals (photo courtesy of Lee Panich).

The publisher gratefully acknowledges the generous
contributions to this book provided by

the Gordon and Betty Moore Fund
in Environmental Studies
and
the General Endowment Fund of
the University of California Press Foundation.

CONTENTS

Preface	ix
Acknowledgments	xiii
RETHINKING CALIFORNIA INDIANS	**1**
Why California Indians Matter	**2**
The Central Role of Fire	**14**
Waves of Migration	**38**
A Landscape of Unparalleled Diversity	**50**
The Uniqueness of California	**72**
The First Fire Managers	**94**
They Are Not Farmers	**124**
Where We Go from Here	**142**
VISUAL GUIDE TO NATURAL RESOURCES	**153**
CALIFORNIA INDIAN USES OF NATURAL RESOURCES	**183**
with contributions by Lee M. Panich, D. Schneider, and K. Elizabeth Soluri	
Northwest Coast Province	**188**
Central Coast Province	**210**
South Coast Province	**252**
Northeast Province	**278**
Great Central Valley and Sierra Nevada Province	**302**
Southern Deserts Province	**340**
Notes	365
General References	391

Resource References by Region and Type   429
Art Credits   451
Index   455

PREFACE

When we were first approached to revise and update Robert Heizer and Albert Elsasser's book, *The Natural World of the California Indians,* first published in 1980, we knew it would be a monumental task. For more than 25 years, it had become one of the mainstays for anyone interested in California Indians and California anthropology. (Our own copy is dog-eared and stained with high-octane tea from many late-night reads.) Redoing this work would no doubt upset some who appreciate the familiarity of its organization, themes, and interpretations. Our original intent was to make relatively few changes to this classic—just update each chapter, leaving the organization of the book pretty much alone. The major exception would be to tack on a natural resources section that would serve as a guide to the primary plants and animals (with color photos) used by Native people across the state.

Once we began to tackle the task, however, it became evident that a new synthesis would be needed to reflect the tremendous amount of research that has taken place by ethnographers, archaeologists, tribal scholars, ecologists, and others since the publication of *The Natural World of the California Indians.* This recent research continues to highlight how different California Indians are from most other indigenous populations in North America. Native California supported the greatest linguistic diversity and highest population density north of Mexico, with people dispersed across the landscape in a plethora of village communities—all without recourse to agriculture (except in the Southern Deserts Province). In writing an introductory book on California Indians and their relationship with natural resources, we chose to focus on why California Indians are unique. We wanted to address how they created a world filled with small, vibrant polities—each boasting its own rich trappings of village life involving chiefs, religious specialists, master craftspeople, dances, feasts, and ceremonies.

In the following pages we outline our perspectives about what makes California Indians different and why this matters today. Our thesis is that they enhanced an already diverse world of natural resources through various management practices centering around prescribed burning.

We introduce a pyrodiversity model that suggests local communities probably implemented a staggered rotation of burns, innovative methods for mass harvesting of terrestrial and coastal resources, and various ways to store goods for winter use, communal gatherings, feasts, and trade. This model is built from the research of others who emphasize the importance of prescribed burning in Native California, as well as the recent findings of fire ecologists who track the history of fire regimes in local regions.

Our perspective on Native fire managers was significantly influenced by compiling the guide to Indian uses of California's natural resources. In working with Lee Panich, Tsim Schneider, and Elizabeth Soluri, we found that many of the plants that served as the primary sources for food, medicine, and raw materials (clothing, baskets, etc.) are fire stimulated. That is, these plant populations are enhanced by fires, primarily through seed germination or sprouting. Furthermore, many of the animals hunted by local groups tend to thrive among the tender browse following fires. Although the resource guide may be used separately, readers will gain much by perusing the first part of the book, which discusses the broader cultural context for understanding how these resources were encouraged, augmented, and exploited by Indian people.

This book is written to be an introduction to California Indians, a resource guide on their use of plants and animals, and a source book on recent literature on Native California. We feel the book is timely. The cultural practices employed by California Indians to increase the diversity and availability of many natural resources have great relevancy for us today. As we grapple with the problems of maintaining habitat diversity, sustainable economies, and managing our wildlands, we can learn much from traditional and contemporary Indian practices as we develop new workable strategies for maintaining native plant and animal populations in the state. It is important that we do not relegate California Indians to a time that has come and gone, but recognize that contemporary Native people and their cultural traditions have much to teach us about the future of California.

ACKNOWLEDGMENTS

Many kind and generous people have contributed to the creation and production of this book. We are indebted to a number of people who read and commented on various sections of the book. They include Sarah Allen, Jim Carlton, Leanne Hinton, Jim Hogue, Ira Jacknis, Roberta Jewett, Patrick Kirch, Peter Moyle, Hans and Pam Peeters, Les Rowntree, John Sawyer, and Scott Stephens. We appreciate greatly the constructive comments provided by Terry Jones, Melissa Nelson, and an anonymous reader who reviewed the book for the University of California Press. Our appreciation for discussions about issues contained in this book and/or field work go to James Allan, Walter Antone, Frank Bayham, Roger Byrne, Meg Conkey, Rob Cuthrell, Glenn Farris, Richard Fitzgerald, Reno Franklin, Andy Galvan, Lynne Goldstein, Sara Gonzalez, Junko Habu, Lori Hager, Christine Hastorf, Bill Hildebrandt, John Holson, Mark Hylkema, Rosemary Joyce, Ed Luby, Malcolm Margolin, Antoinette Martinez, Darren Modzelewski, Breck Parkman, Sherry Parrish, Julia Bendímez Patterson, Matt Russell, Steve Shackley, Chuck Striplen, Nick Tipon, David H. Thomas, Eric Wilder, and Ken Wilson. Our deep thanks to Violet Parrish Chappell and Vivian Wilder for introducing us to the marvels of fresh huckleberry pie, acorn mush, and fried seaweed.

Stephanie Rubin assisted greatly in selecting photographs of plants and animals featured in the book, while Therese Babineau, Jennifer Bai, and Laura Wolfgang helped identify ethnographic photos from the Phoebe Hearst Museum of Anthropology. We appreciate greatly the aid of Victoria Bradshaw and Alicja Egbert at the Phoebe Hearst Museum of Anthropology, Susan Snyder at the Bancroft Library, Karren Elsbernd of the California Academy of Sciences, and Susan Phillips at the Malki

Museum. We are most grateful for the excellent editorial staff at the University of California Press, specifically Jenny Wapner and Scott Norton for their continued assistance, enthusiasm, and undying support, and Kate Hoffman and Meg Hannah for their patience, sage advice, and tremendous work in turning our manuscript into a readable book. The writing of this book was generously supported by the President's Research Fellowship in the Humanities, University of California, and the Humanities Research Fellowship, University of California at Berkeley.

Why California Indians Matter

THE INEVITABLE QUESTION IS COMING. I (K.L.) am standing in front of the California Indian Gallery in the Phoebe A. Hearst Museum of Anthropology on the Berkeley campus of the University of California. A group of undergraduate students from a section of the Introduction to Archaeology course is touring the exhibit. An earnest, but somewhat skeptical looking student, lags behind the others; all signs indicate she is about to launch the relevancy question. "I love all this great old stuff," she gestures animatedly at the brightly colored baskets, soap root brushes, and strings of shell beads collected by ethnographers in the early twentieth century, "but what can you really learn by studying them?" She stops for a moment, adjusting the earpiece and volume of her razor-thin iPod, before continuing. "And what relevancy does studying Indians have for our lives in California today? I mean, this stuff is really ancient history." Before I can find my voice to defend my lifetime efforts of studying this "old stuff," she has turned her attention to her cell phone, on which she is retrieving a slew of text messages. It is going to be another long day on the Berkeley campus.

Ah yes, the relevancy question. This is not an isolated incident. Anyone who works with California Indian materials in classrooms or in public education programs has heard various permutations of this question many times before. Our experience suggests that California Indians are commonly perceived by the denizens of the Golden State to be historical anachronisms that have little relevancy in our fast-paced contemporary world. Museum specimens are all fine and good, but they refer to chapters in the state's history that have little bearing on us today. This common perception is fueled by the widespread untruth that most, if not all, of the "real" Indians suffered extinction in the late eighteenth and nineteenth centuries, following their entanglements with Franciscan missionaries, Russian fur traders, Mexican ranchers, and Anglo-American settlers. Although disease, violence, and homelessness caused massive hardship for all

Indians throughout the state, especially during the dark decades of the 1850s through the 1870s, thousands of Indians *did* survive. After falling to a nadir of an estimated 16,000 to 17,000 in number in 1900, the population has rebounded to about 150,000 people who recognize their Native Californian roots.[1] Furthermore, California boasts the largest number of federally recognized Indian entities for any state in the nation, a total of 108 at last count. In addition, a number of other tribal groups are recognized by state and local agencies but are not yet officially recognized by the federal government. But beyond an occasional visit to an Indian casino, most Californians have limited contact with contemporary Native people and remain largely ignorant of life within Indian communities across the state.

Another factor that has fueled this question of relevancy is an outdated perspective that many of us retain about traditional Indian cultures. Those of us who attended fourth grade in California schools probably built a sugar cube model of one of the 21 Franciscan missions and learned something about the interactions between the padres and Indians. But beyond that, our understanding of past and present Indian people may be pretty sketchy. Moreover, because most Native groups in what is now California traditionally practiced a lifestyle based on the exploitation of wild plants and animals for food, medicine, and raw materials, the general public has a tendency to view Native Californians as historical characters in a play that permanently closed more than a century ago. Portrayed as simplistic hunter-gatherers who foraged for what they needed in the bountiful environment of California, this view has perpetuated a negative stereotype of California Indians as rather primitive, dirty, uninventive, and lazy people (see Rawls 1984). As pointed out throughout this book, nothing could be farther from the truth. But the stereotype lives on.

The truth is, the people of California have always been a little bit different—moving to the beat of a different drum. California Indians, in particular, have always been the exception to the rule.[2] These Pacific Coast people do not fit any of the classic anthropological models devised to explain the evolutionary progression from simple, mobile hunter-gatherers to larger, sedentary, and more complex agrarian societies. In ethnographic summaries of historic hunter-gatherer peoples, they are either ignored or described as being anomalous compared to the more typical small

Figure 1. Indian village near Yuba City by unknown artist in mid-1800s.

nomadic bands of foragers found in other nontemperate regions of the world (e.g., Lee and Devore 1968). Although technically they are hunter-gatherers, many Native California communities exhibited traits more typically associated with well-developed agrarian societies. That is, they enjoyed sizeable population densities, had relatively sedentary villages, amassed significant quantities of stored food and goods, and maintained complex political and religious organizations (fig. 1). We now refer to these kinds of groups as "complex hunter-gatherers" to distinguish them in the anthropological literature from the better known mobile foragers or "generalized hunter-gatherers."[3]

So what makes Native Californians so unique? For one thing, agriculture never played a significant role among California Indians. This is rather exceptional for complex hunter-gatherers worldwide, the majority of whom made the transition to an agrarian base and/or a herding economy in late prehistory. Consequently, the study of complex hunter-gatherers from other temperate regions of the world (eastern North America, Europe, Near East, Southeast Asia) is primarily archaeological in nature. Some scholars, in fact, suggest that the rise of agriculture may have taken place among complex hunter-gatherers in regions of relative abundance (Price and Gebauer 1995b:7–8; Smith 1995). Initially serving as dietary supplements among a broader range of foodstuffs, it is argued that these plant and/or animal domesticates eventually formed the nucleus of intensive food production practices. Most complex hunter-gatherers worldwide either experimented with the domestication of indigenous plants and/ or they eventually adopted foreign domesticates into their mix of hunter-gatherer strategies (see Habu 2004:117–118; Price and Gebauer 1995a).

Yet with the exception of the Southern Deserts Province, agricultural economies never took hold in Native California. Unlike Indian groups in eastern North America who grew "floodplain weeds," such as sunflower, squash, marsh elder, and chenopod (Smith 1995), there is little evidence in California for the widespread domestication of native plants. It is significant that most of the complex hunter-gatherers in eastern North America eventually adopted varying combinations of corn, beans, and squash into their economies. Some hunter-gatherers in the adjacent Great Basin and American Southwest also incorporated these foreign crops into their menus (Keeley 1995:262–263; Wills 1995), making these foods known to people in California through trade and population movements. But with the exception of groups along the Colorado River and adjacent desert areas, Native Californians made little use of them. Consequently, the study of complex hunter-gatherers in California can be based not only on a lengthy archaeological record, but a rich corpus of ethnographic studies, Native oral traditions, and Native histories and observations spanning to the present.

Another thing that stands Native California apart is its population. Even without the infusion of agriculture, California's hunter-gatherers boasted population densities among the highest in any American region north of Mexico at the time of initial European colonization. None of this makes sense according to theoretical models about the rise of agriculture that are predicated on either population pressure or socioeconomic competition, or that view agriculture as an outgrowth of experimentation by complex hunter-gatherers in areas of diverse and rich food supplies (Hayden 1995; Price and Gebauer 1995b:7). Little wonder that at the annual meeting of the Society for American Archaeology when you tell other academic types that you work in California, they typically give you a quick look of pity before moving rapidly away to join colleagues working in less perplexing areas.

Tremendous linguistic and cultural diversity, which defies simplistic summaries or the pigeonholing of groups into the accustomed anthropological constructs, presents another unique

Map 1. Native Californian languages.

characteristic of Native California. One of the most linguistically diverse areas of world, it is estimated that somewhere between 80 to 100 Native languages were spoken about the time of European settlement—approximately 20 percent of all the languages articulated in North America (map 1). Most of the major stocks of North American languages are represented. As a consequence, anthropologists have defined and mapped a complex smorgasbord of ethnolinguistic groupings across the state. There is no surer way to initiate a mass exodus from a college course on California Indians than to require students to memorize ethnographic maps showing the location of these many varied groups.

What complicates the geopolitical landscape of Native California even more is that most of the day-to-day interactions of California Indians took place within polities (political communities) that were small in both spatial area and population size. Thus, what emerges in the study of California Indians is a crowded landscape packed with many modest-sized, semi-autonomous polities, each of which supported its own organization of elites, retainers, religious specialists, craft experts, and commoners. None of this fits neatly into the classic anthropological concepts of bands, tribes, chiefdoms, and states that have been employed to define other Indian groups across the Americas. The difficulty of making sense of the iconoclastic California Indian societies in light of mainstream models and concepts has certainly contributed to the marginalization of their study within the broader fields of North American archaeology and anthropology.

Our purpose in writing this book is to build upon the original work of Heizer and Elssaser (1980) to present a new synthesis of California Indians. The first part addresses why the Native people of the Golden State are different and why this should matter to us today. This front-end information is crucial for understanding the second part of the book—a guide to Indian uses of natural resources in the six provinces of California (Northwest Coast, Central Coast, South Coast, Northeast, Great Central Valley and Sierra Nevada, and Southern Deserts). In taking a fresh look at California Indians, our perspective is that rather than forcing them into models and concepts developed elsewhere, we should pay special attention to those cultural practices and organizational forms that make them different from other complex hunter-gatherer groups and agrarian societies. The seemingly unique hunter-gatherer lifeways that developed in California may have much to contribute to our world today. This rethinking is based largely on a powerful resurgence now taking place among many Native Californian groups, in combination with recent insights provided by historical ecologists, anthropologists, ethnohistorians, and archaeologists. The renewed interest in California Indian histories, cultural practices, spiritual beliefs, languages, arts and crafts, and food ways is profoundly changing our basic understanding of the historical lifeways of our state's first people.

This ongoing research is providing new insights about long-term interactions between California Indians and the environment. Rather than simply exploiting the richness of California's many habitats, it is now generally recognized that indigenous populations helped create and shape much of the ecosystem diversity by means of various kinds of cultural activities and indigenous management practices that can still be seen today. By enhancing the productivity of grasslands, scrub stands, oak woodlands, conifer forests, and montane meadows, California Indians contributed to the construction of a rich network of habitats that provided a cornucopia of foods, medicines, and raw materials for clothing, baskets, houses, dance regalia, and other cultural objects. However, many questions remain about the degree to which Native peoples constructed anthropogenetic landscapes in California's varied topographic and geographic settings, the kinds of techniques they employed to alter the environment, and the overall impacts they had on plant and animal populations.

Most recent perspectives on Californian Indian land-management techniques tend to equate them to agrarian methods employed elsewhere in North America, using concepts such as "protoagricultural," "quasi-agricultural," or "semiagricultural." For example, Kat Anderson (2005:253) has recently argued that protoagricultural management practices employed in Native California "were the same as those utilized in early agriculture to increase yields of the edible parts of domesticated plants." The basic idea is that California Indians practiced protoagricultural economies analogous, for most intents and purposes, to those employed by Indian farmers elsewhere in the Americas. The primary difference for Native Californians was that they were tending and cultivating wild (nondomesticated) crops.

What we propose in this book is an alternative perspective for understanding the hunter-gatherer practices of California Indians and their interactions with the environment. What if California Indians practiced a very different kind of economy, one that was organized in a fundamentally different manner than those of advanced agrarian societies? And in providing a distinct alternative, what if Native California economies offered certain advantages over agrarian systems? In contrast to many highly developed agrarian societies whose members invest considerable labor per unit of area to grow a limited number of domesticates, we argue that Native Californians employed various strategies for enhancing resource diversity over the broader landscape. In this book we depict Native Californians as fire managers (or pyro-diversity collectors, to use the formal anthropological term), which distinguishes them from other agrarian-oriented people in Native North America. Employing this economy of diversification, we argue that Native peoples enjoyed considerable flexibility in choosing suites of plants and animals for exploitation across local regions, depending upon ever-changing environmental conditions and seasonal availability. Although fire management has certain limitations (as outlined later), overall it provides a more balanced menu with less risk and labor intensification than many contemporaneous Native agrarian programs that depended primarily on corn, beans, and squash. Furthermore, this kind of diversified economy has the capability of supporting relatively dense populations, complex political organizations, craft specialization, and sophisticated ceremonial systems.

In presenting a new synthesis on California Indians, we touch upon three major themes throughout the book that make the study of the cultural practices of California Indians and their interactions with the environment relevant to just about any person living in the Golden State today, especially skeptical students touring the amazing California Indian collections in the Phoebe Hearst Museum of Anthropology.

Theme 1: Indigenous Landscape Management

There is no question that California Indians modified the landscape to enhance the production of plant and animal resources. With the pioneering work of Lowell Bean, Henry Lewis, Thomas Blackburn, Florence Shipek, and others in the 1970s, the idea that California Indians have been active agents in augmenting environmental productivity and diversity has been building steam. The most recent and fully articulated rendition of indigenous land management is outlined in Anderson's (2005) seminal book *Tending the Wild: Native American Knowledge and the Management of California's Natural Resources,* a comprehensive discussion of various methods of cultivation employed by California Indians, including pruning and coppicing selected plants, sowing seeds, weeding, prescribed burning, removal of debris from fields and tree groves, and so forth. She argues that it was through close encounters with the environment that Indian communities helped shape the composition and structure of local ecosystems, essentially creating and maintaining some of the state's signature plant communities such as coastal prairies, valley oak savannas, and montane meadows.

But questions are now being raised about the degree to which California Indians actually shaped the local environment. Vale (1998:231) cautions that the former myth of the pre-Columbian wilderness in North America is being replaced with a new exaggerated one: "the myth of the humanized landscape," in which Native people thoroughly modified extensive regions through fire management, cultivation, mound construction, building settlements, harvesting resources, and other such activities. Although he does not question some level of management of the land, Vale (2002) believes that only relatively small areas were typically impacted, and that natural, nonhuman ecological processes continued to shape large components of the environment. Similar points have been made about the vegetation of the Sierra Nevada and California chaparral habitats—that the basic composition and structure of these plant communities can be explained primarily by natural fire regimes, topography, precipitation, and so forth that had little to do with cultural practices of Native Californians (Bendix 2002; Parker 2002). These critiques point out the importance of critically evaluating the nature of the indigenous land-management practices that were employed across space and through time.

This debate is much more than just an academic exercise. In arguing that long-term human management produced, in large part, many of California's coveted vegetation types, Anderson and others maintain that without the infusion of Native knowledge and practices, we are at risk of losing some of our precious landscape resources in the long term. They make a strong case for employing indigenous management techniques to maintain or restore coastal prairies, oak parklands, wetlands, and so on. These scholars raise an important point for Californians to consider today. Should we employ traditional landscape practices, such as intentional burning, to maintain many thousands of hectares of grasslands, woodlands, and forests in public lands across California? This question has significant implications for how we manage our public land reserves in California today.

Theme 2: Sustainable Economies

There is considerable debate about whether traditional Native California economies represented a sustainable program of harvesting wild crops and animal populations that involved minimal environmental degradation over the long run. This view, advocated by Anderson, Bev Ortiz, and other researchers working with contemporary Native people, stresses various conservation practices and cultural rules employed by Indian harvesters. They firmly believe that these cultural conventions, handed down over countless generations, allowed Indian people to live in harmony with the environment. But this position is challenged by some archaeologists whose studies of faunal remains from prehistoric sites indicate that, in some times and places, Native people overharvested animal populations. These scholars argue that the elimination of some of the larger species of marine mammals, terrestrial game, and fishes from local regions forced Native hunters to broaden their diet to include small game and fishes and other sources of food. The implications that overhunting had on local environments over many decades or even centuries is not clear, but it certainly challenges the idea that California Indians were in perfect harmony with the natural world.

Evaluating this complicated debate is important for Californians today. There is much interest about the creation of sustainable economies that can produce food and other resources in an environmentally friendly way. Some of this work on renewable resources is focusing on alternatives to industrial agribusiness farming by stressing smaller-scale organic farms that feature polycultural practices of growing integrated systems of overstory (agroforestry) and understory plant crops, intercropping, natural pest control systems, nontoxic fertilizers and herbicides, and low-flow irrigation systems.[4] But other alternatives to agriculture may also exist for creating sustainable economies, ones that may be of interest to future populations of Californians. Are there lessons to be learned from California Indian pyrodiversity practices in developing such small-scale, sustainable economies that we can incorporate into our lives today?

Theme 3: Harvesting California's Wild Resources

For thousands of years California Indians created regional economies for harvesting food, medicine, and raw materials from local plant communities and animal populations, and for producing objects from stone and clay. In the latter half of this book, we turn to the key resources that fueled the economic engines of Indian communities across different provinces of California. It is important to stress that cultural change and innovation has been an ongoing process in the state for many centuries, and that the tools, techniques, and practices underlining these economies continue to transform over time. Furthermore, Native harvesting economies are still employed across the state, with new innovations continually being introduced to collect and process resources.

Opportunities for many contemporary Indians to harvest foods, medicines, and basketry material are, however, becoming increasingly difficult with the continuing privatization of rural property and the implementation of various harvesting regulations on state and federal lands. This is another important issue for us to think about. Should Native Californians be allowed to continue traditional harvesting practices on public lands? Could these Indian harvesters play a more important role in the education of our state's children by providing a better understanding of the diversity and bounty of California's natural resources? And finally, should we be thinking more seriously about using the immense quantities of diverse wild foods and raw materials produced each year across California that remain largely untouched by humans? Given the high nutritional value of much of the wild foods, they could provide an important supplement to Indian communities and to some highly motivated and energetic non-Indian students and teachers.

So what about the relevancy question? We hope in writing

this book that we all can finally move beyond the question of relevancy and begin a broader dialogue within the state on some important and timely issues that concern California Indians and landscape stewardship practices, sustainable economies, renewable food sources, and the management of public lands. We can learn much about alternative ways of both protecting and using the rich natural resources of California by working with contemporary Native communities and by learning about past Indian cultural practices and lifeways through Native oral traditions, museum collections, archaeology, ethnography, and ethnohistory. In taking this perspective, we look forward in anticipation to the next time a student asks about the relevance of studying California Indian peoples and their material culture.

The Central Role of Fire

DIVERSITY IS THE KEY to understanding California Indians. The original denizens of the Golden State, similar to those in other complex hunter-gatherer and agrarian societies worldwide, could boast of intensive harvesting systems, innovative methods of food storage, some level of sedentary life, high population densities, significant embellishment of material culture, sophisticated ritual systems, and hierarchical relationships of political and religious leaders. But what makes Native Californians so intriguing is that they accomplished all of this by maintaining an exceptional level of resource diversity at the scale of the local region. In working hard to maintain a plethora of distinctive habitats containing varied foods, medicines, and sources of raw materials, they diverged fundamentally from the members of many other complex societies, who increasingly focused their attention on the production of a limited range of crops and specialized goods. One gets the feeling that California Indians reveled in this resource diversity, and that this may be a common thread that ties together many of the distinctive Native cultures of our state.

We have always been intrigued by the astounding range of foods and material culture employed by California Indians. Learning about the first people has involved the study of an impressive array of plants, animals, and artifacts used by indigenous communities. It seems that just about every nook and cranny in the state is characterized by its own particular suite of resources that were harvested by knowledgeable Indian men and women. Even after devoting ourselves to California anthropology and archaeology for more than 20 years, we are still constantly amazed to learn new things about particular plants or animals used by Native people for food, for medicinal purposes, or for the production of a specific basket type or piece of clothing.

The purpose of this chapter is to outline the basic tenets of the fire management (aka pyrodiversity collecting) model. We begin with a brief introduction to the incredible range of foods and material culture that are associated with this kind of economy. We then outline how fire management played a central role in the maintenance and enhancement of plant and animal diversity in local places. It is true that California was already gifted with incredible environmental variability, given its coasts, mountains, valleys, and deserts. Yet with the strategic use of fire and other management practices, Native people contributed greatly to the productivity of this landscape. Food and raw materials, when available en masse, were collected and prepared for immediate consumption by families, for use in communal ceremonies and dances, and for storage in winter villages. We argue that these pyrodiversity practices were well suited for supporting a political economy comprising networks of small polities, each of which had access to sufficient habitat diversity to buffer local fluctuations in environmental conditions.

Keep in mind that tremendous variation can underlie specific Native cultures; the following general outline provides the foundation for more detailed discussions, especially in the resource guide presented in the second half of the book. Aspects of these traditional cultural practices are still employed today by contemporary Native Californian communities, but considerable change has taken place in Native lifeways over the last 250 years with the coming of Spanish, Mexican, Russian, and American colonists, a point we return to later.

Food for Every Occasion

Heizer and Elsasser (1980:83) conservatively estimated that Native Californians harvested more than 500 plant and animal foods. Although earlier generations of ethnographers and archaeologists recognized this diversity, there was a tendency to emphasize a relatively few food staples that centered around the exploitation of acorns, salmon, and large game, such as deer, elk, and antelope (Baumhoff 1963:161–162). While not denying the importance of these resources, much less attention has been paid to the many other kinds of foods that were also significant dietary components of the yearly menu. Depending on the local region, Native people exploited various tree nut crops; gathered seeds of grasses and small flowering plants; plucked fruits and greens; dug for roots, bulbs, corms, tubers, and rhizomes; collected kelp and seaweed along the coast; culled marine and freshwater invertebrates; harvested marine and freshwater fishes; and hunted waterfowl, terrestrial birds, smaller terrestrial game, sea mammals, and even insects (fig. 2).

Figure 2. Two winnowing baskets with crushed (processed) and un-crushed manzanita berries (*Arctostaphylos* spp.), 1918; Western Mono.

In examining the local economies of Native Californians, we should recognize that there is substantial variation across both space and time in the availability of the so-called staples—acorns, salmon, and large game. Not all regions are equally endowed with these resources: the primary salmon streams are found in northern and central California, and the number and productivity of oak species decline significantly as you move into the more arid habitats of southern and northeastern California. More importantly, even in the areas where these resources abounded in the past, acorn crops periodically failed, salmon runs could vary greatly from one migration to the next, and by late prehistory there is archaeological evidence for the overhunting of large game in some places. Consequently, the mix of resources (nuts, seeds, tubers, fruits, birds, fishes, small mammals, large mammals, insects, etc.) used by local Indian communities could vary substantially from season to season, year to year, and through cycles of climatic change, such as during extended droughts and El Niño events. The long-term cultural strategy of Native Californians was to maintain a diverse spectrum of resources that provided considerable flexibility and choice in their diet breadth.

Extraordinary Material Culture

Native Californians also exploited a diverse range of plant, animal, and mineral resources for tools, containers, cordage, clothing, architectural materials, and ceremonial regalia, as well as for medicinal and spiritual purposes. They transformed mineral resources into many important cultural objects. By flaking obsidian and chert nodules, they produced multifunctional tools such as projectile points, knives, and scrapers for hunting and butchering game. Local Indians transformed sandstone, granite, basalt, and other rocks into ground stone implements, including mortars, pestles, milling stones, and handstones. These were used for grinding and pulverizing nuts and seeds into flour (fig. 3). Craftspeople employed other ground stone tools—adzes and mauls—to work wood for houses, canoes, and craft items. In some places (South Coast and Northwest Coast provinces of California), steatite, also called soapstone, was mined for making bowls, tobacco pipes, plates for catching salmon grease, effigy figures, and the ever-enigmatic charmstones. Some Native Californians molded and fired pottery vessels from local clays, which they used for cooking and storing foods and liquids. But full-scale pottery production was relatively rare in Native California; it was adopted only by a relatively few groups in southern California and in east-central California (see, e.g., Jacknis 2004:61–62). Indian groups in southern California, the Great Central Valley, and the North Coast Ranges also exploited local clays to make fired, dried, or baked balls (so called cooking stones), figurines, and tobacco pipes.

Figure 3. Mortar and pestle for pounding or pulverizing plant resources, 1906; Sierra Miwok.

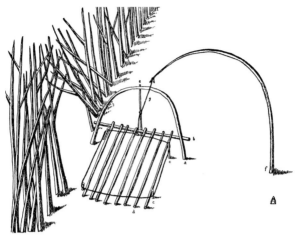

Figure 4. Treadle snare for catching quail; Pomo (from Barrett 1952:136).

But what really sets Native California apart from the remainder of North America is its creation from plant and animal resources of a remarkable perishable material culture that served almost every need of local Indian communities. California Indians skillfully employed wood, plant fibers, animal bones, skins, feathers, and furs to create clothing, houses, house furnishings, food processing tools, storage containers, burden carriers, harvesting implements, and ceremonial regalia. Some of their most notable creations were produced from plant cordage and basketry materials. Plant fibers twisted into two-, three-, or more ply strands of string or rope served as the foundation for the construction of a plethora of different types of nets, snares, traps, and fences for capturing fishes, terrestrial game, waterbirds, and terrestrial birds. Some are works of pure genius. For example, the treadle snare (referred to as a "treddle-type trap" by Barrett [1952:135–138])(fig. 4) is activated by any creature stepping on the wood treadle, which discharges the trigger pin, releasing the spring-pole, catching the animal in the attached noose.

It is in the production of baskets, however, that Native Californians have no peers. Although the method of manufacture varies across the state, from the stately twined baskets of Northwest California to the preference for elegant coiled baskets in

BASKETS FOR EVERY PURPOSE

The forms, functions, and aesthetics of California Indian baskets are truly remarkable. Many tasks in Indian households involving the harvesting, processing, and storage of plant and animal resources, as well as the cooking and consumption of foods, took place with the aid of baskets.

- Burden baskets for transporting materials on the shoulder and back, the shape and size of the stitch (open or closed) dependent on the objects carried (seeds, berries, acorns, etc.)
- Watertight baskets that served as canteens for storing and carrying water
- Watertight baskets that served as cooking vessels, where soups and gruels were heated by placing red-hot rocks into the baskets using wooden tongs and then stirring the contents with special paddles to keep the bottom and sides from burning
- Large and small storage baskets (often with lids) for keeping seeds, nuts, tubers, and nonfood "treasures" dry and safe in houses
- Cradles for carrying infants
- Seed beaters—baskets often shaped like a paddle for harvesting ripe seeds and scooping them into burden baskets attached to the harvester's back
- Trays for winnowing plant foods
- Trays for parching seeds by tossing live coals among the seeds until they turn a delicious crispy brown
- Trays and containers for serving food
- Scoops or dippers for pouring liquids
- Bottomless baskets attached to hopper mortars, designed to keep particles of seeds and nuts from flying away when ground or pulverized into meal with pestles
- Basket hats
- Basket traps for capturing birds, fishes, and small game
- Bags for storing and carrying materials
- Gift or presentation baskets produced specifically for exchange, ceremonies, and funerals

Figure 5. Baskets from a Karuk household in northwestern California, 1930.

southern California, every Indian community produced a broad range of basket types—even those who manufactured pottery vessels. Expertly woven baskets were lightweight, strong, durable, and malleable into many shapes and sizes (fig. 5). A typical extended family could count on having a full suite of basket forms to help perform many daily activities.

A Burning Economy

The primary reason that Native Californians modified the landscape through fire and other cultivation methods was to enhance the growth of economically valuable plants and animals in local regions. Each community initiated an integrated program of land management designed to foster the diversity and production of both food and nonfood resources, especially those that contributed to the production of an abundant perishable material culture. The requirements for manufacturing perishable objects were immense and constant. It is estimated that a medium-sized cooking basket required the harvesting of 3,750 deergrass stalks from 75 plants; a single cradleboard necessitated 500 to

675 straight sourberry stems; while a 12 m long deer net, woven from more than 2,100 m of cordage, demanded an astonishing 35,000 plant stalks (see Blackburn and Anderson 1993b:23). Similarly, it might take hundreds of woodpeckers and flickers to provide the distinctive red and yellow feathers incorporated into headbands and other ceremonial regalia used in a single dance.[1]

Although various methods of cultivation are described in the ethnohistoric and ethnographic literature, the cornerstone of Native California management practices revolved around fires. From the outset, we need to recognize that the Mediterranean climate of California is a classic fire-enabler.[2] The wet winters nurture profuse plant production, which are then followed by long, droughty summers that literally suck the moisture from grasses, bushes, duff, and downed timber, transforming many local areas into tinderboxes. Fires ignited by natural sources (typically lightning) or humans can quickly take hold, often pushed along by seasonal winds and low humidity. Today, we view wildfires primarily in a negative light because they can lead to human casualties, loss of homes and property, and the darkening of many hectares of scenic woodlands. But California Indians recognized many centuries ago that fires can augment the growth and diversity of many economic plants, including roots, tubers, fruits, greens, nuts, and seeds, as well as provide forage that attracts both small and large birds and mammals. Fires control insects and pests, remove detritus from the ground surface, open up pathways in forests and woodlands, and fertilize the soil with nutrients. Fires encourage young, straight sprouts and other useable raw materials that can be incorporated into the production of cordage, baskets, and other household materials. Periodic fires also can facilitate the collection of many resources, such as acorns and mesquite beans, by burning off the underbrush.

Many habitats in California are naturally prone to reoccurring fires. California Indians began to enhance and modify these natural fire regimes by the strategic setting of prescribed burns. It was the combination of natural and human ignitions—what constituted the managed-fire regimes of local Native communities—that greatly promoted pyrodiversity in many regions of the Golden State. We follow Martin and Sapsis (1992) in defining pyrodiversity as landscape heterogeneity and diverse biota that result from various stages of plant succession as those plants recolonize burned areas. The creation of patchy mosaics comprising diverse kinds of plants and animals provided optimal settings for harvesting foods, medicines, and raw materials, especially during times of environmental perturbations, when so-called staple foods, such as acorns and large game, became scarce. Prescribed burning produced edges or transitions between different habitat types and previously burned parcels that greatly enhanced local biodiversity (Lewis 1993:113). The upshot of systematic programs of controlled burns was the creation of fire mosaics that contained a diverse patchwork of habitats containing resources of critical importance to California Indians.

Native Californians initiated management practices at the scale of the local region. As Vale (2002) emphasizes, the most intensive activities probably took place near major settlements, where people would prune, weed, and clear debris from nearby economic habitats. But people traveled frequently across their territories to harvest outlying patches, providing ample opportunities to manage distant habitats containing highly productive nut tree groves, seed crops, and fields of tubers, to tend specific plants that provided medicinal applications, or to enhance the growth of favored raw materials for making baskets or cordage. Travel into the hinterland was facilitated by creating multiple residences during the annual round or by logistical movements—dispatching task groups from the main village, who established short-term camp sites in favored locales where resources could be harvested and processed in bulk and then transported back home.

Vegetation in the local region—grasslands, chaparral, oak woodlands, montane meadows, conifer forests—might be burned at different intervals to augment a patchwork of distinctive habitats with different succession rates of plants and animals. The fire-return intervals for specific habitats depended upon a number factors: the intended mix of economic resources, fuel sources, climatic conditions, the timing and number of natural ignition sources (typically lightning), and the spatial pattern of previous fires. The ultimate goal was to minimize the risk of resource shortages through the creation of diverse habitats and enhancement of food and other economic resources throughout the local region.

Harvesting en Masse

A common economic activity of Native Californians was the bulk or mass collection of important resources when seasonally available. We argue that this activity was facilitated by pyrodiverse landscapes. The creation or augmentation of distinctive patches containing dense concentrations of plant and animal resources in the same stages of succession allowed people to bulk-collect food resources, medicinal supplies, and raw materials. This activity might be casually structured among family members and friends, or it might involve a larger, more structured communal organization.

California Indians went to the trouble to gather food and nonfood resources en masse for three primary reasons: to provide fresh food for meals, to support community gatherings, and to stockpile resources for later or winter use. The recent overview of Native Californian culinary practices by Ira Jacknis (2004) provides an ideal source to learn about Indian foods. Some foods were eaten fresh, while others involved considerable processing and cooking. The basic methods for cooking vegetable foods in Native California included parching in baskets, roasting in coals, simmering or boiling in soups and gruels in cooking baskets or steatite/ceramic vessels, and slow-roasting in earth ovens or pit-hearths.

Indian cooks built earth ovens by excavating pits, lining the bottoms with flat rocks that had been fire-heated (providing a critical heat reservoir), and then placing food items on these rocks in layers sandwiched between a protective lining, such as wild grape leaves. The cooks covered each pit or oven with dirt. They sometimes built a fire over the oven, which they left to burn for several hours or overnight until removal of the succulent food. Earth ovens allowed people to process large quantities of food at one time—enough to feed several families or even an entire community. Pit-baking also provided an essential way of making inulin-rich plants, such as tubers and root crops, digestible and sweet to the taste.[3] Indian chefs also slow-roasted fatty meats in underground ovens, although the more common methods for cooking meats involved broiling on hot coals, seasoning soups and gruels in cooking baskets, or roasting on fire-reddened stones.

A second goal for gathering en masse was to provide vegetables, meats, and craft goods for important community gatherings. Significant quantities of food would be harvested in preparation for multiday feasts, ceremonies, and dances to which people from surrounding communities might be invited. The prestige and social standing of local leaders, leading families, and entire communities were often measured by their generosity during such intercommunity festivals.

The third, and most important, goal for mass harvests was to stockpile food and nonfood resources for later use, especially during winter and early spring months when resource productivity was at its lowest and when inclement weather made it a perfect time for people to stay snugly in warm houses producing and maintaining cordage, baskets, tools, and craft goods. The storage of bulk-harvested foods provided a significant strategy for "overwintering" in Native California.

The bulk harvesting of plant foods typically involved people traveling to specific resource patches to collect large quantities of nut crops, grass seeds, fruits, or roots and tubers when they became ripe. Long poles and climbers knocked nuts to the ground, where harvesters quickly gathered them into burden baskets or woven bags. The gatherers employed seed beaters—fine-mesh baskets shaped like scoops—to knock ripe seeds from plants and into burden baskets on their backs. They picked berries by hand. Fire-hardened, sharpened digging sticks served as ideal implements for exposing roots and tubers. California Indians depended on a variety of sturdy, lightweight baskets to transport and store plant foods in bulk. In some cases, transportation of heavy loads was facilitated by water travel. Local groups employed dugout canoes, tule balsas, and other forms of indigenous watercraft to move across many of the navigable streams, rivers, and lakes across the state. They used plank canoes *(tomols)* and dugouts to venture into ocean waters in some coastal areas, transporting people, foods, raw materials, and cultural objects back and forth between offshore islands and mainland settlements.

Mass collecting of animal foods also took place across Native California. People harvested fishes in rivers and lakes by means of a variety of methods: fish poisons (employed to stupefy prey in fishing holes), hook and line, fish spears, dip nets (fig. 6), and gill nets. But the most effective methods for capturing large numbers of fishes involved seine nets and fish weirs. Long seine nets could be stretched across streams or portions of lakes, often

Figure 6. Dip-net fishing in Yurok Country, 1906.

Figure 7. Salmon fish dam, 1901–1906; Hupa.

with the help of watercraft, and then men, women, and children could drive hundreds of fishes into the nets, where they would be easily captured in shallow water. Fish weirs or fences (fig. 7) built across stream channels yielded many hundreds of kilograms of

Figure 8. Snare trap for harvesting pigeons, 1903; Yokuts.

salmon (*Oncorhynchus* spp.), Pacific Lampreys (*Lampetra tridentata*), Steelheads (*O. mykiss irideus*), and Sacramento Suckers (*Catostomus occcidentalis*) during annual spawning. Although the architectural design, materials employed, and size of the weirs varied greatly in Native California, the basic concept was the same. Periodic openings in the fence would allow swarms of fishes to enter basket traps or shallow corrals where they could be easily captured.

In thinking about hunting in Native California, most of us today conjure up images of the lone Indian in an animal disguise stalking a deer (or other large game), hoping to get close enough to let loose a deadly arrow or two. But Native groups probably obtained much of their game from other kinds of mass collecting methods. Ethnohistoric writings and ethnographic observations describe a wide range of traps, snares, nets, and fences for hunting both large and small game. Communal hunts involved deer or antelope drives, where Indians skillfully chased animals past blinds where carefully camouflaged hunters bided their time. Or they would drive Mule Deer (*Odocoileus hemionus*),

Pronghorn (*Antilocapra americana*), or other game along fences of cordage, brush, or rocks into dead-end corrals where other hunters waited to greet the animals. Some of these fences were structurally analogous to fish weirs in that they contained periodic openings where deer (or other animals) could escape, only to meet lethal snares. The hunters commonly employed fire in these communal drives—they set fires to force animals over cliffs, or they encircled the beasts with fire on hilltops, forcing the game into confined spaces where they could be easily dispatched using clubs or arrows.

California Indians harvested large numbers of rabbits (Leporidae), quails (Odontophoridae), Band-tailed Pigeons (*Patagioenas fasciata*), and other small game in communal hunts. People beat the bushes to force the animals to follow carefully constructed fences with periodic openings containing snares or traps (fig. 8). Rabbits were also driven into long nets, some stretching a hundred or more meters in length, where hunters waited to dispatch the entangled animals. Indians utilized nets of various sizes and configurations to capture waterfowl from lakes and rivers. Some hunters used fire at night to attract birds that could be caught in nets erected on canoes. In other cases, they strategically placed decoys at the bottom of traps to attract birds that could be entangled in nets. Decoys were also placed near hunters waiting patiently in tule blinds. Some hunters were armed with specially constructed wooden projectile points that allowed the entire arrow to skim across the water, greatly increasing the chances of striking ducks (Anatidae) that were taking flight.

California Indians also participated in the mass gathering of insects. After smoking out adult yellowjackets (*Vespula* spp. and *Dolichovespula* spp.), hunters removed the nests and roasted them over a fire. They ate the cooked larvae or dried them for storage. Indians hunted grasshoppers (Caelifera) and crickets (*Anabrus* spp.) en masse with the aid of fire, collecting the scorched insects for immediate consumption or preparing them for storage. Ugan (2005) shows that while the mass collection of small game such as rabbits and quail is rather labor intensive because of the time involved in processing multiple small food items, the return rates for hunting and processing grasshoppers can be quite high, even better than for hunting Mule Deer or Pronghorn (for crickets, see also Sutton 1988).

Figure 9. Harvesting surf or nearshore fishes with nets, 1928; Yurok.

Coastal areas provided additional opportunities for the bulk harvesting of marine foods. Shellfish could be harvested in large numbers. For example, mussels (*Mytilus* spp.) could be systematically stripped from intertidal rocks. Smelt (Osmeridae) swarms along California beaches during the summer months allowed people to harvest many hundreds of kilograms of fishes using dip nets (fig. 9). Nearshore fishes, such as rockfishes (*Sebastes* spp.) and surfperches (Embiotocidae), were taken in large numbers with fishing lines or nets. Ocean-going canoes searched for schooling fishes (anchovies [Engraulididae], Chub Mackerel [*Scomber japonicus*], etc.) that could be harvested with nets. The coast, offshore rookeries, and nearby waters offered the promise of hunting immature cormorants (*Phalacrocorax* spp.) and other species of pelagic birds, as well as porpoises (Delphinidae), Sea Otters (*Enhydra lutris*), Harbor Seals (*Phoca vitulina*), Northern Fur Seals (*Callorhinus ursinus*), Guadalupe Fur Seals (*Arctocephalus townsendi*), California Sea Lions (*Zalophus californianus*), Steller Sea Lions (*Eumetopias jubatus*), and beached Gray Whales (*Eschrichtius robustus*). Kelp (Laminariales) and seaweeds (*Porphyra* spp.), especially after storms, could also be gathered in large quantities off the beach and dried for storage.

Storing for a Winter's Day

In earmarking a portion of their bulk-gathered food and non-food goods for winter and early spring use and ceremonial gatherings, California Indians devised and implemented many innovative methods for the preservation and storage of a diverse range of resources. The methods of preparing plant foods for short- or long-term storage varied with the vegetable material and with the traditions of local communities (see Jacknis 2004).

California Indians typically dried acorns in the sun and stored them in their shells in either outdoor acorn granaries or indoor storage baskets (fig. 10); however, some people stored some species of acorns by shelling them, drying them on rocks or in basket trays, and placing them in large sealed baskets. Before acorns (and buckeyes) can be eaten, the tannic acid must be removed. The simplest way was to bury the acorns in a wet area, such as a riverbank or near a spring, for about a year. This underground aging turned the acorns black, sweet, and ready for

Figure 10. Woman in front of two acorn granaries, 1905–1930; Western Mono.

Figure 11. Woman leaching acorns of tannic acid, 1902; Hupa.

the cooking basket. Another, somewhat more practical, method involved Indians selecting the desired number of acorns for a meal from the storage basket. If the acorns were still in their shell, then the cooks cracked the nuts and removed the meat. They then pounded the shelled acorns in a hopper slab mortar, with the fine particles sifted into a tight, flat basket and then placed in another acorn basket. The Indians took the meal to a sand leaching pit on the riverbank. Sometimes the cooks employed a special leaching basket to keep the acorns separated from the sand. Water was poured over the acorns until the tannic acid leached out (fig. 11). Warm water would leach the meal quicker than cold water. They then removed the acorn meal from the pit, washed the sand out, and put the meal back into the acorn basket, returning home to prepare a meal of gruel or soup or some other dish.[4]

After collecting grass seeds in bulk, Native Californians cleaned them, placing them directly into baskets for making meals, or they winnowed and parched them in preparation for storage. They prepared pine nuts by shelling, roasting, and stor-

Figure 12. Outdoor storage basket for mesquite beans, 1907; Cahuilla.

ing in baskets. Some species of berries were preserved by steaming and/or drying—when ready to eat the cooks reconstituted them with warm water. Berries could also be pounded into a pulp, dried, ground into flour, and then eaten or stored for winter use. Mesquite beans were prepared and placed in storage facilities (fig. 12). Roots and tubers were skinned or peeled, dried, and placed in storage baskets. People sometimes roasted roots and tubers in underground ovens for immediate consumption or dried the roasted food for long-term storage. Greens could be steamed or roasted in underground ovens and dried for storage. Coastal people commonly dried kelp and seaweed for winter storage.

Fishermen typically prepared fishes for storage by splitting and drying them in the sun or by smoking the meat on specially built racks over fires. Family members butchered mammals and birds, and what they did not consume fresh they usually cut into smaller lengths to preserve by sun drying or smoking over fires. Shellfish was also dried for later consumption.

Winter Villages

The diverse kinds of plant and animal foods collected en masse and prepared for storage were often designated for use in winter villages. Local communities tended to aggregate into one or more winter villages where food and other raw materials had been stockpiled for use during the wet, cool (or cold) period of the year (fig. 13) (see also Jacknis 2004:9–10). Storage facilities in winter villages might include outdoor granaries and pit features, separate storehouses, and houses where food was placed in large storage baskets or underground pits or hung from the rafters. As detailed later, the settlement patterns of Indian communities

Figure 13. Chino Village near Hamilton City on the Sacramento River, pencil sketch by Henry B. Brown in 1852. Note the storage facilities at this winter village.

varied greatly across the state. Some groups maintained people in villages throughout the entire annual cycle. In permanently occupied villages, groups of people[5] worked throughout the year to collect and transport foods and raw materials from outlying patches back to the main village. They established small, special-purpose camps[6] in the outlying hinterland, where they harvested and initially processed foods and raw materials in mass quantities. In other cases, elderly men and women or invalids stayed behind at the villages, while younger families left their homes for varying lengths of time, establishing a round of seasonal residences for harvesting food and raw materials some distance from the main settlement. They would periodically transport these goods back to the villages for the elderly and to stockpile foods for use when the rest of the community returned in late fall or early winter.

Still other communities abandoned their winter villages for some period of the annual cycle. It was not uncommon for some groups in the Sierra Nevada or northeastern California to spend late fall, winter, and much of the spring in the winter village. But during the productive seasons of the year (late spring, summer, early fall), the local community might be divided into many small family groups that hunted, gathered, and fished for food and raw materials across their territory. They established one or more small, warm-weather settlements that facilitated the exploitation and maintenance of diverse patches. Food gathered in large quantities would be either cached near these warm-weather residences and then transported back to winter villages when needed, or transported directly to storage facilities in the abandoned winter village sites.

A Land of Small Polities

Foods and raw materials stockpiled at winter villages not only supported people through the lean period of the year, but helped finance and nourish the political organizations and ceremonial programs of local Indian communities. As detailed later, the political organizations of Native California varied in structure, size, and hierarchical arrangement, with house societies dominating the Northwest Coast Province groups, and various forms of tribelet or village communities found primarily in the remainder of the state. The tribelet organizations, often centered around one or more principal winter villages and outlying hamlets, were staffed with headmen, retainers, shamans, ceremonial specialists, and craft experts. Although ceremonies and dances occurred throughout the year, major events took place during times of population aggregation either at winter villages or during communal gatherings involving the bulk collection of resources, such as the first fruit ceremony, first salmon ceremony, acorn festival, and so on. Mass collecting associated with communal hunts or gathering forays supported lavish feasts that took place as part of the ceremonial calendar, while many of the fine baskets, clothing, headdresses, ceremonial regalia, and

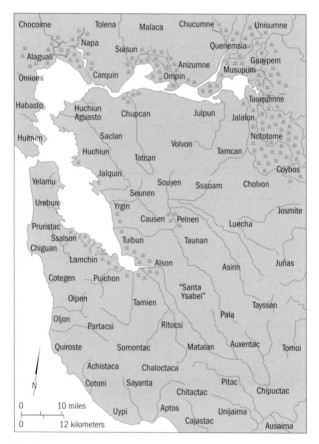

Map 2. A landscape chock full of people: Native polities in the greater San Francisco Bay Area. (From Milliken 1995:229)

musical instruments exhibited during dances and public assemblies were produced from specially tended plant and animal resources within the group's territory.

The size of most Indian communities' territories was large enough to provide sufficient habitat diversity to buffer the unpredictability of environmental perturbations during most years (Keeley 2002:306), but small enough to remain manageable from a few village locations that may have been moved one or a few times a year. The spatial configuration of these territories no doubt varied from generation to generation, depending on population growth or decline, resource fluctuations, and the vagaries of group politics. But what makes Native California truly unique is that not only was it one of the most densely populated regions in all of late prehistoric North America, but the majority of its settlements and polities were fairly small-scale entities. Little evidence exists for large population aggregations—rather, we see a pattern of population dispersal across productive coastal, valley, foothill, mountain, and desert habitats. These habitable places eventually became filled with a plethora of small polities, each of which attempted to maintain access to sufficient habitable diversity to support its moderate populations (map 2).

Relations between People

Local polities were tied into broader regional alliances and exchange systems. Social relationships existed across polity boundaries to allow food and other goods to be exchanged between people from different Native communities. Regional exchange was facilitated by designated trade partners, major ceremonies and dances, and so-called trade fairs that periodically brought people from different communities together. These intercommunity relationships helped minimize local resource shortages by providing social mechanisms for moving food and materials from areas with surplus goods to those facing resource shortages. There is also excellent archaeological evidence for strife and violence between polities, a finding that suggests the common occurrence of warfare and raids between communities.

The creation of Indian "money," a recognized form of currency across much of Native California, also facilitated interpolity exchange. Depending on the local region, dentalium shells, clam-disk beads, magnesite beads or cylinders, and Olive Snail (olivella) shell beads served as standardized mediums of exchange. The size and number of beads or cylinders, usually strung in standardized size lengths, were equated with recognized values that could be used as gifts, as funerary offerings, and for paying off blood-revenge debts or interpersonal acts of violence. Some anthropologists have argued that the production of shell beads created a sort of banking system that allowed Native people in times of surplus to transform food items into bead currency. During times of food shortages, these beads could then be given away as presents to people from regions not facing resource shortages, who would reciprocate by offering presents in foodstuffs equal to or greater than the value of the beads.

Conclusion

In this chapter we present a model of fire management in Native California that revolves around local Indian communities that actively worked to enhance the diversity and productivity of economically important plant and animal resources. Native people implemented prescribed burns that augmented the diversity of landscapes by helping to create a patchwork of heterogeneous habitats containing plants at different stages of succession. Fires fostered the growth of plants used for food and in the creation of perishable material culture. Managed burns also produced new forage that attracted game birds and mammals. The proliferation of economic plant and animal resources in discrete patches across local territories allowed Indian communities to implement harvesting strategies that involved the bulk collection of food, cordage, basketry material, and other kinds of raw materials. Gathering goods en masse and then stockpiling them at winter villages not only sustained people during the lean times of the year, but was instrumental in supporting the profusion of small-scale polities that dotted the landscape of Native California.

Waves of Migration

HOW LONG NATIVE PEOPLE HAVE RESIDED in California is a frequently asked question. Even those students who are skeptical about the relevancy of ethnographic or archaeological collections to our contemporary world are intrigued by the antiquity of Indian material culture. Inevitably, when shown an elegant coiled basket with beautiful black design elements, or a perfectly knapped obsidian projectile point, people want to know how old it is. Addressing when California was first settled and how its material culture evolved over time is critical for understanding cultural diversity among Indian people, as well as providing the time line for the creation of pyrodiversity economies.

An Alien World

The early settlement of California took place during times of massive environmental changes during the Late Pleistocene and Early Holocene.[1] The Late Pleistocene would have been an inspiring but challenging place to behold. Extensive alpine glaciers sculpted the higher mountain terrain of the Sierra Nevada and the Cascade Range. During glacial advances, streams of ice descended down upland valleys, scouring and polishing the granitic batholith, forming what would become the distinctive landscape of Yosemite Valley and other celebrated places in California's high country. When temperatures warmed, the glacial ice retreated to upper mountain slopes and left behind extensive moraines and outwash alluvial deposits. Glacial meltwater and winter precipitation also contributed to expansive freshwater ecosystems across the state, even in the Southern Deserts Province. A plethora of pluvial lakes, produced by rain and meltwater, emerged in lowland basins. Some modern lakes, such as Clear Lake and Tulare Lake, increased greatly their overall size and volume of water during the Late Pleistocene and Early Holocene. Other sizeable Pleistocene lakes, such as Lake Manix, Lake Mojave, and China Lake in the Mojave Desert, have long since been converted into dryland playas as the temperature warmed and precipitation decreased in the later Holocene.

One of the most significant differences between Pleistocene and contemporary California is the drop in sea level. During glacial advances, the ice sheets trapped great quantities of water worldwide, causing the world's oceans to shrink and exposing portions of the continental shelf. During the last glacial maximum, about 18,000 to 20,000 years ago, it is estimated that sea level fell 100 to 125 m (330 to 410 ft) below its present elevation (Erlandson 2002:64; Grayson 1993:47). Along the California coast, this magnitude of Late Pleistocene shoreline change created a strip of dry land totaling an estimated 20,000 km^2 (7,800 mi^2)—land that is sea bottom today (Bickel 1978:16). The most substantial exposure of the California continental shelf took place in the shallowest locations—along the Golden Gate outside of what is now the San Francisco Bay, the Santa Barbara coast, and the Channel Islands.

The colder and wetter environment of the Pleistocene also changed the composition and spatial distribution of plant communities. With snow levels in the Sierra Nevada and Cascade Range a thousand meters lower than today (Jameson and Peeters 2004:21), most vegetation communities shifted their distribution to lower elevations and more southern latitudes.[2] Faunal populations differed dramatically from what we see today.[3]

In California, the Pleistocene animals are best known from the famous tar pits of Rancho La Brea in Los Angeles. Many of the herbivores and carnivores that became extinct at the end of the Pleistocene were considerably larger than their modern cousins. Hence paleontologists and archaeologists often refer to the Pleistocene big game populations as "megafauna." Some of the more spectacular megafauna that disappeared from the California landscape include the Ground Sloth *(Nothrotheriops shastense)*, Dire Wolf *(Canus dirus)*, sabertooth cat *(Smilodon* spp.), and the always popular American Mastodon *(Mammut americanum)* and Columbian Mammoth *(Mammuthus columbia)* (Grayson 1993:67–68; Jameson and Peeters 2004:22).

Multiple Migrations to California

Most Indian groups in California maintain that they have resided in their traditional homelands since the beginning of human time. Although there is considerable debate among archaeologists about this statement, over the course of more than a century of archaeological research in the state, the generally accepted age of human antiquity has been continually pushed back in time.

In the late nineteenth century, a number of claims were made in the media about the existence of "Ice Age Man" in California based on the discovery of human artifacts and skeletal remains found in gold-bearing deposits in the Sierra Nevada, some reported to have been found 60 to 90 m (200 to 300 ft) deep in hard rock mines. Known as "Auriferous Man," investigations of these finds in the early twentieth century under the auspices of the University of California's newly founded University Museum and Department of Anthropology demonstrated that most of these discoveries appeared to have been hoaxes or the accidental mixing of more recent Indian materials with much older geological deposits in the mines (Sinclair 1908). The systematic refutation of other claims of early sites elsewhere eventually eroded support among scientists for the great antiquity of Indian people in North America (Willey and Sabloff 1993:55–57). By the 1910s, most anthropologists publicly subscribed to a short chronology of only several thousand years since the initial entry of people to the continent. This time frame fitted nicely with age estimates for California Indian sites first excavated by archaeologists from the University of California at Berkeley. The large shell mounds of San Francisco Bay, believed at that time to be some of the earliest sites in California, were estimated to be about 3,000 to 4,000 years old based on the volume of shell, ash, and other materials recovered (Kroeber 1925:922–923).

When Heizer and Elsasser first began writing *The Natural World of the California Indians* in the 1970s, the earliest accepted dates for North American sites had been pushed back to about 11,500 years ago. Beginning in the 1920s and continuing through the 1960s, archaeologists carefully excavated and dated a number of sites in the American Southwest and Plains that contained the remains of extinct Pleistocene megafauna and human artifacts. These findings gave rise to the model that big-game hunters, or Paleo-Indians, crossed over Beringia, the celebrated land bridge between the continents exposed by the sea level drop during the Late Pleistocene, by chasing herds of mammoths, saiga antelope, horses, large-horned bisons, and musk-ox from northeastern Asia. The first people to enter the Americas, the so-called Clovis people, named after their signature fluted projectile points associated with mammoths in the earliest sites in North America, followed herds of these massive animals into Alaska. From there the skilled hunters were believed to have hacked and hewed their way down the ice-free corridor between the Laurentide and Cordilleran ice sheets into the heartland of the continental United States, arriving in California, probably about 10,000 years ago (Heizer and Elsasser 1980:1).

This elegant, long-held "Clovis first" model is now in tatters. Both the timing and means of early human migration to the Americas have been challenged. With the discovery of Monte Verde and other possible early sites in South America that predate the Clovis invasion, many archaeologists are now considering the strong possibility that there were multiple migrations, even dribbles of a relatively few people, taking place over time in the Late Pleistocene and Early Holocene. Given the paucity of clearly ancestral Clovis sites in eastern Asia, some scholars advocate that the Clovis tool assemblage may have been a uniquely American innovation that arose from pre-Clovis populations in the American heartland (Meltzer 2002:43). In addition, while some ancestral populations may have come by foot over exposed portions of Beringia, others may have come by water. The widespread deglaciation of the outer coast along the North Pacific Rim by 13,000 to 14,000 years ago opened up potentially rich marine and shoreline habitats and may have enticed people to land-hop down the Pacific coast of North America.

Seafarers in watercrafts may have skimmed along the shoreline and islands of the North Pacific Rim, skirting around jutting masses of glacial ice, and landing in areas that remained ice free (Erlandson 2002). The movement of these early maritime people may have been facilitated by the highly productive kelp forests and associated marine habitats that thrived along the inshore waters of the North Pacific, extending down into Baja California. This so-called kelp highway would have offered ready sources of fishes, sea mammals, seabirds, shellfish, and vegetable foods, as well as raw materials for the sea voyagers (Erlandson et al. 2007). An even more controversial idea has been proposed. Stanford and Bradley (2002) argue that similarities in stone tool production technologies suggest that some ancestors may have come from Iberia rather than northeastern Asia, arriving in North America in small skin boats by dodging the North Atlantic ice sheets.

Sites with Coastal Views

California is a critical player in the evaluation of these proposed migration scenarios, especially that of coastal movements along the North Pacific Rim. The earliest coastal sites in North America that exhibit evidence of maritime economies, dating between 13,000 to 10,000 years ago, are found on the Channel Islands and South Coast Province mainland. The Channel Islands are of particular interest. Even with lower sea levels in the Late Pleistocene, stretches of open ocean still separated the Channel Islands from the mainland, indicating that the earliest people had some kind of oceangoing watercraft. The recent reexamination of the previously excavated skeletal remains at the Arlington Springs site on Santa Rosa Island is now producing AMS (accelerator mass spectrometer) dates of about 13,300 years ago (Johnson et al. 2000). The earliest component at Daisy Cave on San Miguel Island, comprising a handful of chipped stone tools, debitage, and small amounts of marine shell, dates to between about 12,300 and 11,120 years ago (Kennett 2005:113–117; Rick et al. 2001:603). Later components of the Early Holocene occupation of Daisy Cave (ca. 10,300 to 8,500 years ago) have yielded rich deposits of fish remains, shellfish, and perishable material culture, including twined fiber fragments and plied cordage made from sea grass (*Phyllospadix* spp.). The artifacts appear to be the remains of sandals, as well as fragments of fishing lines, nets, or baskets (Connolly et al. 1995).

Recent excavations at Cross Creek near San Luis Obispo on the northern edge of the South Coast Province have unearthed the earliest well-dated coastal site on the California mainland (Jones et al. 2002). In an extensive shell midden with an occupation spanning from about 10,300 to 9,650 years ago, archaeologists recovered a large assemblage of milling stones, handstones, core/cobblestone tools (chopping and scraping implements with heavily battered and rounded edges), hammerstones, and flakestone tools. The analysis of the faunal assemblage yielded mostly shellfish species that once thrived in a nearby estuarine embayment, such as Littleneck Clam *(Leukoma staminea)*, Washington Clam *(Saxidomus nuttalli)*, and Gaper Clam *(Tresus nuttalli)*, with smaller amounts of rocky intertidal species such as the California Mussel *(Mytilus californianus)* and traces of Red Abalone *(Haliotis rufescens)*. Interestingly, vertebrate faunal remains were very scarce, with only one recognizable fragment of an artiodactyl (deer or elk) and a single bone from a rockfish *(Sebastes)*. The analysis of soil samples, using a flotation tank and fine mesh to recover small floral remains and artifacts, yielded charred seeds of seven taxa probably used on the site, including bentgrass (*Agrostis* spp.), fescue (*Vulpia* spp.), ryegrass (*Elymus* spp.), needlegrass (*Stipa* spp.), plantain (*Plantago* spp.), verbena (*Verbena* spp.), and clarkia (*Clarkia* spp.), along with evidence of yucca (*Yucca* spp.) processing and charcoal identified from yucca, pine (*Pinus* spp.), manzanita (*Arctostaphylos* spp.), and an unidentified species of live oak *(Quercus agrifolia* or *Q. wislizenii)*(Jones et al. 2002: 222–224).

Ongoing investigations at Cedros Island, Baja California, have revealed at least five coastal sites that date to the Late Pleistocene. The findings indicate that the roots of the complex hunter-gatherer societies of Cedros Island extend back to archaeological remains of fishing and shellfish collecting that are at least 12,000 years old (Des Lauriers 2006).

Big Game Hunting?

The liberal presence of fluted projectile points, some the same shape and size as Clovis points found in the adjacent American Southwest, have been found in California. They are most commonly reported in the Southern Deserts Province, the southern San Joaquin Valley, and the North Coast Ranges.[4] Interestingly, only a few isolated fluted points have been found in the South Coast Province and South Coast Ranges, and none is from any of the stratified coastal sites with systematically excavated deposits dating to the Late Pleistocene or Early Holocene.[5]

Brian Dillon (2002:123) notes that more than 400 fluted points have now been recorded from over 50 separate locations in 28 California counties. Some of the points have been recovered along the margins of ancient pluvial lakes, such as China Lake, Lake Mojave, and Owens Lake in the Southern Deserts Province or along former shorelines of current lakes and freshwater wetlands, such as Clear Lake and Lake Tulare.[6] A few locations, such as Lake Tulare, have yielded fossil remains of Pleistocene megafauna including mammoths, ground sloths, bisons, camels, and horses (Dillon 2002:116). Unfortunately, many of these points tend to be isolated finds or recovered on surfaces deflated by wind or other environmental processes, which are not directly associated with in situ faunal remains. These kinds of isolated or disturbed geological contexts make detailed chronological studies difficult (but see Fredrickson and Origer 2002). Although some archaeologists propose the ancient hunting of mammoth and other megafauna in California, especially near pluvial lakes, such as China Lake, there is really no concrete evidence yet. The spectacular kill sites containing remains of butchered mammoth and extinct bison in association with fluted points and other artifacts found in the American Southwest and the Plains have yet to be found in California.

Diversification from the Beginning

The early colonization of California involved the rapid diversification of economies and related cultural practices as people settled into divergent ecological habitats during the Holocene (Arnold et al. 2004:10–11). Over 25 shell middens and other types of sites dating to between 12,000 and 8,000 years ago have now been recorded and studied in the northern Channel Islands (Erlandson et al. 2005:680). The findings clearly demonstrate the existence of a paleocoastal fisher-gatherer complex that involved seaworthy boats, shellfish gathering, sophisticated fishing technologies, core and flake stone tool manufacture, shell bead production, and the weaving of basketry and cordage from sea grass. Most sites exhibit a strong pattern of harvesting shellfish from nearby rocky intertidal habitats, with lesser or supplemental use of fishes, sea mammals, and birds. Although California Mussel tends to dominate most mollusk assemblages, one site contains mostly Black Abalone *(Haliotis cracherodii)*, and another is characterized by good evidence of Venus clams (*Chione* spp.), Washington Clam, and California Oyster *(Ostrea conchaphila)* gathered from a nearby extinct estuary (Erlandson et al. 1999; Rick, Kennett, and Erlandson 2005).

Several northern Channel Islands sites exhibit good evidence for harvesting fishes primarily from rocky nearshore and kelp-bed habitats using bipointed fish gorges attached to sea grass fishing lines, as well as nets (Erlandson et al. 1999; Rick et al. 2001:605–606). The analysis of more than 27,000 fish bones from Early Holocene components from Daisy Cave identified 18 different taxa, of which surfperches (Embiotocidae), rockfishes

(*Sebastes* spp.), Cabezon *(Scorpaenichthys marmoratus)*, and California Sheephead *(Semicossyphus pulcher)* dominated. Interestingly, in spite of the contemporary seal (Phocidae) and sea lion (Otariidae) rookeries found on the Channel Islands, there is little direct evidence for the early hunting of sea mammals, although bifacially worked stone tools (known as bifaces) recovered from a site on the south shore of San Miguel Island may signal that such hunting took place and the bones from the butchered animals were deposited elsewhere.[7]

Coastal people living on the mainland of the South Coast Province also emphasized shellfish gathering, but many of the species as exemplified at the Cross Creek site were gathered from large estuaries that appear to have been the focus of many subsistence activities. Coastal dwellers supplemented shellfish with meat from fishes, sea mammals, and some terrestrial game. Erlandson (1994:260–261) estimates that 75 percent of their meat protein came from the sea, especially from shellfish. Compared to the fisher-gatherers on the Channel Islands, the coastal mainlanders exploited a wider variety of terrestrial plants, such as nuts and seeds. The existence of the coastal coniferous forest would have provided nutritious pine nuts, especially the delectable nut of the Torrey pine *(Pinus torreyana)*, which when combined with shellfish and other vegetable foods, provided a balanced and nutritious menu that would please any cardiologist (Erlandson 1991, 1994:261). Current paleoenvironmental data suggest that the Late Pleistocene coastal coniferous forest began to disappear, at least in some places, along the South Coast mainland by the Early Holocene, at the same time that species comprising modern plant communities increased in numbers (Erlandson 1994:32–33).

The discovery of the early milling stone assemblage at Cross Creek and the recovery of charred seed remains also indicate that seed processing took place in the earliest known coastal mainland sites. By 9,000 years ago the increased presence of milling tools along the entire South Coast Province and South Coast Ranges mainland suggests that pine nuts may have become a supplemental food, while small seeds, hard nuts, and other kinds of vegetable foods associated with the more modern vegetation types played a greater role in the menu, along with the continued use of shellfish and other sources of protein (Erlandson 1994: 261; Jones 2003:217–218).

Unfortunately, the poor context of the fluted points recovered from the San Joaquin Valley and Southern Deserts Province as surface finds makes it difficult to say much about possible Late Pleistocene human occupants of the interior. They were probably generalized hunter-gatherers whose economies were geared toward opportunistic hunting of smaller game, snaring waterfowl in freshwater wetlands, fishing, collecting plant foods, gathering freshwater shellfish, and occasionally taking on megafauna when the opportunity presented itself (Erlandson 1994:269–272; Lightfoot 1993:173–177). Findings from archaeological excavations of more definitive sites dating to the Early Holocene suggest that people extensively gathered resources along the margins of lakes, marshes, and sloughs, as well as hunted game in the nearby hinterland. These groups appear to have been generalized hunter-gatherers who used the freshwater wetlands as part of a larger seasonal round that also included other diverse habitats, such as uplands (Sutton 1996:228–230).

Holocene Radiation and Diversification

Some scholars have proposed that California was peopled primarily by a few small donor groups of primitive newcomers who established beachheads along interior pluvial lakes, where they learned on the job how to survive in the Golden State. From these locations they supposedly moved to the coast and other locations across California, and pushed westward as freshwater habitats in the Southern Deserts Province began to dry out after the last ice age. But in reality, the initial settlement of California in the Late Pleistocene and Early Holocene was most likely a product of multiple migrations of people coming from both sea and land. The process of colonization probably involved sophisticated seafarers who were already well attuned to the exploitation of maritime resources (Erlandson 2002; Erlandson et al. 2005; Jones et al. 2002:227–228). It also involved people from the broader Pacific Northwest, Great Basin area, and American Southwest, who had already accumulated much knowledge about a wide range of plant and animal resources in western North America.

From the expansion of populations already here and the recurrent movement of people into the state from elsewhere, Indians radiated out along the California coast and into interior valleys, foothills, and mountains, eventually claiming almost every habitable nook and cranny. This process of population radiation in the Holocene took place against a backdrop of significant environmental change.[8] Rising sea level, resulting from the worldwide shrinking of the great ice masses at the end of the Pleistocene, swallowed former coastlines and wetlands but produced, in combination with tectonic movements, new contours of beaches, rocky headlands, marine terraces, lagoons, and bays. For example, the greater San Francisco Bay system took shape during the height of sea level upswings from 10,000 to 5,000 years ago, when rising ocean waters swamped the Golden Gate and interior river valleys. But this extensive estuarine system continued to expand in the later Holocene, albeit at a much slower pace with the slowdown in sea level rise. The pluvial lakes in the Southern Deserts Province shrank and eventually dried out. Periodic oscillations of global warming and cooling, as well as regional droughts and floods, influenced the distribution and composition of vegetation types across the state.[9]

During the Late Holocene, for example, Native Californians witnessed another shorter interval of global warming known as the Medieval Climatic Anomaly (aka Medieval Warm Period), when increased solar radiation led to pulses of overall milder temperatures and warm summers between AD 800 and AD 1300. This warm interval was then followed by the Little Ice Age, a period of surprisingly cool to cold temperatures beginning about AD 1450 and ending sometime between AD 1850 and 1910, when global warming began to take place again (and which continues at an accelerated rate today)(Caviedes 2001:200–201, 216–217; Jameson and Peeters 2004:23–24). By the beginning of the Late Holocene, about 3,000 years ago, the coastline, riparian corridors, freshwater wetlands, vegetation types, and animal populations that compose our modern world came into focus.

A full discussion of the expansion and radiation of California Indians across the state during the Holocene is beyond this book. Thousands of archaeologists have devoted their careers to the study of regional culture histories and transformations in cultural practices, social organizations, economic strategies, and ceremonial systems of local groups across California. An immense literature now exists.[10] Suffice it to say that the archaeological record is both rich and complex, involving significant regional diversification over time.

Just about every local area in California is characterized by its unique configuration of significant archaeological remains. Some of the most spectacular archaeological remains that we have had the pleasure to visit across California include complex, stratified villages in the far northwest corner of the state; the diverse shell middens along the North and South Coast ranges; the impressive shell mounds of the greater San Francisco Bay; the complicated settlement system of villages, specialized production places, and lithic quarries on the Channel Islands; the remarkable polychrome pictographs of the South Coast Province mainland; diverse fishing sites and hunting blinds in the Modoc Plateau; the incredible shell mounds and dirt mounds of the Sacramento River; the large house-pit villages of the San Joaquin Valley; the complex bedrock mortar sites and obsidian quarries of the Sierra Nevada; the giant intaglio figures of the Southern Deserts Province; and extensive scatters of stone tools and extraordinary petroglyph images of Bighorn Sheep *(Ovis canadensis)*, other animals, animal tracks, and humanlike figures in the nearby Great Basin.[11] There is no question that California boasts one of the most captivating and provocative archaeological records in the world.

Conclusion

We began this book by emphasizing that nowhere else in North America are Indian people distinguished by such an incredible diversity of cultures, polities, and languages. This chapter concludes with three reasons why we feel diversification became a hallmark of Native California.

California Indian societies have been evolving and changing for over 13,000 years. This long time frame provided ample opportunity for the creation and diversification of material culture, economies, ceremonial systems, and political organizations. Social relationships existed between different hunter-gatherer groups, as we discuss later, providing conduits for the spread of new ideas and materials across broad regions, a synergistic process that led to experimentation and the creation of further innovations and developments. Thus, in examining the proliferation of pyrodiversity economies that once existed in late prehistoric and historic times, we need to keep in mind that indigenous management practices were probably developed, used, tested, and refined over many centuries. Indigenous methods employed to augment resource diversity across local landscapes did not come into being overnight, nor were they restricted to relatively few groups.

Over the last 13,000 years or more, many distinctive groups, with their own languages and cultural practices, have migrated to California. The considerable variation in the physical characteristics of California Indians, highlighted by Heizer and Elsasser (1980:7), is probably the consequence of these migrations, as well as biological developments within local populations over many thousands of years. They note, for example, that the tallest (Mojave) and shortest (Yuki) populations of Indian people in North America are found in California. With the coming of new people, unique cultures began to take root as migrants initiated their former practices from elsewhere in new settings, while experimenting with cultural innovations that would transform their cultural traditions over time. Arriving by sea or land, they probably came in dribbles and spurts, creating ripples across the social landscape by enhancing this great cauldron of diversity with periodic infusions of fresh ideas, technologies, and cultural practices.

Diversity in languages, cultures, and polities is the product of long-term interactions with an ever-changing natural world. With the radiation of Native groups into every corner of the state, human interactions with local microclimates, topography, vegetation types, and animal populations would most certainly have enhanced cultural diversity. As people encountered new kinds of habitats, they experimented with innovative ways of harvesting, processing, and using novel resources for foods, medicine, tools, architectural features, and ceremonies, as well as creating new management practices for enhancing and maximizing local resource diversity. Although the environment did not determine the specific cultural practices that arose across the state, California's incredible biodiversity and varied habitats certainly played a significant role in their regional diversification, a point we take up in the next chapter.

A Landscape of
Unparalleled Diversity

CALIFORNIA INDIANS INHERITED and then enhanced a natural world of incredible diversity and productivity. What makes California stand out today to almost anyone visiting from the heartland of America is the fantastic variability that can be found in its topography, climate, geology, and biotic communities within a limited geographic range. For example, on almost any summer day a wide range of temperatures can be enjoyed within an hour's drive of the Berkeley campus of the University of California. In the mood for some blustery fog and cool temperatures? You can stay bundled up on the Berkeley waterfront or drive over to the spectacular Great Highway along the Pacific Ocean in San Francisco, with the car's heater on full blast. In need of some sun and warmth? You can motor out of the San Francisco Bay Area, over the eastern flanks of the Coast Ranges, dropping rapidly into the Great Central Valley. Anywhere along this route you can pull over to savor temperatures increasing from the low 70s to the high 90s to even low 100s (or higher), depending on the particular day and distance you drive.

*Of course, if you really crave summer heat, then take the eight-hour trip south to the small settlement of Furnace Creek in Death Valley, where the highest official air temperature in the Western Hemisphere has been recorded (57 degrees C [134 degrees F]). The ability to enjoy diverse microclimates within limited geographic space is not limited to the greater San Francisco Bay Area or Death Valley, but can be found almost anywhere in the state. The diversity of California's natural world is even more marked when we take into account temporal variation in climatic conditions. The climatic system of the Golden State is complex, dynamic, and ever changing. You may be cruising down to Los Angeles with the top down and the radio blaring a song about it never raining in southern California, but be careful—if you stay long enough you may experience significant El

Niño deluges that can cause floods and mudslides and extensive damage to unsuspecting tourists in convertibles, even in sunny southern California.

In sustaining an intimate relationship with this exquisite, but moody, natural world over thousands of years, Native peoples took advantage of a significant characteristic of California's environment: that substantial resource diversity can be found within limited areas. People had to walk or canoe only relatively short distances to experience exceptionally varied habitats of plants, animals, and minerals. We believe that this may be a critical condition underlying the development of successful pyrodiversity economies: the ability to take an already heterogeneous world and then magnify this diversity through fire management and other cultivation practices. Our purpose here is not to present a detailed environmental overview of California, which has been expertly penned by others,[1] but rather to outline briefly three primary factors—topographic relief, the maritime conditions of the Pacific Ocean, and latitude—that are crucial for understanding habitat diversification in California. The effects of these three factors can still be felt today in the varied microclimates that mark the coastlines, islands, valleys, hills, mountains, and deserts of California. We then conclude with a short discussion about how hunter-gatherer communities have had to cope with an ever-changing world of diversity.

Topographic Relief

Plate tectonic movement over millions of years produced a dynamic landscape of faulting, folding, uplifting, and volcanism that resulted in mountain building and tremendous geological complexity. On the western margin of the North American Plate, California endured the brunt of the geological upheaval caused by the subduction of the Pacific Plate beneath the westward-moving continental plate.[2] Giant chambers of magma, puddled deep below the surface, cooled and crystallized into granitic blocks, known as batholiths. Tectonic movements uplifted gigantic batholith formations along diverging fault zones in eastern and southern California, forming the foundation of the Sierra Nevada, Transverse Ranges, and Peninsular Ranges. Faulting and uplifting also created the geologically diverse rocky uplands of the Klamath Mountains and the multiple ridges and valleys of the 800 km (500 mi) long Coast Ranges. Volcanism in northeastern California produced the Cascade Range, a chain of volcanic mountains that continues into Oregon and Washington, as well as the Modoc Plateau, a spectacularly tortured tableland resulting from repeated lava flows beginning about 5 million years ago.

The ultimate consequence of tectonic movement and volcanic eruptions was the creation of a great ring of mountains that parallel the coastline of the Pacific Ocean on the west and form the backbone of the state on the east. The Klamath Mountains merge with the Coast Ranges to create the coastal mountains, while they, in turn, blend with the Cascade Range and eventually the Sierra Nevada to form a solid rock wall along the eastern side of northern and central California. The great depression in the center of this immense ring of mountains eventually filled with thick alluvial sediments, producing the rich, almost perfectly flat terrain of the Great Central Valley. The Transverse Ranges and Peninsular Ranges form an impressive "tail" to the great ring of mountains, extending the tall peaks down the southern coast and into Baja California.

East of this tall tail are the southern deserts of California—the high-altitude Mojave Desert and the lower-elevation Colorado Desert. The spatial pattern of California's ring of mountains and coastal southern tail resembles a letter Q that has been put on a diet (map 3). This unique configuration resulted in some of the most spectacular and precipitous landscape in the continental United States—the lowest point at Bad Water in Death Valley (87 m [285 ft] below sea level) is located only 128 km [79 mi] from the highest point, Mount Whitney (4,418 m [14,490 ft] above sea level) in the Sierra Nevada.

The implications of this uneven landscape for California Indians is that they did not have to travel far to experience significant variation in topography, ranging from fertile valleys and rolling hills to steep mountains. On the Pacific coast, no matter where Native people stood they were near a magnificent mountain range. Beyond the coastline in most interior places, they experienced hills or steep uplands within short distances. Even in the relatively flat Great Central Valley, its width ranging from about 50 to 150 km (31 to 93 mi), the distance to either the Coast Ranges or the Sierra Nevada was within walking range for energetic hunter-gatherers, especially if they placed their settlements

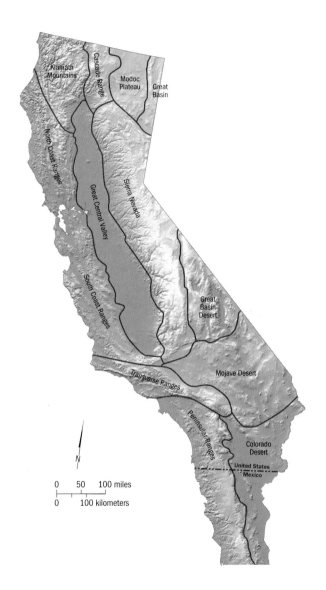

Map 3. Topography of California.

near the base of the mountains on either side of the valley. In the Mojave Desert, people never strayed far from an elevated surface. Tectonic activity created a series of ranges, such as the Clark, Kingston, Ivanpah, Providence, and New York mountains, which rise dramatically from the relatively flat desert pavement.

Maritime Conditions of the Pacific Ocean

The presence of the Pacific Ocean, combined with diverse topographic relief, generates the unique and varied climates of California. In general, the so-called cismontane region to the west of the Cascade Range, Sierra Nevada, Transverse Ranges, and Peninsular Ranges—the area found within the squeezed Q—enjoys a Mediterranean climate of dry, cool summers and wet, mild winters. These conditions are in marked contrast to the more continental climate of the transmontane region east of the mountains, which experiences hot, dry summers and cold winters with relatively little precipitation. The climatic pattern of the cismontane region is greatly influenced by the clockwise circulation pattern of the North Pacific, which brings cold Arctic waters along the west coast of North America via the California Current.[3]

The importance of these maritime conditions for Native Californians is the creation of one of the most productive and diverse fisheries in North America. The southern flow of surface water stimulates upwelling of deep, cold waters off the coast of California, which brings the riches of oxygen, carbon, and other nutrients to the surface to support dense concentrations of microorganisms of plants (phytoplankton) and animals (zooplankton). The plankton blooms, in turn, support a complex marine food chain that includes thousands of small schooling fishes (sardines and anchovies), which in turn are consumed by larger inshore and pelagic fishes, sea mammals, and seabirds. The upwelling cold water also facilitates the growth of productive kelp forests in the inshore waters, which promotes a diverse range of plant and animal life.

Although our pyrodiversity model tends to focus on terrestrial plants and animals most influenced by fire management, it is critical to emphasize the complementary resource diversity of the sea that was also available to coastal California Indians. More than 750 species of fishes and invertebrates, including various rockfishes (*Sebastes* spp.) and mollusks (Mollusca), thrive in the kelp forests of the California coast. At least 125 species of fishes, most spending some time hunting or hiding in the dense kelp, have been identified along the coastline (Schoenherr 1992:653).

Latitudinal Influences

The circulation of the California Current influences many of the weather patterns that Native Californians experienced throughout the state. Precipitation during the winter months occurs primarily from cold, wet storms originating in the North Pacific that follow this current down along the west coast of North America. These potent rain storms, which turn to snow in higher elevations, can hammer northern California with wet weather from October to April, while more sporadic storms may hit southern California from November to March. The storms track down the coast in a south to southeast direction, with the heaviest precipitation falling in the northern latitudes and decreasing as storms move south and east across the state. This storm pattern produces a general north-south gradient in precipitation across the state.

Topographic relief also exerts a tremendous influence on local rainfall patterns. Storms tend to unload precipitation at higher elevations as they rise over the coastal mountains and then rise again on the western side of the Cascade Range and Sierra Nevada, where water vapor condenses into rain or snow in the colder air. These mountains also create a significant rain shadow along the entire eastern border of California. The Cascade Range and Sierra Nevada tend to block precipitation from entering the Great Basin, while the Transverse and Peninsular ranges impede Pacific coast storms, those that make it that far south, from entering the arid Mojave and Colorado deserts. These same mountains also serve as a barrier to the more harsh continental climatic conditions of the transmontane region, buffering the remainder of California from free-flowing hot, dry air in summer and frigid, dry air in winter.

The north to south movement of Arctic storms also influences latitudinal differences in the development of river systems, themselves closely linked to the watersheds that drain winter storms or later snow melt from higher-altitude mountains. The largest rivers and streams in California are associated with the Klamath Mountains, the North Coast Ranges, the Cascade

Range, and the Sierra Nevada.[4] Not only do these rivers cut diverse riparian zones across mountains and valleys, but they are major avenues for seasonal salmon (*Oncorhynchus* spp.) and Steelhead *(O. mykiss irideus)* migrations that remain integral components of some Native cultures in northern and central California.

Coastal moisture is enhanced along the entire California coastline by seasonal fog, especially during summer months, when the warmer land mass causes the colder marine moisture to condense into low-lying clouds. Fog drip, the condensation of moisture on trees and bushes that drips to the ground, can provide much-needed precipitation to some coastal areas, especially during the drought-prone summer months. Fog drip, depending on the time and place, can bring the equivalent of what is estimated to be an extra 25 cm (10 in.) of rain in a year (Ornduff et al. 2003:55).

The typical movement of storms from north to south in the state, resulting in the gradual decrease of precipitation in southern latitudes, combined with high pressure over southern California in the summer, deflects storms to the north. The upshot of these patterns is that far less precipitation falls in southern California than in the remainder of the state. Furthermore, the rain-shadow effect of the Transverse Ranges and Peninsular Ranges limits most of southern California's precipitation to the coastal strip and western slopes of the coastal mountains.[5]

Incredible Environmental Diversity

California is home to more endemic species of plants and animals than any other equivalent-sized area in North America (Schoenherr 1992:x). The authoritative *Jepson Manual: Higher Plants of California* lists 5,867 species known to occur outside of cultivation in California, of which 3,423 species are considered to be native, and another 1,416 species are classified as endemic, that is, they are found only in habitats within the state (Hickman 1993:1315). Nearly 25 percent of all the known plant species in North America north of Mexico are found in California. These include the world's tallest trees, the coast redwood *(Sequoia sempervirens);* the world's largest trees, the giant sequoia *(Sequoiadendron giganteum)*; the world's oldest trees, the western bristle-
continued

EARLY GLIMPSES OF CALIFORNIA'S UNPARALLELED DIVERSITY

One way to grasp the incredible diversity is to peruse the original accounts of European explorers who set eyes on the area for the first time. The earliest known recorded observations, by sailors on four Spanish voyages and one English voyage during the period from 1542 to 1603, provide a unique perspective on California before European colonization (see Lightfoot and Simmons 1998). Although we must be careful about how we interpret these archival documents, since they were written by educated foreign men who often had political and religious motives framing their observations, they provide an important source for examining California at the dawn of the European invasion.

Voyage of Juan Rodriguez Cabrillo

Observation made south of San Diego Bay in September 1542 (diary of voyage by Juan Rodriguez Cabrillo, Quinn 1979a:454):

> This port is called San Mateo. The land appears to be good; there are large savannahs, and the grass is like that of Spain. The land is high and broken. They saw some herds of animals like cattle, which went in droves of a hundred or more, and which, from their appearance, from their gait, and the long wool, looked like Peruvian sheep. They have small horns a span in length and as thick as the thumb. The tail is broad and round and a palm long.

Voyage of Francis Drake

Observation in the Point Reyes region in June 1579 (the "World Encompassed" account of Drake's California visit, Quinn 1979b:475):

> The inland we found to bee far different from the shoare, a goodly Country, and fruitful soile, stored with many blessings fit for the use of man: infinite was the company of very large and fat Deere, which there wee saw by thousands, as wee supposed, in a heard: besides a multitude of a strange kind of Conies, by farre exceeding them in number.

Voyage of Pedro de Unamuno

Observation near and in Morro Bay in October 1587 (Unamuno letter to the Viceroy of Mexico, Quinn 1979c:402):

continued

There is much thick grass around and near the ship, growing out of more than fifteen fathoms of water. These plants are thick and have great leaves and stems, and are the same which sailors say they have seen a hundred leagues at sea floating like great rafts. It is this grass, which grows along all this coast to beyond Isla de Zedros, in latitude full $28\frac{1}{2}°$. It does not grow in rivers, as some have declared, but along the coast, as just stated. . . . In this port there is an unlimited quantity of fish of different kinds, trees suitable for masts, water, firewood, and abundant shell-fish with all of which a ship in need could supply itself.

Voyage of Sebastian Cermeño

Observation of the Drakes Bay region in November 1595 (abstract of Cermeño's journal, Quinn 1979d:410):

They [the local Coast Miwok] produced a seed the shape of an anise seed, only a little thinner, and having the taste of sesame, of which they make the bread they eat. Their food consists of crabs and wild birds, which are in great abundance near where they live, and many deer, as these have been observed going about. They are beyond comparison the largest that have been seen as will be apparent from the horns which were found, of which the Captain carries a sample.

Voyage of Sebastian Vizcaíno

Observation of the Monterey Bay area in December 1602 and January 1603 (Fray António de la Ascensión's brief report, Quinn 1979e: 420):

The land of this country is very fertile and has good pastures and forests, and fine hunting and fowling. Among the animals there are large, fierce bears, and other animals called elks, from which they make elk-leather jackets, and others of the size of young bulls, shaped and formed like deer, with thick, large horns. There were many Castilian roses here. There are pretty ponds of fresh water. The mountains near this port were covered with snow, and that was on Christmas day. On the beach was a dead whale, and at night some bears came to feed on it. There are many fish here, and a great variety of mollusks among the rocks; among them there were certain barnacles, or large shells, fastened to the lowest part of the rocks.

The Indians hunt for them to extract from them their contents to eat. These shells are very bright, of fine mother-of-pearl. All along this coast, there is a great abundance of sea-wolves or dogs, of the size of a yearling calf. They sleep on the water, and sometimes go ashore to take the sun; and there they place their sentinel in order to be secure from enemies.

There are numerous accounts of the amazing diversity of California's habitats by later explorers and settlers who came to California in the late 1700s and early 1800s (see Anderson 2005:13–23). One of our favorites is the little-known account of Otto von Kotzebue, commander of a Russian naval ship, the *Rurik,* who made one of the earliest observations of the Sacramento River (in November 1824) as part of a small flotilla of 20 *baidarkas* (skin kayaks) made up of Native Alaskans and Russians and a Spanish soldier and pilot.

The many rivers flowing through this fruitful country will be of the greatest use to future settlers. The low ground is exactly adapted to the cultivation of rice; and the higher, from the extraordinary strength of the soil, would yield the finest wheat-harvests. The vine might be cultivated here to great advantage. All along the banks of the river grapes grow wild, in as much profusion as the rankest weeds: the clusters were large; and the grapes, though small, very sweet, and agreeably flavoured. We often ate them in considerable quantities, and sustained no inconvenience from them. The Indians also eat them very voraciously.

The chase furnished us with ample and profitable amusement. An abundance of deer, large and small, are to be met with all over the country, and geese, ducks, and cranes, on the banks of the rivers. There was such a super-fluity of game, that even those among us who had never been sportsmen before, when once they took the gun into their hands, became as eager as the rest. The sailors chased the deer very successfully. . . . In the night we were much disturbed by bears, which pursued the deer quite close to our tents; and by the clear moonlight we plainly saw a stag spring into the river to escape the bear; the latter, however, jumped after him, and both swam down the stream till they were out of sight (Kotzebue 1830:143–144).

cone pine *(Pinus longaeva)*; and some of the smallest and most unique plants known to humankind (Ornduff et al. 2003:xv). There are about 1,000 native species of vertebrate animals (540 birds, 214 mammals, 77 reptiles, 47 amphibians, and 83 freshwater fishes), of which about 65 are endemic to California (Schoenherr 1992:x).

The relationship between California Indians and biological diversity can be examined at a number of different spatial scales. At the macro or regional scale, significant differences in plants, animals, and minerals may be observed relative to topography, latitude, distance from the Pacific Ocean, and geology. Geologists and archaeologists have divided California into broad geomorphic provinces based primarily on topography and geology. As Schoenherr (1992:1) notes, "These geomorphic provinces represent natural units within which the boundaries of landforms are remarkably consistent with those of biological communities." We employ six basic geomorphic provinces to organize the guide to California Indian uses of natural resources later in this book. The provinces include the Northwest Coast, Central Coast, South Coast, Northeast, Great Central Valley and Sierra Nevada, and the Southern Deserts (map 4).[6]

There is also great biological diversity at the micro or intraregional scale. Within each of the broad geomorphic provinces there is considerable local variation in flora, fauna, and soils, depending on local elevation, geology, hydrology, slope facing, soil conditions, and shade. For example, sun-tolerant vegetation fares much better on south-facing slopes than in the wetter, cooler conditions on the northern faces of hills or mountains. The upshot, of course, is that California Indians encountered diverse habitats within their local territories. In walking relatively short distances, they might ford riparian corridors, descend into valleys, walk up ridge slopes, and cross over different soil formations, such as those originating from serpentine rocks that produced unique plant communities.

For more than a century, scholars have attempted to make sense of California's biological diversity by defining various classifications of plants and animals.[7] Depending on whether you are a lumper or splitter, you may define relatively few plant communities or vegetation types, as exemplified in the widely used *California Flora and Supplement* (Munz and Keck 1968). Others demarcate many hundreds of vegetation types in California,

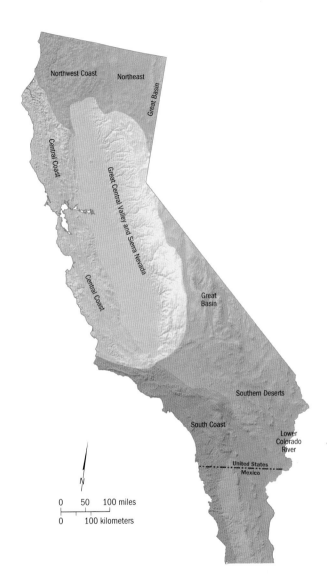

Map 4. Geomorphic provinces of California.

recognizing the unique characteristics of rare plants and their groupings, or differentiating additional riparian, chaparral, and alpine types not distinguished in simpler classificatory systems (see Ornduff et al. 2003:114). In this book we adopt the nomenclature of the companion California Natural History Guide book, *Introduction to California Plant Life,* which lists 23 basic vegetation types. We refer you to this book for a full description of these vegetation types (Ornduff et al. 2003:115–118).

Change Is Inevitable

A significant challenge to hunter-gatherers was that the incredible environmental diversity of California did not exist in a steady-state harmony; rather it was constantly in motion. Over thousands of years of antiquity, Native people experienced not only periods of global warming and cooling as described for the Late Pleistocene and Holocene, but also shorter-term permutations involving El Niños and other related climatic events that contributed to droughts and devastating storms, as well as earthquakes, tsunamis, and volcanic eruptions. Pyrodiversity economies took shape as people continually grappled with ways to address changing climatic conditions, which might include declines in marine and/or terrestrial resource productivity and major environmental catastrophes.

El Niño events take place when the circulation pattern of the equatorial Pacific Ocean reverses itself; the eastern trade winds stop blowing, and ocean currents begin to pump warm ocean waters into the East Pacific, where they accumulate off the coast of North and South America. The consequence of this reversal is an increase in sea surface temperature along the California coast, a reduction in the upwelling of cold, nutrient-rich waters, and often, but not always, the onset of wet, tropical storms and heavy seas (Caviedes 2001:7–14, 79–82). Jones (2003:20) summarizes recent environmental data that show a correlation between El Niño events and rainfall in the South Coast and Southern Deserts provinces, noting that some of these years may be exceptionally wet. He shows that in the South Coast Ranges a strong correlation also holds for historic records documenting higher than normal precipitation and El Niño events, as well as between rainfall and high sea surface temperature.

The warming of sea surface temperature during El Niño

events increases the salinity of upper ocean waters, while at the same time reducing carbon and oxygen levels. These altered water conditions, combined with the cessation of coastal upwelling, decimate the populations of different forms of plankton. This, in turn, can devastate an entire marine food chain, ultimately dependent on plankton, resulting in massive die-offs of fishes, seabirds, and sea mammals. The warmer water temperature can also be detrimental to the growth and health of the kelp forests.[8] Consequently, local cold-water species typically decrease in number during El Niño episodes, and the survivors may shift their territorial ranges to cooler, northern waters. Interestingly, warm-water species from southern latitudes will often appear in more northern waters in unusual numbers.[9]

Although the full consequences of El Niño events for coastal hunter-gatherers probably varied from place to place, depending on the degree of sea surface temperature warming and climatic oscillations, these short-term periods do appear to reduce local marine productivity. As Jones (2003:20) notes, however, reductions in marine productivity may be offset, to some extent, by increased productivity of terrestrial resources that results from higher than normal precipitation.

El Niño events are interspersed with periods, known as La Niña, when colder water flows southward from the North Pacific. This colder water activates the upwelling of deep, nutrient-rich waters along the California coast. These interludes of cold ocean waters provide nourishment to the microscopic plankton and are typically a boon to local fisheries. Intervals of cooler sea surface temperature tend to generate less evaporation of Pacific Ocean waters. This can lead to winter drought conditions in California, and colder winters in continental North America (Caviedes 2001:146–147). The Kennetts' (Kennett 2005:60–71; Kennett and Kennett 2000:383–385) paleoclimatic reconstruction, based on sea cores and oxygen isotopic analysis of plankton species, indicates distinct cycles of warming and cooling patterns of sea surface temperature for the South Coast Province during the Late Holocene. They show that cooler water temperatures tend to be associated with regional decreases in precipitation, based on tree-ring sequences.

El Niño and La Niña events take place in a cyclical fashion along the California coastline, probably related, in some way, to different cycles of solar radiation over time; however, the frequency, timing, and duration of these events are irregular and not yet predictable. Archival records of past events, as well as pertinent paleoclimatic and archaeological data, suggest that El Niños may increase in number and intensity during times of global warming, such as during the Medieval Climatic Anomaly (Caviedes 2001:217–225).

Winter drought conditions in California may be associated with La Niña episodes during relatively cold periods, such as the Little Ice Age. But drought conditions also occur periodically during times of global warming. For example, during the Medieval Climatic Anomaly, much of the American Southwest, the Great Basin, and California experienced intervals of significant drought. In lake level fluctuations documented and dated in the Sierra Nevada, significantly dry conditions are recorded from AD 892 to 1112 and AD 1209 to 1350. Recent paleoclimatic reconstructions of pollen and tree-ring records from the South Coast Province, as well as from other regions of California, support the basic timing of this broadscale drought cycle during the Medieval Climatic Anomaly.[10] We emphasize here that understanding the temporal sequence of major droughts is important in the study of Indian fire managers, since prolonged droughts have significant implications on local fire regimes, as is discussed later.

In addition to periodic and unanticipated periods of droughts and flooding, California Indians have also had to contend with many other kinds of natural hazards, including earthquakes, tsunamis, and volcanism. Undoubtedly, Native communities repeatedly experienced earthquakes, given the many fault systems that permeate the coastal provinces and radiate into the southern Sierra Nevada and the Southern Deserts Province. Much research is now directed at understanding the timing and frequency of large-magnitude earthquakes along different fault lines, and in reconstructing the fault slip rates. These paleoseismic investigations, based on early European observations (such as Franciscan mission records), the excavation of earthquake trenches, and even deep drill holes, demonstrate a long record of major seismic movements along most of California's fault zones.[11] We participated in a paleoseismic study of traces of the San Andreas Fault in the Fort Ross State Historic Park in northern California that incorporated both geological trenching of the fault zone and archaeological investigations of an ancient Kashaya Pomo site.[12]

Fault zones often produce unique geological features and hydrological conditions (sag ponds, scarps, shutter ridges, linear estuaries, etc.), which enhance biological diversity within a region, attracting hunter-gatherers to the multitude of plants and animals residing near these dynamic terrains (Noller and Lightfoot 1997:120). But as anyone living near a major fault zone can tell you, there is a definite downside to living in earthquake country. Large-magnitude earthquakes can destroy Native villages, create destructive landslides, alter drainages, and even contribute to coastal subsidence.

Tsunamis are another unpredictable natural disaster that could wreak havoc on coastal California Indian communities. Typically produced by earthquakes from offshore subsidence, tsunamis can generate massive waves that destroy life and property along low-lying coastal benches and bays.[13] More than 85 percent of the world's tsunamis originate in the Pacific Ocean. California receives its fair share of wave surges from earthquakes that originate off the coast, as well as from subduction-zone earthquakes taking place in Japan, the Aleutian Islands, and coastal Alaska. For example, the Alaskan earthquake of 1964 sent a 6 m (20 ft) high wave into northern California, which caused extensive property damage and killed 11 people (Geist and Rosenthal 2005; Geist et al. 2006). Although California archaeologists have yet to research fully the timing and effects of past tsunamis on Native sites, there is no doubt that occasional wave surges created major problems for coastal California Indians.[14]

Volcanism is another volatile variable that Native people in the northern part of the state have had to cope with for many thousands of years. The recent eruption of Mount St. Helens in Washington, and the activity of Mount Shasta and Mount Lassen within the last two centuries, highlights the dynamic nature of the Cascade Range. As Mount St. Helens demonstrated, volcanic explosions may prove lethal to nearby plant and animal communities, as well as to people caught in the cross fire. But volcanoes and lava flows have implications that extend far beyond the immediate eruption zone. Major volcanic outbursts inject tons of ash, gas, and water vapor into the upper atmosphere, which can absorb incoming solar radiation and affect regional climatic conditions for months or even years afterward (Caviedes 2001: 256–257). In addition, although ash falls may initially be destructive to floral and faunal communities for many kilometers from the eruption, over time they may serve as a natural fertilizer that enhances the growth of certain types of vegetation and increases the biodiversity of the region.

Human Impacts to the Environment

Human interactions with the environment can also create significant changes to local habitats over time, influencing the number, types, and spatial distribution of both plants and animals. Although most discussions of anthropogenic environmental transformations focus on the aftermath of European colonization, it is important to stress that indigenous hunter-gatherers could also generate significant impacts to the environment, a point that is taken up in the next chapter. Suffice it to say here that with the coming of Europeans and other foreigners, a clear trend has taken place in the Golden State—the unrelenting loss of indigenous biodiversity. Many endemic plants and animals have rapidly disappeared as introduced species have aggressively expanded into a landscape transformed by ranching, logging, agriculture, mining, and urbanism.

It is not clear when the first exotic species entered California from Europe, Asia, and Africa. Sailors from the earliest period of European exploration (1542 to 1603) may have unwittingly unleashed some foreign plants into the coastal environments.[15] We have good evidence, however, for intrusive species moving into California prior to the construction of the first Franciscan mission at San Diego in 1769, probably migrating northward from the Jesuit missions in Baja California (Mensing and Byrne 1998). Distinctive pollen grains from a Mediterranean annual, red-stem filaree *(Erodium cicutarium),* have been recovered in sediment cores from the Santa Barbara Basin. The sediments containing the alien pollen, dating between 1755 and 1760, were recovered more than 300 km (186 mi) north of the border between Alta and Baja California.

With the founding of early European colonies,[16] a legion of foreign plants and animals began colonizing the shoreline of California, spreading rapidly into the coastal mountains and interior valleys. Based on the recovery and analysis of botanical remains in sediments from excavation units and adobe bricks from early mission structures, we know that a rapid onslaught of pugnacious weeds took place in coastal California, including prickly sow thistle *(Sonchus asper),* curly dock or yellow dock *(Rumex crispus),* and red-stem filaree. Archaeological research shows that later missions were built in landscapes probably teeming with these weeds, as well as cheeseweed *(Malva parviflora),* common sow thistle *(Sonchus oleraceus),* California burclover *(Medicago polymorpha),* catchfly *(Silene gallica),* and bull mallow *(Malva nicaeensis).*[17]

The Spanish, Russian, and Mexican colonies instituted economic strategies involving the large-scale production of foreign food crops. They attempted to grow wheat and barley crops—along with corn, beans, squash, peas, cabbage, watermelons, potatoes, beets, lettuce, and so on depending on local conditions and preferences—to develop fruit orchards and vineyards, and to graze thousands of head of free-range cattle, as well as sheep, goats, horses, mules, and pigs. The Russians and their Native Alaskan hunters implemented the commercial harvesting of sea mammals along the California coast, especially Sea Otters *(Enhydra lutris),* along with Steller Sea Lions *(Eumetopias jubatus),* California Sea Lions *(Zalophus californianus),* and Harbor Seals *(Phoca vitulina).* They also exploited seabird rookeries on the Farallon Islands for eggs, feathers, and meat, and harvested the northern coastal forest in the hinterland near Fort Ross for redwood, oak, and other woods to construct stockade walls, buildings, furniture, and ships (see Lightfoot 2005).

By the late 1700s and early 1800s, radical changes were under way in the environments of the South Coast Province and Coast Ranges, and even in the Great Central Valley, which had significant implications for California Indians. The rapid spread of Old World weeds, the free-range grazing of livestock that consumed and trampled native grasses, the construction of irrigation systems that altered regional hydrology and watersheds, the local extermination of sea lion and Sea Otter populations, and logging activities in local forests all strikingly altered the composition of local plant and animal communities.[18] While a number of native species, such as spike bentgrass *(Agrostis exarata),* sedges (*Carex* spp.), goosefoots and pigweeds (*Chenopodium* spp.), rushes (*Juncus* spp.), and forget-me-nots (*Cryptantha* spp.) are identified in the adobe bricks from early Spanish missions, these species disappeared in the period immediately postdating the missions. A wave of new intruders are now present, including wild oat *(Avena fatua),* California burclover, and catchfly (Allen 1998:43).

The destruction of indigenous habitats had a deleterious effect on the ability of local hunter-gatherers to pursue traditional subsistence practices and to harvest many of their familiar species used for food, medicine, and raw materials (see Keter 1995:31–32 for a case example). Furthermore, beginning with the Spanish, foreign colonists placed tight restrictions on Indian management practices involving prescribed burns. At the same time that indigenous habitats withered under the onslaught of intrusive people and their foreign plants and animals, Native Californians also faced devastating population losses due to diseases and violence. Some anthropologists believe that it was this combination of indigenous habitat loss, frightening mortality rates, and the decimation of elders and other leaders who maintained the social history of local communities that left many Indians with little choice but to leave their dying villages to join the Franciscan missions and other European settlements, or disappear into the backcountry to join other Native groups.[19]

The commencement of the Gold Rush in 1848 and the occupation of California by the United States ushered in a new period of habitat destruction and reduction of indigenous biodiversity that continues to this day. Significant transformations to the environment were brought about by draining the Great Central Valley; mechanized agriculture; ranching; commercial exploitation of mammals, ducks, and geese for pelts, skins, and feathers; factory fishing; extermination of pests (grizzly bears); placer and hydraulic mining; the damming of rivers as part of water control projects; massive timber harvests; and urban developments. By the early 1900s, the federal government implemented a policy of fire suppression that not only stopped Native prescribed burning, but drastically altered natural fire regimes, leading to changes in the composition and structure of California forestlands. As these points are discussed in detail elsewhere (Anderson 2005:82–121; Preston 1997), we need not repeat them here. Suffice it to say that transmutations of the environment of the California Indians have been profound. More than a thousand foreign plant species have been introduced to California landscapes, and at least 30 native species have become extinct in the last century. Thirty-three percent of the native plants in contemporary California are listed as rare and endangered species by the California Native Plant Society. It is estimated that up to 95 percent of all vernal pools and tidal salt marshes have disappeared;

99 percent of all native grasslands have vanished (Ornduff et al. 2003:6, 284–286).

Despite massive changes in the quantity, spatial distribution, and overall availability of many plants and animals traditionally exploited, California Indians have maintained strong connections to the natural world over the last 250 years. Native Californians are highly adaptive and have modified cultural practices and economic strategies to take advantage of changing conditions. Specific measures are now employed to enhance the growth and health of some traditional resources that may be endangered or locally scarce. California Indians have opportunistically included selected foreign plants and animals into their gathering practices. They also employ new kinds of technologies to harvest wild plants and animals, providing for more efficient exploitation and conservation practices. A cornerstone of Native California societies for many hundreds of years has been their uncanny ability to respond positively to changing circumstances with new ideas, technical innovations, and cultural practices, while still maintaining many of their core values and beliefs.

Conclusion

California is truly blessed with biological diversity at scales ranging from broad geomorphic provinces to small slivers of land and sea. Depending on the intersection of three key variables—topographic relief (elevation), distance from the ocean, and latitude—you may find yourself confronting distinctive microclimates and habitats over relatively short distances. This multifaceted landscape has had significant implications for hunter-gatherers. By walking or canoeing for short stretches across coastlines, valleys, riparian corridors, hills, and mountain slopes, people experienced different environmental conditions and exploited varied mineral resources, plant communities, and animal species. It is with this backdrop of resource heterogeneity that we can fully understand how California Indians developed their pyrodiversity economies. Fire regimes, both natural and cultural, can play a critical role in maintaining and enhancing this kind of local diversity, thereby allowing small communities the opportunity to fulfill many of their subsistence and raw material needs within relatively limited territories. It is within the great ring of mountains and coastal tail—the squeezed Q of California's marked topographic landscape—that we see the most elaborate forms of pyrodiversity practices, a point taken up later in the book.

An uncritical emphasis on California's environmental richness can often send the wrong message, however. California hunter-gatherers are often portrayed as living the good life in a land of plenty—with seeds, fruits, and nuts dropping from heavily laden plants, fishes practically jumping out of the water into their arms, and fat lethargic game ready for the taking. But in reality, the productivity of specific species of plants and animals can vary tremendously from season to season and year to year. Some of this variation is seasonal and relatively predictable given the Golden State's Mediterranean climate of cool, wet winters and warm, dry summers. But other kinds of changes are less predictable, with significant alterations in temperature and precipitation patterns within multiyear cycles. El Niño and La Niña events—often associated with periods of warming and cooling seawater—droughts, and floods can greatly influence resource productivity in local regions, as can other kinds of natural hazards, such as earthquakes, volcanoes, and tsunamis. People can also have significant impacts on environmental diversity, as witnessed by the last 250 years of foreign invasions and landscape modifications. The upshot is that resource availability in local regions varied from year to year, whether it was in the magnitude of salmon runs and acorn crops, in the number of coastal fishes, birds, and sea mammals, or in the accessibility of other important economic resources.

In sum, although California Indians lived in a land of tremendous resource diversity, the availability of foods, medicines, and raw materials for producing baskets and other kinds of material culture must have varied greatly, depending upon the time of the year, whether the region was experiencing cycles of floods or droughts, warm or cool seawater temperatures, or the occurrence of unanticipated natural or human-induced catastrophes. In some times and places, favorite or preferred food resources may have been scarce or not available, resulting in periodic episodes of resource stress for local Indian communities. Consequently, as we see later in this book, Native Californians experimented with pyrodiversity practices in an attempt to diversify plant and animal resources and to minimize the risks of serious food shortages through storage, trade, and mass harvests when resources were plentiful.

The Uniqueness of California

CALIFORNIA ANTHROPOLOGY CUT ITS TEETH on trying to make sense of an unparalleled situation among North American Indian societies. At the time of initial European contact and settlement, California was a world like no other. It not only supported one of the highest population densities north of Mexico, but its people exhibited a truly amazing degree of linguistic and cultural diversity. Hundreds of small polities filled the landscape. The thick smoke from the many households made a strong impression on early European explorers, as did the cadre of chiefs, curing doctors, religious specialists, craft experts, and skilled hunters and gatherers, who often greeted the intruders as they traveled from one polity to another. Since it was not uncommon for neighboring groups to speak different dialects or even languages, community leaders tended to be accomplished orators who could communicate in multiple languages. They played crucial ambassadorial roles in meeting visitors, such as Spanish and Russian exploration parties, and sponsored feasts, mortuary observances, dances, and other communal gatherings. Yet to the surprise of some foreigners, this land of diverse Indian communities sustained itself almost entirely from the plants and meats of the land and sea, without recourse to agriculture.

A sense of the pulsing vitality of Native California at the time of European contact can be appreciated by considering the geography of local communities. Populations of several hundred people might live in one or two principal villages and nearby hamlets, from which they claimed an outlying territory where they maintained use rights to nut and seed crops, game, tubers and roots, valued minerals, basketry materials, and other critical resources. In some places, these polities appear to have been jammed together almost check to jowl; people could reach the outer edges of commonly used tracts after walking only a day or two beyond their principal villages. Thus, the picture that emerges is a dense population that was not aggregated into major cities or towns, but rather dispersed into a plethora of villages and small hamlets packed across a landscape networked together, creating a complex social fabric.

This great jumble of hunter-gatherer humanity in California tends to defy standard anthropological concepts and models that have been applied to Indian people in other areas of the Americas. The classic evolutionary framework of nomadic bands, tribes, chiefdoms, and states does not work here. So what constructs have been devised to better understand the uniqueness that is Native California? This query, if asked among anthropologists today, will no doubt spark some debate and consternation. You can experience this firsthand by attending the annual meeting of the Society for California Archaeology. Just find the nearest bar, buy a few rounds for those bleary-eyed individuals who have not yet made the paper sessions, and ask them the question. You will get many answers, as well as requests for another round of libations to help with the thought process.

Some will no doubt highlight the important work of pioneering ethnographers, linguists, and archaeologists who worked in California in the late nineteenth century. Other anthropologists will point to the major milestone that was crossed when the state founded its inaugural anthropology department at the University of California at Berkeley. With the hiring of Alfred L. Kroeber as instructor in 1901, the department launched the first program dedicated to the systematic study of California Indian cultures. The basic foundation of California anthropology was laid at this time. Finally, after a couple of rounds of Bloody Marys, your informants will no doubt perk up enough to discuss the important contributions of later ethnographers, archaeologists, and Native scholars over the last four decades. California anthropology today is really a product of a Kroeberian foundation that has been modified in recent years by revisionist thinking from a varied assortment of scholars.

Kroeberian Anthropology

Until his retirement from the University of California at Berkeley in 1946, Kroeber directed a field program that amassed a tremendous database on California Indians.[1] It would employ a cadre of faculty members, museum scientists, and graduate students over the next three to four decades. Other scholars, such as C. Hart Merriam and John P. Harrington, also made significant contributions to our understanding of Native California at this time. As a consequence of this fieldwork and subsequent syntheses of information, these pioneering anthropologists created a tripartite conceptual scheme for classifying Indian people by language, culture area, and polity (for a more detailed discussion, see Lightfoot 2005:30–48).

Language

In recognizing California as one of the most diverse linguistic landscapes in the world, a primary objective of early anthropologists and linguists was to classify Native speakers into major language groupings or ethnolinguistic units. These linguistic designations provided a convenient way to classify California Indians into a four-level system of stock, family, language, and dialect. Stocks comprised multiple families, within which were recognized related languages and dialects. For example, the Hokan stock included the Pomoan family, which was further divided into seven distinct languages (Northeastern, Eastern, Northern, Southeastern, Central, Southern, and Southwestern or Kashaya). Today, seven major groupings are recognized for California Indian languages (Hokan, Penutian, Algic, Na-Dené [Athabascan], Uto-Aztecan, Utian, and Yukian), although there is considerable debate about whether some should be classified as stocks, phylums, superfamilies, or families.[2]

This linguistic classificatory system was imposed upon Native California by early scholars to make sense of the region's tremendous linguistic diversity.[3] The ethnolinguistic units defined by anthropologists would probably have had little meaning to people living in traditional Native Californian societies. Although it has become commonplace today to refer to linguistic families or languages as Californian "tribes,"[4] this was never Kroeber's intent. In other regions of North America, a tribe is defined as a social group with a distinct territory, unifying social organization, and language, which is characterized by cultural homogeneity and an integrating political leadership structure (e.g., Winick 1956:546). Ethnolinguistic units, be they stocks, families, or languages, rarely functioned as autonomous sociopolitical entities in traditional Native California. Rather they, in turn, were divided into a number of smaller, independent polities.[5] As William Simmons points out, "To speak of the Pomo 'tribe,' therefore, is really to speak of a large family of languages, not of an actual social group with a leadership structure" (see also Kunkel 1974; Simmons 1997:56).

Culture Area

Another way that Kroeber and colleagues made sense of California Indian diversity was to place the ethnolinguistic units (language families and individual languages) into broader groupings known as culture areas or culture provinces. These "geographical units of cultures" were defined by the correlation of diagnostic cultural traits with natural physiographic regions. From the outset of their ethnographic fieldwork, anthropologists discovered that neighboring people who spoke different languages often shared many similar cultural practices, technologies, and material objects. The classic case identified by Kroeber (1925:5) was how the Yurok (Algic stock/family) "shared this civilization in identical form" to the Karuk (Hokan stock) and Hupa (Na-Dené stock/family). As he remarked when comparing the Karuk and Yurok, "The two peoples are indistinguishable in appearance and customs, except for certain minutiae; but they differ totally in speech" (Kroeber 1925:98). On the other hand, it was recognized that people who spoke related languages, but who lived in disparate places within the state, might diverge considerably in their subsistence patterns, ceremonies, social organization, and material culture.[6]

In recognizing the important roles that social interactions and environment played in the development of cultures, early anthropologists grouped similar-looking societies from specific regions of the state into the same culture areas. Kroeber did not advocate a deterministic relationship between environment and culture, but he did recognize that distinctive environmental conditions helped shape specific cultures.[7] A wide range of diagnostic cultural traits was used to define people into specific culture areas, including material objects (methods of making baskets, basket types, raw materials used in baskets), architectural forms (house types, construction methods), clothing, treatment of the hair, mortuary observances, social organization, ceremonies, and so forth. Early anthropologists believed that significant physiographic features within each culture area probably helped to shape the distinctive cultural traits. For example, the many streams of northwestern California that nurtured dense runs of salmons were thought to have been a significant influence on the development of these cultures.[8]

The first two decades of the ethnographic program resulted in the definition of three to five culture areas in California.[9] By the mid-1930s the number of culture areas increased to six, including the Northwest, Northeast, Central, Southern, Great Basin, and Colorado River.[10] Since the culture areas were based, in part, on physiographic features, it is not surprising to see considerable overlap between these regions and the geomorphic provinces defined for California. For example, in employing geomorphic provinces to organize the resource guide section of this book, the arrangement differs from the classic schema of culture areas only in that the Central California culture area is divided into two (the Central Coast and the Great Central Valley and Sierra Nevada provinces), and the Mojave and Colorado deserts are kept together as a unit (Southern Deserts Province), as opposed to dividing them into the Southern California, Colorado River, and Great Basin culture areas.

Polity

A third way of making sense of California Indians was to define their basic political organizations across the landscape. Kroeber (1925:830) emphasized that no true tribes, as defined elsewhere in North America, are found in California.[11] Instead two basic types of political organizations were recognized—the enigmatic local groupings of the Northwest culture area and the tribelet organization for the remainder of the state. Kroeber viewed Native populations in the Northwest as examples of extreme "political anarchy," having no well-defined village or broader societal political organization.[12] Outside the Northwest culture area, Kroeber recognized the tribelet as the basic political organization of Native California.[13] It was the largest political unit that was autonomous or self-governing.

Each tribelet consisted of a village community composed of a principal village, which often served as the sociopolitical center for several outlying hamlets (fig. 14). Kroeber noted that the tribelet was the largest political entity in which community leaders had recognized authority, their primary duties relegated to presiding over feasts and ceremonies, settling quarrels, hosting visitors, and addressing assemblies (Kroeber 1966:94–95).[14] As the largest land-owning entity, the size of individual tribelets varied across the state. Yet early anthropologists emphasized their diminutive scale, with populations ranging from 100 to 500 people and their territories often measuring less than several hundred square kilometers in size.[15] Kroeber estimated that probably about 500 to 600 tribelets were distributed across

Figure 14. Indian village on the banks of the Feather River, drawn by Fritz Wikersheim between 1845 and 1851. It probably served as one of the principal villages in a tribelet organization. Note the clothes drying on the exterior of the houses and the associated storage facilities.

Native California outside of the Northwest and Colorado River culture areas.

Recent Advances in California Anthropology

Significant changes have been unfolding in the field of California anthropology over the last four decades. New generations of archaeologists and ethnographers, working closely with Native people and employing participant observation methods (along with critical analyses of earlier ethnohistorical and ethnographical observations), are refashioning our understanding of past and present Indian cultures. Although the many contributions of Kroeber's ethnographic program are acknowledged and greatly appreciated, they have raised concerns about some of the interpretations that resulted from the early fieldwork.

The primary purpose of Kroeber's ethnographic program was to reconstruct Native California as it would have looked at the dawn of European contact and settlement (see Simmons 1997: 51). Unlike ethnographic research in other areas of the world, the Berkeley program did not incorporate much participant observation of extant Indian settlements; in other words, the researchers made few observations of the daily lives of people in living communities. Rather, anthropologists initiated a "memory culture" methodology that involved interviews with a few tribal elders about Indian life in their childhood, and in the past generations of their parents, grandparents, and other more distant relatives.[16] The goal of the memory culture methodology was to push back recollections of traditional Indian cultures prior to major disruptions caused by European and American colonialism (see Lightfoot 2005:32–33).

It must be stressed that this was a peculiar kind of anthropology. The memory culture methodology was predicated on the view that Native cultures tended to be static and undynamic. Accordingly, this perspective allowed ethnographers to reconstruct the essence of prehistoric Indian worlds prior to European colonization by using the memories of tribal elders. But it assumed that little culture change had taken place. Unfortunately, this methodology underestimated the magnitude of cultural transformations that took place among Indian cultures during the early years of European exploration and settlement (see Lightfoot 2005:46–47). There was also a tendency to conflate or collapse ethnographic observations into a single monolithic account, a problem that makes using this data difficult in research that considers long-term temporal, or diachronic, changes.[17]

As any member of the Society for California Archaeology can tell you after a drink or two, the pioneering work of Kroeber and others represented a significant watershed in our understanding of the languages, lifeways, and material culture of California Indian groups across the state. But scholars today recognize that this information must be employed in a judicious and discriminating manner. Some constraints underpin its use for evaluating particular kinds of research problems because of how the ethnographic observations were collected and the theoretical models that were employed. Critical rethinking in recent years has led to the exploration of new ideas concerning Native sociopolitical organizations, the management of the regional landscape, and evidence of resource stress and overhunting that may have stemmed from environmental fluctuations and population growth. Much of this recent work focuses on the elaboration of our understanding of complex hunter-gatherer societies in California.

Revisiting Native Polities

Tribelet Organizations

In a series of influential books and papers first published in the 1970s, Lowell Bean and others argued that Kroeber and his colleagues had underestimated the complexity of California Indian sociopolitical organizations by not fully recognizing the existence of powerful hereditary elites who managed local groups by controlling ceremonies, sponsoring feasts, supporting craft specialists and retainers, and maintaining regional exchange networks (see chapters in Bean and Blackburn 1976; Bean and King 1974). This revisionist perspective would prove to be on the cutting edge in advancing new ideas about complex hunter-gatherers in the anthropological literature. The results of more recent ethnographic and archaeological investigations, as well as critical rereadings of earlier ethnographic studies and ethnohistoric observations, suggest that members of local polities or tribelets may have been born into discrete hierarchical classes. It has been argued that some groups were divided into a powerful elite class, whose members were treated very differently from those of the commoner class of people, who in turn were treated differently from captives or slaves. The elite class included political leaders and their family members, who typically managed the production, distribution, and exchange of nonlocal, prestige goods and shell bead wealth, as well as overseeing relationships with elites from other polities. Religious leaders (shamans), political and religious retainers, and economic specialists, such as basket makers, traders, and clam-shell disk bead producers, were also accorded special status within Indian polities, the latter class of people sometimes organized into exclusive craft guilds.

The revisionists believed that in productive environments the populations of tribelets under the administration of powerful leaders could total more than a thousand people. They also argued that tribelet polities could be integrated, at least for short periods, into larger political organizations, such as confederacies and tribelet alliances. Archaeological investigations of cemeteries and regional exchange systems were used to support the new interpretations about tribelet organizations.[18] Moreover, they argued that the spatial extent of tribelet territories could range between 130 and 15,600 km^2 (50 and 6,000 mi^2).

Our perspective is that the size of tribelet territories should have been large enough to provide enough habitat diversity to buffer the vagaries of environmental perturbations during most years (Keeley 2002:306), but small enough to remain manageable from a few village locations that may have been moved once or twice a year.[19] The size and shape of tribelet areas varied greatly across Native California, depending upon local habitat diversity and the nature of the fire management programs. Tribelet areas may have coincided with particular landscape features, such as ridgetops, riparrian corridors, and basalt flows, which may have served as consistent barriers or boundaries for delimiting burn parcels ignited by lightning or by fire managers (map 5). For example, Wills (2006:315) notes how the Great Central Valley is split into two by the Sacramento and San Joaquin waterways and that the east side is partitioned into a number of smaller areas by streams that may have served as effective barriers to low-intensity fires. During drought conditions, however, these same riparian communities may have contributed to the extensive spread of north-south high-severity fires.

House Societies

The 1970s also witnessed the generation of a new model for understanding the sociopolitical organization of complex hunter-gatherers and horticultural societies. Referred to as "house societies," Claude Lévi-Strauss featured the Yurok-speaking people of northwestern California as a crucial case study for his new model.[20] Where Kroeber viewed the Yurok as lacking any kind of broader political organization, Lévi-Strauss argued that they were organized into named houses, corporate bodies that maintained house structures, estates, heirlooms, and other material resources in common. The main points to stress here is that Yurok house groups appear to have had corporate control over a multitude of material resources and that the recruitment of members to specific house units was flexible. Recruitment to specific houses could follow either patrilineal (father's) or matrilineal (mother's) family ties, and distant kin relations and nonkin were typically integrated into these corporate bodies as well.[21] Although some productive harvesting areas may have been owned by individuals, most of the good nut-producing groves and hunting and fishing grounds in Yurok country tended to be controlled by specific houses as part of their corporate estate.[22]

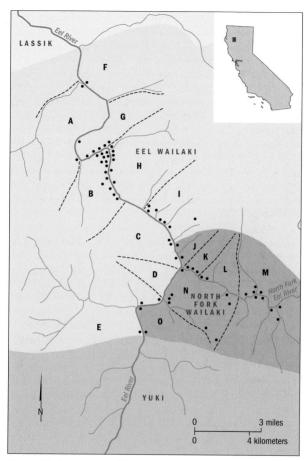

Map 5. Tribelet territories of the Wailaki from northern California. Note how the tribelet boundaries follow drainages. (From Heizer and Elsasser 1980:6.)

Managing the Landscape

Another criticism leveled at the early ethnographic program concerned the common perception that Native Californians were simple hunter-gatherers who passively collected food from a wild, unmodified landscape. In introducing Henry Lewis's (1973, reprinted in 1993) seminal study of Indian burning as a management tool in California, Bean and Lawton (1976) synthesized available information that supported an interpretation of California Indians as nurturing land managers who constructed anthropogenic landscapes through controlled burns, tillage, pruning, seed broadcasting, irrigation, and weeding (see also Shipek 1977). Viewed as an integral component of complex hunter-gatherer societies, they argued that these management strategies increased the productivity of food and raw materials within tribelet territories, providing the necessary surplus to support a burgeoning elite class of polity leaders, retainers, ceremonial professionals, and craft specialists. A significant implication of Bean and Lawton's argument concerns the scale and intent of indigenous management practices—that the modification of the broader landscape by Indian groups increased the productivity and diversity of food and nonfood resources.

Bean and Lawton noted that while acorns and salmon were certainly significant staples for many Native Californians, earlier ethnographic research probably overemphasized their importance at the expense of other resources, such as grass seeds. This highlights one of the problems with the old memory culture methodology—by not taking into account the full effects of colonialism on California Indian populations, there is a strong possibility that the ethnographic studies of the early twentieth century may have overrepresented the use of acorns, deer, and salmon because these resources remained dietary staples well into the historic period (Jacknis 2004:12–13, 113). In fact, at public Indian functions today, such as Pow Wows and Big Times, these resources remain important symbols of Indian identities, especially for people from northern and central California. In contrast, other resources such as seeds and tubers may have been underrepresented in the early ethnographic literature because of economic and social transformations resulting from European and American colonization (Jacknis 2004:12–13). This is particularly apropos for pyrodiversity practices that ceased when widespread prohibitions against prescribed burning were implemented in the early 1900s, as discussed in the next chapter. Since it appears that systematic burning played integral roles in the exploitation of seed and tuber crops, the gathering of these foods may have been greatly curtailed by the time that most early anthropologists were in the field.[23]

In considering explanations for why most California Indians did not adopt agriculture, Bean and Lawton (1976) stressed that the landscape management techniques employed by California Indians represented a kind of protoagriculture (or quasi- or semiagriculture) that was as productive as many indigenous agrarian economies found in other regions of North America. They dismissed earlier ideas about the lack of ingenuity or laziness of Native Californians. They also pointed out weaknesses in Carl Sauer's argument that the winter rain regime of cismontane California prevented the movement of corn, beans, and squash from the American Southwest much beyond the Colorado River and the eastern edge of the Southern Deserts Province. Instead, they argued that the ability of California Indians to enhance the diversity of their already abundant resource base through various protoagricultural methods "made it unnecessary to adapt an agricultural mode, except in some of the marginally productive desert areas" (Bean and Lawton 1976:47).

Our understanding of landscape management practices has been greatly augmented by recent ethnographic fieldwork among basket weavers and other Indian people and through the reanalyses of earlier ethnographic and ethnohistoric observations.[24] These studies provide detailed descriptions of the various methods employed by hunter-gatherers to create anthropogenic habitats by burning, pruning, removing debris, transplanting productive species, coppicing, harrowing, sowing, weeding, digging, and irrigation. Three major points can be gleaned from this most recent and ongoing body of work.

First, indigenous management practices, in enhancing the growth and diversity of various suites of habitats across the landscape, contributed to the production of rich crops of nuts, seeds, grains, greens, fruits, bulbs, corms, rhizomes, taproots, and tubers. Intentional burning of habitats to increase the density and diversity of plant resources also enhanced the number of deer, rabbits, quails, and other economically important animal species who fed off the new vegetation growth.

Second, some scholars claim that several of the signature plant types we know and love in California, such as the coastal prairies, valley oak savannas, open montane forests, and montane meadows, were created and maintained largely through Indian intervention over many hundreds or thousands of years (see Anderson 2005:165–185). The termination of indigenous management practices, because of demographic decline, the

Figure 15. Gathering tule (*Schoenoplectus* spp.) at Clear Lake, 1955–1960; Pomo.

removal of Indian groups to reservations, government policies prohibiting prescribed burning, or by restricting Indian access to private and public lands, typically resulted in the breakdown of these vegetation types as other, less-desirable plants colonized habitat areas. For example, the cessation of regular burning in some grassland environments has been shown to result in the reintroduction of shrubs and trees that would eventually transform these habitats into shrublands or woodlands (Anderson 2005; Keeley 2002:312–313).

Third, ethnographers today emphasize that we cannot understand how Indian people harvest resources without fully recognizing the spiritual and conservation ethics that underpin the exploitation of plant and animal species. Prayers, cultural rules, taboos, and spiritual beliefs are adhered to when gathering plant foods and collecting materials for baskets. These cultural practices assure that resource patches will be regenerated from one year to the next by gathering only a portion of the available seed, nut, and fruit crop or basketry raw material, by wasting nothing during the harvesting process, and by observing specific prohibitions about the collection of resources during certain times of the year or month (fig. 15).[25] It is not clear how long these cultural rules and taboos have been in place among local groups.

The temporal dimension of these conservation practices—for example, how far back in prehistory they were employed, under what social and environmental contexts, and how they may have changed over time—is still not well understood.

The Darker Side of Native California

Arising from recent archaeological research, a third criticism of earlier ethnographic fieldwork questions the common notion that Native California was a primordial paradise before the coming of Europeans. Many of the ethnographic reconstructions generated in the early twentieth century have a timeless quality that depicts California as a healthy land of great abundance and diverse resources, in which people did not have to work hard (for criticisms, see Raab 1996:64–65, 2000). This sense of a timeless paradise is also found in more recent ethnographic work that paints a picture of a rosy, harmonious relationship between people and nature regardless of time and space.

> Although native ways of using and tending the earth were diverse, the people were nonetheless unified by a fundamental land use ethic: one must interact respectfully with nature and coexist with all life-forms. This ethic transcended cultural and political boundaries and enabled sustained relationships between human societies and California's environments over millennia. (Anderson 2005:57)

But a darker, more complicated, story of Late Holocene California is revealed by recent archaeological investigations. The potential to employ highly sophisticated mass harvesting and storage practices and to support larger numbers of people segregated into elite and commoner families did not necessarily translate into a better way of life. We have good evidence that in some times and places Native peoples experienced poor health and hardships brought about by periodic food shortages, parasites, endemic diseases, violence, warfare, and political manipulations.

Paleopathological analyses of human skeletal remains from the South Coast Province indicate increasing nutritional problems and infectious diseases, as evidenced by the occurrence of bone lesions, the frequency of enamel hypoplasia, and the pitting of the orbital roof *(cribra orbitalia)*(Lambert and Walker 1991: 967–969; Walker et al. 1989:353–358). Overall health in later prehistory varied from area to area and even village to village. While the reasons for these health problems are not fully known, Walker, Lambert, and others believe it is tied to population growth, increased sedentarism, and the aggregation of larger numbers of people into villages. The latter may have been especially problematic in that it produced mounting sewage, contaminated water, and increased numbers of parasites.

Walker, Lambert, and others have also shattered the myth of a primordial peaceful Native California. Although the level of physical battery varied greatly in time and space, there is considerable evidence for warfare and violence throughout the prehistoric period in the South Coast Province, based on analyses of lethal and sublethal cranial injuries, and projectile-point wounds. Their findings indicate that violence intensified during the period from AD 300 to AD 1150, probably due to political competition, the appearance of the bow and arrow, and fighting over resource shortfalls possibly caused by increasingly unstable climatic conditions that affected productivity.[26]

Another finding from recent archaeological research is evidence for resource intensification, a concept employed in California archaeology to describe situations where people were forced to work much harder to harvest less-optimal resources. Typically this involved hunter-gatherers working more hours to harvest the same or fewer food calories. Some archaeologists in the South Coast and the Central Coast provinces have observed a general trend where the most highly ranked foods, defined as large species of terrestrial game (deer, elk) and sea mammals (sea lions) decreased markedly in some archaeological sites in late prehistoric times. At the same time, smaller food packages, defined as "secondary resources," increased in the archaeological record.[27] This trend also involved changes in the exploitation of fish resources in the San Francisco Bay Area, where the frequency of large sturgeon declined in relation to smaller fish species (Broughton 1997). This general pattern is interpreted by some scholars as evidence for the overharvesting of large game and fish in some times and places in California.

This pattern of resource intensification in the archaeological record is complex and multifaceted. There is no simple unidirectional trajectory in the shift from the exploitation of large-sized game to smaller species over time (Hildebrandt and McGuire 2002). A variety of social factors, climatic changes, and shifting animal and human demographic conditions appear to have contributed to the variety and kinds of resources harvested in the Early, Middle, and Late Holocene (Broughton and Bayham 2003; Hildebrandt and McGuire 2003; Kennett 2005).

The extensive use of acorns and small seeds in Late Holocene times is also interpreted as evidence for resource intensification. Basgall (1987) makes a convincing argument that full-blown acorn harvesting and processing, which involves pounding acorns into flour and removing tannic acid through some form of leaching, is highly labor intensive. Wohlgemuth's (2004) comprehensive review of available archaeobotanical remains from the archaeological record indicates that acorn use was initiated early in California, at least 10,000 years ago. Thus, acorn exploitation probably took place not long after the first people entered California. But acorn processing in early prehistoric times may have required relatively minimal labor expenditure. Recent archaeological discoveries indicate a casual exploitation of Middle Holocene nuts in the the Sacramento Valley where Indians processed small quantities of nuts placed in water-filled clay pits to remove the tannic acid. This method, while reducing labor output by minimizing the pounding of acorns into flour before the leaching process, increases greatly the time necessary to process nuts and limits markedly the quantity of nuts that can be processed at one time.

By Late Holocene times, about 1,200 years ago, there is evidence for greater use of acorns in the Sacramento Valley. By this time, the water-filled clay pits used to leach acorns disappeared, replaced presumably by the active leaching system observed and described by early ethnographers (see Wohlgemuth 2004:144–147). While much more labor intensive, this processing program allowed people to prepare more nuts for meals in a shorter amount of time. Also, evidence exists from similarly dated archaeological contexts in the Sacramento Valley for significant increases in the use of small seeds. This finding suggests that more intensive methods of bulk harvesting and processing of small seeds were in use. Thus, there appears to be an overall trend toward resource intensification in the Sacramento Valley in Late Holocene times, based on the greater exploitation of both nuts and small seeds (Wohlgemuth 2004:145–146).

Studies of resource intensification suggest that growing populations of hunter-gatherers did have adverse impacts on their local environments in some places over the long term, and that they contributed to the overexploitation of larger species of mammals and fishes (that is, the most highly ranked foods)(see Raab 1996:75–76). This process of overharvesting was probably aggravated by periodic cycles of droughts and above-normal seawater temperatures along the California coast that severely reduced both terrestrial and marine productivity (Jones et al. 1999; Kennett 2005; Kennett and Kennett 2000; Raab and Larson 1997) and forced people to exploit whatever large and small resources were available to ward off famine. Most of these studies also point to the long-term impact of feeding a Native population that continued to grow markedly in late prehistoric times.

The size of human populations, estimated from radiocarbon dating and chronologies based on the hydration rates of obsidian artifacts, appears to have fluctuated across space and time; however, the general trend across Native California was for significant growth spurts during late prehistory up until Spanish colonization (1769). Some local population declines probably took place during the unstable times of the Medieval Warm Period (AD 800 to 1300) and during early European exploration (AD 1542 to 1603), when lethal pathogens may have been unleashed among coastal Indian groups.[28]

The periodic hardships faced by some late prehistoric peoples may have also been exacerbated by the self-serving interests of political elites. The revisionist anthropologists of the 1970s, as noted by Raab (1996, 2000), usually portrayed chiefs as "system serving" regulators who worked for the good of the greater community to buffer the effects of local food shortages by directing harvesting strategies, redistributing stored goods, and facilitating intervillage exchange. While some leaders probably employed their managerial skills to ameliorate local problems, it is likely that others were more self-indulgent, taking advantage of such situations to enhance their own status and political clout.

Archaeologists are now exploring how the political manipulations of elite families and aspiring leaders may have influenced local histories. Arnold (1992, 1995, 2001a), for example, has argued that an extended period of lowered resource productivity on the Channel Islands worked for the benefit of elites who controlled the manufacture and distribution of highly valued shell beads and who owned plank canoes used for pelagic fishing and long-distance trade. Paleopathological evidence from skeletal remains on the Santa Barbara mainland indicates that food short-ages and nutritional stress were not shared equally; members of nonelite families may have suffered the brunt of food shortages (Gamble et al. 2001). Furthermore, competition for leadership positions within families and villages, as well as between rival leaders from antagonistic local communities, may have had un-healthy consequences by stimulating periodic intervals of greater violence and warfare (Lambert and Walker 1991; Raab 2000:17).

Conclusion

Our understanding of California Indians' interactions with the natural world has grown tremendously in the last few years with new insights about the organization of Native groups, the man-agement skills they employed in tending local habitats, and tem-poral changes that took place in their exploitation of food and other resources. However, two very different scenarios about the lifeways of complex hunter-gatherers are being proposed. One scenario, proposed by cultural anthropologists and historical ecologists working primarily with contemporary Native people, is that of nurturing landscape managers who created and main-tained various kinds of productive habitats through fire man-agement, tillage, pruning, seed broadcasting, and weeding. Ac-cording to this scenario, Native peoples maintained sustainable harvesting practices based on cultural rules that stressed conser-vation and a spiritually mediated relationship with the natural world.

The other scenario, painted by archaeologists working with human and animal remains, portrays a much darker story of the ancient history of California, one that suggests Native people, in some times and places, were experiencing poor health and hard-ships brought on by periodic food shortages, parasites, endemic diseases, political manipulations, and violence. A general trend has been observed in the archaeological record in which large game and fish (highly ranked foods) decreased markedly in Late Holocene times, forcing people to use a greater variety of smaller species of animals. This process of resource intensification is at-tributed primarily to human population growth over time. It is argued that with more mouths to feed, Indian groups overhunted the larger animals in their territories, which most certainly had some adverse impacts on local environments. Resource intensification not only concerned the hunting of smaller game, fishes, and birds, but in some places it also involved labor-intensive practices of bulk harvesting and storing and processing acorns and small seeds.

While these two scenarios are not mutually exclusive, the differing interpretations about the health and lifeways of Indian people highlight a crucial problem in California anthropology today. How do we make sense of divergent interpretations about Native California that are constructed from very different lines of evidence and theoretical approaches? The resource intensification model is based primarily on the analysis of animal remains from the archaeological record by ecologically oriented scientists,[29] who are mostly men. The model of harmonious land managers is based mostly on ethnographic work with contemporary Native Californian women who harvest and process indigenous plant foods, along with vegetable materials used in the production of cordage and baskets. This ethnographic work is undertaken by cultural anthropologists and related researchers who are primarily women. Just as we noted about the ethnographic observations in the early twentieth century, in evaluating these two scenarios we must keep in mind that archaeology and contemporary ethnographic accounts have their great strengths, as well as weaknesses, for studying the past.

The great strength of archaeology is that it can provide long-term histories of Native Californians at different spatial scales (individual objects, features, sites, and regions); however, a significant problem with the archaeological record is that we rarely recover perishable material culture except under extraordinary circumstances involving excellent preservation (e.g., waterlogged sites). Consequently, most archaeological interpretations tend to focus on what can be studied—animal bone and shell, artifacts of stone, bone, antler, and shell, and, in some cases, human remains. It is only within the last 30 years or so that archaeologists have attempted to collect charred botanical remains of plants using recently developed techniques, and the recovery of plant foods from sites is still not systematically done in all excavations. But it is the perishable remains of cordage, baskets, nets, clothing, dance regalia, and so on that are rarely unearthed in archaeological contexts. It is a very sobering experience for any archaeologist to compare the rather meager remains from the excavation of an open-air site with the full spectrum of California Indian material culture curated in ethnographic collections, such as at the Phoebe Hearst Museum of Anthropology.

Given the preservation biases of the archaeological record, there is a long tradition of emphasizing stone projectile points in generating interpretations about prehistoric hunting methods. The common view of Native Californians stalking or pursuing deer, elk, and antelope individually with their spears or bows and arrows has certainly been fostered by this archaeological perspective. But as elaborated in this book, many methods for hunting waterfowl and game involved perishable plant materials to make a diverse range of traps, snares, nets, and fences. The mass collecting of fishes, birds, mammals, and insects was probably a common economic activity in the recent past, yet archaeologists are only now examining the full implications of this hunting strategy in their models of prehistory (Broughton and Bayham 2003; Sutton 1988; Ugan 2005). If the collection en masse of small fishes and insects provided higher return rates than the hunting of large-sized game (deer and elk), then how does this affect the expectations of the resource intensification model? Should we not expect to see greater diet breadth and evidence of mass collecting of a diverse range of resources in earlier periods of prehistory?

Ethnographic research with contemporary Native Californian people (mostly women) provides an extremely important perspective on Indian lifeways and material culture today; however, it is not clear how far back in prehistory these cultural practices can be transposed. Certainly, many of the indigenous ways are rooted in cultural traditions that span many generations. Oral traditions handed down from one generation to another have maintained stories, myths, histories, and cultural practices within Indian families for many years. But we must recognize that Indian life today is very different than it was 500 years ago, 300 years ago, or even a century ago. California Indian people and their cultures have survived largely because they have been able to change with the times while still maintaining many of their world views and core values.

Unfortunately, the sense of timelessness that underpinned the early ethnographic studies is still evident in more recent work. Ideals concerning conservation measures and living in harmony with the earth no doubt have deep roots in California Indian cultures. But the implementation of such conservation measures by Native people today may be quite different from implementations in the past. Food used by Indian communities today is still harvested, often for ceremonial use or public gatherings such as Big Times. But food is also readily available in grocery stores. A century ago, Indian people collected wild food sources, while obtaining other necessary resources from ranching and farming activities. Three centuries ago, Indians were completely dependent on what they could gather, fish, and hunt. Conservation measures probably took on added significance when people were completely dependent on what they could harvest. But these cultural practices were probably enacted in a flexible and relative manner, especially during periodic cycles of environmental perturbations, declining resource availability, and warfare. No doubt under these kinds of difficult circumstances, the survival of families was likely to take precedence over the overexploitation of the resource base, a point suggested by recent archaeological research.

In a recent article, Melissa Nelson (2006) emphasizes that past Indian people did occasionally make mistakes or miscalculations that led to the overexploitation of resources and negative impacts to local environments. In fact, a careful listening of many Native oral traditions makes this point very clear.

> Over and over again, the oral traditions of many Indian nations tells [sic] us this same story: In the past, sometimes even in the "before worlds," people stopped honoring the "original instructions" and did not care for the Earth and her creatures. Whenever this selfishness takes over, humans are soon to perish. (Nelson 2006:52)

Nelson notes that because Indian groups were sometimes environmentally destructive in the past, cultural practices, taboos, and laws were enacted (or reenacted) to mitigate this damage and to foster a more balanced relationship between humans and nature. Viewed in this perspective, we may begin to develop a new approach that integrates the recent findings of archaeology with those of ethnographic observations by explicitly recognizing that there were times in the past when California Indians made misjudgments and mistakes about the natural world or were faced with difficult decisions about resource use during periods of devastating droughts or warming seawater temperatures. But these backbreaking times no doubt stimulated the (re)enactment of cultural practices and spiritual values that taught people about the importance of maintaining sustainable human-environment interactions.

As summarized in this chapter, recent interpretations are playing a significant role in revising our understanding of California Indians. The importance of indigenous landscape management, especially prescribed burning, in the creation and maintenance of landscape diversity has been brought to the forefront of California anthropology. Yet, this perspective has been recently critiqued by ecologists and geographers who believe that much of this habitat diversity is due to natural ecological processes, especially natural fire regimes, and not necessarily to Indians creating broadscale anthropogenic landscapes. These points are explored in the following chapter.

The First Fire Managers

IT IS THE SUMMER OF 2007. Smoke is billowing, flames are crackling, and fire crews are defiantly trying to stand their ground. We are watching TV images of people evacuating houses, once again, in the Lake Tahoe area. The camera crew is now panning on the smoldering ruins of a house, its elderly owners grief stricken at their loss. It is a heart-wrenching story that plays out, time and time again, during the summer and early fall months across much of California. As major conflagrations continue to take their toll on wildlands, property, and human lives, it is hard to imagine any forest fire in a positive light. Yet systematic burning of the landscape, when done in a strategic and measured way, can be of immense value to both the environment and the local people. Native Californians learned this lesson many hundreds of years ago, developing sophisticated cultural practices for using fires in a friendly way. Today, while foresters and ecologists are rapidly recognizing the important roles that fire regimes should play in many California habitats, most of us have a long way to go in understanding why we might need to torch wildlands on occasion.

A strong case can be made for widespread use of fire management among California Indians in late prehistoric and early historic times. The frequent references to controlled burning by Native groups in the earliest European explorers' accounts, the ethnographic studies of the early twentieth century, and more recent interviews with Indian elders make a compelling case for this practice throughout much of the state.[1] Despite the considerable literature on prescribed burning, however, there is much that we do not know about the specifics of pyrodiversity practices. Anthropologists and ecologists were slow to recognize that hunter-gatherers in California and elsewhere could significantly manipulate the environment through the strategic use of fire. Consequently, detailed interdisciplinary studies that consider the long-term impacts and implications of the burning practices of Native Californians, using ecological, archaeological, historical, and ethnographic sources of information, are in their infancy.

The first systematic investigation of prescribed fires in Native California came relatively late—initiated by Omer Stewart, a student of Alfred Kroeber's, who published a number of articles on this topic in the 1940s and 1950s. He also wrote an extraordinary synthesis of indigenous burning practices in North America, which unfortunately remained unpublished until 2002 (see Lewis 2002; Lewis and Anderson 2002). But the impact of Stewart's work on the broader anthropological discipline remained relatively minimal prior to the 1970s. His strong plea to consider the implications of Native American burning was largely ignored (Lewis 1982:46).[2]

The memory culture methodology of early California ethnography certainly complicated the study of indigenous burning practices. Few, if any, comprehensive firsthand observations of Native firing practices have been recorded by trained ethnographers—what exists are memory sketches based on interviews with elders, or early ethnohistorical accounts of Indian burning made in passing by European explorers or settlers.[3] Lewis (1993: 80) sums up the situation: "Unfortunately, even the best documented information on the use of fire is all too brief and lies buried within a mass of general ethnographic detail, usually within sections describing subsistence activities or as part of a general description of the precontact environment."

The memory culture methodology is also problematic for evaluating the full magnitude to which prescribed burning took place in late prehistoric and early historic times. Colonial administrators and later American government regulations prohibited Native groups from continuing their traditional practice of prescribed burning, especially near non-Indian settlements. Prohibitions against Indians torching the landscape were enacted as early as 1793 by Spanish colonial administrators (Lightfoot 2005:86–87). Fire control was increasingly implemented in federal forest reserves in California in the late 1800s and early 1900s, first by the U.S. Army, and then later by the U.S. Forest Service (founded as a separate agency in 1905), which established a comprehensive fire-suppression policy (Stephens and Sugihara 2006:433–434). Burning prohibitions probably affected the ability of Native elders to recount details of fire management to early ethnographers, as they were growing up when traditional burning practices were being increasingly curtailed by government agencies.

In some areas, several generations of Indian people have been denied the right to selectively burn vegetation patches across the landscape. A classic example is that of the Chumash speakers in the South Coast Province, where detailed observations by early Spanish explorers and settlers documented the widespread convention of strategic fire broadcasting by local communities. But this practice, first suppressed by local Franciscan missionaries, and then later by Anglo-American settlers, had "long faded from cultural memory" when Harrington and other ethnographers interviewed Indian elders in the early twentieth century (Timbrook et al. 1993:118). Clearly, by relying solely on ethnographic reconstructions, we may seriously underestimate the diversity and extent to which fire management was employed in traditional Native California communities.[4]

The study of indigenous fire ecology went mainstream in North American anthropology in the 1970s, with the growing theoretical interest in ecological anthropology and complex hunter-gatherers. A younger generation of scholars rediscovered Omer Stewart's work, employing some of his observations about Native burning to create a new vision of California Indians as active land managers. With the growing recognition that prescribed burning played an integral role in diversifying and enhancing the productivity of plant and animal resources, the theoretical pendulum began to swing. Interpretations of passive hunter-gatherers gave way to scenarios of California Indians as active human agents who both manipulated and domesticated the natural environment.

Questions have been recently raised about the degree to which fire management was employed by Indian groups in western North America, and the impact it had on local habitats and plant communities. The issue is not whether California Indian groups employed fire in some contexts to stimulate plant growth and to attract some kinds of game. What is being challenged is the scale, intensity, and overall impact of indigenous fire management. Vale (1998, 2000, 2002:6–7) believes that "careless generalizations" are being made by anthropologists who, in rejecting the former myth of the pre-Columbian wilderness in North America, are now pushing a new myth of a "humanized landscape," where Native people actively managed extensive tracts of land. Specifically, Vale (2002), Parker (2002), and Bendix (2002) question whether some of the signature vegetation communities of California, such as chaparral, mixed conifer forests, oak woodlands, and montane meadows were created and maintained by Native Californian cultural practices. They suggest that significant transformations in the composition and structure of vegetation communities attributed to Native Californian fire management can be best explained primarily by natural, nonanthropogenic ecological processes. The fundamental vegetation patterns of California, they believe, would have existed regardless of whether people were present. Furthermore, they contend that recent changes in vegetation patterns that have been attributed to the abolition of Indian burning practices have more to do with state and federal fire cessation policies and subsequent changes in fire regimes across the state.

The remainder of this chapter explores some of the issues raised by Vale and others, considers some of the specific variables that need to be controlled in examining the fire management activities of Indian groups, and outlines a proposed model for pyrodiversity practices in California.

Fire Regimes

The concept of the fire regime is employed by fire ecologists to define the general characteristics or patterns and effects of fires over time within an area (or vegetation type) of interest. Fire regimes are characterized by a number of variables in the ecological literature, but for our purposes we focus on four critical ones: frequency, spatial extent, magnitude, and seasonality.[5] Fire frequency refers to the number of fires per unit of time within a study area. It is often described in terms of fire-return intervals—the length of time between fires in the area of interest (Skinner and Chang 1996:1043; Sugihara, van Wagtendonk, and Fites-Kaufman 2006:66). Spatial extent is the size of the area burned by a fire. Fire magnitude can be described as its intensity (the amount of energy released) and severity (the degree to which the vegetation or ecosystem has been impacted by a fire) (Sugihara, van Wagtendonk, and Fites-Kaufman 2006:68–69). Fire severity may be viewed along a continuum of increasing consequences to the ecosystem. At one end are low-severity fires—light surface burns that consume primarily surface fuels. At the other end of the spectrum are high-severity fires, which may erupt into highly destructive crown fires that consume both

Figure 16. Burning cattails (*Typha* spp.) near Mono Lake. Such burns would rejuvenate wetland vegetation and clean out water sources of debris.

understory vegetation and overstory trees.[6] Seasonality is the season or seasons of the year in which fires burn.

A critical issue explored in this chapter is determining what kinds of fire regimes may have been encouraged by Indians and how these anthropogenic fire regimes may have differed from natural fire regimes. Hunter-gatherers initiated controlled burning for many purposes.[7] They used fires to remove underbrush, thereby facilitating foot travel and resource gathering. They cleansed areas of downed timber and detritus, destroyed diseased plants and pests, and enhanced fertility by recycling nutrients into the soils. Fire management cleared out competing species, such as conifers in oak parklands, and cleaned springs and water holes of vegetation (fig. 16). They also relied on fires in communal hunts to drive animals, birds, and insects into ambushes or traps.

Recent ethnographic work among aboriginal communities in Australia, who still employ prescribed fires to facilitate hunting or to enhance the productivity of economic resources, points to other potential reasons—that Native people often employ fires and specific burn patterns to signal and mark their homelands. People use fires to identify their territories and to claim ownership of specific resources resulting from controlled burns. For example, in Australia's western desert, it appears that the people who set fires maintain control over the resources in those areas for at least two or three years.[8] Closer to home, Tveskov (2007: 435–436) emphasizes how regularized fire management by Native women in southwestern Oregon created strong and lasting identities that tied them to specific landscapes.

The primary reasons for burning in Native California probably revolved around the practice of enhancing the growth and diversity of economically important plant and animal resources. Hunter-gatherers did not typically burn simply to maximize the productivity of a single resource, but rather to stimulate the growth of a broad spectrum of resources (Lewis 1982:51–52). Stewart, Lewis, Anderson, and others stress that California Indians burned a diverse range of patches across the landscape to augment the availability of a variety of plant foods, including tubers, fruits, greens, nuts, and seeds. Native people encouraged the proliferation of sprouts, straight branches, and other useable raw materials that could be incorporated into the production of baskets, cordage, and other household goods. They increased forage that attracted both small and large game such as deer and rabbits. Thus, the burning practices of California Indians created complex environmental mosaics that enhanced landscape heterogeneity, biological diversity, and the availability of economic resources (Hammett 1991:21; Keeley 2002:310–312).

To create these rich environmental mosaics, we propose that California Indians would have encouraged fire regimes with the following characteristics (see also discussion in Hammett 1991: 65).

First, fire frequency would probably have been relatively high. A low fire interval, where burning is staggered between different vegetation stands on a one- to 10-year (or longer) interval, would have allowed people to implement a rotational system of prescribed burns. This would promote diversity by insuring proximate areas were continually under different stages of vegetation succession.

Second, fires would probably have been small in spatial extent. Small fires are ideal for creating and enhancing complex patchworks of unevenly aged habitat types (Lewis 1985b). In staggering the burn intervals of small fires across the landscape, Native people could have produced a dynamic mosaic of ever-changing plant successions and communities even within the same basic vegetation type (Hallam 1985:14–17).

Third, hunter-gatherers would probably have encouraged low-severity surface fires that burned floor debris, grasses, and even shrubs, but would have minimized major damage to the overstory, thereby rapidly promoting increased diversity and productivity within burn areas. Many plants harvested as foods, including seeds, berries, tubers, and roots, as well as those used for manufacturing cordage, baskets, and other material objects, recover quickly after low-intensity fires (e.g., Lathrop and Martin 1982). Low-severity surface fires remove competing plants from oak woodlands. Although even light burns can cause some damage to thin-barked oak species, fire encourages the sprouting of oak saplings and the rejuvenation of oak woodlands (McCarthy 1993:223–224).

Finally, fire seasonality would have varied depending upon considerations of fuel and burning conditions, as outlined below. But Native people would probably have ignited fires during those times of the year when they could have maintained some control over the size and severity of the burn. California Indians appear to have set fires primarily in the late summer to early fall, or in the late spring, depending upon the vegetation type, burning conditions, and the purpose of the burn—whether it was to reduce understory vegetation, to induce sprouting plant species to grow, to facilitate early winter growth of herbaceous plants, or for some other purpose.[9]

In sum, we propose a model of pyrodiversity management that would have encouraged fire regimes consisting of small, frequent, low-severity surface fires. We believe some kind of rotational system would have been practiced by fire managers that facilitated the burning of small patches in a staggered succession over a sequence of years. We stress that the specific characteristics of these fire regimes would have varied across time and space. The multiyear rotational cycles and fire-return intervals for particular patches would no doubt have diverged from one triblet territory to another, depending upon the habitats and resources being burned, fuel accumulations, local burning conditions, topography, and so forth. We illustrate one such hypothetical multiyear rotational cycle for a triblet territory in map 6.

Figure 17. A patchwork of different-aged vegetation stands from successive burns in chaparral country.

Here we depict a rotational cycle where 10 small resource patches are burned in succession over a 10-year period. In reality, many other combinations of burn patterns could be implemented for this same tribelet area when fires are staggered between different patches on a one- to 10-year (or longer) interval. The upshot, however, is that no matter what kind of fire regimes were facilitated in specific tribelet territories, the overall consequence was a tremendous increase in resource diversity at both the local and regional scales (map 6).

The key point we emphasize here is that multiyear rotation cycles of small, frequent, low-severity surface fires would have produced fine-grained vegetation patterns composed of many small stands of plants whose age structure varied from one stand to the next (fig. 17). By employing such rotational cycles, Native people would have ensured that different stages of succession were continually unfolding in distinctive patches of grassland, scrubland, oak woodland, and mixed conifer forests across local regions. For example, the first year after a burn in grassland or chaparral habitats might yield a different mix of herbaceous plants, bulbs, and shrubs, as well as game animals, birds, and insects, than after the second, third, or fourth year (Keeley 2002: 310–312; Lewis 1993; Shaffer and Laudenslayer 2006:129–130). Furthermore, this staggered pattern of burning would have balanced the ever-present need for gathering firewood in Indian communities (King 1993). A fire management program that rotated the burning of nearby parcels of land would have ensured a ready supply of firewood in areas not recently torched.

Not only do these kinds of fire regimes produce rich mosaics of diverse vegetation patches, but they increase the number of edges and open fire yards or corridors between vegetation stands that can support additional plants and animals (Lewis 1991:265). As Lewis (1993:113) notes, strategic burns allowed Indians

> to exploit the ecotones, the transitions or "edges" between forest and brush, between brush and woodland, between woodland and grass. As we know, it is a general principle of ecology that it is the ecotone areas in which the density and variety of life are the greatest . . . Even though the overall environment already provided two and often more natural ecotones, the Indian was able to create a variety of local ecotones within vegetation zones. At the same time, even where natural ecotones already existed— e.g., between woodland-grass and chaparral zones—aboriginal burning pushed back the upper zones of brush or trees to favor a more productive cover of mixed trees, grass, and shrubs.

Furthermore, islands of more mature stands of vegetation offer shelter and forage for many animals. They can also serve as refugia from which both plants and animals colonize recently burned patches (Martin and Sapsis 1992:151). Ultimately, fire regimes characterized by small, frequent fires would have augmented greatly the incredible diversity of the natural world of California already stimulated by topographic relief, the maritime conditions of the Pacific Ocean, and latitude.

Hunter-gatherers should not have encouraged fire regimes characterized by low-frequency, expansive, high-severity crown fires—the kind of burns that result in wholesale stand replacements over extensive areas. These kinds of intense, large-scale fires will produce coarse-grained vegetation patterns in which entire regions may be characterized by vegetation types of the same age and stage of succession.[10] We argue that major conflagrations that foster more homogeneous conditions across large areas would have been antithetical to the anthropogenic fire regimes promoted by fire managers (see also Anderson 2006: 419).

Fire Regimes: The Critical Factors

Fire regimes are influenced primarily by three critical factors: fuel, burning conditions, and ignition sources.[11]

Fuel

Any traditional barbecue master who still uses a Weber grill and charcoal knows the relationship between fuel, fire, and keeping guests happy. In planning either a barbecue or prescribed burn, you must have an adequate supply of dry, burnable fuel. The lower limit of the fire-return interval for a local area or vegetation type is dependent on the minimum fuel needs to support a fire (Pyne 1991:33–36). Fuel load accumulation rates vary greatly depending upon the specific vegetation type, local environmental conditions, and presence of herbaceous plants (Parker 2002:256–257). Fuel types typically consist of dry grasses, litter

---

Map 6 (next spread). The pyrodiversity model in three parts, depicting how fire management in California could have greatly enhanced resource diversity in local Indian territories and across the state.
Left: California is blessed by a landscape of unparalleled diversity that varies with topographic relief, distance from the ocean, and latitude.
Upper right: The natural diversity of California would have been greatly enhanced at the regional scale by individual tribelet groups encouraging multiyear rotational cycles of prescribed burns. This illustration depicts the three land surfaces (A–B, C–D, E–F) at high, medium, and low latitudes. Superimposed across the land surfaces are the hypothetical territories of hunter-gatherer groups who are each employing fire management programs. The tremendous resource diversity that would have resulted at the broader regional scale from the burning practices of numerous tribelet communities, each with its own dynamic fire regime, is a defining characteristic of the pyrodiversity model.
Lower right: The model proposes that hunter-gatherer groups would have encouraged fire regimes characterized by small, staggered, low-severity burns. This illustration shows the hypothetical territory of a hunter-gatherer group with a 10-year rotational cycle of prescribed burns. For the purposes of illustrating this model, we are depicting tribelet territories as approximately 25 km (15 miles) in diameter, but in actuality the territorial ranges of California Indian groups varied considerably. The numbers refer to the year that a particular resource patch was ignited in succession within the 10-year period. We recognize that this is only one of the many combinations of rotational cycles and fire-return intervals that could have been facilitated by local fire managers.

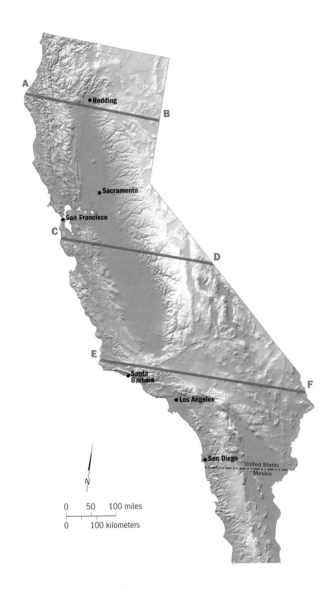

Map 6. Caption on previous page.

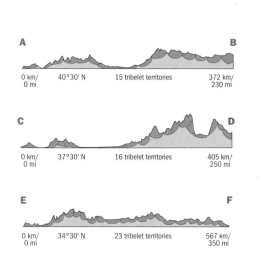

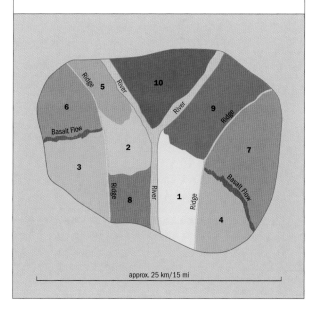

fall (needles and branches from the overstory), and woody materials from shrubs and trees that have died.[12] Fuel load and fuel moisture tend to influence fire magnitude, along with wind speed, slope, and other factors (Miller and Urban 1999b:120–123).

Fires will not occur unless the biota that sustains them recovers sufficiently from past conflagrations to burn again.[13] Some vegetation types, such as valley grassland, coastal prairie, and coastal sage scrub, which tend to be dominated by herbaceous plants, can accumulate sufficient fuel from dead plants and leaf dormancy during summer droughts to support surface fires over short intervals (one or two years). In situations where fuels accrue relatively rapidly, the size and shape of prescribed burns are not constrained by the spatial patterning of previous fires. Rather, the minimum fire-return interval and spatial extent of the fire will depend primarily upon previous precipitation patterns and plant productivity (Minnich 1998:150–155).

Compared to grasslands and sage scrub, woodland and chaparral environments typically take more time to build up adequate fuels for prescribed burns. Montane forests comprising mixed conifers (especially ponderosa pine [*Pinus ponderosa*]), which produce dense leaf litter and support herbaceous plants, may exhibit fire-return intervals of as little as four to five years (Kilgore and Taylor 1979:138–140).[14] Although surface fires can quickly remove floor litter and woody debris, overstory vegetation in these mixed conifer forests can generate future fuel relatively rapidly from pine litter and dead branches, thereby minimizing the fire-return interval (Carle 2008:48; Miller and Urban 1999a:210). Still other vegetation types, such as chaparral and subalpine forests, can take considerable time—sometimes decades—for sufficient fuel to build up to support sizeable prescribed fires.[15]

Fire regimes in many woodland and chaparral vegetation types, especially those with moderate- to long-term fuel load accumulation rates, tend to be self-organizing. That is, previous fires create spatial patterns that influence the size and shape of future fires (Miller and Urban 1999a:210; van Wagtendonk 1986: 6). Once burned, a patch should not burn again until sufficient time has passed to accumulate adequate sources of fuel. Fires should not overlap under these conditions. Rather, they burn out at the boundaries of previous fires for want of fuel (Minnich

1998:153–154). This may result in a classic checkerboard pattern of multiple, small burn parcels, each parcel characterized by its own unique fire history (Minnich 1983:1291–1292).

Burning Conditions

Burning conditions are greatly influenced by such factors as climate and precipitation patterns, fuel moisture, wind, topography, and elevation. Precipitation patterns are critical in defining fire regimes. The Mediterranean climate of California, with its cool, wet winters followed by warm, dry summers, is ideally suited for Indian fire managers. Precipitation during winter and early spring support biotic productivity and fuel accumulation, while the annual drought period of summer and early fall squeezes moisture from annual grasses, litter, dead branches, and logs, making them susceptible to ignition.

Moisture content of fuel is critical. Sufficient fuel may have accumulated over time in a local area to support an intense conflagration, but as long as the fuel remains wet it will be extremely difficult to ignite a prescribed burn. For example, if rains arrive at the wrong time of year or precipitation remains locked within snow or ice at high elevations throughout much of the year, then fires will burn erratically or not at all. Thus, fire seasonality is typically related to fuel moisture (Skinner and Chang 1996:1043). Fuel moisture depends largely on the nature of the fuel and local climatic conditions. Fine dead fuels such as grass may take only a few hours to dry, while large downed logs may require an entire season or prolonged drought conditions (Pyne 1991:35). Summer droughts enhance fuel flammability, and most natural fire regimes in California tend to have their best burns in late summer and early fall.[16]

Severe fire years in California are commonly distinguished by wet winters and early springs, when vegetation flourishes, followed by extreme droughts during the summer and fall, which dry everything out. Hot, dry periods with low humidity are crucial for drying many types of bulky fuel sources. Consequently, there is a strong correlation between big fire years and droughts, especially multiyear droughts, creating conditions that are ideal for widespread conflagrations.[17]

High winds and steep topography can rapidly spread fires, while wind patterns, in combination with fuel availability and distribution, can significantly influence the shape and spatial extent of burns (Minnich 1998:147). As Pyne (1991:37) stresses, the "geography of wind" will often structure the "geography of fire"; however, when winds are absent, fires will take the shape of available fuel. Sprugel (1991:12–13) emphasizes that small increments of temperature over extended periods can have significant impacts on fire regimes. He argues that cooler conditions, such as during the Little Ice Age, can serve to reduce fire frequencies. A similar argument can be made for warmer conditions, such as during the Medieval Climatic Anomaly, when fire frequencies probably increased in many areas of California (see Swetnam 1993:887; van Wagtendonk and Fites-Kaufman 2006:270).

Elevation is an important variable in the mountains, where precipitation increases along an altitudinal gradient, while temperature decreases. Although higher precipitation at upper elevations should support adequate fuel production, the colder temperatures may impede plant growth. Even when fuel is available at high altitudes, there is a good chance that some places in California may be frozen in heavy snow packs for much of the year (see Miller and Urban 1999b:131–132).

Ignition Sources

Although the minimum fire-return interval is determined by fuel accumulation and availability, fires will never burn without sources of ignition. Consequently, the maximum fire-return interval is based primarily on the opportunity for ignition (Pyne 1991:34). Theoretically, the fewer the chances for ignition, then the greater the probability for a long fire-return interval. Conversely, the greater the opportunity for ignitions, the greater the probability of an increased fire frequency rate until the minimum fire-return interval is reached. Ignition sources in California include volcanic activity, meteors, and friction sparks, but the two primary causes of combustion are lightning strikes and humans (fig. 18)(Martin and Sapsis 1992:150; van Wagtendonk 2006:45).

Natural fire regimes are dependent primarily on lightning storms for ignition. In examining the frequency of lightning storms (and natural fires) in California, two significant gradients are recognized: lightning tends to increase with distance from the Pacific Ocean, and in higher elevations (map 7).[18] Consequently, lightning strikes at sea level along the coast are quite rare, while lightning storms in the higher elevations of the Cascade Range and Sierra Nevada are much more common. As

Figure 18. Ishi demonstrating the traditional method for starting a fire using a drill, 1912–1915; Yahi.

noted above, however, low fuel availability and high fuel moisture at the highest elevations tend to counteract the full potential of lightning fires in the upper altitudes of mountains.

Distinguishing Anthropogenic Fire Regimes

Distinguishing natural fires from those ignited by California Indians is not easy (Hammett 1991:208–209; Martin and Sapsis 1992:152). Research in Australia shows that Native people managed the size and magnitude of controlled burns by setting them at the optimal time of the day and season in order to take advantage of wind conditions, humidity, fuel availability, and fuel moisture, especially if the goal was small, low-severity surface fires (Lewis 1985a:22–26, 1991:266–268). For example, using prevalent wind patterns, it is possible to "aim" fires toward areas already burned to limit their spread. It is true that California Indians, similar to Australian aboriginal groups, had no real method for extinguishing or suppressing fires once they began to spread across the landscape (Bowman 1998:390).

The size and spatial configuration of fires could be controlled to some degree by past fire histories that produced patchy distributions of recently burned parcels that might impede the progress of low-intensity fires. This patchwork quilt of past fires,

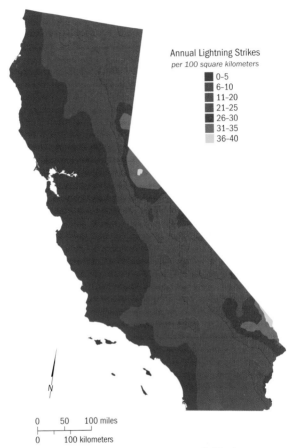

Map 7. The frequency of lightning strikes across California.

when combined with natural barriers, may have facilitated the creation of relatively small burn areas with definable boundaries.[19] Skinner and Taylor (2006:218) emphasize the importance of understanding local topographic conditions "as a control on fire regimes." Specific kinds of natural features could have served as barriers to the diffusion of low-intensity fires across local landscapes that had been ignited by lightning or people.

In reality, California Indians could have modified natural fire regimes only in two basic ways. One was to increase fire frequency by igniting burns whenever fuel availability and moisture were adequate, especially in lowland elevations near the ocean, where lightning rarely strikes (Anderson 2002:50–52; Greenlee and Langenheim 1990:245; Stephens et al. 2007:212). The other was to expand the seasons of fire ignition beyond the period of frequent natural fires caused by the annual arrival of thunderstorms (Lewis 1993:94). No matter how hard they might have tried, however, hunter-gatherers could not have ignited fires more frequently than the minimum fire-return interval for a particular vegetation type, nor could they have set prescribed burns in seasons when fuels were wet.

We argue that Native fire managers would have initiated a rotational system of burning small patches within local areas, depending upon burning conditions and the minimum fire-return intervals for different vegetation types. As noted above, fire-return intervals might vary from one to two years for valley grasslands and coastal prairies, a few years for coastal sage scrub, from four to five years for some montane forests, and 10 or more years for other montane forests, chaparral, and subalpine forests. Clearly, fire managers did not have to set fires to every patch within their territory on a yearly schedule to produce highly productive mosaics. Depending on the resources being exploited, fuel loads, and fuel moisture, the optimal burn interval appears to have varied among vegetation types in a rotational cycle of one to 10 (or more) years.

For example, prescribed burning to increase the edges of chaparral and coastal sage scrub, as well as to enhance productive grassland vegetation, would have been ideally applied at an interval of between one and five years to allow herbaceous plants to take hold and create islands of shrubs that resprout with high yields of fruit. Furthermore, the continued burning of chaparral or coastal sage scrub at this interval could convert these patches to more open mixtures of herbaceous plants, perennial grasses, and some remnant shrubs (Keeley 2002:308–309, 311). This practice would not only have increased seed, bulb, and fruit production, but it would have augmented the biodiversity of local patches. Ecological studies estimate that burning can increase the number of different species from about two dozen to more than 80 following fires.[20] The one- to five-year burn interval would also be ideal for game management. It could have multiplied deer browse 40-fold, supporting not only a three- to fivefold boom in the deer population, but a significant increase in the quantity of quails (Odontophoridae), rodents (Rodentia), rabbits (Leporidae), Mourning Doves *(Zenaida macroura)*, ravens (Corvidae), owls (Tytonidae and Strigidae), woodpeckers (Picidae), Golden Eagles *(Aquila chrysaetos)*, and Peregrine Falcons *(Falco peregrinus)*.[21] Other studies indicate that the optimal timing for burns to maintain bunchgrass habitats ranges between three and five years.[22] Quick (1962:102–103) observes that gooseberry plants that colonized in a burn area in the Sierra Nevada took about five years to fruit, and that each successive year after this five year interval, they bore more fruit. It is not clear what the ideal burn interval is for maintaining open oak woodlands, and for keeping nearby conifers from colonizing such habitats, as has been documented for Yosemite Valley (McCarthy 1993:220–224); however, burn intervals of two to five or even 10 years do not seem unreasonable for removing conifer seedlings and detritus from the ground.

Evidence for Anthropogenic Fire Regimes

What evidence exists for anthropogenic fire regimes in Native California, characterized by frequent, small, low-severity surface burns? Studies of historical and prehistoric fire regimes are based on various lines of evidence: historical accounts of Indian burning, ethnobotanical remains, the contents of pack rat nests, pollen, charcoal, fire-scar dating (employing dendrochronology), stand age profiles, and aerial photography.[23] While this is not the place to review these methods, we note that historical fire ecology is a relatively new field in which findings from field and laboratory research are accelerating rapidly. Considerable debate currently exists about the interpretation of fire-scar patterns at the scale of individual trees, groups of trees, and the broader region, as well as the interpretation of charcoal and pollen recovered from soil columns (see Bowman 1998).[24]

We have good evidence that anthropogenic fire regimes were implemented by hunter-gatherers in Late Holocene California. Employing the most current data on past (presuppression) fire-return intervals for different California vegetation types, Stephens et al. (2007:210–212) estimate that the amount of area that burned annually varied from 1,814,614 to 4,838,293 ha (7,000 to

18,700 mi^2) or about 6 to 16 percent of the state (excluding the dry Southern Deserts Province). Their findings indicate that not only a large portion of the state burned each year, but that Native Californians must have had a significant hand in promoting fires. The monumental synthesis on California fire ecology by Sugihara and others (Sugihara, van Wagtendonk, Shaffer, et al. 2006) features individual chapters detailing the current state of knowledge about past (and present) fire regimes for each of the major geomorphic provinces (see also Carle 2008:37–80). Four points can be gleaned from this work that are germane to our discussion.

First, past fire regimes varied significantly in time and space. Fire regimes changed in relation to environmental conditions (temperature, precipitation), elevation, aspect, distance from the ocean, vegetation types, and so on. Despite this considerable range of variation, Late Holocene fire regimes at mid- to low elevations have a tendency to be characterized by small, frequent, low-severity surface fires.[25]

Second, although the authors recognize the potential importance of burning by California Indians as a significant factor in past fire regimes, most are candid in admitting that the full impact of anthropogenic fires is not yet known.[26]

Third, in listing the fire responses for important plant species for the major geomorphic provinces of California, the authors identify whether they are fire stimulated. Fire-stimulated plants are those whose populations are enhanced by fires, primarily through seed germination or sprouting, while plants whose populations are either little impacted by fires or adversely impacted are defined as fire neutral or fire inhibited, respectively (see Fites-Kaufman et al. 2006:104–105). What immediately struck us in perusing these tables is that the great majority of species used by Native Californians are fire stimulated. This becomes quite evident when the trees, shrubs, and grasses listed as fire stimulated in the tables are compared to those commonly employed by Indians (see the resource guide section of this book).[27]

Fourth, with the advent of fire suppression practices, especially after 1905, the nature of the fire regimes changed dramatically across California, with fewer, larger, and more severe fires. Fires still occur through natural and human ignitions, but most are quickly suppressed by vigilant fire fighters. Fire suppression has greatly altered the composition and structure of local habitats, often producing increases in stand density, the accumulation of floor debris, a decrease in native plant biodiversity, and the spread of fire inhibited species.[28] When fires do erupt, they are either small and quickly put out, or they tend to explode into major firestorms, which under the right burning conditions, feed upon the high fuel loads (Sugihara, van Wagtendonk, and Fites-Kaufman 2006:72). Major fires, when they do ignite, create considerable damage and produce coarse-grained, homogeneous patch structures across broad areas. They have also resulted in the spread of less fire tolerant plants into local regions.[28]

A number of fire ecology case studies provide substance to the importance of Native burning in the Late Holocene. Keeley (2002) provides a detailed and balanced evaluation of Native-controlled burning in coastal California. In evaluating data on lightning strikes for the Central Coast Province, he shows that their numbers are few. Yet in synthesizing available pollen and charcoal information from soil cores, there is evidence for relatively high fire frequencies that could only have been caused by humans. For example, the 560-year record of pollen and charcoal from a sediment column collected in the Santa Barbara Basin shows a regular interval of large fires, probably enhanced by Santa Ana weather conditions, before, during, and after Spanish colonization, with an average interval of 21, 29, and 23 years, respectively. Humans are believed to have been the cause of most fires, although lightning is also an important ignition source (Mensing et al. 1999:303). This study also demonstrates that smaller fires were quite common and would probably have created an anthropogenic mosaic of productive habitats.

Greenlee and Langenheim's (1990) study of historic fire events in the Monterey Bay area also shows that the fire-return interval in late prehistoric times is higher than would be expected from lightning ignitions alone. In the northern coastal forest, dominated by coast redwood *(Sequoia sempervirens)*, they estimate that the mean fire interval, based on lightning strikes alone, would have been about 135 years, and that with the advent of Native-managed burning the fire interval dropped to roughly 50 years (Greenlee and Langenheim 1990:245). A recent fire history study of redwood trees from several locations in the Santa Cruz Mountains found even shorter fire-return intervals, ranging on average from nine to 16 years during the time span of about 1650 to 1860—a finding that strongly points to Native American and possibly early Euro-American burning (Stephens and Fry 2005). The study of pollen cores, opal phytoliths (microscopic silica bodies produced in plants), ethnohistoric sources, and other kinds of data indicate that coastal prairies and valley grasslands, most likely maintained by regular Indian-controlled burning, were once more common along the coastline of the Coast Ranges and have now been encroached on by forests and scrublands (Anderson 2005:168; Greenlee and Langenheim 1990:250).

Anderson and Carpenter's (1991) study of pollen and charcoal samples from Yosemite Valley suggests that major fires may have initially cleared conifers from the valley bottom about 700 years ago, allowing an increase in oak trees. They believe that low-severity surface fires regularly set by local Indian groups maintained mixed oak woodlands and grasslands and kept the pines from regenerating. Kilgore and Taylor's (1979:138–140) analysis of fire-scar patterns in the Sequoia and Kings Canyon national parks over the last 400 to 500 years reveal a pattern of frequent surface fires that burned small, irregularly shaped areas. Although they conclude that the frequency of fire events is greater than can be attributed to lightning strikes alone (a strong indicator of Native-managed burning), they also note the strong influence of climate in the Sierra Nevada fire regimes. Broadscale fire events did occur during prolonged drought conditions.

Firestorms in Native California

If fire managers habitually set small, frequent, surface fires that burned off surface litter, duff, dead wood, and grasses, then it is commonly assumed that this practice would have curtailed the periodic occurrence of major firestorms, in contradistinction to the modern fire regimes created under fire suppression policies.[29] Yet a growing body of data indicates that large infernos periodically swept across late prehistoric and early historic Native California (see Parker 2002:246–251). These firestorms tend to be associated with severe fire weather characterized by droughts and hot, dry winds, such as the infamous Santa Ana winds of southern California. These winds, originating from the sweltering Great Basin during the fall season, have been clocked at speeds of over 100 km per hour (62 mi per hour). They can sustain significant fire spread, on the order of 30,000 ha (115 mi^2) in a single day (Keeley 2006:352). Fire ecologists note that during periods of severe fire weather, checkerboard burn patterns and natural barriers (ridgetops, riparian corridors) that may impede low-intensity burns will do little to stop these kinds of infernos.[30] The upshot is that large, scorching, high-severity crown fires that burned everything in their path could have wiped out complex pyrodiversity mosaics within hours.

The ecological research by Mensing et al. (1999) in the Santa Barbara region showed that extensive firestorms erupted occasionally, especially at the end of wet periods and at the beginning of significant droughts. Some of these massive burns were probably driven by the onset of the dry, gusty Santa Ana winds (see also Keeley 2006:370). Periodic oscillations between wet intervals, followed by dry periods that sucked moisture from fuels, provided the right conditions for large fires to burn on a regular basis. Mensing et al. note that neither chronic burning by Chumash Indians nor modern fire suppression was able to curtail these large, stand-replacement blazes.

Minnich et al.'s research (2000:120–121) in northern Baja California shows that infrequent, intense surface fires (at an interval of about 50 years), which destroy pole-sized trees, can whip through the landscape, creating open, parklike forests; however, other smaller, more frequent, low- to moderate-severity fires may have also influenced the structure or composition of the Baja California forests (Stephens et al. 2003). Minnich (1998: 147–148) emphasizes in his research in the South Coast Province that severe weather conditions, epitomized by the Santa Ana winds, can enable high-energy, destructive firestorms. These infernos consume not only old-growth chaparral stands, but also young, recently burned patches where little fuel has had time to accumulate.

Caprio and Swetnam's (1995) analysis of fire histories over the last 300 to 400 years along the west slope of the Sierra Nevada identifies periodic eruptions of coherent and widespread fire events that cut across a broad range of elevations. This finding contrasts with the basic pattern of small, patchy fires reported for the same time period by Kilgore and Taylor (1979).[31] Caprio and Swetman found that fire frequencies increased in the 1700s, decreased from 1800 to 1830, increased again from 1830 to 1850, and then decreased thereafter with the decline of Indian populations, the advent of cattle grazing, and fire suppression policies.

The reoccurrence intervals of widespread fires during the 1700s and 1800s ranged from 15 to 44 years (Caprio and Swetnam 1995:175). They also show that lower elevations in the Sierra Nevada experienced much higher fire frequencies than upper elevations. The mean interval for all fires in the lower elevations ranged from about four to 5.5 years, a record that indicates a pattern of many small and spotty fire events punctuated by a few large firestorms.

Swetnam (1993), using tree ring data from giant sequoia *(Sequoiadendron giganteum)* trees in the Sierra Nevada spanning many centuries, emphasizes the dynamic nature of fire histories. He shows that the cycle of large fires in multiple giant sequoia groves in the Sierra Nevada tended to be associated with dry years, a finding supported by others (van Wagtendonk and Fites-Kaufman 2006:280). Conversely, during wet years, the frequency of fires declined. Swetnam argues that during times of high fire frequencies, fuel accumulation remained limited and the patchy mosaic of small fires produced a fine-grained spatial distribution of vegetation. During times of low fire frequency, fires were more intense and widespread, resulting in a more homogeneous and coarse-grained pattern of habitats.

Conclusion

Current findings from fire ecology studies present mixed results for evaluating our model of indigenous fire managers. We propose that California Indians would have instigated anthropogenic fire regimes characterized by frequent, small, low-severity surface burns that were staggered across local areas in some kind of multiyear rotational cycle. We suggest that individual resource patches may have been burned in a staggered rotation on a one- to 10-year (or longer) interval. We recognize that a diverse array of fire regimes, rotational schedules, and patch fire-return intervals would have been facilitated by Native fire managers across California in Late Holocene times, depending upon local conditions and changing environmental circumstances (droughts, precipitation, El Niño and La Niña events, and so forth). Multiyear rotational cycles would have enhanced biological diversity and productivity through the creation and enhancement of environmental mosaics—complex quiltlike environments with multifaceted habitats—teeming with varied kinds of food, medicinal, and basketry resources. The already in-credible diversity of the natural world of Native California would have been multiplied many times over by Indian com-munities regularly burning many small separate parcels at dif-ferent intervals.

Native California did experience many small surface burns in late prehistoric and early historic times; the fire-return interval, spatial extent, and exact magnitude of these fires appear to have varied greatly across space and time. There is little doubt that Indians started a good portion of the fires, while others resulted from natural ignition sources. The periodic setting of many small fires would have created patchy environmental mosaics that enhanced biological diversity and availability of food and nonfood resources exploited by Indian communities. This basic fire regime appears to be most evident in the cismontane region along the Pacific watershed of the Cascade Range, Sierra Nevada, Transverse Ranges, and Peninsular Ranges. Thus, the squeezed Q ring of mountains, valleys, and coastline constituted the heart-land of pyrodiversity collecting in California.

Yet, there is also growing evidence for fire histories in which periodic widespread firestorms punctuated the normal record of frequent, diminutive surface burns. Quite frankly, we did not ex-pect to see these large, high-magnitude infernos as regular com-ponents of the anthropogenic fire regimes of Native California. These conflagrations varied greatly in frequency, but current data indicate that they occurred in a regular cycle of about 20 to 50 years in the South Coast Ranges, South Coast Province, and Sierra Nevada. These fires appear to have been severe enough to replace the understory and some overstory vegetation. This im-plies that the patchy environmental mosaics carefully created and enhanced over time by fire broadcasting were occasionally modified by spontaneous holocausts.

It is possible that major fire events were an intentional part of the plans of indigenous fire managers. Native people might have ignited high-severity fires to replace older, less-productive tree stands with a succession of grasses, shrubs, and younger trees. High-severity fires would have also triggered the germina-tion of some kinds of plants that might not be affected by low-intensity surface burns (Bendix 2002:288). What is more likely, however, is that major fire events were an outcome of the inter-play between natural and anthropogenic fire regimes in Native

California. Fire in California has a dynamic element that cannot always be controlled, even in today's world of high-tech surveillance and communication, specialized fire-fighting crews, slurry bombers, and so forth. Lightning storms or human ignitions under severe drought conditions (following a wet period of intense biotic productivity) and windy conditions have always been a possibility.

Indigenous fire management was always in the process of making. Large firestorms could have periodically wiped the environmental slate clean at moderate spatial scales in local regions. This would have forced fire managers to start over, creating a fine-grained patchy environment from the coarse-grained structure that results from major fires. In starting over, they probably experimented with different fire-return intervals and rotational cycles that might have produced different kinds of patchlike environmental mosaics. The dynamic nature of California fire regimes suggests that the organization and structure of plant and animal types across the landscape were never static, but ever changing.

We believe it is best to recognize that the fire management practices of California Indians were embedded within natural ecological processes (see also van Wagtendonk 2006:45). In reality, fire managers could have altered natural fire regimes only by increasing the opportunity for ignitions and by expanding the seasons of fires. Anthropogenic fire regimes were ultimately dependent on natural processes involving fuel accumulation, fuel moisture, and burning conditions. Native people learned to take advantage of natural ecological conditions and to make the most of fires ignited by natural causes. In some regions of California, such as in the Sierra Nevada, frequent lightning strikes (e.g., Vale 1998:233) might have facilitated the creation of fire mosaics by local Indian groups. In other places, such as the Central Coast Province, where natural lightning fires are less frequent (e.g., Keeley 2002:305–306), a greater initial effort might have been involved in creating fire mosaics.

We feel that the current dichotomous debate about whether Late Holocene fire regimes can be primarily attributed to natural causes or to human motivations may not be fruitful. It is almost impossible to separate anthropogenic fire regimes from natural ecological processes. As Martin and Sapsis (1992:152) have commented,

The role of Native Americans in modifying fire regimes is often considered unnatural and not part of a "natural" fire regime. Yet we can not separate their role over the last 12,000 to 17,000 years from "natural" agents. Changes in climate have contributed to changes in fire regimes, as have Native Americans. Along with all this, the biota has gone through many generations, which might have led to changes to genetic strains more adapted to the recent fire regimes.

In sum, indigenous fire managers worked closely within the natural world, augmenting natural fire regimes by increasing the opportunities for ignitions and extending the seasons of fires—all of which were dependent on natural ecological processes in-

A NEW GENERATION OF ECOARCHAEOLOGICAL RESEARCH

A pioneering study of Indian landscape management practices in Late Holocene and historic times is under way at the Año Nuevo State Park in the South Coast Ranges (Diekmann et al. 2007). A collaboration of the California Department of Parks and Recreation, the Amah Mutsun Tribal Band of Ohlone/Costanoan Indians, University of California at Berkeley, University of California at Santa Cruz, and

Figure 19. Archaeological investigations at Año Nuevo State Park with Rob Cuthrell (UC Berkeley), Rico Miranda (Rumsen Ohlone), and Chuck Striplen (UC Berkeley; Amah Mutsun Ohlone).

volving fuel accumulation, fuel moisture, and burning conditions. Clearly, future research needs to be devoted to understanding better the past fire regimes in Native California. More detailed studies need to be undertaken within each geomorphic province to examine the frequency, spatial extent, magnitude, and seasonality of fires over time for specific vegetation types and habitats, to build upon the pioneering synthesis presented by Sugihara, van Wagtendonk, K. E. Shaffer, et al. (2006). This will require interdisciplinary work that takes into account multiple lines of evidence—paleoecological remains (pollen, charcoal, ethnobotanical remains), fire-scar dating, stand age profiles, historical aerial photography, ethnohistorical accounts, ethnography, Native oral traditions and oral histories, and archaeology.

the San Francisco Estuary Institute (fig. 19), the project involves Native scholars, archaeologists, and ecologists working together to develop an integrated ecoarchaeological approach for investigating past fire regimes and the pyrodiversity practices of hunter-gatherer peoples. The research involves the collection of on-site and off-site archaeological samples that will allow fine-grained analyses of pollen, charcoal, opal phytoliths, and other paleobotanical remains, as well as the integrated use of historic photographs, maps, sequential aerial imagery, fire-scar dating, and Native oral traditions. One team member, Chuck Striplen, is evaluating whether local Indians served as "ecosystem engineers" by altering species diversity, distribution, and abundance across the local region in late prehistoric and historic times. Another team member, Rob Cuthrell, is experimenting with new methods for extracting opal phytoliths and plant remains, such as starches from tubers and roots, from well-dated archaeological contexts.

Other ongoing archaeological research on the pyrodiversity practices of hunter-gatherer peoples in the western United States, directed by James O'Connell of the University of Utah, involves prescribed burning of experimental plots in the northern Great Basin to rigorously evaluate increases in densities and distributions of economical tubers, as well as experimental work on the energy costs and returns of harvesting yampah (*Perideridia* spp.)(O'Connell et al. 2008; Trammell et al. 2008).

Archaeology can play a much more important role in examining past fire regimes of specific regions and specific Native groups. Although considerable archaeological fieldwork is taking place across California today, few studies explicitly attempt to recover evidence of fire regimes and to evaluate how indigenous burning influenced long-term interactions between human populations and the environment. We recognize, however, that using archaeological data to address past fire regimes is anything but straightforward. As Bowman (1998:394–395) notes for Australia, evidence of aboriginal fires can be practically invisible in the archaeological record.[32] Archaeologists will need to develop new, innovative methods for comparing archaeological remains (artifacts, faunal materials, floral remains) recovered from Native residential places with paleoecological data on past fires (i.e., charcoal, pollen, fire-scar information, opal phytoliths) from off-site locations to develop a more comprehensive framework for examining the implications of pyrodiversity on past human populations and environments.

They Are Not Farmers

I (K.L.) AM PRESENTING A BRIEF INTRODUCTION about the pyrodiversity practices of California Indians in a public symposium on the Berkeley campus. It is hot and muggy in the cramped lecture hall. My lecture is going pretty well, at least in my estimation, even though I am trying to appear cool and collected without breaking a sweat in my new, bright red Hawaiian shirt with the dancing Hula women. I am a little apprehensive—today is the first time that I am lecturing about my perspective on how fire management was commonly employed by local hunter-gatherer communities to enhance and diversify wild food crops, medicines, and raw materials. A hand shoots up from an astute elderly gentleman in the second row. "So then, were California Indians not practicing agriculture?" I curtly reply, "No, they were not," and quickly press on with the lecture. My newfound friend responds rapidly, as he stands up, "But why not? What is different about this so-called pyrodiversity economy, or whatever you call it, and agriculture?" He looks a little agitated, as if I was trying to sidestep his questions. Looking out across the room, I notice a flurry of about dozen hands now in the air, several of them pumping up and down in anticipation. Ah, this should be a fun afternoon.

Since this initial lecture about fire management, a number of provocative, and sometimes heated, discussions revolving around this issue have taken place with scholars, students, tribal people, and interested lay people. Should we view fire management as simply a variation of more traditional methods of agriculture? Since Jones's (1969) classic article on "fire-stick farming" in Australia, there has been a tendency to view hunter-gatherer fire managers as analogous to farmers (e.g., Pyne 1991: xii). Lewis, Bean, and Lawton, for example, explored in the 1970s the idea that prescribed burning in Native California resembled swidden farming as practiced in other areas of the world, since they both used fire to produce changes in plant successions (Bean and Lawton 1976:40–41). This idea is becoming increasingly popular among scholars who link the concept of proto-agriculture to Native economies, arguing that California Indians were essentially practicing agriculture using wild crops.[1]

We disagree.[2] Many scholars view protoagriculture as an intermediate stage along an evolutionary path between hunting-gathering and agriculture, with its cultivation techniques transitional to the adoption of full-scale agriculture (see Smith 2001: 23–25; Yen 1989). This perception conjures up the idea that had Native Californians only been given a little more time before the commencement of European colonization, then the process of domestication would have eventually led to some kind of agrarian economy, not unlike what happened to most other complex hunter-gatherers around the world. But does this kind of thinking give short shrift to the innovative and distinctive cultural practices of California Indians? Native California is one of the few places on earth where complex hunter-gatherers in a temperate environment did not make the shift to agriculture. What if their pyrodiversity practices differed fundamentally in structure, scale, and labor investments than many types of intensive agrarian systems? What if they were following a divergent path, one that would not lead to the eventual adoption of full-blown agriculture (e.g., Yen 1989:69–71)?

Defining Characteristics

We propose that there are four defining characteristics of California Indian pyrodiversity practices that, when considered together, compose a very different kind of economic system than that found among advanced agrarian societies.

Diversification

Fire managers participated in an economic program of diversification. Although the specific suite of resources employed by local groups varied greatly from one region to the next, a common characteristic of California Indians is their ability to use a broad mix of different resources during the annual cycle. In our pyrodiversity model, we argue that they employed a regional rotation system of prescribed burns to promote and exploit a diverse range of plant and animal species for food, as well as for medicines, baskets, building materials, ceremonial regalia, and so on. Coastal people also developed a suite of innovative fishing techniques and harvesting methods to draw on a diverse range of shellfish, fishes, marine plants, and sea mammals.[3] Kroeber (1925:523–525) noted that California Indians were among the most "omnivorous group of tribes on the continent" and that unlike other Native people in North America, they tended not to specialize in a relatively few crops or foods. "Further, the food resources of California were bountiful in their variety rather than in their overwhelming abundance along special lines. If one supply failed, there were a hundred others to fall back on" (Kroeber 1925:524).

An important contribution of recent ethnographic and archaeological research is the growing identification of the amazing diet breadth of California Indians and the diverse range of resources exploited, especially seeds, berries, greens, fruits, roots, bulbs, tubers, corms, rhizomes, game, shellfish, insects, and fishes.[4]

Cultivating a Regional Landscape

California Indians employed various cultivation methods to manage landscapes at the scale of the local region. Techniques besides fire broadcasting, documented among contemporary California Indians and in some of the early ethnographic literature, include pruning, coppicing, weeding, digging, and removing debris from around plants. They were undoubtedly employed by ancestral populations as well, but evaluating the extent of their use across California over the last few centuries or millennia is difficult. Small-scale irrigation, where water from springs was channeled to specific areas to enhance plant growth, may also have been incorporated into the management of the landscape, but its use in the distant past is also difficult to evaluate. The only well-documented case involving extensive use of irrigation for cultivating wild foods in California took place among the Owens Valley Paiute, where dams, ditches, and canals measuring over three to five km (2 to 3 mi) long were constructed to water yellow nut-grass *(Cyperus esculentus)*, wild-hyacinth *(Dichelostemma pulchella)*, and other crops (Lawton et al. 1993:361–363).

The sowing or seeding of wild plants is widely reported in Native California. Most ethnographic reports of sowing describe the tending of wild tobacco (*Nicotiana* spp.) patches, especially in the Northwest Coast, Great Central Valley and Sierra Nevada,

Figure 20. Woman gathering leaves from a tobacco patch, 1932; Tubatulabal.

and Southern Deserts provinces. These cultivation practices involved burning areas, sowing tobacco seeds, and pruning individual plants (fig. 20)(Anderson 2005:173–174).[5] The cultivated plots provided a steady supply of strong tobacco, which was smoked in ceremonial and social contexts, as well as by individuals for recreational and other uses (Keeley 1995:265).

Interestingly, the relatively widespread tending of garden plots of an addictive drug (nicotine) stands in sharp contrast to the much more restricted practice of sowing seeds to grow wild plant foods in Native California.[6] In his cross-cultural analysis of complex hunter-gatherers, Keeley (1995:263–264) found that only six of the 39 California groups in his sample exhibited any evidence for seed sowing (Diegueño, Modoc, Cahuilla, Luiseño, East Shasta, Eastern Achumawi). As Keeley points out, the six seed-sowing groups are all located in relatively marginal regions with very low rainfall (33 cm [13 in.] of rain per year or less). Anderson would expand this group of seed-sowing people somewhat, but the basic association of finding these groups in arid environments appears to hold.[7] The spatial pattern indicates that seed sowing was limited primarily to the Southern Deserts

Province and places adjacent to the Great Basin—areas along the margins of the cismontane region of California.

Thus, California Indians did employ various cultivation methods in the management of the regional landscape. But they reserved the most labor intensive methods per unit area primarily to tend nonfood resources—growing tobacco and cultivating specific plants for basketry and cordage materials. Food plants appear to be a different matter. Pruning, clearing debris, and transplanting plants to new habitats no doubt took place; however, there is relatively little evidence for the widespread storage, sowing, and planting of seeds to produce future food crops—the kinds of practices that would make growing wild food crops analogous to farming.

Maintaining Flexibility

Most anthropologists draw a distinction between cultivation and domestication.[8] Price and Gebauer (1995b:6) define the latter as "a biological process that involves changes in the genotypes and physical characteristics of plants and animals as they become dependent on humans for reproductive success." The process of domestication involves a burgeoning dependency between people and domesticates as specific kinds of attributes (e.g., larger seed size, thinner seed coats, shatter-resistant seed dispersal mechanisms, quicker growing plants) are selected over time. As human intervention continues, a point is reached when domesticated species (or domesticates) can no longer successfully reproduce on their own, but must be dispersed and cared for by people to ensure that they reach maturity and maximum productivity.

Agriculture is the cultivation of domesticated crops.[9] Therefore, most agrarian practices incorporate a growing dependency relationship between resources and humans as the reproduction and survival of domesticates become ever more dependent on people.[10] Little evidence has been found that Native people domesticated indigenous plants in California.[11] We argue that this kind of dependency relationship is antithetical to the cultural practices of Native Californians who cherished flexibility—the ability to use different suites of resources and habitats from one season to the next, depending upon environmental conditions and resource availability. Native Californian harvesting methods, such as seed beating, enabled people to harvest and broadcast seeds in an efficient manner, but they did not initiate a dependency relationship over time.[12] If people did not return to a specific resource patch for several years, then it posed no long-term problem, as the plants continued to thrive without constant or sustained human interaction.

Maintaining a flexible relationship with local resources may have been a strategic way for California Indians to cope with environmental perturbations in a land of diversity caused by El Niño events, La Niña episodes, droughts, and unpredictable catastrophes such as earthquakes, volcanoes, and tsunamis, which often effect the productivity of some, but not necessarily all, resources in local regions. Oscillations in precipitation, sea surface temperature, and land temperature can differentially influence the availability of resources from nearshore waters, fisheries, and kelp forests, as well as terrestrial plant and animal foods in seasonal, yearly, or multiyear cycles.

But as outlined earlier, while warming seawater temperatures caused by El Niño conditions may adversely affect marine productivity, this warming may at the same time increase the availability of some nearby terrestrial resources due to increased precipitation. Similarly, during periods of droughts instigated by La Niña events, lower seawater temperatures may actually increase nearby marine productivity.

Flexibility may also have also been advantageous given the cyclical nature of seed, fruit, and nut productivity associated with many California plant foods. Although the cyclical pattern of high and low yields can often be associated with changing local climatic conditions, various genetic factors, as well as seed dispersal, diseases, and predator relationships, may also influence the yields of wild crops. The classic case of cyclical production is that of acorn harvests. California boasts 18 species of *Quercus* (oaks) and one species of *Lithocarpus* (tan-oak), of which nine are commonly used by California Indians (Baumhoff 1963:162; McCarthy 1993:214). Oak trees tend to produce good mast crops every two to five years, depending on the species, geographic location, and local environmental conditions (Baumhoff 1963:164–166; Koenig et al. 1994; McCarthy 1993). Considerable variability exists in the acorn production of individual trees within and between species. Some trees may regularly produce few or no acorns, while others may be superproducers that yield bumper crops in consecutive years.[13] There is little consensus among scientists about why such variation in oak masts takes place in time and space.[14] Acorns are not an anomaly; many other food crops extensively used by California Indians also experienced considerable variation in yields from one year to the next.[15]

The point we stress here is that it made little sense for California Indians to develop a dependency relationship with one particular resource type or specific habitat given frequent fluctuations in productivity across space and time. Flexibility is the key to long-term success under these kinds of conditions. In taking a regional-scale approach to resource management, California Indians could have monitored different resource patches early in the growing season, such as during La Niña years, to evaluate the potential productivity of nut crops, seeds, roots, tubers, and fruits, and the availability of marine and freshwater fishes, shellfish, insects, and game. Depending upon what resources looked promising, local groups would have planned their seasonal movements and harvesting strategies accordingly and built up their stored supply of goods.

Timing of Labor

Shipek (1993:381) observes for the Kumeyaay speaking people, that outside the occasional harvesting of large oak groves, pine groves, and agave patches, the workload was fairly evenly distributed throughout the year. This can be contrasted with full-scale agrarian peoples who characteristically invest considerable time and energy during the peak planting, growing, and harvesting times of the year. California hunter-gatherers, in general, may have been able to distribute much of their workload throughout the year. Fires were probably set in the late summer, fall, and spring months, depending upon fuel availability and moisture and burning conditions. Certainly there were some peak times of high labor investment when resources such as acorns (fall) and salmon (major runs in fall through spring), which might involve the construction of fish weirs, could be harvested and processed in bulk. But Indians could have implemented hunting forays, freshwater fishing, and the gathering of freshwater and marine shellfish throughout much of the year, while plant food harvesting took place in the spring, summer, and fall, with a decrease in harvesting activities in the winter months, when families increasingly relied upon stored foods.

A Different Kind of Emphasis

So what are the basic differences that distinguish pyrodiversity collectors in California from advanced agrarian societies? Similar to many farmers, California Indians modified the landscape, used fires strategically to clear areas and enhance productivity, and initiated strategies of bulk harvesting and storage to provide food and other resources for times of scarcity, especially during the winter months. What makes California Indians unique is how they accomplished this.

First, California Indians maintained a flexible relationship with local food resources. Plants and animals did not become dependent on human intervention for their reproductive success and survival. In contrast to farmers, they did not commonly sow seeds to produce food crops outside the Southern Deserts Province. Consequently, they did not need to tend specific food crops throughout the growing season but could incorporate them into the management of the landscape on a multiyear rotational cycle.

Second, families and local groups in Native California tended to emphasize the management of resources at a regional scale. In contrast, the primary producers (individual farmers, families, cooperatives) in field agriculture focused their attention on individual fields and possible tree crops, as well as potentially some hunting and gathering in outlying areas. While some of these fields may have been placed in diverse habitats to minimize risks from environmental perturbations, as exemplified by Hopi farmers in Arizona, the unit of production tended to be the individual field and not the broader landscape per se. In contrast to the more macroscale emphasis of pyrodiversity economies, the scale of per capita production for agrarian families and other primary producers tended to be at the microscale—labor investment in individual fields, with some fields dispersed across the landscape to minimize risk (Watson and Watson 1971:5).

Third, among many agrarian societies, the process of resource intensification involves increasing specialization, in which greater labor and time are invested in the production of a relatively narrow suite of resources. In contrast, California Indians maintained a strong commitment to the diversification of many resources spread across diverse habitats, rather than focusing the majority of their attention on a relatively few food crops, such as corn, beans, and squash.[16] Of course, agricultural intensification involving increased labor input to produce more food per unit of area can involve a mix of resources. Pacific island societies intensified production using a variety of methods and species, including fishpond aquaculture, taro irrigation, short fallow dry farming of yams and sweet potatoes, and arboriculture (bread fruit, coconut)(Kirch 1994). Prehistoric Hohokam farmers in nearby Arizona initiated labor-intensive irrigation systems but also maintained a diverse range of other kinds of agrarian and wild food exploitation, although there was a strong trend toward regional specialization of specific crops (Gasser and Kwiatkowski 1991a, 1991b). But within the last 300 years of agrarian development, the world has witnessed a dramatic shift toward hyperspecialized agrarian economies, with individual growers participating in agribusiness farm programs that focus on the production of one or two species (Bird and Ikerd 1993; Harris 1969:5; Matson et al. 1997). Clearly, the advent of monocropping is antithetical in both practice and philosophy to the pyrodiversity practitioners of Native California.

Spatial Organization of Managed Regional Landscapes

Another potential difference between California Indians and many agrarian societies is how human populations are distributed across the landscape. A detailed exploration of this topic is beyond this book, but it deserves serious attention in the future. We believe that a truly unique characteristic of Native California was its dense mass of humanity distributed across the landscape in numerous small settlements and polities. In comparing Native California to agrarian societies in the American Southwest, Southeast, and Midwest, we have detailed elsewhere significant differences in the spatial scale and elaboration of regional settlement systems (see Lightfoot 1993:182–185). Many of the agrarian polities are composed of complex settlement hierarchies consisting of large primary and secondary centers centrally placed in relation to numerous outlying hamlets and homesteads. The hamlets and homesteads are typically interpreted as places where families and other social groups resided while tending outlying agrarian fields. It is believed that the large settlements served as political and religious centers for the outlying population, as is suggested by their elaborate public structures, plazas, sophisticated domestic structures, exotic goods, and large-scale storage facilities. The settlement hierarchies tend to be found in distinctive site clusters; that is, the distribution of the primary centers, secondary centers, hamlets, and homesteads composing a single settlement hierarchy are clustered together in an area spanning about 10 to 50 km (6 to 31 mi) or more in diameter. When viewed at the regional scale, these settlement hierarchies or site clusters tend to be separated by extensive tracts of vacant land, or buffer zones. It is not uncommon for individual settlement hierarchies in the Southwest and Southeast to be separated by buffer zones of up to 70 km (44 mi) or more.

In contrast, there is little evidence in the archaeological record of Native California for extensive, well-developed settlement hierarchies, separated by broadscale buffer zones. The majority of Native people lived in relatively small villages, most probably containing no more than a few hundred individuals, as Kroeber initially estimated. In some places, such as the Santa Barbara coast and Channel Islands, substantial aggregates of people did live in very large settlements. While the spatial patterning, size, and configuration of villages varied greatly across California, there is little evidence for multitiered settlement hierarchies. The most elaborate settlement hierarchies consisted of some form of settlement cluster, typically composed of one or two larger sites and a handful of smaller ones in the nearby hinterland.[17]

Some of these larger settlements may be associated with nondomestic architecture and communal open areas that are much more embellished than in the smaller, outlying sites. These larger settlements probably served as political and religious centers for the greater settlement cluster. The villages may have been occupied throughout much of the year, or used primarily as winter villages, with other settlements being established and used throughout the annual cycle. Rather than the well-developed settlement hierarchies and extensive buffer zones that have been documented in the American Southwest and elsewhere, what we see primarily for late prehistoric coastal California is an archaeological record of individual villages and settlement clusters that were tightly packed across the inhabitable tidal coastlines, bay shores, riparian corridors, oak parklands, valley grasslands, and foothill woodlands of the state (see Lightfoot 1993:184). We believe this kind of dispersed settlement pattern would have facilitated the management of regional landscapes using pyrodiversity methods. A relatively modest-sized tribelet could have managed the local region using fire ecology in the following three ways.

First, by employing multiyear rotational cycles for burning resource patches, a relatively small population could have maintained a sequence of prescribed fires that would have kept resource diversity and productivity high. Individual resource patches did not need to be burned every year. Depending upon the types of resources to be promoted, fuel availability, and burning conditions, fires might be set in outlying areas once every few years.

Second, villages and hamlets could be moved, depending upon the spatial distribution and availability of resources throughout the seasonal cycle of the year. Early European accounts note that the locations of Indian villages often shifted from the coast to the interior (or vice versa), depending on the season of the year (Lightfoot and Simmons 1998:150–151). The movement of villages and hamlets to more distant locations within the tribelet territory would have expedited the staggered sequence of burning of outlying resource patches. Furthermore, it would have encouraged the management of nonfood resources in the hinterland that were periodically tended by individuals and families. Tobacco fields could be burned, sowed, and individual plants pinched to enable growth, while patches of grasses and willows used in the production of basketry materials and cordage could be weeded and cleared of debris, individual plants pruned to shape stems, and so on (Anderson 2005; Peri and Patterson 1993).

Third, even in cases where villages and hamlets remained tethered to one place throughout the annual cycle, logistical movements of people from villages to outlying areas were frequently undertaken to harvest and process food and other resources en masse. The dispersal of people in the hinterlands of principal villages, either on foot or by watercraft (see Ames 2002), would have enabled people to monitor resource patches across the tribelet territory and, if fuels and burning conditions were favorable, ignite prescribed burns. Anthropogenic fires tend to be set along corridors of movement and occupation, as noted in Australia (Lewis 1985b:78), indicating that the pathways of logistical travel provided an excellent opportunity for spreading fires into more distant corners of tribelet territories.

The diminutive spatial scale of tribelets has contributed to a common view of Native Californians as being extremely provincial—that most people did not travel more than a few kilometers from their birthplace, that they did not interact much with "foreigners," and that social networks did not extend much beyond the tribelet boundary.[18] That most people would never venture more than 15 to 25 km (9 to 16 mi) from where they were born may have made sense when we perceived Native California to be a lush paradise where no one went hungry and where elite families worked as system-serving regulators for the good of everyone. But this model makes very little sense in light of recent findings about environmental perturbations, resource stress, warfare, and violence. Furthermore, recent archaeological and ethnohistorical findings are painting a very different interpretation in regards to the relative isolation of Native California polities—one in which many people were plugged into broader social networks that cut across village communities and regions. These studies indicate that local and regional exchange of shell ornaments, obsidian tools and raw material, and other goods was relatively ubiquitous across much of California, that intermarriage was fairly common between people from different village communities and even across linguistic boundaries, and that religious organizations, such as the Kuksu Cult and 'Antap Society, linked together people from across broad regions.[19]

If the local polity consisted of a village community, then we can imagine a number of discrete lines radiating out from these settlements that connected individuals and families to people in the near and distant hinterland. These external social relations would have provided critical safety nets for hunter-gatherers experiencing localized hardships. Not only could they have obtained food and other goods through exchange with trade partners and participation in regional trade fairs or "fiestas," where food was brought from the surrounding countryside, or through exchange relationships between people from different communities using shell bead currency,[20] but they may have used these social connections to move their residences to new places. Thus, we believe the boundaries between polities would have been much more porous or "fuzzy" than traditionally conceived.[21]

The concept of tribelets as tiny nations evokes a picture of discrete political entities with international borders that were defended from any unauthorized intrusion. In a few cases, territorial boundaries may have been defended against neighboring groups by the entire polity. But in most cases, a much more nuanced and complex situation probably existed regarding the joint sharing and defense of resource patches. It may be fruitful in the future to consider late prehistoric and early historic California not so much as a series of distinctive, inflexible, and rigidly bounded tribal nations, but rather as a more open network of individuals, families, and local groups intertwined across the landscape through various social, kin, political, and religious relationships. Some outlying areas may have been claimed and used by several local groups. Management of resource patches on a one- to 10-year or longer interval may have been jointly shared and the areas used by a larger network of people, while patches of productive oak groves and rich fishing spots may have been owned and regulated by individuals and families. This model, which deemphasizes clear-cut polity boundaries in favor of a networked fabric of social relationships radiating across the landscape, will be the focus of future research, along with its comparison to the political economies of indigenous farmers in the American Southwest and elsewhere in North America.

Conclusion

In creating sophisticated and robust lifeways tailor-made for sustaining themselves in the natural worlds of California, Native people implemented pyrodiversity practices designed to increase the variety of local resources by enhancing the productivity of wild tree crops, shrubs, grasses, roots, tubers, and populations of large and small terrestrial game. With fire ecology as the primary management tool, they tended regional landscapes, maintained flexible and dynamic relationships with both plants and their habitats, and supported dense human populations whose members were spatially dispersed into many small groups. They also created innovative methods for harvesting a diverse array of shellfish, fishes, sea mammals, and marine plants along the coast. The periodic movement of villages and the logistical organization of workers facilitated the management of moderately large tracts of land by relatively small numbers of people. Viewed in this light, we believe it is misleading to describe the economies of California Indians as protoagricultural.[22] Not only does this send the wrong message about the incredibly rich, distinctive cultural practices of Native Californians, but it downplays important distinctions between their pyrodiversity economies and the many kinds of agricultural systems that have flourished across the world.

True, some horticultural people share some commonalities with California Indians. This is especially true for people who maintained many hunting and gathering practices during the annual round, but who selectively appended domesticates to their overall subsistence package to enhance resource diversity in relatively marginal, arid environments. We may want to refer to these mixed hunter, gatherer, and horticultural groups as "protopyrodiversity" people. Indian groups in the Southern Deserts Province who experimented with seed sowing and the growing of foreign plants are classic examples of people who augmented the diversity of their resource base by adding domesticates (such as corn) to the greater mix of plant foods available to them.[23] In other words, they fashioned their own version of a pyrodiversity economy designed specifically for the arid environments of the Colorado Desert and Mojave Desert. This involved sporadic burning of resource patches, since fuel sources are often limited in low-elevation desert settings, and adding domesticates to the subsistence mix.

But farmers involved in advanced agrarian systems that are intensifying food production per unit of land are fundamentally different than California Indians. Pyrodiversity practitioners emphasize resource diversification, landscape management at the regional scale, minimal seed sowing, flexible relationships with specific plant species and habitats, and relatively modest labor inputs throughout the year. This contrasts with intensified growers who stress resource specialization, field management, extensive planting of seeds, strong dependency relationships between growers and crops, and high labor investments during the growing and harvesting seasons. Nothing about the economic strategies or lifeways of California fire managers makes them protoagricultural when compared to these specialized, labor-intensive agrarian economies. The ethos of California Indians is entirely different, as this quote from a Karuk elder makes perfectly clear. "Our kind of people never used to plow, they never used to grub up the ground, they never used to sow anything, except tobacco. All that they used to do was to burn the brush at various places, so that good things will grow up" (Harrington 1932:63).

Much ink has been spilled by scholars about the paucity of agriculture practiced in Native California (see Bean and Lawton 1976). Why did not more advanced agrarian economies take hold here as they did in some other regions of Native North America? Climatic conditions (especially the paucity of summer rainfall) may have been a factor in why corn, beans, and squash did not move readily westward across the Colorado River or the Sierra Nevada from the Great Basin and the American Southwest. But what gives us pause about environmental explanations is the variety and extent of dry farming and irrigation agriculture practiced in historic California by Franciscan missionaries, Russian merchants, Mexican ranchers, and later Anglo-American farmers, suggesting that the Mediterranean climate alone cannot be the primary factor in explaining the paucity of indigenous agriculture. Furthermore, it is perfectly clear that local Native groups knew about agrarian practices. Not only did they trade with farmers along the Colorado River and Great Basin, but they employed agrarian-like methods in the sowing of tobacco crops in various places across California.

Rather than developing or adopting agriculture like most other complex hunter-gatherers eventually did across the globe, California Indians remained wedded to their cultural traditions of gathering, fishing, and hunting. The specific reasons why these traditions were maintained over thousands of years may vary from group to group, but we suspect it is related to the development of pyrodiversity practices that were tailor-made for the environmental diversity of California. Future research will need to address the question of why California Indians deliberately chose not to adopt agriculture. Following are some considerations regarding why Native people may have been leery about committing to agriculture.

California Indians enjoyed a greater mix of food resources, which may have translated in the long run into more nutritious and balanced diets. Native Californians may have been indisposed toward full-scale agriculture because of the varied tastes and menus that they enjoyed as fire managers. A significant problem that some Native Californians experienced in joining the historic Franciscan missions and participating in intensive agrarian and ranching practices was a much more mundane and monotonous diet. Some scholars suggest the agrarian diet, which not only reduced variety but also nutritional balance, may have had serious consequences for the health of mission Indian populations (Hoover 1989:399–400; Walker et al. 1989:354–355).

California Indians maintained a more balanced workload throughout the year than their agrarian counterparts. Although detailed comparative studies of labor expenditures have not been done for fire managers, future work needs to evaluate Florence Shipek's idea that California hunter-gatherers may have worked fewer hours overall than full-time farmers and that workloads were probably spaced more evenly over the year.

California Indians sustained flexible and dynamic relationships with the natural world, a strategy that proved beneficial for buffering periods of environmental perturbations. Hyperspecialized farmers are in big trouble if their crops fail. Either they must resort to stored goods from previous productive years or they must depend on neighbors and others to help them out. Native Californians could also cushion periods of low productivity by depending on stored goods and neighbors. But creating and maintaining access to diverse plant and animal resources within the regional landscape helped them manage periods of environmental perturbations and localized crop failures. Since wild California food crops did not require continuous human intervention or tending, prescribed burning and other management methods could be integrated into a multiyear rotational cycle. Consequently, relatively modest-sized groups could tend or manage small regions in ways that maximized the diversity and availability of food and nonfood resources. This would allow local groups the utmost flexibility for dealing with periodic cycles of El Niño and La Niña events, sea surface temperature warming, droughts, early frosts, and spatial and temporal variations in fish runs, marine productivity, game availability, and nut, grass, fruit, and other wild plant food crops.

Ultimately we wonder if the practice of fire management may have served as a deterrent to the adoption of agriculture. It will be provocative to examine the specific case studies where Native people sowed and/or raised food crops in California. In general, it appears that most of these groups are found in the Southern Deserts Province and along the edges of the Great Basin. These places tend to be characterized by rather distinctive fire regimes, often with lower incidences of fire frequency when compared to the heartland of Native fire management within the squeezed Q ring of mountains and coastal tail. This is not to say that Indian people in the lowland deserts and Great Basin did not employ prescribed burns. They certainly did. But the extent and magnitude that fires played in the ecological relationship between people and resources appear to be different in these areas. Low-elevation desert regions cannot maintain frequent, surface burns because of limited fuel loads and the discontinuous distribution of fuel across the landscape. Great Basin environments associated with juniper and pinyon woodlands are by definition characterized by long fire intervals, otherwise these fire-inhibited species could not survive and would be replaced by other, more fire-stimulated plant communities. Future work will need to address whether the sowing of food seeds or adoption of agriculture in these particular places is linked to their relatively limited utility for practicing full-scale pyrodiversity methods.

In outlining some of the benefits of fire management, we caution that there are some significant constraints as well. It is not clear, for instance, how well pyrodiversity practices would work in regions with significantly less environmental variation. Furthermore, this kind of economy requires sufficient territory for small groups to be able to gain access to varied habitats throughout much of the year. Finally, while pyrodiversity economies can maintain relatively high population densities, given the packing of many small groups across the landscape, it will typically not, unlike many advanced agrarian systems, support substantial population aggregates (towns, cities) in specific places for any substantial period of time unless supplemented by other resources that allow larger, long-term settlements (e.g., marine resources in certain coastal areas).

Where We Go from Here

I (K.L.) AM MEETING WITH A SMALL GROUP of sixth grade students from the Roosevelt Middle School in Oakland, California. It is part of an innovative program that brings university students and professors into an after school curriculum to facilitate the teaching of literacy skills through the study of archaeology.[1] In serving as mentors and coaches, we work with the younger students as they create digital stories about topics that interest them. I am continually amazed at the creativity and hard work of the students who produce inspiring story lines about living in the inner city. But one of the significant challenges for me is to make Native California—its archaeology, history, and contemporary people—pertinent to this diverse group of students, many of whom are recent immigrants to this country. They are getting a nice exposure to Native California history in school, especially in the fourth grade. But what I am discovering is that most have never talked to a California Indian, have not yet had the pleasure to dine on wild huckleberry pie, fried seaweed, and acorn mush, or fully appreciated the unique combination of artistry and functionality that characterizes indigenous cultural objects—whether they are intricately woven baskets with their delicate earth-tone designs, expertly carved antler purses, strings of Olive Snail shell (olivella) and clam-disk beads, impressive obsidian tools, or elaborate nets and traps made from cordage, among other treasures.

In discussing issues about Native California, it is not uncommon for me (K.L.) to lose the attention of not only my young charges, but the undergraduate students and other members of the teaching team, especially when I launch into some jargon-laden babble concerning an arcane academic debate. I know that this is the case when more are lined up to go to the bathroom than to listen to me. What they really want to know is quite simple. What can we learn from Native Californians that is pertinent to our lives today? Yes, the relevancy question; it rears its head once again. After giving this question considerable thought, we believe that there are four reasons why the study and appreciation of California Indians is so very crucial to the citizens of the Golden State—more so now than ever before.

Lessons on Tending the Land

First, we stress that California is blessed with indigenous populations who generated many unique cultural traditions centering around pyrodiversity economies—specific kinds of practices employed by complex hunter-gatherers that emphasize diversity and flexibility in their engagement with food and nonfood resources. Taking advantage of a remarkably diverse natural world shaped by topographic relief, the maritime conditions of the Pacific Ocean, and latitudinal differences, local groups embellished the quantity, quality, and variety of economically important plant and animal resources. California Indians initiated a plethora of methods to manage and cultivate resources across local landscapes, including the careful pruning of individual plants, transplanting sprouts and seeds to new habitats, clearing areas of debris, and some limited sowing of seeds (mostly in the cultivation of nonfood resources, such as tobacco [*Nicotiana* spp.]). The primary management tool, however, appears to have been prescribed burning.

Fire managers implemented a strategic system of burning that took into account natural ecological processes involving fuel loads and moisture, burning conditions, and ignition sources, especially those resulting from lightning storms. They accentuated local fire regimes by setting fires, most likely in some kind of staggered rotation across varied vegetation patches and habitats. In this book, we hypothesize that the ideal management program for producing diverse fire mosaics is to produce fire regimes characterized primarily by small, frequent, low-severity fires with fire-return intervals of one to 10 (or more) years, depending upon the vegetation type, burning conditions, fuels, and so forth. Although there are some data to support this model, past fire regimes in Native California appear to have been more complex and more unpredictable than we originally thought. Increasing paleoecological evidence is coming to light for recurrent firestorms that swept across some areas of prehistoric and historic Native California of significant size and intensity to destroy understory and some upperstory vegetation. The implications of these destructive conflagrations are significant—they would have periodically established new ground zeros from which hunter-gatherers would have had to work to create a fine-grained, patchy environment from the coarse-grained structure resulting from major fires.

Current estimates suggest that literally millions of hectares were burned annually in California in late prehistoric and early historic times—a staggering 6 to 16 percent of the state (not including the Southern Deserts Province). Calculations of smoke emissions from this magnitude of burning suggest that a distinct haze would have hung in many places in California during the summer and fall months (Stephens et al. 2007:213). In augmenting natural fire regimes by increasing the sources of ignition and season(s) of burns, California Indians increased the density and diversity of important food plants (seeds, tubers, roots, nut crops, greens, fruits) and small and large game, as well as nonfood resources (basketry material, cordage, medicines, ceremonial regalia). In addition, through creative harvesting methods and new technologies (boats, fishhooks), coastal hunter-gatherers increased greatly the diversity of shellfish, fishes, plants, and sea mammals that they harvested from the sea. The following section of the book—the guide to Indian uses of California's natural resources—features a sample of the amazing array of fire-enhanced terrestrial species and coastal plants and animals employed by local groups in the six provinces of the state.

Pyrodiversity practices, in turn, provided the foundation for local Native groups to collect food and nonfood resources en masse throughout much of the year using a profusion of innovative harvesting methods implemented by families and larger communal groups. They processed some portion of the food resources for preservation and storage, a critical practice that allowed them to overwinter during the period of the year when resources might be scarce. The bulk-collected resources supported winter villages, seasonal cycles of ceremonies, dances, and feasts, community political organizations, and craft production and interregional trade.

Lessons on Working with the Natural World

Second, we need to stress the close interaction that California Indians maintained with the natural world. In making the point that they were not passive hunter-gatherers, revisionist anthropologists beginning in the 1970s painted a picture of activist land managers who modified and restructured the natural environment, producing an artificial landscape not unlike that created by many agrarian people. While this was an important point to make three decades ago, it may be time to reevaluate this perspective. Native Californians crafted successful management programs thoroughly embedded within the natural world. The basic principle of pyrodiversity economies is not to transform the natural world into a humanly constructed artifact, but rather to enhance the diversity, productivity, and availability of the wild resource base by complementing and working with ongoing natural ecological processes.

This principle of working closely with mother nature would seem to have great applicability for the future management of the many thousands of hectares of public lands in California. Recognition is growing among land stewards and park administrators that strict fire-suppression policies need to be reevaluated, that native and endangered species need to be encouraged, and that maintaining or even increasing indigenous plant and animal biodiversity would be a positive development. Limited prescribed burning is now being experimented with and undertaken on some federal, state, and local parklands (fig. 21) to reduce heavy fuel loads, to clear ground debris, and to enhance native vegetation, such as bear grass *(Xerophyllum tenax)*;[2] however, considerable debate continues to swirl around prescribed burns, given the potential for fires to escape and cause significant loss of life and property damage, the problems of meeting

Figure 21. Prescribed burning at Yosemite National Park to help maintain valley meadows.

ever more stringent smoke restrictions, the difficulties of obtaining permits, and the unintended consequences of fires that could have adverse impacts to specific kinds of historic settings, vegetation, wildlife, endangered or at-risk species, and habitat types.[3] Some land stewards believe that the "natural" role of fires needs to be reintroduced—that is, allowing lightning-ignited fires to burn so long as life and property are not put at risk—but they are reluctant to employ Native fire management because it is not clear how far we should go.

> Moreover, if Indians are taken to be a "natural" component of the primitive landscape at the time Europeans first saw it—the Leopold standard for scene management—then by what logic does one stop at that particular element? One must seek to replicate Indian hunting and acorn gathering, the effect of the California grizzly bears, and so on. (Parsons et al. 1986:23)

The point is that it is very difficult to separate natural fire regimes from those created by Native fire managers. Rather than trying to make this distinction, it makes more sense to explore the use of prescribed burning methods embedded within natural processes, in combination with the latest research in forestry and land use practices, in developing new approaches for managing public lands. As van Wagtendonk and Fites-Kaufman (2006:290) emphasize, our success at managing wildlife habitats in the Sierra Nevada and most of California is "contingent on our ability and willingness to keep fire an integral part of these ecosystems. To not do so is to doom ourselves to failure; fire is inevitable and we must try to manage only in harmony with fire."

In light of the ever-tightening budgetary constraints and limited personnel available to most state and federal agencies, the California Indian model of land management involving relatively few people tending local regions may be of particular interest. We may want to experiment with rotational systems of small, low-intensity burns with fire-return intervals of between one and 10 (or more) years, depending upon the specific environmental parameters, land use policies, and so forth. This kind of management practice could maintain dynamic, diverse, and productive habitats in California without huge expenditures of time, funding, or people. What is needed now is a concerted collaborative research effort involving Native scholars, fire ecologists, archaeologists, paleoecologists, land managers, and others to understand better historic fire ecologies and prescribed burning strategies across different regions of California. We can then consider whether it is feasible for past pyrodiversity fire regimes to be revived in specific regions, and then modified according to the latest findings in forestry and land use research in order to create a new generation of efficient and economical landscape management practices.

Lessons on Sustainable Economies

Third, traditional Native practices may provide important insights in the development of sustainable economies in California. The ongoing debate about the degree to which California Indians may have adversely impacted the environment suggests that we should not view the past as a harmonious utopia within which interactions between Indians, plants, and animals remained suspended in a timeless equilibrium. There is good evidence for overhunting, warfare, violence, and even substantial clouds of smoky haze in some times and places. Significant cultural and environmental changes took place over time; human and environmental interactions remained dynamic for many thousands of years. It is not clear, for example, that indigenous management practices necessarily maintained some of California's signature plant communities—coastal prairies, valley oak savannas, and montane meadows—relatively unchanged for hundreds of years. Periodic firestorms in some regions may have restructured local environments and habitats, providing opportunities for Native groups to create new kinds of fire mosaics, and for new associations of plants and animals to unfold over time.

What is clear, however, is that Native Californians were able to maintain strong cultural traditions and successful economies for thousands of years. They handcrafted small-scale economies that were tailor-made to the specific environmental parameters of local places in order to weather El Niño events, droughts, and periods of global warming and cooling. This emphasis on local, small-scale enterprises that are ecologically sensitive may be prudent for us to consider in developing sustainable food production economies in California today. This is a hot topic. Although there are many dimensions of sustainable agriculture, we follow Matson et al.'s (1997:508) lead in defining sustainability "as meeting current production goals without compromising the future in terms of resource degradation or depletion." A significant literature now exists on the looming crisis involving the continued intensification of agrarian methods to feed an ever growing human population. Most studies warn that we are paying a heavy price in implementing this process of intensification on local environments. The negative environmental consequences include erosion, groundwater pollution, salinization by irrigation water, toxic pesticide accumulation, decreasing soil fertility and the use of unhealthy fertilizers, and critical reductions in biodiversity. Much research is now being undertaken on food production systems that might serve as alternatives to the superspecialized, monocropping programs of modern industrial agribusinesses (factory farming).[4]

One avenue of research concerns sustainable organic farming that emphasizes smaller-scale owner-operated enterprises featuring polycropping, mixed overstory (tree crops) and understory production, integrated pest management systems (which rely partly on natural predators to control pests), natural pollinators (wild bees, etc.), and integrated nutrient management systems. There is movement in California toward smaller-scale organic-based farms and ranches as environmentally friendly alternatives to industrial agriculture's large-scale monocropping enterprises. Some of these small farms are being incorporated into the urban landscape to create a more sustainable local community.[5] Traditional agricultural knowledge is now receiving some attention by researchers as having potential for integration into revised farming practices (Matson et al. 1997:508). But as Jacknis laments (2004:116), indigenous Native Californian foods and economies have been largely ignored in addressing this issue of sustainability.

It makes good sense to also consider pyrodiversity practices in conceptualizing what the future of food production could look like in California. At the very least, it may make us pause to reconsider alternative ways of managing the landscape that are not so destructive to the environment and yet still highly nurturing to plant, animal, and human populations. The monocropping practices of California agribusiness have not only minimized biodiversity, but created artificial agrarian landscapes in which native vegetation has been largely removed. One only has to take a drive to the wine producing counties of California or the farms of the Great Central Valley to see what is happening to the once abundant oak woodlands, grasslands, and riparian habitats. We are not suggesting a return to yesterday and the re-creation of pyrodiversity landscapes in place of our current agrarian lands. But it may be prudent to explore the potential benefits of introducing some vestiges of these native habitats within our contemporary farms.

Is it possible in envisioning twenty-first-century food production in California that we consider small pyrodiversity plots within farmlands, where wild foods could be reintroduced, especially along the boundaries of our modern agrarian landscapes? Rather than cutting down oak, buckeye and other native trees, they could become part of the modern farm, providing habitats for birds that could help control destructive insects and pests feeding on crops (Matson et al. 1997:507). Matthew Wheeland (2007:25), in his recent piece on "Wilding the Farm," discusses the use of towering hedgerows comprising complex mixes of native grasses, shrubs, and trees as one successful alternative in California. The mix of both domesticated and wild resources as part of the development of these smaller-scale farms would increase not only biodiversity, but the production of varied economic crops. It might be worth exploring whether niche markets might exist for native foods, such as wild berries, acorns, onions, tubers, and so forth, and experimenting with pyrodiversity methods in enhancing these wild crops. These kinds of new economic enterprises could potentially be developed in collaboration with nearby Indian groups.

However, recent attempts in California to implement wildlife habitat and water-quality programs within and around farms have met with skepticism. Professional growers and food processors are concerned that wildlife habitats will increase rodents and other predators of crops. More significantly, wildlife can introduce (through animal feces) deadly bacteria, such as *E. coli* or salmonella, to commercially grown foods. This latter problem has led to the introduction of "clean farming techniques," which encourage removal of native habitats and the creation of "clean, bare earth" around crops (Martin 2006). The introduction of native habitats into commercial farmlands is a very touchy situation that will require further research and field studies. Yet, in considering possible alternative strategies to the bare-earth practice, it may be prudent to consider pyrodiversity options that involve frequent, low-severity fires of native woodlands that will produce clean surfaces and understories, while maintaining economically useful upperstories.

Lessons on Cultural Survival

Fourth, the greater public needs to recognize and respect the fact that contemporary Native peoples continue to harvest and use wild foods and nonfood resources. Acorns, salmon, berries, and other foods are collected for ceremonies, feasts, dances, Pow-Wows, and Big Times, and also for making favorite meals or special desserts. Plant parts, shell, antler, and other materials are very much in demand for making Native arts and crafts, including baskets, shell beads, elkhorn spoons, and so on. Anthropological museums, art galleries, tribal cultural centers, and Indian casinos can do a much better job of promoting and marketing Native California crafts, not unlike what museums and other cultural institutions in Arizona and New Mexico have done for Southwestern Indian arts over the last 60 years. In recognizing the importance of Native harvesting today, we must also be sensitive and responsive to the significant problems Native Californians face. Indian people experience restricted access to resources on both public and private lands, cumbersome permit processes to harvest wild plants, the wrath of unsympathetic landowners, encounters with dangerous herbicides and pesticides, litter and garbage dumped in undeveloped areas, and the continuing loss of significant habitats containing economic plants and animals (Anderson 2005:318–325; Ortiz 1993:205–210).

But positive changes are in the making. Federal, state, and local government agencies are increasingly working with California Indian groups to facilitate gathering of traditional foods and nonfood resources. In some cases, formal agreements are being negotiated between Indian organizations and federal, state, or local government agencies, allowing specific kinds of plants to be harvested or the continuation of traditional management practices. Examples of this include pruning or tending to honey mesquite *(Prosopis glandulosa)* or single-leaf pinyon pine *(Pinus monophylla)* groves in Death Valley National Park, and prescribed burns to augment bear grass habitats in the Klamath, Shasta-Trinity, and Six Rivers national forests.[6] The California Department of Parks and Recreation has implemented an innovative program that allows California Indians to gather natural resources on state property for use in their traditional cultural practices, such as weaving baskets, crafting dance regalia, and so forth. Permits are available from the district superintendent of the specific unit of the state park system where the gathering activities will occur. A new interagency policy is being introduced for Bureau of Land Management and Forest Service lands in California and Nevada to allow tribal members to gain access and gather plant and fungal materials in such a manner that utilizes traditional management practices and promotes ecosystem health. Traditional management techniques include, "but are not limited to, burning, pruning and coppicing." The new policy stipulates that local managers of agencies "shall work in collaboration with Tribes, tribal communities, tribal organizations, and traditional practitioners to identify, restore, and enhance traditionally important plant resources" (U.S. Bureau of Land Management 2006).

We believe that a critical agenda in California's schools is to continue developing educational opportunities for our youth about Indian groups and pyrodiversity economies. Teaching about California Indians is an opportunity to stress California's great environmental diversity, and to emphasize that human cultures can work hand in hand with natural ecological processes to maintain and even enhance biodiversity. Native management practices are important in teaching our youth about the amazingly diverse indigenous food and nonfood resources that still flourish in the Golden State. We should be promoting programs that involve students' harvesting, processing, and consuming of wild foods and gathering the raw materials for producing indigenous crafts, in direct consultation with Native elders of local Indian groups. Tribal cultural centers, casinos, and traditional museums, such as the Phoebe Hearst Museum of Anthropology, can play a more critical role in providing such programs about California Indian material culture and cultural practices to school-age children. In developing such programs, we might even be able to create and expand niche markets for specific kinds of wild foods that could become available from innovative organic farmers and Native tribal organizations.

The time for appreciating and understanding Native California is now. Our state's future could be a little brighter if we look to and learn from the cultural practices and ways of working with the environment that California Indians have created and fostered over many thousands of years.

VISUAL GUIDE TO NATURAL RESOURCES

Plants

Animals

The following plates depict animals and plants once and sometimes currently used by Native Californians. We have tried to use representative species with broad ranges in California; however, in some cases, a species may not have been present in the province in which it is discussed, but instead, it represents the genus or family that did occur there.

Plate 1 *(top)*. Bracken fern (*Pteridium aquilinum*).

Plate 2 *(middle left)*. Bull kelp (*Nereocystic leutkeana*).

Plate 3 *(middle right)*. Giant bladder kelp (*Macrocystis pyrifera*).

Plate 4 *(bottom)*. Sea grass (*Phyllospadix torreyi*).

Plate 5 *(top left)*. Bear grass *(Xerophyllum tenax)*.

Plate 6 *(top right)*. Broad-leaved cattail *(Typha latifolia)*.

Plate 7 *(bottom left)*. Camas *(Camassia quamash)*.

Plate 8 *(bottom right)*. Chia *(Salvia columbariae)*.

Plate 9 *(top left)*. Coyote tobacco *(Nicotiana attenuata)*.

Plate 10 *(top right)*. Dogbane *(Apocynum cannabinum)*.

Plate 11 *(bottom left)*. Elegant brodiaea *(Brodiaea elegans)*.

Plate 12 *(bottom right)*. Ground iris *(Iris macrosiphon)*.

Plate 13 *(top left)*. Indian milkweed
(Asclepias eriocarpa).

Plate 14 *(top right)*. Ithuriel's spear
(Triteleia laxa).

Plate 15 *(bottom left)*. Pigweed
(Amaranthus fimbriatus).

Plate 16 *(bottom right)*. Red maids
(Calandrinia ciliata).

Plate 17 *(top right)*. Soap plant *(Chlorogalum pomeridianum)*.

Plate 18 *(middle left)*. Swamp onion *(Allium validum)*.

Plate 19 *(middle right)*. Toloache *(Datura wrightii)*.

Plate 20 *(bottom)*. Tules (*Schoenoplectus* spp.).

Plate 21 *(top)*. Arrowweed *(Pluchea sericea)*.

Plate 22 *(first left)*. Bigberry manzanita *(Arctostaphylos glauca)*.

Plate 23 *(second left)*. California bay *(Umbellularia californica)*.

Plate 24 *(right)*. Blue elderberry *(Sambucus mexicana)*.

Plate 25 *(bottom)*. California black walnut *(Juglans californica)*.

Plate 26 *(top)*. California blackberry *(Rubus ursinus)*.

Plate 27 *(middle left)*. California buckeye *(Aesculus californica)*.

Plate 28 *(middle right)*. California huckleberry *(Vaccinium ovatum)*.

Plate 29 *(bottom)*. California wild grape *(Vitis californica)*.

Plate 30 *(top)*. Coast redwood *(Sequoia sempervirens)*.

Plate 31 *(left)*. Honey mesquite *(Prosopis glandulosa)*.

Plate 32 *(right)*. Holly-leafed cherry *(Prunus ilicifolia)*.

Plate 33 *(top left)*. California juniper (*Juniperus californica*).

Plate 34 *(bottom)*. Western juniper (*Juniperus occidentalis* var. *occidentalis*).

Plate 35 *(top right)*. Narrowleaf willow (*Salix exigua*).

Plate 36 *(top).*
Black oak
*(Quercus
kelloggii).*

Plate 37 *(middle).*
Blue oak *(Quercus
douglasii).*

Plate 38 *(bottom).*
California scrub
oak *(Quercus
berberidifolia).*

Facing page:

Plate 39 *(top)*. Coast live oak *(Quercus agrifolia)*.

Plate 40 *(middle left)*. Interior live oak *(Quercus wislizeni)*.

Plate 41 *(middle right)*. Oregon oak *(Quercus garryana)*.

Plate 42 *(bottom left)*. Valley oak *(Quercus lobata)*.

Plate 43 *(bottom right)*. Tan-oak *(Lithocarpus densiflorus)*.

This page:

Plate 44 *(top left)*. Sierra gooseberry *(Ribes roezlii)*.

Plate 45 *(bottom left)*. Single-leaf pinyon *(Pinus monophylla)*.

Plate 46 *(right)*. Sugar pine *(Pinus lambertiana)*.

Plate 47 *(top)*. Western redbud *(Cercis occidentalis)*.

Plate 48 *(middle left)*. Yerba santa *(Eriodictyon californicum)*.

Plate 49 *(middle right)*. Beavertail cactus *(Opuntia basilaris)*.

Plate 50 *(bottom)*. Buckhorn cholla *(Cylindropuntia acanthocarpa)*.

Plate 51 *(top left)*.
California barrel cactus
(Ferocactus cylindraceus).

Plate 52 *(top center)*.
Desert agave *(Agave
deserti)*.

Plate 53 *(top right)*.
Our Lord's candle *(Yucca
whipplei)*.

Plate 54 *(bottom)*. Mojave
yucca *(Yucca schidegera)*.

Facing page:

Plate 55 *(top left)*. Black Abalone *(Haliotis cracherodii)*.

Plate 56 *(top right)*. Red Abalone *(Haliotis rufescens)*.

Plate 57 *(middle left)*. Black Turban Snail *(Chlorostoma funebralis)*.

Plate 58 *(middle right)*. California Mussel *(Mytilus californianus)*.

Plate 59 *(bottom left)*. Washington Clam *(Saxidomus nuttalli)*.

Plate 60 *(bottom right)*. Western Pearlshell *(Margaritifera falcata)*.

This page:

Plate 61 *(top)*. Ceanothus Silk Moth *(Hyalophora euryalus)*.

Plate 62 *(middle)*. Grasshopper *(Melanoplus* spp.).

Plate 63 *(bottom)*. Western Yellowjacket *(Vespula pennsylvanica)*.

Plate 64 *(top).* Anchovies (Engraulididae).

Plate 65 *(middle).* Pacific Barracuda *(Sphyraena argentea).*

Plate 66 *(bottom left).* Yellowtail *(Seriola lalandi).*

Plate 67 *(bottom right).* Cabezon *(Scorpaenichthys marmoratus).*

Plate 68 *(top)*.
California Sheephead
(Semicossyphus pulcher).

Plate 69 *(upper middle)*.
Kelp Rockfish *(Sebastes atovirens)*.

Plate 70 *(lower middle)*.
Lingcod *(Ophiodon elongatus)*.

Plate 71 *(bottom)*.
Striped Surfperch
(Embiotoca lateralis).

Plate 72 *(top).* Chinook Salmon *(Oncorhynchus tshawytscha).*

Plate 73 *(middle).* Pacific Lamprey *(Lampetra tridentata):* adult *(above)* and larva *(below).*

Plate 74 *(bottom).* White Sturgeon *(Acipenser transmontanus).*

Plate 75 *(top)*. Hardhead *(Mylopharodon conocephalus)*.

Plate 76 *(middle)*. Hitch *(Lavinia exilicauda)*.

Plate 77 *(bottom)*. Sacramento Perch *(Archoplites interruptus)*.

Plate 78 *(top)*. Sacramento Splittail *(Pogonichthys macrolepidotus)*.

Plate 79 *(middle)*. Sacramento Sucker *(Catostomus occidentalis)*.

Plate 80 *(bottom)*. Western Pond Turtle *(Clemmys marmorata)*.

Plate 81 *(top left)*. American Coot
(Fulica americana).

Plate 82 *(top right)*. California Gull
(Larus californicus).

Plate 83 *(middle left)*. Canada Goose
(Branta canadensis).

Plate 84 *(middle right)*. Common Loon
(Gavia immer).

Plate 85 *(bottom left)*. Brandt's
Cormorant *(Phalacrocorax penicillatus)*.

Plate 86 *(bottom right)*. Double-crested
Cormorant *(Phalacrocorax auritus)*.

Plate 87 *(top left)*. Pelagic Cormorant *(Phalacrocorax pelagicus)*.

Plate 88 *(top right)*. Cinnamon Teal *(Anas cyanoptera)*.

Plate 89 *(second right)*. Green-winged Teal *(Anas crecca)*.

Plate 90 *(second left)*. Mallard *(Anas platyrynchos)*.

Plate 91 *(third right)*. Ruddy Duck *(Oxyura jamaicensis)*.

Plate 92 *(bottom)*. Western Grebe *(Aechmophorus occidentalis)*.

Plate 93 *(top)*. White Pelican *(Pelecanus erythrorhynchos)*.

Plate 94 *(middle left)*. Acorn Woodpecker *(Melanerpes formicivorus)*.

Plate 95 *(middle right)*. Band-tailed Pigeon *(Patagioenas fasciata)*.

Plate 96 *(bottom left)*. Common Raven *(Corvus corax)*.

Plate 97 *(bottom right)*. Golden Eagle *(Aquila chrysaetos)*.

Plate 98 (top left). Northern Flicker (Colaptes auratus).

Plate 99 (top right). California Quail (Callipepla californica).

Plate 100 (middle). Gambel's Quail (Callipepla gambelii).

Plate 101 (bottom). Red-tailed Hawk (Buteo jamaicensis).

Plate 102 *(top)*. California Sea Lion *(Zalophus californianus)*.

Plate 103 *(middle)*. Common Dolphin *(Delphinus delphis)*.

Plate 104 *(bottom)*. Pacific White-sided Dophin *(Lagenorhynchus obliquidens)*.

Plate 105 (top). Gray Whale (Eschrichtius robustus).

Plate 106 (middle). Harbor Seal (Phoca vitulina).

Plate 107 (bottom). Northern Fur Seal (Callorhinus ursinus).

Plate 108 (top). Bighorn Sheep (Ovis canadensis).

Plate 109 (middle left). Black-tailed Jackrabbit (Lepus californicus).

Plate 110 (middle right). Roosevelt Elk (Cervus elaphus roosevelti).

Plate 111 (bottom). Tule Elk (Cervus elaphus nannodes).

Plate 112 *(top)*. Mule Deer
(Odocoileus hemionus).

Plate 113 *(middle)*. Golden-
mantled Ground Squirrel
(Spermophilus lateralis).

Plate 114 *(bottom)* Western
Gray Squirrel *(Sciurus griseus)*.

CALIFORNIA INDIAN USES
OF NATURAL RESOURCES

Kent G. Lightfoot, Lee M. Panich, Tsim D. Schneider, and K. Elizabeth Soluri

THE PURPOSE OF THIS GUIDE is to introduce the plants, animals, and minerals utilized by California Indians for foods, for medicinal and spiritual purposes, and for producing their sophisticated material culture, including cordage, clothing, tools, weapons, architectural materials, and ceremonial regalia. It is not meant to be comprehensive, but rather representative of the primary natural resources employed by Native people within each of California's six geomorphic provinces (map 8).[1] Furthermore, we restrict our discussion to those resources used from the early twentieth century to about 500 years ago. Information is derived primarily from archaeological investigations, Native oral traditions, and ethnographic studies.[2] Since most Native groups today continue to harvest natural resources as integral components of their Indian cultures, a separate guide focusing on contemporary uses of the natural world will need to be written in the future to complement this one. We present tantalizing glimpses of the tremendous depth and richness of contemporary Indian practices in sidebars for each geomorphic province.

The resources guide is organized into broad categories of plants, animals, and minerals that make sense from the perspective of hunter-gatherer people who emphasized pyrodiversity practices. Citations about specific resources for further reading are included in the text. Extensive citations are marked by an asterisk (*); these readings can be found in the back matter (see Resource References by Region and Type). They are listed separately for each region by individual subject matter or resource type. The organization for plants includes mosses and ferns, marine plants, herbaceous plants, trees and shrubs, and cacti and succulents. In provinces where we report multiple species of oaks and pines, these are grouped together in separate subcategories. For animals the major categories are shellfish, crustaceans and other water invertebrates, insects and other terrestrial invertebrates, fishes (pelagic, nearshore, anadromous, freshwater), birds (marine/water, terrestrial), and mammals (marine, terrestrial). Important rocks and minerals are also included.

This guide is written to be more than just a historical overview of the primary resources used by California Indians. We hope it will foster a closer look at the vegetation and creatures that we tend to take for granted in our own backyards, local parks, and wildlands across the state. In the hustle and bustle of our busy lives, many of us appear to be experiencing a growing

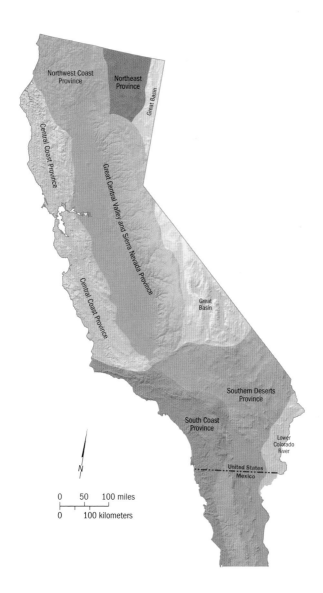

Map 8. Six geomorphic provinces of California.

disconnect with the natural environments of California. You can observe this on any workday morning, when hordes of cars and trucks rumble along Highway 101 from Marin County to San Francisco over the Golden Gate Bridge. Sullen drivers clutch their coffee cups, barely looking up from the vehicle in front of them. It is truly amazing what a constant routine and early hour can do to your senses. There probably are no more beautiful stretches of highway anywhere on the planet than those from the North Coast Ranges to the entrance of the San Francisco Bay to the South Coast Ranges. Yet navigating through the mass of humanity tends to jade the best of us to the magnificence that surrounds us—we are simply driving through it to get somewhere else.

What we find most disheartening, however, is the growing nonchalance about the natural world exhibited by children and young adults who have grown up in the Golden State. Trying to pry some students loose from their technological devices—high-definition TV, laptops, Nintendo, iPods, and so on—to experience the outdoors can be difficult, as many parents know, but we have found that some young students would rather download images of California's natural resources than to actually walk among them. Recent studies have documented an alarming trend of youth alienation concerning open spaces with wild plants and animals.[3] One manifestation of this alienation, which we have observed during field trips, lectures, and museum tours, is where students exhibit a sharp detachment between their lives and the natural environment identified with Indians—as if these represent two very separate and distinct worlds. It is clear that we need to do a better job getting the point across that Indians exploited resources from almost every place imaginable in California, including what are now our cities, towns, and suburbs.

True, California is a different place than it was only 50 or 100 years ago, and a profound sea change has transformed the state's environment since its colonization by non-Indian people. Nonetheless, what must be underscored is that the same basic conditions (latitude, distance from the ocean, and topographic relief) that produced the diverse microclimates and vegetation patterns in the past are still very much with us today. Furthermore, we must stress that change has always been part of the California landscape. Native Californians devised innovative tools, techniques, and cultural practices to cope with and survive ever-changing environmental and social conditions throughout Late Pleistocene and Holocene times to the current day. That California ever existed as a wild and pristine place is really a myth—it has been impacted and molded by people for thousands of years. Our world today is a continuation of human interactions with the environment that have long-term roots in California.

California landscapes continue to encompass incredible variety; most of the food and nonfood resources listed in this guide are still out there, even if the structure and composition of local habitats have changed—in some cases dramatically. The key point we want to emphasize with this resources guide is that all of us can rediscover the amazing diversity of California and its many uses by Indian people. All we need to do is take the time to identify some of the native plants and animals found in local parks, open spaces, and even our own backyards, and to reflect upon how they may have been utilized by California Indians. Of course, any use or consumption of these resources should not be undertaken without the assistance and consultation of local Indian elders, as some are poisonous unless processed properly.

An asterisk (*) denotes that a resource is discussed in more detail in other references. See Resource References by Region and Type in back matter.

Coastal strand, coastal prairie, northern coastal scrub, closed-cone pine forest, northern coastal forest, montane forest, riparian woodland.

Na-Dené stock or family: Chilula, Hupa, Tolowa, Whilkut languages; Algic stock or family: Wiyot, Yurok languages; Hokan stock: Chimariko, Karuk, Shasta languages.

The people of the Northwest Coast Province are renowned for their distinctive architecture, economy, and social organization. Archaeological and ethnographic information documents a plethora of late prehistoric and early historic villages dispersed along the lower reaches of rivers and streams, at the confluences of upper drainages, and along the ocean coast, especially near bays, lagoons, and places where rivers and streams entered into the Pacific. Settlements varied in size from a few structures to major villages consisting of 15 or more family houses, one or two sweathouses, menstrual huts, a dance ground, outdoor hearths, and cooking and food preparation areas. The family or living houses, built of redwood planks near the coast and of cedar planks in the interior mountainous areas, were rectangular structures with pitched roofs and unique, small circular doors only about .6 m (2 ft) in diameter. Yurok, Hupa, and neighboring people dug pits about a meter or more deep as central features in their houses. The house pits featured a central hearth and space enough for cooking and sleeping. Furniture included wooden stools around the hearth, carved wooden headrests, and sleeping mats. Wood planks supported an earthen bank around the central pit where many items were stored: a typical household would be equipped with a full range of twined baskets for serving food, cooking gruels, and storing food, water, valuables, and tobacco; hopper mortars; stone, bone, and shell tools; and clothing. The area around the house was typically paved with river cobbles. In most villages they built semisubterranean sweathouses consisting of plank-lined structures with a gabled roof, polished wooden floor, a hearth and sacred post, and a sunning porch of flat river cobbles off the rear exit door. People entered the sweathouse through a rectangular door in the roof (Nabokov and Easton 1989:288–293; Pilling 1978).

Women and children slept in the family houses, while men and older boys spent much of their time in the nearby sweathouses smoking tobacco, telling stories, mending nets and snares, manufacturing tools, and preparing for ceremonies and dances. The males began the day with a sweat, while women prepared a morning meal communally eaten in the family house, after which people pursued various activities throughout the day. When the sun began to set, the men and older boys returned to the sweathouse for another sweat then joined the remainder of the family in the living house for a second meal cooked by the women. After dinner the male relatives retired to the sweathouse to smoke by passing around several pipes, to talk, to make plans for the next day, and to sleep, at the same time that the women cleaned up after the meal, put the children to bed, and enjoyed each others' company (Harrington 1932).

The primary political entity was not the village but the house, which served as a corporate unit for undertaking economic tasks; claiming use rights to fishing spots, oak groves, and hunting places; maintaining social relations with people from other villages; and preparing for and financing ceremonies, dances, and feasts. Large, influential houses were led by so-called rich men, renowned and powerful individuals who had amassed large numbers of wealth items, including Dentalium shells traded from the north, woodpecker scalps, white deerskins, and large obsidian blades. These house societies maintained relatively fluid membership, with influential men and women recruiting family members, distant relations, and nonkin to join specifically named houses. The names of former houses, reduced to only pits in the ground, were remembered for two or three generations after the structures had been abandoned.

Major houses and their allies from the surrounding region took turns sponsoring World Renewal ceremonies, which were conducted in early fall and late spring to "maintain the established world," thereby insuring an abundance of food and the prevention of major catastrophes. Although local religious observances took place, the major ceremonies focused around the Jumping Dance, which involved elaborate headdresses, each having up to 70 redheaded woodpecker scalps, and dance baskets. Another major ceremony was the White Deerskin Dance, which featured the display of skins from rare albino deer and large obsidian and chert bifaces. The dances—performed in specially built religious structures, in large houses in prominent villages, and in dance grounds—featured songs, a set pattern of dance steps, and recitations of sacred formulas, which were conducted in various sequences over a period of up to five to 16 days (Kroeber 1925:53–75; Kroeber and Gifford 1949; Pilling 1978).

The foundation of the Northwest Coast Province economy rested on the management of the fisheries, exploiting a varied range of coastal and interior plant and animal resources, and enhancing local biodiversity through prescribed burns (see especially Harrington 1932:63–65; Stewart 2002:274–278). Travel across the landscape was facilitated by dugout canoes along the major rivers. Hunting and gathering parties also exploited nearshore coastal waters and visited offshore rocks using oceangoing canoes. The greatest labor expenditure involved the construction of large and small fish dams (weirs) across rivers and streams to capture salmon (*Oncorhynchus* spp.) and lampreys (*Lampetra* spp.) making their annual run up the rivers to spawn. Waterman and Kroeber (1938) described in detail the considerable undertaking involved in building the Kepel fish dam across the Klamath River, where a tight fence of poles and stakes was driven into the river bed, forcing thousands of salmon to enter multiple traps or corrals where fishes were removed using dip nets. Throughout the construction of the dam over a 10-day period, a series of strict religious observances and rules were applied to the several hundred men cutting stakes, the 70 men pounding poles and stakes into the river, and the large number of women feeding the work crews. Swezey and Heizer (1993) argued that many of the ritual observances, such as the First Salmon Ceremony and the use of the fish dams for only a relatively few days out of the salmon run (after which they were torn down), was part of a concerted effort to manage the anadromous fisheries in the Northwest Coast Province. For example, no one could harvest or eat salmon until the formulist or priest undertook a formal ritual, which

> may have served a distinct conservational or management purpose. In allowing the salmon to run freely during the initial period of ritual restriction (the duration and timing of which was controlled by the formulist, and generally appears to have lasted from several days to two weeks), riverine tribes maintained a productive inventory of spawning salmon each spring, which ensured successful reproduction and return of the king salmon runs in following years. (Swezey and Heizer 1993:324)

The First Salmon Ceremony usually took place during the spring run of Chinook Salmon *(Oncorhynchus tshawytscha)*, also known as King Salmon. Following the spring run, house groups might be involved in gathering roots, tubers, and early berries in late spring and summer, and for those near the coast, the harvesting of sea lions (Otariidae) and smelts (Osmeridae). The people returned to the riverbanks in late summer and early fall for the second run of the Chinook Salmon and the appearance of Coho Salmon *(O. kisutch)*, also known as Silver Salmon, and lampreys. If the acorn crop was good, then local groups estab-

CONTEMPORARY CARVING ART
IN NORTHWESTERN CALIFORNIA

The Klamath River region boasts one of the most sophisticated carving traditions in Native California, if not greater North America. Employing primarily wood, as well as elk antler or stone, artisans carved impressive dugout canoes, house elements (ladders, doors, and posts), furniture (stools, pillows, storage boxes), and other household and personal accoutrements (acorn mush paddles, spoons, hairpins, combs, purses, smoking pipes, serving platters, and bowls). As detailed by Jacknis (1995:7) and Kelly (1930), the Phoebe Hearst Museum of Anthropology is privileged to be the repository of perhaps the largest, most comprehensive collections of ethnographic examples of Klamath River carved objects in the world.

Today this carving art is alive and well. But like much of California Indian culture today, while the carving tradition has deep roots that draw energy, inspiration, and knowledge from ancestral people, it is continually undergoing change and refinement in the hands of contemporary Indian carvers. For example, most of the ethnographic pieces in the museum appear to have been manufactured using iron-tipped tools, which allowed for greater efficiency and creativity in carving various types of objects (Jacknis 1995:31). Although some materials are still carved for local use in Indian houses and for ceremonies and feasts, most of the intricate objects are produced for sale in the fine arts market specifically for non-Native collectors. The combination of the creative genius of Indian artisans and the ever-changing Indian art market has created significant innovations in traditional forms such as wooden mush paddles, spoons of antler

lished camps in the uplands for harvesting and processing acorns and for hunting deer and elk. If the acorn crop was paltry or failed, then late berries, seeds, tubers, roots, and laurel nuts were incorporated into the seasonal round, along with shellfish near the coast, which could be harvested year-round. By the early winter, people had returned to the winter villages from which they might fish for Steelhead *(O. mykiss irideus)* and hunt for game, while spending most of their time socializing, mending gear, participating in dances, and gambling (Drucker 1937a:231–232; Gould 1975:161–162).

or wood, purses, pipes, and even canoes. Jacknis (1995: 43–63) offers an intimate look at two contemporary artists, George Blake (Hupa/Yurok) and Frank Gist (Yurok), who are producing both traditional forms and new kinds of forms, such as the figurative carvings of Indian people.

A detailed description of how George Blake carves full-scale Yurok-style redwood canoes is available (Ortiz 1990/1991). Blake uses modern tools, such as chisels, gouges, and electric grinders, for producing traditional forms, including the Yurok boat. When

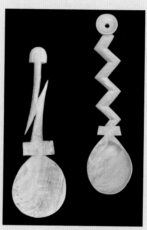

Figure 22. Wooden (maple) spoons carved by George Blake.

people question his use of nontraditional tools and methods, he is quick to reply, "When people come to buy a canoe in a covered wagon, I'll make it with old-time tools" (Ortiz 1990/1991:14). Most recently, George Blake has established a green wood furniture workshop on the Hoopa Reservation that blends Native Californian artistic traditions with Old World manufacturing methods and forms to produce eye-popping works of beauty from local oak, redwood, and fir timber (fig. 22)(Margolin 2006).

MOSSES AND FERNS

BRACKEN FERN   *Pteridium aquilinum*
Plate 1
The fronds of this fern could be pulverized and employed in making a poultice for treating poison-oak *(Toxicodendron diversilobum)* reactions. In traditional houses, the fern fronds were collected for use as plates for serving and covering fish. The fern fronds were also useful for cleaning salmon (*Oncorhynchus* spp.) and lampreys (*Lampetra* spp.)(Baker 1981:48).

CALIFORNIA MAIDEN-HAIR FERN   *Adiantum jordanii*
The characteristic black patterns in the twined baskets from the Northwest Coast Province were produced from the California maiden-hair fern. Harvested in June and July (after August the plants become too brittle), the black stalks of this fern were kept in bundles until ready for use. The stalks were then soaked in water, and the red underside was separated from the black outer side of the stalk. The stems of woodwardia or chain fern *(Woodwardia fimbriata)* were also widely used in twined baskets (O'Neale 1932: 23–24).

MARINE PLANTS

SEA LETTUCE   *Ulva lactuca*
Sea lettuce was probably eaten (Baker 1981:99).

SEAWEED   *Porphyra lanceolata*
This species of seaweed was picked in the spring, preferably in February or March for optimal taste; it could be dried and then eaten (Baker 1981:47).

HERBACEOUS PLANTS

BEAR GRASS or WHITE GRASS   *Xerophyllum tenax*
Plate 5
A member of the lily family, the clumps of grasslike leaves from this herbaceous perennial were widely used in the past as overlay in twined baskets, and they serve the same purpose today. Yurok and Karuk women harvest the highest-quality leaves from the center of clumps that are well shaded in northern coastal forests. It usually takes two to three days of drying the leaves, along with the removal of the barbed midrib from the leaf, before bear grass can be used as twining material in baskets. Indian weavers interviewed in the late

1920s and the early 1930s noted that the quality of bear grass improved greatly with periodic burns.

The thick rhizomes of bear grass could be harvested for food, often boiled or slow roasted in an earth oven for two days (Anderson 2005:192–193; O'Neale 1932:21–23).

CAMASES or INDIAN POTATOES   *Camassia* spp.
Plate 7

Local groups harvested these bulbs with digging sticks and cooked them in earth ovens (about 60 cm [2 ft] in diameter) with alternating layers of California wild grape leaves and camas bulbs (Baker 1981:21–22).

COLTSFOOT   *Petasites frigidus* var. *palmatus*

This plant used to be steamed to provide medicine for a sick child. A formula was recited as part of the treatment (Schenck and Gifford 1952:390).

IRISES   *Iris* spp.
Plate 12

Ethnographic reports indicate iris leaves were used for making cordage in fish nets, deer nets or snares, and other traps. Craftspeople dried the leaves, scraped them with mussel shells, and separated the two outer fibers. After cleaning and drying the fibers, they twisted them along the front of their thigh to make lengths of cord (Schenck and Gifford 1952:381).

MILKWEEDS   *Asclepias* spp.
Plate 13

Indians picked milkweeds, breaking the stem to extract the "milk," which they heated and stirred, often with salmon or deer fat, for use as chewing gum. It was commonly chewed at the World Renewal Ceremony (Schenck and Gifford 1952:388).

SOAP PLANT   *Chlorogalum pomeridianum*
Plate 17

People slow roasted the harvested soap plant bulbs in an earth oven. They lined the pit with rocks, started a fire, and then waited for the wood to turn to embers. After sweeping away the coals, the cooks placed alternating layers of leaves—from poison-oak *(Toxicodendron diversilobum)*, California huckleberry *(Vaccinium ovatum)*, and California wild grape *(Vitis californica)*—and soap plant bulbs on top of the hot rocks, filling up the pit. They added a final layer of sand and ashes to seal in the food, and built a fire over the earth oven. They cooked the soap plant bulbs all night until they were tender and juicy.

Fibers from the bulbs were used to make small brushes for sweeping the inside of the basket hopper during acorn processing. The bulb, when pounded and mixed with water, also served as a detergent for cleaning clothes (Schenck and Gifford 1952:380).

SWEET CICELY *Osmorhiza chilensis*

The root of this plant served as an important medicine for many kinds of ailments. It was harvested, cured, and then stored in the living house. When used as a medicine, it required the recitation of a formula. Local Indians chewed the dried root for headaches, placed sweet cicely in hearths to fumigate houses when someone had been sick, and placed it under their pillows at night to keep sickness away. Someone mourning over the loss of a loved one was bathed with medicine made from the root.

The leaves of sweet cicely could be eaten as greens in the spring (Schenck and Gifford 1952:386–387).

TARWEEDS *Madia* **spp.,** *Hemizonia* **spp., and** *Blepharizonia* **spp.**

Tarweeds were collected by the Hupa, as reported in the ethnographic literature (Drucker 1937a:231).

TIGER LILY or *Lilium paradalinum*
LEOPARD LILY subsp. *paradalinum*

This bulb, harvested in the fall using digging sticks, is reported in the ethnographic literature to be one of the local favorites. It was cooked in underground ovens, in much the same way as soap plant *(Chlorogalum pomeridianum)*(Schenck and Gifford 1952:381). Anderson (2005:349) cites historical documents indicating how well tiger lily bulbs flourish in open areas that are burned periodically, and how they disappear in fire-suppressed places as taller plants begin to shade them out.

WILD TOBACCOS *Nicotiana* **spp.**
Plate 9

Harrington (1932) presented a detailed discussion of traditional wild tobacco use among the Karuk speakers: how they burned garden plots and upslope areas, their methods of cultivation, how they cured and then stored tobacco in special baskets in living houses, when and how men smoked tobacco in wood and steatite pipes, and tobacco use among women doctors.

TREES AND SHRUBS

CALIFORNIA BAY or LAUREL   *Umbellularia californica*
Plate 24

California bay nuts were harvested in the fall; the shelled nuts were placed in large storage baskets in the living house. Cooked on a fire, people cracked the parched nuts and then ate them directly or mixed them in acorn gruels or soups.

Young Indian children once (and probably still do) enjoyed throwing the leaves into the fire, where they made a loud cracking noise.

The boughs of the tree, used to fumigate living houses after someone had been sick, were buried in the coals of the hearth. Sometimes the leaves were simply burned in houses (Baker 1981:59; Schenck and Gifford 1952:383).

CALIFORNIA BLACKBERRY   *Rubus ursinus*
Plate 26

California blackberries were eaten raw and were not preserved. Young shoots were boiled to make tea (Baker 1981:52; Schenck and Gifford 1952:384).

CALIFORNIA HAZEL   *Corylus cornuta*

California hazel sticks are one of the most common foundation materials for making twined baskets. Young shoots from recently burned patches are widely recognized as providing the highest-quality foundation material. In the old days, local basket weavers burned California hazel groves in summer or early fall. They did not cut the young sprouts in the burned areas until their second year of growth, when the young shoots had reached between 30 and 90 cm (1 and 3 ft) in length. The weavers harvested the young shoots in spring, cured them for a day or two in the sun, and then graded them into different sizes. They carefully rolled the shoots from the same size classes together, placing them in a tule mat until needed.

California hazelnuts were once gathered for food. Harvesters dried the nuts and stored them for winter use in large baskets in the living house. Similar to acorns, they were pounded into gruel flour, which was of "special value" to invalids.

The wood could be used for making fish nets and the frames for snowshoes. (Baker 1981:25–26; O'Neale 1932:15–16; Schenck and Gifford 1952:382).

CALIFORNIA HUCKLEBERRY or EVERGREEN

Vaccinium ovatum

Plate 28

People harvested the berries in fall after the first frost, when they were sweet to the taste. The berries were eaten raw. Traditionally, people stored California huckleberries in baskets in the living house.

The leaves were also useful in separating foods, such as the soap plant *(Chlorogalum pomeridianum)*, in earth ovens (Schenck and Gifford 1952:388).

CALIFORNIA WILD GRAPE

Vitis californica

Plate 29

The grapes were eaten raw and reportedly not preserved. Smaller vines were used to make rope, while the small roots could be prepared as twining elements in baskets. The leaves were commonly used to separate foods (tubers, meats, etc.) roasted in earth ovens (Schenck and Gifford 1952:386).

COAST REDWOOD

Sequoia sempervirens

Plate 30

The coast redwood served as an important raw material, especially for people near the coast. People utilized downed trees or driftwood, although trees were occasionally cut down using elk horn axes or adzes, with the help of stone mauls. A cut was made large enough to allow a person to chisel his or her way through the tree.

Craftspeople constructed dugout canoes from large logs for river travel and for traveling to offshore islands. Traditional methods of canoe manufacture involved splitting the logs into two halves, then carving out one of the halves with the aid of fire and stone-handled adzes of mussel shell. Steel quickly replaced the mussel shell for adzes beginning in the late 1800s. The canoe makers plugged holes and cracks with pitch to make the dugout watertight. Although the length and breadth of the canoes varied somewhat, Kroeber observed in the early 1900s that the standard size was about 5.5 m (18 ft). Carved paddles, measuring 1.8 to 2.4 m (6 to 8 ft) in length, were used to push off rocks, for steering, and for paddling.

Coast redwood logs continue to be used today for planks in the construction of "special" houses and sweathouses. In ancient times, home builders used elk horn wedges to split logs and planks, with the aid of a pear-shaped maul made of basalt or some other hard stone.

The Yurok constructed small cylindrical boxes by hollowing out sections of coast redwood logs about .6 to 1.2 m (2 to 4 ft) in length. The boxes were used to store wealth objects and dance regalia in houses. From slabs of wood, craftsmen carved rectangular platters or trays for serving deer meat, and handsome finger bowls for use after meals. Small round block stools, from 8 to 23 cm (3 to 9 in.) high, crafted from coast redwood and other local woods, provided seats for high-ranking men. The pillow or headrest, a square-shaped block with a curved area for the head or neck, which used to be standard furniture in any family house or sweathouse, was also carved from coast redwood.*

Coast redwood roots are still used as twining elements in the weaving of baskets; they are especially good for making cooking baskets, since they expand when wet and can hold water. Other woods used for making planks in the construction of houses and furniture, especially along interior drainages, included incense-cedar *(Calocedrus decurrens)* and Port Orford cedar *(Chamaecyparis lawsoniana)*.

Oaks

Several species of oaks in the Northwest Coast Province served as sources of food, medicine, and raw materials.

BLACK OAK *Quercus kelloggii*
Plate 36
These acorns, collected in fall, were viewed as second rate when compared to acorns from tan-oak *(Lithocarpus densiflorus)*, but they were still consumed by local people (Schenck and Gifford 1952:382).

OREGON OAK *Quercus garryana*
Plate 41
Oregon oak acorns were collected in the fall. Ethnographic reports indicate they were not as tasty as tan-oak acorns. Consequently, local Indians did not use it much unless other oak species failed. Family cooks also found it harder to pound into meal.

They used the bark on either side of knots as medicine for expectant mothers. The bark could be pounded and then rubbed on the woman's body, or it could be served in warm water (Schenck and Gifford 1952:382).

TAN-OAK or TANBARK-OAK *Lithocarpus densiflorus*
Plate 43
By all accounts tan-oak, although not a true oak, produced the best-tasting acorns in the Northwest Coast Province. Harvests took place in early fall, usually in October. Families had their favorite groves where they established acorn camps. The people of the Northwest Coast Province employed various methods for removing tannic acid, as outlined in the chapter "The Central Role of Fire." Merriam (1967:200) described how women placed fresh acorn flour on a

porous cloth and let water sprinkle through it all night so that it was ready to eat the next day. Once the tannic acid was removed, the acorn chefs cooked the meal in several basic ways. One involved warming gruel or soup in a cooking basket with hot rocks, stirring the contents occasionally with a wooden paddle. They often flavored the acorn gruel with venison, herbs, and other additions. Another way involved the preparation of acorn bread cooked in underground rock-lined ovens. Today, acorn bread is often baked in modern stoves. Acorn paste could also be made into patties and cooked in hot coals.

Tan-oak bark was used as a dye for fishing nets, so that the fishes "could not see them." The oak flats were set on fire after the harvests to reduce underbrush (Baker 1981:35–36; Gould 1975:156; Schenck and Gifford 1952:382).

PACIFIC MADRONE   *Arbutus menziesii*

Pacific madrone berries, harvested in the fall by vigorously shaking the tree's branches, used to be steamed in an acorn-cooking basket with a little water and hot rocks. The cooks dried the steamed berries on a basket platter and then placed them in storage baskets in the living house. Once prepared for storage, the berries could be soaked in warm water before eating. Pacific madrone berries were also edible after roasting over an open fire.

As with leaves of other plants, Pacific madrone leaves were used in earth ovens to separate layers of food. Pacific madrone leaves were also used during puberty ceremonies, where young girls picked and tossed the leaves over their shoulders for good luck as they prepared to take a cold water bath.

Northwest Coast Province people harvested Pacific madrone wood specifically to cook salmon in the First Salmon Ceremony. In the past and today, the wood is also recognized as excellent material for carving objects. The inner bark of this plant was also used in the past to make an "every-day dress" (Baker 1981:17; Schenck and Gifford 1952:387–388).

SALMONBERRY   *Rubus spectabilis*

Salmonberries were eaten fresh. Long shoots of salmonberry were harvested and eaten with seaweed and lampreys (*Lampetra* spp.) (Baker 1981:51).

STRAGGLY GOOSEBERRY   *Ribes divaricatum var. pubiflorum*

Straggly gooseberries were eaten raw (Schenck and Gifford 1952: 384).

SUGAR PINE   *Pinus lambertiana*
Plate 46

Sugar pine "nuts" (the seeds of the plant) were gathered in fall. Men climbed the trees to shake the limbs with the aid of a hook to knock off the large pine cones. As the cones fell, people on the ground quickly gathered them. They roasted the sugar pine cones in underground ovens to extract the nuts. The nuts could be eaten or stored.

The wood of the sugar pine was used in the construction of planks for houses and sweathouses. The pitch of the pine could be used as an adhesive, and the sweet sap was eaten raw. Pine nuts are still used in making jewelry today (Baker 1981:44; Schenck and Gifford 1952:378–379).

WESTERN CHOKE-CHERRY   *Prunus virginiana* var. *demissa*

As with the California blackberry, the berries of western choke-cherry were eaten raw and were not preserved (Schenck and Gifford 1952:384).

WILLOWS   *Salix* spp.
Plate 35

The roots of several different species of willow, including narrowleaf willow *(S. exigua)*, Sitka willow *(S. sitchensis)*, and Scouler's willow *(S. scouleriana)*, are still used as twining elements in the production of baskets (Baker 1981:52–53). O'Neale (1932:18–19) described how the roots used to be harvested and processed. A .9 to 1.2 m (3 to 4 ft) length of root, identified as having excellent attributes for basket weaving, was slowly cooked for 12 to 14 hours by mixing hot coals into the sand around the roots. The weavers then cut the roots, splitting them into eighths, and soaking them overnight. After soaking, the roots were split into ribbons and smoothed using a mussel shell, bone spoon, or case knife. A variety of other roots, including those of coast redwood *(Sequoia sempervirens)*, sugar pine *(Pinus lambertiana)*, ponderosa pine *(P. ponderosa)*, alders *(Alnus* spp.), and California wild grape *(Vitis californica)*, were processed and used as twining elements in local baskets.

The roots of the Sitka willow were employed in making fire drills, while the twigs served nicely for drying salmon *(Oncorhynchus* spp.).

YERBA SANTA or   *Eriodictyon californicum*
MOUNTAIN BALM
Plate 48

Yerba santa can be harvested as a medicine for treating colds, pleurisy, and tuberculosis. The leaves were boiled in a cooking basket with hot rocks. Today, syrup is produced by boiling the leaves and adding some sugar or mixing it with the pitch of the sugar pine *(Pinus lambertiana)*. Traditional medicinal practices involved the recitation of formulas as part of the treatment. The leaves could also be chewed, along with water, making a "sweet and soothing" relaxant (Baker 1981:30; Schenck and Gifford 1952:388).

SHELLFISH

Plate 59

In addition to the shellfish species described below, other species also gathered include Littleneck Clam *(Leukoma staminea)*, Rock Scallop *(Crassadoma gigantea)*, Northern Razor Clam *(Siliqua patula)*, Washington Clam *(Saxidomus nuttalli)*, Giant Chiton or Gumboot *(Cryptochiton stelleri)*, sea urchins (*Strongylocentrotus* spp.), and various species of barnacles (Gould 1975:155).

CALIFORNIA MUSSEL   *Mytilus californianus*

Plate 58

The primary shellfish species collected on the northwest coast of California was California Mussel. Local Indians still collect them from the intertidal rocky coastline in large numbers. They are available year-round, but during the summer months a marine dinoflagellate *(Alexandrium catenella)* makes the meat poisonous to humans. The meat was roasted, and the shells employed as spoons, especially by women, for eating acorn gruel and other kinds of soups (Gould 1975:155; Kroeber 1925:93).

DENTALIUM or TUSK SHELL   *Antalis pretiosum*

The shell of this mollusk provided the most-valued shell money in the Northwest Coast Province. Indians graded Dentalium shells by length and kept them on strings. Much of the shell probably came (via trade networks) from Vancouver Island and the nearby environs (Kroeber 1925:22–25).

INSECTS AND OTHER TERRESTRIAL INVERTEBRATES

The Indians of the Northwest Coast Province were among the few reported in the state who did not regularly include insects in their diet, apparently due to the abundance of other food resources. As Kroeber (1925:84) writes, "The food supply was unusually ample along both coast and river, and the Yurok ordinarily did not have to condescend to the grasshoppers, angle-worms, and yellow-jacket larvae whose nourishing qualities other tribes of the State exploited." The same was true of other groups in the Northwest Coast Province, but the indigenous peoples of the region likely did consume some insects in times of scarcity.

BANANA SLUG   *Ariolimax columbianus*

Banana Slugs were considered a starvation food among the Yurok and Karuk (Driver 1939:376; Kroeber 1925:84).

CRICKETS   *Anabrus* spp.

Crickets were an important source of protein in the Shasta Valley. Women were the primary gatherers of these insects, which were ground into meal for storage (Silver 1978:216; Voegelin 1942:177).

GRASSHOPPERS   **Suborder Caelifera**

Plate 62

Only the Chilula and Shasta groups are reported to have eaten grasshoppers, although not in large numbers. Grasshoppers were boiled among the Shasta (Driver 1939:310; Voegelin 1942:177).

HONEYBEE   *Apis mellifera*

The Wiyot collected wild honey from the introduced Honeybee in postcontact times (Driver 1939:376).

YELLOWJACKET LARVAE   *Vespula* spp. and

Plate 63   *Dolichovespula* spp.

While not as popular in this province as in other parts of the state, yellowjacket larvae were occasionally eaten by the Tolowa, Yurok, Wiyot, and Shasta (Driver 1939:310; Voegelin 1942:59).

FISHES
Nearshore Fishes

Plates 69, 70

Coastal northwestern California boasts a rich offshore fishery. It was exploited by local Native people with nets and fishing lines from the shore or in dugout canoes when the sea was relatively calm. Some of the more important species included rockfishes (*Sebastes* spp.), California Halibut *(Paralichthys californicus),* sculpins (Cottidae), and Lingcod *(Ophiodon elongatus).* Redtail Surfperch and smelts, described below, were also important catches.

REDTAIL SURFPERCH   *Amphistichus rhodoterus*

This fish, which might weigh as much as 34 kg (75 lb), could be caught off the beach (Gould 1975:159).

SMELTS   **Family Osmeridae**

Smelts are small, silvery fishes that thrive in large shoals or schools. Both marine and freshwater species of smelts are native to California. Nearshore smelts were caught in large numbers along beaches using V-shaped dip nets. Local fishermen could often tell when the fishes were running because of the large number of gulls (*Larus* spp.) feeding on the schools. Gould observed that the size of smelt runs varied along local beaches from year to year. Fishes not eaten fresh were initially dried on driftwood in the sun, and then in the sand. The curing process for preparing the bulk-harvested smelts for storage took several days (Drucker 1937a:233; Gould 1975:158–159; McGinnis 2006:196–203).

Anadromous Fishes

| **CHINOOK SALMON or KING SALMON** | *Oncorhynchus tshawytscha* |

Plate 72

Chinook Salmon make runs upstream from the ocean in great numbers to spawn in the spring and fall. The spring run may take place between March and June, while the fall run typically occurs anywhere between September and January, depending on the timing of winter rains, which increase water flow and lower the water temperature. After putting on weight in the sea, the Chinook Salmon return upstream to gravelly stream places to spawn; at that time they typically measure between a half and a meter long. Traditional methods of fishing involved dip netting from fishing places or platforms; the use of seines, gill nets, or harpoons; or bulk harvesting in fish traps built into fish weirs. Salmon were also hunted at night from canoes using torches and harpoons or by wading out into the river. The Chinook Salmon were prepared by splitting with a wood-handled chert knife; they were then smoked for storage. Ethnographic observations suggest the fishes from the river mouths were higher in fat and, when dried, richer and tastier; the fishes harvested from upstream locations, whose meat was leaner, stored longer after they were cured. But the fat content depended on the runs as well. Fishes in spring runs of Chinook were often fatter than those coming up the rivers and streams in the fall to spawn.*

| **COHO SALMON or SILVER SALMON** | *Oncorhynchus kisutch* |

This species swims upstream in the fall, to spawn. Their migration is usually triggered by the first major storm with heavy rainfall. Although the timing of the run overlaps with that of the Chinook Salmon *(O. tshawytscha)*—sometime between September and November, depending on when the first hard rains come—the Coho Salmon prefers the smaller, cooler streams, in contrast to the Chinook Salmon. At sea the fish spends most of its time in coastal areas close to its natal streams, growing in size from 6 to up to 10 kg (13 to 22 lb). Recent research indicates that less than half of the over 600 coastal streams and rivers that once supported Coho Salmon runs in

California are still spawning places today. Old-timers employed similar methods of harvesting and processing this fish as those described for Chinook Salmon (McGinnis 2006:149–152; Schoenherr 1992:614; Swezey and Heizer 1993).

EULACHON or CANDLEFISH   *Thaleichthys pacificus*

This smelt species is technically an anadromous species, spending nearly three years in ocean waters and then spawning up coastal creeks and rivers (especially the Klamath River) in spring and summer. It attains a length of almost 30 cm (1 ft). The male and female Eulachon school separately during the spawning run. The female fishes, which have a high fat content because of their eggs, were processed by local Natives into a flavorful oil. The high oil content of the Eulachon allowed them to be used for candles (Gould 1975:158; McGinnis 2006:202–203).

PACIFIC LAMPREY   *Lampetra tridentata*
Plate 73

Schools of Pacific Lampreys ascend the rivers from the ocean to spawn in large numbers between late spring and the end of summer. Dip nets, lamprey nets, and lamprey traps (round or conical) were used to harvest the fishes, some measuring almost 60 cm (24 in.) in length. Local Indians constructed special weirs with V-shaped fences across streams and small rivers, where they harvested the Pacific Lamprey en masse, preparing them for meals or storage by splitting them in two using bone awls (Drucker 1937a:233; Kroeber 1925:85; McGinnis 2006:127).

RAINBOW TROUT   *Oncorhynchus mykiss,*
formerly Salmo gairdneri

Rainbow Trout may be found year-round in the large rivers of the Northwest Coast Province. Some are anadromous, spending an average of two years in the sea, while others never leave their natal streams and rivers. The anadromous subspecies of the Rainbow Trout, *O. m. irideus,* known as the Steelhead, makes its spawning run up coastal streams and rivers in fall/winter or spring. Some of these fishes returning to their home rivers and creeks may weigh over 9 kg (20 lb). Unlike the Chinook and Coho Salmon *(O. tshawytscha and O. kisutch),* the Rainbow Trout does not die after spawning but returns to the ocean, although modern tagging studies indicate only about 10 to 20 percent of the individuals return for a second spawning run. The Rainbow Trout migration was greeted along the rivers and streams by Native people with gill nets and spears (McGinnis 2006:167–176; Swezey and Heizer 1993).

BIRDS
Marine Birds and Waterbirds

Coots and cormorants were the primary species taken, but Gould noted that various species of ducks (Anatidae), geese (Anatidae), rails (Raillidae), and murres (Alcidae) were also hunted as minor constituents of the annual round (Gould 1975:161).

AMERICAN COOT   *Fulica americana*
Plate 81

Old-timers hunted this species on Lake Earle when they were unable to fly during the molting of their major flight feathers. At this time they could be clubbed easily from canoes (Drucker 1937a:234).

CORMORANTS   *Phalacrocorax* spp.
Plates 85–87

These sea birds used to be hunted on offshore sea stacks, rocks, and sea cliffs during the nesting season in midsummer. Dugout canoes brought hunters to the nests, where the young birds, unable to fly, could be easily clubbed (Gould 1975:158).

Terrestrial Birds

CALIFORNIA QUAIL   *Callipepla californica*
Plate 99

This bird was hunted using a trap of sticks fashioned like a crib (Drucker 1937a:234).

WOODPECKERS   **Family Picidae**
Plate 94

The scalps of woodpeckers were highly valued in Native California, serving as important components of dance regalia. Species included the Pileated Woodpecker *(Dryocopus pileatus)* and the Acorn Woodpecker *(Melanerpes formicivorus)*(Kroeber 1925:26; Merriam 1967: 199).

MAMMALS
Marine Mammals

GRAY WHALE   *Eschrichtius robustus*
Plate 105

Stranded whales, highly valued as food and raw material, would bring the entire community to the beach. Rich men and their families divided the coast into discrete zones near their villages, where they would claim whales that drifted ashore. The Gray Whale was probably the most common species, but a Humpback Whale *(Meg-*

aptera novaeangliae), Blue Whale *(Balaenoptera musculus)*, or perhaps Northern Right Whale *(Eubalaena glacialis)* might also drift to shore (Drucker 1937a:228, 245).

SEA LIONS and SEALS   Families Otariidae and Phocidae
Plates 102, 106, 107

Excellent archaeological evidence has been found for late prehistoric hunting of several species of sea lions: Steller Sea Lion *(Eumetopias jubatus)*, Northern Fur Seal *(Callorhinus ursinus)*, and California Sea Lion *(Zalophus californianus)*. In addition, an excavation of a ritual site on an offshore rock near Patrick's Point uncovered a thousand or more complete sea lion crania (Heizer 1951). Prehistoric hunting of pinniped species historically known to avoid the coast may have also led to the development of watercraft (Hildebrandt and Jones 1992). The Steller Sea Lion is a local migrant and frequents the offshore islands of the Northwest Coast Province, where this species historically had rookeries, but now those areas are mostly used as resting sites. The California Sea Lion is a known migratory species that has rookeries mostly south of Point Conception. Mostly males migrate north along northern California, where they pursue hake, squid, salmon, and other prey.

Oceangoing dugout canoes were once employed to bring hunters to offshore islands, especially rookeries where they hunted adults and pups. Ethnographic descriptions indicate that some men used bear or deer skins as disguises, with the hunters hiding behind rocks waiting for the sea lions to make landfall. In other cases, Indians would sneak up to sleeping animals. Hunters used to kill sleeping Harbor Seals *(Phoca vitulina)* on the beach with clubs (Drucker 1937a:234). Larger mature animals were either clubbed or dispatched with a harpoon tied to a shaft that was thrown with some accuracy for short distances. The shaft was then retrieved, and the hunters followed the seal or sea lion out to sea in their canoe. Eventually the hunters fired more shots and closed in to club the tiring animal. The animal was either brought on board or towed to the mainland. Good places for hunting sea lions were claimed by rich men from major villages.*

Terrestrial Mammals

BLACK-TAILED DEER   *Odocoileus hemionus columbianus*
Traditional methods of hunting Black-tailed Deer (the coastal subspecies of Mule Deer) included the use of snares and pits to capture them. Drucker (1937:233) described the snares as a "running noose of twisted or braided hide suspended between 2 trees in the runway, tied to springy sapling to prevent breaking." Pits were dug deep

enough, with poles laid across the opening, so that when an animal fell through its legs could not touch the bottom of the pit. The poles were covered with branches and duff to disguise the pits from deer herds. The hunters also drove deer into rivers or lakes where they shot or clubbed the animals from canoes.

Local people employed deer hides to make clothing for both men and women, as well as moccasins. Skins of white (albino) deer were highly valued and used in the White Deerskin Dance of the World Renewal Ceremony. Old-timers employed deer bone and antler for crafting awls, harpoons, fish gorgets, and other tools.*

ROOSEVELT ELK or WAPITI *Cervus elaphus roosevelti*
Plate 110

Traditional methods of hunting this animal also included the use of snares and pits, as described above, as well as driving them into ravines or streams, where they could be shot with arrows from canoes.

Elk horn was coveted in the past for manufacturing a diverse range of utensils and tools, including the points of stone tools, elaborately carved spoons used in eating acorn gruel, and purses used to hold dentalium *(Antalis pretiosum)* and other dance regalia. Craftspeople excelled at designing cylindrical purses or money boxes with lids that could be lashed into place. Elk horn also served as wedges for splitting logs and as chisels for finishing planks in house structures.

Elk hide sometimes served as armor for catching or deflecting arrows. People also employed elk bone and antlers for making awls, harpoons, and other tools (Kroeber 1925:93–94; Merriam 1967: 171). Today there is a strong revival of employing elk horn in the production of Northwest Coast Province Indian crafts and art objects, such as intricately carved spoons.

ROCKS AND MINERALS

OBSIDIAN

Skilled craftspeople who made stone tools (known in the anthropological literature as lithic knappers) relished black and red obsidian for making tools and elaborately flaked ceremonial objects. The latter were exemplified by stunningly crafted, symmetrically bipointed artifacts that had been intricately knapped on both sides (defined by archaeologists as bifaces). These impressive works of art, measuring up to 76 to 84 cm (30 to 33 in.) in length, were used in the World Renewal Ceremony. Red obsidian bifaces had the highest value (Kroeber 1925:26–27). Chemical methods for determining the source of obsidian found in archaeological sites indicates that material used for making projectile points came from the Medicine Highlands about 280 km to the east, while the large bifaces used in ceremonies originated from the Warner Mountains in northwestern Nevada and southern Oregon, more than 400 km (250 mi) away (Hughes 1982).

STEATITE or SOAPSTONE
People of the Northwest Coast Province mined steatite from local sources to produce carved dishes for catching grease from roasting salmon and other foods (Bright 1978:183).

CENTRAL COAST PROVINCE VEGETATION TYPES

Coastal strand, coastal salt marsh, freshwater marsh, coastal prairie, coastal sage scrub, northern coastal scrub, closed-cone pine forest, northern coastal forest, valley and foothill woodland, valley grassland, riparian woodland, chaparral.

CENTRAL COAST PROVINCE ETHNOLINGUISTIC UNITS

Yukian stock or family: Yuki, Wappo languages; Hokan stock: Pomo, Salinan, Esselen languages; Utian (Penutian) stock or family: Lake Miwok, Coast Miwok, Costanoan (Ohlone) languages; southern Na-Dené stock or family: Mattole, Nongatl, Sinkyone, Lassik, Wailaki, Cahto languages.

The Central Coast Province is widely recognized for its spectacular scenery of varied ocean, mountain, and valley landscapes, and its people created sophisticated technologies, cultural practices, and social organizations for supporting large numbers of Native communities. Taking full advantage of the amazing array of plants and animals available in local areas, Indian people maintained a carefully orchestrated settlement pattern designed to exploit seasonal resources. Local communities typically moved their residences from river shores or oceanfront property in the summer to inland and often elevated areas during the cool and rainy winter, where they often established winter villages. Following this pattern, they usually constructed brush huts or open ramadas in the summer and built more labor intensive enclosed tule or bark houses for winter use.*

The architecture of the Central Coast Province varied depending on the resources available and the distinctive cultural traditions of local areas. Redwood bark offered a readily available siding to many homes in the North Coast Ranges. People built the classic conical redwood bark house by excavating a central pit, erecting house poles, and then attaching strips of redwood bark and grasses to this framework. Tules (*Schoenoplectus* spp.), also called bulrushes, and other marsh grasses provided an alternative thatching for groups living near estuaries or riverine or coastal environments. Here, tules, ferns, and other plants were woven across domed frameworks of bent poles. Additional buildings constructed in major settlements, especially winter villages, included sweathouses, menstrual huts, multifamily houses, and assembly or ceremonial houses. Semisubteranean assembly houses became permanent features of large villages and could be used for various social gatherings and ceremonies.*

Local communities sponsored important communal activities such as dances, religious observances, and feasts for which they invited people from surrounding areas to attend. These ceremonies tended to be centered in the larger villages containing assembly houses or specially built dance houses or outdoor brush enclosures. Central Coast Province people also worked communally in the bulk harvesting of game. These hunts often targeted large game, such as Black-tailed Deer (*Odocoileus hemionus columbianus*), Elk (*Cervus elaphus*), and Pronghorn (*Antilocapra americana*); however, most groups also communally hunted rabbits (Leporidae). Hunters equipped with bows and arrows, slings, and other items would work together to flush animals from the woods and drive them to kill locations. Game could be driven toward a specific hunter who waited in ambush with bow and arrow, or toward fences, snares, and multiple hunters. Groups of hunters drove smaller game, such as rabbits, into a series of nets designed to trap the animals, where the entangled creatures could be clubbed or shot with arrows. Although individual hunters procured many species of game, communal hunting figured prominently in the procurement of game, providing an important means for bulk harvesting of food for immediate consumption, such as during intervillage feasts and dances, or for winter storage.[*]

The ownership of resource patches varied among groups. Among some people, families and individuals did not own specific resources or places, making these resources communal property readily available to the broader social group (Gifford 1967:13; Sawyer 1978:262). Among other groups the recognition of private property allowed some resource procurement by single families or individuals (Beard 1977:50; Collier and Thalman 1996:126, 193–195; McLendon and Lowry 1978:310). For example, Coast Miwok people practiced private ownership of oak trees (*Quercus* spp.), where they passed down rights to specific trees or groves from parents to children over multiple generations (Collier and Thalman 1996:193–194). By maintaining ownership to productive trees, some families could have been insured a steady supply of acorns, even though they probably shared their crop with other members of the tribelet (Collier and Thalman 1996:193). People also owned fields with known bulb or seed resources, clam beds, fishing locations, and boat landings. These approaches to ownership, in addition to the communal hunting discussed above, reflect the numerous ways, both family-based and communal, that Native Californians procured their resources.

Land management practices played a central role in the procurement of resources in the Central Coast Province. Costanoan and Wappo groups managed their landscapes through controlled burning of fields. Periodic burns limited undergrowth and the risk of wildfires, fostered the growth of desired wild plants, and created habitats that would attract sought-after game, such as deer.* However, the nature and degree to which pyrodiversity collecting was achieved has yet to be fully evaluated. For example, it is not clear if all groups practiced controlled burns. Little ethnographic evidence exists for Coast Miwok people torching fields, but they did practice another form of landscape management in that they intentionally transplanted small California bay trees *(Umbellularia californica)* to new habitats (Collier and Thalman 1996:37). It is claimed that the Wappo intentionally scattered seeds from desired plants to increase plant yields in specific locations (Beard 1977:52). These various approaches to land management would have allowed Native Californians to actively control the availability of key resources. Through diverse hunting and gathering methods, ownership of productive resource patches, and controlled burning and other landscape management practices, Native Californians throughout the Central Coast Province actively engaged with one another and their natural surroundings to obtain the resources they desired.

MOSSES AND FERNS

FERNS   Phylum Pteridophyta
Plate 1

Central Coast Province groups typically exploited locally available ferns to make designs in basketry. Bracken fern *(Pteridium aquilinum)*, the California maiden-hair fern *(Adiantum jordanii)*, and the common maiden-hair fern *(A. capillus-veneris)* are among the ferns employed by the Coast Yuki, Wappo, Kashaya Pomo, and Salinan.*

Costanoan peoples used to employ ferns as thatch for structures (Levy 1978a:492). The Coast Miwok also utilized western sword fern *(Polystichum munitum)* to thatch structures (Collier and Thalman 1996:178). The Kashaya Pomo extracted the juice from the young,

LANGUAGE REVITALIZATION IN NATIVE CALIFORNIA

A significant challenge in California Indian country is the revitalization of its many languages. Although 80 to 100 (or more) different languages may have been spoken at the time of European contact, only about 50 still have Native speakers today. Many of these languages are now endangered, as they are no longer used at home and children are not learning them. Furthermore, many of these languages have only one or, at most, a few fluent speakers remaining. As Leanne Hinton (1994:13–14) emphasizes, California Indian languages are in a "life-and-death struggle" — we may see "ninety percent of these languages, or perhaps all of them, disappear in our lifetimes." Facing this catastrophic situation, a number of Indian and non-Indian people have mobilized to support language training among Native people across California. One such nonprofit organization, The Advocates for Indigenous California Language Survival (www.aicls.org), established in 1992, is working to keep California Indian languages alive by providing small grants to assist Indians in learning endangered languages, by pairing elder speakers with younger Indians in "master-apprentice" learning teams, and by sponsoring various meetings and workshops that facilitate the revitalization of Native Californian languages.

With the support of the Advocates for Indigenous California Language Survival, Professor Hinton directs the Breath of Life workshop program, which provides in-depth training to Indians who are studying endangered languages. This program, taught on the Berkeley campus of the University of California, provides access to the vast holdings of linguistic information housed in the Bancroft Library, the Phoebe Hearst Museum of Anthropology, and the Department of Linguistics (where the Survey for California and Other Indian Languages, and the Audio Archive of Linguistic Fieldwork in the Berkeley Language Center are situated). Indian scholars can access field notes of ethnographers and linguists from 1901 onward, as well as recordings of songs, stories, and vocabularies originally made on wax cylinders, in addition to later sound information available on tapes and compact discs from more contemporary linguistic studies.

The Breath of Life program, typically taught in the summer, offers a crash course in linguistics and teams apprentice language learners with mentors, usually Department of Linguistics graduate students or seasoned Indian scholars (fig. 23). Significantly, this language training program is applicable not only for endangered languages, but also for the so-called dormant languages, which are no longer spoken by any living person. One of the great success stories is that of Quirina Luna-Costillas, whose ancestors once spoke the Mutsun language, one of eight languages within the Costanoan language family. The Mutsun speakers inhabited an extensive homeland that extended west from the Monterey Bay environs well into the Coast Ranges. The last recorded speaker of the Mutsun language died around 1930; however, with the help of a 1977 dissertation on the Mutsun language by Marc Okrand (who went on to devise the Klingon language for the *Star Trek* TV show), Luna-Costillas and her mentor, Natasha Warner (now a professor at the University of Arizona), produced an English-Mutsun dictionary, a phrase book of common expressions, and a translated version of Dr. Seuss's classic *Green Eggs and Ham*. Luna-Costillas is able to carry on conversations in Mutsun and is teaching the language to her children. For more information on Mutsun language revitalization see the Mutsun Language Foundation (www.mutsunlanguage.com).

Figure 23. Language training in the 2008 Breath of Life workshop on the Berkeley campus of the University of California.

uncurled fronds of the bracken fern as a deodorant (Goodrich et al. 1980:44–45).

Kashaya Pomo groups placed a stem of the five-finger fern *(A. aleuticum)* in an ear piercing to prevent the hole from closing (Gifford 1967:11; Goodrich et al. 1980:45–46). They also employed California maiden-hair fern in the same way.

MARINE PLANTS

KELPS   Order Laminariales
Plate 2

Central Coast Province Indians still gather various species of kelp for food. Some groups not living right near the coast make special trips to the ocean to obtain kelp. In the old days, the Western Pomo dried kelp and considered it a delicacy. The Kashaya Pomo processed bull kelp *(Nereocystic leutkeana)* by cooking the stalks in ovens or hot ashes before eating, or by cutting the stalks into strips and sun-drying them for storage. The Coast Yuki cooked stalked kelp *(Pterygophora californica),* also called winged kelp, in hot coals before consumption.*

In addition to eating bull kelp, the Kashaya Pomo utilized it medicinally: people with colds would suck dried bits to soothe sore throats and clear mucus. They also manufactured cordage from partially dried kelp strips for use in fishing lines (Goodrich et al. 1980: 124–125).

SEA PALM   *Postelsia palmaeformis*

The Kashaya Pomo chewed this plant raw or cooked it on a flat rock or in hot ashes before consumption (Gifford 1967:10). The Coast Yuki also gathered sea palm. They did not eat the leaves of this plant, instead preferring the stalks, which were typically cooked but sometimes eaten raw (Gifford 1965:18).

SEAWEEDS   *Porphyra* spp.

Costanoan peoples collected seaweeds primarily for salt, while the Salinan, Coast Miwok, Lake Miwok, Wappo, Kashaya Pomo, Yuki, and Coast Yuki gathered seaweeds more as a regular food source. The Kashaya Pomo collected two seaweeds in particular *(P. lanceolata* and laver *[P. perforata]).* Both species could be baked and eaten right away or could be sun-dried and stored for later use as large cakes (about 30 cm [12 in.] in diameter). The dried cakes could later be removed from storage and baked in ovens or fried before being eaten. Coast Yuki peoples also collected laver. Gathered primarily in the summer, it was dried in the sun and heated before being eaten to prevent it from being too tough. The Coast Miwok collected seaweeds at low tide then dried the plants in the sun or near a fire. The dried seaweeds could be eaten without further preparation or pounded and eaten with acorn mush.*

HERBACEOUS PLANTS

Similar to the other regions of California, herbaceous plants in the Central Coast Province served as critical resources for food, medicine, and raw materials. Seeds, in particular, were a very important resource. Native people collected and ground wild seeds to make a meal called pinole. Pinole seed meal was usually boiled with water and eaten as mush (Holmes 1975:22–23); however, the Coast Miwok used to eat their pinole as a dry seed meal, with water as an accompanying drink (Collier and Thalman 1996:147). For some peoples, such as the Costanoan, pinole was a significant component of the menu; it was consumed year-round and supplemented by seasonally available fish, meat, shellfish, and plants (Morrow 1982:21). The Eastern and Southeastern Pomo used to collect wild seeds for pinole in August and September from the near hinterland of their main villages.* The seeds used in pinole included those from chia, wild oats, peppergrasses, tarweeds, and various wildflower seeds.

ANGELICA   *Angelica tomentosa*

The Kashaya Pomo have many medicinal uses for angelica. Small pieces of root were chewed to prevent sore throats and bad breath, a practice still sometimes done today. The root was also boiled and the liquid used to wash sores. A tea made from the boiled root eased menstrual cramps, regulated menses, relieved discomfort associated with menopause, and treated stomachaches and colds (Goodrich et al. 1980:20). The Lake Miwok also used angelica medicinally, making a poultice of angelica and tree bark to treat sore spots (Callaghan 1978:272). Coast Miwok peoples chewed the root to alleviate stomachaches (Collier and Thalman 1996:394).

The Kashaya Pomo ate the young green shoots of this plant uncooked (Goodrich et al. 1980:20), and the Wappo relished angelica as an after-bath oil (Beard 1977:53; Driver 1936:189). Wappo groups also rubbed angelica on their arrows for good luck (Driver 1936: 191). The Coast Miwok smeared angelica leaves on their bodies to cover their scent and to bring them luck in hunting (Collier and Thalman 1996:132). The Lake Miwok tied angelica leaves together to make a ball for playing (Callaghan 1978:268).

BROAD-LEAVED CATTAIL   *Typha latifolia*
Plate 6

It has been noted that many peoples of the Coast Ranges consumed the "roots" of the broad-leaved cattail; however it is likely that the consumed structure was actually the underground stem of this plant, called a rhizome. The Wappo either ate the roots raw or roasted them before consumption. Among the Kashaya Pomo, young shoots of cattail could be eaten, but it was taboo for young girls and women to go near where cattails grew.*

Pomo groups living near Clear Lake used broad-leaved cattail as a thatching material in constructing dwellings (Barrett 1975:40). Wappo groups employed the leaves and stems to make matting (Beard 1977:53).

BRODIAEAS
Brodiaea spp., _Dichelostemma_ spp., _and Triteleia_ spp.

Plates 11, 14

It is often noted that Wappo, Pomo, Coast Miwok, and Costanoan peoples once ate brodiaea bulbs, although these "bulbs" are likely to have been corms rather than true bulbs. The Kashaya Pomo baked the bulbs in hot ashes or boiled them before consumption. They did not usually store these bulbs because they tended to go bad and start sprouting soon after they were removed from the ground.* Brodiaea remains have been recovered from archaeological sites in this region (Hammett and Lawlor 2004:297).

The Kashaya Pomo also featured Brodiaea flowers in wreaths for the Strawberry Festival dance (Goodrich et al. 1980:25–26).

CAMASES OR INDIAN POTATOES
Camassia spp.

Plate 7

Costanoan peoples crushed camas bulbs to create a poultice, which they applied to the body to treat boils, bruises, and sprains (Morrow 1982:35). Although not specifically mentioned as a food source in the ethnographic literature that we reviewed, it was probably eaten as well.

CHIA
Salvia columbariae

Plate 8

Wappo, Costanoan, and Salinan groups collected and ate chia seeds. The Wappo processed and consumed these seeds specifically as pinole, and Costanoan groups often roasted chia seeds in baskets with hot coals before eating them.*

CLOVERS
Trifolium spp.

Most Central Coast Province peoples relished fresh clover leaves. In the past, the Eastern and Southeastern Pomo gathered clovers in April and early May primarily from near their main village sites. The Wappo sometimes burned fields within their territories to encourage the growth of clovers.*

The Kashaya Pomo recognized the medicinal value of clovers in boiling the flowers of the plant to make a drink for treating vomiting (Gifford 1967:13).

DOGBANE OR INDIAN HEMP   *Apocynum cannabinum*
Plate 10

Dogbane is a common cordage material throughout the Coast Ranges. Salinan, Esselen, Costanoan, Wappo, Lake Miwok, Yuki, and some Pomo groups all made use of this plant in producing cordage.*

GRASSES   **Family Poaceae**

Central Coast Province peoples used various grasses as basketry material (Beard 1977:58; Morrow 1982:25). Grasses served as thatch in building houses, and as raw materials for making ceremonial headdresses, pillows, and arrow quivers. The Western and Northeastern Pomo also ate fresh grass seeds and stored grass seeds for later consumption.*

IRISES   *Iris* **spp.**
Plate 12

Iris leaf fibers are another common material used as cordage and basketry material.* The Costanoan once used Iris plants to make bolas for hunting (Margolin 1978:23), and the Pomo took advantage of Iris leaves to line acorn-leaching areas and earth ovens (Holmes 1975:22). Iris flowers were used in Strawberry Festival dance wreaths by the Kashaya Pomo (Goodrich et al. 1980:62). The Coast Miwok peoples made a tea from Iris leaves for cleansing the stomach, and prepared boiled roots (probably rhizomes) as a poison (Collier and Thalman 1996:42).

MARIPOSA LILIES   *Calochortus* **spp.**

Wappo, Pomo, and Costanoan peoples identified mariposa lily bulbs as food. Among the Wappo, these bulbs were baked in earth ovens before being eaten. Similarly, the Kashaya Pomo baked mariposa lily bulbs in hot ashes before consuming them.* Remains of mariposa lilies have been found at archaeological sites in this region (Hammett and Lawlor 2004:297).

MILKWEEDS   *Asclepias* **spp.**
Plate 13

Milkweeds were once widely used to make general cordage and fish nets.* Milkweed roots and leaves could also be eaten, the latter as greens (Driver 1936:187; Margolin 1978:50).

MULE EARS   *Wyethia* **spp.**

Costanoan people relished the shoots of these plants as fresh greens (Margolin 1978:50), while the Kashaya Pomo processed the seeds as pinole (Goodrich et al. 1980:74–75). The Coast Miwok used to eat mule ears seeds raw, though they sometimes roasted them (Collier and Thalman 1996:56–57).

PEPPERGRASSES   *Lepidium* spp.

Some Costanoan groups relished the seeds from peppergrasses in making pinole. They ground the seeds into meal, added water, and consumed the mixture as mush (Morrow 1982:20–21).

RUSHES   *Juncus* spp.

Costanoan, Esselen, and Salinan groups employed rushes in basketry. The Kashaya Pomo did not use this material in their baskets, but wire rush *(J. balticus)* was relegated to young girls in play basketmaking. However, because wire rush grows in moist, swampy areas, it was taboo for Kashaya Pomo women who were menstruating to go near where it grows.*

The Costanoan made women's front aprons out of rushes (Morrow 1982:14). The Kashaya Pomo utilized wire rush to keep clamshell beads together while they were rolled and smoothed (Gifford 1967:12; Goodrich et al. 1980:100). Coast Miwok peoples sometimes used rushes to cover structures (Collier and Thalman 1996:42).

SEDGES   *Carex* spp.

Central Coast Province groups commonly enlisted the roots of assorted sedge species as basketry materials, and the Esselen, at one time, processed sedge roots for cordage.* The Kashaya Pomo preferred the white center roots of Santa Barbara sedge *(C. barbarae)* in particular for basketry (Goodrich et al. 1980:103–104). It is likely that the sedge "roots" often described in the ethnographic literature are actually the plants' rhizomes rather than true roots.

Kashaya Pomo groups cut, dried, and bundled sedge leaves to make torches that could be carried while traveling after dark. The tighter they wound the torch bundles, the longer they would burn (Gifford 1967:11–12).

SOAP PLANTS OR AMOLES   *Chlorogalum* spp.
Plate 17

Soap plants were once used as a fish poison by several groups in the Central Coast Province.* For example, the Kashaya Pomo pounded the "root" (i.e., the bulb) and placed this messy pulp into baskets for immersion into creeks, streams, or tidepools. The juice from the roots stunned fishes and caused them to float to the surface, where they could be collected.

The most common additional usage of soap plants was in the manufacture of brushes for combing hair, for processing acorns, and for cleaning residences.* The roots and shoots of the plant could be eaten, the juice employed as an adhesive, and the roots processed as soap for washing hair, body, and utensils.* Soap plant remains have been recovered from archaeological sites in this region (Hammett and Lawlor 2004:297).

TARWEEDS   *Madia* **spp.,** *Hemizonia* **spp.,**
                                  and *Blepharizonia* **spp.**

Many Native Californians in the Central Coast Province used to eat
tarweed seeds. They roasted the seeds in basket trays with hot coals,
pounded the seeds into meal, and prepared them as pinole. Tarweed
seeds could be stored for use throughout the year. Kashaya Pomo
groups stored the seeds raw, parching and pounding them just before they were to be eaten.*

TULES OR BULRUSHES   *Schoenoplectus* **spp.**
Plate 20

In the past, some Costanoan, Esselen, and Salinan peoples employed
tules as basketry material, however the ethnographic record does not
indicate this was a common use of these plants in the Coast Ranges.*

More often, where available in the region, tule was used in the
construction of buildings, in the weaving of tule pads into sanitary
napkins, and in making boats, mats for various purposes, and clothing.* Margolin (1978:54) notes tules were valuable construction material for the Costanoan because they were easy to work with and
readily available in much of their territory.

Some Costanoan groups also ate tule roots and pollen—the latter formed into balls and baked before being dined upon—while the
Wappo and Coast Miwok enjoyed tule sprouts and tule roots, respectively.*

WILD GINGER   *Asarum caudatum*

The Kashaya Pomo warmed wild ginger leaves before making a
poultice for use at night to "draw a boil to a head" (Gifford 1967:13).
The Coast Yuki applied a poultice of warmed wild ginger leaves to
sore parts of the body to alleviate pain (Gifford 1965:18).

WILD MUSTARDS   **Family Brassicaceae**

The presence of many mustard genera in California today is the result of their historic introduction to the area, thus these genera (such
as *Brassica*) were not available until after their introduction. Several
other genera within the mustard family (including *Descurainia*) are
native to California and would have been available to California Indians even in the deep past. The Kashaya Pomo ate various kinds of
wild mustards. In the old days, they savored the flowers and young
leaves raw or prepared them by boiling and then frying. The flowers
and young leaves could be collected in different seasons: the leaves in
late winter and early spring, the flowers in spring (Goodrich et al.
1980:76). Costanoan peoples collected and ate tansy mustard species
(*Descurainia* spp.). They ate both the seeds and the leaves of these
wild mustards (Margolin 1978:48).

WILD OATS *Avena* **spp.**

The species of wild oats in the Coast Ranges are naturalized European species brought into the area with Spanish-Mexican cattle in the 1800s. These species flourish in the inland fields of the region. Many of the Native Californians in the Central Coast Province used to collect, process, store, and eat the seeds from these wild oats. In the recent past, Pomo groups gathered these seeds in June or July using seed-beaters and baskets. The seeds were then winnowed in basket trays, parched in baskets with hot coals, pounded, and eaten as pinole. Wild oats seeds could often be stored for use throughout the year.*

WILD ONIONS *Allium* **spp.**

Plate 18

Wild onion bulbs were eaten by Pomo and Costanoan groups (Goodrich et al. 1980:86–87; Levy 1978a:491). The Kashaya Pomo ate both the greens and bulb of this plant raw; they also cooked the bulbs with other foods as flavoring (Goodrich et al. 1980:86–87). Wild onion remains have also been found at archaeological sites in the Central Coast Province (Hammett and Lawlor 2004:297).

WILD STRAWBERRIES *Fragaria* **spp.**

Wild strawberries are still a favorite among Central Coast Province Indians. In the old days, some groups, such as the Pomo and Coast Yuki, preferred to eat the berries fresh during the short harvest season in June. Other groups, such as the Costanoan, ate them fresh, cooked, dried, or made into cider. Coast Miwok people dried wild strawberry fruits and stored them for winter use.*

The Kashaya Pomo featured wild strawberries in the flower dance performed by young girls at the Strawberry Festival. This dance took place each year before wild strawberries could be eaten (Goodrich et al. 1980:110).

WILD TOBACCOS *Nicotiana* **spp.**

Plate 9

Many groups in the Central Coast Province once collected and smoked wild tobaccos.* Beard (1977:54) observes that the Wappo used to intentionally scatter wild tobacco seeds near village sites. This seed sowing indicates some control over the plant and its growth patterns. Interestingly, similar kinds of management practices for wild tobacco plants are not found in the ethnographic literature for non-Wappo groups in the Central Coast. Instead, we see accounts like the one provided by Gifford (1967:15) in which the Kashaya Pomo collected the leaves and stems of wild tobacco plants from their natural habitats, often some distance from village locations, where the tobacco would eventually be transported for curing, storing, and smoking.

YERBA BUENA   *Satureja douglasii*

The Kashaya Pomo made a tea from yerba buena that once served as a blood purifier, as well as a treatment for upset stomachs for people who were losing weight (Gifford 1967:15). The Coast Miwok also served yerba buena tea to treat various internal problems (Collier and Thalman 1996:396). Coast Yuki people chewed yerba buena to relieve various pains, particularly stomach problems (Gifford 1965:26).

TREES AND SHRUBS

ALDERS   *Alnus* spp.

In the past, Central Coast Province peoples relied on several species of alder for medicinal remedies. The Costanoan made a tea from the bark of white alder *(A. rhombifolia)* for the treatment of stomachaches and diarrhea (Morrow 1982:35). The Kashaya Pomo boiled the bark of white alder or red alder *(A. rubra)*, using the liquid to wash skin irritations such as diaper rash (Gifford 1967:12; Goodrich et al. 1980:19).

Wappo and Costanoan groups also selected alder wood to make arrow shafts and flutes (Beard 1977:52; Driver 1936:191; Levy 1978a: 490). The Coast Yuki processed alder roots to make red designs in basketry (Gifford 1965:62).

CALIFORNIA BAY OR LAUREL   *Umbellularia californica*
Plate 24

Wappo peoples ate California bay leaves with clovers (*Trifolium* spp.) to prevent bloating. They also kept the leaves inside their dwellings to repel insects (Beard 1977:53). The Kashaya Pomo heated California bay leaves to make a poultice for treating rheumatic pain (Gifford 1967:13). They also made a tea from the leaves to wash sores, or the tea could be drunk to treat colds, sore throats, menstrual cramps, and clotting (Goodrich et al. 1980:90–91). Lake Miwok people gathered California bay leaves to make a poultice that was applied to the cheek in the treatment of toothaches (Callaghan 1978:272). The Coast Miwok made a tea from the leaves to relieve stomachaches, and they applied fresh leaves to the head to treat headaches (Collier and Thalman 1996:395).

Various groups in the Central Coast Province consumed the "nuts" (i.e., the seeds) of the California bay, sometimes after roasting them first.* Some Costanoan people coveted the wood of this tree to make split-stick clapper instruments and fences for dance circles

(Levy 1978a:490, 492; Morrow 1982:42). California bay remains are common at archaeological sites in the Central Coast Province (Hammett and Lawlor 2004:297).

CALIFORNIA BUCKEYE — *Aesculus californica*
Plate 27

Many groups in the Central Coast Province harvested, processed, and ate California buckeye "nuts" (i.e., the seeds). Buckeye nuts, like acorns, have tannins that must be removed before they can be eaten. Thus, many groups pounded, leached, and made the nuts into mush in a manner similar to the processing of acorns. The Kashaya Pomo collected ripe nuts from the ground, peeled them, and then roasted them in hot ashes. The roasted nuts were then crushed and leached in a sandy area near a stream by repeatedly pouring stream water over the crushed nuts for about five hours. Nuts were also stored and eaten year-round, much like acorns. Among the Costanoan, California buckeye nuts tended to be used when acorn crops failed. The Esselen reserved consumption primarily for times of food shortage (Breschini and Haversat 2004:121); however, this treatment of California buckeye nuts as a less desirable, fall-back food is not seen in the literature for other groups in the region.*

Central Coast Province people also selected California buckeye wood for making fire-drills and bows, and prepared the nuts as a fish poison.*

CALIFORNIA HAZEL — *Corylus cornuta* var. *californica*

Yuki, Wappo, Kashaya Pomo, Coast Miwok, and Costanoan groups ate hazelnuts.* Hazelnuts have been recovered from archaeological sites in the Central Coast Province (Hammett and Lawlor 2004:297).

California hazel is still a key component in some California Indian baskets. The wood could also be employed to make storage granaries, fish weirs, arrow shafts, and bows.*

CALIFORNIA WILD GRAPE — *Vitis californica*
Plate 29

The California wild grape is found throughout much of the Central Coast Province, particularly in the North Coast Ranges. It tends to grow in moist areas around streams and creeks. Ethnographic observations detail Costanoan, Pomo, and Wappo groups collecting and eating the grapes.*

California wild grape vines could be used for various purposes. Some Pomo groups produced a twine from these vines as the support for a foot drum. The twine was stretched between two stakes over a pit in the ground. With the drum sitting on the stretched twine it created a resonating chamber beneath the instrument.

Kashaya Pomo groups also used the cordage to tie goods together for traveling, to attach thatch to houses, and for other similar purposes. The Yuki employed California wild grape vines in basketry.*

COAST REDWOOD   *Sequoia sempervirens*
Plate 30

People in the Central Coast Province used coast redwood primarily for its bark. Pomo groups shredded the bark to make clothing for both men and women. Yuki, Pomo, Coast Miwok, and Costanoan groups living near coast redwood forests used the bark slabs in constructing dwellings and other buildings, such as storage structures. The roots were employed by the Coast Yuki to make red designs in basketry.*

The Kashaya Pomo used coast redwood for medicinal purposes. They collected the new growth of the foliage and prepared it as a poultice for earaches. They also soaked the sap in water to fix a drink for people feeling run down (Gifford 1967:11).

ELDERBERRIES   *Sambucus* **spp.**
Plate 23

Yuki, Wappo, Coast Miwok, Costanoan, and Esselen groups used to eat the berries of these species fresh, cooked, or made into cider. The berries were also dried and stored for use in winter.* While Gifford (1967:15) suggests the Kashaya Pomo did not eat elderberries, Goodrich et al. (1980:42–43) note that the berries were eaten fresh.

Elderberry wood was used to make musical instruments, such as clappers and whistles, and pipes for smoking tobacco.* Some Pomo groups used elderberry medicinally. The roots were boiled, and the resulting liquid was employed to treat open sores and cuts. Both the Kashaya Pomo and the Coast Miwok made tea from elderberry flowers for reducing fevers. The Lake Miwok utilized elderberry branches to make splints for injuries.*

HOLLY-LEAFED CHERRY or ISLAY   *Prunus ilicifolia*
Plate 32

A large pit is found within the holly-leafed cherry fruit, and pits were often collected and ground into a meal that was later eaten or used for flavoring other dishes. Archaeological remains of holly-leafed cherry have been recovered from the western peninsula of San Francisco Bay and the coast extending southward from there, where it seems to have been an even more important resource (Hammett and Lawlor 2004:297).*

HUCKLEBERRIES
Plate 28

Vaccinium spp.

Yuki, Coast Yuki, Kashaya Pomo, and Costanoan groups ate huckleberries fresh, cooked, or as cider. The berries could also be dried and
stored for later use. The Kashaya stored sun-dried berries in baskets
and boiled them in cooking baskets before consumption. Today, they
still eat fresh huckleberries raw.*

The Kashaya Pomo not only consumed berries from the California huckleberry *(V. ovatum)*, but prepared a tea from its leaves for
treating diabetes (Goodrich et al. 1980:60–61).

MADRONE

Arbutus menziesii

Many Pomo groups, including the Kashaya, ate fresh madrone
berries or parched the berries and stored them for later consumption. Wappo, Costanoan, and Esselen groups also consumed madrone berries in various fresh and prepared forms similar to those
for other berries.*

Kashaya Pomo groups prepared tea from madrone bark to wash
sores and as a gargle for sore throats (Gifford 1967:14; Goodrich et
al. 1980:67). The Esselen made a lotion from madrone bark that was
used to bathe sores and wounds, and they also produced a tea made
from madrone bark for stomachaches (Breschini and Haversat 2004:
121).

MANZANITAS
Plate 22

Arctostaphylos spp.

Manzanita berries of various species were eaten or made into a cider
and drunk by most groups in the Central Coast Province.* For
example, in the old days, Kashaya Pomo groups dried, pounded,
and stored the berries of the Eastwood manzanita *(A. glandulosa)*.
The stored berries were then made into pinole or mixed with water
and eaten (Gifford 1967:14; Goodrich et al. 1980:68–69). The Lake
Miwok dried and pounded manzanita berries. They could later re-
hydrate the stored berries with water, rolling them into balls, and
eating them like candy (Callaghan 1978:265). Manzanita remains
have been recovered from archaeological sites in the Central Coast
Province (Hammett and Lawlor 2004:297).

Wappo groups utilized manzanita wood to make digging sticks
and bows (Beard 1977:53; Driver 1936:190), and the Kashaya Pomo
employed the wood of Eastwood manzanita and hairy manzanita
(A. columbiana) to make awl handles (Goodrich et al. 1980:68–69).

The Coast Miwok used fire-hardened manzanita wood to make
arrow points (Collier and Thalman 1996:188). Medicinally, some
Pomo groups made a tea from hairy manzanita bark that is said to
have relieved diarrhea (Gifford 1967:14; Goodrich et al. 1980:69).

Oaks

Oaks are an incredibly valuable resource to the peoples of the Central Coast Province. Many ethnographic studies highlight the importance of acorns to the traditional Indian communities of the Central Coast.* Various oak species are sought and used by Native Californians in the Coast Ranges, depending on what species are available and preferred. For example, in the old days, the Costanoan preferred black oak acorns and tan-oak acorns, but they also utilized the acorns of coast live oak and valley oak. Preferences for certain species over others are important because, in many areas, people would travel a long way to a single tree of a preferred species while ignoring nearby groves of less-desirable species.

The acorn harvest played a large role in shaping the lifeways of the people of the Central Coast Province. During the fall acorn harvest, whole villages would move to temporary camps near the desired oak groves. The people would work together to harvest the acorns and bring them back to their winter villages. Here, the acorns would often be dried, shelled, and stored in baskets, storerooms, or special acorn granaries for use throughout the rest of the year. When Indians used stored acorns later in the year, they pounded the acorns in mortars and poured water over the flour to leach away the tannic acid. The leached acorn flour, sometimes after being further ground, was then made into acorn mush or bread.*

BLACK OAK   *Quercus kelloggii*

Plate 36

Black oak is common throughout the Coast Ranges up to elevations of 2,100 m (6,900 ft). Ethnographers observed that acorns from the black oak were among the preferred acorns of the Costanoans, and other Central Coast Province groups (Kashaya Pomo, Coast Miwok, Yuki, Wappo) also enjoyed eating these nuts.*

The Coast Miwok considered the wood of young black oak trees among the best wood for making drums (Collier and Thalman 1996: 223).

COAST LIVE OAK   *Quercus agrifolia*

Plate 39

Coast live oak is distributed in various forested and woodland areas of the Coast Ranges up to elevations of approximately 1,200 m (3,950 ft). Coast Miwok and Pomo groups consumed acorns from the coast live oak, and some Pomo groups preferred them to the acorns of several other oak species. The Costanoan peoples also ate coast live oak acorns and valued this oak because of the high acorn yields.*

TAN-OAK or TANBARK-OAK   *Lithocarpus densiflorus*
Plate 43

Tan-oak can be found in most of the Coast Ranges region. Although it is not a true oak, it produces tasty acorns. Pomo, Coast Miwok, Costanoan, and Wappo peoples still prefer tan-oak acorns to those of most true oak species.* Tan-oak remains have been recovered from archaeological sites in this area (Hammett and Lawlor 2004:297).

The Lake Miwok boiled tan-oak bark as a dye for coloring fish nets (Callaghan 1978:266). The Coast Yuki procured the wood as a construction material for dwellings (Thomsen and Heizer 1964:52).

VALLEY OAK or WHITE OAK   *Quercus lobata*
Plate 42

Valley oak is widely distributed in the foothill areas of the Coast Ranges up to 600 m (1,950 ft) elevation. Early ethnographers noted that Costanoan, Lake Miwok, Coast Miwok, and Yuki people ate valley oak acorns, but they were not necessarily preferred. The Costanoan valued some valley oak trees because of their high yields, while the Kashaya Pomo tended not to use valley oak nuts.*

Some Pomo groups used the wood from valley oaks to make support poles in the construction of assembly or dance houses (Barrett 1975:48).

Pines

Central Coast Province people employed pine trees as sources of food, medicine, and raw materials. Below we highlight two species.

FOOTHILL PINE or GRAY PINE   *Pinus sabiniana*

The foothill pine grows in foothills up to 1,370 m (4,500 ft) in elevation, so it is available to most groups in the Central Coast Province. Wappo, Yuki, and Costanoan groups consumed foothill pine "nuts" (i.e., the seeds), occasionally roasting them beforehand. Costanoan groups, in particular, valued these pine nuts. The Kashaya Pomo ate foothill pine nuts fresh or dried, similarly to the way they dined on sugar pine nuts.*

The Wappo used the pitch from this pine medicinally and as an adhesive. They also employed foothill pine roots in basketry (Beard 1977:54, 58; Driver 1936:187).

SUGAR PINE   *Pinus lambertiana*
Plate 46

The sugar pine is not as widely distributed in the Central Coast Province as the foothill pine *(P. sabiniana);* the sugar pine is limited to the northern and southern reaches of the province, not found in the immediate San Francisco Bay Area.

The Kashaya Pomo ate the "nuts" (i.e., the seeds) from inside sugar pine cones fresh. They also stored the nuts for the winter, when they were eaten whole or pounded and mixed with pinole (Goodrich et al. 1980:93). Among the Kashaya, men would climb the trees to get the cones, using a hook of wood and deer antler to loosen the cones from the trees. Fathers of newborn babies, however, were prohibited from doing this around the time of their child's birth. Sugar pine nuts were also eaten by Lake Miwok, Yuki, and Wappo peoples (Callaghan 1978:265; Driver 1936:187; Foster 1944:166, 226).

The Lake Miwok relied on the sugar from sugar pines to treat colds (Callaghan 1978:272).

POISON-OAK   *Toxicodendron diversilobum*
Costanoan and Coast Yuki groups employed poison-oak vines in basketry (Gifford 1965:62; Morrow 1982:25), and the Wappo extracted juice from this plant to make a black dye for baskets (Beard 1977:54).

The Wappo turned to poison-oak leaves as an antidote for rattlesnake poison (Beard 1977:54). Kashaya Pomo and Coast Miwok peoples burned poison-oak and utilized the charcoal or ashes as a pigment for tattooing (Collier and Thalman 1996:175; Gifford 1967:14; Goodrich et al. 1980:81–82; Kelly 1978:417). Esselen children reportedly ate poison-oak leaves to help develop immunity to poison-oak rashes, and they continued this practice as adults (Breschini and Haversat 2004:124).

SALTBUSH   *Atriplex californica*
The Wappo gathered the roots of saltbush for soap (Beard 1977:54). They also prepared saltbush seeds as pinole (Beard 1977:54).

THIMBLEBERRY   *Rubus parviflorus*
Central Coast Province people usually ate thimbleberries fresh, but they sometimes cooked or dried them, depending on particular traditions.[*] The Kashaya Pomo used thimbleberry leaves to wrap other foods for baking in earth ovens (Goodrich et al. 1980:113–114).

TOYON   *Heteromeles arbutifolia*
Indian people in the Coast Ranges enjoyed toyon berries either fresh or cooked, or made a tea from the plant's leaves and bark.[*]

WESTERN REDBUD   *Cercis occidentalis*
Plate 47
Yuki, Wappo, and Kashaya Pomo groups used western redbud bark in basketry (Beard 1977:58; Goodrich et al. 1980:96–97; Kroeber

1925:171). A few years ago, the Kashaya Pomo utilized both the brown bark and the inner, white woody material—left after the bark was peeled away—to make different-colored designs in baskets (Goodrich et al. 1980:96–97).

WILD ROSE or ROSE   *Rosa californica*

Several Pomo and Wappo groups ate the fruit of the wild rose. The Kashaya Pomo preferred collecting and eating the fruit just after the first frost of autumn, when the fruit tasted best (Beard 1977:54; Goodrich et al. 1980:99; Holmes 1975:22).*

Wappo groups gathered wood from the wild rose to make arrow shafts (Beard 1977:54).

WILLOWS   *Salix* spp.

Plate 35

Willow shoots were a common basketry material for most Central Coast Province groups.*

Various groups once shredded willow bark to make clothing for men and women, while willow branches were used in the construction of dwellings, acorn caches, arrows, and fish weirs.*

The Kashaya Pomo also gathered the bark or leaves of the sandbar willow *(S. hindsiana)*, also called white willow, for medicinal purposes. They boiled the parts and produced a tea to relieve sore throats or laryngitis (Goodrich et al. 1980:118–119).

WORMWOODS or MUGWORTS   *Artemisia* spp.

The Kashaya Pomo boiled the leaves of wormwood *(A. douglasiana)* to create a drink for treating excessive menstruation, stomachaches, and cramps related to diarrhea (Gifford 1967:15; Goodrich et al. 1980:119–120). The Coast Miwok also made a tea from the same species for treating stomachaches (Collier and Thalman 1996:54). The Kashaya Pomo groups also harvested the leaves from this plant to treat newborn babies; some years ago, after birth, a baby's umbilical cord was severed with an obsidian blade, and wormwood leaves were repeatedly placed on the baby's belly for several days until the remaining cord fell off (Gifford 1967:15; Goodrich et al. 1980:119–120). The Yuki treated earaches by wrapping wormwood leaves around hot coals and allowing the steam to enter the ears. They also drank a tea from wormwood bark to relieve stomachaches and sore throats, and they washed sore eyes with a wormwood bark infusion (Foster 1944:174).

YERBA SANTA or MOUNTAIN BALM   *Eriodictyon californicum*
Plate 48

Costanoan peoples brewed a tea from yerba santa to relieve coughs, colds, and sore throats (Morrow 1982:35). The Coast Miwok brewed their yerba santa tea to calm stomachaches (Collier and Thalman 1996:57).

SHELLFISH

ABALONES   *Haliotis* **spp.**
Plates 55, 56

Red Abalone *(H. rufescens)* and Black Abalone *(H. cracherodii)* are indigenous to rocky intertidal shores along the central California coast and occur from Oregon to Baja California.

Abalone was collected using a specialized wooden spatula, a precursor to the modern stainless steel abalone bars employed by abalone divers today. The spatula, usually made from a hard wood, such as western azalea *(Rhododendron occidentale)* or coast silktassel *(Garrya elliptica)*, measured about .9 m (3 ft) in length. It was fire-hardened and sharpened into a chisel shape using mussel-shell knives. Abalone could be collected at low tide, using the wooden spatula to pry the creatures from the rocks and to separate the meat from the shell. Another method involved quickly striking the abalone with a stick to knock it from its rock.* Abalone meat could be eaten fresh, dried for storage, or sometimes used as bait for Rainbow Trout *(Oncorhynchus mykiss)* and other fishes.* The strikingly iridescent abalone shell is widely used today, as it was in the past, to make ornaments for baskets or jewelry. The abalone shell was broken into pieces, ground into desired shapes using water and sandstone, and perforated using a pump drill. Abalone ornaments were traded widely. The shape of an abalone shell made it a handy scoop or container.*

BLACK TURBAN SNAIL   *Chlorostoma funebralis*
and BROWN TURBAN SNAIL   and *C. brunnea*
Plate 57

Black Turban Snails, with their conspicuously shaped shells, were gathered, then cooked in hot ashes, cracked on an anvil, winnowed to separate the shell from the meat, and consumed, sometimes with acorn mush. According to ethnographers, Black and Brown Turban Snails were never dried or stored (Gifford 1965:41, 1967:21).

CALIFORNIA OYSTER   *Ostrea conchaphila*

A native to the central California coast, oysters were commonly harvested by Native Californians in estuaries (Greengo 1952; Margolin 1978:36). California Oyster remains from archaeological sites along the central California coast appear in the earliest deposits and decrease in frequency through time. In San Francisco Bay sites, oysters are replaced by mussels and later by clams (Jones 1992:4).

CHITONS   *Cryptochiton stelleri* and *Katharina tunicata*

The Coast Yuki used to cook chitons in hot ashes, removing the hard dorsal plates and viscera before eating. They sometimes prepared the foot, along with the intestines, for storage—the dried meat could then be rehydrated for winter meals (Gifford 1965:41; Greengo 1952). In the old days, the Kashaya Pomo heated chitons in hot ashes to loosen the plates, which were later scraped off. After the meat was cooked in hot coals or an earth oven, the intestines were removed, and the rest of the animal was eaten or dried. Dried meat was boiled before eating (Gifford 1967:21).

CLAMS   Class Bivalvia

Plate 59

Several clam species were (and still are) gathered by Native Californians in the Central Coast Province. These include Washington Clam (*Saxidomus nuttalli*), Nuttall's Cockle (*Clinocardium nuttallii*), Bent-nose Clam (*Macoma nasuta*), Pismo Clam (*Tivela stultorum*), Littleneck Clam (*Leukoma staminea*), and Long-neck Clam (*Tresus nuttallii*). Clams were collected during low tide where siphon holes marked their presence in the sandy or muddy flats along shorelines; once located, the clam gatherers dig for the burrowing creatures—with shovels today and sharpened digging sticks in the past (Collier and Thalman 1996:125–126; Driver 1936:184; Greengo 1952). Some clam beds were privately owned, measuring about 100 m (330 ft) long and delineated using sticks stuck upright in the ground (Collier and Thalman 1996:194). While clamshells were exchanged and outsiders might pay to gather at certain clam beds, the clam beds were never sold.

Shellfish in general and clams in particular were a very important food resource and prized for their shells in the manufacture of shell-disk beads.* The traditional method of preparing clam meat was to roast the entire clam in hot ashes until the shells opened. Families dried the meat from some clam species for winter storage (Driver 1936:185). Clamshell-disk beads used to be a ubiquitous component of Native California material culture and are still the foundation of a brisk, and sometimes intense, exchange market. The traditional method of manufacturing the beads involved breaking and chipping pieces of the large Washington Clam shells into nickel-sized pieces, grinding the pieces smooth — requiring hours of strenuous labor — before piercing the pieces using a pump drill with a flint tip to make dime-sized disk beads (Gifford 1967:21). The Yuki prized clamshells from Bodega Bay, in addition to magnesite, dentalia, and olivella shells, as these items often adorned ceremonial regalia (Collier and Thalman 1996:170–71; Foster 1944:173). Clamshell-disk beads were once an active currency used to purchase venison, obsidian, magnesite, and other items (Kelly 1978:419).

LIMPETS   Family Lottidae

Limpets were cooked in hot ashes or in baskets with hot rocks, and sometimes accompanied with acorn mush. They were never dried or stored (Gifford 1965:41, 1967:20).

MUSSELS   *Mytilus* spp.
Plate 58

Native Californians collected and consumed Bay Mussels *(M. trossulus),* found in the San Francisco and San Pablo bays, and California Mussels *(M. californianus),* which were collected at low tide from open coast rocky intertidal shores. Mussels, clams, and oysters are three of the most prominent shellfish types found in shell midden sites around the San Francisco Bay Area (Gifford 1916; Greengo 1951; Lightfoot 1997:134). Mussels were exchanged up and down the central California coast, as well as with interior groups such as the Yokuts (Levy 1978a:488; Miller 1978:255). In the old days, people collected mussels by hand or hammered them off rocks using a hard stick (Collier and Thalman 1996:127; Driver 1936:184). The Coast Miwok carried bear bones when collecting mussels to ensure a good load of mussels (Collier and Thalman 1996:127).

Mussels were consumed only from October to May to avoid the harmful effects of the toxic phytoplankton that the shellfish consumed during the summer months (Gifford 1967:21; Greengo 1952:85–90). Mussels could be roasted, boiled, or steamed until the shell opened exposing the cooked meat inside. Once removed, the meat was eaten or skewered on twigs or strung on grass for drying, and for storage in winter villages. Dried mussels could later be rehydrated and cooked again.[*]

Mussel shells were crafted into fishhooks and occasionally shell beads. Mussel shell spoons were once common — the Wappo perforated their spoons and attached them to a necklace for quick access. The Yuki and Coast Yuki once used mussel shell thumbnails to separate fibers of the ground iris *(Iris macrosiphon)* for cordage, a time-intensive task. The Costanoan employed a pair of mussel shells as one would a pair of tweezers to remove unwanted facial hair.[*]

OLIVE SNAIL   *Callianax biplicata,* formerly *Olivella biplicata*
The Olive Snail was used almost exclusively for its shell, although some groups did eat the snail meat. For example, the Coast Yuki cooked Olive Snails in ashes and picked out the meat. They did not produce shell-disk beads, but instead the ends of the shells were ground and strung into necklaces.[*]

Other snails were also eaten. The Garden Snail *(Helix aspersa)* is not native to California, but may have been consumed. Driver (1936: 186) writes that land snails used to be picked from the ground, roasted, and eaten. Many native snails, including the California Horn Snail *(Cerithidea hegewischii californica),* are common in marsh environments and were also eaten. Intensification of California Horn Snail harvests in South San Francisco Bay may relate to gathering practices in between seasonal mussel harvests (Milliken et al. 2007:109).

CRUSTACEANS AND OTHER WATER INVERTEBRATES

CRABS   *Cancer antennarius* and *C. productus*
Crabs are still collected year-round at low tide by hand, with the use of baited lines and nets, or captured by swimming. In the old days, crabs could be stepped on, impaled with a sharp stick, or caught by thrusting a stick in a tide pool. The crab, angered by this offense, would seize the stick and could be quickly pulled from the water. The traditional method for preparing crabs involved boiling, roasting, or baking in hot sand. The flesh and roe were consumed.[*]

GOOSENECK BARNACLE   *Pollicipes polymerus*
Gooseneck Barnacles were collected and cooked in hot ashes. After cooking, its stalk was removed and eaten or stored (Gifford 1965:39, 1967:20; Margolin 1978:36). Acorn Barnacles *(Balanus nubilus)* also occur on the central California coast. The Pomo would build fires over barnacle beds at low tide, which would be extinguished with the following high tide, allowing the gatherers to remove the barnacles for immediate consumption or for transportation back to camp (Greengo 1952; Loeb 1926:164; Stewart 1943:60).

OCTOPUSES   *Octopus spp.*
Like crabs, octopuses can be captured by plunging a stick into a tide pool for the octopus to seize. Octopuses were also obtained by spearing, by poisoning them in small tide pools, or by scavenging them off the beach. The animals were then roasted over a fire or baked in an earth oven. They were usually not dried. Only the tentacles were eaten.[*]

SEA ANEMONES   *Anthopleura* spp.

Sea anemones were removed from rocks using abalone wedges, cleaned to remove sand and detritus attached to them, and cooked in hot ashes (Gifford 1965:42, 1967:20; Greengo 1952). Prior to refrigeration, the Pomo were able to keep sea anemones alive for several days by wrapping them in leaves and dry grass. The creature hardens when cooked but softens again when soaked and reheated (Greengo 1952). Omer Stewart (in Greengo 1952) mused that sea anemones have "a texture like calves' brains and, except for the usual 'sea flavor' and the sand which could not be removed, might have been mistaken for them."

SEA URCHINS   *Strongylocentrotus* spp.

Tom Smith, a Bodega Miwok, commented that sea urchins are "good to eat" (Collier and Thalman 1996:127). Sea urchins were placed in a fire to burn off the inedible spines. The eggs and gonads, the only edible portions, were eaten raw and never dried. They were consumed only twice annually, when the sea urchins produced eggs.*

INSECTS AND OTHER TERRESTRIAL INVERTEBRATES

ANTS   *Pogonomyrmex* spp.

The Salinan used to allow red ants to sting parts of their body afflicted by pain. J. Alden Mason (1912:165) noted that this is an example of "fighting fire with fire."

ARMY WORMS   Family Noctuidae

Native Californians used to collect and eat the larvae of several species of noctuid moths known as army worms. The insects were caught with baskets or by digging trenches around the base of trees. As the worms "marched" from tree to tree, they would slip on a ring of dry sand around the rim of the trench. Roasting army worms over hot coals sweetened them (Barrett 1936:5; Foster 1944:166, 226; Miller 1978:253).

CALIFORNIA GALL WASP   *Andricus quercuscalifornicus*

Parasitic gall wasps cause galls, or tumors, on the leaves of various oak species as they feed. The galls contain tannic acid, which was once used among the Lake Miwok as ink for tattooing (Callaghan 1978:266). The Yuki used the tannic acid in oak galls as an eyewash for sore eyes and cataracts (Foster 1944:174), whereas the Coast Miwok chewed fresh oak galls to clean their teeth (Collier and Thalman 1996:211).

CATERPILLARS   Order Lepidoptera

Indians considered roasted caterpillars, the larvae of butterflies and moths, a delicacy.*

CEANOTHUS SILK MOTH   *Hyalophora euryalus* and
and POLYPHEMUS MOTH   *Antheraea polyphemus*
Plate 61

Moth cocoons were once used to make ceremonial rattles. Several cocoons were attached to one or both ends of a stick, which was sometimes decorated with feathers. Surviving examples are all made from the cocoons of the Ceanothus Silk Moth, although the Polyphemus Moth would also have been available to Native groups in the region.*

GRASSHOPPERS   Suborder Caelifera
Plate 62

In historic times, communal grasshopper hunts took place with people using fire to herd them into pits. The grasshoppers were either roasted in the fire or intentionally cooked by bunching the insects together where they could be covered by grass that was then lit and burned until the grasshoppers were lightly toasted.*

WESTERN BLACK WIDOW SPIDER   *Latrodectus hesperus*

The egg sacs of Western Black Widow spiders were dried, ground into a fine powder, and used by the Lake Miwok to poison arrows (Callaghan 1978:267).

YELLOWJACKET LARVAE   *Vespula spp.* and
Plate 63   *Dolichovespula*
spp.

Larvae were collected after smoke had been blown into the nests to stupefy the adult insects. The grubs were usually roasted and eaten. They are said to taste sweet "like young maize" (Gifford 1965:42).*

FISHES

Native people captured fishes in streams, rivers, and lakes using weirs, basketry traps, dip nets, seines, gigs, harpoons, clubs, and various poisons from soap plants (*Chlorogalum* spp.), tarweed (*Madia* spp., *Hemizonia* spp., and *Blepharizonia* spp.), California buckeye *(Aesculus californica)*, turkey mullein *(Eremocarpus setigerus)*, and California manroot *(Marah fabaceus)*.* Fishing could take place at night, as exemplified by the Yuki who tossed white rocks into the stream to be able to see the silhouettes of fishes better (Foster 1944:164). Some fishing spots were privately owned (Collier and

Thalman 1996:194). Offerings were commonly made during harvests to the animal deities that created fishes. The Wappo are said to have tied clamshell-disk beads to fish baskets or tossed clamshell-disk beads into the water for Coyote to bring good luck (Driver 1936:186). Fishes were normally gutted, split, dried, and eaten later as the main entree or as an accompaniment to acorn mush or pinole.* Local Indians occasionally employed fish bones to make tools such as combs (Foster 1944:168).

Nearshore Fishes

CABEZON
Scorpaenichthys marmoratus
Plate 67

Cabezon is prevalent along coastal California along with other sculpins. Archaeologically, the Brown Irish Lord *(Hemilepidotus spinosus)*, Pacific Staghorn Sculpin *(Leptocottus armatus)*, and Cabezon were harvested widely by Central Coast Province groups (Gobalet and Jones 1995:816).

PACIFIC HERRING
Clupea pallasi

Pacific Herring was netted on communal fishing trips. Fishermen strung nets with stone sinkers between two tule balsas and dragged the nets through the water (Collier and Thalman 1996:143; Morrow 1982:17). Pacific Herring was also collected off the beach, as this fish was often cast ashore, especially after storms (Gifford 1965:36).

ROCKFISHES
Sebastes spp.
Plate 69

Several species of rockfishes can be taken along the central California coast (Gobalet and Jones 1995; Love 1996). The rockfishes were often beheaded, gutted, and split for drying during the summer, providing a good source of meat for the winter. The Coast Yuki used to smoke rockfishes and then snack upon them as they traveled inland for the winter (Gifford 1965:39). Over half of 77,000 fish remains recently studied from 51 archaeological sites included rockfishes and other large nearshore species (Gobalet and Jones 1995).

SHARKS and RAYS
Subclass Elasmobranchi

A variety of sharks and rays are known primarily from archaeological findings. These include sharks (families Carcharhinidae and Triakididae), skates (*Raja* spp.), stingrays (family Dasyatidae), and the Bat Ray *(Myliobatus californica)*. While they appear to be important components of specialized prehistoric coastal and bayshore fisheries (Gobalet and Jones 1995; Gobalet et al. 2004), they are mysteriously absent from many Central Coast Province ethnographies.

SILVERSIDES
Family Atherinopsidae

At Elkhorn Slough and Morro Bay, prehistoric fisheries include primarily the remains of small schooling fish such as from the Atherinopsidae family. These include Jacksmelt *(Altherinopsis californiensis)* and Topsmelt *(A. affinis)*, which have been identified from archaeological sites (Gobalet and Jones 1995).

SMELTS
Family Osmeridae

Surf Smelt *(Hypomesus pretiosus)* and Night Smelt *(Spirinchus starski)* are common to the California coastline. The Kashaya Pomo fished for smelts at ebb tide during the morning or afternoon using baskets and, more recently, nets. Smelts were baked overnight in earth ovens, while the eggs were usually cracked open and dried in the sun to prevent spoilage (Collier and Thalman 1996:140; Gifford 1967:19–20). Among the Coast Yuki, Gifford (1965:36–38) describes smelts as "one of the most important food fishes." They captured smelts with specially engineered nets that featured mesh the thickness of one's index finger. Smelts were washed only with saltwater, as freshwater caused the fishes to shrink when they were cooked, then dried in the sun. Afterward, Indians covered the fishes in redwood bark in preparation for smoking. Smoked smelt represented a significant resource carried to winter villages. There they stored the dried fish in pits lined with redwood branches (Gifford 1965:36).

SURFPERCHES
Family Embiotocidae

Plate 71

Many species of surfperches have been recorded in archaeological excavations (Gobalet and Jones 1995:816). Ethnographic descriptions indicate people harvested surfperches by swimming underwater with nets, fishing off rocks onshore using rounded nets, or scattering poisons in tide pools. Indian cooks prepared surfperches in hot ashes or baked them in earth ovens. They were not dried, although inland groups traded for the coastal fishes.*

Anadromous Fishes

PACIFIC LAMPREY
Lampetra tridentata

Plate 73

Plentiful eel hauls gave the Eel River its name. Pacific Lampreys were collected using bare hands but could also be flipped onto shore using a gaff bone hook or by raking the bottom of shallow streams as they lay coiled at night. The Coast Miwok poisoned lampreys using California manroot *(Marah fabaceus),* which would be attached to a long stick and introduced to a crevice where the lampreys were thought to live. Lampreys were cut into small pieces and boiled in stew—

chefs took care not to boil the meat for too long, as this would make it too soft.*

Huchnom dancers used lamprey grease to style their hair (Foster 1944:227).

RAINBOW TROUT   *Oncorhynchus mykiss,*
                                     formerly *Salmo gairdneri*

Rainbow Trout are fished in streams throughout the Coast Ranges today using fishing poles. In the past, Indians depended on spears, nets, weirs, or poison. Both the anadromous (Steelhead *[O. m. irideus]*) and nonanadromous subspecies of Rainbow Trout were fished in coastal flowing streams and rivers. The Wappo and Kashaya Pomo used baited hooks. The Wappo tied grasshoppers (Caelifera) to a strand of hair, which they attached to the fishing line. When the fish swallowed the bait, the hair got tangled in its teeth. The Coast Yuki also used human hair to catch Rainbow Trout. The Kashaya Pomo preferred abalone meat or entrails for bait.*

SALMON   *Oncorhynchus spp.*
Plate 72

Chinook Salmon *(O. tshawytscha)*, also called King Salmon, and Coho Salmon *(O. kisutch)*, also called Silver Salmon, are two primary salmon species that are fished by Native Californians throughout the Central Coast Province (Gobalet et al. 2004). Traditional methods of salmon fishing included the use of spears and harpoons, sometimes made from deer or elk antler. Nets, traps, weirs, bow and arrow, or poison were also used to catch salmon.* The Wappo constructed weirs by hammering several posts into a streambed. Willow and hazel shoots provided a latticework for the weir, and gaps in the dam were filled with nets or baskets to catch the fishes. Communal salmon fishing among the Wappo involved people driving fishes toward two men holding a net across the stream. To drive fishes from deep pools, people would dive into the water and frighten the fishes with a stick with pepperwood branches attached to it (Driver 1936:184–185). The Coast Miwok sang to the salmon for good luck, as well as to coax them out of holes (Collier and Thalman 1996:142). Indians broiled or dried salmon, while salmon eggs could be boiled as a delicacy (Collier and Thalman 1996:140; Gifford 1965:38). Among the Lake Miwok, pregnant women refrained from eating salmon since doing so might cause sores on their baby's head or eyes (Callaghan 1978:268).

STURGEONS   *Acipenser spp.*
Plate 74

Green Sturgeon *(A. medirostris)* and White Sturgeon *(A. transmontanus)* are both bottom-dwelling fishes and are native to California

(Love 1996). Prehistoric sturgeon fisheries are especially well documented in the San Francisco Bay estuary (Gobalet et al. 2004). White Sturgeon is the largest freshwater fish in North America, and in California it is most abundant in the San Francisco Bay estuary. This fish swims up large rivers, such as the Sacramento and San Joaquin rivers, to spawn. Green Sturgeon is usually smaller than White Sturgeon and is generally more marine oriented. Historically, Green Sturgeon spawned in the Eel River but is now concentrated in northwestern California in the Klamath and Trinity Rivers (McGinnis 2006:139–140; Moyle 2002:110).

Freshwater Fishes

RAINBOW TROUT *Oncorhynchus mykiss,*
formerly Salmo gairdneri

Rainbow Trout, both the anadromous subspecies, Steelhead *(O. m. irideus),* and nonanadromous varieties were fished in coastal streams and rivers (Kniffen 1939:376; Nomland 1938:112–113).

SACRAMENTO SUCKER *Catostomus occidentalis*
Plate 79

Sacramento Suckers were fished using nets (Driver 1936:184; Mason 1912:122; McLendon and Lowry 1978:309).

AMPHIBIANS AND REPTILES

LIZARDS Suborder Sauria

Lizards were caught using grass snares (Hester 1978a:497). They were sometimes eaten and were also used in shamanistic practices (Foster 1944:163). The Lake Miwok consider lizards with forked tongues good luck, especially in gambling (Callaghan 1978:271–272).

SALAMANDERS Order Caudata

In the old days, dried salamanders were ground into a poison by malevolent people. This poison supposedly burned a victim like fire (Gifford 1965:91). Shamans administered salamander blood to cure patients who had been poisoned by dried salamanders (Gifford 1965:91–92).

SNAKES Suborder Serpentes

People sometimes hunted snakes with sticks and cooked them in hot ashes (Mason 1912:122, 124). Others refrained from eating snakes, as they were believed to be the source of irrevocable disaster. According to Lake Miwok oral traditions, the sight of a snake would cause cramps for a woman during menstruation. It was considered bad luck to keep rattlesnake rattles or to wear snakeskin belts (Callaghan 1978:268, 272). Shamans used to capture snakes for various purposes (Foster 1944:163).

TURTLES Order Testudines
Plate 80

People enjoyed eating turtles and turtle eggs. One method of cooking a turtle involved removing the shell and boiling the meat (Collier and Thalman 1996:128). Another method was to place the creature upside down in a depression and then cover it in hot ashes. After cooking, the diners cracked open the shell, exposing the edible meat.*

BIRDS
Marine Birds and Waterbirds

AMERICAN COOT *Fulica americana*
Plate 81

The American Coot inhabits coastal saltwater and freshwater marshes, ponds, and brackish water. Nets were once commonly used to capture this species. One netting method set the four corners of a net on sticks, which were pulled when the birds flew or swam underneath (Collier and Thalman 1996:129). The birds were scorched whole to remove the feathers, cleaned, then either cooked or dried (Collier and Thalman 1996:145; Gifford 1967:18; Levy 1978a:491). The Coast Miwok made sure to throw leftover bones into the campfire to ensure good luck in hunting (Collier and Thalman 1996:133).

CORMORANTS *Phalacrocorax* spp.
Plates 85–87

Double-crested Cormorant *(P. auritus)*, Pelagic Cormorant *(P. pelagicus)*, and Brandt's Cormorant *(P. penicillatus)* are common to the California coast, while the Double-crested Cormorant also frequents marshes and rivers in the Great Central Valley. Cormorant remains are also prevalent in prehistoric shell middens; Double-crested Cormorants in particular were hunted intensively, causing the extirpation of island-based colonies (Broughton 2004; Broughton et al. 2007). Consumption of these birds, as well as their eggs, varied between Indian groups (Gifford 1967:18; Margolin 1978:37). The Coast Yuki used long poles to knock young birds off rocky coastal rookeries and cooked them on hot coals (Gifford 1965:33).

DUCKS Family Anatidae
Plates 90, 91

Ducks were hunted communally using decoys, bolas, slings, or nets. The primary species include Mallard *(Anas platyrynchos)* and Ruddy

Duck *(Oxyura jamaicensis),* while many more species are winter visitors to the San Francisco Bay region. People relished having skins, feathers, and down in their blankets and robes, ceremonial cloaks, ceremonial belts, and basketry. Duck meat sometimes supplemented acorn mush and dried fish, and duck eggs were widely consumed.*

GEESE Family Anatidae
Plate 83

Native Californians throughout the Central Coast Province have long hunted the Canada Goose *(Branta canadensis),* Snow Goose *(Chen caerulescens),* and Greater White-fronted Goose *(Anser albifrons).* The birds used to be hunted with slings and stones, nets, and decoys. One goose net was described as being approximately 23 m (75 ft) long. It was spread above the surface of the water and camouflaged with grass. When geese attempted to fly low across the water, they would become entangled in the net. Indians enjoyed the flavor of goose meat and eggs, while goose down, like our contemporary down comforters, provided excellent sources of warmth during cooler winter months as either blankets or capes.* Excavations from the Emeryville shell mound indicate intensive hunting of geese prehistorically, with a sharp decline in goose remains through time (Broughton 2004).

GULLS *Larus* spp.
Plate 82

Several species of gulls inhabit the shores of California. Eggs and young gulls, which didn't smell as fishy as older gulls, were collected from offshore rookeries (Collier and Thalman 1996:128; Gifford 1965:33). Gulls were caught with clam- or abalone-intestine-baited gorges and were typically eaten only during food shortages (Collier and Thalman 1996:129; Gifford 1967:18). The Kashaya Pomo crafted manzanita wood hooks with barbs for catching gulls (Gifford 1967:18), and, when eaten, they cooked them whole on a fire until burned; the meat was never dried (Collier and Thalman 1996:129). Eggs were boiled or cooked in hot ashes; some groups did not eat eggs containing gull fetuses (Collier and Thalman 1996:128; Gifford 1965:33).

PELICANS *Pelecanus* spp.
Plate 93

The White Pelican *(P. erythrorhynchos)* and Brown Pelican *(P. occidentalis)* are native to the California coast, with the former also on large lakes. They were usually shot with bow and arrow near water or scavenged from the beach. Although the birds were sometimes eaten (Gifford 1965:33), the skins of Brown Pelicans figure prominently in some Native Californian ceremonial practices. Pelican skins were even traded inland to groups such as the Yokuts, who used them to wrap babies (Gayton 1948a:49). On the coast, after a pelican was killed or collected, the skin was removed and taken to a chief, who sprinkled acorn flour on it (Collier and Thalman 1996:195, 414, 418). People made coats from the skin of the Brown Pelican and added abalone shell buttons. The coats might be used in the Pelican Dance, while feathers were prominently displayed in ceremonial headpieces (Collier and Thalman 1996:167, 413). The Kashaya Pomo did not eat Brown Pelicans but carried their feathers to prevent rattlesnake bites (Gifford 1967:18). Sinew from the Brown Pelican was used to strengthen Coast Miwok bows (Kelly 1978:418), while the humerus, radius, or ulna could be shaped into whistles (Collier and Thalman 1996:218).

Terrestrial Birds

Terrestrial birds were once hunted widely using bird blinds, poisoned seed, nets, bow and arrow, slings, snares, and sometimes clubs.* Some birds served as a ready source of protein, while hunters captured others solely for their feathers, and in some instances, released them back into the wild.

BAND-TAILED PIGEON
MOURNING DOVE
Patagioenas fasciata and
Zenaida macroura

Plate 95

The Band-tailed Pigeon can be hunted with bow and arrow while it feeds, but it can also be snared or captured in a large openwork basket. A hunter hidden behind a blind dropped the basket on birds as they drank from a spring. The Costanoans used bolas, but they also hurled stones from slings at flying flocks. Among the Kashaya Pomo, only the elderly would eat Band-tailed Pigeons and Mourning Doves, since consuming this meat was thought to cause deafness.*

BLACKBIRDS
Family Icteridae

These birds could be hunted with bolas and probably bow and arrow (Margolin 1978:12). In addition to being a source of food for some (Foster 1944:163), the feathers were widely used in basketry and ceremonial regalia (Collier and Thalman 1996:162, 171). Basket makers especially prized the red feathers from the Red-winged Blackbird *(Agelaius phoeniceus)*(Margolin 1978:120).

CALIFORNIA CONDOR
Gymnogyps californianus

The California Condor, once found in the arid foothills, mountains, and coast of the Central Coast and South Coast provinces, was captured by placing a gorge in deer meat. The hunters harvested the highly prized feathers for use in feather cloaks that replicated the bird's majesty and size (Collier and Thalman 1996:409–410).

CROWS AND RAVENS   Family Corvidae

Plate 96

The American Crow *(Corvus brachyrhynchos)* and Common Raven *(C. corax)* were typically not eaten. The feathers, however, were once used to decorate ceremonial regalia, especially men's dance skirts (Collier and Thalman 1996:162; Foster 1944:163, 226; Margolin 1978: 152).

GOLDEN EAGLE   *Aquila chrysaetos*

Plate 97

The Golden Eagle was not usually eaten, but its feathers were saved when found (Foster 1944:163, 225). The Coast Miwok kept Golden Eagle feathers in their houses for good luck (Collier and Thalman 1996:195).

GOLDFINCHES   *Carduelis* spp.

The Lesser Goldfinch *(C. psaltria)*, Lawrence's Goldfinch *(C. lawrencei)*, and American Goldfinch *(C. tristis)* were supposedly captured in baited nets. The golden yellow feathers were used, along with woodpecker feathers, in deer skin belts, which they made by covering the belt in pine pitch to adhere the feathers (Collier and Thalman 1996:169, 419).

HAWKS   Family Accipitridae

Plate 101

Hunters selected the feathers of the Red-tailed Hawk *(Buteo jamaicensis)* for use as arrow fletching and for dance regalia (Collier and Thalman 1996:161; Gifford 1967:18; Margolin 1978:26). Hawks were sometimes hunted with bolas (Levy 1978a:491) but were also captured alive, kept in cages, and used when needed (Gifford 1967:18).

HUMMINGBIRDS   Family Trochilidae

The Huchnom did not bother hummingbirds as they were regarded as symbols of good luck, especially in gambling (Foster 1944:226). The hummingbird is also a mythological creature that stole fire for the Coast Miwok: it flew up the coast to steal a chunk of fire and flew back to the Coast Miwok carrying the fire under its throat (Collier and Thalman 1996:423, 434).

QUAILS   Family Odontophoridae

Plate 99

The California Quail *(Callipepla californica)* is found throughout the Central Coast Province, while the Mountain Quail *(Oreortyx pictus)* is more localized, generally at higher elevations. Both were hunted using bow and arrow, slings, fences, nets, bent-sapling traps, and bolas. Quails hunted during a rainstorm were unable to fly and could be captured with one's bare hands. Hunters would also imitate quail calls to lure them into an ambush or wild oat–baited trap.* Quails could be roasted on coals, and quail eggs were viewed as a delicacy. Quail feathers are still used by basket weavers as decorative accents. Some people raise quails to obtain a steady supply of feathers and food.*

WOODPECKERS
Plates 94, 98

Family Picidae

Several species of woodpecker inhabit the Central Coast Province. Common species of the Picidae family include the Acorn Woodpecker *(Melanerpes formicivorus)*, Northern Flicker *(Colaptes auratus)*, Red-breasted Sapsucker *(Sphyrapicus ruber)*, Nuttall's Woodpecker *(Picoides nuttallii)*, Downy Woodpecker *(P. pubescens)*, and Hairy Woodpecker *(P. villosus)*. The Northern Flicker includes the subspecies Red-shafted Flicker *(Colaptes auratus cafer)*. While the Pileated Woodpecker *(Dryocopus pileatus)* occurs in this area, oral traditions among some people suggest it was bad luck to disturb or harm this bird; however, the red scalps and red feathers of the other woodpeckers were widely used in ceremonial regalia such as feather headbands. Woodpeckers were trapped in baskets as they deposited acorns in trees. Taking advantage of this habit, some Native Californians would raid dead trees riddled with small holes within which woodpeckers had deposited an acorn. Lake Miwok women did not eat woodpecker meat for fear that their babies would cry a lot. Northern Flickers were sometimes eaten, but only by adults, as children might become spotted. Interestingly, Salinan descendents have no record of using flicker feather headbands, or other feather work and ornaments common to other California Indian groups.*

MAMMALS
Marine Mammals

GRAY WHALE
Plate 105

Eschrichtius robustus

As in the Northwest Province, stranded Gray Whales found on the beach or near the shore were scavenged and eaten. The Coast Miwok ate only a portion off each side of the jaw (Collier and Thalman 1996:139). The Kashaya Pomo used only the rib bones, which were chipped, sprinkled on hot coals, and covered with branches of California coffeeberry *(Rhamnus californica)*, also called pigeon-berry. Patients suffering from paralysis or rheumatism would be treated by lying on the branches and hot coals. Some people carried whale bones to protect against rattlesnakes (Gifford 1967:17). The Coast Yuki cut whale meat into strips and hung it in house rafters to smoke (Gifford 1965:30–31). When eaten, a small piece was sliced off, soaked in water to remove any fat or odors, and then roasted (Gifford 1965:31). Whale blubber was dried in baskets using hot stones and stored. Seaweed could be dipped in whale grease and eaten (Gifford 1965:31).

| **HARBOR SEAL** | *Phoca vitulina* |

Plate 106

Harbor Seals were once harpooned, clubbed, or shot with bow and arrow.* Skilled seamstresses could make fine blankets from sealskins (Gifford 1965:21).

| **SEA LIONS** | **Family Otariidae** |

Plate 102, 107

Steller Sea Lion *(Eumetopias jubatus)*, California Sea Lion *(Zalophus californianus),* and Northern Fur Seal *(Callorhinus ursinus)* were hunted or scavenged on the rocky shores and offshore islands of California. Hunters took them with bows and arrows, spears, harpoons with flint or elk bone points, or clubs. The Coast Yuki clubbed sea lions as they slept on rocks. It is reported that skilled swimmers could seize a sea lion's flippers in the water and crush its face with a stone, although this seems to be a bit of an exaggeration. Sea lions were butchered and cooked on the seashore. The skin was retained for bedding, or cooked along with the seal meat and fat in a fire, washed, then baked in an earth oven.*

| **SEA OTTER** | *Enhydra lutris* |

The dense fur of the Sea Otter produced luxuriant and warm blankets, robes, and other articles of clothing.* An increase in the demand for Sea Otter pelts lured the Russian-American Company to the shores of present-day Sonoma County in the early nineteenth century. Commercial harvesting decimated Sea Otter populations along the central California coast to the point of near extinction.

Terrestrial Mammals

| **BEARS** | *Ursus* **spp.** |

The Black Bear *(U. americanus)* and Grizzly Bear *(U. arctos horribilis)* were once found throughout California. Some groups hunted bears, often smoking them out of their den as they hibernated in the winter, while other tribelets avoided bears and killed them only when threatened. The meat was usually roasted, baked in an earth oven, or dried. The Kashaya Pomo considered young bears especially delicious, drying or broiling the meat on coals, while the Lake Miwok believed the meat good for patients suffering from tuberculosis. Others considered the hide more valuable than the meat. Hides were valued for warm winter blankets and for burial shrouds, while the hides of cubs were sometimes used to make quivers. The cubs were sometimes kept as pets.*

BLACK-TAILED DEER   *Odocoileus hemionus columbianus*

The Black-tailed Deer, the coastal subspecies of Mule Deer, was the chief game animal among Native residents of the Central Coast Province. A hunter normally refrained from sleeping with his wife prior to a hunt and especially during her menstruation, and also around the time when a child was born. Hunters ate a special meal of acorn mush or nothing at all in the days leading up to the hunt and would sweat, bathe, and rub angelica root or scorched pepperwood leaves on their bodies to mask any body odors and to propitiate the spirits. While in pursuit, a hunter might chew angelica root or tobacco (*Nicotiana* spp.) to retard the deer's sensibilities, or poke sticks in deer tracks to impair the animal's health.*

The hunt could be accomplished individually or communally. Black-tailed Deer would be flushed out of the forests using slings and clay balls, chased down, or stalked carefully using a stuffed deer head decoy. Nets, fences, and snares were once common methods for harvesting deer en masse, with the bow and arrow or club used to dispatch captured individuals. During a Coast Yuki hunt, an animal might be chased onto a beach where it could be shot, drowned at sea, or killed in the water by hunters.* When hunters killed one or more deer, they observed various rituals.*

Indian cooks either roasted venison over a fire or dried the meat. The bone marrow was commonly consumed. The Lake Miwok used to mix deer blood with ground rabbit bones, allowing the mixture to congeal, and then they baked it into the consistency of a crumbly cottage cheese. Blood sausage was made by filling the deer paunch with blood and scraps of the heart, liver, other entrails, and salt, then roasting it. Indians pounded the vertebrae into a paste that could be roasted. They singed the feet to remove hair, then skinned, dehoofed, and pounded the remaining pieces in preparation for roasting. The elderly tended to be the only ones who ate deer brains, as it was believed they turned one's hair white.*

Deer skins were used primarily for clothing and blankets, as well as for making slings, quivers, and pouches. Leg sinew was once important for making sinew-backed and sinew-wrapped bows. Bones were commonly used to make awls and other tools. Marrow made excellent hair grease. A deer scrotum could be cleaned, stuffed with gravel, sewn shut, and used as a child's ball, perhaps like a hacky sack. The Coast Miwok kept the skin of an albino deer for good luck. They employed knuckles as gambling game pieces.*

BOBCAT and MOUNTAIN LION   *Lynx rufus* and *Puma concolor*

Indians once hunted Bobcats and Mountain Lions primarily for their pelts, but the cats were sometimes eaten. They would be smoked out of their dens and shot with arrows or ambushed. Pelts were used to make blankets and quivers.[*]

BOTTA'S POCKET GOPHER   *Thomomys bottae*

Native Californians hunted Botta's Pocket Gopher using baited snares (Gifford 1967:17); however if left alone this rodent could bite through the snare lines. People sometimes kept the skins to make blankets, but they were otherwise singed, skinned, eviscerated, and roasted on coals (Bean and Theodoratus 1978:292; Gifford 1967:17; Margolin 1978:24).

COYOTE and FOXES   Family Canidae

The Coyote *(Canis latrans)*, Gray Fox *(Urocyon cinereoargenteus)*, and Kit Fox *(Vulpes macrotis)* were hunted for their hides, but rarely eaten. Fox skin quivers were once frequently made by beheading the animal and allowing the skin to dry in the sun.[*]

ELK   *Cervus elaphus*

Plates 110, 111

Tule Elk *(C. e. nannodes)* and Roosevelt Elk *(C. e. roosevelti)* were once hunted communally with snares, bow and arrow, and often by chasing to exhaustion. The animals were usually butchered and the meat roasted where slain, a practical decision considering the weight of mature individuals. Bones were broken to extract the marrow. Antlers were frequently used as wedges for prying bark off trees for houses, as digging tools, and as spoons, while the hide could be used for making slings and armor, and as a burial shroud.[*]

HARES and RABBITS   Family Leporidae

Plate 109

The Black-tailed Jackrabbit *(Lepus californicus)*, Desert Cottontail *(Sylvilagus audubonii)*, and Brush Rabbit *(S. bachmani)* are common to the central California coast. In traditional times, hunters utilized slings to stun the animals, or they hunted them in communal drives using fences. They also clubbed them, shot them with arrows, and snared them. People roasted the meat on a stick; after communal hunts they dried and stored some of the meat for later use. Indian seamstresses turned the furs into fine winter blankets and clothing.[*]

PRONGHORN   *Antilocapra americana*

Pronghorn were once a common sight in valleys throughout the Central Coast Province. Indian groups hunted the animals in communal drives with bows and arrows (Bean and Theodoratus 1978: 290; Margolin 1978:24–25).

RACCOON   *Procyon lotor*

The Raccoon could be smoked out of hollow trees and shot with arrows, snared, clubbed, or crushed in deadfall traps. Indian cooks roasted the animals over hot coals, their backbones pounded to prevent the carcass from bending. The fur was used to make bags. The animals were also kept as pets.*

SKUNKS   Family Mephitidae

Two species of skunk are found within the Central Coast Province: the Western Spotted Skunk *(Spilogale gracilis)* and the Striped Skunk *(Mephitis mephitis)*. Indians either ate them or diligently avoided them. Hunters clubbed the animals as they grubbed for food or stunned them with a hurled stick, then clubbed them. The Huchnom are the only people reported to eat skunk during times of illness, at which time the creature's fat and scent glad would be eaten. Skunk meat could be cooked in hot ashes; the grease was dried and used as hair gel, as it was believed to prevent balding and gray hair. The Coast Miwok believed the skins would bring good luck for a house, and the Wappo kept the striped animals as pets. Although the scent glad had to be removed to eliminate any foul odors, it supposedly behaved like a domestic cat.*

SQUIRRELS   Family Sciuridae
Plate 114

Tree squirrels found in the Central Coast Province include the Western Gray Squirrel *(Sciurus griseus)* and Douglas Squirrel *(Tamiasciurus douglasii)*; the Beechey Ground Squirrel *(Spermophilus beecheyi)* is also prevalent. Tree squirrels were dispatched using bows and arrows, slings, or clubs. They were also netted or snared, but these rodents could bite through snares if left alone. Ground squirrels chased on foot, snared in a baited spring trap, or smoked out of their burrows could be killed with clubs or arrows. Small game was usually pulverized into meal or roasted whole. Squirrel skins were sometimes used in baby baskets, and the bones could be sharpened into awls or other implements. The Wappo sometimes kept them as pets.*

WOODRATS   *Neotoma* spp.

Woodrats gather sticks and plant cuttings to form conical homes, which were set on fire by hunters. They also hunted the animals with bows and arrows and slings (Driver 1936:186; Foster 1944:163). Young Lake Miwok children and pregnant women refrained from eating woodrat for fear that its nest might appear on top of the child's or baby's head (Callaghan 1978:268).

ROCKS AND MINERALS

ASPHALTUM or BITUMEN

Asphaltum—natural tar—can be collected from beaches (Breschini and Haversat 2004:119). In the past, Indians employed it primarily as an adhesive for hafting projectile points or for adhering sundry items. The Salinan, however, chewed asphaltum like chewing gum (Harrington 1942:9).

CLAY

Clay was added to acorn mush as a leavening agent (Driver 1936: 187; Foster 1944:165). A white clay and pitch mixture was placed on the singed hair of grieving Lake Miwok widows (Callaghan 1978: 268). Kashaya Pomo once made clay pipes for smoking tobacco (*Nicotiana* spp.)(Gifford 1967:15).

MAGNESITE

As Tom Smith, a Coast Miwok descendant, stated, magnesite is "our gold" (Collier and Thalman 1996:198). The intrinsic value manifest in magnesite can be seen in the widespread use of magnesite beads as a medium of exchange and monetary symbol. To the Coast Miwok, a single magnesite bead used to be worth about 1.8 m (6 ft) of clam-shell disk beads.[*]

OBSIDIAN and CHERT

Both obsidian and chert were important resources for making many kinds of stone tools, including stone points, tattoo needles, and scrapers, as noted in many archaeological and ethnographic studies. Obsidian sources exist in the North Coast Ranges, but some of the obsidian found in archaeological sites was traded from as far away as the eastern Sierra Nevada. Some people believed obsidian was blessed with curative properties. It supposedly could bring good luck during hunting (Collier and Thalman 1996:137, 397, 462).

SALT

When the salt from seaweed was not sufficient, salt crystals could be collected from coastal pools where sea spray had evaporated or from inland deposits. Some groups made annual trips to the coast to gather salt. Salt was also traded; in fact Native Californians maintained a heavy salt traffic up and down the coast, as well as to the interior of California.[*]

Coastal strand, coastal sage scrub, valley grassland, valley and foothill woodland, chaparral, montane forest, alpine fell-field.

Chumash languages; Hokan stock: Diegueño languages (Ipai, Kumeyaay, Tipai); Uto-Aztecan stock or family: Tataviam, Luiseño, Gabrielino (Tongva), Juaneño, Fernandeño languages.

It is tough to generalize about the Indians of the South Coast Province, whose settlements once spanned the offshore Channel Islands, the coastal mainland from the Santa Barbara Channel to Baja California, and the western slopes of the Transverse and Peninsular ranges, which form the backbone of this province. Suffice it to say that significant variation occurred in the settlement patterns, social organizations, ceremonies, and economies of local communities. At the time of Spanish exploration and initial colonization, large populations of people lived in villages near water sources on the islands; along the mainland coast, especially near estuaries, lagoons, and streams; and along drainages in upland valleys. The traditional settlement pattern of the coast and lower valleys focused on a few larger villages, which typically functioned as ceremonial and political centers for smaller hamlets and house clusters in the nearby hinterland. The large villages typically contained dome-shaped thatched houses, semisubterranean sweat lodges, fenced ceremonial enclosures, shrines, work areas, ramadas, menstrual huts, and formal cemeteries. Chumash people marked individual graves in cemeteries with painted poles and whale bones. Archaeological and ethnohistorical research on Chumash villages indicates some of the largest settlements may have housed over 1,000 people during some seasons of the year. Village space might be segregated into large open ceremonial areas, well-demarcated cemeteries, and outlying house clusters, or in some cases, what appears to have been streets with rows of houses.[*]

Although traditional Chumash houses may have been somewhat larger and taller than domestic structures to the south, the basic architectural plan of the South Coast Province was the domed grass or brush house. The builders placed cut saplings into the ground about a meter apart in a large circle, lashing them together at the top to form the roof of the house. Horizontal stringers tied to the saplings provided the framework for anchoring roof thatching (the materials varying among sea grasses [*Phyllospadix* spp.], grasses [Poaceae], tules [*Schoeno-plectus* spp.], or brush, depending upon the location), with spaces left open for one or two doors, a large smoke hole, and sometimes windows. Mats, typically woven from tule or other available cordage, hung from the door, while other mats were fastened to the roof to create partitions within the house. Among the Chumash and Tongva communities, large houses measuring more than 18 m (59 ft) in diameter might hold up to three or four related families. Whale bone was often used in constructing houses on the Channel Islands. In some Luiseño and Dieguiño settlements, houses might be semisubterranean. The domestic houses were usually inhabited by women and children, while men and older boys spent much of their leisure time smoking and discussing issues of importance in the sweat lodges. Weavers created a diverse range of twined and coiled baskets for cooking, processing, serving, and storing food and other items. Some of the southern communities (Luiseño, Dieguiño) manufactured ceramic vessels in gray, brown, and red colors (Bean and Shipek 1978; Bean and Smith 1978b; Nabokov and Easton 1989:310–315).

The political organization of most of the South Coast Province communities revolved around tribelets composed of patrilineal lineages or clans, although mission records provide good evidence that the core residential groups in Chumash settlements consisted of matrilineally related families. Tribelets and villages sponsored ceremonies, dances, and feasts that brought together South Coast communities. Among the Chumash, Tongva, and possibly other South Coast groups, a formal religious organization, known as the '*antap,* comprising initiated members of elite families, performed dances and other observances at major ceremonies. The Chinigchinich cult, involving the ingestion of the toloache plant *(Datura wrightii),* also called jimsonweed, played a particularly important role among Tongva and Luiseño communities in early historic times, as observed by Spanish explorers and missionaries. The drug produced hallucinations and visions among participants, and it was widely used in the initiation rites of young boys and girls, as well as in the initiation rites of new members into the Chinigchinich cult. Various ceremonies centering around the Chinigchinich cult typically involved the construction of a shrine or alter, which might include various offerings such as feathers, coyote skins, arrows, and the remains of raptors. In front of the shrine, one or more participants created one or more intricate, colorful sand paintings depicting various aspects of the universe. The participants destroyed the painting(s) at the end of the ceremony.*

Recent archaeological and ethnohistorical research on the Chumash has documented the most elaborate social and political hierarchies in California. There are convincing data from cemetery excavations and bioarchaeological analyses for the rise of elite families or lineages who maintained differential access to bead wealth and other key resources as a consequence of ascribed status. Large villages were organized into complex political organizations staffed by chiefs, religious leaders, retainers, and craft specialists. The archaeological record provides ample evidence for the specialized production of stone microblades, shell beads, steatite ollas, bowls, and effigies that people traded for across the islands, coastal mainland, and interior communities of the South Coast Province. Extensive steatite mines existed near Tongva settlements on Santa Catalina Island, and recent archaeological research on Santa Cruz Island has documented intensive shell bead production among the Chumash islanders, including hundreds of thousands of pieces of olivella shell bead parts and detritus from bead-making locales. There is also good evidence for the specialized manufacture of chert microblades used in shell bead manufacture.

Elite or chiefly families probably owned the costly plank canoes *(tomols)* employed in long-distance trade and in the harvesting of pelagic fishes and sea mammals. The large, curved seagoing *tomols* constructed from planks sewn and glued together, measuring 3.6 to 9 m (12 to 30 ft) or longer in length, were propelled by long double-bladed oars. Some of the larger boats had a two ton cargo capacity. There is great deliberation among archaeologists about when the first plank canoes appeared in the South Coast Province. There is also considerable debate about whether the inspiration for these complex boats arose locally in South Coast communities or from contacts with Polynesian sea voyagers who arrived on the Santa Barbara coast hundreds of years ago.*

Many questions still remain to be answered about these South Coast Province maritime societies. A healthy debate is now taking place about when complex political organizations first arose and the causal factors that may have stimulated their development. It is still not clear how the coastal villages were organized into local polities, how these polities might have been incorporated into broader political confederacies or chiefdoms, and how much power and authority was actually invested in political and religious leaders.*

The economy of the people on the Channel Islands emphasized the sea, with the Chumash and Tongva islanders highly adept at exploiting shellfish, fishes, sea mammals, and sea vegetables, using a diverse range of tools and harvesting strategies. The cold, upwelling waters along the Santa Barbara channel support a rich fishery and kelp forest system, a point emphasized by the recent identification of more than 131 different genera or species of fishes recovered in archaeological sites on Santa Cruz Island alone (Colten 2001:202). The *tomol*s were used for deepsea fishing, hunting pelagic fishes and sea mammals, and transporting people and cargoes between the Channel Islands and the mainland. Coastal mainland people also focused on the bounty of the sea but incorporated a greater percentage of their menu from terrestrial plants and animals. It appears that deep-sea fishing may have been restricted primarily to Chumash people along the Santa Barbara Channel (Gamble and Russell 2002:114). Indian populations living in interior valleys and mountains emphasized the harvesting and processing of terrestrial resources, although visits to the coast and extensive trade across the islands, mainland, and interior locales allowed them access to marine foods as well.

Some seasonal movements took place during the course of the year, with logistical task groups and residential units leaving the major coastal villages to exploit resources in the hinterland or to participate in ceremonies and dances at other communities. Early Spanish accounts document pyrodiversity practices among the South Coast Province people.

TRIBAL MUSEUMS AND CULTURAL CENTERS
IN SOUTHERN CALIFORNIA

An important development in California Indian country is the creation of tribal museums and cultural centers dedicated to the perpetuation of Native Californian cultures, languages, foods, and ceremonies. These Indian-run organizations offer educational programs that stress not only ancestral traditions, but the diverse livelihoods of Californian Indian people today. Many tribal museums function as community centers for local Indian people, where they can enjoy each others' company while participating in communal feasts and dances, lectures, classes, and workshops. Elders and tribal scholars teach classes on local Indian languages, the production of Native crafts and art objects, Indian resource management skills, and Native culinary practices. Some organizations are dedicated to Native groups across the Golden State, such as the proposed California Indian Heritage Center in Sacramento and the vibrant California Indian Museum and Cultural Center (www.cimcc.org) in Santa Rosa, which provides a diverse array of programs, museum exhibits, and lectures for educating the public about California Indian cultures.

Most Indian museums and cultural centers, however, focus on specific regions or Indian groups within California. Southern California is home to some outstanding examples of what Indian-run organizations can accomplish in educating people about local Native communities. The Malki Museum (www.malki.museum.org), the oldest all-Indian museum in southern California, located on the Morongo Indian Reservation, is exemplary for its many educational programs about Cahuilla speakers, as well as other Indian people that span the South Coast and Southern Deserts provinces. Chartered in 1964, the Malki Museum produces museum displays on the ethnography and archaeology of the region and supports a flourishing ethnobotanical garden that provides information on the foods, medicine, and materials used in craft and art production. The museum also boasts an excellent publication program that features booklets, monographs, and books on the Indians of southern California, as well as a student research center that assists college students carrying out field research in the area. The annual Malki Fiesta attracts large crowds of both Indians and non-Indians to the reservation, who sample local Native foods, view and buy Indian crafts, and enjoy Indian dances (fig. 24).

continued

The Museum also sponsors many other communal gatherings including the Agave Harvest and Roast, and the Fall Gathering (see Farmer 2003; Magallanes and Thompson 2003).

Other fine organizations can be found in the South Coast Province. One is the Satwiwa Native American Indian Culture Center (www.satwiwa.org), which is a partnership between Native groups including the Chumash and Tongva and the National Park Service. Located in the Santa Monica Mountains National Recreation Area near Thousand Oaks, Satwiwa hosts a diverse range of lectures and workshops featuring both traditional and contemporary arts. Another is the Barona Cultural Center and Museum on the Barona Indian Reservation near Lakeside (www.baronamuseum.org). The goal of the museum is to showcase and preserve the culture, language, and history of the Kumeyaay/Diegueño peoples of southern California. The museum's exhibits explore Kumeyaay culture, past and present, through archaeological artifacts, contemporary crafts, and discussions about modern indigenous identity. The Barona Cultural Center and Museum also offers school tours and special classes and sponsors many other community activities.

Figure 24. Eagle dancer at the Malki Fiesta.

MARINE PLANTS

FEATHER BOA KELP   *Egregia menziesii*
Feather boa kelp is a common kelp that could be eaten raw, cooked, or dried (Clarke 1977:153–154).

GIANT BLADDER KELP   *Macrocystis pyrifera*
Plate 3
This kelp grows in extensive stands along the coastline, with some plants attaining lengths of 60 m (200 ft); they produce a dense canopy of multibranching fronds with blades held up by gas bladders. The fastest growing plant known, it can grow over 35 cm (14 in.) per day (Schoenherr 1992:652). The young blades are tender and delectable—they can be eaten raw, cooked, or dried. While fishing in offshore waters, Indians once anchored their canoes by pulling living fronds onto the boat and securing them. Dried kelp was also "carried for protection against people who were carrying dangerous magical substances" (Clarke 1977:155; Timbrook 1990:245).

SEA GRASSES or SURF-GRASSES   *Phyllospadix* spp.
Plate 4
Found in archaeological sites on the Channel Islands, sea grasses could be used for thatching structures and for manufacturing cordage for use in ropes, fishing lines, nets, bags, mats, and skirts (Martin and Popper 2001:255; Timbrook 2007:139–141).

HERBACEOUS PLANTS

BLUE DICKS   *Dichelostemma capitatum*
Harvested with digging sticks in the spring, the "bulbs" (probably corms) were roasted in cooking fires in houses or in underground ovens. Some ovens could be quite spacious, cooking extensive amounts of food for people during communal gatherings (Martin and Popper 2001:257; Timbrook 1990:247, 2007:75–77).

CALIFORNIA BUCKWHEAT   *Eriogonum fasciculatum*
Parts of this semiwoody shrub could be mixed into a drink for treating irregular menstruation, rheumatism, and stomach problems. The patient also bathed in a solution (Timbrook 1990:248, 2007:84–85).

CANARYGRASSES   *Phalaris* spp.
Canarygrass seeds are commonly found in some archaeological deposits in Orange County and San Diego County (Byrd and Reddy 2002:58; Koerper et al. 2002:72; Reddy 1999:39).

CATTAILS   *Typha* spp.
Plate 6

Southern cattail *(T. domingensis)*, narrow-leaved cattail *(T. angusti-folia)*, and broad-leaved cattail *(T. latifolia)* stems were used for thatching structures and for making twined mats.

Bread was made from the roots, and the roots and seeds were used to make pinole (Grant 1978:516; Timbrook 1990:246, 2007: 219–220).

CHIA   *Salvia columbariae*
Plate 8

The highly valued and nutritious seeds of the chia plant were collected in late spring and summer with seed-beaters or by pulling up entire plants. The seeds were stored in large baskets in houses; when needed they were toasted, ground into flour, and then mixed with cold water to make a drink, mush, or cakes and loaves, depending on the consistency of the mixture. The stalks of young plants and leaves were eaten.

People also employed the seeds to remove unwanted particles from the eyes and as a poultice for wounds. The seeds functioned as important ceremonial offerings or trade items. The plant was commonly used by Indian communities across the South Coast Province (Martin and Popper 2001:254–255; Reddy 1999:39; Timbrook 2007: 188–193).

DEATH CAMAS or   *Zigadenus fremontii*
FREMONT'S STAR-LILY

Similar to soap plant *(Chlorogalum pomeridianum)*, the death camas is another member of the lily family (Liliaceae), sporting a large bulb. The bulb is poisonous, however, and typically not used as food, although it was commonly mashed into a poultice and placed on sores. Sorcerers are reputed to have used this bulb to murder people (Munz et al. 2004:24–25; Timbrook 1990:246, 2007:230).

DOGBANE or INDIAN HEMP   *Apocynum cannabinum*
Plate 10

Dogbane was one of the most important fiber plants used by the Chumash. Collected in the summer or early fall, the stalks were dried and the fiber extracted to make cordage for bowstrings, lashings for the plank canoes, fishing lines, nets, bags, belts, headbands, and necklaces, among other things. The fibers were also incorporated into dance regalia, including feather headbands and dance skirts (Timbrook 2007:31–34).

MARIPOSA LILIES   *Calochortus* spp.

The corms or bulbs of these lilies were gathered, prepared, and eaten in the same way as blue dicks *(Dichelostemma capitatum)*(Timbrook 2007:49).

MILKWEEDS   *Asclepias* spp.
Plate 13

Among the Chumash, milkweeds were second only to dogbane *(Apocynum cannabinum)* as a fiber plant. Timbrook identifies two species in Chumash country: broad-leaved milkweed *(A. eriocarpa)* and narrow-leaved milkweed *(A. fascicularis)*. The stems were cut while green, allowed to dry, and then the fiber extracted. The cordage was used to make carrying nets and tumplines for light objects, cradle bands, men's belts, dance aprons, and other materials. The congealed sap was chewed as gum, and the plant could be used as a purgative (Timbrook 2007:40–42).

MUGWORT or WORMWOOD   *Artemisia douglasiana*

Chumash doctors twisted dried leaves of mugwort into small cones that were lit and placed on patients to cauterize wounds and treat sores and rheumatism. The leaves were prepared in a plaster for sore muscles and as a poultice for headaches and toothaches. The plant could also be prepared as a remedy for poison-oak rash (Timbrook 2007:37–39).

NATIVE BARLEY   *Hordeum intercedens*

Native barley seeds are commonly recovered from some Late Holocene archaeological sites, especially in Orange and San Diego counties. Some evidence suggests that Late Holocene harvesting practices may have produced morphological changes in the seeds (Byrd and Reddy 2002:58; Koerper et al. 2002:72; Reddy 1999:39).

PEPPERGRASS   *Lepidium nitidum*

The small, yellow seeds of peppergrass were harvested and used to make pinole. The ground seeds could be mixed with cold water to treat diarrhea or dysentery (Timbrook 1990:248, 2007:111).

PITSEED GOOSEFOOT   *Chenopodium berlandieri*

Pitseed goosefoot seeds were harvested and prepared as food, and the young plants were eaten as greens (Martin and Popper 2001: 252; Timbrook 1990:248, 2007:55). Seeds identified to the genus *Chenopodium* are commonly recovered from archaeological sites in Orange and San Diego counties (Koerper et al. 2002:72; Reddy 1999: 38).

RED MAIDS   *Calandrinia ciliata*

Plate 16

The diminutive, shiny seeds of this annual could be harvested from early spring to early summer and stored in large baskets. When needed, they were parched and ground for food. The greens were also eaten by the Luiseño.

The seeds served as important ceremonial offerings and were associated with burial rituals among some South Coast Province people. The seeds have been recovered from archaeological excavations (burials) throughout Chumash lands. The Chumash burned grasslands to increase the supply of red maids seeds (Hammett and Lawlor 2004:339–340; Martin and Popper 2001:252; Timbrook 1990: 248, 2007:46–48). Red maids seeds have been recovered from archaeological sites in this region, and the people in this area probably relied more on these seeds than did the people living in coastal areas to the north (Hammett and Lawlor 2004:297).

RUSHES   *Juncus* **spp.**

An important raw material for South Coast Province people; rush stems were employed widely for making a variety of twined and coiled baskets, mats, brooms, and dance headdresses, and for polishing shell bead money. Timbrook describes the specific uses of spiny rush *(J. acutus)*, bog rush *(J. effusus)*, wire rush *(J. balticus)*, and Indian rush *(J. textilis)*(Bean and Smith 1978b:542; Timbrook 1990: 246, 2007:97–108).

SOAP PLANT   *Chlorogalum pomeridianum*

Plate 17

Collected with digging sticks in the spring, soap plant bulbs were roasted in underground ovens. The bulbs were also crushed to make fish poison, soap for washing clothes, a shampoo, and a mixture for preparing hides. The outer fibers of the bulbs made excellent brushes; they were also incorporated into bear shaman costumes. The young shoots were eaten (Grant 1978:516; Timbrook 1990:246, 2007:56–57).

TARWEEDS   *Madia* **spp.,** *Hemizonia* **spp.,**
                                            and *Blepharizonia* **spp.**

The small black seeds of tarweeds were collected in the summer, dried, winnowed, and then ground into flour. The flour could be made into pinole, a gruel, or a cake that could be eaten raw. Tarweed seeds are found in archaeological sites on Santa Cruz Island and San Diego County (Martin and Popper 2001:255; Reddy 1999:38; Timbrook 1990:253, 2007:90–91).

The plants were tied together into bundles and used as brooms.

TOLOACHE or JIMSONWEED
Plate 19

Datura wrightii

The roots or leaves of this plant were gathered, pounded in a small mortar, soaked in cold water, and allowed to settle. A small portion of the strained toloache mixture was eaten or prepared as a drink. It was ingested for three basic purposes: to connect with the supernatural world, to become clairvoyant, and for medicinal purposes. Ritual specialists took the drug to communicate with spirits while experiencing visions in a trancelike state. It served as a hallucinogenic drink for various ceremonies, especially puberty and initiation rites associated with the Chinigchinich cult. Various taboos, including sexual abstinence and dietary restrictions, were typically observed when taking the drug. Toloache was prepared in a drink as a painkiller for serious injuries, and for treating hemorrhoids, tapeworms, and as a poultice for wounds (Kroeber 1925:668–671; Timbrook 1990:252, 2007:65–73).

TULES or BULRUSHES
Plate 20

Schoenoplectus spp.

Stems of common tule *(S. acutus)* and California bulrush *(S. californicus)* were employed in the manufacture of baskets, clothing, mats, duck traps, balsa canoes, archery targets, dance headdresses, and so on, and as thatching for houses. The roots were also eaten.

Ashes from burned stems could be used to treat poison-oak rash and for application on a baby's navel. Stems were also reportedly used for making sponges for "sucking up tobacco liquid" (Timbrook 1990:246, 2007:203–206).

WILD CUCUMBER

Marah macrocarpus

A paste from the seeds of wild cucumber was prepared for pregnant women and as a purgative for babies and children. The plant was also prepared in a mixture to help with wounds, cataracts, inflammations, and urinary problems. It reportedly was used as a cure for baldness (Martin and Popper 2001:253; Timbrook 1990:252, 2007:122–124).

Charred seeds were employed in making paints for pictographs among the Luiseño (Anderson 2005:50; Timbrook 2007:124). Wild cucumber seeds have been recovered from archaeological sites in Orange (Koerper et al. 2002:72) and San Diego counties (Reddy 1999:38).

WILD TOBACCOS
Plate 9

Nicotiana spp.

Timbrook identifies three native wild tobacco species for the Chumash territory: *N. clevelandii* from the Channel Islands and coast, and coyote tobacco *(N. attenuata)* and Indian tobacco *(N. quadri-valvis)* from the interior mountains and valleys. People gathered wild tobacco leaves in the spring, drying them in the sun or on heated stones. As a recreational drug, primarily men would ingest it as a drink. A mixture of tobacco and lime (from a powder produced from heated mussel, abalone, or oyster shells) was prepared into small cakes that could be stored. As needed, the tobacco mixture was added to water and consumed as a drink, often in a social setting of men before dinner. Sometimes the tobacco and lime mixture was eaten, but it would inevitably cause vomiting. Tobacco was smoked in tubular steatite pipes primarily by ritual specialists in various curing and ceremonial settings. Tobacco served as an important ceremonial offering. Tobacco mixed with lime can relieve stomach pains; it can also be prepared as a poultice for use as a topical anesthetic or rubbed onto sore muscles (Timbrook 1990:252, 2007:126–132).

YERBA MANSA or LIZARD'S TAIL   *Anemopsis californica*
Yerba mansa has been an important medicinal plant for South Coast Province people. The "root" (probably rhizome) was gathered (often in spring), boiled, and prepared as a tea to combat colds, coughs, asthma, kidney problems, and venereal disease; it could also be used as a solution for treating cuts and sores, in preparing hot baths to sooth rheumatism, and as a blood purifier. The roots were chewed or prepared in a tea as part of a ceremony of ritual purification (Timbrook 1990:247, 2007:29–31).

TREES AND SHRUBS

BLUE ELDERBERRY   *Sambucus mexicana*
Plate 24
Blue elderberry fruits could be eaten.

The wood was favored for making bows. Stems were crafted into tobacco containers, smoking pipes, dance wands, flutes, clapper-sticks, bull-roarers, fire drills, and other objects. Fibers could be extracted from the bark.

The plant had many medicinal uses. A tea made from the flowers induced sweating, served as a blood purifier, and helped fight colds and fevers. A tea made from the roots served as a laxative. Remains of various species of *Sambucus* have been recovered from archaeological sites in San Diego County (Reddy 1999:38; Timbrook 1990: 252, 2007:197–198).

CALIFORNIA BAY or LAUREL   *Umbellularia californica*
Plate 24

California bay leaves were boiled and served as a drink to treat colds and diarrhea. Leaves mixed with lard served as a headache medicine, and bathing in a hot bath with the leaves helped with rheumatism.

Hunters burned the leaves before a hunt to acquire a smell that would attract or stupefy deer. Some sources indicate that there is little evidence that the Chumash used the "nuts" (i.e., the seeds) for food (Timbrook 1990:248, 2007:220–221); other sources suggest nuts were harvested and roasted (Grant 1978:516–517).

CALIFORNIA BLACK WALNUT   *Juglans californica*
Plate 25

The sweet, oil-rich nuts of this tree were considered a delicacy.

The nutshells were used as gaming pieces. The bark might be used in baskets (Martin and Popper 2001:247–248; Timbrook 1990: 247, 2007:95–97). Walnut remains have been recovered at archaeological sites in the South Coast Province, and they seem to have been a more important resource to people living here than they were to people living in more northern coastal areas (Hammett and Lawlor 2004:297).

CALIFORNIA BLACKBERRY   *Rubus ursinus*
Plate 26

These berries were collected and eaten. California blackberry roots could be boiled and made into a tea for treating diarrhea or dysentery (Timbrook 1990:249, 2007:174).

CALIFORNIA COFFEEBERRY   *Rhamnus californica*

California coffeeberry leaves were used to treat rheumatism and poison-oak rash, while the bark was boiled into a tea that served as a laxative and purgative (Timbrook 2007:164–165).

CALIFORNIA JUNIPER   *Juniperus californica*
Plate 33

South Coast Province people collected California juniper berries during the fall months along the Transverse and Peninsular ranges. The berries were usually molded into cakes and eaten, although it is reported that some people ate the berries fresh or prepared them in mush.

The wood was used for firewood and for making sinew-backed bows. A medicinal decoction was also used to treat rheumatism and urinary problems (Timbrook 1990:246, 2007:108–110).

CALIFORNIA WILD GRAPE   *Vitis californica*
Plate 29

The fruit of this plant was collected as food; it was probably not native to the entire South Coast Province (Timbrook 1990:250, 2007: 224–225).

COAST REDWOOD   *Sequoia sempervirens*
Plate 30

People procured coast redwood logs as driftwood along the coast. Canoe builders chose the best pieces for constructing *tomols.* The logs were split into planks using bone wedges and hammerstones and carefully shaped to fit together in the canoes. Family members marked graves in cemeteries with designs painted in bright colors on coast redwood mortuary poles. Driftwood not suitable for other uses was burned as firewood (Timbrook 1990:245, 2007:208–210).

COASTAL SAGEBRUSH   *Artemisia californica*

The leaves of this shrub were prepared as a remedy for headaches, while breathing the steam from boiling leaves could help patients with paralysis. The plant was also used for ritual purification, such as when someone had died in a house, or after a funeral. The wood was used to make foreshafts of composite arrows, to construct windbreaks around dance grounds, and as firewood (Timbrook 2007: 36–37).

COTTONWOODS   *Populus* spp.

Fremont cottonwood *(P. fremontii)* and black cottonwood *(P. balsamifera)* were widely used as materials for making house poles, boxes, bowls, trays, and even dugout canoes. The inner bark was also shredded to make women's skirts.

The bark and leaves were prepared in a poultice or wash for treating bruises and other injuries (Timbrook 1990:247, 2007:149–150).

CURRANTS and GOOSEBERRIES   *Ribes* spp.
Plate 44

Fruits of some current and gooseberry species were eaten; the Chumash differentiated those plants with spines from those without spines (Timbrook 1990:249, 2007:170–171).

HOLLY-LEAFED CHERRY or ISLAY   *Prunus ilicifolia*
Plate 32

The fruits of this tree were gathered in the summer and the pits removed, cracked open, and the kernels carefully extracted. Dried kernels could be stored in large baskets until needed. Before eating, the hydrocyanic acid had to be leached away; following the leaching process the kernels were boiled, mashed, and rolled into balls (often with pinole flour). The cherry kernel balls could be eaten within a week's time. The fruit pulp could also be eaten fresh, or mashed and dried in the sun.

The kernels were once commonly used as ceremonial offerings. They have been recovered from archaeological sites in San Diego County (Hammett and Lawlor 2004:297; Reddy 1999:40; Timbrook 1990:249, 2007:151–154).

LEMONADEBERRY *Rhus integrifolia*

The fruits of lemonadeberry were collected, pounded, dried, winnowed, and eaten. Some South Coast Province people made a drink from the berries.

The berries have medicinal uses as well (Martin and Popper 2001:253–254; Timbrook 1990:249–250, 2007:165–166).

MANZANITAS *Arctostaphylos* **spp.**

Plate 22

The fruits of various species, especially bigberry manzanita *(A. glauca)*, were collected in summer, dried, and ground into flour. The flour could then be made into pinole or mixed with water to make a beverage (Reddy 1999:38; Timbrook 1990:250, 2007:34–35).

Oaks

Acorns from various oak species were collected, dried outdoors, shelled, and then further dried in preparation for long-term storage in large baskets in houses. Before eating, the cooks would pound the acorns into flour, then remove the bitter tannic acid by repeatedly bathing the acorn flour in a wooden bowl or by using basketry or sand leaching basins. The acorns were typically prepared in a mush or soup. Oaks also provided a variety of other uses for South Coast Province people, as Harrington's (1942) work among the Chumash demonstrates. For example, in the old days, acorns were used as toys, strung together on necklaces, chewed and rubbed on the body for protection against the sun, used as a dye in making baskets, and employed as ceremonial offerings (Timbrook 1990:247, 2007:155–160). Charred acorn remains have been recovered from sites in this region (Hammett and Lawlor 2004:297)

BLACK OAK *Quercus kelloggii*

Plate 36

The Luiseño people preferred the taste of black oak acorns over other species (Martin and Popper 2001:249).

CALIFORNIA SCRUB OAK   *Quercus berberidifolia*
Plate 38

The acorns of California Scrub Oak were harvested and eaten, but they were not the preferred acorns of Chumash people. The wood was utilized for crafting bows, arrow foreshafts, and thatching needles (Timbrook 1990:247, 2007:162–163).

COAST LIVE OAK   *Quercus agrifolia*
Plate 39

Chumash people appear to have preferred this oak's acorn for cooking mush or soup.

Craftspeople used the wood to construct handsome bowls, mush-stirrers, and plank boxes. The twigs were employed in cradle making, the oak shoots for making bows and hoops for the hoop-pole game. The bark served as firewood and as dye for hides, while the green bark could be prepared as charcoal and mixed into a drink for treating indigestion and bowel disorders. Boils and pustules could be treated by preparing a drink soaked in oak bark or by applying the fresh juice of oak galls. Hemorrhoids were treated with charred oak galls. Bark coals were once used to parch seeds and to trim hair (Grant 1978:515; Timbrook 1990:247, 2007:160–162).

VALLEY OAK or WHITE OAK   *Quercus lobata*
Plate 42

While the acorns of this oak were harvested and cooked, it was not the preferred species of Chumash people (Timbrook 1990:247, 2007:163–164).

POISON-OAK   *Toxicodendron diversilobum*

The juice of poison-oak was prepared to remove warts, corns, and calluses, to treat sores, skin cancer, and wounds, and to stop bleeding. The roots could be boiled in a tea to fight dysentery or diarrhea (Timbrook 1990:250, 2007:215–217).

SINGLELEAF PINYON   *Pinus monophylla*
Plate 45

Significant stands of these trees are found in the Transverse Ranges and in some locations of the Peninsular Ranges. Pine "nuts" (i.e., the seeds) were collected by Chumash people as early as August; the cones were knocked loose with short poles. The cones were then roasted in aboveground roasting ovens until the resin was removed, the cones opened, and the nuts could be extracted. The nuts were dried for two to three days and made ready to eat, usually by toasting in a basket with hot coals and cracking the nuts with mortar and pestle, or they could be stored for later use.

People crafted bows from the wood, used the pitch as an adhesive or caulking material (such as for attaching arrow points to wooden shafts and for sealing the plank canoes), and chewed the pitch as gum (Timbrook 1990:245, 2007:142–146).

TOYON   *Heteromeles arbutifolia*
The fruit of this tree was harvested, then either toasted or dried and mashed. Before eating, the prepared fruit was usually left in a vessel to sit for several days as it softened and sweetened.

Shoots of the hard wood could be used for making various utensils, such as arrow and harpoon shafts, bows, awls, wedges, scrapers, digging sticks, cradle frames, pestles, pegs for *tomols,* game sticks, balls, and headdress pins. The wood was once widely employed for making bowls and feathered offering poles. It could also be used to smoke fish (Timbrook 1990:249, 2007:91–94).

WILD ROSE or ROSE   *Rosa californica*
The fruit of the wild rose could be eaten raw and was also used for making necklaces and earrings. The petals were dried, powdered, and applied to skin rashes on babies. A tea was made from the petals and used to help with stomach pains and colic or to wash sore eyes (Timbrook 1990:249, 2007:172–174).

WILLOWS   *Salix* spp.
Plate 35
South Coast Province people used willow woods for making houses, furniture (sleeping platforms, storage platforms, storage bins), ceremonial enclosures, ladders for sweathouses, dugout canoes, baskets, fire sticks, and bull-roarers. They also were preferred as firewood. Shoots of red willow *(S. laevigata)* were employed in basketry. The bark was used for crafting fiber belts, skirts, sandals, tumplines, bags, nets, carrying rings, and brushes. The wood was fashioned into mush-stirring sticks, spoons, digging sticks, and probably bowls. Shoots of arroyo willow *(S. lasiolepis)* were also used in basketry, and strips of bark were useful as lashing material.

Leafy branches from arroyo willow were placed on beds to cool people with fevers. Willow bark tea could be useful for treating fevers and sore throats (Timbrook 1990:247, 2007:176–183).

CACTI AND SUCCULENTS

OUR LORD'S CANDLE   *Yucca whipplei*
Plate 53
Leaf fibers from this plant were fashioned into cordage for use in fishing lines and nets and for making sandals. The needles served as tattooing instruments and for ear piercing.

Our Lord's candle and other *Yucca* species were an important food source for the Chumash and other South Coast Province people: fresh flower stalks and the basal portion of the plant were roasted in underground ovens and eaten. The flower stalks could also be cooked in hot ashes. The dried stalk was used as tinder, and charcoal made from this plant served as a pigment for body tattoos (Timbrook 1990:247, 2007:226–229). Yucca-roasting ovens are well documented in the archaeological literature for the South Coast Province (Shackley 2004). Yucca was also an important exchange item (Gamble and Zepeda 2002:73–74).

PRICKLY-PEARS   *Opuntia* spp.
Plate 49

People harvested the fruit of prickly-pears for food; the pads were also eaten. The thorns could be used as tattoo needles and to pierce ears. Artisans prepared the fruits for use as paints or dyes (Timbrook 1990:250, 2007:133–135).

SHELLFISH

ABALONES   *Haliotis* spp.
Plates 55, 56

Various species of abalone were gathered by South Coast Province people for both food and sources of raw material for making ornaments, spangles for clothing, and inlays for art objects made of stone, bone, and wood. Abalones were once commonly employed for making circular fishhooks, and as eating dishes when the siphon holes were filled with asphaltum (Arnold and Graesch 2001:90–97, 108–111; Grant 1978:516). Black Abalone *(H. cracherodii)* appears to be the most common species found in most Late Holocene shell middens, although Red Abalone *(H. rufescens)* and Green Abalone *(H. fulgens)* have also been found.

BEAN CLAM   *Donax gouldii*
A small shellfish that frequents sandy beaches, the Bean Clam is commonly recovered from Late Holocene shell midden sites in places along the Orange County and San Diego coastline (Byrd and Reddy 2002:57; Koerper et al. 2002:71).

BLACK TURBAN SNAIL   *Chlorostoma funebralis*
Plate 57

The Black Turban Snail is common in coastal archaeological sites. On San Clemente Island, discrete shell-bearing sites containing high percentages of crushed Black Turban Snails have been recorded, possibly reflecting the bulk harvesting of snails for making some kind of soup during times of resource stress (Raab et al. 2002:20). Glassow

(1996:135, 2002:188–189) also documents the common presence of this snail in Late Holocene archaeological sites along the northern shores of the South Coast Province.

CALIFORNIA MUSSEL — *Mytilus californianus*
Plate 58

Native Californians ate California Mussel meat, and mussels are among the most common shellfish in coastal archaeological sites along the rocky shoreline of the South Coast Province.

Archaeological findings indicate that J-shaped fish hooks and beads were once manufactured from California Mussel shells (Arnold and Graesch 2001:103–106, 108–111; Greenwood 1978:522).

LITTLENECK CLAM or ROCK COCKLE — *Leukoma staminea*

This distinctive, ridged-lined, chalky-shelled clam is found in shell middens near sheltered beaches and gravel habitats throughout the South Coast Province (Byrd and Reddy 2002:58; Gamble and Russell 2002:112).

OLIVE SNAIL — *Callianax biplicata,* formerly *Olivella biplicata*

Shell from the Olive Snail was a critical source for the manufacture of various forms of shell beads. Significant late prehistoric manufacturing sites have been excavated on Santa Cruz Island, where over 150,000 pieces of Olive Snail shell detritus per square meter have been recovered from shell bead production sites. Other shell bead production sites have been found on other northern Channel Islands; some shell bead manufacturing also took place on the Santa Barbara mainland as well (Arnold and Graesch 2001:74–75; Erlandson and Rick 2002:175–177).

PISMO CLAM — *Tivela stultorum*

The meat from the Pismo Clam was eaten. The shells were suitable for making beads and disks, while clam tubes were worn as nasal piercings (Arnold and Graesch 2001:97–103; Grant 1978:516).

THICK SCALLOP — *Argopecten ventricosus*

This sand-adapted form of scallop was harvested near lagoons from Santa Barbara to southern Baja California (Byrd and Reddy 2002:58–60; Erlandson and Rick 2002).

VENUS CLAMS or HARDSHELL COCKLES — *Chione* spp.

Several species from this genus of sand-flat clams are commonly found in Late Holocene archaeological sites throughout the South Coast Province (Byrd and Reddy 2002:58–60; Erlandson and Rick 2002; Gamble and Russell 2002:112).

INSECTS AND OTHER TERRESTRIAL INVERTEBRATES

APHIDS   **Superfamily Aphidoidea**
Chumash and Fernandeño peoples collected honeydew from aphids and other scale insects. This sticky sweet substance was likely used as a condiment (Harrington 1942:9; Landberg 1965:81).

CATERPILLARS   **Order Lepidoptera**
The Western Diegueño (Kumeyaay) and Luiseño consumed dried caterpillars, the larvae of butterflies and moths. Some Chumash groups preferred caterpillar chrysalids (Drucker 1937b:9; Harrington 1942:8).

GRASSHOPPERS   **Suborder Caelifera**
Plate 62
Grasshoppers were eaten by many Native groups. Young wingless grasshoppers were driven into pits and roasted. The insects could also be dried (Drucker 1937b:9; Harrington 1942:8; Kroeber 1925:652).

HARVESTER ANTS   *Pogonomyrmex* **spp.**
Among the Luiseño, an important boys' initiation rite was the Ant Ordeal. Young men were placed on ant hills or had their bodies covered with ants. Special songs were sung during this secretive ceremony, and the ants were whipped from the young men's bodies at its conclusion (Drucker 1937b:35; Kroeber 1925:672).

YELLOWJACKET LARVAE   *Vespula* **spp. and**
Plate 63   *Dolichovespula* **spp.**
Several South Coast Province groups consumed yellowjacket larvae (Drucker 1937b:9; Harrington 1942:8).

FISHES
Pelagic Fishes
Plates 64–66
In late prehistoric and early historic times, open-water marine fishes were captured primarily from boats using harpoons, fish arrows, hooks and lines, and nets, although some fishing may have taken place from the shoreline of the Channel Islands near deep water. Most of the South Coast Province ethnographies were written in the early and mid-twentieth century, after the indigenous groups of this area had lost much of their traditional coastal access to Spanish, Mexican, and American colonists. Accordingly, information on the marine resources used by these groups is particularly scarce. Conse-

quently, much of our information on specific species once fished come from archaeological investigations. Most of the evidence for deepwater fishing is associated with Channel Island sites and Chumash sites on the coastal mainland of the Santa Barbara Channel. A diverse range of species was exploited. A few of the more common pelagic fishes recovered from Late Holocene archaeological excavations include anchovies (Engraulididae), Chub Mackerel *(Scomber japonicus)*, Pacific Bonito *(Sarda chiliensis)*, Leopard Shark *(Triakis semifasciata)*, Pacific Angel Shark *(Squatina californica)*, Pacific Barracuda *(Sphyraena argentea)*, Pacific Sardine *(Sardinops sagax)*, Shovelnose Guitarfish *(Rhinobatos productus)*, Soupfin Shark *(Galeorhinus galeus)*, and Yellowtail *(Seriola lalandi)*.*

SWORDFISH   ***Xiphias gladius***

Swordfish meat was eaten. Interestingly, Swordfish remains once played an important role in Chumash ritual, where a Swordfish Dancer wearing a headdress fashioned from a Swordfish skull participated in ceremonies. Excavations along the Santa Barbara mainland revealed the renowned "Swordfish Man" burial, including a headdress made from the skull and bill of a Swordfish, and a cape decorated with abalone ornaments. Swordfish images are also depicted in Chumash rock art (Davenport et al. 1993; Erlandson and Rick 2002:174; Pletka 2001:229).

Nearshore Fishes
Plates 67–69, 71

A diverse range of nearshore marine fishes was once harvested by South Coast Province people using hooks and lines, nets, traps, beach seines, gorges, and spears from shore, as well as hooks and lines from boats. Some of the more prominent species identified in archaeological sites include Cabezon *(Scorpaenichthys marmoratus)*; California Sheephead *(Semicossyphus pulcher)*, relatively common in archaeological sites on the Channel Islands and the coastal mainland; surfperches (Embiotocidae), various species common in coastal sites across the province; rockfishes (*Sebastes* spp.), various species common in coastal sites across the province; Kelp Bass *(Paralabrax clathratus)*; Señorita *(Oxyjulis californica)*, common in Late Holocene Orange County sites; Blacksmith *(Chromis punctipinnis)*, common in Late Holocene Orange County sites; Bat Ray *(Myliobatis californica)*; Soupfin Shark *(Galeorhinus galeus)*; and small clupeids, including the Pacific Sardine *(Sardinops sagax)*.*

Freshwater Fishes

RAINBOW TROUT *Oncorhyncus mykiss,* formerly *Salmo gairdneri*

Sparkman reports that the Luiseño obtained "mountain trout" from the upper San Luis Rey River. Traditionally, the Rainbow Trout were immobilized through the use of a fish stupefacient and were taken using a fish scoop or basket (Sparkman 1908:200).

BIRDS
Marine Birds and Waterbirds
Plates 81, 84, 88–91

Waterbirds were probably hunted along lakes and lagoons near the coast using nets and arrows. People on the Channel Islands also hunted some species. A few of the species reported from Late Holocene archaeological sites include Common Loon *(Gavia immer),* Green-winged Teal *(Anas crecca),* Cinnamon Teal *(A. cyanoptera),* Ruddy Duck *(Oxyura jamaicensis),* American Coot *(Fulica americana),* Mallard *(A. platyrynchos),* and White-winged Scoter *(Melanitta fusca).**

BROWN PELICAN *Pelecanus occidentalis*

Brown Pelican remains have been recovered from archaeological sites throughout the South Coast Province and Channel Islands (Colten 2001:209; Gamble and Russell 2002:113).

CORMORANTS *Phalacrocorax* spp.
Plates 85–87

Double-crested Cormorant *(P. auritus),* Pelagic Cormorant *(P. pelagicus),* and Brandt's Cormorant *(P. penicillatus)* are found in archaeological sites on the mainland and Channel Islands (Colten 2001: 209; Gamble and Russell 2002:113; Glassow 2002:191).

GULLS *Larus* spp.
Plate 82

Various species of gulls are found in archaeological sites throughout the South Coast Province and Channel Islands, with the California Gull *(L. californicus)* being the most common species identified (Colten 2001:209; Gamble and Russell 2002:113; Glassow 1996:68).

Terrestrial Birds

CALIFORNIA QUAIL
Callipepla californica

Plate 99

In southern California, quails were hunted with snares and traps. The California Quail has been identified in archaeological sites (Byrd and Reddy 2002:58; Glassow 1996:68).

RAPTORS
Order Falconiformes

Plates 97, 101

Birds of prey played an especially significant role in the symbolic meanings and creation stories of South Coast Province people. Spanish accounts indicate that raptors were incorporated into various ceremonies, dances, and feasts. A central ritual of the Chinigchinich cult included the Eagle Ceremony or Dance, which involved a dance that concluded with the sacrifice of an eagle (often raised in captivity), its feathers removed, the body cremated or buried, and the bird mourned as part of the rite. Interestingly, archaeological findings of raptors, including the Golden Eagle *(Aquila chrysaetos)* and Red-tailed Hawk *(Buteo jamaicensis),* in late prehistoric and historic sites indicate that Native ceremonies involving the birds continued in the Franciscan missions.*

MAMMALS
Marine Mammals

SEA LIONS
Family Otariidae

Plates 102, 107

California Sea Lion *(Zalophus californianus),* Guadalupe Fur Seal *(Arctocephalus townsendi),* and Northern Fur Seal *(Callorhinus ursinus)* were hunted in southern California, especially on the Channel Islands. California Sea Lions established rookeries on the Channel Islands during the summer, when they gave birth to pups; there is some disagreement about whether the fur seals did the same. All these species may have used local haul outs along the mainland coast as well (Glassow 2002:189–190). During the breeding season, they could be harvested using clubs. A large percentage of the Guadalupe Fur Seals and California Sea Lions found in early archaeological sites on San Clemente Island are juveniles and females, probably taken during the breeding season. In the Late Holocene, overhunting probably made them more difficult to hunt, and some were captured using the combination of harpoons and plank canoes (Colten 2001: 203; Hildebrandt and Jones 1992; Kennet 2005:196–198; Moss et al. 2006:168–169; Raab et al. 2002:18–19).

DOLPHINS and PORPOISES   Family Delphinidae
Plates 103, 104

Various species of dolphins are found in archaeological sites on the Channel Islands, including Pacific White-sided Dolphin *(Lagenorhynchus obliquidens),* Common Dolphin *(Delphinus delphis),* and Bottlenose Dolphin *(Tursiops truncata)*(Colten 2001:203).

GRAY WHALE   *Eschrichtius robustus*
Plate 105

Stranded Gray Whales were once claimed by local coastal villages. Whale bones were used for wedges, abalone pries, and burial markers, and as building material for houses (Grant 1978:516).

HARBOR SEAL   *Phoca vitulina*
Plate 106

Harbor Seals have been found in archaeological sites on the mainland and Channel Islands (Colten 2001:203; Gamble and Russell 2002:113).

NORTHERN ELEPHANT SEAL   *Mirounga angustirostris*

There is archaeological evidence for the hunting of this sea mammal, especially on the Channel Islands (Kennet 2005:196; Stewart et al. 1994:30).

SEA OTTER   *Enhydra lutris*

The remains of Sea Otters are found in coastal archaeological sites on the California mainland and on the Channel Islands (Byrd and Reddy 2002:58; Colten 2001:203; Gamble and Russell 2002:113).

Terrestrial Mammals

GROUND SQUIRRELS   *Spermophilus* spp.

Ground squirrels, probably Beechey Ground Squirrel *(S. beecheyi),* have been recovered from archaeological sites throughout the South Coast Province (Gamble and Russell 2002:113).

HARES and RABBITS   Family Leporidae
Plate 109

South Coast Province people hunted hares and rabbits with snares and deadfalls. They also initiated communal hunts using "flat, curved throwing sticks" to knock down animals. Although not always distinguished by species in archaeological excavations, they probably include the Black-tailed Jackrabbit *(Lepus californicus)* and Desert Cottontail *(Sylvilagus auduboni)*(Gamble and Russell 2002: 113; Glassow 1996:68; Grant 1978:517).

MULE DEER   *Odocoileus hemionus*

Plate 112

The Mule Deer was hunted with bow and arrow (Gamble and Russell 2002:113; Grant 1978:517).

WOODRATS   *Neotoma* spp.

Woodrats, probably the Dusky-footed Woodrat *(N. fuscipes)* and Desert Woodrat *(N. lepida),* have been recovered in archaeological sites throughout the South Coast Province (Gamble and Russell 2002:113).

ROCKS AND MINERALS

ASPHALTUM or BITUMEN

A widely used material found in seeps along the coast, this natural tar served as caulking for planked canoes, a sealant for water bottles and baskets, a suitable material for hafting projectile points, and an ideal medium for inlaying shell beads and other materials into steatite effigies and other art objects (Grant 1978:515).

STEATITE or SOAPSTONE

Steatite was used for making ollas, comals, bowls, beads, tobacco pipes, medicine tubes, and effigies of various animals, such as whales. Archaeologists have recorded large quarry sites in the Pots Valley on Santa Catalina Island (Grant 1978:514; Heizer 1972).

Northeast Province

Freshwater marsh, riparian woodland, montane forest, chaparral, pinyon-juniper woodland, sagebrush scrub.

Hokan stock: Achumawi (Pit River), Atsugewi languages; Utian stock or family: Modoc language.

At the crossroads of three broad culture areas—California, the Great Basin, and the Plateau—the people of the Northeast Province created a sophisticated lifeway centering around winter villages, fire management of grassland, meadow, and upland resources, and the exploitation of diverse foods from an extensive wetland system of streams, lakes, seasonal marshes, and swamps. As the primary social unit, the winter village was organized into discrete house clusters, where related families established homes, cookhouses, storage facilities, and sweathouses. Each house cluster within the village was usually represented by a headman, with one leader from a particularly powerful family serving as the village's chief. Large Atsugewi villages comprised 20 to 25 houses, often divided into several house clusters, which might be spatially separated by as much as .4 km (.25 mi). A typical large settlement contained several semisubterranean earth lodges with associated cookhouses, a number of mat lodges or dome-shaped houses for smaller or less-wealthy families, and a handful of sweathouses. People living in the smaller hamlets of a few houses or one- or two-house clusters tended to be associated with one of the larger villages (Garth 1953:176; Ray 1963; Stern 1998).

Spacious earth lodges served as the residences of chiefly families or the homes of other wealthy or influential people in the winter village. The impressive earth lodges, measuring about 5 to 15 m (16 to 49 ft) in diameter, might house up to six to eight families, with the central space near the hearth reserved for communal use, and the places along the walls assigned to specific families. Modoc houses, dug to a depth of .9 to 1.2 m (3 to 4 ft) with digging sticks and burden baskets, featured four main posts rising out of the sunken floor, which supported a conical roof of poles running from the earthen wall to the center of the house. The builders sealed the roofs with several insulating layers of tule mats and brush, followed by a thick layer of earth. Household members gained entrance through a central roof hatchway and ladder; with a central hearth, grass-covered floor, and comfortable sleeping mats, the earth lodge provided a cozy place to spend cold winter nights. During the day, household members rolled up their personal items in sleeping mats and set them against the wall. Large earth lodges not only served as winter residences, but also places for hosting communal gatherings where dances, feasts, and some ceremonies took place. It does not appear that large assembly or dance houses were constructed in traditional winter villages in the Northeast Province.*

Families and individuals also built smaller mat lodges, bark houses, or dome-shaped structures in the winter villages. Mat lodges consisted of wooden superstructures built over shallow earth pits, covered with several layers of tule mats. The bark houses and dome-shaped structures consisted of wooden structures cloaked in bark, or a conical framework of willow poles covered with either mats and/or bark. Poorer families tended to live in the bark or dome-shaped houses, as well as elderly people who could no longer climb in and out of the roof entrances of earth lodges. The latter buildings also served as cookhouses— multipurpose structures built adjacent to earth lodges for storage, cooking, and other indoor work activities. Sweathouses varied in design—some were dome-shaped structures of willow poles thatched with insulating layers of tule mats; others maintained a distinctive long and narrow shape, with a sunken floor and a sloping roof of earth. Modoc sweathouses differed from others in California, with fires burning outside the entrance to heat rocks, which when carried to an interior pit and sprinkled with water, produced plenty of steam.*

While in residence during the winter, women rotated the cooking duties for large multifamily groups in earth lodges, serving two meals a day: a morning breakfast of boiled roots and seeds, and an afternoon dinner with meat and other available foods. Women spent considerable time in the nearby cooking or utility houses, where they prepared meals, bringing them over to the earth lodges where the entire multifamily household would eat. The cooking houses served as work rooms for women where they not only prepared and fixed meals, but manufactured tule mats, sewed clothing, and wove a diverse range of twined basket types (coiled basketry manufacture is recent). The cooking houses also served as menstrual huts, places for childbirth, and locations where women could get away from men and other people in the village. Men and older boys spent some of their free time in the sweathouses, which served as male clubhouses in the villages. But the use of the sweathouses for sweats or other social activities appears to have been rather casual and sporadic. Men enjoyed passing a pipe full of lit tobacco around after dinner and chatting about the day's events. The after-dinner smoke might take place in one of the earth lodges or in the nearby sweathouse (Ray 1963:158–162; Stern 1998:451).

Ceremonies, dances, and feasts took place within the villages, usually sponsored by the chief or another influential and wealthy person or family. The most elaborate events were Big Times, where people from nearby villages were invited for several days of festivities, including food donations, gambling, trading, and competitive sweat dances. Religion played an important role in the social life of winter villages, with people recognizing a complex mix of spirits inhabiting the natural and supernatural world. Guardian spirits looked out for the welfare of individuals; influential shamans enjoyed the protection and assistance of a number of powerful spirits, with specific ones conferring distinctive kinds of power and capabilities to these religious specialists. The shamans served as doctors for curing sick or injured people by sucking out painful objects and/or by singing; however, they could also poison people (Garth 1953:171–172, 186–192; Ray 1963:31–71).

Winter villages broke up in the spring, with people separating into smaller groups to pursue available resources in the local region. The east slope of the Cascade Range supports oak groves and salmon (*Oncorhynchus* spp.), although salmon runs terminate at the confluence of the Pit and Fall rivers. The lowlands of the Modoc Plateau support a surprising number of lakes, seasonal freshwater habitats, and meadows, which eventually make the transition to the arid sagebrush country of the Great Basin. The strategic use of fire in various habitats greatly enhanced the biodiversity of useful resources across the region (see especially Olmsted and Stewart 1978). A detailed description of the Modoc seasonal round is provided by Ray (1963:180–183) and Stern (1998:448–449). Leaving behind elderly and invalid people in the winter villages, most able-bodied people established a series of small camps across the tribelet's territory from March to October, during which time they fished for Rainbow Trout *(Oncorhynchus mykiss)* and Sacramento Suckers *(Catostomus occidentalis)*, gathered roots in wetland meadows, collected seeds in grasslands, and hunted game and harvested berries in the uplands. Much of this food was specifically prepared for winter stores, either cached for later pick up, carried to elderly relatives left at home, or transported back to the primary winter residences in early fall.

INDIAN MANAGEMENT OF LOCAL FISH POPULATIONS

The built landscape of northeastern California features elaborate stone fish traps used by local Indians over hundreds of years to capture Sacramento Suckers (Catostomus occidentalis) and other freshwater fishes. The best documented fish traps are found in the crystal clear waters of the greater Pit River drainage, particularly where cold spring waters flow from the twisted but magnificent lava fields into the Tule River, Harr Pond, and Big Lake wetlands. These waters attract large numbers of Suckers, particularly during the months of late January to July, when they spawn in the gravels of the shallow ponds. The local Ajumawi Indians constructed extensive fish weirs from volcanic rocks that incorporated these shallow ponds into their design. A solid outer wall with one or more openings directed fishes into an enclosed area where smaller rock alignments created shallow water pens or corrals where they could spawn. During harvests, the openings in the outer wall were shut, leaving fishermen to spear selected fishes, to capture them with basket scoops, or to catch them with bare hands and throw them onto the bank.

Today, Native fishermen still maintain and use these intricate traps (fig. 25). Built, modified, and reconfigured over time, these fish weirs are places where contemporary Indian people literally work with the handicraft of their ancestors. As John Foster (2000:268) observes, the most complex traps may consist of "an elaborate maze of interior channels, chambers, rock piles and outer wall [that] direct the spawning fishes into very shallow water. During the peak spawning season, the preoccupied fishes can be touched from the bank as they deposit eggs on the gravels." It is reported that during a single run, more than 100 fishes may be harvested from one fish weir or trap. This represents a bountiful harvest, as each large fish may weigh between 1.8 and 3.1 kg (4 and 7 lb). Fishermen may return to a single fish weir as many as three to six times during the spawning season, depending upon the fish supply and local water conditions.

MOSSES AND FERNS

Gathered from pine trees, dried, and ground, black moss *(Alectoria fremontii)* was usually boiled and then used as a poultice for reducing swelling (Garth 1953:140; Olmsted and Stewart 1978:230). The leaves and/or stalks of bracken fern *(Pteridium aquilinum)* were once eaten raw or cooked (Garth 1953:139).

John Foster emphasizes that these fish traps are part of a broader strategy of resource conservation that Indians employ to manage the Sacramento Sucker population as a fishery. He points out that when sufficient fishes are harvested, the trap is reopened so that the remaining fishes can escape after they have spawned. More importantly, the labyrinth of inner chambers is specifically designed to maximize the extent of gravel area where the cold spring water nurtures the fish eggs. An important activity of local Native fishermen, both past and present, is to remove debris from the fish traps, to rebuild walls so that rocks are removed from the spawning gravels, and to reconstruct channels that direct the cold spring water to the spawning grounds. All of these efforts help to ensure that future spawning events are successful (see Foster 2000).

Figure 25. Upper rock alignments of a fish weir used for capturing Sacramento Suckers in northeastern California.

CALIFORNIA MAIDEN-HAIR FERN　　　*Adiantum jordanii*

Basket makers used California maiden-hair fern for weaving distinctive design elements into the twined baskets of the Northeast Province (Garth 1953:148–149; Olmsted and Stewart 1978:229).

HERBACEOUS PLANTS

Garth (1953:139) identifies several species of plants whose leaves and/or stalks—tender and delectable in the early spring months—were once eaten either raw or cooked: Gray's licorice-root *(Ligusticum grayi)*, elk thistle *(Cirsium scariosum)*, as well as common lomatium *(Lomatium utriculatum)*, and *L. nudicaule* (see also Olmsted and Stewart 1978:227–228).

BALSAM-ROOT　　　*Balsamorhiza sagittata*

Balsam-root seeds could be harvested and processed in the same way as the seeds of wild sunflowers (*Helianthus* and other genera). Balsam-root thrives in burned-over patches (Garth 1953:139; Ray 1963:199).

BEAR GRASS or WHITE GRASS　　　*Xerophyllum tenax*
Plate 5

This tawny-colored member of the lily family was widely used by weavers for making distinctive designs in twined baskets (Garth 1953:148–149). As noted by Anderson (2005:194), bear grass responded well to fires, putting out new healthy growth from its woody rhizomes, giving it the nickname "fire lily."

BLAZING STAR　　　*Mentzelia albicaulis*

Blazing star seeds were harvested and eaten (Ray 1963:199).

CAMAS or QUAMASH　　　*Camassia quamash*
Plate 7

Another important food crop, camas plants flourish in moist meadows and can be harvested after epos *(Perideridia oregana)* in June or July. Women used digging sticks to break the soil around the roots, and the strenuous harvest season lasted about a month. They dried and cleaned the bulbs in root-digging camps near the meadows, then carried the camas back to the winter villages for storage. Mono women cooked the bulbs in earth ovens, dried the cooked bulbs on tule mats, and then placed them in storage bags in pits until needed in winter (Ray 1963:181, 198).

The Atsugewi processed the bulbs by placing them in a rock-lined earth oven, in which a fire was lit and allowed to burn down to coals. The coals were then swept out, and pine needles were placed on the hot rocks, followed by camas bulbs. The cooks then placed another layer of pine needles on top of the bulbs, followed by a layer of dirt. A fire was then built on top of the oven, and the roots were allowed to cook overnight. The next day, they removed the bulbs from the oven, mashed them well, and made them into cakes. The discriminating chefs then placed the cakes back in the rock-lined pit, where they were baked until sweet to the taste. The cakes could be eaten or dried and stored for later use. When needed, a person simply added water to the dried cakes to reconstitute them.*

Anderson (2005:296, 302) cites how burning the meadows improved the quality and quantity of camas bulbs.

COW PARSNIP   *Heracleum lanatum*
In the old days, people depended on cow parsnip to treat many medical problems. The roots were chewed or brewed as a beverage for colds, coughs, and pulmonary congestion. The plant could be processed for use as a salve for bruises and swelling. An infusion made from cow parsnip was taken for headaches. A root compress worked well for sore eyes (Ray 1963:219).

DELTOID BALSAM-ROOT   *Balsamorhiza deltoidea*
The seeds of this plant could be harvested and processed in the same way as seeds of wild sunflowers (*Helianthus* and other genera). Deltoid balsam-root also grows well in recently burned areas. Other nearby Indian groups (Maidu) in the Great Central Valley and Sierra Nevada Province also prepared the roots for food (Garth 1953:139; Strike 1994:27).

DESERT PARSLEY   *Lomatium canbyi*
An early root crop available in April and May, the Modoc Indians once dug for this prolific turnip-like tuber in the sagebrush scrub near Tule Lake. The tubers could be either dried for winter storage or cooked and eaten fresh (Ray 1963:181, 198). Another species *(L. triternatum)* was gathered by the Atsugewi, had a similar taste to the epos root, and was cooked in earth ovens (Garth 1953:139).

DOGBANE or INDIAN HEMP   *Apocynum cannabinum*
Plate 10
Ethnographers reported that the fibers of this perennial herb were collected and widely used for making twine in nets, lines, and various other materials.*

EPOS or IPOS   *Perideridia oregana**
Recognized as one of the significant traditional foods of the region, local people harvested large quantities of the tuberous roots of epos

with digging sticks before they bloomed in spring (usually in May). A hard-working woman could dig a burden basketful of roots in a day. The roots had to be processed while fresh, about every three or four days during the harvest, which might last for three or four weeks. Women removed the skins by placing the roots in damp sand in a shallow basket. They then worked the roots back and forth with their feet. The skinned roots were dried on rocks and stored for the winter, probably in storage baskets. When needed, Indian cooks pounded the dried roots in basket hoppers in preparation for making soup or bread. The bread could be wrapped in grass, hung up to dry, and then stored.* Garth (1953:138) also noted that fresh epos roots had a "fine meaty flavor," and could be processed using a mano and metate.

FIDDLENECKS   *Amsinckia* spp.
Fiddleneck seeds could be harvested and processed in the same way as the seeds of wild sunflowers (*Helianthus* and other genera). Garth (1953:139) identified this plant as *A. parviflora,* but see Mead (1972: 14). Strike (1994:12) warned that *Amsinckia* seeds can have a "cumulative poisonous effect."

HARVEST BRODIAEA   *Brodiaea coronaria*
Harvest brodiaea corms were harvested, then either boiled in water or cooked in underground ovens (Garth 1953:138; Kniffen 1928:301).

LAMB'S-QUARTERS   *Chenopodium fremontii*
People in this province harvested and ate lamb's-quarters seeds (Ray 1963:199).

MANNAGRASSES   *Glyceria* spp.
Mannagrass seeds were harvested and eaten (Ray 1963:199).

MOUNTAIN TARWEED   *Madia glomerata*
Mountain tarweed seeds were among the important seeds harvested and eaten by people in the Northeast Province (Ray 1963:199).

SULPHUR FLOWER   *Eriogonum umbellatum*
Sulphur flower seeds were harvested and eaten (Ray 1963:199; Strike 1994:59–60).

TIGER LILY   *Lilium pardalinum*
Tiger lily bulbs were harvested and cooked in earth ovens overnight until ready to eat (Garth 1953:138; see also Olmsted and Stewart 1978:227). Anderson (2005:349) emphasizes how the tiger lily responds positively to prescribed burning.

TULES or BULRUSHES   *Schoenoplectus* spp.
Plate 20

Various species of tules provided important sources of raw material for making baskets, mats for houses, and clothing, among other objects. A primary species mentioned in the literature is common tule *(S. acutus)*. Basket types included decorative baskets, gambling baskets, storage baskets, and hats, especially in the eastern section of the Northeast Province, where other kinds of basketry materials might be scarce. Tule used to be a critical material for making various types of mats, some used in the construction of houses or insulation in sweathouses, others as sleeping mats, and so forth. In the old days, tule was also employed to make winter shoes, aprons, robes, and other clothing; twines for nets, lines, and so on; and even rafts for use on shallow waters.[*]

Young tule shoots can be eaten in spring when they first sprout (Kniffen 1928:301; Olmsted and Stewart 1978:227).

WHITE BRODIAEA or   *Triteleia hyacinthina*
WHITE-FLOWERED GRASS-NUT

White brodiaea corms were harvested, prepared, and cooked like the bulbs of camas *(Camassia quamash)* in earth ovens (Garth 1953: 138).

WHITE CAMAS or DEATH CAMAS   *Zigadenus venenosus*

Another important root crop of the Mono people, the white camas thrives within moist grassy flats in the montane forests. Traditional gatherers included white camas into their seasonal round, extending the root harvest season into late July. The one drawback with white camas is that poisonous toxins in the bulbs had to be leached out. Once brought back to the winter village, the bulb's skin was removed, the rest of the bulb was dried, and it was placed in a tule sack. The sack was then immersed in a flowing stream for three days to remove the toxins. The bulbs were carefully dried and then stored for use in winter (Ray 1963:181, 199).

WILD PARSLEY   *Ligusticum grayi*

Wild parsley was widely recognized as a remedy for colds, coughs, and stomachaches. Roots could be chewed, or they could be dried, scraped, and added to warm water as a soothing drink. Wild parsley could also be employed as a poultice for application to the chest or to the back to prevent a cold. In the old days, the medicinal potential of the plant caused some Indians to view it as magical (Garth 1953: 140; Olmsted and Stewart 1978:230).

Wild parsley leaves were harvested in spring when tender, soaked in water, cooked in earth ovens, and either eaten or stored.

WILD STRAWBERRIES *Fragaria* spp.

Wild strawberries were harvested and eaten (Ray 1963:200).

WILD SUNFLOWERS *Helianthus* and related genera

Several different sunflower species are available in the Northeast Province. The seeds of these plants are typically ripe for the picking in July. Traditional gathering tools included the seed-beater and burden basket, which in the hands of a skilled gatherer could result in extensive seed harvests over a two-week period. A woman could collect a basketful of seeds in one day. Food connoisseurs processed the seeds by parching them in a flat tray, removing the skins in another basket with a rock, and then winnowing the seeds and grinding them into flour with a milling stone and handstone. The flour was then stored or eaten, often formed into ready-to-eat biscuit-sized cakes. Wild sunflower plants grow profusely in burned-over areas. (Garth 1953: 139; Ray 1963:199). Ray (1963:217) listed Cusick's sunflower *(H. cusickii)* and Nuttall's sunflower *(H. nuttallii)* as species used by the Modoc.

WILD TOBACCOS *Nicotiana* spp.

Plate 9

Wild tobacco plants flourished in areas that had been burned near old village sites. It is reported that some Atsugewi people used to sow wild tobacco seeds in burned areas. During harvest season, they uprooted the plants, tying them in bundles, and drying them under the shade of a tree. The dried leaves were pulverized and smoked in pipes carved out of steatite or sandstone, with cane, elderberry, or wild rose stems. Carved wooden pipes were also used (Garth 1953: 175).

WOOLY MULLEIN *Verbascum thapsus*

Prepared as a cure for colds and rheumatism, the leaves of wooly mullein were boiled and the soothing tea slowly sipped. The leaves could also be pounded and placed on cuts as a poultice (Garth 1953:140; Olmsted and Stewart 1978:230).

YELLOW POND-LILY *Nuphar lutea* subsp. *polysepala*

The marshes and shallow lakes of the eastern lowlands of the Northeast Province supported many hectares of this species of water lily, whose seeds were once intensively harvested by Klamath Indians to the north and some Modoc groups, especially around Tule Lake and Lower Klamath Lake. Local Indians exploited the seeds in late July,

August, or September as they ripened, gathering the seed pods in tule bags, which were brought back to camp. There the gatherers separated the seeds, lightly hulling them using a metate and horned (two-handled) milling stone. After the milled seeds had been winnowed, they were prepared for winter storage (Barrett 1910:242–243; Ray 1963:182; Stern 1998:449).

TREES AND SHRUBS

BARBERRY · *Berberis aquifolium* var. *repens*
A salve could be prepared from the root of this plant to treat sore throat or infection (Ray 1963:219).

BLUE ELDERBERRY · *Sambucus mexicana*
Plate 24
Blue elderberries were harvested and eaten (Ray 1963:200).

BUCKTHORNS · *Rhamnus* spp.
Buckthorn fruit was harvested when ripe and eaten fresh (Olmsted and Stewart 1978:229). Garth (1953:139) identifies one of the species used by local Indians as Sierra coffeeberry *(R. rubra),* but there are several other species of buckthorn native to the Northeast Province.

CASCARA · *Rhamnus purshiana*
Leaves or bark from this plant were once prepared as a beverage that served as a laxative. The berries were also eaten as an emetic (Ray 1963:219).

CURRANTS · *Ribes* spp.
Currants were harvested when ripe and eaten (Garth 1953:139). The currants used in the Northeast Province include golden currant *(R. aureum)* and wax currant *(R. cereum)*(Stuart and Sawyer 2001:348–350).

GOOSEBERRIES · *Ribes* spp.
Plate 44
Gooseberries were harvested when ripe and eaten fresh (Garth 1953:139; Olmsted and Stewart 1978:229). In addition to the distinctive Sierra gooseberry *(R. roezlii),* two other species of gooseberry are native to the Northeast Province: straggly gooseberry *(R. divaricatum* var. *pubiflorum)* and mountain gooseberry *(R. montigenum)*(Stuart and Sawyer 2001:350–353). The distinctive, big "hairy" berries of the Sierra gooseberry were harvested fresh and eaten, the bristles removed by rolling them between two rocks (Garth 1953:139).

GREENLEAF MANZANITA   *Arctostaphylos patula*
Greenleaf manzanita berries were collected in July and August, using a stick to knock them into burden baskets. In traditional times, local groups stored them in earth pits (presumably in the cookhouse), processing them when needed by pounding and sifting the berries into a fine flour. They made cakes the size of biscuits, which could be eaten plain or placed in water to make a beverage. Sometimes they added a mixture of wild plum flour to spice up the biscuits. Family cooks also made cider by pounding the berries into mush and adding water; a deer tail sop was used to drink it (Garth 1953:138; Kniffen 1928:301; Olmsted and Stewart 1978:229).

Greenleaf manzanita was widely recognized for its medicinal value (Olmsted and Stewart 1978:230). The leaves were once pounded and boiled for application on burns and cuts (Garth 1953:140). Some forms of this manzanita will sprout from burls after fires, and seeds can remain dormant in the soil for many years (Stuart and Sawyer 2001:161–163).

HUCKLEBERRIES   *Vaccinium* spp.
Huckleberry fruit was harvested when ripe and eaten (Garth 1953:139). The primary species used in the Northeast Province include dwarf huckleberry *(V. caespitosum),* thinleaf huckleberry *(V. membranaceum),* and red huckleberry *(V. parvifolium)*(Olmsted and Stewart 1978:229; Stuart and Sawyer 2001:404–408).

KLAMATH PLUM or SIERRA PLUM   *Prunus subcordata*
The traditional way of preparing the Klamath plum fruit was to remove the stones and dry the pulp, which was then pounded into flour and made into cakes. The cakes could be eaten or stored for winter use.*

MOUNTAIN-MAHOGANIES   *Cercocarpus* spp.
Mountain-mahogany wood is preferred for crafting spear shafts, arrows, digging sticks, or any item that is best made from a hard, durable wood (Barrett 1910:247). Two species are found in the Northeast Province: birch-leaf mountain-mahogany *(C. betuloides* var. *betuloides)* and curl-leaf mountain-mahogany *(C. ledifolius)* (Ray 1963:194; Stuart and Sawyer 2001:204–207).

Oaks

Two species of oaks are found primarily in the western part of this province. In addition to providing acorns, building material, and firewood, oak bark could be boiled to make a drink that women used to prevent blood poisoning or catching a cold during childbirth (Garth 1953:140).

BLACK OAK   *Quercus kelloggii*
Plate 36

This oak provided the preferred acorn crop for Atsugewi people; the acorns were dried in their shell, stored in pits or granaries, or shelled and stored in large storage baskets in the cookhouse. Native cooks depended on hopper mortars to grind shelled acorns into flour, which could be used to make a gruel heated in a cooking basket with hot rocks or for making acorn bread cooked in underground ovens (Garth 1953:137–138).

OREGON OAK   *Quercus garryana*
Plate 41

Acorns from the Oregon oak were harvested in fall, although many people preferred the nuts of the black oak *(Q. kelloggii),* if they were available (Garth 1953:137).

PACIFIC YEW   *Taxus brevifolia*

Pacific yew was widely recognized as providing the very best wood for making bows in the Northeast Province (Garth 1953:153; Kniffen 1928:301; Olmsted and Stewart 1978:229).

Pines

The wefts of twined baskets can be made from prepared pine roots. Weavers dug up 90 cm (35 in.) or longer lengths of pine roots and then buried them in hot ashes for a half to a full day. Using a digging stick or stone chopper, they split the cooked root sections into halves about the thickness of a pencil. After cutting one end with a knife, the weaver held the root section in her mouth and, using one hand, carefully pulled a thin piece off that was suitable for making a basket. The specific species of pines used in the twined baskets are not specified (Garth 1953:148–149; Olmsted and Stewart 1978:229).

FOOTHILL PINE or GRAY PINE   *Pinus sabiniana*

Foothill pine "nuts" (i.e., the seeds) were once widely harvested and prepared in similar fashion as those of the sugar pine *(P. lambertiana)*. The one difference was that after burning the cones, they were hit with a rock to release the nuts (Garth 1953:138; Olmsted and Stewart 1978:229).

PONDEROSA PINE   *Pinus ponderosa*

Local craftspeople manufactured shovel-nosed dugout canoes from ponderosa pine wood. They used wedges to split large logs, employed fire and hot rocks to carve out the interior of the canoe, and then, using sharpened sticks or horn picks, removed the burned wood (Garth 1953:154–155; Stern 1998:452). The wood was also an important source of firewood. Households probably employed ponderosa pine wood for major support structures and poles in traditional earth lodges, but the specific species of pine is not identified in ethnographic reports (Ray 1963:149–151).

SUGAR PINE   *Pinus lambertiana*

Plate 46

Sugar pine "nuts" (i.e., the seeds) are still a favorite source of food. Cones are shaken from the tree and then collected on the ground. The traditional method for processing the nuts involved placing the cones on end and burning them with dry grass. The nuts could then be separated by pulling back the spine of the cone. The sugar pine nuts were then cooked in earth ovens, removed, and either eaten directly or stored in baskets for winter use (Garth 1953:138; Olmsted and Stewart 1978:229).

SAGEBRUSH   *Artemisia tridentata*

Widely recognized for its medicinal value, sagebrush was applied to aches and pains as a pulp solution, or prepared as a beverage to reduce pain or fever (Olmsted and Stewart 1978:230; Ray 1963:219).

Sagebrush was employed in the construction of short-term windbreaks, especially in spring or fall camps, providing protection from cold winds. Sagebrush fibers were also used for making cordage or rope (Ray 1963:157, 186).

SKUNKBUSH   *Rhus trilobata*

Harvested in midsummer, skunkbush berries were washed, dried, and then stored. When needed, people pounded them into flour in a hopper mortar, mixing the concoction with manzanita flour and water to make a beverage. Today the skunkbush berry produces a delicious local jam (Garth 1953:139; Olmsted and Stewart 1978:229).

TWINBERRY   *Lonicera involucrata*

People in the Northeast Province harvested and ate twinberries (Ray 1963:200).

WESTERN CHOKE-CHERRY   *Prunus virginiana* var. *demissa*

Local gatherers harvested the fruit when ripe, using tule baskets within which they mashed the cherries into paste by adding water.

The paste could be eaten without further preparation or cooked (Garth 1953:139; Olmsted and Stewart 1978:229; Ray 1963:200).

Basket weavers employed second-growth choke-cherry stems for making the rim of burden and hopper baskets (Garth 1953:149). The plant also has some beneficial medicinal properties. People collected the green leaves for making a paste in a hopper mortar—this served as a poultice that was applied to cuts, sores, bruises, and black eyes in the morning and evening until the wounds healed. The bark of the choke-cherry was also scraped, pounded, and boiled, then used to bathe wounds, thereby quickening the healing process (Garth 1953: 140).

WESTERN JUNIPER   *Juniperus occidentalis var. occidentalis*
Plate 34

Western juniper berries were harvested, eaten fresh or dried, pounded and mixed with flour, and stored for winter use (Garth 1953:139).

The roots and limbs of western juniper could be used to make sturdy, utility ware types of baskets, including fishing and root-cleaning baskets, carrying and storage baskets, fish traps, cradles, and seed-beaters. The wood was split into squarish strands about 90 cm (35 in.) long, after having been roasted on hot coals. Western juniper still represents an important source of firewood (Garth 1953: 150; Olmsted and Stewart 1978:229).

Western juniper was also used to treat a wide range of ailments. Smoke from burning juniper branches could be inhaled to treat colds, coughs, sore throats, and pulmonary congestion. An infusion from the leaves soothed colds and coughs, and an infusion of the berries or leaves was concocted to help with urinary problems (Ray 1963:219).

WESTERN REDBUD   *Cercis occidentalis*
Plate 47

Basket weavers coveted western redbud for making designs in twined baskets. They preferred second-growth stems, collected in fall, which they peeled, split, and stored in coils until ready to use. Before using, the coils were soaked in water (Garth 1953:148–149; Olmsted and Stewart 1978:229).

WESTERN SERVICE-BERRY   *Amelanchier alnifolia*

Western service-berry fruit was once mashed and made into an edible paste, as described for choke-cherry fruit. The fruit could also be dried and stored for later use. People would then add water to reconstitute the berries (Garth 1953:139; Olmsted and Stewart 1978: 229; Ray 1963:200).

WHITE FIR   *Abies concolor*

The Modoc appear to have preferred white fir logs for making dugout canoes (Barrett 1910:247).

WILLOWS   *Salix* spp.

Plate 35

Slender willow ends are collected in spring to serve as the warps of twined baskets. The willow pieces can be peeled and used unsplit. Garth (1953:148–149) identified narrowleaf willow *(S. exigua)* as one of the species used by basket weavers (see also Barrett 1910:256; Olmsted and Stewart 1978:229).

Willow poles were once used in the construction of *wickiups* or dome-shaped houses used in summer camps or winter villages (Barrett 1910:244; Ray 1963:156–157).

YERBA SANTA or MOUNTAIN BALM   *Eriodictyon californicum*

Plate 48

For treating rheumatism, the patient was wrapped in a blanket and then placed over a fire pit on a bed composed of both pine needles and yerba santa branches and leaves. The steam from the yerba santa soothed the symptoms of rheumatism. People also chewed this plant to fight colds and whooping cough (Garth 1953:140; Olmsted and Stewart 1978:230).

SHELLFISH

WESTERN PEARLSHELL   *Margaritifera falcata*

Plate 60

Shellfish could be gathered along the Pit River, Lost River, and their tributaries (Ray 1963:193). Fairly extensive shell middens are found along the Pit River from past shellfish harvesting and consumption. In addition to the Western Pearlshell, local Indians probably harvested California Floater *(Anodonta californiensis)* and Western Ridged Mussel *(Gonidea angulata).*

INSECTS AND OTHER TERRESTRIAL INVERTEBRATES

GRASSHOPPERS   Suborder Caelifera

Plate 62

These insects were commonly eaten when available. The Native inhabitants of the Northeast Province searched for grasshoppers in the early morning, when the cold, lethargic insects could be easily knocked into burden baskets. Another harvesting method involved weaving together a 9 to 12 m (30 to 39 ft) long willow strip interspersed with dry grass bunches. In setting the grass bunches on fire, two people ran across a field of grasshoppers, holding the willow strip between them, forcing the little creatures into the flames. The hunters then gathered the singed grasshoppers, preparing them for immediate consumption or storage in the same way as they prepared Mormon Crickets *(Anabrus simplex)*(Garth 1953:139; Olmsted and Stewart 1978:228; Sutton 1988:11–22).

HARVESTER ANTS — *Pogonomyrmex* spp.
Harvester ant nests were dug for eggs and larva. Ants served as a food source primarily in the eastern half of the Northeast Province (Garth 1953:139; Olmsted and Stewart 1978:228).

MORMON CRICKET — *Anabrus simplex*
Swarms of Mormon Crickets occasionally intruded into the Northeast Province. By carefully monitoring their movement, Atsugewi and Achumawi people located the swarms in the early morning, when the insects were numb and docile from the cold. They then scraped the little creatures off plants and rocks with sticks, placing them into baskets where they were transported to earth ovens. After roasting for an hour or so, they were dried for two days. The dried insects could then be eaten or stored for later consumption. In some cases, the intrepid Mormon Cricket hunters encircled the insect swarms with fire. The burned and roasted crickets were eaten directly or prepared for storage (Garth 1953:139; Olmsted and Stewart 1978:228). Sutton (1988:32) emphasized how the exploitation of Mormon Crickets could provide "huge returns for labor invested."

SALMON FLIES — Order Plecoptera
Along streams and shallow water, the Atsugewi and Achumawi hunted for the ubiquitous salmon flies in spring mornings before the wind kicked up. They separated and discarded the wings, boiling the insect bodies until ready to eat (Garth 1953:139; Olmsted and Stewart 1978:228). Sutton (1988:50–51) noted that salmon flies may have been an important food resource among the Modoc, Wintu, and Achumawi people. He further suggested that salmon fly procurement probably had a favorable cost-benefit ratio.

YELLOWJACKET LARVAE — *Vespula* spp. and *Dolichovespula* spp.
Plate 63

Yellowjackets are a traditional food of the Northeast Province. Ethnographic observations note that local Indians employed a white flower and grasshopper leg as bait to attract individual yellowjackets, then followed the insects to their nests. Once they located a nest, they prepared a fire fueled by pine needles to smoke out the insects and to kill those that remained behind. Using a digging stick or some other implement, they dug the nest up and then roasted it over coals until both sides browned to a nice crisp. The cooked grubs were eaten with relish (Garth 1953:139; Olmsted and Stewart 1978:228).

FISHES
Anadromous Fishes

SALMON   *Oncorhynchus* spp.
Plate 72

Yoshiyama et al. (2001:148–152) present an excellent discussion on past and present distributions of salmon in the Pit River drainage as part of their overview of the Sacramento and San Joaquin river basins. The Achumawi are reported to have fished 80 km (50 mi) of salmon streams in their territory. Salmon were reportedly not found east of the Fall River tributary on the Pit River (Kniffen 1928:302). Atsugewi people east of this area sometimes participated with Achumawi groups in fishing for salmon. Traditional methods of harvesting salmon involved the construction of fish weirs and the use of fish harpoons (Garth 1953:136). Farther north, salmon are not found in Modoc country, so the Modocs often joined Klamath groups along the Klamath River in fishing expeditions, or they traded with the Klamath and other Indian people to the west for fish (Ray 1963:192). Chinook or King Salmon *(O. tshawytscha)* appears to have been the primary salmon species found in the Pit River and upper drainages of the Klamath River.

Freshwater Fishes

RAINBOW TROUT   *Oncorhynchus mykiss,*
                                   formerly *Salmo gairdneri*

In spring, significant numbers of Rainbow Trout migrate out of local lakes and enter smaller streams and creeks to spawn. Some of the fishes may weigh as much as 6 to 7 kg (13 to 15 lbs) or more. Fishing parties in ideal locations harvested large numbers of Rainbow Trout by harpooning them from shore, using dip nets, setting gill nets across the streams, or capturing them in fish weirs (see the descriptions for the Sacramento Sucker *[Catostomus occidentalis]*). Some fishes were eaten fresh, but most were prepared by removing the heads, splitting the bodies to remove the innards and backbone, and stringing them on poles to dry in the sun. The dried fish could then be moved to winter villages in large burden baskets and then placed in storage pits in the cookhouse until needed (Garth 1953:136; Ray 1963:192–193). Rainbow Trout could also be fished in the winter by cutting holes in the ice. The Cutthroat Trout *(O. clarki)* was probably harvested in Northeast Province waters as well (McGinnis 2006:183–188).

SACRAMENTO PIKEMINNOW — *Ptychocheilus grandis*

This impressive "minnow" can grow to over 1.0 m (3.3 ft) in length and weigh up to 14.5 kg (32 lb). It can tolerate relatively high temperatures, which allows it to survive in intermittent pools in creek beds throughout the summer. Local people fished for it using one or more of the techniques described for the Sacramento Sucker *(Catostomus occidentalis).**

SACRAMENTO SUCKER — *Catostomus occidentalis*
Plate 79

Reaching a length of 50 cm (20 in.) or more, Sacramento Suckers initiate spawning runs in early spring to upstream gravel-bed sites. The Sucker migration begins around late January and continues through early June. Indian fishermen lined the banks of streams and shallow waters during fish swarms, catching many hundreds of kilograms of fish using a wide range of fishing techniques. These fishing methods included the use of large A-frame nets attached to the prow of dugout canoes or rafts. Operated by two people, they literally scooped fishes out of the water by the tens or hundreds.

Many Sacramento Suckers and other resident fishes were captured in various types of basketry or net traps set at night across stream bottoms and then checked in the morning. One was the funnel trap. Measuring about 1.5 m (5 ft) long and anchored to the stream bottom with willow poles, a small enclosed basket allowed fishes to swim into, but not out of, the funnel trap. Another trap involved bow-type nets anchored to stream bottoms with willow rods. Yet another trap featured large gill nets, typically measuring 4.5 to 9 m (15 to 30 ft) in length and more than .9 m (3 ft) in height, strung across a river or stream. In some instances, people drove Suckers into these traps using canoes or by walking along the stream bottom. Archaeological and ethnographic studies also describe elaborate weirs of stone and/or wood to catch Sacramento Suckers and other freshwater fishes; some are still used today (see sidebar).

Local people still spear fish from shore with special composite harpoon points or multipronged spears. Sacramento Suckers are sometimes fished at night using a torch to attract the fishes, which are then netted or speared. Hook and line are also used to fish for Suckers (and other stream or lake fishes). Bulk-collected fishes were traditionally prepared by gutting, cleaning, and drying for winter stores.*

TUI CHUB   *Siphateles bicolor*

A medium-sized minnow, 20 to 30 cm (8 to 12 in.) in length, the Tui Chub frequents lakes and slower moving streams. This fish was harvested using one or more of the techniques described for the Sacramento Sucker *(Catostomus occidentalis).* Fishermen specifically employed large sacklike nets, with a rectangular mouth, propped open at each side by a pole, to catch Chubs.*

BIRDS
Marine Birds and Waterbirds
Plates 81, 83, 90, 92

Large flocks of waterbirds, attracted to the meadows, freshwater swamps, and lakes of the Northeast Province, were widely hunted, especially in the spring, summer, and fall months. Traditional hunting methods involved the use of large nets of dogbane cordage measuring about 3 by .9 m (10 by 3 ft) in size, which were staked out with poles along the margins of wetlands where waterbirds congregated. The nets, set up by hunters at night, often had duck decoys of feathers and/or buckskin attached to the bases. The hunters in their morning rounds gathered the birds that had become entangled in the nets. Hunters also relied on large triangular nets, erected on the prow of dugout canoes at night, to capture curious birds attracted to fires from torches on the boats. Decoys enticed birds to land near hunters who, hidden in thick tule stands or in tule blinds, were disguised in tule camouflage and antelope head skins. They shot the birds with bows and arrows. Barrett (1910:247) described in detail a special "ring-arrow," sporting a ring of sinew and pitch placed around the foreshaft, which allowed it to skip across the water and hit unsuspecting waterbirds. A series of snares or nooses were also set about a meter high above a stream or pond using poles; ducks were caught in the snares when flying across the water. Waterbirds were eaten for food, while the feathers and skins provided important raw materials for winter capes, clothing, and ornaments.* A few of the many species of waterbirds hunted in the Northeast Province include Northern Pintail *(Anas acuta),* speared at night by torchlight; Mallard *(A. platyrynchos),* their eggs collected in spring; Canada Goose *(Branta canadensis);* Tundra Swan *(Cygnus columbianus);* American Coot *(Fulica americana),* their eggs collected in spring, and the birds hunted from rafts in the fall and clubbed on the ice in winter; and various species of grebes (Podicipedidae).

Terrestrial Birds

Local Indians hunted small birds such as Western Meadowlark *(Sturnella neglecta)*, American Robin *(Turdus migratorius)*, and several genera of blackbirds (Icteridae), with blunt-pointed arrows (Garth 1953:135).

GREATER SAGE GROUSE   *Centrocercus urophasianus*

The Greater Sage Grouse was another commonly hunted bird. In the old days, hunters captured them with blunt-pointed arrows, with snares, and by driving them into nets. They also hunted them during nuptial displays. Their eggs were collected (Garth 1953:135; Olmsted and Stewart 1978:228).

QUAILS   **Family Odontophoridae**
Plate 99

California Quail *(Callipepla californica)* and Mountain Quail *(Oreortyx pictus)* were widely hunted. Hunters used to dress in Pronghorn disguises to surprise the birds (Ray 1963:189).

MAMMALS
Terrestrial Mammals

AMERICAN PORCUPINE   *Erethizon dorsatum*

This animal was once hunted for meat and quills, the latter woven into baskets as design elements. The tails served as combs (Barrett 1910:254, 258; Garth 1953:134).

CHIPMUNKS and SQUIRRELS   **Family Sciuridae**
Plates 113, 114

Chipmunks could be hunted with bows and arrows (Garth 1953:134). Species harvested in the Northeast Province probably included the Yellow-pine Chipmunk *(Tamias amoenus)* and Least Chipmunk *(T. minimus)*. The Western Gray Squirrel *(Sciurus griseus)* was once hunted with bows and arrows after being attracted by special whistling (Garth 1953:134). The Douglas Squirrel *(Tamiasciurus douglasii)* was probably also hunted. Ground squirrels *(Spermophilus* spp.) were run down with dogs, smoked out of holes or trees, then gutted and roasted in ashes (Garth 1953:134). The indigenous species of ground squirrel include the Beechey Ground Squirrel *(S. beecheyi)*, Belding's Ground Squirrel *(S. beldingi)*, and the Golden-mantled Ground Squirrel *(S. lateralis)*.

HARES and RABBITS   Family Leporidae
Plate 109

Black-tailed Jackrabbits *(Lepus californicus),* White-tailed Jackrabbits *(L. townsendii),* and Mountain Cottontail *(Sylvilagus nuttalli)* were hunted communally. People drove animals into long nets, where they clubbed those that became entangled. They were tracked in the snow during the winter and taken with bows and arrows. Fires were also set to smoke Mountain Cottontails from their burrows. The meat was eaten and the fur used to make winter robes (Garth 1953:134; Ray 1963:189).

MULE DEER   *Odocoileus hemionus*
Plate 112

Several methods were employed to hunt this critical game animal. Hunters, dressed in deer head and hide disguises, quietly stalked individual animals with bows and arrows or waited near game trails in ambush. They also dug pits or set nooses along game trails, entrapping deer, which could then be strangled or shot. Communal hunts took place with men driving a herd of deer, often by setting fires, into a group of screaming women holding one or more long ropes. The corralled and disoriented animals could then be shot or bludgeoned with clubs. Using fires, the hunters worked together to force herds of deer to the top of hills where the agitated, rope wielding women were positioned. Deer were also driven by dogs into shallow water, where hunters with clubs and arrows killed them. Animals were stalked in the winter snow by hunters on snowshoes, who then killed them with clubs. The deer were butchered and the meat cooked and eaten or dried for winter use. The skin was used to make many types of clothing, robes, and bags (Garth 1953:132–133; Ray 1963:182; Stern 1998:449).

PRONGHORN   *Antilocapra americana*

Found primarily in the eastern half of the Northeast Province, people worked together to drive Pronghorns into ambushes during the winter months. The hunters set fires in strategic places to drive herds into enclosures constructed of sagebrush, where women holding long sagebrush-fiber ropes waited. Hunters killed the animals with clubs in the enclosure as the women distracted the Pronghorn by yelling and waving their arms up and down. They were also stalked in the winter by hunters wearing snowshoes. Hides were used to make quivers, blankets, caps, and clothing (Garth 1953:133; Olmsted and Stewart 1978:228; Ray 1963:186–187).

WOODRATS   *Neotoma* **spp.**

A common method of hunting woodrats was to disturb their nests, then capture the animals as they tried to escape (Garth 1953:134). The indigenous species include Bushy-tailed Woodrat *(N. cinerea)* and Dusky-footed Woodrat *(N. fuscipes).*

ROCKS AND MINERALS

OBSIDIAN

High-grade obsidian sources, including Little Glass Mountain and Glass Mountain near Medicine Lake, were exploited along the borders of traditional Modoc and Achumawi territories (Olmsted and Stewart 1978:229).

Valley grassland, riparian woodland, freshwater marsh, alkali sink scrub, valley and foothill woodland, chaparral, montane forest, subalpine forest, montane meadow, and alpine fell-field.

Hokan stock: Yana, Washo languages; Uto-Aztecan stock or family: Mono (Monachi), Tubatulabal languages; Penutian stock: Wintuan family (Wintu, Nomlaki, Patwin), Maiduan family (Northeastern Maidu, Konkow, Nisenan) of languages; Utian stock or family: Miwokan family (Plains Miwok, Northern Sierra Miwok, Central Sierra Miwok, Southern Sierra Miwok), Yokutsun family of languages.

The people of the Great Central Valley and Sierra Nevada Province are distinguished by relatively dense populations, large impressive villages marked by many houses, granaries, underground assembly or dance houses where important ceremonies and group gatherings took place, and bountiful stores of food from plants, fishes, waterbirds, and terrestrial game. The incredibly diverse ecology and cultural variation of this extensive province makes it difficult to neatly summarize. The traditional political organization for most of the province was the tribelet, typically consisting of one primary village and several smaller satellite villages. Moratto (1984:173) noted most settlements were inhabited permanently except during the fall acorn harvest, when families spent time away from the permanent village to collect acorns. Some groups, however, such as the Nomlaki and Northern Foothills Yokuts, inhabited large communal villages during the winter but dispersed to smaller family-based camps during other times of the year.* These scattered familial camps provided great flexibility in pursuing diverse resources across local territories, as well as managing the landscape through prescribed burning. In spring, summer, and fall, individual families worked hard to amass foods and other resources to build up their winter reserves. When fresh resources became scarce in the late fall and winter months, people aggregated back into large villages where they could enjoy the bounty of their many hours of labor, share time and goods with others, and participate in community-wide ceremonies, dances, and other social activities.

The traditional architecture of this province included single-family houses, communal structures sheltering multiple families, sweathouses, summer shade shelters, granaries, menstrual huts, and formidable semisubterranean assembly houses. Native architects constructed circular or oval-shaped single-family homes using materials available locally. For example, groups having access to pine, redwood, or cedar bark constructed single-family houses using pole frames and bark siding, while groups living closer to wetland environments constructed houses using wood frames, tule matting, and brush.* The house structures tended to be dwarfed by the roomy semisubterranean buildings constructed of complex frameworks of stout posts, roof frames, and stringers, typically finished off with packed earth roofs. The assembly or dance houses served as communal and ceremonial gathering places, as well as residences during cold winter months.*

Many groups in the Great Central Valley and Sierra Nevada foothills recognized ownership of particular resources or resource-rich places. The Nisenan, Nomlaki, and other Sierra foothills groups maintained individual or family-level ownership of oak trees (*Quercus* spp.) and the acorns they produced. The Patwin, on the other hand, owned oak groves at the broader tribelet level, rather than recognizing ownership of trees by families or individuals. Oak trees, while a particularly valuable possession, were not the only resource owned by families or individuals. Tulare Lake Yokuts women and Patwin families commonly claimed productive seed-gathering places. Similarly, Nomlaki, Nisenan, and Patwin families or individuals often owned important fishing sites. The various approaches to resource ownership certainly influenced the way individuals, families, and tribelets obtained resources. Resource ownership also factored into the social organization of local groups, as Jackson (1991) and Mayer (1976:20–21) discuss.*

Families and tribelet members cultivated wild foods, medicinal plants, basketry materials, and other important raw materials, primarily by implementing a routine of prescribed fires, pruning plants, and removing debris from the understory (Anderson 2006). People worked together to harvest many foods en masse, such as in the communal hunting of Mule Deer *(Odocoileus hemionus)*, rabbits (Leporidae), and squirrels (Sciuridae). They drove Mule Deer into large sturdy nets where they could be easily dispatched, or they chased them into ambush sites where hunters waited to shoot the disoriented animals with bows and arrows. Communal hunts also focused on rabbits, and occasionally squirrels, by driving the small game into nets where the hunters clubbed them to death. In addition to providing large sources of protein for winter stores, communal hunting served a critical role in supporting community events and social activities. For example, the Nisenan and Nomlaki instigated communal hunting of rabbits to provide meat for community-wide feasts, known as Big Times.*

BASKET WEAVING: A VIBRANT ART FORM IN NATIVE CALIFORNIA TODAY

Not long ago, basket weaving—the quintessential art form of California Indians—was in serious decline across the state. By the late 1980s, only a few women elders remained active weavers, mostly isolated from each other in their respective communities. As it was rare to find younger people learning the intricate art of basket making, increasing concern was voiced in California Indian country about losing this traditional knowledge base with the passing of these basketry experts. A statewide gathering of basket weavers took place in 1991, which led to the establishment the following year of the California Indian Basketweavers Association (www.ciba.org), an energetic organization whose mission is to "preserve, promote, and perpetuate California Indian basketweaving traditions while promoting a healthy physical, social, spiritual, and economic environment for basketweavers." Since its founding, CIBA has been instrumental in providing a forum for basket weavers across the state. The organization is a true success story, as it now hosts local, statewide, and regional gatherings of basket weavers, administers scholarship funds for facilitating basket-weaving activities (trips to classes, basketry collections, etc.), promotes younger weavers working with more advanced experts, advocates environmental research and management that advance the healthy regeneration of native plants, and supports the activities of an estimated 650 California Indian basket weavers of varying expertise and age, from young children to elders (Brawley 2006/2007; CIBA 2001; News from Native California 1999; Willie 2002).

continued

The current headquarters of CIBA is in historic downtown Nevada City in the foothills of the Sierra Nevada; a field office has also been opened on Willow Creek in the Northwest Province. Although we emphasize here that the membership of CIBA spans the entire state and that talented basket weavers are found throughout California, the Great Central Valley and Sierra Nevada Province is an especially active area for basket weaving today. Julia Parker (fig. 26), one of the most celebrated basket weavers—possibly in the country—has employed the resources of this province to make baskets featured in numerous exhibitions, documentaries, and publications. As a Coast Miwok/Kashaya Pomo woman who married into a family of Sierra Miwok and Mono Lake Paiute people, she has combined the traditional weaving knowledge of the coast with that of the mountains by working with some of the legendary basket weavers of Native Cali-

Figure 26. Julia Parker (seated) and her family of basket makers featured in the 2006 poster celebrating California Archaeology Month.

fornia—Lucy Telles, Mabel McKay, and Elsie Allen. She has been giving back to the Native California community for more than four decades, not only by nurturing her daughters, such as Lucy Parker, who has served as chairwoman of CIBA, to become skilled artisans, but in giving countless public demonstrations and workshops at the Yosemite Museum in Yosemite National Park that promote the traditional values and skills involved in the manufacture of Native Californian material culture (Brawley 2006/2007; Valoma 2004).

A significant activity of CIBA is its resource protection program, which advocates for the perpetuation of and access to basketry resources and gathering sites on both private and public lands. The majority of Native California communities lack sufficient land bases from which to manage and gather their own plants and animals for subsistence and medicinal purposes, as well as for cordage manufacture, regalia production, and other tradition-based activities. CIBA works with a diverse range of local, state, and federal agencies to foster greater access to public lands for Native uses, and to advocate for tradition-based resource management practices. The organization is particularly concerned about the use of pesticides and herbicides in public and private wildlands, the use of which can have dire health consequences for Indian gatherers. For example, the membership of CIBA has been working with representatives of the Eldorado National Forest in the Sierra Nevada to dissuade them from a proposed plan to use herbicides to reduce fuels on forestland. They are suggesting that various alternatives to herbicides exist for fuel reduction, such as prescribed burning, mulching, mowing, and goat grazing (CIBA 2001: 13–14).

MOSSES AND FERNS

CALIFORNIA MAIDEN-HAIR FERN   *Adiantum jordanii*
Groups in the northern part of the province used California maiden-hair fern as a basketry material (Du Bois 1935:132; Kroeber 1925:415; Riddell 1978:376; Wilson and Towne 1978:392).

HERBACEOUS PLANTS
In the past, central California Indians made use of a vast array of seeds. Harvesters obtained seeds from plants by beating the plants with seed-beaters and collecting the loosened seeds in tightly woven

burden baskets. These seeds could then be dried, winnowed, and stored. Seeds pulled from storage during the lean winter months, or anytime of the year, were pounded into a meal. Family cooks often added water to this meal to produce a nutritious mush.*

BEAR GRASS or WHITE GRASS   *Xerophyllum tenax*
Plate 5
Groups in the northern valley and foothills employed bear grass as an important basketry material (Du Bois 1935:131; Duncan 1963:63; Kroeber 1925:415; Riddell 1978:376).

BRODIAEAS   *Brodiaea* spp., *Dichelostemma* spp.,
Plate 11   **and** *Triteleia* spp.
People across the Great Central Valley and Sierra Nevada Province used a variety of Brodiaea "bulbs" (i.e., corms) as a food source.* Remains of brodiaea bulbs, identified to the genus level, have been recovered from prehistoric and protohistoric archaeological sites in the interior of central California (Wohlgemuth 2004:75). Some of the specific species identified in the ethnographic literature include golden brodiaea *(T. ixioides)* and elegant brodiaea *(B. elegans)*, which Maidu and Miwok peoples roasted in earth ovens until they were tender and succulent (Duncan 1963:35; Levy 1978b:402).*

CANARYGRASSES   *Phalaris* spp.
Canarygrass seeds appear in considerable numbers in late prehistoric sites in interior central California, as well as in the Sierra Nevada foothills (Rosenthal et al. 2006:37–39; Wohlgemuth 2004:79, 102); however, the use of these seeds is not readily identified in the ethnographic literature.

CATTAILS   *Typha* spp.
Plate 6
Kroeber (1925:415) noted that in the past, Maidu people employed broad-leaved cattail *(T. latifolia)* for making mats for seats, beds, and the roofs and doors of mobile camp structures.

The Maidu peeled the white root of southern cattail *(T. domingensis)* for a source of food, and the stems of broad-leaved cattail could also be eaten (Duncan 1963:76). The Southern Valley Yokuts made flour from cattail "roots" (possibly rhizomes), and they used the flowers to make yellow bread (Gayton 1948a:49).

CLARKIAS or FAREWELL-TO-SPRING   *Clarkia* spp.
Several species of clarkias, also called farewell-to-spring, were traditionally harvested in the Great Central Valley and Sierra Nevada Province. In the past, the Nisenan used manzanita wood sickles to

cut the plants, which they bunched together for drying until the seeds fell out. The seeds could be prepared as pinole or made into large loaves of bread (Duncan 1963:64). Native people today emphasize how the density of clarkias increases substantially after burns (Anderson 2005:138–139, 183, 264). Clarkia seeds show up in large numbers in archaeological sites in interior central California, the upper Sacramento Valley, and the Sierra Nevada foothills (Rosenthal et al. 2006:37–39; Wohlgemuth 2004:79, 102, 111, 113).

CLOVERS   *Trifolium* spp.

A number of different kinds of clovers were recognized and used by Indian groups. Some of the species mentioned in the ethnographic literature include *T. barbigerum,* foothill clover *(T. ciliolatum), T. variegatum,* and *T. wormskioldii.* Widely anticipated after the long winter, clovers are the first fresh crop available in early spring. Though usually eaten raw with a little salt, while young and succulent, clovers could also be parched with coals. Many Yokuts groups relished raw clovers as an accompaniment to acorn mush. Indian people in the past and today recognize that regular burning of meadowlands increases the quality and quantity of clover crops. Among the Nisenan, the clover harvest was traditionally associated with the annual spring gathering, a time of communal dances and ceremonies. Typically held in April when many species bloomed, this gathering is also known as the Flower Dance because girls danced in the fields with flower wreaths and belts. In preparation for the spring gathering, community members cut large quantities of clovers with wooden knives, collecting them in piles and cooking them in earth ovens. After the clover was cool and dry, people feasted on it and/or prepared it for winter storage. When used as a stored food in winter villages, family cooks ground the dried clover into flour for use in mush dishes. Clover seeds have been recovered from archaeological excavations in interior central California, the upper Sacramento Valley, and the Sierra Nevada foothills.*

DANDELIONS   *Taraxacum* spp.

The milky root of dandelions, boiled and prepared as tea, was traditionally served as a remedy for kidney trouble. The typical dosage was one cup (Duncan 1963:45).

DOGBANES or INDIAN HEMPS   *Apocynum cannabinum*
Plate 10   **and *A. androsaemifolium***

Periodic burning increases the density and growth of dogbanes. Burned patches produce long, straight stems that are ideal for making cordage. People rolled the inner bark of the plant on the thigh to make string. The Yokuts used it to make the "finest" string for tumplines, carrying and head nets, belts, and strings for beads. Dogbane cordage was also used to make ropes for deer drives, nets for communal rabbit hunts, clothing, fish nets, carrying nets, and generic string and rope. Among the Patwin, dogbanes provided the material for manufacturing burial rope used in wrapping the dead.*

GOOSEFOOTS   *Chenopodium* spp.
Duncan (1963:42) noted that, in the past, the Nisenan cooked this entire plant in earth ovens, while the Mountain Maidu prepared the plant as greens. Goosefoot seeds have been recovered from archaeological excavations in interior central California, the upper Sacramento Valley, and the Sierra Nevada foothills (Rosenthal et al. 2006: 37–39; Wohlgemuth 2004:79, 102, 113).

ITHURIEL'S SPEAR or GRASS-NUT   *Triteleia laxa*
Plate 14
The small nutty bulbs of this plant were once highly prized. Yokuts people gathered, roasted, and then consumed these bulbs whole or mashed into flour. The Maidu also roasted the bulbs in great quantities (Duncan 1963:35; Gayton 1948a:16).

MARIPOSA LILIES   *Calochortus* spp.
Earlier generations of California Indians used digging sticks to harvest several different species of mariposa lily bulbs, including butterfly mariposa *(C. venustus),* also called white mariposa lily, and white fairy lantern *(C. albus),* also called white globe lily. Yokuts families gathered mariposa lily when in bloom in April and May, removing the skin by rubbing it across an open twined basket. They then boiled the skinned bulbs. Some Central Foothill Yokuts considered this bulb "a favorite dish" (Gayton 1948a:77). Maidu and Miwok people gathered large quantities of the bulbs in the past, which were cooked in earth ovens or roasted on hot ashes; however, Tubatulabal peoples traditionally ate the bulbs raw. They also dried and pounded the bulbs, mixing this concoction with water to make a flavorful mush.*

MILKWEEDS   *Asclepias* spp.
Plate 13
Milkweed stems, collected in early winter, were peeled and shredded by hand to reveal the strong fibers used for making cordage or twine. Objects made from this fiber include wide carrying bands; tying cords; fish, rabbit, and duck nets; and bowstrings, fishing lines, and trap strings. The Yokuts used milkweed cordage for lashing thatch to their conical houses.*

The milky juice of the plant was applied to warts and other skin problems, including cancer. The plant was eaten as a green. The Sierra Miwok sometimes added milkweed to manzanita cider as a thickening agent.*

MINER'S LETTUCE   *Claytonia perfoliata*

Miner's lettuce, collected in February and March, was eaten raw or cooked as greens. The seeds were also eaten. Miner's lettuce seeds have been recovered from archaeological excavations in interior central California, the Sierra Nevada foothills, and the upper Sacramento Valley (Duncan 1963:66; Levy 1978b:403; Rosenthal et al. 2006:37–39; Wohlgemuth 2004:79, 102, 113).

MONKEYFLOWER   *Mimulus guttatus*

Monkeyflower was harvested and eaten like lettuce before it flowered in April (Duncan 1963:74; Levy 1978b:403). The Sierra Miwok used to make a tea from monkeyflower roots to treat diarrhea (Barrett and Gifford 1933:171).

NATIVE BARLEYS   *Hordeum* spp.

Native barley seeds have been recovered in some quantity from archaeological sites in the interior of central California and in a few protohistoric archaeological excavations in the Upper Sacramento Valley; however, they are not readily identified in the ethnographic literature for this province (Wohlgemuth 2004:79, 113).

NIGHTSHADES   *Solanum* spp.

Black-colored nightshade berries were eaten fresh. Nightshade berries have been recovered from archaeological excavations in interior central California and the upper Sacramento Valley (Duncan 1963: 75; Levy 1978b:403; Wohlgemuth 2004:75, 109).

The Sierra Miwok used black nightshade *(S. nigrum)* to make an eyewash for sore eyes (Barrett and Gifford 1933:173).

RED MAIDS   *Calandrinia ciliata*
Plate 16

The small, oily, but edible seeds of red maids used to be greatly prized by Yokuts; the seeds could be crushed, rolled into a ball, and eaten like candy. Central Sierra Miwok and Maidu groups also ate red maids seeds. The seeds are found in archaeological sites in interior central California, the Sierra Nevada foothills, and the upper Sacramento Valley.*

SEDGES   *Carex* spp.

Patwin and Nomlaki groups utilized sedges as a basketry material (Goldschmidt 1951:427; Johnson 1978:356).

SOAP PLANTS or AMOLES   *Chlorogalum* spp.

Plate 17

Soap plants were once used to treat sores. For example, the Wintu mashed the plant into a poultice for application on poison-oak rashes and warts (Du Bois 1935).

The bulb produced a liquid soap, which was used for washing hair, baskets, and clothing. Brushes were made from the fibrous bulb coating. Soap plants were also used to stupefy fishes by pounding the bulb into pulp, mixing it with soil and water, and then placing the mixture upstream of the fishing hole. Some Yokuts people used to roast and eat the roots. Soap plant remains have been identified from at least one prehistoric site in interior central California.*

TARWEEDS   *Madia* spp., *Hemizonia* spp.,
                                              and *Blepharizonia* spp.

After the plants bloomed in July, tarweed seeds were picked, parched on circular basket trays, and then pulverized in deep mortar holes by the Yokuts. The Sierra Miwok and Maidu also ate tarweed seeds. Seeds from tarweed species have been recovered from archaeological excavations in interior central California, the upper Sacramento Valley, and the Sierra Nevada foothills.*

In the past, some Yokuts groups used tarweed branches for thatching houses (Gayton 1948b:186).

TOLOACHES or JIMSON WEEDS   *Datura* spp.

Plate 19

These plants were used to treat almost any painful injury. The healer mashed the roots to form a poultice, which he or she placed on the injury. Mashed leaves were also put on sores. Some Southern Valley Yokuts groups used the plants to treat syphilitic sores. The patient or healer would remove a bit of the sore and bring it to a growing toloache plant whose root had been carefully exposed. A small cut was made in the root, where the sore material could be placed. Once inserted into the root, the sore material was allowed to become part of the plant as it continued to grow. Among some Yokuts groups, these plants also played a focal role in religious ceremonies and initiation rites, as we noted for the people of the South Coast Province (Gayton 1948a:16, 47, 49, 52–53, 118–120, 1948b:150–151, 158, 173, 245–247, 281–283; Kroeber 1925:502).

TULES or BULRUSHES   *Schoenoplectus* spp.
Plate 20

Once commonly found in the extensive wetlands of the Great Central Valley, tules served as an important raw material for many people. Tule leaves were used to thatch houses and other structures near wetlands; to weave mats that served as wall partitions, doors, sleeping pads, and seats in houses; to make aprons, skirts, and dance headdresses; and to weave twined baskets. Families sought tules to build balsa boats, small watercrafts made by bundling together the lightweight tule stems and leaves, for use in slow moving rivers and lakes. Powered by one or two men poling the craft along, the average-sized boat held four to six people and their belongings. These boats remained in service until recent times at Tulare Lake.*

Tule roots were collected, dried, and pounded into flour for mush; the seeds were also collected and eaten. In some areas of the San Joaquin Valley, where wood was scarce, tules served as firewood. Tule seeds have been recovered from archaeological excavations in interior central California, the upper Sacramento Valley, and the Sierra Nevada foothills (Gayton 1948a:15, 16; Rosenthal et al. 2006: 37–39; Wohlgemuth 2004:79, 102, 113).

TURKEY MULLEIN   *Eremocarpus setigerus*

Like soap plants (*Chlorogalum* spp.), turkey mullein could also be used to stupefy fishes in localized fishing places (Goldschmidt 1951: 406–407; Wilson and Towne 1978:389).

WILD OATS   *Avena* spp.

These grasses are not native to California; rather, after being introduced through European settlement, they spread widely across areas of California, providing another food crop for local Indians. Wild oats were gathered with seed-beaters and burden baskets—the plants were beaten to loosen the seeds, which were then caught and transported in the baskets. The seeds were then dried on rocks and winnowed. When ready to eat, the seeds could be parched in a basket with hot coals, pounded in a bedrock mortar, and then mixed with water to make biscuits, which could be cooked in hot ashes. Among the Patwin and Eastern Miwok, wild oat gathering areas could be owned by families who returned to the same places regularly (Gayton 1948b:179; Johnson 1978:355; Levy 1978b:402).

WILD ONIONS   *Allium* spp.

Plate 18

Various species of the *Allium* genus, including the swamp onion *(A. validum)*, thrive in moist foothill and mountain valley habitats. Clarke (1977:70) reports there are 38 species of wild onions in California. Native gatherers today recognize that the wild onion responds well to burning (Anderson 2005:138).

The plants could be eaten raw or steamed until fully cooked, then mashed and salted into a nice meal. The leaves were also eaten as fresh greens (Duncan 1963:34–35; Wilson and Towne 1978:389).

WILD STRAWBERRIES   *Fragaria* spp.

The berries were eaten raw, with wild strawberry patches intentionally burned to increase productivity (Anderson 2005:138; Brubaker 1926:77; Duncan 1963:70).

WILD SUNFLOWERS   *Helianthus* spp.

In the past, Nomlaki peoples collected, dried, and stored sunflower seeds for later consumption. Nomlaki harvesters could collect two sacks of seeds in a day's work. The Patwin also traditionally collected and dried the seeds, which could then be pounded into a meal and prepared for consumption. Sunflower seeds have been recovered from archaeological excavations in interior central California and the upper Sacramento Valley (Goldschmidt 1951:409; Johnson 1978:355; Wohlgemuth 2004:79, 113).

WILD TOBACCOS   *Nicotiana* spp.

Plate 9

Tobacco plants grow wild, especially in places that have been recently burned. Some Yokuts and Western Mono people tended specific plants by pinching the tips of the plants in March and April, by watering the plants if they became too dry, and by removing worms. Kroeber (1925:419) observed that some Mountain Maidu people may have grown wild tobacco on the roofs of earth-covered lodges. Duncan (1963:74–75) described how the Nisenan and Mountain Maidu sowed wild tobacco seeds in patches. Nisenan people did little else with wild tobacco patches until they harvested the plants. There is little indication that other Indian people in the province cultivated or pruned wild tobacco in the past. The leaves were harvested around June or July when they turned yellow. The pyrodiversity collectors did not typically save or sow the seeds, although some Wintu reportedly seeded areas after harvest. Most Native groups dried the leaves under the shade of a tree for about two weeks. The dried leaves could then be crumpled up or pounded into a powder, ready for smoking in pipes. Some years ago, the Yokuts dried the harvested leaves on flat rocks and then pulverized them in special mortars to produce tobacco powder. In making a paste from the powder mixed with liquid, the Yokuts produced long-lasting tobacco cakes for storage. Tobacco was generally smoked, but it could also be mixed with lime and eaten to induce vomiting. A tobacco and lime mixture was also used as a salve or poultice to treat sore spots on the body. Traditionally, some doctors used wild tobacco to cure patients—by first chewing the substance, then blowing and squirting it on the patient.[*]

WORMWOODS or MUGWORTS   *Artemisia* spp.

Northern Foothills Yokuts extracted juice from wormwood plants, which they rubbed on body areas suffering from rheumatic pain. The plants could also be prepared in a bath for the treatment of rheumatic pain. The Sierra Miwok used wormwoods to treat headaches, as well as rheumatic pain. They used the plant spiritually to keep ghosts away and to prevent personal injury (Barrett and Gifford 1933:167; Gayton 1948b:182).

TREES AND SHRUBS

BIG-LEAF MAPLE   *Acer macrophyllum*

Big-leaf maple is a common tree along stream banks and canyons in the foothills and mountains up to 1,500 m (4,900 ft). Maple bark strips could be hung on shrubs and trees to form funnel-shaped deer fences used in communal hunts. In the past, the Nomlaki and Nisenan also used shredded maple bark in skirts and aprons.

The leaves were used to wrap meat or acorn bread, keeping the food moist and tender in earth ovens (Duncan 1963:32–34; Goldschmidt 1951:425; Wilson and Towne 1978:390).

CALIFORNIA BAY or LAUREL   *Umbellularia californica*
Plate 24

The California bay is found primarily in the Sierra Nevada foothills up to 1,600 m (5,250 ft) in elevation. The medicinal uses of this plant are many. Traditional practices involved harvesting the "fruit kernels" (i.e., the seeds) and parching them lightly in baskets. Consumption of the parched kernels supposedly prevented indigestion. Women not feeling well used to eat one roasted California bay nut a month. California bay remains have been recovered from archaeological sites in interior central California, the Sierra Nevada foothills, and the upper Sacramento Valley (Brubaker 1926:79; Hammett and Lawlor 2004: 338; Rosenthal et al. 2006:37–39; Wohlgemuth 2004:75, 99, 107, 109).

Some Indian people found it helpful to place a California bay leaf in their nostril to relieve headaches. Some groups used the leaves in footbaths. They also purified their houses by burning sprigs of California bay (Brubaker 1926:79; Duncan 1963:57–58). In the past, the Western Mono used California bay wood to make bows (Gayton 1948b:218; Spier 1978b:429).

CALIFORNIA BLACKBERRY *Rubus ursinus*
Plate 26
The fruit of the California blackberry was usually eaten fresh; however, the Patwin used to dry the berries, which could then be pounded into a meal and boiled. California blackberry remains have been recovered from archaeological excavations in interior central California, the Sierra Nevada foothills, and the upper Sacramento Valley.*

CALIFORNIA BUCKEYE *Aesculus californica*
Plate 27
Many groups in the region harvested California buckeye "nuts" (i.e., the seeds). Kroeber (1925:527) described the traditional Yokuts method of processing the nuts: they were broken apart and soaked in water for a day; the nuts were then pounded into flour and placed in leaching pits where water removed the tannic acid. The resulting flour could be cooked like acorn mush. It was not uncommon for groups such as the Miwok to rely more on buckeye nuts when acorn crops failed. Buckeye remains have been recovered from archaeological sites in interior central California and the Sierra Nevada foothills.*

In the past, Northern Foothills Yokuts and Western Mono groups also used the wood from California buckeye trees as the hearths for fire-making drills (Gayton 1948b:185, 224, 266).

CALIFORNIA HAZEL *Corylus cornuta* var. *californica*
This deciduous tree is common in the western Sierra Nevada. Its nuts were harvested and prepared as food. California hazelnut remains have been recovered from archaeological sites in interior central California and in early prehistoric deposits in the upper Sacramento Valley.*

California hazel stems were employed as basketry material among the Konkow, Nisenan, and Maidu. The sticks were also traditionally used to make snowshoe frames and bows.*

CALIFORNIA WILD GRAPE *Vitis californica*
Plate 29
California wild grapes were picked fresh and eaten, not dried for storage. The harvesters sometimes crushed the grapes to make a red

juice beverage. Grape remains have been recovered from Late Period archaeological sites in interior central California and the upper Sacramento Valley, as well as earlier deposits in the Sierra Nevada foothills.*

The vines could be used to bind fish weirs and to tie materials together in the construction of granaries and other structures. The leaves could be used to wrap acorn bread for baking in earth ovens, while the Nisenan placed the leaves in earth ovens with grasshoppers to season baked foods.*

ELDERBERRIES   *Sambucus* spp.
Plate 24

Elderberry plants are various small trees or shrubs found throughmuch of California, varying by species. The Northern Foothill Yokuts gathered blue elderberries *(S. mexicana)* in the mountains at the same time as sugar pine nuts. They harvested the berries around August, preparing them for storage by drying them on rocks. Transported back to the winter villages, the dried berries were boiled before being eaten. Local groups dined on the boiled dried berries about once a week in the winter. Gayton (1948b:180) noted that the dried berries "kept a long time." Miwok, Nomlaki, and Northern Valley Yokuts peoples also harvested elderberries. Elderberry remains have been recovered from archaeological sites in interior central California, the Sierra Nevada foothills, and the upper Sacramento Valley.*

Elderberry wood was commonly used to make split-stick clappers, tobacco pipes, and flutes.*

GREENLEAF MANZANITA   *Arctostaphylos patula*
In the past, Maidu people mixed greenleaf manzanita leaves with a local black moss to make a poultice for sores that would not heal. The berries were supposedly not eaten (Duncan 1963:49).

INCENSE-CEDAR   *Calocedrus decurrens*
Incense-cedar bark was used as waterproof roofing for traditional Maidu houses and granaries, and the logs were hollowed out to make dugout canoes. In the past, the bark of this tree was also used by Mono, Nisenan, and Yokuts groups in house construction, either to line the interior of the structures or as an exterior covering (Beals 1933:344; Gayton 1948b:161, 260).

The tips of the branches could be used to break the flowing water in acorn leaching pits and add a pleasant flavor to the acorns. The bark also provided a blue dye for body tattooing (Duncan 1963:30–31).

MANZANITAS *Arctostaphylos* **spp.**

Species of manzanita mentioned in the literature include common manzanita *(A. manzanita)*, pinemat manzanita *(A. nevadensis)*, and whiteleaf manzanita *(A. viscida)*. Manzanita berries were collected when ripe. The traditional method included raking the area clean beneath and around the shrub, after which women knocked the berries to the ground and collected them into baskets, taking care to winnow leaves, twigs, and other debris from the berries. The berries were further cleaned and laid out on rocks to dry. Once dried, they could be mashed into pulp, placed into a sieve basket to remove the seeds, and then sacked for storage in the winter village. To produce cider, several handfuls of berries were placed in water within a water-tight basket to soak. The berries were squeezed and placed within a sieve basket, and then water was poured over the berry pulp to produce the refreshing cider. Among the Nisenan, a special dance was performed to increase the harvest of whiteleaf manzanita berries. Many Indians in this region regularly burned manzanita shrubs to encourage fruit productivity (Anderson and Moratto 1996:198). The berries are well represented in archaeological sites from interior central California, the Sierra Nevada foothills, and the upper Sacramento Valley.*

People preferred manzanita woods for making hot fires with little smoke. The hard woods were also ideal for making digging sticks and other wooden implements, such as sickles. The Nomlaki used manzanitas medicinally, making a tea from the leaves to treat diarrhea.*

MOUNTAIN DOGWOOD *Cornus nuttallii*

The Sierra Miwok prepared mountain dogwood bark as a remedy for fevers (Brubaker 1926:79).

Oaks

Various oak species thrived in this province, depending upon the specific habitat (valley floor, foothills, and lower mountains); however, acorns were not readily available to Southern Valley Yokuts. Indians knocked nearly ripe acorns off trees with poles and/or shook branches. Some acorns were harvested green, their shells pulled off with the teeth and hands, and then sun-dried. Supposedly, the green acorns would last longer in storage (up to five years) than mature acorns kept in their shell in acorn granaries. Wilson (1972:36) reported that a Nisenan family would typically need about 10 to 12 sacks, each weighing 22 kg (50 lb), of acorns to see them through the winter. In addition to being a major food resource, acorns could be traded to neighboring peoples for other foodstuffs and material goods. Considerable quantities of acorn remains have been recovered from archaeological sites in interior central California, the Sierra Nevada foothills, and the upper Sacramento Valley. These can mostly be assigned only to the genus level, as identification to the species level is difficult in most archaeological settings.

Oaks also provide building materials (post supports and poles) for sweathouses, earth lodges, dance houses, and other significant structures, as well as firewood. Some Yokuts and Mono groups also traditionally used oak wood for arrow shafts and digging sticks. Oak trees and the resources they provide were incredibly important to most people in the Great Central Valley and Sierra Nevada Province. Single trees or groves of trees could be owned by individuals or families who returned to the same trees annually for many years.*

BLACK OAK   *Quercus kelloggii*
Plate 36

The black oak is a common oak in the foothills and lower mountains from 600 to 1,800 m (2,000 to 5,900 ft). Yokuts people picked black oak acorns green, then peeled the shells off, pounding the remaining meat into flour, which was leached in a basin with water and heated in cooking baskets. Ethnographic descriptions indicate that very fine flour made better acorn mush than coarser flours. Today, coffee grinders are sometimes used to obtain the desired fine flour (Duncan 1963:50). The Wintu considered black oak acorns a preferred acorn for making acorn bread, and black oak was generally the favorite acorn of many Yokuts, Nisenan, Maidu, and Sierra Miwok people. In the past, ripe black oak acorns were stored in their shells in acorn granaries.*

BLUE OAK   *Quercus douglasii*
Plate 37

The blue oak grows well in various foothill habitats and along the valley borderlands below 1,000 m (3,300 ft). It produced one of the preferred acorns of the Sierra Miwok groups (Levy 1978b:402; Mayer 1976:5). The blue oak acorns, described as "little rocks," were difficult to process in mortars, and they were not popular among Nisenan women in the past. But men enjoyed the flavor they gave to mush and insisted that they be served. The reluctant women cooks soaked the acorns to soften them for processing. They often added a handful of blue oak acorns to black oak acorn mush for flavor (Duncan 1963:50).

CANYON LIVE OAK   *Quercus chrysolepis*

This oak is dispersed up drainages and canyons in the foothills and mountains up to 2,700 m (8,850 ft). It produces acorns that were among the top three species enjoyed by the Maidu (Dixon 1905:181; Kroeber 1925:411).

INTERIOR LIVE OAK   *Quercus wislizeni*
Plate 40

This is another common oak found along the border of the valley and foothills, up to about 1,500 m (4,900 ft). It provided one of the acorns preferred by the Maidu and Sierra Miwok.*

OREGON OAK   *Quercus garryana*
Plate 41

Small groves of Oregon oak are found along the western slope of the Sierra Nevada to an elevation of about 1,200 m (4,000 ft). The acorns, once harvested, are difficult to keep from spoiling. In the past, Yokuts people shelled them immediately and then dried them for storage in sacks, keeping the stored acorns in the dwelling house or storehouse (Gayton 1948b:179, 187).

VALLEY OAK or WHITE OAK   *Quercus lobata*
Plate 32

Once common in the Sacramento Valley and northern San Joaquin Valley, these impressive trees can yield up to 225 kg (500 lb) of acorns from one productive tree. During productive years, the valley oak represented a significant source of food to Northern Valley Yokuts, Sierra Miwok, Plains Miwok, and other valley groups to the north. The Wintu preferred the valley oak for making acorn bread.*

The Sierra Miwok traditionally pulverized the bark of this oak to treat sores and made tea from the bark for bad coughs (Barrett and Gifford 1933:172).

Pines

Several species of pines distributed across the foothills and mountains provided excellent sources of food, construction and craft materials, and firewood.

FOOTHILL PINE or GRAY PINE   *Pinus sabiniana*

Found along the margins of the Great Central Valley and in the northern foothills up to about 2,100 m (6,900 ft), foothill pine "nuts" (i.e., the seeds) were usually harvested in fall. Yokuts and Konkow people ate the nuts whole and raw or treated them like seeds, winnowing them in scoop-shaped baskets and grinding them into a fine flour, which was then ready to cook. The Sierra Miwok and Wintu traditionally harvested foothill pine nuts in spring when green, as well as in fall, when they were mature; however, the Nisenan tended to harvest the nuts in July. Foothill pine remains have been recovered from archaeological excavations in interior central California, the Sierra Nevada foothills, and the upper Sacramento Valley.*

In the past, the Maidu and Konkow made beads from foothill pine nut shells; and the Sierra Miwok used the needles for bedding and thatch, the twigs for basketry, and the cones for pitch. The Sierra Miwok also applied foothill pine charcoal medicinally to sores and abrasions (Barrett and Gifford 1933:149; Riddell 1978:374).

PONDEROSA PINE   *Pinus ponderosa*

Ponderosa pine "nuts" (i.e., the seeds) were harvested and eaten plain or in soups and patties (Riddell 1978:374).

Ponderosa pine wood could be used in construction and as firewood; the needles could be placed in leaching pits to give acorns flavor; and the roots could be harvested as basketry material (Duncan 1963:29–30; Wilson and Towne 1978:392). Kroeber (1925:414) observed that, in the past, the Maidu buried the root fibers with charcoal and mud in order to produce a black design on baskets.

SUGAR PINE   *Pinus lambertiana*
Plate 46

Sugar pine tends to grow well in the foothills and mountains from about 1,200 to 3,000 m (4,000 to 9,850 ft). Sugar pine "nuts" (i.e., the seeds) were harvested in August, when families camped in the higher elevations to pick pine nuts, hazelnuts (*Corylus* spp.), and elderberries (*Sambucus* spp.). When ripe, men knocked the sugar pine cones off the trees, which women gathered as they hit the ground. The Nomlaki used two poles in harvesting pine nuts—a hooked one for climbing and a shorter one for knocking down the cones. They roasted the pine cones in fires fueled with pine needles to remove the pitch. After the cones cooled, the harvesters split the cones to remove the nuts. They then parched the nuts in basket trays. The parched nuts could be eaten separately, added to soups, or stored for winter use. Sometimes family chefs pounded sugar pine nuts into pulp in mortars, and the resulting greasy mess was rolled into balls and eaten with acorn mush.*

SIERRA GOOSEBERRY   *Ribes roezlii*
Plate 44

Many groups in the province ate gooseberries. The Yokuts people preferred to eat them fresh, not dried for storage.*

SKUNKBUSH   *Rhus trilobata*

Skunkbush offered a traditional medicine for people experiencing a variety of minor illnesses. The remedy was prepared by mashing the sour berries on a ground-stone metate and adding water. This could be drunk straight or combined with acorn mush. The typical dosage for most problems consisted of drinking or eating a cup of the potent medicine. Among the Maidu, a prayer was said and the medicine sprinkled in four directions before drinking (Duncan 1963:37–38).

TOYON   *Heteromeles arbutifolia*

Local Indians harvested toyon berries in the fall or winter. The Nisenan cooked them on hot rocks, mashing them with their hands after the berries began to simmer. Toyon berries have been recovered from archaeological sites in interior central California, the Sierra Nevada foothills, and the upper Sacramento Valley (Duncan 1963: 70; Levy 1978b:403; Wohlgemuth 2004:75, 99, 109).

WESTERN REDBUD   *Cercis occidentalis*
Plate 47

Western redbud was widely used for making red and white designs, such as plain or herringbone patterns, in baskets.*

WHITE FIR   *Abies concolor*

The Konkow mixed the inner bark of white fir with rattlesnake heads in a mortar to produce a poison. A spiteful person administered the poison to an intended victim by a slap on the back, which released the poison via the small wood slivers. The antidote to this poison was similar to that for a rattlesnake bite and involved rubbing wormwood juice over the afflicted area (Duncan 1963:28).

WILLOWS   *Salix* spp.
Plate 35

Gathered in the fall, the bark of willow branches was peeled off and the knots worked out. Basket makers utilized this material to make rods in coiled baskets; they favored the split willow in twined conical burden baskets. Willow bark was also used to make cordage.*

Local Indians employed willow poles as construction material in houses, other architectural structures, and fish weirs. They used pliable willow pieces for attaching poles together in conical houses and small branches to thatch houses. People gathered branches of any size for use as firewood, especially in the Great Central Valley. Women made aprons and skirts from shredded willow bark. The Nisenan also used willow to make snowshoe frames, and various groups converted willow branches into arrows and spears.*

YERBA SANTA or MOUNTAIN BALM *Eriodictyon californicum*
Plate 48

This plant had several known uses in the past. By combining yerba santa and hot rocks in a basket, Indian doctors produced a therapeutic vapor for treating tuberculosis and dizziness. They also brewed tea with yerba santa that comforted people suffering nasty coughs and colds (Barrett and Gifford 1933:169; Duncan, 1963:55; Goldschmidt 1951:389).

SHELLFISH

FRESHWATER CLAMS   Family Sphaeriidae

The Nisenan and Miwok collected freshwater clams from local watercourses, ate the meat, and used the shells in necklaces (Levy 1978b:403; Wilson and Towne 1978:389, 391).

FRESHWATER PEARL MUSSEL   *Margaritifera margaritifera*
and WESTERN RIDGED MUSSEL   and *Gonidea angulata*

These freshwater mussels are found in the Great Central Valley; they were once collected from the beds of larger rivers, and the Wintu dove for them. The collected mussels were roasted or boiled and sometimes dried. The Nisenan used mussel shells as knives, and mussel shell could also be ground down for lime and added to chewing tobacco.* Freshwater shellfish remains in some Central Valley archaeological sites increase from early- to late-period deposits, suggesting changes in settlement pattern and resource use through time (Heizer 1949:12). Careful study of freshwater mussel shells indicates season of occupation for some Central Valley archaeological sites (Broughton 1994b:508; Meyer and Rosenthal 1998:14; White 2003:171).

CRUSTACEANS AND OTHER WATER INVERTEBRATES

CRAYFISH   Family Astacidae

The Yokuts captured crayfish together with freshwater mussels (Gayton 1948a:14).

INSECTS AND OTHER TERRESTRIAL INVERTEBRATES

ANGLEWORMS or EARTHWORMS   *Lumbricus* **spp.**

Angleworms were obtained in winter and cooked in steatite, or soapstone, dishes with a little water added to make gravy. Angleworms could be dried and stored for later use (Gayton 1948b:181; Kroeber 1925:527).

ANTS   **Family Formicidae**

Ants were sometimes eaten (Wilson and Towne 1978:390).

CALIFORNIA GALL WASP   *Andricus quercuscalifornicus*

The parasitic Gall Wasp causes galls, or tumors, on the leaves of various oak species as they feed. The galls contain tannic acid, which was once used as an eyewash (Barrett and Gifford 1933:192).

CATERPILLARS   **Order Lepidoptera**

Representing the larval stage of several insects, caterpillars could be skinned, roasted, and eaten (Gayton 1948a:14).

CEANOTHUS SILK MOTH   *Hyalophora euryalus*
and POLYPHEMUS MOTH   **and** *Antheraea polyphemus*

Plate 61

Moth cocoons were attached to twigs to be used as rattles. Pebbles were usually inserted inside the cocoon to make a rustling sound when shaken. Cocoon rattles were typically used for ceremonial purposes and were sometimes decorated with feathers. Cocoons from the Ceanothus Silk Moth were used most commonly, but the Polyphemus Moth would also have been available to local Native groups.*

GRASSHOPPERS   **Suborder Caelifera**

Plate 62

Grasshoppers were once eaten across the province. To catch grasshoppers, a pit was excavated in the middle of a meadow. A fire set around the meadow was used to drive the grasshoppers inward toward the pit. The fire singed off their wings, keeping them on the ground and easy to collect. Grasshoppers were dried at home or roasted on a tray with live coals. Among the Wintu, grasshoppers could be boiled or steamed, dried, sometimes mashed, and eaten with salt as a side dish to acorn mush. The Wintu also enjoyed toasted grasshoppers with acorn mush. They could be gathered, salted, covered with rocks, and heated in a trench, then enjoyed as tasty finger food. Dried grasshoppers could also be stored for winter use.*

HONEYBEE   *Apis mellifera*

In postcontact times, the introduced Honeybees were smoked out of their hives with a damp tule smudge, then the larvae picked out and eaten (Gayton 1948a:14).

HORSEFLIES   **Family Tabanidae**

Horsefly grubs could be eaten (Gayton 1948a:14).

SALMON FLIES   **Order Plecoptera**

Considered a "great delicacy" by the Wintu, salmon flies swarm near the edge of rivers. They used to be gathered on summer mornings, boiled, and, if the catch was large, dried for the winter (Du Bois 1935:15).

YELLOWJACKET LARVAE   *Vespula* **spp. and**
Plate 63   *Dolichovespula* **spp.**

Yellowjacket larvae used to be a favorite accompaniment to manzanita berries. To locate a yellowjacket nest, the entrance holes of nests were scouted at night. Another method of finding nests is cited in the ethnographic literature on the Miwok. They attached a dry piece of the flower of velvet grass *(Holcus lanatus)*, an introduced species, to a grasshopper leg. Attracted to the grasshopper leg, a wasp would collect the leg and return to the nest, with the hunters, following the larger, easily spotted velvet grass flower, in close pursuit. The following morning, the hunters would build a fire of pine needles over the nest, the smoke from which would stupefy the yellowjackets and render them harmless. After removing the nest, the hunters roasted it on hot coals. The cooked nest was shaken to release the larvae, which were then washed, placed in a cooking basket, boiled in water, drained, and eaten—sometimes with acorn gruel or mixed with manzanita berries.*

FISHES
Anadromous Fishes

LAMPREYS   *Lampetra* **spp.**
Plate 73

Lampreys are mentioned consistently in the ethnographic literature as important food items. Pacific Lamprey *(L. tridentata)* was one of the primary species harvested by Native people. This anadromous species made seasonal runs (late spring to late summer) in large numbers into the greater Sacramento River and San Joaquin River basin drainages (McGinnis 2006:127–129; Yoshiyama 1999:199). Considered a delicacy by the Nisenan, they obtained dried lamprey through trade or fished for them at waterfalls. One method of capturing them involved the placement of special fishing baskets in strategic places along watercourses, and then allowing the lampreys to accumulate in the baskets over a week. Lampreys could also be speared; the meat was split and dried for winter storage. In preparing the meat for meals, the animal was usually diced and stewed. Young lampreys were believed to be poisonous by the Wintu and not eaten. Stepping on a lamprey in the mud was considered as harmful as a snake bite.*

SALMON   *Oncorhynchus* spp.
Plate 72

Salmon were an important food resource for some people of the Great Central Valley and Sierra Nevada Province. Ronald Yoshiyama has written excellent overviews on the tremendous quantity of salmon harvested in the Central Valley drainage of California by Indians and early commercial fishermen, who established up to 21 canneries in the region by the early 1880s (Yoshiyama 1999; Yoshiyama and Fisher 2001). He emphasizes that the primary species of salmon harvested in these waters in great numbers was Chinook Salmon *(O. tshawytscha)*. Depending on the specific water conditions and drainage, the Chinook Salmon could make up to four runs a year (winter, spring, fall, and late fall)(Yoshiyama et al. 2001).

Traditional methods for the bulk harvesting of salmon varied. The Konkow Maidu caught salmon in the spring and fall months with toggle-headed spears, as well as with gigs fashioned from bone and antler. The Nisenan captured salmon using nets and spears at lower elevations, while the Patwin relied on the construction of fish weirs of various sizes and shapes. The Yokuts used nets and spears from a darkened booth constructed above a watercourse to procure salmon. The Wintu employed harpoons, nets, and clubs at night to fish for Chinook Salmon.

Salmon were eaten fresh and often dried, sometimes made into a powder, and then stored in baskets for later use, especially during the winter months. Among the Maidu and Miwok, the vertebrae were pounded and eaten raw, while the Miwok consumed the eggs. The Wintu considered those fishes caught later in the year to be less greasy and more suitable for drying. Among the Wintu, salmon were usually split, dried, folded into quarters, and stored for the winter. The head, entrails, tails, and bones could also be dried, pounded into flour, and stored for the winter in baskets lined with maple leaves. Indian people mixed dried salmon roe and pine nuts with the salmon flour, creating a valuable trade item often exchanged for salt and clamshell-disk beads from the coast.*

WHITE STURGEON   *Acipenser transmontanus*
Plate 74

Found in estuaries and along the shoreline of slow moving rivers, White Sturgeon was eaten by Plains Miwok, Sierra Miwok, Patwin, and Nisenan groups. Cora Du Bois (1935:21) noted that in the past the Wintu did not eat sturgeon. Sturgeon could be caught using nets, spears, and fish weirs.*

Freshwater Fishes

Numerous prehistoric fisheries in the Great Central Valley indicate consumption of many freshwater fish species (Gobalet et al. 2004; Moratto 1984:183; Rosenthal et al. 2006:35; White 2003). These include most notably Sacramento Perch, Thicktail Chub, Sacramento Sucker, Sacramento Blackfish *(Orthodon microlepidotus)*, Hitch *(Lavinia exilicauda)*, Tule Perch *(Hysterocarpus traski)*, and, to a lesser extent, the now-endangered Delta Smelt *(Hypomesus transpacificus)*(Gobalet et al. 2004).

Indians in the Central Valley employed a variety of methods for bulk-harvest fishing. Fishermen dragged fishnets between the shore and a tule balsa boat, moving in an arc toward the shoreline and trapping fishes against the shore. They caught fishes with nets while diving or wading in waterways. Communal fish harvests focused on the use of fish weirs, often built of willow wickerwork, set into place in shallow waters using willow stakes and tule twining. Communal fish drives in lakes and slow moving streams involved groups of people arranged in a semicircle, who slowly walked through the water toward the weir, driving the fishes along until the swarming mass became trapped between the weir and shore. In the shallow water, men, women, and children quickly scooped out the struggling fishes with open-mesh baskets. In the more rapidly moving streams of the foothills, fishermen built fish traps within weir structures. For example, the Northern Foothill Yokuts manufactured cone-shaped nets of milkweed (*Asclepias* spp.) as traps, setting them into fish weirs so that they faced upstream to catch fishes driven into them. Fishes might also be caught in shallow pools with open-bottom baskets, or by poisoning fish holes. Specially built rafts with holes in the hull were also used for gigging fishes. Scaffolding constructed from poles and branches over good fishing holes provided handy places to net or harpoon fishes. Fish harpoons might sport sharpened pelican wing bones lashed to a detachable foreshaft with sinew, while other fish harpoons could be as long as 2 to 3.6 m (6.5 to 12 ft), depending on water depths, made from local woods, and tipped with two pointed deer tibia.

Indian ways of cooking fishes included boiling, but more often the cooks split the fishes ventrally, laying the pieces on hot coals. By covering the fish with a layer of sand and grass, then a final layer of coals, the juicy meat cooked evenly from bottom to top. At other times, fishes would be split ventrally and hung, unsalted, along slender poles set on forked sticks to dry. Meat could also be cut in strips to be dried and turned every two to three days.*

HARDHEAD   *Mylopharodon conocephalus*
Plate 75
Native to the Great Central Valley, the Nomlaki and Patwin were noted for catching and preparing this particular fish (Goldschmidt 1951:401; Johnson 1978:355). This species is also identified in archaeological samples (Broughton 1994b; Ragir 1968:421).

SACRAMENTO PERCH   *Archoplites interruptus*
Plate 77
Sacramento Perch, native to the Great Central Valley, was once extremely abundant and commercially fished in the 1800s; its population has declined dramatically in native habitats in recent years. It can reach lengths of 60 cm (23 in.) and weigh up to 1.6 kg (3.5 lb) (McGinnis 2006:308-310). The Nomlaki, Patwin, and Yokuts, in particular, caught and ate this fish species.*

SACRAMENTO SPLITTAIL   *Pogonichthys macrolepidotus*
Plate 78
Splittails are a large (45 cm [18 in.]) migratory minnow native to low-elevation waters in the Great Central Valley and are typically found in the Sacramento and San Joaquin rivers and their tributaries, as well as in the Russian River and streams that enter the San Francisco Bay (Moyle 2002:185–186). They have been identified in archaeological sites of the region (Broughton 1994b; White 2003:168).

SACRAMENTO SUCKER   *Catostomus occidentalis*
Plate 79
Sacramento Sucker is native to the Great Central Valley. Sacramento Sucker fisheries are documented archaeologically near slow moving waters in the Great Central Valley (Gobalet et al. 2004). The Wintu organized fish drives in August to bulk-collect this fish. Wintu groups along the McCloud River encouraged their children to spear these animals with miniature spears as practice, while adults speared salmon (*Oncorhynchus* spp.) nearby. Suckers were also eaten by the Nisenan, Nomlaki, Patwin, and Yokuts.*

THICKTAIL CHUB   *Gila crassicauda*
An extinct species of fish once one of the most abundant fishes in the Great Central Valley, it was fished for by the Patwin and Yokuts (Broughton 1994b:504; Gayton 1948a:14; Johnson 1978:355; Ragir 1968:421; White 2003:168).

TROUTS   *Oncorhynchus* spp.
Considered an important source of food, trout are fished in rivers and streams of the Great Central Valley, the Sierra Nevada, Coast Ranges foothills, and in higher elevations.

Rainbow Trout *(O. mykiss)* was the primary species harvested by Native people. This included both the nonandromous variety and its closely related anadromous relative known as Steelhead *(O. m. irideus)*. The latter made substantial seasonal runs into the Central Valley drainage. Traditional fishing methods involved the use of weirs, nets, harpoons, bone hooks and lines, and poison. Trout, like many other species of fish, could be roasted, steamed with greens, dried, or pounded into meal for soups or cakes.*

AMPHIBIANS AND REPTILES
Although several species of salamander, frog, turtle, lizard, and snake make the Great Central Valley home, very little is known about their use by Native Californians, perhaps because most groups avoided them.*

TURTLES   Order Testudines
Plate 80
Of all reptiles, turtles were eaten consistently (Broughton 1994b:503; Ragir 1968:421). Hunters carried sharp sticks to plunge into the throat of the Western Pond Turtle *(Clemmys marmorata)*. After roasting the turtle, its shell and larger entrails could be removed (Gayton 1948a: 14; Goldschmidt 1951:401; Johnson 1978:355).

WESTERN RATTLESNAKE   *Crotalus viridis*
Poison for arrow points could be made by teasing a Western Rattlesnake to bite a putrescent deer liver. The Maidu rubbed Brewer's angelica *(Angelica breweri)* on their legs to keep these snakes at bay, or chewed Brewer's angelica and spit or blew it in the direction of the snake to blind it. Rattlesnake weed *(Euphoria ocellata)*, sanicles *(Sanicula* spp.), and snake roots *(Osmorrhiza* spp.) could be used as poultices for snake bites. The Yokuts hold a rattlesnake ritual in April to prevent rattlesnake injuries and spread tobacco juice on their legs to deter rattlesnakes when walking in the countryside.*

BIRDS

Marine Birds and Waterbirds

The remains of ducks and geese are abundant in many Central Valley archaeological assemblages (Broughton 1994b:503; Ragir 1968: 419; White 2003:173). Waterbirds could be prepared for meals by broiling or roasting the meat. For example, the Nisenan prepared them by plastering the birds in mud and roasting them on coals. Birds provided not only much-desired sources of nutritious food, but also feathers for clothing, basketry, and ceremonial accouterment. Some groups in the Central Valley used duck and goose down for blankets and robes, while feathers were used to decorate Konkow Maidu and Miwok dancing implements, headdresses, and belts.*

DUCKS   Family Anatidae

Plates 88, 89, 90

Many duck species are prevalent in the Great Central Valley, including Wood Duck *(Aix sponsa)*, Mallard *(Anas platyrynchos)*, Green-winged Teal *(Anas crecca)*, Northern Pintail *(Anas acuta)*, Northern Shoveler *(Anas clypeatra)*, and Cinnamon Teal *(Anas cyanoptera)*.

Ducks were once caught with snares and nets set up among patches of tule *(Schoenoplectus* spp.) bordering water. Some Indians used innovative tule balsa blinds, which allowed the hunters to approach their prey without detection. The floating hunting blinds were made from two logs that formed the foundation of a raft, camouflaged with tule stalks (about 1.2 to 1.8 m [4 to 6 ft] tall) attached to the bottom of the logs and tied off at the top. The hunters moved the blind silently across the water with the use of poles. Bows and arrows were used to shoot birds in close range. It is reported that hunters also used snares, described as spring traps, or nooses of string, that were set with a trigger to ensnare the limbs of unsuspecting prey (although these types of traps were more common for capturing mammals). Nets with decoys used to be very effective for capturing ducks.* Duck meat is consumed and the green feathers used by Miwok in baskets (Barrett and Gifford 1933:238).

GEESE   Family Anatidae

Plate 83

The Canada Goose *(Branta canadensis)* and Brant *(B. bernicla)* are found in the Great Central Valley. The ethnographic literature reported that Yokuts consumed "white, brown, and black geese" (Gayton 1948a:49). They captured geese by lighting fires in strategic spots in the marshes; the birds, attracted to the fire's light, flew into the fire and supposedly immolated themselves.

GREBES
Plate 92   **Family Podicipedidae**

Grebes were hunted in local waterways. Five grebe species are found in the Great Central Valley (some seasonally), including the Pied-billed Grebe *(Podilymbus podiceps)*, Horned Grebe *(Podiceps auritus)*, Eared Grebe *(Podiceps nigricollis)*, Western Grebe *(Aechmophorus occidentalis)*, and Clark's Grebe *(A. clarkii)*.

LOONS
Plate 84   **Family Gaviidae**

Exploited when available; three species of loon are found in central California, including the Common Loon *(Gavia immer)*, Pacific Loon *(G. pacifica)*, and Red-throated Loon *(G. stellata)*.

RAILS
Plate 81   **Family Rallidae**

The Rallidae family includes Virginia Rail *(Rallus limicola)*, Sora *(Porzana carolina)*, Common Moorhen *(Gallinula chloropus)*, and American Coot *(Fulica americana)*. Coots used to be caught in nets. The Yokuts stitched coot skin strips together to make blankets (Gayton 1948a:17).

Terrestrial Birds

BAND-TAILED PIGEON and MOURNING DOVE
Plate 95

Patagioenas fasciata and *Zenaida macroura*

Hunters reportedly snared the birds or captured them from specially built pigeon booths. They were excellent sources of food. The Nisenan used pigeon feathers as fletching in arrows.*

BLACKBIRDS
Family Icteridae

In addition to being a source of food for some Native Californian groups, blackbird feathers were widely used in basketry. For example, red feathers from the Red-winged Blackbird *(Agelaius phoeniceus)* and black feathers from Brewer's Blackbird *(Euphagus cyanocephalus)* were incorporated as decoration in Miwok baskets (Barrett and Gifford 1933:238; Goldschmidt 1951:401).

CROWS and RAVENS
Plate 96   **Family Corvidae**

Feathers from the American Crow *(Corvus brachyrhynchos)* were woven into the ceremonial dress of the Nisenan, Western Mono, Miwok, and Yokuts, while the Patwin used feathers from the Common Raven *(C. corax)* in their ceremonial dress.*

FALCONS   **Family Falconidae**

Falcon species found in the Great Central Valley include the American Kestrel *(Falco sparverius)*, Prairie Falcon *(F. mexicanus)*, and Peregrine Falcon *(F. peregrinus)*, along with the seasonally available Merlin *(F. columbarius)*. The Yokuts used falcon feathers as ear ornaments (Gayton 1948a:69).

GOLDEN EAGLE   *Aquila chrysaetos*

Plate 97

Usually hunted for feathers through the use of snares, people commonly incorporated Golden Eagles into their ceremonial regalia. Among the Yokuts, eagle down was used in dance skirts, or sometimes scattered during ceremonial gatherings. Eagle feathers were highly prized by powerful Nisenan dancers, while the Nomlaki, Yokuts, and Western Mono used leg bones for whistles. According to oral traditions, the Miwok never ate eagles, and the Konkow Maidu never hunted eagles. In the past, some groups might have practiced a catch-and-release program for eagles, much like the Nisenan, who collected feathers from the Northern Flicker *(Colaptes auratus)* in this manner, while other groups kept eagles for display during dances.[*]

GREATER ROADRUNNER   *Geococcyx californianus*

The Western Mono once consumed Greater Roadrunner meat, using the feathers in ceremonial dress. While feathers from the Red-tailed Hawk *(Buteo jamaicensis)* were de rigueur as arrow fletching, the Miwok considered Greater Roadrunner feathers to be ideal for making fast-moving arrows, given the quickness on foot of this bird species (Barrett and Gifford 1933:218).

GROUSES   **Family Phasianidae**

The Nisenan coveted feathers from the Greater Sage Grouse *(Centrocercus urophasianus)* and Dusky Grouse *(Dendragapus obscurus)* for arrow fletching. The Miwok saved the bones to make whistles. The skins were sometimes used by the Southern Valley Yokuts to make cloaks (Barrett and Gifford 1933:226–228; Beals 1933:340–341; Gayton 1948a:49).

HAWKS   **Family Accipitridae**

Plate 101

Hawk feathers, especially from the Red-tailed Hawk *(Buteo jamaicensis)*, were used widely in ceremonial regalia and as arrow fletching. The Monache employed the feathers to make fans for fires.[*]

JAYS
Family Corvidae

The Western Scrub-Jay *(Aphelocoma californica)* is common to the Great Central Valley, and the Steller's Jay *(Cyanocitta stelleri)* to the foothills and mountains. The Nisenan once caught jays using bird blinds, which they constructed from several poles covered with branches. Hunters attracted the birds to their blinds by imitating bird calls or by placing an imitation bird's nest made from pine needles and feathers on a pole near the blind. The Nomlaki, Western Mono, and Yokuts ate jays and used the feathers in ceremonial dress (Beals 1933:349; Gayton 1948b:178, 218; Goldschmidt 1951:401).

OWLS
Families Tytonidae and Strigidae

The use of these birds by Native Californians was restricted almost entirely to ceremonial practices. For example, the Miwok did not eat the Great Horned Owl *(Bubo virginianus),* but the feathers were highly coveted by dancers. This cultural practice might hold for most, if not all, of the tribelets in the Great Central Valley. Among the Nisenan, powerful dancers favored owl feathers, while the Yokuts of the central foothills collected down and breast feathers for ceremonial dress (Barrett and Gifford 1933:226–228; Gayton 1948a:69; Levy 1978b:403).

QUAILS
Family Odontophoridae

Plate 99

California Quail *(Callipepla californica)* and Mountain Quail *(Oreortyx pictus)* were hunted for food and for feathers. Hunters captured them with bows and arrows, nets, snares, and fences. Quail fences were generally 20 to 23 cm (8 to 9 in.) high and ran diagonally up hill slopes. Women donated their hair to make snares, which were placed in openings in the fence to capture the quails as they moved uphill. Miwok people along the Sierra foothills viewed quails as their most important game birds. Quail topknots were highly prized in decorating baskets. Topknots also have a long tradition as body decoration. Yokuts ear piercings often have quail feathers attached to stick earplugs. Konkow Maidu women used ear plugs with quail topknots and woodpecker scalps, while feather plume-sticks could be made by tying bird scalps and quail plumes around a small manzanita stick.*

WOODPECKERS
Family Picidae

Plates 94, 98

The Miwok ate woodpeckers and used the feathers to decorate the buckskin belts of the daughters of tribelet chiefs. The Miwok also employed red feathers from the Acorn Woodpecker *(Melanerpes formicivorus)* and Pileated Woodpecker *(Dryocopus pileatus)* to adorn baskets. Feathers could also be used as body ornamentation, especially for the head. Konkow Maidu women, for example, plugged their ears with bone decorated with woodpecker scalps and quail topknots, while Konkow Maidu men sported feathers as part of their nasal septum piercing.* The feathers of the Northern Flicker *(Colaptes auratus)* were used widely in dance regalia, such as feather headbands, and they once served as a medium of exchange. The Nisenan caught flickers, removed their feathers, and released them, while the Miwok ate flickers along with other terrestrial birds.*

YELLOW-BILLED MAGPIE   *Pica nuttallii*
Hunted in the Great Central Valley, this bird's black iridescent feathers were used almost exclusively for dance regalia, including headdresses and skirts. Konkow Miadu tribal boundaries were patrolled in the past by pairs of men with single magpie feathers stuck upright on top of their heads.*

MAMMALS
Terrestrial Mammals

BEARS   *Ursus* spp.
Black Bear *(U. americanus)* and Grizzly Bear *(U. arctos horribilis)* were once found throughout most of the Great Central Valley and Sierra Nevada. Local Indians once hunted bears by torching their dens while they slumbered during hibernation. The animals would either die from smoke inhalation, or the waking beasts would exit the den to be shot by arrows or spears. The Yana hunted bears and Mule Deer *(Odocoileus hemionus)* with dogs. Several Native California groups did not eat bears. The Miwok, for example, believed the feet looked too human. Many Indians prized bear hides because they made perfect burial shrouds, dance regalia, bedding, and winter robes. The Wintu savored every bite of fresh bear meat but considered it too greasy to be dried. If a piece of bear meat dropped on the ground, then everyone ducked quickly as if avoiding a blow from the bear they were consuming.*

CHIPMUNKS   *Tamias* spp.
Chipmunks and other small game could be hunted using blunt arrows, traps, snares, nets, and fire. The Yokuts often dried small game for storage (Gayton 1946:256, 1948a:75; Wilson and Towne 1978: 389).

FOXES *Vulpes* **spp. and** *Urocyon* **spp.**

The Red Fox *(V. vulpes)*, Kit Fox *(V. macrotis)*, and Gray Fox *(U. cinereoargenteus)* may have been eaten. People employed trained dogs to tree the Gray Fox, which could then be shot with arrows. The Patwin coveted fox furs for tobacco sacks, while the Yokuts used fox furs for quivers.*

GOPHERS **Family Geomyidae**

Gophers were trapped and eaten. The Nisenan cooked gophers in hot ashes (Beals 1933:349; Gayton 1948a:75, 1948b:180).

HARES and RABBITS **Family Leporidae**
Plate 109

The Black-tailed Jackrabbit *(Lepus californicus)*, Desert Cottontail *(Sylvilagus audubonii)*, and Brush Rabbit *(S. bachmani)* are common throughout the Great Central Valley. The animals were once hunted communally with nets, fences, snares, and clubs or smoked out of their burrows. Dogs used to be specially bred to participate in the hunts. The skins, made into blankets and robes, served as excellent sources of warmth in the colder months. They were also made into dance costumes. Cottontail rabbit toes, strung on necklaces with beads, once served as Miwok love charms.

To prepare rabbit and hare meat, the fur was removed, and then the entrails and larger bones removed. Next, the animal was pounded with a flat rock and then roasted flat on coals. Another method was to boil, pound, and roll the meat into edible balls. The Nisenan often consumed rabbits during dance feasts by covering the animal in mud and setting it on coals to roast.*

MULE DEER *Odocoileus hemionus*
Plate 112

Mule Deer could be hunted individually year-round, while communal drives took place in fall. Hunters working in tandem drove deer herds into hunters with bows and arrows or off cliffs. Fire rings, snares, nets, hunting blinds, and pits or deadfalls were also used. Some hunters employed disguises made from the deer head, antlers, and skin to stalk animals. They often attempted to imitate deer movements by propping their arms up with two long sticks. In such a fashion, they mimicked a four legged creature so as to approach the unsuspecting prey at a distance close enough to shoot with an arrow.

Miwok deer hunters used to bathe in Brewer's angelica *(Angelica breweri)* to eliminate odors, and if no deer were taken then hunters cleansed themselves in a decoction of balsam-root *(Balsamorhiza* *sagittata).* Deer brush *(Ceanothus integerrimus)* was also monitored to locate deer browsing areas.*

Most, if not all, of the animal was eaten or used in some manner. After skinning and butchering at the place of the hunt, the meat was taken back home to be distributed. Indian cooks typically roasted the meat, while some of it might be boiled or jerked. To dry venison, the meat was cut into strips, rubbed with rock salt, hung over trees, and turned daily until dry. The Patwin pounded dried venison into meal to be stored for later use. Cora Du Bois (1935:9–11) described, in rich detail, past Wintu deer hunting and butchering practices. After a deer was skinned and quartered outside, the hunters would wash their hands. The meat was then passed inside to women who would distribute the meat to separate households. Venison was roasted in strips over a fire that would have been stirred with a fir poker. Wintu cooks roasted deer heads separately, and this cut of meat remained forbidden food for young women. The elderly could eat head meat but not with salt, water, or hot mush, while all who ate head meat washed their hands in a communal container of water that was later dumped back onto the rocks covering the deer remains. The lower jaw would be cleaned and hung from a tree to attract more deer.*

Deer bone could be used to make harpoons and awls for basket making. Hooves could serve as rattles, while deer brains were used to dress animal skins. After being stretched and fleshed, the skins were used for many important daily items, including bedding, clothing, blankets, floor mats, roof coverings, moccasins, and quivers. The Maidu depended on deerskin leggings to protect the calf when walking in rattlesnake country. Deer sinew was used to secure sundry household and daily items, such as fastening snowshoes to one's feet or lashing poles together to make the frame for a house. Sinew was also used widely to strengthen bows. Young Wintu men were discouraged from eating sinew as it might cause them to shine at night and catch the attention of a Grizzly Bear *(Ursus arctos horribilis).**

PRONGHORN   *Antilocapra americana*

Pronghorn could be hunted by using disguises or in communal drives, as for Mule Deer *(Odocoileus hemionus).* People ate the meat, employed the skins for making clothing and household items, and fashioned the horns into storage containers for tobacco. In the past, the Yokuts distinguished animals with unusual antlers as "singing antelopes," sparing them from death.*

SQUIRRELS
Family Sciuridae

Plate 114

Squirrels found in the province include the Western Gray Squirrel *(Sciurus griseus),* Douglas Squirrel *(Tamiasciurus douglasii),* and Beechey Ground Squirrel *(Spermophilus beecheyi).* Tree squirrels were trapped communally, hunted with bows and arrows or slings, or caught by specially bred hunting dogs. The Nisenan once prized the Western Gray Squirrel, which was chased from trees and shot with arrows or clubbed.* Hunters trapped Beechey Ground Squirrels in nets as they escaped from flooded or smoking burrows. The Monache used long flexible sticks to twist the fur of the Beechey Ground Squirrel to extract it from its burrow. To eat a ground squirrel, they broke the tail off, singed the entire animal on coals, and then slow roasted it, sometimes in its burrow, much like an earth oven.*

TULE ELK
Cervus elaphus nannodes

Plate 111

Another significant source of meat and protein, Tule Elk was once hunted with snares or bows and arrows. The animal might be chased until exhausted and slowed down enough for a clear shot. Stiff elk hides and mountain-mahogany sticks could be used as armor to repel arrows during armed confrontations (Du Bois 1935:124; Kroeber 1925:400, 528; Riddell 1978:380).

WOODRATS
***Neotoma* spp.**

Woodrats were hunted by the Wintu in the winter, supposedly when they were sluggish (Du Bois 1935:14). The animals were either shot with arrows or clubbed. Small rodents such as woodrats were cooked by singing off the fur, cutting off the tail and paws, and then roasting the animal on coals. Later, the head was removed, along with any larger bones, which were pounded into meal (Du Bois 1935:14).

ROCKS AND MINERALS

BASALT

People utilized basalt to make stone tools such as knives and spears. Its durability and strength made this material a suitable choice for mortars, pestles, and other milling implements (Dixon 1905:132; Riddell 1978:374; Wilson and Towne 1978:391).

CHERT

Chert was a common source of chipped stone tools (Johnson 1978: 357).

CLAY

Local Indians sometimes added clay to oats or acorn mush as a sweetener or to absorb acids. It was also a good source of essential minerals. Red and white clays could be used to make paint, while the Western Mono, Tubatulabal, and Southern Valley Yokuts obtained clay for manufacturing pottery and clay pipes.*

HEMATITE

Also known as red ochre, cinnabar, or red stone, local people used hematite to create red paint (Riddell 1978:376; Wilson and Towne 1978:391).

MAGNESITE

The intrinsic value manifest in magnesite is demonstrated by the widespread use of magnesite beads as a medium of exchange and as a monetary symbol.*

OBSIDIAN

Obsidian was an important resource for many kinds of stone tools, including stone points, tattoo needles, and scrapers. Obsidian was procured directly and frequently traded.*

SALT

Salt was obtained through trade or procured directly from ponds and springs and from plants. Although some groups did not use salt extensively, other groups burned umbelliferous plants or other salty plants to release salts.*

STEATITE or SOAPSTONE

Steatite was used to make dishes, arrow straighteners, tobacco pipes, and beads.*

SOUTHERN DESERTS PROVINCE VEGETATION TYPES

Creosote bush scrub, alkali sink scrub, shadscale scrub, pinyon-juniper woodland, chaparral.

SOUTHERN DESERTS PROVINCE ETHNOLINGUISTIC UNITS

Hokan stock: speakers of the southern Diegueño (Kumeyaay, Ipai/Tipai), Paipai, Kiliwa languages who inhabit noncoastal desert environs; Uto-Aztecan stock or family: Cupeño, Luiseño, Serrano, Cahuilla, Kitanemuk languages.

In our consideration of the Southern Deserts Province, we employ the term "California Indian" as a cultural designation rather than a strictly geographical one. Thus, some groups whose homelands are located within the modern political boundaries of the state of California are excluded, while some groups living in Mexico are incorporated into this discussion. Among those whose practices are not included are those indigenous groups living on the northern and eastern boundaries of the Southern Deserts Province, including groups of Kawaiisu, Western Shoshone, and Southern Paiute peoples, whose traditional cultural affiliation and environment were more closely related to that of the Great Basin, as well as groups living along the Lower Colorado River, such as the Cocopa, Quechan, Halchidhoma, and Mojave, who have strong ties to the American Southwest. Looking southward, the distribution of the Native peoples and environmental zones of the Southern Deserts Province does not stop at the international border. Accordingly, information is included below about the indigenous groups of northern Baja California, such as the Kiliwa, Paipai, and those Kumeyaay groups whose territory lies south of the international line.

Traditionally, the Native inhabitants of the Southern Deserts Province shared similar lifeways, characterized by the exploitation of diverse environmental zones in seasonal, east-west procurement ranges that included desert, montane, and coastal environments. These people, though culturally very similar, can be broken into ethnolinguistic units belonging to two major language families: the Takic-speaking (Uto-Aztecan stock or family) Serrano, Kitanemuk, Luiseño, Cupeño, and Cahuilla; and the Yuman-speaking (Hokan stock) Kumeyaay, Paipai, and Kiliwa.

Today, these linguistic divisions mirror the modern tribal identities of Native Californian groups living in southern California and northern Baja California. In the past, however, political and social organization was based on patrilineal, exogamous lineages. Lineages were typically made up of several extended families, and the members of each lineage were related to one another through the male line. No firm consensus exists as to the size of traditional lineages, but it is likely that most lineages contained between 70 and 120 individuals. Lineages maintained specific homelands, which included areas that produced large quantities of food resources during significant portions of the year. Each localized lineage owned certain highly productive areas, but the intervening land could be used by anyone for either hunting or gathering. During various times of the year, families or even entire lineages would move to seasonal villages or camps that were in close proximity to particular food resources. Of course, this picture of the lineage is somewhat idealized. The degree to which lineages owned specific resources varied between the different ethnolinguistic groups, and the composition of specific lineages changed over time. In some cases, such as among the Cahuilla, larger sociopolitical units likely existed that included members of multiple lineages. Despite local variations, seasonally mobile lineages appear to have been the basic social and political unit throughout the region.*

In the old days, political authority within a particular lineage resided in a hereditary leader. This office passed from a father to his eldest son, or if no heir was available, to his brother. The lineage leader presided over ceremonies, resolved intralineage disputes, and maintained trade relationships with outside groups. The leader commonly had one or more assistants. Shamans were powerful figures but were not necessarily political leaders. Drawing upon their knowledge of the supernatural, shamans cured the sick and performed important ceremonial duties.*

Native settlements in this region range from permanent villages to temporary campsites. Large villages were located in areas close to important plant and animal resources, as well as a reliable source of water. Within settlements, family households typically dispersed themselves across a relatively large area. Domestic structures varied widely between and among ethnolinguistic groups. House forms included conical, dome-shaped, or gabled structures with circular, oval, or rectangular footprints. Floors could be dug out, creating a house pit of varying depth. Walls were constructed of various locally available materials including palm fronds, willow boughs, tules, or other plants. House struc-

CONTEMPORARY CERAMIC ARTS
IN THE SOUTHERN DESERTS

The indigenous art of pottery making is alive and well in the Paipai community of Santa Catarina. Located in the mountains of northern Baja California, Santa Catarina is home to several families of artisans who have transformed the region's thousand-year ceramic tradition into a contemporary art form (fig. 27). These artisans

Figure 27. Daria Mariscal working on a ceramic bowl in the Paipai community of Santa Catarina in Baja California.

continued

sell their pottery and other crafts at events in both Mexico and the United States, as well as to visitors who make the trip to Santa Catarina. While many modern Paipai vessels resemble those made in pre-contact times, local potters have created new forms and elaborated old ones to create a diverse array of ceramic vessels that are both durable and beautiful. In addition to bowls and jars, other ceramic objects created by artisans in Santa Catarina include pipes, rattles, and dolls.

To produce their wares, Paipai potters use local clays, which are ground into a fine powder on a stone metate. Water is then added, and the mixture is kneaded thoroughly. Once the clay has been prepared, the potter begins to construct the pot by producing a circular, flat sheet of clay that is then molded around the base of a gourd or broken pot. Clay is added to the edges in a series of separate coils, and a wooden paddle and clay anvil are then used to shape the vessel and thin its walls. The finished product is left to dry, and it is later polished with a smooth stone. Pots are fired in a shallow pit, using dried yucca stalks as fuel. Firing usually occurs in the evening, and the vessels are left overnight in the coals before being collected in the morning. Due to the nature of the firing conditions, pottery from Santa Catarina is characterized by rich colors and distinctive fire clouds, which are valued for their aesthetic quality by the Paipai and non-Indian consumers alike.

tures contained a small hearth, and smoke escaped via the door or a hole in the roof. Ramadas were common, as most daily activities took place outside. Large villages contained ceremonial structures and sweathouses. Ceremonial structures resembled their domestic counterparts but were larger in size. Sweathouses were covered entirely with earth. Granaries tended to be located on platforms or on top of houses or boulders.*

Traditionally, the indigenous groups of this region all practiced some version of the seasonal round, in which they exploited resources available in different environmental zones at different times of the year. It is difficult to generalize about the seasonal round, as the movements of a particular lineage depended in large measure on its location within the landscape. Within its homeland, each lineage had access to one or more high-yield food resources such as agave (*Agave* spp.), mesquite, or acorns (Hicks 1963:199). Of these primary food plants, agave was most palatable during the early spring; mesquite ripened in the summer months; and acorns were harvested in the autumn. These foods, as well as pinyon (*Pinus* spp.), were collected during large, communal harvests. Seeds, fruits, and berries were also important summer foods but were often collected by smaller parties. Native peoples in this province also collected a vast array of other plants and animals for food, medicine, and ceremonial purposes, as well as for raw materials for basketry and construction. The homelands of many lineages contained a majority of the group's plant and animal needs, although pinyon and marine resources typically required movement outside of the lineage homeland (Bean 1972:74; Hicks 1963:201; Meigs 1939:21). Many food resources were stored for later use, especially during the winter months.

As part of their traditional subsistence strategies, the indigenous groups of the Southern Deserts Province used various techniques to manipulate the environment. For example, Eastern Kumeyaay groups living in the Imperial Valley practiced floodplain agriculture in aboriginal times. Among other crops, the Eastern Kumeyaay grew maize, beans, and melons; but they also collected wild foods, and domesticates were just one part of their overall subsistence strategy. As such, the cultivation of these crops likely represented a strategy designed to diversify hunting and gathering practices rather than a heavy investment in agriculture. As in other areas of California, wild tobaccos (*Nicotiana* spp.) were widely managed in the past. They were tended and/or grown from seed by many ethnolinguistic groups in the region. The Cahuilla and Kumeyaay both may have also planted other species in the past, including desert palms. Although perhaps less prevalent in this region, fire was an important management tool for Native people. It increased the yields of certain plants such as chia *(Salvia columbariae)* and was employed to hunt rabbits (Leporidae) and other animals. Traditionally, grasslands were most commonly burned, but the Cahuilla also used fire to thin mesquite groves and to rid palm stands of insects.*

HERBACEOUS PLANTS

BUCKWHEATS *Eriogonum* **spp.**

The seeds of various species of buckwheat were eaten and gathered in the summer months. Desert dwellers also ate the young shoots of this plant.

A decoction of buckwheat leaves would alleviate headaches and stomach pain. The flowers were used to make an eyewash (Barrows 1900:78; Bean and Saubel 1972:72; Luomala 1978:600).

CHIA *Salvia columbariae*

Plate 8

This herb occurs widely in the Southern Deserts Province, usually below 1,800 m (5,900 ft). Chia seeds were once an important Native food resource, available in the summer months. To gather the chia seeds, women used a seed-beater to knock the seeds from the plant into a basket. Alternatively, the seed-bearing stems could be cut and later beaten against a container to remove the seeds. The seeds were then hulled, parched, and ground. Varying amounts of water could be added to the resulting meal in order to make a beverage or mush or cakes to be eaten. The meal was also boiled. Whole seeds could be stored for later use. Among the Cahuilla, stands of chia were burned in the past to increase yields.

Mush produced from chia seeds was used as a poultice to treat infections.*

DEERGRASS *Muhlenbergia rigens*

This tall grass, which grows along drainages, has been an important material for making several different types of baskets (Hohenthal 2001:163; Kroeber 1908a:41; Sparkman 1908:204).

GOOSEFOOTS *Chenopodium* **spp.**

The seeds of these common plants were parched and then ground to make mush or cakes. The shoots of young plants were also boiled and eaten as greens.*

PIGWEEDS or AMARANTHS *Amaranthus* **spp.**

Plate 15

These plants produce small, edible seeds. After being collected, the fruiting parts were dried, pounded with sticks, and winnowed to extract the seeds. The seeds were then parched and ground into a meal for making mush. The dried seeds could be stored. Young plants were also eaten as greens.*

RUSHES   *Juncus* spp.

Many different species of rushes live in this region, usually in moist environments. These plants were commonly employed in basketry. Rush plants of different colors were used to make designs in the baskets.*

SALTBUSHES   *Atriplex* spp.

These species occur primarily in the deserts of this region. Native peoples collected the seeds by beating the plants with a seed-beater. The seeds were hulled in a wooden mortar, winnowed, and soaked, then placed in a pit lined with hot rocks. After baking for several hours, the seeds were removed from the pit, parched, and ground. The meal was mixed with water before eating.*

Owen (1962:109) reported that the Paipai used a liniment of saltbushes to treat bone and muscle pain.

STINGING NETTLE   *Urtica dioica*

The stinging property of nettle leaves and stems offered relief for a number of ailments such as rheumatism and muscle pain. Native healers wrapped the affected area in nettles, which would act as a counterirritant.

Nettles (probably their fibrous stems) were used for basketry and cordage. Apparently, young shoots could be eaten raw or boiled.*

TOLOACHE or JIMSONWEED   *Datura wrightii*
Plate 19

This common plant is easily recognized by its trumpet-shaped flowers. It was widely used in the past for its hallucinogenic properties. All parts of the plant could produce such effects, and different portions of the plant were used for different purposes. Great care must be taken in its preparation, however; otherwise its ingestion could prove fatal. For traditional boys' puberty rites, dried toloache root was specially ground, and the resulting decoction played an important role in the initiation of boys into manhood. Native peoples employed toloache in many other rituals and ceremonies, usually in small doses. The use of toloache was also considered to be part of the process through which individuals acquired the skills necessary to become a shaman. Not all shamans used toloache, but those who did were able to transcend reality. Hohenthal (2001:206) reported that only the part of the root that pointed north could be utilized for shamanistic purposes. Toloache root was additionally chewed while gambling in order to enhance perception and for luck.*

Toloache leaves were placed on boils to cause them to open and drain. The root could be toasted, ground, and made into a tea to treat gonorrhea (Owen 1962:135).

TULES or BULRUSHES   *Schoenoplectus* spp.
Plate 20

The roots of these wetland plants were roasted whole in hot coals. Individuals removed the outer covering before dining on the roots.

Hohenthal (2001:180) indicated that tule balsas were used along the Pacific coast in Baja California during precontact and mission times. Tules were also used for house thatching and for mats.*

WILD TOBACCOS   *Nicotiana* spp.
Plate 9

Native peoples used wild tobaccos, sometimes called coyote tobacco, for both medicinal and spiritual purposes, and plants can often be found growing in and around former Indian settlements. Among the Kumeyaay, wild tobaccos played an important role in girls' puberty rites and in the Eagle Dance. The smoke itself could additionally cure sickness during shamanistic healing ceremonies, and for many groups this herb held greater ceremonial importance than toloache *(Datura wrightii)*. Yet most Native groups also smoked wild tobacco leaves casually, often in ceramic pipes or reed cigarettes. Perhaps ironically, it was smoked to alleviate coughs and asthma. People made a poultice from the leaves to treat wounds. Traditionally, tobacco leaves were a prized trading commodity. The Kumeyaay appear to have cultivated wild tobaccos; groups living in the United States report that it was grown from seed, while those living south of the border in Baja California indicate only that it was watered and weeded. In Cahuilla territory, individual shamans owned their own tobacco plots.*

YERBA MANSA or LIZARD'S TAIL   *Anemopsis californica*

This popular medicinal plant has a peppery odor and taste. The roots were boiled and used to treat colds, ulcers, and respiratory ailments. A powder made from dried yerba mansa could be used as a disinfectant. A poultice was also made from the leaves and applied to the forehead for headaches.

The seeds of this plant were occasionally eaten. They were ground in a mortar and cooked as a mush or cakes (Bean and Saubel 1972: 38–39; Gifford 1931:24; Meigs 1939:10).

TREES AND SHRUBS

ARROWWEED — *Pluchea sericea*
Plate 21

The stems of this herb were interwoven to construct granaries, as well as being used for the thatching of ramadas, houses, and ceremonial structures. Its stems could be used for the shafts of arrows or fire drills. Arrowweed gum was used to fletch arrows.*

BLUE ELDERBERRY — *Sambucus mexicana*
Plate 24

The berries of this shrub were gathered in the summer months. The berries could be eaten fresh but were also dried, ground, and prepared as a sauce or mush.

A tea from blue elderberry flowers was used to treat fever, measles, smallpox, and other ailments. A paste of the boiled plants could also ease pain from rheumatism. The flowers are used as basket dyes.*

CALIFORNIA FAN PALM — *Washingtonia filifera*

The California fan palm is common on the northern and western edges of the Colorado Desert, usually occurring in moist environments below 1,000 m (3,300 ft). The Cahuilla used this palm as both a food resource and a construction material. The small, datelike fruits were collected from midsummer through fall and could be eaten fresh or stored for later use. The palm fronds were used to thatch the roofs of houses or ramadas. They could also be used for sandals. The Cahuilla and the Kumeyaay used the seeds of the fruit for rattles. Research on modern populations of California fan palm north of the international border, estimated to be about 11,000 individual plants, indicates low levels of genetic variation. This low genetic differentiation appears to support reports that the Cahuilla and other local Indians dispersed California fan palm seeds to suitable habitats where they would grow.*

CALIFORNIA JUNIPER — *Juniperus californica*
Plate 33

This large evergreen shrub is common throughout the region. Local Indians view California juniper wood as superior for the construction of houses and fences, since it is considered to be stronger and more resistant to rotting than any other locally available construction material. Hohenthal (2001:137) reported that the Kumeyaay of northern Baja California avoided using it for firewood.

Juniper berries could be eaten fresh or boiled, although they were not a highly esteemed source of food. They could also be ground into a meal for mush or cakes. The Paipai made a tea from California juniper that served as a general therapeutic (Hicks 1963:144; Meigs 1939:9; Owen 1962:109).

CHAMISE or GREASEWOOD   *Adenostoma fasciculatum*
Chamise is a common evergreen shrub that grows in the chaparral zones of this region. People employed its trunk as a construction material, and its branches for arrows, fences, and ramadas. The wood was also used for making bull-roarers, a type of musical instrument. The gum from the plant could be used as a glue.

When boiled, chamise leaves and branches made a solution that was used to treat various pains and wounds.*

CREOSOTE BUSH   *Larrea tridentata*
This common desert shrub was widely known for its medicinal properties in treating a host of ailments. In particular, a tea made from the leaves could alleviate stomach discomfort and coughs (Bean and Saubel 1972:83; Meigs 1939:10; Owen 1962:111).

DESERT-WILLOW   *Chilopsis linearis*
Wood from the desert-willow was utilized in the construction of traditional houses. It proved to be a popular wood for making bows (Bean and Saubel 1972:53–54; Hooper 1920:358).

FREMONT COTTONWOOD   *Populus fremontii*
Desert people employed the wood of these trees to make mortars and house poles.

The leaves and bark could be boiled together to make a solution to relieve headaches. A poultice of the same materials was used to treat muscle strain (Bean and Saubel 1972:106; Gifford 1931; Hohenthal 2001:181).

HOLLY-LEAFED CHERRY or ISLAY   *Prunus ilicifolia*
Plate 32
Holly-leafed cherry is common in mountainous areas below 1,200 m (3,900 ft). This evergreen chaparral shrub produces a cherrylike fruit with a large pit. Although the flesh of the fruit is edible, most Native groups more commonly ate the seed it contained. The seeds, however, had to be processed before they could be consumed, and wide variation existed in the manner in which particular groups prepared holly-leafed cherry seeds. In all cases, the seeds were crushed or ground and then leached to remove their bitter flavor. Most cooks employed the meat of the seeds to make a mush, which was usually boiled.*

The Kumeyaay made syrup from the fruit, which they used to treat coughs or stomach discomfort (Hohenthal 2001:277). Owen (1962:131) observed that the Paipai used the leaf of the plant to make a tea for treating colds.

HONEY MESQUITE   *Prosopis glandulosa*

Plate 31

This abundant tree typically occurs below 1,000 m (3,300 ft) and its range includes the Colorado River Valley, the Colorado Desert, and the Colorado Desert foothill zones. The long, beanlike pods of the honey mesquite were once one of the most important Native food resources in the arid regions of the Southern Deserts Province. Honey mesquite was particularly valuable for Cahuilla lineages, who maintained sole access to particular groves. Mesquite gathering took place in the summer months and lasted for several weeks. Both green and older, naturally dried pods could be collected. The green pods were pounded in a wooden or stone mortar, resulting in a juicy pulp that was enjoyed as a beverage. Green pods could also be left to dry in the sun for a period of several days. Dried pods were pounded; typically the pods and their seeds were pounded together, but the pods could also be separated and soaked in water prior to eating. The seeds, or seed and pod combination, could be further ground into a meal for making cakes or mush, neither of which was cooked. Honey mesquite was traded widely and could be stored for long periods of time in large granaries. In the event of the occasional infestation of insect larvae, the insects were ground and consumed along with the mesquite. Mesquite blossoms, which occur in late spring, were also eaten. Cicadas (Cicadidae) and grasshoppers (Caelifera) live in honey mesquite groves and were collected and eaten by the Cahuilla. Such groves were also burned—both as a way to increase future yields and as a method for catching small game such as rabbits (Leporidae).*

Native peoples used the honey mesquite for a host of additional purposes. The Cahuilla employed the trunk of the tree to make mortars, and for house construction. The wood served as a source of firewood, particularly for firing pottery. Mesquite wood was used for clubs and shovels; bows were made from smaller branches. Fiber from the inner bark could be spun into string. Traditionally, the thorns could be used for tattooing, and the bark was used for clothing. Honey mesquite gum served as an adhesive. Diluted gum was once used as a shampoo and to treat wounds. For a purge, a tea could be made from the bark. Owen notes that the Paipai used a solution of boiled leaves to treat inflamed eyes.*

JOJOBA   *Simmondsia chinensis*

This shrub produces a bitter "nut" (i.e., seed) similar to the acorn. Native peoples ground the nut to create a meal, which was then parched and added to water. Jojoba nuts apparently do not require leaching (Bean and Saubel 1972:139; Hicks 1963:162; Meigs 1939:9).

The oil obtained from roasted nuts could be used to dry out persistent sores (Hohenthal 2001:278).

MANZANITAS   *Arctostaphylos* spp.

Plate 22

Many species of this shrub occur in this region, ranging from the chaparral zones to the higher elevations. The berries could be eaten raw or prepared as a drink with water and sometimes honey. People ground the seeds into a meal for making mush or cakes.

Manzanita wood was a favored firewood among many groups. Indians also gathered the roots as fuel, since they produced less smoke when burned. The roots were additionally made into a tea to treat stomach trouble.*

MORMON TEAS   *Ephedra* spp.

These distinctive-looking shrubs are common throughout southern California and northern Baja California. Traditional healers made a tea from Mormon tea twigs as a general therapeutic, although drinking the tea too regularly was considered dangerous. They boiled the roots in water to give to individuals suffering from venereal disease.

The seeds of this plant could be ground and eaten as mush (Bean and Saubel 1972:70; Hohenthal 2001:277; Meigs 1939:9; Owen 1962: 110).

MULE FAT or SEEP-WILLOW   *Baccharis salicifolia*

This shrub occurs along watercourses, typically at elevations below 460 m (1,500 ft). A poultice of the mule fat leaves soothed boils and sores. The leaves were also used to treat kidney ailments and other aches and pains (Hohenthal 2001:279; Meigs 1939:10; Owen 1962: 111).

Mule fat was used to thatch traditional dwellings. Its wood was also used for fire-making drills (Hinton and Owen 1957:91; Hohenthal 2001; Meigs 1939:29).

Oaks

Plate 40

40 oak species exist in the Southern Deserts Province, any of which could be used to supplement the variable yields of acorns from the preferred oak species, coast live oak and black oak. For example, the interior live oak *(Quercus wislizeni)* and Engelmann oak *(Q. engelmannii)* occur in the region. Like the scrub oaks, however, their acorns were considered less desirable by local peoples (Hicks 1963: 136; Sparkman 1908:193).

BLACK OAK   *Quercus kelloggii*

Plate 36

The black oak is an important source of acorns for Native groups living in southern California, particularly the Cahuilla and Luiseño.

Its range is restricted to higher elevations, and it does not extend far into Baja California. Although this oak does not produce acorns every year, it offers an abundant crop, and people used to travel long distances to gather its acorns. The acorns required leaching and were processed in much the same way as those from the coast live oak *(Q. agrifolia)*. Bean and Saubel (1972) reported that the Cahuilla produce two different grades of acorn meal, a fine meal for making acorn bread and a coarser meal for acorn mush. When preparing mush, meal from other oak species can be added to achieve the desired consistency. In the past, acorns were stored in granaries located in the main winter villages and were an important exchange item.*

CANYON LIVE OAK *Quercus chrysolepis*

Canyon live oak commonly occurs in small groves among the mountainous canyons and arroyos of this region, up to an elevation of approximately 2,000 m (6,550 ft). Though edible, the acorns of this species were not a popular food resource. The acorns were prepared in the same manner as those from other species of oaks, although Hicks (1963:134) indicated that the Paipai did not leach them. The acorns could be stored for long periods of time (Bean and Saubel 1972:123; Hicks 1963:134).

COAST LIVE OAK *Quercus agrifolia*
Plate 39

This oak species occurs in large groves and provides an abundant supply of acorns for local Native groups. Acorns were harvested in the fall, although not all trees produced acorns every year. Like other oak species, the acorns of the coast live oak required leaching to remove bitter tannic acid before they could be eaten. Indians pounded the acorns and removed the shells. The acorn meat was dried and ground into meal, which was then leached by pouring warm water over it. They ground the meal again after the leaching. The finished acorn meal was combined with water and cooked into a mush that had a gelatin-like consistency. Hicks (1963:130) reported that the Paipai make a sour mush from acorn meal allowed to stand for several days after leaching. Traditionally, all groups in this region stored unshelled acorns, typically in granaries woven from plant material.*

The Kiliwa used the green wood of the coast live oak for throwing sticks (Meigs 1939:28).

SCRUB OAKS *Quercus dumosa* and *Q. turbinella*
These species of scrub oak occur primarily in the chaparral zone, below 1,400 m (4,600 ft). Many Native groups ate scrub oak acorns, particularly Nuttall's scrub oak *(Q. dumosa)*, but they were not preferred. Desert Indians leached and processed the acorns like those of

other oak species. Scrub oak acorns could be used to stretch supplies of acorns from more highly esteemed oaks.*

Among the Tipai (Kumeyaay), the scrub oak insect gall was crushed and used to treat sores and toothaches (Hohenthal 2001: 277).

PINYON PINES *Pinus* **spp.**

Plate 45

Singleleaf pinyon *(P. monophylla)* is common in the Peninsular and Transverse ranges at elevations of 1,200 to 1,500 m (3,900 to 4,900 ft), although it is sometimes found as low as 600 m (1,950 ft). Parry pinyon *(P. quadrifolia)* typically grows at higher altitudes and consequently has a more restricted distribution. The "nuts" (i.e., the seeds) of both species were an important food resource for the Native peoples of this region, with harvests typically beginning in late summer. In the old days, pinyon harvests could last several weeks. Large groups of people moved to the pine groves, which could be located many kilometers from the homeland of a particular lineage. During the harvest, men and boys knocked the cones from the trees, while the women and children processed the pine nuts. Once collected, they roasted the cones or left them to dry, which caused the cones to open and the nuts to loosen inside. The cones could also be beaten to extract the nuts. A time-tested method for removing the "hulls" (i.e., seed coats) involved lightly grinding the nuts on a metate, then winnowing the shelled nuts. Pine nuts were usually roasted, then eaten whole or ground into a meal for mush. Roasted nuts could be stored for up to two years. Pinyon pine nuts were also an important trade item; they could be exchanged for acorns or, more recently, sold to others for cash. Although pinyon pines were highly prized, harvests were not always reliable from year to year. Due to the unpredictability of the harvest, individual pinyon groves were not owned by specific lineages.*

Pine needles were used for basketry, and pine pitch might be employed as an adhesive. Among the Paipai, pinyon pine gum was used to cure a number of ailments, including headaches, coughs, and colds (Bean and Saubel 1972:104–105; Owen 1962:113).

SAGEBRUSHES *Artemisia* **spp.**

These evergreen shrubs served as the principal medicinal plant of the Southern Deserts Province, particularly in terms of women's health. Traditional Cahuilla women would take a tea prepared from this plant to induce menstruation each month. It was also essential for the passing of girls into puberty and for ensuring a woman's safety in childbirth. The leaves could be chewed or smoked to relieve colds, or made into a tea for colic. A liniment made from this plant could be used to alleviate bone and muscle pain.

In Cahuilla territory, sagebrushes were also a common construction material for granaries used to store mesquite beans. Branches were used for fashioning arrows.*

SCREWBEAN
Prosopis pubescens

This tree is related to honey mesquite (*P. glandulosa*), although its distribution is more restricted. Screwbean is commonly found near the Lower Colorado River and in certain areas of the Colorado Desert. As its name suggests, the seed pod of this tree is tightly coiled. Screwbean pods also differ from those of honey mesquite in that they require special processing before they can be consumed. The traditional method for eliminating the bitterness of the pods was to place them in a pit lined with reeds. Native cooks covered the screwbeans with more reeds and applied water to the pit, which they then covered in soil. The screwbeans were left for a period of roughly six weeks, during which time they became soft and sweeter tasting. Once removed from the pit, the screwbeans were processed in a manner similar to honey mesquite pods. The cooks dried and pounded the pods in a mortar. They then toasted the meal and ground it to make mush. Like honey mesquite, screwbeans can be stored for long periods of time.

Screwbean wood was used for rabbit sticks, as well as for clubs and bows.*

SUMACS
Rhus spp.

Native Californians living in the Southern Deserts Province used various species of this common plant. Skunkbush (*R. trilobata*) was important for basketry. The berries of several sumac species were also a food resource. They could be eaten whole or ground into a meal. They were not cooked.*

WESTERN CHOKE-CHERRY
Prunus virginiana var. *demissa*

Western choke-cherry occurs in the mountainous regions of southern California; its range does not extend far into Baja California. Although the seed can be ground into meal, it appears that Native peoples exploited the plant primarily for its fleshy fruit. The fruit ripens in late summer or early fall. It was eaten fresh or left for several days after harvesting, as among the Luiseño.*

WHITE SAGE
Salvia apiana

White sage, one of the most common sages in this region, was used by Native people for many purposes. To treat colds, the leaves could be smoked, eaten, or boiled into a tea. A poultice made from the aromatic leaves could also be used as a deodorant. According to Waterman (1910:286), white sage featured prominently in the girls' puberty ritual among the Kumeyaay.

White sage seeds were collected in the late summer and eaten whole or ground into mush.*

WILLOWS   *Salix* **spp.**

Plate 35

Various species of willows are found along watercourses below 900 m (2,950 ft). They were used for making baskets and granaries, bows, and women's willow bark skirts.* The inner bark could be made into cordage.

YERBA SANTAS   *Eriodictyon* **spp.**

Several species of this common shrub occur in the Southern Deserts Province including thickleaf yerba santa *(E. crassifolium)* and hairy yerba santa *(E. trichocalyn)*. Indians made tea from the leaves for treating sore throats or coughs. The leaves were also used as a poultice for wounds. When heated, they also served as a hot compress for rheumatism (Bean and Saubel 1972:71; Hohenthal 2001:278; Owen 1962:122–123).

CACTI AND SUCCULENTS

AGAVES   *Agave* **spp.**

Plate 52

These plants, often called mescal, were a principal food source in the Southern Deserts Province, particularly in the lower elevations. Two common species are desert agave *(A. deserti)* and coastal agave *(A. shawii),* a larger species. Agave heads—the inner part of the basal rosette–were typically roasted in large pits, often several dozen at a time. To obtain the head, the agave gatherers removed the stalk and root, along with the outer leaves. Meanwhile, a pit was dug and a fire built inside of it. They allowed the fire to burn down and placed large stones on top of the embers, although in some cases, the pit was lined with rocks first. The agave heads were placed in the pit and covered with brush before the pit was refilled with earth. The heads were then left to roast for a period of one to three days. The finished product has a smoky sweet taste with a tender, if somewhat fibrous, consistency. The flower stalk could be roasted along with the heads, and for the Cahuilla, the stalk was apparently preferred. To facilitate storage, roasted agave heads or stalks could be pounded into thin cakes and left to dry in the sun. Agave flowers were also edible, usually after parboiling. The leaves could be eaten fresh.

The leaves of agave plants were an important source of fiber, which was used for the manufacture of a number of items, including nets, sandals, fishing line, bowstrings, brushes, and cordage. Among other uses, agave nets proved instrumental in communal rabbit drives.*

CALIFORNIA BARREL CACTUS   *Ferocactus cylindraceus*
Plate 51

Species of this cactus genus are common in nearly all areas of the region below 1,500 m (4,900 ft), ranging from the Pacific coast to the Colorado Desert. The flower buds and small fruits of California barrel cactus ripen in late spring and early summer. The buds were usually boiled. The flesh of the cactus itself could be eaten raw or boiled. The Paipai also collected the seeds from the cactus fruit, which could be stored for later use.*

According to Gifford, Kumeyaay living in the Imperial Valley used spines from this cactus as fishhooks (Gifford 1931:26).

CHOLLAS   *Cylindropuntia* spp.
Plate 50

Various species of chollas share the same unique appearance; most are erect plants with cylindrical, spiny branches or joints. A common species is the buckhorn cholla *(C. acanthocarpa)*. The fruits can be eaten fresh, cooked, or dried for later use. The blossoms and seeds are also edible.

The root of the cholla could be made into a tea and used as a purge or to treat diarrhea. Ashes from the stems were used to promote the healing of wounds.*

HEDGEHOG CACTI   *Echinocereus* spp.

These low, clumping cacti produce a fruit that is eaten by some Native groups in this region, particularly in Baja California. The fruit is eaten fresh.

The juice of these plants could be used as a fish stupefacient (Hicks 1963:128; Hohenthal 2001:138; Meigs 1939:9).

PRICKLY-PEARS   *Opuntia* spp.
Plate 49

The prickly-pears are differentiated by their large, flat pads. Although Spanish settlers introduced the common tuna cactus *(O. ficus-indica)*, several species of prickly-pears are native to California. The pulpy fruits remain an important food resource and can be eaten fresh in the late summer months when they are juicy and sweet. The fruits and/or their seeds were also ground into a fine meal for making mush or cakes. After grinding, the fruits could be stored. The fruits of the beavertail cactus *(O. basilaris)* are dry, and the buds were consequently cooked or steamed by Indians for several hours. The pads of prickly-pears can be eaten after boiling, although little evidence exists for their use prior to the arrival of Europeans.*

Traditionally, the spines were used as tattoo needles. The Paipai used toasted pads for splints, and such pads when sliced open would draw out thorns or soothe festering wounds (Owen 1962:123; Spier 1923:342).

YUCCAS   *Yucca* spp.
Plates 53, 54

The Native groups of this region used three main species of yucca: Our Lord's candle *(Y. whipplei)*, Spanish bayonet *(Y. baccata)*, and Mojave yucca *(Y. schidegera)*. The basal rosettes, or heads, of these species were prepared in much the same way as agave heads. Cooks removed the leaves and roasted the heads in a rock-lined pit. The cooked heads could be stored after being dried and pounded into cakes. The flower stalk and flowers of Mojave yucca were also eaten. The cooks roasted the stalks and boiled the flowers. Mojave yucca produces a fleshy fruit that could be roasted and eaten.

Yuccas were an important source of fiber for rope, nets, baskets, and sandals. The fiber of the Mojave yucca is considered to be superior. Yucca roots were also used as soap.*

INSECTS AND OTHER TERRESTRIAL INVERTEBRATES

Traditionally, the indigenous groups of the Southern Deserts Province consumed various insects including species of ants, cicadas, caterpillars, and grubs; however, information about specific species or methods of preparation is scarce.*

GRASSHOPPERS   Suborder Caelifera
Plate 62

In the past, grasshoppers, where available, contributed to the diet of many Native groups. The Cahuilla collected them from mesquite groves. Swarming grasshoppers were driven into a pit, where they were roasted. Some grasshoppers are not considered edible. Gifford reported that Kumeyaay groups in the Imperial Valley used grasshoppers as fish bait.*

HONEYBEE   *Apis mellifera*

Since the introduction of the Honeybee to California in the 1850s, wild honey has become a highly esteemed food in the Southern Deserts Province. Native people collect wild honey from beehives located in small caves and dead trees. Often the opening of caves and rock crevices are manipulated to facilitate honey gathering. (Hinton and Owen 1957:96; Meigs 1939:25; Michelsen and Smith 1967).

FISHES

Pelagic Fishes

Some groups living in Baja California, such as the Kiliwa and Paipai, made fishing trips to the Gulf of California near the present-day city of San Felipe. The Kiliwa did not use boats and instead practiced shore fishing. The fishes could be dried and stored. Unfortunately no information exists on the type of fishes caught during these trips (Hohenthal 2001:53, 148; Meigs 1939:21, 27).

Freshwater Fishes

BONYTAIL CHUB   *Gila elegans*

This white minnow, reaching lengths of 40 cm (about 16 in.), was once common in the Colorado River drainage. Gifford indicated it was eaten among the eastern Kumeyaay (Gifford 1931:26).

COLORADO PIKEMINNOW   *Ptychocheilus lucius*

This large minnow can reach a length of roughly 90 cm or more (35 in.) and can weigh up to 9 kg (20 lb). This fish is common in the territory of eastern Kumeyaay groups, who in the past harvested it through the use of fish scoops, hooks, and seines. (Gifford 1931:26; Hicks 1963:170).

RAZORBACK SUCKER   *Xyrauchen texanus*
or HUMPBACK SUCKER

The Kumeyaay ate this freshwater fish, which measures up to 60 cm (about 24 in.) long. Gifford reports that the Razorback Sucker was the only species killed through the use of the bow and arrow. It was also caught in the same manner as the Colorado Pikeminnow (*Ptychocheilus lucius*)(Gifford 1931:26; Hicks 1963:170).

AMPHIBIANS AND REPTILES

The Native groups of this region used some species of snakes and lizards as a secondary food resource. Few accounts, however, give specific information on species or hunting techniques (Hohenthal 2001:157; Luomala 1978:601; Meigs 1939:25).

RATTLESNAKES   *Crotalus* spp.

Rattlesnakes were eaten, at least among the Cahuilla.

Traditionally, the Kumeyaay used Rattlesnake venom to poison arrows. Hohenthal (2001:144) reported that arrows poisoned in this way were used only for war and not for hunting game. Rattlesnake skin could be used to treat rheumatism when tied around the affected appendages (Bean 1972:61; Hohenthal 2001:274; Spier 1923:353).

SEA TURTLES   Families Cheloniidae and Dermochelyidae

Hohenthal indicated that in the past both the Kumeyaay and the Paipai hunted sea turtles along the coast of the Gulf of California (Hohenthal 2001:53, 148).

BIRDS
Terrestrial Birds

DOVES   *Zenaida* spp. and *Columbina* spp.

Doves are common in this region, and Native peoples utilized several species, including the Common Ground-Dove *(C. passerina)*. Spier noted that among some Kumeyaay groups only elders were allowed to eat doves. Gifford suggested that the eastern Kumeyaay did not eat the Mourning Dove *(Z. macroura)* because the birds were believed to be reincarnated souls.*

EAGLES   Family Accipitridae
Plate 97

Few ethnographic accounts from this region indicate which species of eagles Native people used in the past. Both the Golden Eagle *(Aquila chrysaetos)* and Bald Eagle *(Haliaeetus leucocephalus)* would have been available to most groups. Eagle feathers featured prominently in the dancing regalia of several groups, particularly the Luiseño and Kumeyaay. In the Kumeyaay Eagle Dance, a bird was sacrificed to commemorate the death of important persons. Perhaps due to their former ceremonial importance, Kumeyaay people interviewed by Hohenthal in the 1940s specified that eagles were not to be killed.*

HAWKS   *Accipiter* spp. and *Buteo* spp.
Plate 101

Hawk feathers were commonly used for fletching arrows. They were also part of some groups' ceremonial ornamentation. Hawks were usually not eaten (Hohenthal 2001; Kroeber 1908a:62; Spier 1923: 352).

QUAILS   Family Odontophoridae
Plates 99, 100

Quails once comprised an important part of the diet for the groups of this region. Most groups had access to California Quail *(Callipepla californica)* and some probably to Mountain Quail *(Oreortyx pictus)*. Gambel's Quail *(C. gambelii)* was available to groups living in the Colorado Desert. Birds were driven into nets located at the convergence of two brush fences. Hunters also shot them with bows and arrows. Family cooks roasted the quails on coals and prepared the eggs to be eaten.*

MAMMALS
Terrestrial Mammals

BEARS   *Ursus* spp.

Before European colonization, bears were more common in this region than they are today. Hohenthal suggested that the Kumeyaay would eat bear, but Sparkman reported that the Luiseño killed them only for their skins and claws. The claws were used as ornaments (Hohenthal 2001:147; Sparkman 1908:199).

BIGHORN SHEEP   *Ovis canadensis*
Plate 108

This rare and shy species was eaten by the Native peoples of the region, although probably infrequently. Great patience was required to ambush Bighorn Sheep, typically at watering places. They were also driven into ambush sites with the aid of strategically placed rocks that were fashioned to look like humans. The meat, when obtained, was highly esteemed.*

COYOTE   *Canis latrans*

Coyote meat is not considered edible. Coyote hides were used to make quivers and other pouches (Hohenthal 2001:147; Spier 1923:353).

HARES and RABBITS   **Family Leporidae**
Plate 109

For the Native groups of this region, hares and rabbits made up the most abundant and most easily obtainable source of meat. Ethnographic evidence suggests that the Desert Cottontail *(Sylvilagus audubonii)* and Black-tailed Jackrabbit *(Lepus californicus)* were the primary game animals for most groups, although today the Desert Cottontail is preferred. They could be caught in communal drives, which might include the use of nets, brush fences, and/or intentionally set fires. The hunters dispatched the animals using a rabbit stick, a type of nonreturning boomerang, or bows and arrows with wooden foreshafts. Snares were also used. The animals were roasted in coals or over a fire. They were also cooked in an earth oven, after which the bones and flesh could be ground together to create pemmican for later use. Hohenthal (2001:144–145) indicated that the meat was avoided in the autumn months because the animals develop boils.

Blankets and clothing were made from the skins of both species.*

MULE DEER
Odocoileus hemionus

Plate 112

To overcome the relatively short range of the traditional bow and arrow, Native people employed several methods of hunting Mule Deer. Deer were ambushed at watering holes, and also chased to the point of exhaustion by men running them in a zig-zag pattern or in a relay with other hunters. Communal deer drives were used to flush the animals toward waiting hunters. Stuffed deer head decoys were also utilized in the past. Some groups used pitfalls or large snares. The meat was roasted on hot coals or cooked in an earth oven. Cooked venison could be ground to facilitate storage, and slabs of dried venison were also stored for future consumption. Deer bones could also be ground to a paste and eaten.

Deer vertebral sinew was used to make bow cords. Deerskin could be used for breechclouts and archers' wrist guards. The brains were used to tan animal skins. People once made tools, such as awls, from the bones. Deer hoof rattles were used for the girls' puberty ritual and other ceremonies.*

PRONGHORN
Antilocapra americana

Pronghorns used to inhabit parts of the Southern Deserts Province and were eaten by Native peoples. Separate groups of hunters chased the herds in relays in order to exhaust the animals or to drive them to an area where they could be more easily killed (Bean 1972:57; Hicks 1963:185; Hohenthal 2001:147).

SQUIRRELS
Family Sciuridae

Squirrels provided another source of meat for the Native groups of this region. Several species may have been captured in specific southern desert habitats, including Antelope Ground Squirrel *(Ammospermophilus leucurus),* Rock Ground Squirrel *(Spermophilus variegatus),* and Round-tailed Ground Squirrel *(S. tereticaudus).* Little information is available on hunting techniques other than the use of deadfalls.*

WOODRATS
Neotoma **spp.**

These common nocturnal rodents once represented an important source of meat in the Southern Deserts Province. The species hunted by Native peoples probably included the Desert Woodrat *(N. lepida)* and Dusky-footed Woodrat *(N. fuscipes).* To catch woodrats, the nests were set on fire while the hunters waited to club the animals or shoot them with arrows as they fled. People also caught woodrats by forcing them from their nests with sticks. Alternatively, these creatures could be killed using a deadfall with bait such as quail eggs or acorn meal. They were prepared in the same manner as rabbits (Leporidae).*

ROCKS AND MINERALS

CLAY

The indigenous groups of this region were among the few in California to make pottery before the arrival of Europeans. Many continue to make pottery today. Clay for ceramics is carefully selected and processed, and pottery is made using the paddle-and-anvil technique. In the past, finished pots were used for cooking and to store seeds and water. Decoration is uncommon, especially in the southern areas. Pipes and rattles were also made from clay. Certain clays were used for face painting.*

GRANITE

Granite could be used to make grinding implements such as mortars and pestles, or metates and manos. Some mortars have basketry hoppers to keep the contents from spilling during grinding or pounding. Native peoples also used bedrock outcrops to create mortars and grinding surfaces. Other metamorphic or granitic rocks were also used for grinding implements (Bean and Shipek 1978:553; Kroeber 1908a:51; Luomala 1978:602).

OBSIDIAN

This volcanic glass was highly prized in the production of projectile points and other stone tools. Two geologic sources of obsidian occur in southern California, one in the Bristol Mountains in San Bernardino County and one at Obsidian Butte in Imperial County. Other sources occur near the Mexican town of San Felipe on the Gulf of California coast. Traditionally, obsidian was obtained by direct procurement as well as through long-distance trade (Hohenthal 2001:289).

QUARTZ

Quartz was used as a raw material for stone tools. Quartz crystals were also an important part of a shaman's toolkit, especially if they contained tourmaline inclusions (Bean and Shipek 1978:552–553; Hohenthal 2001:288–289).

SALT

In the old days, groups who had access to the coast collected salt in tidal pools. It was commonly traded to interior groups. It could also be obtained from certain other low-lying areas, especially in the Colorado Desert.*

NOTES

Why California Indians Matter

1. For sources on California Indian populations in historic times, see Anderson 2005:309; Castillo 1978:118; Heizer and Almquist 1971; Lightfoot 2005. The figure of 150,000 California Indians is from Anderson who cites a personal communication from the California Native American Heritage Commission. In the 2000 federal census, 333,346 people living in California listed their only race as American Indian or Alaskan Native; for those who listed more than one race, 627,562 people identified either American Indian or Alaskan Native. The 2000 census also counted 51,707 people living on Indian reservations or federally held trust land in the state of California.

2. This point is also true for the Native groups of the Northwest Coast of America, including Oregon, Washington, British Columbia, and southern Alaska.

3. For excellent introductions and overviews on complex hunter-gatherers, see Fitzhugh and Habu 2002; Habu et al. 2003; Price and Brown 1985.

4. A large and growing literature addresses recent research on sustainable economies. For examples, see Bird and Ikerd 1993; Lubchenco et al. 1991; Matson et al. 1997; Wartzman 2007.

The Central Role of Fire

1. It is not clear whether massive bird kills took place for feathers or whether local groups employed catch-and-release methods to pluck feathers from living birds, which were then set free.

2. The critical role that fires play in the majority of California's habitats is outlined in some detail later in the book. For those who cannot wait, please refer to the recent magnum opus on this topic by Sugihara, van Wagtendonk, Shaffer, et al. (2006).

3. Wandsnider (1997:18) details how fructan-rich foods, containing significant amounts of inulin, when slow-cooked in earth ovens or pit-hearths, can provide up to a 100 percent increase in energy. Inulin can not normally be digested very well without this heat treatment. Cooks can prepare large quantities of different kinds of foods that require similar heat and moisture demands in ovens or pit-hearths. She notes that earth ovens are especially useful for cooking large packages of fatty meats along with vegetable foods.

4. For more on acorn processing, see various citations listed in the guide to resources section of this book.

5. These are designated as "logistically organized task groups" in the anthropological literature.

6. Often referred to as "logistical encampments" by archaeologists.

Waves of Migration

1. The Quaternary Period in California, divided into the Pleistocene (2 million to 10,000 years ago) and Holocene (10,000 years ago to present) epochs, is characterized by divergent, and sometimes rapid, oscillations in climatic conditions. During the Pleistocene Epoch, often referred to as the Ice Age, more than 20 glacial episodes of conditions cooler and wetter than today's took place on a global scale. During those periods of lower temperature, giant ice sheets formed in the Northern and Southern hemispheres, covering more than 30 percent of the Earth's land surface. Interglacial periods of warmer temperatures, in which the spatial extent and thickness of ice masses diminished worldwide, periodically ameliorated the harsh glacial episodes. California was probably settled sometime during the last ice age episode of the Late Pleistocene, from about 25,000 to 10,000 years ago. The maximum glacial advance took place about 18,000 years ago, at which time two massive ice sheets stretched across much of North America. The Laurentide Ice Sheet spread from Labrador to the eastern Rockies, having a maximum thickness of about 3,300 m (10,800 ft), and the Cordilleran Ice Sheet extended from the Canadian Rockies through the mountains in British Columbia.

2. For example, palynological research indicates that a much more extensive Pleistocene coniferous forest once existed along the South Coast Province (Erlandson 1994:30–32), montane forests dominated by coast redwood *(Sequoia sempervirens)* extended farther south in latitude along the coast, and montane forests in the Sierra Nevada descended into the lower foothills.

3. Grayson (1993:63) notes that the Late Pleistocene to Holocene

transition witnessed the extinction of 35 genera of mammals and 19 genera of birds in North America. While the most notable large mammals died out, many species of fishes, birds, shellfish, and smaller game that we know and love today survived.

4. Not all of these fluted points fit the classic typological definition of the Clovis points. Many appear to be smaller versions of the later so-called Folsom points, which in the American Southwest are associated with Paleo-Indian, who hunted extinct bison and other game. For more information on the location and description of California fluted points, see Arnold et al. 2004:42–44; Dillon 2002; Jenkins 2005; Moratto 1984:79–88; Sutton 1996:227–228.

5. See a map of fluted projectile point locations in California, published by Dillon (2002:122). Erlandson (1994:175) describes the surface find for a fluted point recovered from a site (CA-SBA-1951) along the Santa Barbara coast.

6. See Dillon's (2002:113–114) list of fluted point locations and Moratto's (1984:77) map of Late Pleistocene and Early Holocene sites and pluvial lakes.

7. See, for example, Erlandson et al. 1999:261, 2005:682; Kennett 2005:125.

8. Although the upper boundary of the Holocene is drawn at the end of the last glacial period, usually considered to be about 10,000 years ago when global warming severely reduced the size and extent of glacial sheets, it ushered in anything but a stable climatic regime. Paleoclimatic research in California indicates that there were significant oscillations in precipitation across both space and time, as well as in air and ocean water temperatures. While the average air temperature of the Holocene may have been statistically warmer than that of the Late Pleistocene, later climatic conditions, especially in areas away from the Pacific coast, were characterized by greater extremes in winter and summer temperatures and rainfall patterns. This would have had a significant effect on the distribution and reorganization of plant communities, creating ecological disruptions in some times and places (Grayson 1993:72).

9. The Holocene is often divided into a tripartite scheme of climatic regimes, originally outlined by Antevs (1955), which begins with relatively cool and moist conditions in the Early Holocene, followed by a hot and dry period, known as the Altithermal, in the Middle Holocene (ranging from 8,000 to 3,000 years ago), and the onset of milder temperatures and moderate precipitation beginning between 6,000 to 4,000 years ago, with modern conditions taking hold by the Late Holocene, beginning about 3,000 years ago (see Erlandson 1994: 31; Raab and Larson 1997:319–320). These macroclimatic regimes

exhibited considerable variation in climatic conditions for specific locations over time. Douglas Kennett (2005:41–71) provides an excellent synthesis of significant oscillations in precipitation and seawater temperatures during the Holocene that had significant impacts on the fisheries and terrestrial resources of people along the southern California coast.

10. See syntheses by Arnold et al. 2004; Chartkoff and Chartkoff 1984; Erlandson 1997; Erlandson and Colten 1991; Erlandson and Jones 2002; Fagan 2003; Jones and Klar 2007; Moratto 1984.

11. For further information on these sites, see Arnold 2001b; Gould 1966; Grant 1965; Grant et al. 1968; Jackson 1991; Lightfoot 1997; Lightfoot and Luby 2002; Napton and Greathouse 2005; Waechter 1995.

A Landscape of Unparalleled Diversity

1. See, for example, Jameson and Peeters 2004; Kavanagh 2005; McGinnis 2006; Ornduff et al. 2003; Schoenherr 1992.

2. Sometime between 25 and 15 million years ago, much of this subduction action began to be transformed into strike-slip movements as the two plates touched along the west coast of central and southern California. Along the emerging San Andreas Fault zone, the Pacific Plate slipped, with an occasional major jolt, northward against the North American Plate, producing a right-lateral strike-slip fault system. In the ensuing years, faults radiating out across much of California provided the blueprint for how subsequent landscape modification would take place. Seismic activity along some of these faults raised or subsided extensive blocks of land in what is known as dip-slip movement. In other cases, extensive blocks of land moved sideways or northward in a strike-slip movement (see Schoenherr 1992: 58–68; Sloan 2006:27–45).

3. The water is then pumped down to the equator, where it is heated and then transported to the western Pacific, following the famous equatorial easterlies or trade winds. As this warm Equatorial Current flows off the coast of Asia, waters are circulated northward along the North Pacific Current, where they are eventually cooled in the northern latitudes and sent back to coastal North America by means of the California Current (see Caviedes 2001; Schoenherr 1992:33–46).

4. The Klamath Mountains, given their northern latitude and elevation, can receive over 300 cm (118 in.) of precipitation a year, while the other northern mountains enjoy considerable rainfall or snow, depending on the year. The Smith, Klamath, Trinity, and Mad rivers

drain the Klamath Mountains; the Eel and Russian rivers originate in the North Coast Ranges; while the Pit River flows through the Modoc Plateau and Cascade Range. Snowmelt in late spring and early summer in the Sierra Nevada feeds many western-flowing streams and rivers, including the Butte, Feather, Yuba, Bear, American, Cosumnes, Mokelumne, Stanislaus, Tuolumne, Merced, and Kings rivers. The Sierra Nevada waters converge into the San Joaquin and Sacramento rivers; together they carry 40 percent of California's water through the Delta, the San Francisco Bay system, and then out to the Pacific Ocean.

5. The deserts east of the South Coast Province's mountains do receive periodic torrential thunderstorms from the Gulf of California during the summer months. But southeastern California is a dry place. The southern end of the Great Central Valley receives less than 25 cm (10 in.) of rain a year, while some places in the Mojave Desert may not receive any measurable rainfall for extended periods. Bagdad, a deserted settlement in the Mojave Desert, is reported to be the driest place in the continental United States, having no recorded precipitation over a period of 25 months (Schoenherr 1992:ix). Aside from the Colorado River and the related Salton Sea in the Colorado Desert, which receives occasional runoff from the Colorado River, southeastern California has no major river systems.

6. For the purposes of this book, we do not include the Great Basin and Lower Colorado River as geomorphic provinces of Native California. The Native people of these regions are described in detail elsewhere. Known as the cold desert because most of its precious precipitation falls in winter as snow, a strip of the Great Basin sits along the eastern border of California, meeting the Modoc Plateau and then tumbling down the steep eastern escarpment of the Sierra Nevada. Peppered with north-south-trending fault-block ranges and deep valleys, which give the region its characteristic basin-and-range topography, the broader province extends across a significant area sandwiched between the Columbia Plateau, the Wasatch Mountains of Utah, and the Colorado Plateau of the American Southwest. Along the California margin, a number of significant ranges are found: the Warner Mountains, with their characteristic mahogany-colored obsidian, east of the Modoc Plateau; the White and Inyo mountains, east of the Owens Valley; and the Panamint Range, west of Death Valley. Owens Valley, situated in a deep depression between the eastern Sierra Nevada and the western slopes of the White and Inyo mountains, is usually included in the Great Basin (Heizer and Elsasser 1980: 29). The people of the Lower Colorado River are typically included in the greater American Southwest culture area.

7. Heizer and Elsasser (1980:9–10) employed the concept of life zones, first defined by C. Hart Merriam in the 1890s, to describe Boreal, Transition, Upper Sonoran, and Lower Sonoran zones across California. They emphasized that California Indians would "stake out their tribal territory so as to cover several life zones." More recent classifications have employed the concept of biomes, based on temperature and precipitation patterns that correspond to broad assemblages of flora and fauna, better known as plant communities. Some botanists are now questioning the concept of plant communities defined as an interacting group of plants dominated by one or more species, because it is unclear in many situations how specific species depend on or interact with one another to create an integrated community. Consequently, there is a trend in recent classifications to replace "plant community" with the more neutral term "vegetation type." For further discussion, see Ornduff et al. 2003:113–115; Schoenherr 1992:46–47.

8. See, for example, Arnold 1992:69–70; Kennett 2005:60–61; Kennett and Kennett 2000:381.

9. For example, in the El Niño events of 1982/1983 and 1997/1998, salmon runs failed to materialize in any numbers from California to British Columbia, but fishermen caught nonnative, warmwater yellowfin tuna, skipjack, marlin, albacore, and yellowtail off the California coast (Caviedes 2001:23). See discussion of this issue for prehistory by Arnold et al. 1997; Raab et al. 1995.

10. See, for example, Jones et al. 1999; Kennett and Kennett 2000: 385; Raab and Larson 1997:324–325; Stine 1994.

11. For example, see Grant and Sieh 1994; Lemey 2005; Niemi and Hall 1992.

12. The Indian village had been built along the fault. By carefully measuring and dating distinctive strata that crossed the San Andreas, we estimated the amount of strike-slip movement that had taken place over the last 3,000 years (Noller and Lightfoot 1997).

13. The power and devastation of tsunamis were demonstrated all too well by the December 26, 2004, mammoth wave event that killed more than 225,000 people around the Indian Ocean.

14. For an example of recent research addressing past tsunamis and landslides along the Oregon coast, using archaeology and Native oral traditions, see Byram 2007.

15. Bicknell and Mackey (1998) believe that the sea fig (*Carpobrotus chilensis*), originally indigenous to South Africa, probably came to California during the period between early exploration (1500s) and Spanish colonization (1800s), possibly from dumping ballast from one or more ships in California ports. They identify several potential

ships that may have brought the sea fig to the California coast, including Francis Drake's *Golden Hind* (1579) and Sebastian Rodriguez Cermeño's *San Agustin* (1595).

16. These early settlements included the Spanish (and later Mexican) chain of 21 Franciscan missions, four military presidios, three civilian pueblos, and numerous private ranchos (1769 to 1830s), as well as the establishment of the Russian outpost of Colony Ross (1812 to 1841); see Lightfoot 2005.

17. For discussions on the evidence of early weeds in California, see Allen 1998:43–46; Hendry 1931; Honeysett 1989:178–179; West 1989. An account by the French sea captain Auguste Duhaut-Cilly, riding over free-range land near the Pueblo of Los Angeles in September 1827, highlights the insidious nature of the early onslaught of these invaders.

> Leaving this plain, we came to nothing less than a forest of mustard [fennel?] whose great stalks stood higher than the head of a horseman and formed something like a thick wall on each side of the route. In recent years this plant has become a terrible scourge in parts of California, invading the finest pasture lands and threatening to spread over the entire country. In the beginning the people could have fought off this enemy by eradicating the first troublesome plants, but their negligence has allowed the evil weed to increase in such a way that it may no longer be controllable by such a small population. Fire has been tried but without success. When the stalks are dry enough to burn they have already spread most of their seeds, and fire only renders the soil more suitable to reproduction of the plant they wish to destroy. (Duhaut-Cilly 1999:144)

18. For summaries of these significant changes to California's environment, see Allen 1998; Anderson 2005:71–78; Preston 1997.

19. For further discussion, see Lightfoot 2005:86–88; Milliken 1995.

The Uniqueness of California

1. Much of this information is published in two series: *University of California Publications in American Archaeology and Ethnology* and *University of California Anthropological Records,* as well as Kroeber's (1925) seminal monograph, *Handbook of the Indians of California.* These publications on the material objects, cultural practices, ceremonial systems, languages, and political organizations of hundreds of Indian communities remain significant sources for any scholar working in Native California today.

2. Chumash languages were once affiliated with the Hokan stock or phylum but are now treated as a classificatory isolate (Golla 2007: 80–81). Some scholars today recognize the Utian language group as its own distinctive stock or superfamily, others do not. Yukian, Uto-Aztecan, Algic, and Na-Dené are similarly defined as either stocks, superfamilies, or families, depending on the linguistic classification (Golla 2007; Hinton 1994:83–85; Moratto 1984:533–534; Shipley 1978; Simmons 1997:56).

3. Roland Dixon and Alfred Kroeber (1913, 1919), along with Edward Sapir (1917, 1921, 1921–1923), pioneered the linguistic classificatory system in California when they first identified and defined the extensive Hokan and Penutian stocks. Almost from the outset, however, questions were raised about the validity of these linguistic groupings that encompass a large and diverse range of California Indian languages. Today a healthy debate continues about the Hokan and Penutian stocks, as well as the placement and rearrangement of specific family groups and languages within the greater classificatory system (Golla 2007; Hughes 1992:325; Shipley 1978).

4. See, for example, Heizer and Elsasser 1980:10–24.

5. As Kroeber remarked (1966:100),

> In any strict sense, the word "tribe" denotes a group of people that act together, feel themselves to be a unit, and are sovereign in a defined territory. Now, in California, these traits attached to the Masut Pomo, once again to the Elem Pomo, to the Yokaia Pomo, and to the 30 other Pomo tribelets. They did not attach to the Pomo as a whole, because the Pomo as a whole did not act or govern themselves, or hold land as a unit. In other words, there was strictly no such tribal entity as "the Pomo": there were 34 miniature tribes.

6. For example, the Karuk, Kashaya Pomo, and southern Diegueño languages are classified within the Hokan stock, but the speakers of these languages deviate greatly in their lifeways and cultural practices.

7. See, for example, Kroeber 1939:1–6. He believed that environments tended to stabilize cultures over time. Once a culture took hold in a particular environment, it would change very little unless something major upset the human–environment stasis. In their discussion of culture areas, Heizer and Elsasser (1980:28) elaborated upon this point:

> Although culture areas can be geographically delineated, they are more than mere geographic areas, for in each one there lived a series of tribes that shared among themselves a way of life distinctly different from that prevailing in neighboring culture areas. The

features that set off one culture area from another were often direct reflections of the potentiality of the environment and the ways in which people learned to utilize it.

8. In central California, they argued that the valley environments and oak woodlands were critical for acorn harvests and related cultural practices. In southern California it was the productive coastline and islands that provided the basis for a maritime economy. For the Lower Colorado River area, it was the Colorado River that flowed through the desert country, replenishing rich alluvial soils after winter flooding and providing opportunities for floodwater agriculture.

9. For more on the early description of culture areas in California, see Kroeber 1904, 1920, 1925:898–902.

10. A new program of culture element surveys had been instituted at the Berkeley campus of the University of California, whereby ethnographers asked Native informants about the presence or absence of cultural traits from a standardized list of 1,000 to 1,100 items. The trait lists were then statistically analyzed to better define the spatial pattern of culture areas and to examine the genetic relationship of Native groups. For further information on the trait list approach, see Gifford and Kroeber 1937; Klimek 1935; Kroeber 1936.

11. The primary exceptions are the large, agrarian-based societies of the Lower Colorado River, exemplified by the Yuman speaking people (Quechan, Mojave). At the time of initial Spanish settlement in Alta California, they each numbered upward of 2,000 to 2,500 people who spoke the same dialect and recognized a broader nation of shared identity and political organization (Kroeber 1925:830). As we are focusing on the pyrodiversity collectors of California, the Lower Colorado River farmers are not discussed in any detail in this book.

12. Kin ties and individual social connections seemingly bisected any kind of larger village or community organization.

> In practice a northwestern settlement was likely to act as a body, but it did so either because its inhabitants were kinsmen or because it contained a man of sufficient wealth to have established personal relations of obligation between himself and individual fellow townsmen not related to him in blood. The Yurok, Karok, and Hupa, and probably several of the adjacent groups, simply did not recognize any organization which transcended individuals and kin groups. (Kroeber 1925:830)

13. Initially described as "village communities" in earlier writings, Kroeber later developed the concept of the tribelet more fully beginning with his 1932 publication, *The Patwin and their Neighbors* (Kroeber 1932). For a more detailed discussion about tribelets, see Lightfoot 2005:42–43.

14. Kroeber (1966:106–108) suggested that these chiefs had "next to no true authority," and that they led more by example and by skilled oration.

15. Kroeber (1925:830–831) initially defined the population of most village communities (except the Yokuts) as averaging only about 100 people. In later years, after more fieldwork had been completed, he argued that the size of most tribelets ranged between 100 and 500 people, usually averaging about 200 to 250 individuals (Kroeber 1966:92).

16. During these interviews, the ethnographers asked questions about traditional material culture, ceremonies, political organization, subsistence practices, myths, and so forth. They collected linguistic information for different Native languages using word lists and early sound recordings.

17. As noted elsewhere (Lightfoot 2005:46–47),

This conflation of time renders these ethnographic reconstructions notoriously difficult to use in the study of culture change. I have become frustrated on more than one occasion because it is not clear whether specific observations depicting social practices, house types, or ceremonial gatherings were about the early twentieth, late nineteenth, or mid-nineteenth centuries, or even earlier times (see for example, Lightfoot et al. 1991:121–145). In reality, the memory culture methodology probably reveals more about the generation of Indians and anthropologists of the late nineteenth and early twentieth century than about some idealized precolonial past.

18. For more information on these archaeological studies, see Fredrickson 1974; C. King 1974; L. King 1969; T.F. King 1970, 1974.

19. Analysis of early European accounts and missionary records indicate the territorial extent of some coastal village communities was not very extensive, with estimates measuring anywhere from 13 to 19 km (8 to 12 mi) across in the San Francisco Bay area (Milliken 1995: 21–24) and from about 15 to 30 km (9 to 19 mi) across in the Santa Barbara Channel area (Johnson 1988:278–281).

20. For details on the house society model, see Lévi-Strauss 1982, 1987. Gillespie (2000) presents an excellent up-to-date overview of house societies (also see other chapters in Joyce and Gillespie 2000), while Joyce (2000) outlines new insights about the Yurok case in particular.

21. House members justified their membership by claiming ties through real or imagined genealogies to ancestors who founded house pedigrees, by inheriting house names that had been used by

deceased members, and by participating in ceremonies, dances, and other public functions that were sponsored by specific houses.

22. Yurok house groups also owned dance regalia, wealth objects, and even the formulas sung at major dances. Social ranking took place within houses, based on such factors as wealth and influence. Houses were also ranked in relation to one another within the village and broader region.

23. There is also a strong possibility that some activities involving entire village communities may not have been fully recorded in twentieth-century ethnographies because by that time many Indian groups had split apart into smaller family groups and no longer functioned as larger social entities (see Lightfoot 2005:chapter 8). As a consequence, early ethnographic descriptions of some kinds of community social gatherings, and communal plant harvesting and hunting activities may not be given the full attention that they deserve.

24. For detailed studies, see chapters in Blackburn and Anderson 1993a; also see Anderson 1996, 2005; Anderson and Moratto 1996; Fowler 1996, 2000; Fowler et al. 2003; Ortiz 2006; Shipek 1989.

25. For excellent sources, see Anderson 2005:55–56; Ortiz 1993, 2006; Peri and Patterson 1993:182–184; Swezey and Heizer 1993:324.

26. See Kennett 2005:183–186; Lambert and Walker 1991:970; Walker et al. 1989:359.

27. See studies by Broughton 1994a; Hildebrandt and Jones 1992; Raab 1996; Raab et al. 2002.

28. For sources on regional population trends, see Glassow 1996:99–103; Jones 2002:8–9; Lambert and Walker 1991:965; Lightfoot and Simmons 1998; Lightfoot et al. 1991:110–112.

29. Most of these studies incorporate tenets of human behavioral ecology or evolutionary ecology into their analyses (see Broughton and O'Connell 1999; Kennett 2005:10–40).

The First Fire Managers

1. For syntheses and case studies about prescribed burning by California Indians, see Anderson 2005; Hammett and Lawlor 2004: 291–291, 343–344; Keter 1995; Lewis 1993; Stewart 2002; Timbrook et al. 1993:121–134. See also Tveskov 2007 for coastal Oregon.

2. Lewis attributes this inattention to the dominant theoretical perspective that viewed fires as largely destructive and hunter-gatherers as passive harvesters of an unmodified natural world (Lewis 1991:264, 2002:21–28).

3. Anderson (2006:419) also points out that Indian burning and its positive ecological purposes for economic plants may have been underrecorded by early ethnographers, as they primarily interviewed Indian men.

4. For example, there are few ethnographic observations of Coast Miwok people involved in pyrodiversity practices (Collier and Thalman 1996). It is not clear whether the paucity of evidence is because the Coast Miwok chose not to participate in prescribed burning, or whether these practices may predate later ethnographic accounts. There is excellent evidence of pyrodiversity activities directly north of Coast Miwok country, where merchants and sailors from the Russian-American Company outpost of Colony Ross observed Kashaya Pomo (and possibly Coast Miwok?) torching parcels of land near the colony. Fedor Lütke (1989:257) described the following account on September 4, 1818.

> When it was completely dark we had a very interesting spectacle: a certain extent of land near the settlement was all afire. The Indians who live in this area eat a wild plant which resembles rye, for which reason our settlers call it *rozhnitsa* [*rozh,* rye]. When the kernels of the rozhnitsa have been harvested, the straw which remains is generally burned. This procedure makes the next year's crop bigger and more flavorful. The fires continued throughout the night.

5. See, for example, Martin and Sapsis 1992:150–152; Skinner and Chang 1996:1043; Sugihara, van Wagtendonk, and Fites-Kaufman 2006.

6. See Miller and Urban 1999a:203; Skinner and Chang 1996: 1043–1044; Sugihara, van Wagtendonk, and Fites-Kaufman 2006: 68–69.

7. For overviews on the benefits of prescribed burning for Indians, see Anderson 2005:135–137, 144–154; Bird et al. 2005; Fowler 1996:91–93; Hallam 1985:13–17; Hammett 1991:21; Jones 1969:226–227; Lewis 1982:50–52; McCarthy 1993:220–224.

8. Consequently, Native foragers pay close attention to each burn: "Most adults can recount when, where and by whom every fire was lit (with details of fire intensity and progression) over at least the three previous seasonal cycles within a radius of about 100 km from the three Outstations" (Bird et al. 2005:449).

9. For more on fire seasonality, see Fowler 1996:92; Lewis 1993: 66, 73, 93–94, 103–105; Timbrook et al. 1993:147.

10. See Miller and Urban 1999a:203; Swetnam 1993:888. Crown fires can quickly spread in windy conditions through long-distance spotting, where particles of burning fuel loft above the canopy and

torch trees in a chain reaction that instantaneously spreads the conflagration (Pyne 1991:37).

11. For more detailed discussions, see Martin and Sapsis 1992: 150; Pyne 1991:42; van Wagtendonk 1986:5, 2006.

12. Mediterranean climates like California's tend not to be conducive to the rapid decomposition of many woody fuels (van Wagtendonk 2006:38).

13. See Pyne 1991:39 for an Australian example.

14. It was probably more common, however, for montane forests in the lower elevations of the Sierra Nevada to have experienced return intervals of eight to 12 years (Lewis 1982:57; Miller and Urban 1999a:210; van Wagtendonk 1986:6).

15. For sources on fire intervals in different vegetation types, see Bendix 2002:286–288; Miller and Urban 1999b:115; Minnich 1998; van Wagtendonk 1986:5–6.

16. See, for example, Kilgore and Taylor 1979:138 for the Sierra Nevada. As Pyne (1991:35–36) elucidates,

> Burning is patchy, combustion incomplete, and the more complex the fuel, the more complicated the fire. Under normal circumstances fires will burn more fiercely in summer than in winter, along exposed ridges better than within sheltered ravines, in open forests more vigorously than in closed. Only during times of severe droughts—when all fuels, living and dead, small and large, are drained of moisture—can a fire burn with relative disregard for local nuances of fuel moisture. Under such conditions everything burns, and fire intensity correlates closely with fuel quantity. Where the climate makes fire routinely possible, where ignition is abundant and reliable, fire history follows fuel history.

17. See Kilgore and Taylor 1979:138–139; Minnich 2006:33–35; Swetnam 1993:887–888.

18. For more detail, see Carle 2008:13–14; Keeley 2002:304–305; Minnich 2006:20–24; van Wagtendonk 1986:4–5; Wills 2006:296.

19. Recent fire ecology research indicates that some kinds of natural features, such as ridgetops, riparian corridors, aspect changes, basalt flows, and debris flows, can influence local fuel loads, fuel moisture, and the spread of fires (Skinner and Taylor 2006:203, 213; Skinner et al. 2006:179; Wills 2006:313).

20. This is based on species diversity for shrubland (per tenth hectare) under pre- and postfire conditions, as reported by Keeley (2002:310). For an Australian example see Pyne 1991:40.

21. For more information see Bean and Lawton 1976:39; Keeley 2002:311; Lewis 1993:72; Shaffer and Laudenslayer 2006:129, 135.

22. See Anderson 1996:417–418; Menke 1992:24; Timbrook et al. 1993:138–144.

23. For more information on these methods, see Anderson 2002: 48; Carle 2008:30–32; Kilgore and Taylor 1979:130–133; Minnich et al. 2000; Skinner and Chang 1996:1043–1044; van Wagtendonk and Fites-Kaufman 2006:270.

24. For example, there is some controversy as to whether low-severity surface fires will be reflected in the fire scar and dendro-chronological records from old trees and stumps (Anderson 2002:54; Bowman 1998:392). Concerns have also been raised about the dating of past fire events. Some scholars advocate the use of master fire chronologies that dendrochronologically cross-date fire events across broad regions, a method that allows investigators to track fires across adjacent patches (Caprio and Swetnam 1995:175–176). Questions also exist about the interpretation of charcoal recovered from sediments—about whether small, low-severity surface fires can be detected and whether the advent of regular burning practices by hunter-gatherers would result in high or low charcoal concentrations (Hallam 1985:11–13; Timbrook et al. 1993:146).

25. See, for example, Carle 2008:47, 67; Riegel et al. 2006:243, 248; Skinner and Taylor 2006:201–202; Skinner et al. 2006:176; Stuart and Stephens 2006:152–153; van Wagtendonk and Fites-Kaufman 2006:270, 278, 280; Wills 2006:300–303, 307. The one major exception is the Southern Deserts Province, where low fuel loads and discontinuous distributions of fuels at low elevations can hinder fire spread, resulting in patchy spatial patterns of burns with long return intervals (Brooks and Minnich 2006:397, 402; Stephens et al. 2007: 208). Our perception is that the nature of the fire regimes of the Southern Deserts Province and adjacent Great Basin vary significantly from those found within the more cismontane region of California—the squeezed Q of the great ring of mountains and its coastal tail.

26. See, for example, Carle 2008:14–17; Davis and Borchert 2006: 333; Riegel et al. 2006:238; Skinner et al. 2006:176; Wills 2006:300.

27. Since fire is an integral part of ecological processes in most plant communities in California (Fites-Kaufman et al. 2006:94), one might simply dismiss this association between economically important plants and fire-stimulated species as fortuitous. But it raises an important question beyond the scope of this book. Is the strong relationship a product of a long-term coevolutionary process stimulated by the pyrodiversity practices of hunter-gatherers over many hundreds of years on the resources that they had come to rely on? Significantly, this kind of relationship does not appear to be evident

east of the cismontane region (the squeezed Q topographic landscape) of California, such as in the adjacent Great Basin borderlands, where important economic resources, such as the juniper and pinyon woodlands, are fire inhibited and will not survive fire regimes characterized by frequent burns (Brooks and Minnich 2006:406–407).

28. See, for example, Brooks and Minnich 2006:407; Carle 2008: 41–42, 48–50, 68, 73; Riegel et al. 2006:230, 239–242; Skinner and Taylor 2006:220; Skinner et al. 2006:178–179; Stuart and Stephens 2006:164; van Wagtendonk and Fites-Kaufman 2006:273, 280; also see Keter 1995. Case examples are presented about how fire-suppression practices have influenced the spread of conifers in oak woodlands, chaparral into grasslands, and juniper woodlands or juniper and pinyon woodlands into sagebrush steppe communities. Other factors that make contemporary fire regimes very distinctive from those of the past are the invasive nonnative plants, livestock grazing, and modern landscape modifications that have altered the timing, spread, and intensity of fires (Sugihara and Barbour 2006: 6–7).

29. See, for example, Anderson 2006:419; Kilgore and Taylor 1979: 138; Lewis 1993:74–77; van Wagtendonk 1986:6.

30. See Keeley 2006:382; Skinner et al. 2006:179; Wills 2006:313–315.

31. Caprio and Swetnam (1995) attribute this difference of interpretation to their use of cross-dating techniques that allowed them to connect fire events across elevational gradients and vegetation types.

32. For example, studies of Tasmanian hunter-gatherers indicate that there is no necessary relationship between the complexity of tool kits and the sophistication of Native fire management programs.

They Are Not Farmers

1. "Protoagriculture" is technically defined as the "the cultivation of morphologically wild plants by hunter-gatherers" (Keeley 1995:245). Heizer (1958:20–23) wrote some years ago that Native California was in a "Preformative stage" (or possibly even Formative stage) during late prehistory based on the productive, dependable acorn economy, supplemented by "hunting, fishing, fowling, root, greens, and small-seed collecting." Given the abundant and assured food supply, he believed that California could be defined as "semi-agricultural." Ziegler (1968:64) referred to the acorn-salmon complex in north-central California as "quasi-agricultural," affording Native Californians the leisure time and the opportunity to pursue "non-vital occupations," as did many agrarian societies. In a similar vein,

Bean and Lawton (1976:48) argued that the hunter-gatherer economies in California "may have been analogous to many primitive agriculture societies elsewhere." Anderson (2005) builds on these earlier works and makes a strong case for protoagricultural practices in Native California in her new book.

> Most if not all of the cultural groups in aboriginal California could claim an intermediate spot in this gradation [between foraging and farming] because they enhanced and intensified food resources by practicing various forms of resource and land management. Many of these management practices, along with selective harvesting strategies, were the same as those utilized in early agriculture to increase yields of the edible parts of domesticated plants. The protoagricultural techniques used by native people altered natural environments enough to put artificial selective pressures on many species of desirable plants, setting them on the path to domestication. In a few cases (e.g., devil's claw, discussed in Chapter 5), domesticated varieties of desirable plant species may have actually been created by the time Euro-Americans began to settle California, and many other species were arguably in a state of incipient or intermediate domestication. (Anderson 2005:252–253)

2. See also the discussion by Baumhoff 1963:229–230.

3. See, for example, Gamble 2002; Kennett 2005:188–193; Rick, Erlandson, et al. 2005; Rick et al. 2001, 2002.

4. In a recent overview of over 150 plant taxa documented from charred seeds and nut fragments recovered from archaeological sites across the state, Hammett and Lawlor (2004:296) succinctly state: "Overall, California ethnobotanical diversity is astounding." Wohlgemuth's (2004:71–72, 141) massive synthesis of ethnobotanical remains from prehistoric archaeological contexts largely supports an observation of increasing diversification in late prehistory. Acorn nutshells are more common than remains of other plant taxa in many local regions, but this varies by time and space. Some seed plants, such as fescues (*Vulpia* spp.), goosefoots (*Chenopodium* spp.), maygrasses (*Phalaris* spp.), native barleys (*Hordeum* spp.), and hairgrasses (*Deschampsia* spp.), which are fairly common in archaeological samples in some provinces, are barely mentioned in the ethnographic literature. Conversely, some berries, greens, and roots, now recognized as important food sources by ethnographers, are underrepresented in archaeological contexts, most likely due to the slim chance that these resources would have been charred in food preparation and then preserved in the archaeological record.

Wohlgemuth's (2004) summary of archaeological data from a

plethora of site reports demonstrates that there is great regional variation in the kinds of plant resources used by California Indian groups (see also Hammett and Lawlor 2004). In examining the ubiquity or presence of nuts, berries, roots, fruit capsules, and seeds in archaeological samples, there is a clear trend in most regions for increasing diversity of species from early prehistoric periods to the late prehistoric and early historic periods, the latter beginning about 1,200 years ago. It is amazing how many different species are represented in archaeological samples dating to this later time span. For example, samples from the Great Central Valley dating to either the Lower or Upper Emergent phases contain seven species of nuts, seven species of berries, two root species, one fruit capsule (clarkia [*Clarkia* sp.]), and 39 species of seeds.

There is also good evidence for the increasing diversification of animal resources in archaeological sites in late prehistory, as noted in the discussion of resource intensification in the chapter "The Uniqueness of California." Native hunters captured large game and anadromous fishes, whenever available, but also harvested a wide range of smaller game, birds, fishes, shellfish, and insects. New technologies in marine fishing along some areas of the coast also allowed for the exploitation of a wider range of marine fishes. This point is exemplified along the South Coast Province, where innovations in boat design and fishing technology provided the ability to go after an increasing number of deepwater fishes, such as tunas (*Thunnus* spp.), Swordfish (*Xiphias gladius*), and mako sharks (Lamnidae) (see Rick, Erlandson, et al. 2005:209–210). Thus, Native Californian subsistence practices in late prehistory and early historic times are characterized by an increase in diet breadth and the continued diversification of both plant and animal resources.

5. As Harrington (1932:9) noted,

Their agriculture consisted of producing potash for raising tobacco by burning logs and brush at the site of the garden to be sometime previous to the sowing, of scattering the seeds at the right season, of harrowing the seed in, of weeding the plants, and of harvesting the leaves, stems and seeds with careful attention, extending over a considerable period. What they did not do was to till the soil about the plants, which was unnecessary and closely approached in process by their dragging a bush over the sown ground and by weeding, and to irrigate or water them, which was unnecessary.

6. See, for example, Keeley 1995:263–265. As Harrington (1932:9) emphasized for one of the groups he studied,

This sole position in Karuk agriculture was occupied, not by a food plant, but by a drug; not by a plant lost to nature, but by one still growing wild all over the Karuk country, but which the Indians were cultivating and endeavoring to breed along a different road from the wild tobacco by always sowing seed taken from their tobacco gardens, solely for the purpose of making it "*ikpihan*" ("strong").

7. Anderson (2005:262), in her citation of California Indians who sowed seeds to produce wild plant foods, relies on the original synthesis of Driver and Massey (1957:225, 228), who identified seven groups (Modoc, Eastern Shasta, Achumawi, Northestern Maidu, Nisenan, Mojave, and Quechan). Unfortunately, these groups are simply listed in a footnote in the Driver and Massey publication, and no information is presented on the kinds of cultivation practices employed. Anderson also lists other ethnographic sightings of seed broadcasting among the Chumash, Wappo, and the Paiute on the east side of the Sierra Nevada. Keeley (1995:264), however, does not include the Northeastern (Foothill) Maidu and the Nisenan because the information is uncertain. We question the degree to which seed sowing was regularly integrated into the annual schedule of most Chumash people, given the paucity of information on this cultivation practice in ethnohistorical and ethnographic accounts. The Wappo, situated in the North Coast Ranges of Napa Valley, are clearly an interesting outlier when considering the arid habitats of most of the other seed-sowing groups.

8. For example, see definitions in Harris 1989:19–20; Price and Gebauer 1995b:6; Yen 1989.

9. See, for example, Harris 1989:19; Wills 1988:2. Smith (2001:1) recognizes agriculturalists as people who "strongly depend on domesticated species as food sources."

10. In discussing maize agriculture in the adjacent American Southwest, Wills (1988) stresses that Native farmers had to carefully tend and monitor their crops to make sure they were not consumed by insects, birds, and animals or hurt by competition from other plants.

> It is not surprising that New World ethnographic data provide abundant evidence that corn production involves nearly constant monitoring by cultivators….A careful reading of the ethnohistory of certain North American groups does not support the assumption that they practiced untended maize cultivation. (Wills 1988:40)

11. In their comprehensive review of ethnobotanical remains from archaeological sites, Hammett and Lawlor (2004:345) conclude that "little unequivocal archaeobotanical evidence exists for plant

domestication or the use of domesticated plants in Native California." Anderson (2005:160) cites the devil's claw *(Proboscidea parviflora)* as an example of indigenous domestication in the American Southwest, Great Basin, and California. But it appears this plant was first domesticated in southern Arizona by the Akimel O'odham and Tohona O'odham (Desert Papago) people for basketry fiber, probably in the late 1800s, as the demand for baskets increased among non-Indian settlers (Nabhan and Rea 1987:60–61). It was then introduced shortly thereafter to Native peoples in the Great Basin and the Southern Deserts Province of California, probably as part of the broader Sonoran Desert complex of domesticates that were adopted and experimented with in late prehistoric and historic times.

Wohlgemuth (2004:125–133) identifies native barley and maygrass as two other possible indigenous domesticates in Native California (see also Hammett and Lawlor 2004:345; Koerper et al. 2002: 72). Metric analysis of plant remains recovered from archaeological contexts shows marked increases in seed size over time. These changes may have resulted from cultural selection for larger seed volume, which may have precipitated genetic transformations in native barley and maygrass plants. Wohlgemuth also notes, however, that these changes could have resulted from other factors, such as a regularized regime of controlled burning or the movement of plants to new habitats as part of settlement shifts. He concludes, "There is no means to determine which alternative best accounts for the increase in seed size based on current metric data" (Wohlgemuth 2004:134).

12. In a classic paper, Wilke et al. (1972) argue that the traditional harvesting methods widely used by Native people in California and the Great Basin may have selected against the domestication of indigenous seed crops. The use of seed beaters, either a wooden or basket paddle, to knock ripened seeds into baskets is widely documented in Native California. As outlined by Wilke et al., this harvesting method not only disperses some seeds through spillage across the local habitat, but it selects for plants that have wild genetic characteristics that enhance natural seed dispersal, thus ensuring that wild genotypes will be perpetuated. Even if the seeds from these plants are harvested, then used the following year to reseed plots, the characteristics of the wild plant population will continue to thrive in the local area.

Hillman and Davies's (1990:172–173) experimentation with different methods of harvesting wild wheats and barleys in the Near East showed that seed beating is among the most efficient harvesting techniques in dry weather. It involves the least stooping and effort and yet produces the greatest yields per unit of time. Their research empirically supports the points outlined by Wilke et al. (1972).

Some spikelets from brittle-rachised ears invariably fall to the ground during harvest, and if the farmer relies on these for next year's crop, this will be of the wild type. Likewise, new plots sown from the harvested seed will be entirely of the wild type. Harvesting by beating thus selects strongly in favor of the wild type and against tough-rachised forms, regardless of what other husbandry practices accompany it. (Hillman and Davies 1990:172)

13. Koenig et al. (1994:105), in a study of five oak species in the Central Coast Province, observed an individual tree *(Quercus lobata)* producing good harvests 10 out of 12 years. But this level of production is relatively rare—most trees may produce a bumper crop, then a year or two of small or mediocre crops before yielding another good or bumper supply of acorns.

14. Although local climatic conditions may play a role, other factors such as wind pollination, predator satiation, and seed dispersal issues may also be important (Koenig et al. 1994). Whatever the local causes, Native Californians had to cope with variable acorn production. McCarthy (1993:215–216) stresses that in local regions supporting only one or two species of harvestable oak trees, there may be serious shortages of acorns between good or bumper years. Even in regions where five species are found, such as in the study area investigated by Koenig et al., there may be some years when few acorns are available. In examining the data for their 12-year study, we note that for two years (1983, 1991) the average yields for all five species of oak trees were low to nonexistent (see Koenig et al. 1994:fig. 1).

15. Large game (deer, Elk, Pronghorn, *[Odocoileus* spp., *Cervus elaphus, Antilocapra americana]*), anadromous fishes (Chinook Salmon, Coho Salmon, Steelhead *[Oncorhynchus tshawytscha, O. kisutch, O. mykiss irideus]*), and various pine nuts (including pinyon pines *[Pinus* spp.] in the Southern Deserts Province and Great Basin) are recognized as important resources because of their potential for producing bulk harvests that can be processed en masse for storage. But they can all vary greatly in productivity across time and space. In late prehistoric times, the overexploitation of large game in some regions made deer, Elk, and Pronghorn increasingly difficult and costly to obtain. Salmon and Steelhead runs also vary in intensity from year to year and stream to stream, depending upon water flow, water temperature, and other critical conditions (Baumhoff 1963: 170–171; Gould 1975:162). And not unlike acorn masts, pine nut harvests are notorious for their significant variation in location and abundance from year to year (Bettinger 1976:92; Farris 1993; Thomas 1974).

16. In comparing Native Californian subsistence practices with agrarian economies, it is important to stress that there are many types

of agriculture, some of which emphasize species diversity in food production. Some scholars believe that the initial experimentation with and adoption of early domesticates among complex hunter-gatherers took place in order for groups to augment resource diversity by adding new resources to their mix of wild plant and animal foods (Price and Gebauer 1995b:7–8; Smith 1995:212–213). Flannery (1969) among others, defined this process of diversifying subsistence strategies in the initial stages of agrarian production as part of the "broad-spectrum" revolution. In considering the adoption of domesticates in the American Southwest, Wills (1988, 1995:241–242) emphasizes that hunter-gatherer groups added these resources to an already diverse range of plant and animal foods primarily to reduce risk and uncertainty in the face of environmental perturbations. He notes that hunter-gatherer people did not initially adopt domesticates to become farmers, but rather to maintain themselves as effective foragers. Thus, there is some evidence to support the idea that farming took place among hunter-gatherers as a means of diversifying their resource base. In some cases, domesticated species may serve simply as replacements for wild plants that occupy similar niches in the understory and overstory, where herbs, shrubs, climbers, and tree crops are grown, along with wild species that thrive in disturbed settings (Harris 1969:6–7). Archaeological and ethnographic research has shown that it is not uncommon for some societies to maintain so-called mixed economies or low-level food production that involves some components of hunting and gathering along with the raising of domesticates in small-scale gardens or through swidden agriculture (Harris 1989:19–20; Smith 2001; Tucker 2006; Winterhalder and Kennett 2006:4).

17. For a more detailed discussion of this settlement pattern, see Beaton 1991; Fredrickson 1989; Lightfoot 1997:136; Lightfoot et al. 1991:112–114. A possible exception to this pattern may be found among the Chumash people in the South Coast Province. Jeanne Arnold et al. (Arnold 2001b) have made a strong case for arguing that some of the late prehistoric and early historic Chumash communities were organized into simple chiefdoms with hereditary leaders who controlled access to labor, the production of shell beads and other objects of wealth, ownership of ocean-going canoes, and trade routes between the mainland and islands. Although no one doubts the political complexity of the Chumash, there is some debate about how they were organized on a regional scale. Johnson's (2000) investigation of the regional distribution of Chumash mainland and island settlements concludes that they may have been characterized by a heterarchical organization, in which politically autonomous villages

and even households participated individually in economic specialization, exchange, and resources exploitation. Kennett's (2005: 110) detailed settlement analysis for historic Chumash villages on the northern Channel Islands suggests that these settlements were "relatively autonomous politically."

> These data also suggest that the economic force of diversification dominated the economic and political system. That is, relatively small autonomous villages are scattered across the landscape, maximizing access to resource locations and raw material sources. Political autonomy neither rules out economic interdependence between individuals in different villages in Chumash territory nor the periodic integration of villages into larger political units as suggested by the ethnohistoric record. (Kennett 2005:101–111)

Although the studies by Johnson and Kennett do not preclude the existence of broader political confederacies or chiefdoms, their analyses do not suggest that well-defined settlement hierarchies, such as those found among agrarian societies in the American Southwest and elsewhere, are characteristic of Chumash societies.

18. No one has said this better than Robert Heizer (1978:649):

> California...was a region holding a large number of societies that had limited knowledge, understanding, experience, and tolerance of neighboring peoples. California Indians, while perhaps knowing individuals in neighboring tribelets, for the most part lived out their lives mainly within their own limited and familiar territory. Nothing illustrates more the deep-seated provincialism and attachment to the place of their birth of California Indians than the abundantly documented wish for persons who died away from home to have their bodies (or their ashes if the distance was too great) returned for burial at their natal village. Living out the span of existence from birth to death within an area bounded by a horizon lying not more than 10 or 15 miles from one's village and not having talked to more than 100 different persons in a whole life must have made one's world small, familiar, safe and secure.

19. See, for example, Bean and Theodoratus 1978; Ericson 1977; Hollimon 2000; Hudson and Blackburn 1978; Hughes 1989; Johnson 1988:252–272, 2000; King 1976; Milliken 1995:23–24, 30.

20. See, for example, Gamble 1991; Johnson 2000:311; King 1976: 301–302; Vayda 1967.

21. We base this idea, in part, on the difficulties that archaeologists have experienced in detecting discrete boundaries between ethnographically described tribal entities using various classes of material

culture, especially in examining the distribution of obsidian artifacts across space (see Lightfoot and Martinez 1995:480–481).

22. Smith (2001:15, 30–33) defines complex hunter-gatherers such as found in California as groups that practiced low-level food production without domesticates. He emphasizes that this kind of management of plant resources may represent a relatively long-term stable pattern that did not result in the development of more intensive forms of agriculture.

23. For example, Wallace (1980:271) emphasizes that the adoption of domesticates by the Timbisha Shoshone of Death Valley did not revolutionize traditional hunting and gathering activities but was merely incorporated into them.

> Whatever its source, crop raising made no great impress on Death Valley Indian life and culture. To be sure, its introduction meant a little more food and a more diversified diet. But native gardens did not produce enough to allow for abandonment of or even substantial alteration in the foraging-hunting pattern of subsistence that had endured for centuries. Nor did the addition of horticulture to the native economy result in a sudden elaboration of technology. Mostly, implements and techniques already in use were adapted to the needs of farming and the processing of its products.

Shackley (2004:32) notes that the Eastern Kumeyaay simply included corn and other domesticates into the seasonal round of local groups.

> It appears that cultigens were simply seen as another storable food resource like agave or acorns, and little investment in time was devoted to an agricultural lifeway (Shackley 1981, 1984, 1990). Groups regularly practicing agriculture in the Mexicali Valley would just as regularly harvest agave in the desert foothills 60 km west and acorns in the mountains 100 km west, and exploit marine resources at San Diego Bay 200 km west, whenever the floodwaters were insufficient for farming. Apparently, after planting in the late spring, the fields were not necessarily tended, particularly if the agave harvest was especially good that year.

Where We Go from Here

1. The Expedition Program at Roosevelt Middle School, sponsored by University-Community Links at University of California, Berkeley, was established by Charles Underwood and Tamara Sturak

of the University of California Links Office, and Professors Ruth Tringham and Margaret Conkey of the Department of Anthropology, University of California, Berkeley.

2. For some recent examples, see Anderson 2005:312–318; Carle 2008:122–128; Husari et al. 2006:460–462; Menke 1992; Nicola 1995; Ortiz 2006:33; Parsons et al. 1986.

3. In addition to the issues listed, a particularly troublesome problem involving prescribed burning is the continued construction of housing in former wildlands, thereby expanding the wildland-urban interface. As this interface continues to grow throughout much of California, the difficulty of implementing prescribed burning programs increases. Another difficult issue concerns air quality regulations and the limited window that is available to many land managers in scheduling prescribed burns. But as Husari et al. (2006:457) emphasize, small, low-severity controlled burns produce much less smoke than uncontrolled wild fires. For various perspectives on prescribed burning and problems facing its systematic implementation across the state, see Ahuja 2006; Brooks and Minnich 2006:408–413; Carle 2008:125–126, 131–132; Davis and Borchert 2006:345; Husari et al. 2006; Keeley 2006:381–382; Menke 1992; Riegel et al. 2006:256; Shaffer 2006; Skinner and Taylor 2006:220; van Wagtendonk and Fites-Kaufman 2006:289–290; Wills 2006:316.

4. See, for example, Bird and Ikerd 1993; Lubchenco et al. 1991; Matson et al. 1997; Wartzman 2007.

5. This particular movement is known as the New Ruralism (see Wartzman 2007:18).

6. See Fowler et al. 2003; Nicola 1995; Ruppert 2003.

California Indian Uses of Natural Resources

1. The six geomorphic provinces include the Northwest, Central Coast, Southern Coast, Northeast, Great Central Valley and Sierra Nevada, and Southern Deserts. As discussed in the chapter "A Landscape of Unparalleled Diversity," we are not including the Great Basin or Lower Colorado River provinces in this book about California hunter-gatherers.

2. We recognize that the specific temporal relationship for the use of some resources may be ambiguous. For example, the rich descriptions of some of the early ethnographic reports may be referencing early twentieth-century cultural practices, while other studies employing the memory culture methodology may be referring to tools, techniques, and resources employed by much earlier generations of Native people. Furthermore, we are aware that the twentieth-century

ethnographic descriptions were written after major disruptions had already occurred in the so-called traditional Native communities, as colonial encounters resulted in significant environmental transformations, horrific population decline, loss of Indian lands, and government prohibitions of pyrodiversity practices. Thus, we look at this guide as a work in progress—many of the ethnographic observations, archaeological findings, and Native oral traditions still need to be critically evaluated to provide better temporal placement. We use the past tense to describe the so-called late prehistoric/early historic traditional pyrodiversity collecting practices, but employ the present tense when relating these practices to contemporary Indian groups in California.

3. A recent poll by the Public Policy Institute of California indicates that almost 50 percent of teenagers either did not participate at all or participated only once in an outdoor nature activity such as hiking, backpacking, or camping during the summer of 2007. This is part of a documented national trend in which our youth are spending less and less time outdoors. Known as the "nature deficit disorder," polls and interviews have shown that young people today would rather spend time in a mall or in front of a video screen than experience a national or state park, "where there is nothing to do." *San Francisco Chronicle* writer Peter Fimrite quoted one 15-year-old as saying, "I'd rather be at the mall because you can enjoy yourself walking around looking at stuff as opposed to the woods....In Yosemite and other parks the only thing you look at is the trees, grass, and sky." The fact that many children are no longer playing outside or appreciating what nature has to offer has spawned a national "children and nature" movement. Spurred on by Richard Louv's influential book, *Last Child in the Woods: Saving our Children from Nature-Deficit Order,* this movement has initiated the "Leave No Child Inside" campaign in an attempt to reconnect our youth to the natural environment. For information on these studies and the children and nature movement, see Fimrite 2007; Children and Nature Network, www.cnaturenet .org; Public Policy Institute of California, www.ppic.org.

GENERAL REFERENCES

Acken, C.S. 1976. How Indians caught wild pigeons. In *A collection of ethnographical articles on the California Indians,* edited by R.F. Heizer, 56. Ballena Press Publications in Archaeology, Ethnology, and History, no. 7. Ramona, CA: Ballena Press.

Ahuja, S. 2006. Fire and air resources. In *Fires in California's ecosystems,* edited by N.G. Sugihara, J.W. van Wagtendonk, K.E. Shaffer, J. Fites-Kaufman, and A.E. Thode, 481–498. Berkeley: University of California Press.

Allen, R. 1998. *Native Americans at Mission Santa Cruz, 1791–1834: Interpreting the archaeological record.* Perspectives in California Archaeology, vol. 5. Los Angeles: Institute of Archaeology, University of California.

Ames, K.M. 2002. Going by boat: The forager-collector continuum at sea. In *Beyond foraging and collecting: Evolutionary change in hunter-gatherer settlement systems,* edited by B. Fitzhugh and J. Habu, 19–52. New York: Kluwer-Plenum Publishing Corp.

Anderson, M.K. 1996. The ethnobotany of deergrass, *Muhlenbergia rigen* (Poaceae): Its uses and fire management by California and Indian tribes. *Economic Botany* 50 (4): 409–422.

Anderson, M.K. 2002. An ecological critique. In *Forgotten fires: Native Americans and the transient wilderness,* edited by H.T. Lewis and M.K. Anderson, 37–64. Norman: University of Oklahoma Press.

Anderson, M.K. 2005. *Tending the wild: Native American knowledge and the management of California's natural resources.* Berkeley: University of California Press.

Anderson, M.K. 2006. The use of fire by Native Americans in California. In *Fires in California's ecosystems,* edited by N.G. Sugihara, J.W. van Wagtendonk, K.E. Shaffer, J. Fites-Kaufman, and A.E. Thode, 417–430. Berkeley: University of California Press.

Anderson, M.K., and M.J. Moratto. 1996. Native American land-use practices and ecological impacts. In *Assessments and scientific basis for management options,* 187–206. Vol. 2 of *Sierra Nevada*

Ecosystem Project: Final report to Congress. Davis: University of California, Davis, Centers for Water and Wildland Resources.

Anderson, R.S., and S.L. Carpenter. 1991. Vegetation change in Yosemite Valley, Yosemite National Park, California, during the protohistoric period. *Madrono* 38 (1): 1–13.

Antevs, E. 1955. Geologic-climatic dating in the West. *American Antiquity* 20 (4): 317–335.

Arnold, J.E. 1992. Complex hunter-gatherer-fishers of prehistoric California: Chiefs, specialists, and maritime adaptations of the Channel Islands. *American Antiquity* 57 (1): 60–84.

Arnold, J.E. 1995. Transportation innovation and social complexity among maritime hunter-gatherer societies. *American Anthropologist* 97:733–747.

Arnold, J.E. 2001a. The Chumash in world and regional perspectives. In *The origins of a Pacific Coast chiefdom: The Chumash of the Channel Islands,* edited by J.E. Arnold, 1–20. Salt Lake City: University of Utah Press.

Arnold, J.E., editor. 2001b. *The origins of Pacific Coast chiefdom: The Chumash of the Channel Islands.* Salt Lake City: University of Utah Press.

Arnold, J.E., R. Colten, and S. Pletka. 1997. Contexts of cultural change in insular California. *American Antiquity* 62 (2): 300–318.

Arnold, J.E., and A.P. Graesch. 2001. The evolution of specialized shellworking among the Island Chumash. In *The origins of a Pacific Coast chiefdom: The Chumash of the Channel Islands,* edited by J.E. Arnold, 71–112. Salt Lake City: University of Utah Press.

Arnold, J.E., M.R. Walsh, and S.E. Hollimon. 2004. The archaeology of California. *Journal of Archaeological Research* 12 (1): 1–74.

Baker, M.A. 1981. The ethnobotany of the Yurok, Tolowa, and Karok Indians of Northwest California. M.A. thesis, Humboldt State University, Arcata, CA.

Barrett, S.A. 1910. The material culture of the Klamath Lake and Modoc Indians of northeastern California and southern Oregon. *University of California Publications in American Archaeology and Ethnology* 5 (4): 239–293.

Barrett, S.A. 1936. The army worm: A food of the Pomo Indians. In *Essays in anthropology presented to A.L. Kroeber on his sixtieth birthday, June 11, 1936,* edited by R.H. Lowie, 1–5. Berkeley: University of California Press.

Barrett, S.A. 1952. *Material aspects of Pomo culture.* Parts 1 and 2. Bulletin of the Public Museum of the City of Milwaukee, 20. Milwaukee, WI: Public Museum of the City of Milwaukee.

Barrett, S.A. 1975. Pomo buildings. In *Seven early accounts of the Pomo Indians and their culture,* edited by R.F. Heizer, 37–63. Berkeley: University of California Archaeological Research Facility.

Barrett, S.A., and E.W. Gifford. 1933. *Miwok material culture.* Milwaukee, WI: Public Museum of the City of Milwaukee.

Barrows, D.P. 1900. *The ethno-botany of the Coahuilla Indians of southern California.* Chicago: University of Chicago Press (reprinted in 1971 by Malki Museum Press).

Basgall, M.E. 1987. Resource intensification among hunter-gatherers: Acorn economies in prehistoric California. *Research in Economic Anthropology* 9:21–52.

Baumhoff, M.A. 1963. Ecological determination of aboriginal California populations. *University of California Publications in American Archaeology and Ethnology* 49 (2): 155–236.

Baumhoff, M.A. 1978. Environmental background. In *Handbook of North American Indians,* vol. 8: *California,* edited by R.F. Heizer, 16–24. Washington, DC: Smithsonian Institution.

Beals, R.L. 1933. Ethnology of the Nisenan. *University of California Publications in American Archaeology and Ethnology* 31 (6): 333–414.

Bean, L.J. 1972. *Mukat's people: The Cahuilla Indians of southern California.* Berkeley: University of California Press.

Bean, L.J., and T.C. Blackburn, editors. 1976. *Native Californians: A theoretical retrospective.* Ramona, CA: Ballena Press.

Bean, L.J., and T.F. King, editors. 1974. *'Antap: California Indian political and economic organization.* Ramona, CA: Ballena Press.

Bean, L.J., and H. Lawton. 1976. Some explanations for the rise of cultural complexity in Native California with comments on proto-agriculture and agriculture. In *Native Californians: A theoretical retrospective,* edited by L.J. Bean and T.C. Blackburn, 19–48. Menlo Park, CA: Ballena Press.

Bean, L.J., and K.S. Saubel. 1972. *Temalpakh: Cahuilla Indian knowledge and usage of plants.* Banning, CA: Malki Museum Press.

Bean, L.J., and F.C. Shipek. 1978. Luiseño. In *Handbook of North American Indians,* vol. 8: *California,* edited by R.F. Heizer, 550–563. Washington, DC: Smithsonian Institution.

Bean, L.J., and C.R. Smith. 1978a. Cupeño. In *Handbook of North American Indians,* vol. 8: *California,* edited by R.F. Heizer, 588–591. Washington, DC: Smithsonian Institution.

Bean, L.J., and C.R. Smith. 1978b. Gabrielino. In *Handbook of North American Indians,* vol. 8: *California,* edited by R.F. Heizer, 538–549. Washington, DC: Smithsonian Institution.

Bean, L.J., and C.R. Smith. 1978c. Serrano. In *Handbook of North American Indians*, vol. 8: *California*, edited by R.F. Heizer, 570–574. Washington, DC: Smithsonian Institution.

Bean, L.J., and D. Theodoratus. 1978. Western Pomo and Northeastern Pomo. In *Handbook of North American Indians*, vol. 8: *California*, edited by R.F. Heizer, 289–305. Washington, DC: Smithsonian Institution.

Beard, Y.S. 1977. *The Wappo: A report.* Banning, CA: Malki Museum Press, Morongo Indian Reservation.

Beaton, J.M. 1991. Extensification and intensification in central California prehistory. *Antiquity* 65:946–952.

Bendix, J. 2002. Pre-European fire in California chaparral. In *Fire, native peoples, and the natural landscape*, edited by T.R. Vale, 269–293. Covelo, CA: Island Press.

Benedict, R. 1924. A brief sketch of Serrano culture. *American Anthropologist* 26 (3): 366–392.

Bettinger, R.L. 1976. The development of pinyon exploitation in central eastern California. *Journal of California Anthropology* 3 (1): 81–95.

Bickel, P. 1978. Changing sea levels along the California coast: Anthropological implications. *Journal of California Anthropology* 5:6–20.

Bicknell, S.H., and E.M. Mackey. 1998. Mysterious nativity of California's sea fig. *Fremontia* 26 (1): 3–11.

Bird, D.W., R.B. Bird, and C.H. Parker. 2005. Aboriginal burning regimes and hunting strategies in Australia's Western Desert. *Human Ecology* 33 (4): 443–464.

Bird, G.W., and J. Ikerd. 1993. Sustainable agriculture: A twenty-first-century system. *Annals of the American Academy of Political and Social Sciences* 529:92–102.

Blackburn, T.C. 1976. Ceremonial integration and aborigional interaction in aboriginal California. In *Native Californians: A theoretical retrospective*, edited by L.J. Bean and T.C. Blackburn, 225–244. Menlo Park, CA: Ballena Press.

Blackburn, T.C., and K. Anderson, editors. 1993a. *Before the wilderness: Environmental management by native Californians.* Menlo Park, CA: Ballena Press.

Blackburn, T.C., and K. Anderson. 1993b. Introduction: Managing the domesticated environment. In *Before the wilderness: Environmental management by native Californians*, edited by T.C. Blackburn and K. Anderson, 15–25. Menlo Park, CA: Ballena Press.

Blackburn, T.C., and L.J. Bean. 1978. Kitanemuk. In *Handbook of North American Indians,* vol. 8: *California,* edited by R.F. Heizer, 564–569. Washington, DC: Smithsonian Institution.

Bowman, D.M.J.S. 1998. The impact of aboriginal landscape burning on the Australian biota. *New Phytologist* 140:385–410.

Brawley, S. 2006/2007. Sixteenth annual basketweavers' gathering. *News from Native California* 20 (2): 37–40.

Breschini, G.S., and T. Haversat. 2004. *The Esselen Indians of the Big Sur country: The land and the people.* Salinas, CA: Coyote Press.

Bright, W. 1978. Karok. In *Handbook of North American Indians,* vol. 8: *California,* edited by R.F. Heizer, 180–189. Washington, DC: Smithsonian Institution.

Brooks, M.L., and R.A. Minnich. 2006. Southeastern Deserts bioregion. In *Fires in California's ecosystems,* edited by N.G. Sugihara, J.W. van Wagtendonk, K.E. Shaffer, J. Fites-Kaufman, and A.E. Thode, 391–414. Berkeley: University of California Press.

Broughton, J.M. 1994a. Declines in mammalian foraging efficiency during the Late Holocene, San Francisco Bay, California. *Journal of Anthropological Archaeology* 13 (4): 371–401.

Broughton, J.M. 1994b. Late Holocene resource intensification in Sacramento Valley, California: The vertebrate evidence. *Journal of Archaeological Science* 21:501–514.

Broughton, J.M. 1997. Widening diet breadth, declining foraging efficiency, and prehistoric harvest pressure: Ichthyofaunal evidence from the Emeryville shellmound, California. *Antiquity* 71:845–862.

Broughton, J.M. 2004. Prehistoric human impacts on California birds: Evidence from the Emeryville shellmound avifauna. Ornithological Monographs, no. 56. McLean, VA: American Ornithologists' Union.

Broughton, J.M., and F.E. Bayham. 2003. Showing off, foraging models, and the ascendance of large-game hunting in the California Middle Archaic. *American Antiquity* 68 (4): 783–789.

Broughton, J.M., D. Mullins, and T. Ekker. 2007. Avian resource depression or intertaxonomic variation in bone density? A test with San Francisco Bay avifaunas. *Journal of Archaeological Science* 34 (3): 374–391.

Broughton, J.M., and J.F. O'Connell. 1999. On evolutionary ecology, selectionist archaeology, and behavioral archaeology. *American Antiquity* 64:153–165.

Brubaker, F. 1926. Plants used by Yosemite Indians. *Yosemite Nature Notes* 5 (10): 73–79.

Byram, R.S. 2007. Tectonic history and cultural meaning: Catastrophe and restoration on the Oregon coast. *Oregon Historical Quarterly* 108 (2): 167–180.

Byrd, B.F., and S.N. Reddy. 2002. Late Holocene adaptations along the northern San Diego Coast: New perspectives on old paradigms. In *Catalysts to complexity: The Late Holocene on the California coast,* edited by J. Erlandson and T. Jones, 41–62. Los Angeles: Costen Institute of Archaeology, UCLA.

Callaghan, C.A. 1978. Lake Miwok. In *Handbook of North American Indians,* vol. 8: *California,* edited by R.F. Heizer, 264–273. Washington, DC: Smithsonian Institution.

Caprio, A.C., and T.W. Swetnam. 1995. Historic fire regimes along an elevational gradient on the west slope of the Sierra Nevada, California. In *Proceedings: Symposium on fire in wilderness and park management.* General Technical Report, INT-320. Ogden, UT: U.S. Department of Agriculture, Forest Service.

Carle, D. 2008. *Introduction to fire in California.* California Natural History Guides, no. 95. Berkeley: University of California Press.

Castetter, E.F., and W.H. Bell. 1951. *Yuman Indian agriculture: Primitive subsistence on the Lower Colorado and Gila rivers.* Albuquerque: University of New Mexico Press.

Castillo, E.D. 1978. The impact of Euro-American exploration and settlement. In *Handbook of North American Indians,* vol. 8: *California,* edited by R.F. Heizer, 99–127. Washington, DC: Smithsonian Institution.

Caviedes, C.N. 2001. *El Niño in history: Storming through the years.* Gainsville: University Press of Florida.

Chartkoff, J.L., and K.K. Chartkoff. 1984. *The archaeology of California.* Stanford, CA: Stanford University Press.

CIBA. 2001. CIBA: Where we've been, where we're going. *Roots and Shoots Newsletter* 38 (Spring 2001): 1–16.

Clarke, C.B. 1977. *Edible and useful plants of California.* California History Guides, no. 41. Berkeley: University of California Press.

Collier, M.E.T., and S.B. Thalman. 1996. *Interviews with Tom Smith and Maria Copa: Isabel Kelly's ethnographic notes on the Coast Miwok Indians of Marin and southern Sonoma counties California.* MAPOM Occasional Papers, no. 6. San Rafael, CA: Miwok Archaeological Preserve of Marin.

Colten, R.H. 2001. Ecological and economic analysis of faunal remains from Santa Cruz Island. In *The origins of a Pacific Coast chiefdom: The Chumash of the Channel Islands,* edited by J.E. Arnold, 199–219. Salt Lake City: University of Utah Press.

Connolly, T.J., J.M. Erlandson, and S. Norris. 1995. Early Holocene basketry and cordage from Daisy Cave, San Miguel Island, California. *American Antiquity* 60 (2): 309–318.

Davenport, D., J.R. Johnson, and J. Timbrook. 1993. The Chumash and the Swordfish. *Antiquity* 67 (255): 257–272.

Davis, F.W., and M.I. Borchert. 2006. Central Coast bioregion. In *Fires in California's ecosystems,* edited by N.G. Sugihara, J.W. van Wagtendonk, K.E. Shaffer, J. Fites-Kaufman, and A.E. Thode, 321–349. Berkeley: University of California Press.

Des Lauriers, M.R. 2006. Terminal Pleistocene and Early Holocene occupations of Isla de Cedros, Baja California, Mexico. *Journal of Island and Coastal Archaeology* 1 (2): 255–270.

Diekmann, L., L. Panich, and C. Striplen. 2007. Native American management and the legacy of working landscapes in California. *Rangelands* 29 (3): 46–50.

Dillon, B.D. 2002. California PalaeoIndians: Lack of evidence, or evidence of a lack? In *Essays in California archaeology: A memorial to Franklin Fenenga,* edited by W.J. Wallace and F.A. Riddell, 110–128. Contributions of the University of California Archaeological Research Facility, no. 60. Berkeley: University of California Archaeological Research Facility.

Dixon, R.B. 1905. The Northern Maidu. *Bulletin of the American Museum of Natural History* 17 (3): 119–346.

Dixon, R.B., and A.L. Kroeber. 1913. New linguistic families in California. *American Anthropologist* 15 (4): 647–655.

Dixon, R.B., and A.L. Kroeber. 1919. Linguistic families of California. *University of California Publications in American Archaeology and Ethnology* 16:47–118.

Driver, H.E. 1936. Wappo ethnography. *University of California Publications in American Archaeology and Ethnology* 36 (3): 179–220.

Driver, H.E. 1939. Culture element distributions, X: Northwest California. *University of California Anthropological Records* 1 (6): 297–433.

Driver, H.E., and W.C. Massey. 1957. Comparative studies of North American Indians. *Transactions of the American Philosophical Society* 47 (2): 1–456.

Drucker, P. 1937a. The Tolowa and their southwest Oregon kin. *University of California Publications in American Archaeology and Ethnology* 36 (4): 221–300.

Drucker, P. 1937b. Culture Element Distribution, V: Southern California. *University of California Anthropological Records* 1(1): 1–52.

Du Bois, C.A. 1935. Wintu ethnogeography. *University of California Publications in American Archaeology and Ethnology* 36 (1): 1–148.

Duhaut-Cilly, A. 1999. *A voyage to California, the Sandwich Islands, and around the world in the years 1826–1829*. Translated and edited by A. Fruge and N. Harlow. Berkeley: University of California Press.

Duncan, J.W. 1963. Maidu ethnobotany. M.A. thesis, Sacramento State University.

Ericson, J.E. 1977. Egalitarian exchange systems in California: A preliminary view. In *Exchange systems in prehistory,* edited by T.K. Earle and J.E. Ericson, 109–126. New York: Academic Press.

Erlandson, J.M. 1991. Shellfish and seeds as optimal resources: Early Holocene subsistence on the Santa Barbara coast. In *Hunter-gatherers of Early Holocene coastal California,* edited by J.M. Erlandson and R. Colten, 89–100. Los Angeles: Institute of Archaeology, University of California.

Erlandson, J.M. 1994. *Early hunter-gatherers of the California coast.* New York: Plenum Press.

Erlandson, J.M. 1997. The Middle Holocene along the California coast. In *Archaeology of the California coast during the Middle Holocene,* edited by J. Erlandson and M. Glassow, 1–10. Los Angeles: Institute of Archaeology, University of California.

Erlandson, J.M. 2002. Anatomically modern humans, maritime voyaging, and the Pleistocene colonization of the Americas. In *The first Americans: The Pleistocene colonization of the New World,* edited by N.G. Jablonski, 59–92. Memoirs of the California Academy of Sciences no. 27. San Francisco: California Academy of Sciences.

Erlandson, J.M., T.J. Braje, T.C. Rick, and J. Peterson. 2005. Beads, bifaces, and boats: An early maritime adapation on the south coast of San Miguel Island, California. *American Anthropologist* 107 (4): 677–683.

Erlandson, J.M., and R. Colten, editors. 1991. *Hunter-gatherers of Early Holocene coastal California.* Los Angeles: Institute of Archaeology, University of California.

Erlandson, J.M., M.H. Graham, B.J. Bourque, D. Corbett, J.A. Estes, and R.S. Steneck. 2007. The kelp highway hypothesis: Marine ecology, the coastal migration theory, and the peopling of the Americas. *Journal of Island and Coastal Archaeology* 2 (2): 161–174.

Erlandson, J.M., and T. Jones. 2002. *Catalysts to complexity: The Late Holocene on the California coast.* Los Angeles: Costen Institute of Archaeology, UCLA.

Erlandson, J.M., and T.C. Rick. 2002. Late Holocene cultural developments along the Santa Barbara coast. In *Catalysts to complexity: The Late Holocene on the California coast,* edited by J. Erlandson and T. Jones, 166–182. Los Angeles: Costen Institute of Archaeology, UCLA.

Erlandson, J.M., T.C. Rick, R.L. Vellanoweth, and D.J. Kennett. 1999. Maritime subsistence at a 9300 year old shell midden on Santa Rosa Island, California. *Journal of Field Archaeology* 26 (3): 255–265.

Fagan, B. 2003. *Before California: An archaeologist looks at our earliest inhabitants.* Lanham, MD: Rowman and Littlefield Publishers.

Farmer, J. 2003. Agave roast and the Malki Museum. *News from Native California* 16 (4): 4–5.

Farris, G. 1993. Quality food: The quest for pine nuts in northern California. In *Before the wilderness: Environmental management by native Californians,* edited by T.C. Blackburn and K. Anderson, 229–240. Menlo Park, CA: Ballena Press.

Fimrite, P. 2007. Nature deficit disorder. Growing worry: Youths conquer virtual world, overlook real one. *San Francisco Chronicle,* October 22: A1, A10.

Fites-Kaufman, J., A.F. Bradley, and A.G. Merrill. 2006. Fire and plant interactions. In *Fires in California's ecosystems,* edited by N.G. Sugihara, J.W. van Wagtendonk, K.E. Shaffer, J. Fites-Kaufman, and A.E. Thode, 94–117. Berkeley: University of California Press.

Fitzhugh, B., and J. Habu, editors. 2002. *Beyond foraging and collecting: Evolutionary change in hunter-gatherer settlement systems.* New York: Kluwer-Plenum Publishing.

Flannery, K.V. 1969. Origins and ecological effects of early domestication in Iran and the Near East. In *The domestication and exploitation of plants and animals,* edited by P.J. Ucko and G.W. Dimbleby, 73–100. Chicago: Aldine Publishing Co.

Foster, G.M. 1944. A summary of Yuki culture. *University of California Anthropological Records* 5 (3): 155–244.

Foster, J.W. 2000. Ajumawi fish traps: Harvesting and managing suckers in the springs of the Pit River drainage. *Proceedings of the Society for California Archaeology* 13:266–272.

Fowler, C.S. 1996. Historical perspectives on Timbisha Shoshone land management practices, Death Valley, California. In *Case studies in environmental archaeology,* edited by E.J. Reitz, L.A. Newsom, and S.J. Scudder, 87–101. New York: Plenum Press.

Fowler, C.S. 2000. "We live by them": Native knowledge of biodiversity in the Great Basin of western North America. In *Biodiversity and native America,* edited by P.E. Minnis and W.J. Elisens, 99–132. Norman: University of Oklahoma Press.

Fowler, C.S., P. Esteves, G. Goad, B. Helmer, and K. Watterson. 2003. Caring for the trees: Restoring Timbisha Shoshone land management practices in Death Valley National Park. *Ecological Restoration* 21 (4): 302–306.

Fredrickson, D. 1974. Social change in prehistory: A central California example. In *'Antap: California Indian political and economic organization,* edited by L. J. Bean and T. F. King, 55–73. Ramona, CA: Ballena Press.

Fredrickson, D. 1989. Spatial and temporal patterning of obsidian materials in the Geyers region. In *Current directions in California obsidian studies,* edited by R. Hughes, 95–110. Contributions of the University of California Archaeological Research Facility, no. 48. Berkeley: University of California Archaeological Research Facility.

Fredrickson, D. A., and T. M. Origer. 2002. Obsidian hydration in the Borax Lake Basin, Lake County, California. In *Essays in California archaeology: A memorial to Franklin Fenenga,* edited by W. J. Wallace and F. A. Riddell, 148–165. Contributions of the University of California Archaeological Research Facility, no. 60. Berkeley: University of California Archaeological Research Facility.

Gamble, L. H. 1991. *Organization of activities at the historic settlement of Helo': A Chumash political, economic, and religious center.* Ph.D. dissertation, Department of Anthropology, University of California, Santa Barbara.

Gamble, L. H. 2002. Archaeological evidence for the origin of the plank canoe in North America. *American Antiquity* 67:301–315.

Gamble, L. H., and G. S. Russell. 2002. A view from the mainland: Late Holocene cultural developments among the Ventureño Chumash and Tongva. In *Catalysts to complexity: The Late Holocene on the California coast,* edited by J. Erlandson and T. Jones, 101–126. Los Angeles: Costen Institute of Archaeology, UCLA.

Gamble, L. H., P. L. Walker, and G. S. Russell. 2001. An integrative approach to mortuary analysis: Social and symbolic dimensions of Chumash burial practices. *American Antiquity* 66 (2): 185–212.

Gamble, L. H., and I. C. Zepeda. 2002. Social differentiation and exchange among the Kumeyaay Indians during the Historic Period in California. *Historical Archaeology* 36 (2): 71–91.

Garth, T. R. 1953. Atsugewi ethnography. *Anthropological Records* 14 (2): 129–212.

Gasser, R. E., and S. M. Kwiatkowski. 1991a. Food for thought: Recognizing patterns in Hohokam subsistence. In *Exploring the Hohokam: Prehistoric desert peoples of the American Southwest,* edited by G. J. Gumerman, 417–459. Dragoon, AZ: Amerind Foundation

Gasser, R. E., and S. M. Kwiatkowski. 1991b. Regional signatures of Hohokam plant use. *Kiva* 56 (3): 207–226.

Gayton, A. H. 1946. Culture-environment integration: External references in Yokuts life. *Southwestern Journal of Anthropology* 2 (3): 252–268.

Gayton, A. H. 1948a. Yokuts and Western Mono ethnography I: Tulare

Lake, Southern Valley, and Central Foothill Yokuts. *Anthropological Records* 10 (1): 1–142.

Gayton, A.H. 1948b. Yokuts and Western Mono ethnography II: Northern Foothill Yokuts and Western Mono. *Anthropological Records* 10 (2): 143–302.

Geist, E.L., and A. Rosenthal. 2005. Bay Area tsunamis: Are we at risk? *USGS General Information Product* 21:7.

Geist, E.L., V.V. Titov, and C.E. Synolakis. 2006. Tsunami: Wave of change. *Scientific American* 294 (January): 56–63.

Gifford, E.W. 1916. Composition of California shellmounds. *University of California Publications in American Archaeology and Ethnology* 12 (1): 1–29.

Gifford, E.W. 1931. The Kamia of Imperial Valley. In *Bureau of American Ethnology Bulletin,* no. 97. Washington, DC: Smithsonian Institution.

Gifford, E.W. 1932. The Northfork Mono. *University of California Publications in American Archaeology and Ethnology* 31 (2): 15–65.

Gifford, E.W. 1965. *The Coast Yuki.* Sacramento Anthropological Society Papers, no. 2. Sacramento: Sacramento Anthropological Society.

Gifford, E.W. 1967. Ethnographic notes on the Southwestern Pomo. *University of California Anthropological Records* 25:1–48.

Gifford, E.W., and A.L. Kroeber. 1937. Culture element distributions: IV, Pomo. *University of California Publications in American Archaeology and Ethnology* 37 (4): 117–254.

Gillespie, S.D. 2000. Lévi-Strauss: Maison and société à maisons. In *Beyond kinship: Social and material reproduction in house societies,* edited by R.A. Joyce and S.D. Gillespie, 22–52. Philadelphia: University of Pennsylvania Press.

Glassow, M.A. 1996. *Purisimeno Chumash prehistory: Maritime adaptations along the southern California coast.* Fort Worth, TX: Harcourt Brace College Publishers.

Glassow, M.A. 2002. Late Holocene Prehistory of the Vandenberg region. In *Catalysts to complexity: The Late Holocene on the California coast,* edited by J. Erlandson and T. Jones, 183–204. Los Angeles: Costen Institute of Archaeology, UCLA.

Gobalet, K.W., and T.L. Jones. 1995. Prehistoric Native American fisheries of the central California coast. *Transactions of the American Fisheries Society* 124 (6): 813–823.

Gobalet, K.W., P.D. Schulz, T.A. Wake, and N. Siefkin. 2004. Archaeological perspectives on Native American fisheries of California, with emphasis on steelhead and salmon. *Transactions of the American Fisheries Society* 133 (4): 801–833.

Goldschmidt, W. 1951. Nomlaki ethnography. *University of California Publications in American Archaeology and Ethnology* 42 (4): 303–443.

Golla, V. 2007. Linguistic prehistory. In *California prehistory: Colonization, culture, and complexity,* edited by T.L. Jones and K. Klar, 71–82. New York: AltaMira Press.

Goodrich, J., C. Lawson, and V.P. Lawson. 1980. *Kashaya Pomo plants.* Los Angeles: American Indian Studies Center, UCLA.

Gould, R.A. 1966. *Archaeology of the Point St. George site and Tolowa prehistory.* University of California Publications in Anthroplogy, vol. 4. Berkeley: University of California.

Gould, R.A. 1975. Ecology and adaptive response among the Tolowa Indians of northwest California. *Journal of California Anthropology* 2 (2): 148–170.

Grant, C. 1965. *The rock paintings of the Chumash.* Berkeley: University of California Press.

Grant, C. 1978. Eastern Coastal Chumash. In *Handbook of North American Indians,* vol. 8: *California,* edited by R.F. Heizer, 509–519. Washington, DC: Smithsonian Institution.

Grant, C., J.W. Baird, and J.K. Pringle. 1968. *Rock drawings of the Coso Range, Inyo County, California.* Maturango Museum Publication 4. China Lake, CA: Maturango Museum.

Grant, L.B., and K. Sieh. 1994. Paleoseismic evidence of clustered earthquakes on the San Adreas Fault in the Carrizo Plain, California. *Journal of Geophysical Research* 99 (B4): 6819–6841.

Grayson, D.K. 1993. *The desert's past: A natural prehistory of the Great Basin.* Washington, DC: Smithsonian Institution Press.

Greengo, R.E. 1951. Molluscan species in California shell middens. *Reports of the University of California Archaeological Survey* 13: 1–29.

Greengo, R.E. 1952. Shellfish foods of the California Indians. *Kroeber Anthropological Society Papers* 7:63–114.

Greenlee, J.M., and J.H. Langenheim. 1990. Historic fire regimes and their relation to vegetation patterns in the Monterey Bay area of California. *American Midland Naturalist* 124 (2): 239–253.

Greenwood, R.S. 1978. Obispeño and Purisimeño Chumash. In *Handbook of North American Indians,* vol. 8: *California,* edited by R.F. Heizer, 520–523. Washington, DC: Smithsonian Institution.

Habu, J. 2004. *Ancient Jomon of Japan.* Cambridge: Cambridge University Press.

Habu, J., J.M. Savelle, S. Koyama, and H. Hongo, editors. 2003. *Hunter-gatherers of the north Pacific rim.* Senri Ethnological Studies, no. 63. Osaka, Japan: National Museum of Ethnology.

Hallam, S. J. 1985. The history of aboriginal firing. In *Fire ecology and management in Western Australian ecosystems,* edited by J. R. Ford, 7–20. WAIT Environmental Studies Group Report, no. 14. Perth: Western Australian Institute of Technology.

Hammett, J. E. 1991. *Ecology of sedentary societies without agriculture: Paleoethnobotanical indicators from Native California.* Ph.D. dissertation, Department of Anthropology, University of North Carolina, Chapel Hill.

Hammett, J. E., and E. J. Lawlor. 2004. Paleoethnobotany in California. In *People and plants in ancient western North America,* edited by P. E. Minnis, 278–366. Washington, DC: Smithsonian Books.

Harrington, J. P. 1932. *Tobacco among the Karuk Indians of California.* Smithsonian Institution Bureau of American Ethnology Bulletin 94. Washington, DC: Smithsonian Institution.

Harrington, J. P. 1942. Culture element distributions, XIX: Central California coast. *University of California Anthropological Records* 7 (1): 1–46.

Harris, D. R. 1969. Agricultural systems, ecosystems and the origins of agriculture. In *The domestication and exploitation of plants and animals,* edited by P. J. Ucko and G. W. Dimbleby, 3–16. Chicago: Aldine Publishing Co.

Harris, D. R. 1989. An evolutionary continuum of people-planting interactions. In *Foraging and farming: The evolution of plant exploitation,* edited by D. R. Harris and G. C. Hillman, 11–26. Boston: Unwin Hyman.

Hayden, B. 1995. A new overview of domestication. In *Last hunters–first farmers: New perspectives on the prehistoric transition to agriculture,* edited by T. D. Price and A. B. Gebauer, 273–299. Santa Fe, NM: School of American Research Press.

Heizer, R. F. 1949. The archaeology of central California, I: The Early Horizon. *University of California Anthropological Records* 12 (1): 1–84.

Heizer, R. F. 1951. A prehistoric Yurok ceremonial site (HUM-174). *Reports of the University of California Archaeological Survey* 11: 1–4.

Heizer, R. F. 1958. Prehistoric central California: A problem in historical-developmental classification. *University of California Archaeological Survey Reports* 41:19–26.

Heizer, R. F. 1972. *Mines and quarries of the Indians of California.* Ramona, CA: Ballena Press.

Heizer, R. F. 1978. Natural forces and native world view. In *Handbook of North American Indians,* vol. 8: *California,* edited by R. F. Heizer, 649–653. Washington, DC: Smithsonian Institution.

Heizer, R. F., and A. F. Almquist. 1971. *The other Californians: Preju-
dice and discrimination under Spain, Mexico, and the United States
to 1920.* Berkeley: University of California Press.

Heizer, R. F., and A. B. Elsasser. 1980. *The natural world of the California Indians.* California Natural History Guides, no. 46. Berkeley:
University of California Press.

Hendry, G. W. 1931. The adobe brick as a historical source. *Agricultural History* 5:110–127.

Hester, T. R. 1978a. Esselen. In *Handbook of North American Indians,*
vol. 8: *California,* edited by R. F. Heizer, 496–499. Washington,
DC: Smithsonian Institution.

Hester, T. R. 1978b. Salinan. In *Handbook of North American Indians,*
vol. 8: *California,* edited by R. F. Heizer, 500–504. Washington,
DC: Smithsonian Institution.

Hickman, J. C., editor. 1993. *The Jepson manual: Higher plants of California.* Berkeley: University of California Press.

Hicks, F. N. 1963. Ecological aspects of aboriginal culture in the Western Yuman area. Ph.D. dissertation, Department of Anthropology, University of California, Los Angeles.

Hildebrandt, W. R., and T. L. Jones. 1992. Evolution of marine mammal hunting: A view from the California and Oregon coasts. *Journal of Anthropological Archaeology* 11:360–401.

Hildebrandt, W. R., and V. A. Levulett. 2002. Late Holocene emergence
of marine-focused economies in northwest California. In *Catalysts to complexity: The Late Holocene on the California coast,* edited by J. Erlandson and T. Jones, 303–319. Los Angeles: Costen
Institute of Archaeology, UCLA.

Hildebrandt, W. R., and K. R. McGuire. 2002. The ascendance of
hunting during the California Middle Archaic: An evolutionary
perspective. *American Antiquity* 67:231–256.

Hildebrandt, W. R., and K. R. McGuire. 2003. Large-game hunting,
gender differentiated work organization, and the role of evolutionary ecology in California and Great Basin prehistory: A reply
to Broughton and Bayham. *American Antiquity* 68 (4): 790–792.

Hillman, G. C., and M. S. Davies. 1990. Measured domestication rates
in wild wheats and barley under primitive cultivation, and their
archaeological implications. *Journal of World Prehistory* 4 (2):
157–222.

Hinton, L. 1994. *Flutes of fire: Essays on California Indian languages.*
Berkeley, CA: Heyday Books.

Hinton, T. B., and R. C. Owen. 1957. Some surviving Yuman groups in
northern Baja California. *América Indígena* 17 (1): 87–102.

Hohenthal, W. D. 2001. *Tipai ethnographic notes: A Baja California In-*

dian community at mid-century. Ballena Press Anthropological Papers, no. 48. Novato, CA: Ballena Press.

Hollimon, S.E. 2000. Archaeology of the 'Aqi: Gender and sexuality in prehistoric Chumash Society. In *Archaeologies of sexuality,* edited by R.A. Schmidt and B.L. Voss, 179–196. London: Routledge.

Holmes, W.H. 1975. Pomo Reservation, Mendocino County [1902]. In *Seven early accounts of the Pomo Indians and their culture,* edited by R.F. Heizer, 21–23. Berkeley: University of California Archaeological Research Facility.

Honeysett, E.A. 1989. Seed remains from Santa Inés Mission. In *Santa Inés Mission excavations: 1986–1988,* edited by J.G. Costello, 177–179. Salinas, CA: Coyote Press.

Hooper, L. 1920. The Cahuilla Indians. *University of California Publications in American Archaeology and Ethnology* 16 (6): 316–380.

Hoover, R.L. 1989. Spanish-native interaction and acculturation in the Alta California Missions. In *Columbian consequences,* vol. 1: *Archaeological and historical perspectives on the Spanish borderlands west,* edited by D.H. Thomas, 395–406. Washington, DC: Smithsonian Institution Press.

Hudson, J.W. 1975. Pomo wampum makers: An aboriginal double standard [1897]. In *Seven early accounts of the Pomo Indians and their culture,* edited by R.F. Heizer, 9–20. Berkeley: University of California Archaeological Research Facility.

Hudson, T., and T. Blackburn. 1978. The integration of myth and ritual in south-central California: The "northern complex." *Journal of California Anthropology* 5 (2): 225–250.

Hughes, R.E. 1982. Age and exploitation of obsidian from Medicine Lake Highland, California. *Journal of Archaeological Science* 9 (2): 173–185.

Hughes, R.E., editor. 1989. *Current directions in California obsidian studies,* no. 48. Berkeley: University of California Archaeological Research Facility.

Hughes, R.E. 1992. California archaeology and linguistic prehistory. *Journal of Anthropological Research* 48:317–338.

Husari, S., H.T. Nichols, N.G. Sugihara, and S.L. Stephens. 2006. Fire and fuel management. In *Fires in California's ecosystems,* edited by N.G. Sugihara, J.W. van Wagtendonk, K.E. Shaffer, J. Fites-Kaufman, and A.E. Thode, 444–465. Berkeley: University of California Press.

Jacknis, I. 1995. *Carving traditions of northwest California.* Berkeley: Phoebe Apperson Hearst Museum of Anthropology, University of California.

Jacknis, I. 2004. Notes toward a culinary anthropology of Native

California. In *Food in California Indian culture,* edited by I. Jacknis, 1–119. Berkeley: Phoebe Hearst Museum of Anthropology, University of California.

Jackson, T.L. 1991. Pounding acorn: Women's production as social and economic focus. In *Engendering archaeology,* edited by J.M. Gero and M.W. Conkey, 301–328. Cambridge: Basil Blackwell.

Jameson, E.W., Jr., and H.J. Peeters. 2004. *Mammals of California.* California Natural History Guides, no. 68. Berkeley: University of California Press.

Jenkins, R.C. 2005. A fluted point from Siskiyou County, California. In *Archaeology without limits: Papers in honor of Clement W. Meighan,* edited by B.D. Dillon and M.A. Boxt, 61–68. Lancaster, CA: Labyrinthos.

Joël, J. 1976. Some Paipai accounts of food gathering. *Journal of California Anthropology* 3 (1): 59–71.

Johnson, J.R. 1988. *Chumash social organization: An ethnohistoric perspective.* Ph.D. dissertation, Department of Anthropology, University of California, Santa Barbara.

Johnson, J.R. 2000. Social responses to climate change among the Chumash Indians of south-central California. In *The way the wind blows: Climate, history and human action,* edited by R.J. McIntosh, J.A. Tainter, and S.K. McIntosh, 301–327. New York: Columbia University Press.

Johnson, J.R., T.W. Stafford, H.O. Ajie, and D.P. Morris. 2000. Arlington Springs revisited. In *Proceedings of the Fifth California Islands Symposium,* edited by D.R. Browne, K.L. Mitchell, and H.W. Chaney, 541–545. Washington, DC: U.S. Department of the Interior.

Johnson, P.J. 1978. Patwin. In *Handbook of North American Indians,* vol. 8: *California,* edited by R.F. Heizer, 350–360. Washington, DC: Smithsonian Institution.

Jones, R. 1969. Fire-stick farming. *Australian Natural History* 16: 224–228.

Jones, T.L. 1992. Settlement trends along the California coast. In *Essays on the prehistory of maritime California,* edited by T.L. Jones, 1–37. Publication no. 10. Davis: Center for Archaeological Research, University of California.

Jones, T.L. 2002. Late Holocene cultural complexity on the California coast. In *Catalysts to complexity: The Late Holocene on the California coast,* edited by J. Erlandson and T. Jones, 1–12. Los Angeles: Costen Institute of Archaeology, UCLA.

Jones, T.L. 2003. *Prehistoric human ecology of the Big Sur coast, California.* Contributions of the University of California Archaeological Research Facility, no. 61. Berkeley: University of California Archaeological Research Facility.

Jones, T.L., G.M. Brown, J. McVicar, L.M. Raab, D.J. Kennett, G. Spaulding, and A. York. 1999. Environmental imperatives reconsidered: Demographic crises in western North America during the Medieval Climatic Anomaly. *Current Anthropology* 40 (2): 137–170.

Jones, T.L., R.T. Fitzgerald, D.J. Kennett, C.H. Miksicek, J.L. Fagan, J. Sharp, and J.M. Erlandson. 2002. The Cross Creek site (CA-SLO-1797) and its implications for New World colonization. *American Antiquity* 67 (2): 213–230.

Jones, T.L., and K.A. Klar. 2005. Diffusionism reconsidered: Linguistic and archaeological evidence for prehistoric Polynesian contact with southern California. *American Antiquity* 70 (3): 457–484.

Jones, T.L., and K.A. Klar. 2007. *California prehistory: Colonization, culture, and complexity.* Lanham, MD: Alta Mira Press.

Joyce, R.A. 2000. Heirlooms and houses: Materiality and social memory. In *Beyond kinship: Social and material reproduction in house societies,* edited by R.A. Joyce and S.D. Gillespie, 189–212. Philadelphia: University of Pennsylvania Press.

Joyce, R.A., and S.D. Gillespie, editors. 2000. *Beyond kinship: Social and material reproduction in house societies.* Philadelphia: University of Pennsylvania Press.

Kavanagh, J. 2005. *The nature of California: An introduction to familiar plants, animals, and outstanding natural attractions.* Phoenix, AZ: Waterford Press.

Keeley, J.E. 2002. Native American impacts on fire regimes of the California Coastal Ranges. *Journal of Biogeography* 29:303–320.

Keeley, J.E. 2006. South Coast bioregion. In *Fires in California's ecosystems,* edited by N.G. Sugihara, J.W. van Wagtendonk, K.E. Shaffer, J. Fites-Kaufman, and A.E. Thode, 350–390. Berkeley: University of California Press.

Keeley, L.H. 1995. Protoagricultural practices among hunter-gatherers: A cross-cultural survey. In *Last hunters–first farmers: New perspectives on the prehistoric transition to agriculture,* edited by T.D. Price and A.B. Gebauer, 243–272. Santa Fe, NM: School of American Research Press.

Kelly, I.T. 1930. The carver's art of the Indians of northwest California. *University of California Publications in American Archaeology and Ethnology* 24 (7): 343–360.

Kelly, I.T. 1978. Coast Miwok. In *Handbook of North American Indians,* vol. 8: *California,* edited by R.F. Heizer, 414–425. Washington, DC: Smithsonian Institution.

Kennett, D.J. 2005. *The Island Chumash: Behavioral ecology of a maritime society.* Berkeley: University of California Press.

Kennett, D.J., and J.P. Kennett. 2000. Competitive and cooperative responses to climatic instability in coastal southern California. *American Antiquity* 65 (2): 379–395.

Keter, T.S. 1995. *Environmental history and cultural ecology of the North Fork of the Eel River Basin, California.* U.S. Department of Agriculture, Forest Service, Pacific Southwest Region, R5-EM-TP-002. Washington, DC: U.S. Government Printing Office.

Kilgore, B.M., and D. Taylor. 1979. Fire history of a sequoia–mixed conifer forest. *Ecology* 60 (1): 129–142.

King, C. 1974. Explanations of differences and similarities among bead use in prehistoric and early historic California. In *'Antap: California Indian political and economic organization,* edited by L.J. Bean and T.F. King. Ramona, CA: Ballena Press.

King, C. 1976. Chumash inter-village economic exchange. In *Native Californians: A theoretical retrospective,* edited by L.J. Bean and T.C. Blackburn, 289–318. Menlo Park, CA: Ballena Press.

King, C. 1990. *Evolution of Chumash society: A comparative study of artifacts used for social system maintenance in the Santa Barbara Channel region before A.D. 1804.* New York: Garland Publishing.

King, C. 1993. Fuel use and resource management: Implications for the study of land management in prehistoric California and recommendations for a research program. In *Before the wilderness: Environmental management by Native Californians,* edited by T.C. Blackburn and K. Anderson, 279–298. Menlo Park, CA: Ballena Press.

King, L. 1969. The Medea Creek cemetery (LAn-243): An investigation of social organization from mortuary practices. *UCLA Archaeological Survey Annual Review* 11:23–58.

King, T.F. 1970. *The dead at Tiburon.* Occasional Paper 2. Daly City: Northwestern California Archaeological Society.

King, T.F. 1974. The evolution of status ascription around San Francisco Bay. In *'Antap: California Indian political and economic organization,* edited by L.J. Bean and T.F. King, 35–54. Ramona, CA: Ballena Press.

Kirch, P.V. 1994. *The wet and the dry: Irrigation and agricultural intensification in Polynesia.* Chicago: University of Chicago Press.

Klimek, S. 1935. Culture element distributions: I, The structure of California Indian culture. *University of California Publications in American Archaeology and Ethnology* 37 (1): 1–70.

Kniffen, F.B. 1928. Achomawi geography. *University of California Publications in American Archaeology and Ethnology* 23 (5): 297–332.

Kniffen, F.B. 1939. Pomo geography. *University of California Publications in American Archaeology and Ethnology* 36 (6): 353–400.

Koenig, W.D., R.L. Mumme, W.J. Carmen, and M.T. Stanback. 1994. Acorn production by oaks in central coastal California: Variation within and among years. *Ecology* 75 (1): 99–109.

Koerper, H.C., R.D. Mason, and M.L. Peterson. 2002. Complexity, demography, and change in Late Holocene Orange County. In *Catalysts to complexity: The Late Holocene on the California coast,* edited by J. Erlandson and T. Jones, 63–81. Los Angeles: Costen Institute of Archaeology, UCLA.

Kotzebue, O.V. 1830. *A new voyage round the world, in the years 1823, 24, 25, and 26,* 1 and 2. London: Henry Colburn and Richard Bentley.

Kroeber, A.L. 1904. Types of Indian culture in California. *University of California Publications in American Archaeology and Ethnology* 2 (3): 81–103.

Kroeber, A.L. 1908a. Ethnography of the Cahuilla Indians. *University of California Publications in American Archaeology and Ethnology* 8 (2): 29–68.

Kroeber, A.L. 1908b. Notes on the Luiseño. *University of California Publications in American Archaeology and Ethnology* 8 (3): 174–186.

Kroeber, A.L. 1920. California culture provinces. *University of California Publications in American Archaeology and Ethnology* 17 (2): 151–169.

Kroeber, A.L. 1925. *Handbook of the Indians of California.* Bulletin 78, Bureau of American Ethnology, Smithsonian Institution. Washington, DC: U.S. Government Printing Office.

Kroeber, A.L. 1932. The Patwin and their neighbors. *University of California Publications in American Archaeology and Ethnology* 29 (4): 253–423.

Kroeber, A.L. 1936. Culture element distributions: III, Area and climax. *University of California Publications in American Archaeology and Ethnology* 37 (3): 101–116.

Kroeber, A.L. 1939. Cultural and natural areas of Native North America. *University of California Publications in American Archaeology and Ethnology* 38 (2): 1–242.

Kroeber, A.L. 1966. The nature of land-holding groups in aboriginal California. In *Aboriginal California: Three studies in culture history,* edited by R.F. Hiezer, 82–120. Berkeley: University of California Archaeological Research Facility.

Kroeber, A.L., and E.W. Gifford. 1949. World renewal: A cult system of Native northwest California. *Anthropological Records* 13 (1): 1–156.

Kunkel, P.H. 1974. The Pomo Kin group and the political unit in aboriginal California. *The Journal of California Anthropology* 1 (1): 7–18.

Lambert, P.M., and P.L. Walker. 1991. Physical anthropological evidence for the evolution of social complexity in coastal southern California. *Antiquity* 65:963–973.

Landberg, L.C.W. 1965. *The Chumash Indians of southern California.* Southwest Museum Papers 19. Los Angeles: Southwest Museum.

Lathrop, E., and B. Martin. 1982. Fire ecology of deergrass *(Muhlenbergia rigens)* in Cuyamaca Rancho State Park, California. *Crossosoma* 8 (6): 1–4, 9–10.

Lawton, H.W., P.J. Wilke, M. DeDecker, and W.M. Mason. 1993. Agriculture among the Paiute of Owens Valley. In *Before the wilderness: Environmental management by Native Californians,* edited by T.C. Blackburn and K. Anderson, 329–378. Menlo Park, CA: Ballena Press.

Lee, R., and I. Devore, editors. 1968. *Man the hunter.* Chicago: Aldine Publishing Co.

Lemley, B. 2005. Drilling San Andreas. *Discover* March:53–56.

Lévi-Strauss, C. 1982. *The way of the masks.* Translated by S. Modelski. Seattle: University of Washington Press.

Lévi-Strauss, C. 1987. *Anthropology and myth: Lectures 1951–1982.* Translated by R. Willis. Oxford: Blackwell.

Levy, R. 1978a. Costanoan. In *Handbook of North American Indians,* vol. 8: *California,* edited by R.F. Heizer, 485–495. Washington, DC: Smithsonian Institution.

Levy, R. 1978b. Eastern Miwok. In *Handbook of North American Indians,* vol. 8: *California,* edited by R.F. Heizer, 398–413. Washington, DC: Smithsonian Institution.

Lewis, H.T. 1973. *Patterns of Indian burning in California: Ecology and ethnohistory.* Ramona, CA: Ballena Press.

Lewis, H.T. 1982. Fire technology and resource management in aboriginal North America and Australia. In *The Regulation of environmental resources in food collecting societies,* edited by E. Hunn and N.M. Williams, 45–67. Boulder, CO: Westview Press.

Lewis, H.T. 1985a. Burning the "top end": Kangaroos and cattle. In *Fire ecology and management in Western Australian ecosystems,* edited by J.R. Ford, 21–31. WAIT Environmental Studies Group Report no. 14. Perth: Western Australian Institute of Technology.

Lewis, H.T. 1985b. Why Indians burned: Specific versus general reasons. In *Proceedings: Symposium and Workshop on Wilderness Fire,* edited by J.E. Lotan, B.M. Kilgore, W.C. Fischer and W.R. Mutsch, 75–80. Ogden, UT: Intermountain Forest and Range

Experiment Station, U.S. Department of Agriculture, Forest Service.

Lewis, H.T. 1991. Technological complexity, ecological diversity, and fire regimes in northern Australia: Hunter-gathererer, cowboy, ranger. In *Profiles in cultural evolution,* edited by A.T. Rambo and K. Gillogly, 261–288. Anthropological Papers, no. 85. Ann Arbor: Museum of Anthropology, University of Michigan.

Lewis, H.T. 1993. Patterns of Indian burning in California: Ecology and ethnohistory. In *Before the wilderness: Environmental management by Native Californians,* edited by T.C. Blackburn and K. Anderson, 55–116. Menlo Park, CA: Ballena Press.

Lewis, H.T. 2002. An anthropological critique. In *Forgotten fires: Native Americans and the transient wilderness,* edited by H.T. Lewis and M.K. Anderson, 17–36. Norman: University of Oklahoma Press.

Lewis, H.T., and M.K. Anderson. 2002. Introduction. In *Forgotten fires: Native Americans and the transient wilderness,* edited by H.T. Lewis and M.K. Anderson, 3–16. Norman: University of Oklahoma Press.

Lightfoot, K.G. 1993. Long-term developments in complex hunter-gatherer societies: Recent perspectives from the Pacific Coast of North America. *Journal of Archaeological Research* 1 (3): 167–201.

Lightfoot, K.G. 1997. Cultural construction of coastal landscapes: A Middle Holocene perspective from San Francisco Bay. In *Archaeology of the California coast during the Middle Holocene,* edited by J. Erlandson and M. Glassow, 129–141. Los Angeles: Institute of Archaeology, University of California.

Lightfoot, K.G. 2005. *Indians, missionaries, and merchants: The legacy of colonial encounters on the California frontiers.* Berkeley: University of California Press.

Lightfoot, K.G., and E.M. Luby. 2002. Late Holocene in the Greater San Francisco Bay Area: Temporal trends in the use and abandonment of shell mounds in the East Bay. In *Catalysts to complexity: The Late Holocene on the California coast,* edited by J. Erlandson and T. Jones, 263–281. Los Angeles: Costen Institute of Archaeology, UCLA.

Lightfoot, K.G., and A. Martinez. 1995. Frontiers and boundaries in archaeological perspective. *Annual Review of Anthropology* 24: 471–492.

Lightfoot, K.G., and W.S. Simmons. 1998. Culture contact in proto-historic California: Social contexts of Native and European encounters. *Journal of California and Great Basin Anthropology* 20 (2): 138–170.

Lightfoot, K.G., T.A. Wake, and A.M. Schiff. 1991. *The archaeology and ethnohistory of Fort Ross, California,* vol. 1: *Introduction.* Contributions of the University of California Archaeological Research Facility, no. 49. Berkeley: University of California Archaeological Research Facility.

Loeb, E.M. 1926. Pomo folkways. *University of California Publications in American Archaeology and Ethnology* 19 (2) 149–405.

Love, M. 1996. *Probably more than you want to know about the fishes of the Pacific.* Santa Barbara, CA: Really Big Press.

Lubchenco, J., A.M. Olson, L.B. Brubaker, S.L. Carpenter, M.M. Holland, S.P. Hubbell, S. Levin, J.A. MacMahon, P.A. Matson, J.A. Melillo, H.A. Mooney, C.H. Peterson, H.R. Pulliam, L.A. Real, P.J. Regal, and P.G. Risser. 1991. The sustainable biosphere initiative. An ecological research agenda: A report from the Ecological Society of America. *Ecology* 72 (2): 371–412.

Luomala, K. 1978. Tipai and Ipai. In *Handbook of North American Indians,* vol. 8: *California,* edited by R.F. Heizer, 592–609. Washington, DC: Smithsonian Institution.

Lütke, F.P. 1989. September 4–28, 1818. From the Diary of Fedor P. Lütke during his circumnavigation aboard the Sloop Kamchatka, 1817–1819: Observations on California. In *The Russian American colonies: Three centuries of Russian eastward expansion, 1798–1867,* vol. 3: *A documentary record,* edited by B. Dmytryshyn, E.A.P. Crownhart-Vaughan, and T. Vaughan, 257–285. Portland: Oregon Historical Society Press.

Magallanes, F., and S. Thompson. 2003. What's cooking at the Malki Museum? *News from Native California* 16 (4): 6–7.

Margolin, M. 1978. *The Ohlone way: Indian life in the San Francisco–Monterey Bay area.* Berkeley, CA: Heyday Books.

Margolin, M. 2006. Green Furniture Workshop finds a home at Hoopa. *News from Native California* 19 (4): 29–31.

Martin, G. 2006. Farms may cut habitat renewal over E. coli fears. In *San Francisco Chronicle,* December 19, A1, A4.

Martin, R.E., and D.B. Sapsis. 1992. Fires as agents of biodiversity—pyrodiversity promotes biodiversity. In *Proceedings of the Symposium on Biodiversity of Northwestern California, October 1991,* edited by R.R. Harris and D.C. Erman, 150–157. Berkeley: Division of Agricultural and Natural Resources, University of California.

Martin, S.L., and V.S. Popper. 2001. Paleoethnobotanical investigations of archaeological sites on Santa Cruz Island. In *The origins of a Pacific Coast chiefdom: The Chumash of the Channel Islands,* edited by J.E. Arnold, 245–259. Salt Lake City, UT: University of Utah Press.

Mason, J.A. 1912. The ethnology of the Salinian Indians. *University of California Publications in American Archaeology and Ethnology* 10 (4): 97–240.

Matson, P.A., W.J. Parton, A.G. Power, and M.J. Swift. 1997. Agricultural intensification and ecosystem properties. *Science* 277 (5325): 504–509.

Mayer, P.J. 1976. *Miwok balenophagy: Implications for the cultural development of some California acorn-eaters.* Berkeley: University of California Archaeological Research Facility.

McCarthy, H. 1993. Managing oaks and the acorn crop. In *Before the wilderness: Environmental management by Native Californians,* edited by T.C. Blackburn and K. Anderson, 213–228. Menlo Park, CA: Ballena Press.

McClenaghan, L.R., and A.C. Beauchamp. 1986. Low genetic differentiation among isolated populations of the California fan palm (*Washingtonia filifera*). *Evolution* 40 (2): 315–322.

McGinnis, S.M. 2006. *Field guide to freshwater fishes of California.* California Natural History Guides, no. 77. Berkeley: University of California Press.

McLendon, S., and M.J. Lowry. 1978. Eastern Pomo and Southeastern Pomo. In *Handbook of North American Indians,* vol. 8: *California,* edited by R.F. Heizer, 306–323. Washington, DC: Smithsonian Institution.

Mead, G.R. 1972. *The ethnobotany of the California Indians: A compendium of the plants, their users, and their uses.* Occasional Publications in Anthropology, Ethnology Series, no. 30. Greenley, CO: University of Northern Colorado, Museum of Anthropology.

Meigs, P.I. 1939. The Kiliwa Indians of lower California. In *Ibero Americana,* vol. 15. Berkeley: University of California Press.

Meltzer, D.J. 2002. What do you do when no one's been there before? Thoughts on the exploration and colonization of new lands. In *The first Americans: The Pleistocene colonization of the New World,* edited by N.G. Jablonski, 27–58. Memoirs of the California Academy of Sciences, no. 27. San Francisco: California Academy of Sciences.

Menke, J.W. 1992. Grazing and fire management for native perennial grass restoration in California grasslands. *Fremontia* 20 (2): 22–25.

Mensing, S., and R. Byrne. 1998. Pre-mission invasion of *Erodium cicutarium* in California. *Journal of Biogeography* 25:757–762.

Mensing, S.A., J. Michaelson, and R. Byrne. 1999. A 560-year record of Santa Ana fires reconstructed from charcoal deposited in the Santa Barbara basin, California. *Quaternary Research* 51:295–305.

Merriam, C. H. 1967. Ethnographic notes on California Indian Tribes, II: Ethnological notes on northern and southern California Indian tribes, compiled and edited by Robert F. Heizer. *Reports of the University of California Archaeological Survey* 68 (2): 167–256.

Meyer, J., and J. S. Rosenthal. 1998. An archaeological investigation of artifacts and human remains from CA-CCO-637, Los Vaqueros Project area, Contra Costa County, California. Rohnert Park, CA: Archaeological Studies Center, Sonoma State University Academic Foundation.

Michelsen, R. C. 1974. Ethnographic notes on agave fiber cordage. *Pacific Coast Archaeological Society Quarterly* 10 (1): 39–47.

Michelsen, R. C. 1977. The construction of a Kiliwa house. *Pacific Coast Archaeological Society Quarterly* 13 (1): 21–27.

Michelsen, R. C., and M. K. Michelsen. 1979. A piñon harvest by Paipai Indians. *Pacific Coast Archaeological Society Quarterly* 15 (1): 27–31.

Michelsen, R. C., and H. C. Smith. 1967. Honey collecting by Indians in Baja California, Mexico. *Pacific Coast Archaeological Society Quarterly* 3 (1): 53–57.

Miller, C., and D. L. Urban. 1999a. Interactions between forest heterogeneity and surface fire regimes in the southern Sierra Nevada. *Canadian Journal of Forest Research* 29:202–212.

Miller, C., and D. L. Urban. 1999b. A model of surface fire, climate, and forest pattern in the Sierra Nevada, California. *Ecological Modelling* 114:113–135.

Miller, V. P. 1978. Yuki, Huchnom, and Coast Yuki. In *Handbook of North American Indians*, vol. 8: *California*, edited by R. F. Heizer, 249–255. Washington, DC: Smithsonian Institution.

Milliken, R. 1995. *A time of little choice: The disintegration of tribal culture in the San Francisco Bay Area 1769–1810.* Menlo Park, CA: Ballena Press.

Milliken, R., R. T. Fitzgerald, M. G. Hylkema, R. Gorza, T. Origer, D. G. Bieling, A. Leventhal, R. S. Wiberg, A. Gottsfield, D. Gillette, V. Bellifemine, E. Strother, R. Cartier, and D. A. Fredrickson. 2007. Punctuated culture change in the San Francisco Bay Area. In *California prehistory*, edited by T. L. Jones and K. A. Klar, 99–123. Walnut Creek, CA: Alta Mira Press.

Minnich, R. A. 1983. Fire mosaics in southern California and northern Baja California. *Science* 219 (4590): 1257–1294.

Minnich, R. A. 1998. Landscapes, land-use and fire policy: Where do the large fires come from? In *Large Forest Fires*, edited by J. M. Moreno, 133–158. Leiden, Netherlands: Backhuys.

Minnich, R. A. 2006. California climate and fire weather. In *Fires in*

California's ecosystems, edited by N.G. Sugihara, J.W. van Wagtendonk, K.E. Shaffer, J. Fites-Kaufman, and A.E. Thode, 13–37. Berkeley: University of California Press.

Minnich, R.A., M.G. Barbour, J.H. Burk, and J. Sosa-Ramirez. 2000. California mixed-conifer forests under unmanaged fire regimes in the Sierra San Pedro Martir, Baja California, Mexico. *Journal of Biogeography* 27:105–129.

Moratto, M.J. 1984. *California Archaeology.* Orlando, FL: Academic Press.

Morrow, B. 1982. *People at the edge of the world: The Ohlone of central California.* Berkeley, CA: B. Morrow.

Moss, M.L., D.Y. Yang, S.D. Newsome, C.F. Speller, I. McKechnie, A.D. McMillan, R.J. Losey, and P.L. Koch. 2006. Historical ecology and biogeography of North Pacific pinnipeds: Isotopes and ancient DNA from three archaeological assemblages. *Journal of Island and Coastal Archaeology* 1 (2): 165–190.

Moyle, P.B. 2002. *Inland fishes of California.* Berkeley: University of California Press.

Muir, J. 1911. *The mountains of California.* 9th ed. New York: The Century Co.

Munz, P.A., and D.D. Keck. 1968. *A California flora and supplement.* Berkeley: University of California Press.

Munz, P.A., D. Lake, and P.M. Faber. 2004. *Introduction to California spring wildflowers.* California Natural History Guides, no. 75. Berkeley: University of California Press.

Nabhan, G.P., and A. Rea. 1987. Plant domestication and folk-biological change: The Upper Piman/devil's claw example. *American Anthropologist* 89 (1): 57–73.

Nabokov, P., and R. Easton. 1989. *Native American architecture.* Oxford: Oxford University Press.

Napton, L.K., and E.E.A. Greathouse. 2005. Archaeological research in the Central Valley: Stanislaus, Merced, and San Joaquin counties, California. In *Archaeology without limits: Papers in honor of Clement W. Meighan,* edited by B.D. Dillon and M.A. Boxt, 113–126. Lancaster, CA: Labyrinthos.

Nelson, M. 2006. Ravens, storms, and the ecological Indian at the National Museum of the American Indian. *Wicaso Sa Review* 21 (2): 41–60.

News from Native California. 1999. Western regional indigenous basketweavers gathering, June 17–20, 1999. *News from Native California* 13 (1): 21–43.

Nicola, S. 1995. Beargrass burning spreads. *California Indian Basketweavers Association* 13:11.

Niemi, T.M., and N.T. Hall. 1992. Late Holocene slip rate and recurrence of great earthquakes on the San Andreas Fault in northern California. *Geology* 20:195–198.

Noller, J.S., and K.G. Lightfoot. 1997. An archaeoseismic approach and method for the study of active strike-slip faults. *Geoarchaeology* 12 (2): 117–135.

Nomland, G.A. 1938. Bear River ethnography. *Anthropological Records* 2 (2): 91–126.

O'Connell, J., J. Trammell, C. Parker, S. Grant, and L. Hunsaker. 2008. Experimental assessment of resource rank: Handling costs for *Perideridia* (epos, yampa) in the North Great Basin. Poster session presented at the Annual Meeting of the Society for American Archaeology, Vancouver, BC.

Olmsted, D.L., and O.C. Stewart. 1978. Achumawi. In *Handbook of North American Indians,* vol. 8: *California,* edited by R.F. Heizer, 225–235. Washington, DC: Smithsonian Institution.

O'Neale, L.M. 1932. Yurok-Karok basket weavers. *University of California Publications in American Archaeology and Ethnology* 32 (1): 1–184.

Ornduff, R., P.M. Faber, and T. Keeler-Wolf. 2003. *Introduction to California plant life.* Revised ed. California Natural History Guides, no. 69. Berkeley: University of California Press.

Ortiz, B.R. 1990–1991. A rich red hue: Yurok dugout canoes. *News from Native California* 5 (1): 12–16.

Ortiz, B.R. 1993. Contemporary California Indian basketweavers and the environment. In *Before the wilderness: Environmental management by Native Californians,* edited by T.C. Blackburn and K. Anderson, 195–211. Menlo Park, CA: Ballena Press.

Ortiz, B.R. 2006. Wild garden: How Native Americans shaped local landscapes. *Bay Nature* 6 (1): 12–15, 33.

Owen, R.C. 1962. The Indians of Santa Catarina, Baja California Norte, Mexico: Concepts of disease and curing. Ph.D. dissertation, University of California, Los Angeles.

Owen, R.C. 1965. The patrilineal band: A linguistically and culturally hybrid social unit. *American Anthropologist* 67:675–690.

Parker, A.J. 2002. Fire in Sierra Nevada forests: Evaluating the ecological impact of burning by Native Americans. In *Fire, native peoples, and the natural landscape,* edited by T.R. Vale, 233–267. Covelo, CA: Island Press.

Parsons, D.J., D.M. Graber, J.K. Agee, and J.W.V. Wagtendonk. 1986. Natural fire management in national parks. *Environmental Management* 10:21–24.

Peigler, R.S. 1994. Non-sericultural uses of moth coccoons in diverse cultures. *Proceedings of the Denver Museum of Natural History* 3 (5): 1–20.

Peri, D.W., and S.M. Patterson. 1993. "The basket is the roots, that's where it begins." In *Before the wilderness: Environmental management by Native Californians,* edited by T.C. Blackburn and K. Anderson, 175–193. Menlo Park, CA: Ballena Press.

Perry, J. 1988. Yurok fishing. *News from Native California* 2 (3): 13–15.

Pilling, A.R. 1978. Yurok. In *Handbook of North American Indians,* vol. 8: *California,* edited by R.F. Heizer, 137–154. Washington, DC: Smithsonian Institution.

Pletka, S. 2001. The economics of Island Chumash fishing practices. In *The origins of a Pacific Coast chiefdom: The Chumash of the Channel Islands,* edited by J.E. Arnold, 221–244. Salt Lake City, UT: University of Utah Press.

Preston, W. 1997. Serpent in the garden: Environmental change in colonial California. *California History* 76 (2/3): 260–298.

Preziosi, A.M. 2001. Standardization and specialization: The Island Chumash microdrill industry. In *The origins of a Pacific Coast chiefdom: The Chumash of the Channel Islands,* edited by J.E. Arnold, 151–164. Salt Lake City, UT: University of Utah Press.

Price, T.D., and J. Brown. 1985. *Prehistoric hunter-gatherers: The emergence of cultural complexity.* Orlando, FL: Academic Press.

Price, T.D., and A.B. Gebauer, editors. 1995a. *Last hunters–first farmers: New perspectives on the prehistoric transition to agriculture.* Santa Fe, NM: School of American Research Press.

Price, T.D., and A.B. Gebauer. 1995b. New perspectives on the transition to agriculture. In *Last hunters–first farmers: New perspectives on the prehistoric transition to agriculture,* edited by T.D. Price and A.B. Gebauer, 3–19. Santa Fe, NM: School of American Research Press.

Pyne, S.J. 1991. *Burning bush: A fire history of Australia.* New York: Henry Holt.

Quick, C.R. 1962. Resurgence of a gooseberry population after fire in mature timber. *Journal of Forestry* 60 (2): 100–103.

Quinn, D.B. 1979a. 1542–1543. The voyage of Juan Rodríguez Cabrillo (João Rodrigues Cabrilho) up the Pacific coast. In *New American world: A documentary history of North America to 1612,* vol. 1: *America from conception to discovery: Early exploration of North America,* edited by D.B. Quinn, 450–461. New York: Arno Press and Hector Bye.

Quinn, D.B. 1979b. "The world encompassed," account of Drake's California visit. In *New American world: A documentary history of North America to 1612,* vol. 1: *America from concept to discovery:*

Early exploration of North America, edited by D.B. Quinn, 467–476. New York: Arno Press and Hector Bye.

Quinn, D.B. 1979c. December 1, 1587. Pedro de Unamuno to the Marqués de Villamanrique, Viceroy of Mexico. In *New American world: A documentary history of North America to 1612,* vol. 5: *The extension of settlement in Florida, Virginia, and the Spanish Southwest,* edited by D.B. Quinn, 401–408. New York: Arno Press and Hector Bye.

Quinn, D.B. 1979d. November 30, 1595. Abstract of the journal of Sebastian Cermeño on his voyage up the California coast. In *New American world: A documentary history of North America to 1612,* vol. 5: *The extension of settlement in Florida, Virginia, and the Spanish Southwest,* edited by D.B. Quinn, 408–413. New York: Arno Press and Hector Bye.

Quinn, D.B. 1979e. May 5, 1602. Fray António de la Ascensión's "brief report" of the voyage of Sebastian Vizcaíno up the California coast. In *New American world: A documentary history of North America to 1612,* vol. 5: *The extension of settlement in Florida, Virginia, and the Spanish Southwest,* edited by D.B. Quinn, 413–426. New York: Arno Press and Hector Bye.

Raab, L.M. 1996. Debating prehistory in coastal southern California: Resource intensification versus political economy. *Journal of California and Great Basin Anthropology* 18 (1): 64–80.

Raab, L.M. 2000. Remodeling California prehistory: Notes on the changing roles of ethnohistory in archaeology. *Proceedings of the Society for California Archaeology* 13:11–26.

Raab, L.M., K. Bradford, and A. Yatsko. 1994. Advances in southern Channel Islands archaeology: 1983–1993. *Journal of California and Great Basin Anthropology* 16 (2): 243–270.

Raab, L.M., and D.O. Larson. 1997. Medieval Climatic Anomaly and punctuated cultural evolution in coastal southern California. *American Antiquity* 62 (2): 319–336.

Raab, L.M., J.F. Porcasi, and W.J. Howard. 1995. Return to Little Harbor, Santa Catalina Island, California: A critique of the marine paleotemperature model. *American Antiquity* 60:287–308.

Raab, L.M., A. Yatsko, T.S. Garlinghouse, and J.F. Porcasi. 2002. Late Holocene San Clemente Island: Notes on comparative social complexity in coastal southern California. In *Catalysts to complexity: The Late Holocene on the California coast,* edited by J. Erlandson and T. Jones, 13–26. Los Angeles: Costen Institute of Archaeology, UCLA.

Ragir, S.R. 1968. *The Early Horizon in central California prehistory.* Berkeley: University of California.

Rawls, J.J. 1984. *Indians of California: The changing image.* Norman: University of Oklahoma Press.

Ray, V.F. 1963. *Primitive pragmatists: The Modoc Indians of northern California.* Seattle: University of Washington Press.

Reddy, S. 1999. Plant usage and prehistoric diet: Paleoethnobotanical investigations on Camp Pendleton, southern California. *Pacific Coast Archaeological Society Quarterly* 35 (4): 25–44.

Rick, T.C., J.M. Erlandson, and R.L. Vellanoweth. 2001. Paleocoastal marine fishing on the Pacific coast of the Americas: Perspectives from Daisy Cave, California. *American Antiquity* 66 (4): 595–613.

Rick, T.C., J.M. Erlandson, R.L. Vellanoweth, and T.J. Braje. 2005. From Pleistocene mariners to complex hunter-gatherers: The archaeology of the California Channel Islands. *Journal of World Prehistory* 19:169–228.

Rick, T.C., D.J. Kennett, and J.M. Erlandson. 2005. Preliminary report on the archaeology and paleoecology of the Abalone Rocks Estuary, Santa Rosa Island, California. In *Proceedings of the Sixth California Islands Symposium, Ventura, California, December 1–3, 2003,* edited by D.K. Garcelon and C.A. Schwemm. Arcata, CA: National Park Service, Institute for Wildlife Studies.

Rick, T.C., R.L. Vellanoweth, J.M. Erlandson, and D.J. Kennett. 2002. On the antiquity of the single-piece shell fishhooks: AMS radiocarbon evidence from the southern California coast. *Journal of Archaeological Science* 29:933–942.

Riddell, F.A. 1978. Maidu and Konkow. In *Handbook of North American Indians,* vol. 8: *California,* edited by R.F. Heizer, 370–386. Washington, DC: Smithsonian Institution.

Riegel, G.M., R.F. Miller, C.N. Skinner, and S.E. Smith. 2006. Northeastern Plateaus bioregion. In *Fires in California's ecosystems,* edited by N.G. Sugihara, J.W. van Wagtendonk, K.E. Shaffer, J. Fites-Kaufman, and A.E. Thode, 225–263. Berkeley: University of California Press.

Rosenthal, J.S., J. Meyer, J. Nelson, D. Furlong, T. Carpenter, and E. Wohlgemuth. 2006. Results of limited geoarchaeological and archaeological study of CA-CCO-18/548, John Marsh Historic Park, Brentwood, California. Sacramento: California Department of Parks and Recreation.

Rosenthal, J.S., G.G. White, and M.Q. Sutton. 2007. The Central Valley: A view from the catbird's seat. In *California prehistory,* edited by T.L. Jones and K.A. Klar, 147–163. Walnut Creek, CA: Alta Mira Press.

Ruppert, D. 2003. Building partnerships between American Indian tribes and the National Park Service. *Ecological Restoration* 21 (4): 261–263.

Sapir, E. 1917. The position of Yana in the Hokan Stock. *University of California Publications in American Archaeology and Ethnology* 13 (1): 1–34.

Sapir, E. 1921. A bird's-eye view of American languages north of Mexico. *Science* 54 (1400): 408.

Sapir, E. 1921–1923. A characteristic Penutian form of stem. *International Journal of American Linguistics* 21 (1–2): 58–67.

Sawyer, J.O. 1978. Wappo. In *Handbook of North American Indians,* vol. 8: *California,* edited by R.F. Heizer, 256–263. Washington, DC: Smithsonian Institution.

Schenck, S.M., and E.W. Gifford. 1952. Karok ethnobotany. *Anthropological Records* 13 (6): 377–392.

Schoenherr, A.A. 1992. *A natural history of California.* Berkeley: University of California Press.

Shackley, M.S. 1981. Late prehistoric exchange network analysis in Carrizo Gorge and the far Southwest. M.A. thesis, San Diego State University.

Shackley, M.S. 1984. *Archaeological investigations in the western Colorado Desert: A socioecological approach.* Salina, CA: Coyote Press.

Shackley, M.S. 1990. Early hunter-gatherer procurement ranges in the Southwest: Evidence from obsidian geochemistry and lithic technology. Ph.D. dissertation, Department of Anthropology, Arizona State University.

Shackley, M.S. 2004. Prehistory, archaeology, and history of research. In *The early ethnography of the Kumeyaay,* edited by M.S. Shackley, 12–35. Berkeley: Phoebe Hearst Museum of Anthropology, University of California.

Shaffer, K.E. 2006. Fire and at-risk species. In *Fires in California's ecosystems,* edited by N.G. Sugihara, J.W. van Wagtendonk, K.E. Shaffer, J. Fites-Kaufman, and A.E. Thode, 520–537. Berkeley: University of California Press.

Shaffer, K.E., and W.F. Laudenslayer. 2006. Fire and animal interactions. In *Fires in California's ecosystems,* edited by N.G. Sugihara, J.W. van Wagtendonk, K.E. Shaffer, J. Fites-Kaufman, and A.E. Thode, 118–144. Berkeley: University of California Press.

Shipek, F.C. 1977. A strategy for change: The Luiseño of southern California. Ph.D. dissertation, Department of Anthropology, University of Hawaii.

Shipek, F.C. 1989. An example of intensive plant husbandry. The Kumeyaay of southern California. In *Foraging and farming: The evolution of plant exploitation,* edited by D.R. Harris and G.C. Hillman, 159–170. London: Unwin-Hyman.

Shipek, F.C. 1993. Kumeyaay plant husbandry: Fire, water, and erosion management systems. In *Before the wilderness: Environmental management by Native Californians,* edited by T.C. Blackburn and K. Anderson, 379–388. Menlo Park, CA: Ballena Press.

Shipley, W.F. 1978. Native languages of California. In *Handbook of North American Indians,* vol. 8: *California,* edited by R.F. Heizer, 80–90. Washington, DC: Smithsonian Institution.

Silver, S. 1978. Shastan peoples. In *Handbook of North American Indians,* vol. 8: *California,* edited by R.F. Heizer, 211–224. Washington, DC: Smithsonian Institution.

Simmons, W.S. 1997. Indian peoples of California. *California History* 76 (2/3): 48–77.

Sinclair, W.J. 1908. Recent investigations bearing on the question of the occurrence of Neocene man in the auriferous gravels of the Sierra Nevada. *University of California Publications in American Archaeology and Ethnology* 7 (2): 107–131.

Skinner, C.N., and C. Chang. 1996. Fire regimes, past and present. In *Sierra Nevada Ecosystem Project: Final report to Congress,* vol. 2: *Assessments and scientific basis for management options,* 1041–1069. Davis: Centers for Water and Wildlife Resourses, University of California.

Skinner, C.N., and A.H. Taylor. 2006. Southern Cascade bioregions. In *Fires in California's ecosystems,* edited by N.G. Sugihara, J.W. van Wagtendonk, K.E. Shaffer, J. Fites-Kaufman, and A.E. Thode, 195–224. Berkeley: University of California Press.

Skinner, C.N., A.H. Taylor, and J.K. Agee. 2006. Klamath Mountain bioregion. In *Fires in California's ecosystems,* edited by N.G. Sugihara, J.W. van Wagtendonk, K.E. Shaffer, J. Fites-Kaufman, and A.E. Thode, 170–194. Berkeley: University of California Press.

Sloan, D. 2006. *Geology of the San Francisco Bay region.* Berkeley: University of California Press.

Smith, B.D. 1995. Seed plant domestication in eastern North America. In *Last hunters–first farmers: New perspectives on the prehistoric transition to agriculture,* edited by T.D. Price and A.B. Gebauer, 193–213. Santa Fe, NM: School of American Research Press.

Smith, B.D. 2001. Low-level food production. *Journal of Archaeological Research* 9 (1): 1–43.

Smith, C.R. 1978. Tubatulabal. In *Handbook of North American Indians,* vol. 8: *California,* edited by R.F. Heizer, 437–445. Washington, DC: Smithsonian Institution.

Sparkman, P.S. 1908. The culture of the Luiseño Indians. *University of California Publications in American Archaeology and Ethnology* 8 (4): 187–234.

Spier, L. 1923. Southern Diegueño customs. *University of California Publications in American Archaeology and Ethnology* 20 (16): 295–358.

Spier, R.F.G. 1978a. Foothill Yokuts. In *Handbook of North American Indians,* vol. 8: *California,* edited by R.F. Heizer, 471–484. Washington, DC: Smithsonian Institution.

Spier, R.F.G. 1978b. Monache. In *Handbook of North American Indians,* vol. 8: *California,* edited by R.F. Heizer, 426–436. Washington, DC: Smithsonian Institution.

Sprugel, D.G. 1991. Disturbance, equilibrium, and environmental variability: What is "natural" vegetation in a changing environment? *Biological Conservation* 58:1–18.

Stanford, D., and B. Bradley. 2002. Ocean trails and prairie paths? Thoughts about Clovis origins. In *The first Americans: The Pleistocene colonization of the New World,* edited by N.G. Jablonski, 255–272. Memoirs of the California Academy of Sciences, no. 27. San Francisco: California Academy of Sciences.

Stephens, S.L., and D.L. Fry. 2005. Fire history in coast redwood stands in the northeastern Santa Cruz Mountains, California. *Fire Ecology* 1 (1): 2–19.

Stephens, S.L., R.E. Martin, and N.E. Clinton. 2007. Prehistoric fire area and emissions from California's forests, woodlands, shrublands, and grasslands. *Forest Ecology and Management* 251:205–216.

Stephens, S.L., C.N. Skinner, and S.J. Gill. 2003. Dendrochronology-based fire history of Jeffrey pine—mixed forests in the Sierra San Pedro Martir, Mexico. *Canadian Journal of Forest Research* 33: 1090–1101.

Stephens, S.L., and N.G. Sugihara. 2006. Fire management and policy since European settlement. In *Fires in California's ecosystems,* edited by N.G. Sugihara, J.W. van Wagtendonk, K.E. Shaffer, J. Fites-Kaufman, and A.E. Thode, 431–443. Berkeley: University of California Press.

Stern, T. 1998. Klamath and Modoc. In *Handbook of North American Indians,* vol. 12: *Plateau,* edited by D.E. Walker Jr., 446–466. Washington, DC: Smithsonian Institution.

Stewart, B.S., P.K. Yochem, H.R. Huber, R.L. DeLong, R.J. Jameson, W.J. Snydeman, S.G. Allen, and B.J. Le Boeuf. 1994. History and present status of the Northern Elephant Seal population. In *Elephant seals: Population ecology, behavior and physiology,* edited by B.J. Le Boeuf and R.M. Laws, 29–48. Berkeley: University of California Press.

Stewart, O.C. 1943. Notes on Pomo ethnogeography. *University of*

California Publications in American Archaeology and Ethnology 40 (2): 29–62.

Stewart, O.C. 2002. *Forgotten fires: Native Americans and the transient wilderness.* Norman: University of Oklahoma Press.

Stine, S. 1994. Extreme and persistent drought in California and Patagonia during Medieval time. *Nature* 369:546–549.

Strike, S.S. 1994. *Ethnobotany of the California Indians,* vol. 2: *Aboriginal uses of California's indigenous plants.* Champaign, IL: Koeltz Scientific Books.

Strong, W.D. 1929. Aboriginal society in southern California. *University of California Publications in American Archaeology and Ethnology* 26:1–358.

Stuart, J.D., and J.O. Sawyer. 2001. *Trees and shrubs of California.* California Natural History Guides, no. 62. Berkeley: University of California Press.

Stuart, J.D., and S.L. Stephens. 2006. North Coast bioregion. In *Fires in California's ecosystems,* edited by N.G. Sugihara, J.W. van Wagtendonk, K.E. Shaffer, J. Fites-Kaufman, and A.E. Thode, 147–169. Berkeley: University of California Press.

Sugihara, N.G., and M.G. Barbour. 2006. Fire and California vegetation. In *Fires in California's ecosystems,* edited by N.G. Sugihara, J.W. van Wagtendonk, K.E. Shaffer, J. Fites-Kaufman, and A.E. Thode, 1–9. Berkeley: University of California Press.

Sugihara, N.G., J.W. van Wagtendonk, and J. Fites-Kaufman. 2006. Fire as an ecological process. In *Fires in California's ecosystems,* edited by N.G. Sugihara, J.W. van Wagtendonk, K.E. Shaffer, J. Fites-Kaufman, and A.E. Thode, 58–74. Berkeley: University of California Press.

Sugihara, N.G., J.W. van Wagtendonk, K.E. Shaffer, J. Fites-Kaufman, and A.E. Thode, editors. 2006. *Fires in California's ecosystems.* Berkeley: University of California Press.

Sutton, M.Q. 1988. *Insects as food: Aboriginal entomophagy in the Great Basin.* Ballena Press Anthropological Papers, no. 33. Menlo Park, CA: Ballena Press.

Sutton, M.Q. 1996. The current status of archaeological research in the Mojave Desert. *Journal of California and Great Basin Anthropology* 18 (2): 221–257.

Swetnam, T.W. 1993. Fire history and climate change in giant sequoia groves. *Science* 262:885–889.

Swezey, S.L., and R.F. Heizer. 1993. Ritual management of salmonid fish resources in California. In *Before the wilderness: Environmental management by Native Californians,* edited by T.C. Blackburn and K. Anderson, 299–327. Menlo Park, CA: Ballena Press.

Thomas, D.H. 1974. An archaeological perspective on Shoshonean bands. *American Anthropologist* 76:11–23.

Thomsen, H.H., and R.F. Heizer. 1964. The archaeological potential of the Coast Yuki. *University of California Archaeological Survey Reports* 63:45–83.

Timbrook, J. 1990. Ethnobotany of Chumash Indians, California, based on collections by John P. Harrington. *Economic Botany* 44 (2): 236–253.

Timbrook, J. 2007. *Chumash ethnobotany: Plant knowledge among the Chumash people of southern California.* Santa Barbara Museum of Natural History Monographs, no. 5. Berkeley, CA: Heyday Books.

Timbrook, J., J.R. Johnson, and D.D. Earle. 1993. Vegetation burning by the Chumash. In *Before the wilderness: Environmental management by Native Californians,* edited by T.C. Blackburn and K. Anderson, 117–149. Menlo Park, CA: Ballena Press.

Trammell, J., S. Bush, J. O'Connell, C. Parker, and P. Borghi. 2008. After the fire: Thoughts on Pre-Columbian and Post-Apocalyptic western North American landscapes. Poster session presented at the Annual Meeting of the Society for American Archaeology, Vancouver, BC.

Tucker, B. 2006. A future discounting explanation for the persistence of a mixed foraging-horticulture strategy among the Mikea of Madagascar. In *Behavioral ecology and the transition to agriculture,* edited by D.J. Kennett and B. Winterhalder, 22–40. Berkeley: University of California Press.

Tveskov, M.A. 2007. Social identity and culture change on the southern Northwest Coast. *American Anthropologist* 109 (3): 431–441.

Ugan, A. 2005. Does size matter? Body size, mass collecting, and their implications for understanding prehistoric foraging behavior. *American Antiquity* 70 (1): 75–89.

U.S. Bureau of Land Management. 2006. Draft: Interagency Indian traditional gathering policy. Sacramento, CA: U.S. Department of the Interior, Bureau of Land Management.

Vale, T.R. 1998. The myth of the humanized landscape: An example from Yosemite National Park. *Natural Areas Journal* 18 (3): 231–236.

Vale, T.R. 2000. Pre-Columbian North America: Pristine or humanized—or both? *Ecological Restoration* 18 (1): 2–3.

Vale, T.R. 2002. The pre-European landscape of the United States: Pristine or humanized? In *Fire, native peoples, and the natural landscape,* edited by T.R. Vale, 1–39. Covelo, CA: Island Press.

Valoma, D. 2004. The past in present tense: Four decades of baskets by Julia Parker. *News from Native California* 18 (1): 4–6.

van Wagtendonk, J.W. 1986. The role of fire in the Yosemite wilderness. In *Proceedings of the National Wilderness Research Conference: Current research,* 2–9. General Technical Report INT-212. Ogden, UT: U.S. Department of Agriculture, Forest Service.

van Wagtendonk, J.W. 2006. Fire as a physical process. In *Fires in California's ecosystems,* edited by N.G. Sugihara, J.W. van Wagtendonk, K.E. Shaffer, J. Fites-Kaufman, and A.E. Thode, 38–57. Berkeley: University of California Press.

van Wagtendonk, J.W., and J. Fites-Kaufman. 2006. Sierra Nevada bioregion. In *Fires in California's ecosystems,* edited by N.G. Sugihara, J.W. van Wagtendonk, K.E. Shaffer, J. Fites-Kaufman, and A.E. Thode, 264–294. Berkeley: University of California Press.

Vayda, A.P. 1967. Pomo trade feasts. In *Tribal and peasant economies,* edited by G. Dalton, 495–500. Garden City, NY: Natural History Press.

Voegelin, E. 1942. Culture element distributions, XX: Northeast California. *University of California Anthropological Records* 7 (2): 47–252.

Waechter, S.A. 1995. *The Brazil mound: Archaeology of a prehistoric village.* Davis, CA: Far Western Anthropological Research Group.

Walker, P.L., P. Lambert, and M.J. DeNiro. 1989. The effects of European contact on the health of Alta California Indians. In *Columbian consequences,* vol. 1: *Archaeological and historical perspectives on the Spanish borderlands west,* edited by D.H. Thomas, 349–364. Washington, DC: Smithsonian Institution Press.

Wallace, W.J. 1978a. Northern Valley Yokuts. In *Handbook of North American Indians,* vol. 8: *California,* edited by R.F. Heizer, 462–470. Washington, DC: Smithsonian Institution.

Wallace, W.J. 1978b. Southern Valley Yokuts. In *Handbook of North American Indians,* vol. 8: *California,* edited by R.F. Heizer, 448–461. Washington, DC: Smithsonian Institution.

Wallace, W.J. 1980. Death Valley Indian farming. *Journal of California and Great Basin Anthropology* 2:269–272.

Wandsnider, L. 1997. The roasted and the boiled: Food composition and heat treatment with special emphasis on pit-hearth cooking. *Journal of Anthropological Archaeology* 16:1–48.

Wartzman, R. 2007. Can the city save the farm? *California* 118 (3): 17–24.

Waterman, T.T. 1910. The religious practices of the Diegueño Indians. *University of California Publications in American Archaeology and Ethnology* 8 (6): 271–358.

Waterman, T.T., and A. Kroeber. 1938. The Kepel fish dam. *University of California Publications in American Archaeology and Ethnology* 35 (6): 49–80.

Watson, R.A., and P.J. Watson. 1971. The domesticator of plants and animals. In *Prehistoric agriculture,* edited by S. Stuever, 3–11. Garden City, NY: The Natural History Press.

West, G.J. 1989. Early historic vegetation change in Alta California: The fossil evidence. In *Columbian consequences,* vol. 1: *Archaeological and historical perspectives on the Spanish borderlands west,* edited by D.H. Thomas, 333–348. Washington, DC: Smithsonian Institution Press.

Wheeland, M. 2007. Wilding the farm. *California* 118 (3): 23, 25, 26.

White, G.G. 2003. *Population ecology of the prehistoric Colusa Reach.* PhD. dissertation, University of California, Davis.

Wilke, P.J., R. Bettinger, T.F. King, and J.F. O'Connell. 1972. Harvest selection and domestication in seed plants. *Antiquity* 46 (183): 203–209.

Willey, G.R., and J.A. Sabloff. 1993. *A history of American archaeology.* 3rd ed. New York: W.H. Freeman and Co.

Willie, E. 2002. Nothing to do but weave: A basketweavers' retreat. *News from Native California* 16 (1): 12–14.

Wills, R. 2006. Central Valley bioregion. In *Fires in California's ecosystems,* edited by N.G. Sugihara, J.W. van Wagtendonk, K.E. Shaffer, J. Fites-Kaufman, and A.E. Thode, 295–320. Berkeley: University of California Press.

Wills, W.H. 1988. *Early prehistoric agriculture in the American Southwest.* Santa Fe, NM: School of American Research Press.

Wills, W.H. 1995. Archaic foraging and the beginning of food production in the American Southwest. In *Last hunters–first farmers: New perspectives on the prehistoric transition to agriculture,* edited by T.D. Price and A.B. Gebauer, 215–242. Santa Fe, NM: School of American Research Press.

Wilson, N.L. 1972. Notes on traditional Foothill Nisenan food technology. *University of California Center for Archaeological Publications* 3:32–38.

Wilson, N.L., and A.H. Towne. 1978. Nisenan. In *Handbook of North American Indians,* vol. 8: *California,* edited by R.F. Heizer, 387–397. Washington, DC: Smithsonian Institution.

Winick, C. 1956. *Dictionary of anthropology.* New York: Philosophical Library.

Winterhalder, B., and D.J. Kennett. 2006. Behavioral ecology and the transition from hunting and gathering to agriculture. In *Behavioral ecology and the transition to agriculture,* edited by D.J. Kennett and B. Winterhalder, 1–21. Berkeley: University of California Press.

Wohlgemuth, E. 1998. Archaeobotanical investigation of the Spillway Outlet feature at CA-CCO-637. In *An archaeological investigation of artifacts and human remains from CA-CCO-637, Los Vaqueros Project area, Contra Costa County, California,* edited by J. Meyer and J.S. Rosenthal, B1–B2. Rohnert Park, CA: Archaeological Studies Center, Sonoma State University Academic Foundation.

Wohlgemuth, E. 2004. The course of plant food intensification in Native central California. Ph.D. dissertation, Department of Anthropology, University of California, Davis.

Yates, L.G. 1975. Notes on the Indians of Clear Lake [1875]. In *Seven early accounts of the Pomo Indians and their culture,* edited by R.F. Heizer, 1–3. Berkeley: University of California Archaeological Research Facility.

Yen, D.E. 1989. The domestication of environment. In *Foraging and farming: The evolution of plant exploitation,* edited by D.R. Harris and G.C. Hillman, 55–75. Boston: Unwin Hyman.

Yoshiyama, R.M. 1999. A history of salmon and people in the Central Valley region of California. *Reviews in Fisheries Science* 7 (3/4): 197–239.

Yoshiyama, R.M., and F.W. Fisher. 2001. Long time past: Baird Station and the McCloud Wintu. *Fisheries* 26 (3): 6–22.

Yoshiyama, R. M., E. R. Gerstung, F. W. Fisher, and P. B. Moyle. 2001. Historical and present distribution of Chinook Salmon in the Central Valley drainage of California. *In* Fish Bulletin 179: Contributions to the biology of Central Valley salmonids, edited by R. L. Brown, 71–176, vol. 1. Sacramento: California Department of Fish and Game.

Ziegler, A.C. 1968. Quasi-agriculture in north-central California and its effect on aboriginal social structure. *Kroeber Anthropological Society Papers* 38:52–67.

RESOURCE REFERENCES BY REGION AND TYPE

Northwest Coast Province (pages 188–209)

PLANTS

Coast redwood: Baker 1981:55; Kroeber 1925:92–94; Merriam 1967: 174; O'Neale 1932:17; Schenck and Gifford 1952:379

ANIMALS

Black-tailed Deer: Bright 1978:181; Drucker 1937:234; Hildebrandt and Levulett 2002:310; Merriam 1967:185

Chinook Salmon: Drucker 1937:233; Kroeber 1925:85; McGinnis 2006:153–158; Perry 1988; Schoenherr 1992:612–613; Swezey and Heizer 1993

HUNTING

Sea lions: Drucker 1937:228, 234; Gould 1975:154; Hildebrandt and Levulett 2002; Kroeber 1925:86

Central Coast Province (pages 210–251)

FERNS

Ferns: Beard 1977:58; Gifford 1965:18, 19, 62, 1967:11; Goodrich et al. 1980:44–46; Margolin 1978:117; Mason 1912:149; Morrow 1982:25

MARINE PLANTS

Kelps, uses: Bean and Theodoratus 1978:290; Foster 1944:167; Gifford 1965:17–18, 1967:10; Goodrich et al. 1980:124–125; Hudson 1975:11; Kelly 1978:415

Seaweeds, uses: Callaghan 1978:265; Collier and Thalman 1996:124, 148; Driver 1936:187; Foster 1944:167; Gifford 1965:17–18; Goodrich et al. 1980:125–126; Harrington 1942:8; Margolin 1978:50; Morrow 1982:21; Sawyer 1978:260, 261

HERBACEOUS PLANTS

Broad-leaved Cattails, as food: Beard 1977:53; Goodrich et al. 1980: 32; Levy 1978a: 491; Margolin 1978:50; Morrow 1982:20

Brodiaeas: Collier and Thalman 1996:39; Driver 1936:187; Goodrich et al. 1980:25–27; Margolin 1978:50

Chia: Beard 1977:53; Harrington 1942:8; Levy 1978a:491; Mason 1912:120

Clovers: Beard 1977:52; Collier and Thalman 1996:120–121; Driver 1936:187; Gifford 1967:13; Goodrich et al. 1980:35–38; Levy 1978a:491; Margolin 1978:50; McLendon and Lowry 1978:310; Morrow 1982:20

Dogbane: Bean and Theodoratus 1978:291; Beard 1977:53, 58; Breschini and Haversat 2004:124; Callaghan 1978:267; Foster 1944: 170; Harrington 1942:1; Levy 1978a:493; Margolin 1978:52

Grasses, as raw material: Barrett 1975:38; Bean and Theodoratus 1978:290–292; Beard 1977:45–46; Collier and Thalman 1996:190; Morrow 1982:13, 15; Sawyer 1978:261

Irises: Bean and Theodoratus 1978:291; Beard 1977:53; Driver 1936:191; Gifford 1965:19, 58–59; Kroeber 1925:214; Morrow 1982:25; Thomsen and Heizer 1964:55

Mariposa lilies: Beard 1977:53; Goodrich et al. 1980:63; Margolin 1978:50; Morrow 1982:20

Milkweeds, for cordage and nets: Bean and Theodoratus 1978:291; Beard 1977:53, 58; Breschini and Haversat 2004:51; Callaghan 1978: 267; Driver 1936:191; Harrington 1942:1; Levy 1978a:493; Mason 1912:124; McLendon and Lowry 1978:311; Morrow 1982: 26

Pinole: Beard 1977:53–54; Collier and Thalman 1996:146–148; Foster 1944:226; Gifford 1967:15; Goodrich et al. 1980:85–86; McLendon and Lowry 1978:310; Morrow 1982:20–21

Rushes, uses: Breschini and Haversat 2004:62; Gifford 1967:12; Goodrich et al. 1980:100; Harrington 1942:23; Levy 1978a:493; Morrow 1982:22, 25

Sedges: Beard 1977:58; Breschini and Haversat 2004:82; Callaghan 1978:266; Collier and Thalman 1996:39, 60, 158; Gifford 1965:18, 62, 1967:11–12; Goodrich et al. 1980:103–104; Kroeber 1925:171; Margolin 1978:117; Morrow 1982:25

Soap plants, brushes: Collier and Thalman 1996:173, 192; Foster

1944:169; Gifford 1967:12; Goodrich et al. 1980:107–108; Harrington 1942:12; Levy 1978a:493; Margolin 1978:43

Soap plants, as fish poison: Beard 1977:50, 52–53; Driver 1936:185; Gifford 1967:12; Goodrich et al. 1980:107–108; Levy 1978a:492

Soap plants, uses: Beard 1977:52–53; Collier and Thalman 1996:121, 148; Driver 1936:187; Foster 1944:166; Gifford 1967:12; Goodrich et al. 1980:107–108; Levy 1978a:491; Margolin 1978:50; Morrow 1982:21

Tarweeds: Beard 1977:54; Collier and Thalman 1996:147; Foster 1944:226; Gifford 1967:15; Goodrich et al. 1980:111–112; Holmes 1975:22; Levy 1978a:491; Margolin 1978:48

Tules, as basketry material: Breschini and Haversat 2004:122; Gifford 1965:62; Harrington 1942:23; Hester 1978a:498; Levy 1978a:493; Mason 1912:150

Tules, as building material etc.: Barrett 1975:40, 43; Bean and Theodoratus 1978:291, 292; Beard 1977:48; Collier and Thalman 1996: 160, 177–178, 210; Foster 1944:170; Hester 1978a:497–498; Holmes 1975:23; Kelly 1978:417, 419; Levy 1978a:492, 493; Margolin 1978:37, 54; Mason 1912:125; McLendon and Lowry 1978: 307, 310–312; Yates 1975:3

Tules, as food: Collier and Thalman 1996:121–122, 496; Driver 1936: 187; Levy 1978a:491; Morrow 1982:20

Wild oats: Collier and Thalman 1996:148; Gifford 1965:26, 1967:11; Goodrich et al. 1980:85–86; Hester 1978b:501; Mason 1912:120; Thomsen and Heizer 1964:54; Yates 1975:3

Wild strawberries, as food: Collier and Thalman 1996:123; Gifford 1965:19, 26, 1967:13; Goodrich et al. 1980:109–110; Levy 1978a: 491; Margolin 1978:50

Wild tobaccos: Beard 1977:54; Collier and Thalman 1996:151–152; Driver 1936:187; Gifford 1967:15; Goodrich et al. 1980:115; Margolin 1978:52; Miller 1978:252; Morrow 1982:47

TREES AND SHRUBS

Black oak acorns, for food: Collier and Thalman 1996:38, 47; Driver 1936:186; Foster 1944:165, 226; Gifford 1965:20, 1967:12; Goodrich et al. 1980:79–80; Margolin 1978:42

California bay nuts: Beard 1977:53; Collier and Thalman 1996:119, 146; Gifford 1965:20, 25, 1967:13; Goodrich et al. 1980:90–91; Holmes 1975:22; Levy 1978a:491; Margolin 1978:50; Morrow 1982:20

California buckeye, nonfood uses: Beard 1977:53; Breschini and Haversat 2004:121; Collier and Thalman 1996:186; Driver 1936:190, 192; Gifford 1967:14; Goodrich et al. 1980:27–28; Mason 1912:124

California buckeye nuts, ethnographic observations: Bean and Theodoratus 1978:290; Beard 1977:53; Breschini and Haversat 2004: 121; Collier and Thalman 1996:146; Driver 1936:187; Foster 1944: 166, 226; Gifford 1965:25, 1967:14; Goodrich et al. 1980:27–28; Harrington 1942:8; Hester 1978a:497; Holmes 1975:22; Kelly 1978:417; Levy 1978a:491; Margolin 1978:43; Mason 1912:120; McLendon and Lowry 1978:310; Sawyer 1978:261; Thomsen and Heizer 1964:54

California hazel, as food: Beard 1977:53; Collier and Thalman 1996: 120; Driver 1936:187; Foster 1944:166; Goodrich et al. 1980: 55–56; Levy 1978a:491; Margolin 1978:50

California hazel, as raw material: Beard 1977:53; Callaghan 1978:267; Collier and Thalman 1996:44, 187–188, 500; Driver 1936:191; Gifford 1965:46; Goodrich et al. 1980:55–56; Kroeber 1925:171; Morrow 1982:25; Thomsen and Heizer 1964:52

California wild grape, as cordage and basketry material: Barrett 1975:51; Gifford 1967:14; Goodrich et al. 1980:51–52; Kroeber 1925:172

California wild grape, as food: Driver 1936:187; Goodrich et al. 1980: 51–52; Levy 1978a:491; Margolin 1978:50

Coast live oak: Collier and Thalman 1996:47; Gifford 1967:12; Goodrich et al. 1980:80; Holmes 1975:22; Levy 1978a:491; Margolin 1978:41

Coast redwood, uses: Barrett 1975:37; Bean and Theodoratus 1978: 291–292; Collier and Thalman 1996:177–178; Gifford 1965:24, 62, 1967:11; Goodrich et al. 1980:97–98; Levy 1978a:492; Miller 1978:255; Thomsen and Heizer 1964:52

Elderberries, as food: Beard 1977:53; Breschini and Haversat 2004:62; Collier and Thalman 1996:122; Driver 1936:187; Foster 1944:166; Levy 1978a:491; Margolin 1978:50

Elderberries, medicinal uses: Callaghan 1978:272; Collier and Thalman 1996:391, 394; Gifford 1967:15; Goodrich et al. 1980: 42–43

Elderberries, as wood: Beard 1977:53, 61; Breschini and Haversat 2004:62; Callaghan 1978:267, 270; Collier and Thalman 1996:151, 219; Foster 1944:168, 171; Gifford 1965:65, 1967:15; Goodrich et al. 1980:42–43; Harrington 1942:27; Kelly 1978:417; Mason 1912:158

Foothill pine nuts: Beard 1977:53–54; Foster 1944:166, 226; Goodrich et al. 1980:92–93; Levy 1978a:491; Margolin 1978:49

Holly-leafed cherry: Breschini and Haversat 2004:122; Hammett and Lawlor 2004:297; Hester 1978a:497; Levy 1978a:491; Margolin 1978:50

Huckleberries, as food: Foster 1944:166, 226; Gifford 1965:20, 1967: 15; Margolin 1978:50

Madrone berries: Beard 1977:53; Breschini and Haversat 2004:121; Goodrich et al. 1980:67–68; Holmes 1975:22; Levy 1978a:491; Margolin 1978:50

Manzanita berries, as food and cider: Beard 1977:53; Breschini and Haversat 2004:122; Callaghan 1978:265; Collier and Thalman 1996:123; Driver 1936:187; Foster 1944:166, 226; Gifford 1965:18; Goodrich et al. 1980:68–69; Holmes 1975:22; Levy 1978a:491; Margolin 1978:50; Morrow 1982:20

Oak acorns, harvests, processing, storage, and cooking: Barrett 1975:43–44; Bean and Theodoratus 1978:290; Beard 1977:51; Gifford 1965:24; Goodrich et al. 1980:83–84; Holmes 1975:22; Levy 1978a:491; Margolin 1978:42–44; McLendon and Lowry 1978:310; Morrow 1982:19, 28; Yates 1975:3

Oak acorns, importance: Baumhoff 1978; Bean and Theodoratus 1978: 290; Holmes 1975:22; Levy 1978a:491; Margolin 1978:41; McLendon and Lowry 1978:310; Miller 1978:255; Morrow 1982:19, 21

Tan-oak acorns: Collier and Thalman 1996:119; Driver 1936:186; Gifford 1967:12; Goodrich et al. 1980:83–84; Holmes 1975:22; Kelly 1978:416; Levy 1978a:491; Margolin 1978:42

Thimbleberries, as food: Collier and Thalman 1996:123; Gifford 1967:13; Goodrich et al. 1980:113–114; Margolin 1978:50

Toyon berries, as food: Beard 1977:54; Collier and Thalman 1996: 115–116; Driver 1936:187; Gifford 1967:13; Levy 1978a:491; Margolin 1978:50

Valley oak acorns: Callaghan 1978:265; Foster 1944:165, 226; Gifford 1965:20, 1967:12; Goodrich et al. 1980:84–85; Kelly 1978:416; Levy 1978a:491; Margolin 1978:41

Wild rose: Beard 1977:54; Goodrich et al. 1980:99; Holmes 1975:22

Willows, as basketry material: Beard 1977:54, 58; Breschini and Haversat 2004:121; Callaghan 1978:266; Collier and Thalman 1996:158–159; Gifford 1967:12; Goodrich et al. 1980:118–119; Harrington 1942:23; Kroeber 1925:171; Levy 1978a:493; Margolin 1978:117; Mason 1912:145; Morrow 1982:25

Willows, as building material: Barrett 1975:44; Bean and Theodoratus 1978:291; Beard 1977:50, 54; Callaghan 1978:267; Collier and Thalman 1996:177; Hester 1978b:501; Holmes 1975:23; Levy 1978a:492; Margolin 1978:54; Morrow 1982:13

SHELLFISH

Abalone shell, for jewelry and other objects: Bean and Theodoratus 1978:292; Beard 1977:49; Breschini and Haversat 2004:119;

Driver 1936:188; Gifford 1965:56; Levy 1978a:488, 494; Margolin 1978:46, 120; Mason 1912:129, 131; Morrow 1982:25–26

Abalones, gathering: Collier and Thalman 1996:125; Driver 1936:184; Gifford 1965:40; Greengo 1952:74; Miller 1978:255

Abalones, processing and cooking: Collier and Thalman 1996:125; Gifford 1965:28, 1967:21; Hester 1978a:497; Levy 1978:492; Margolin 1978:36; Mason 1912:122

Clams, as food and for beads: Beard 1977:49; Callaghan 1978:267; Driver 1936:188; Harrington 1942:16; Hester 1978b:500; Hudson 1975:11; Kelly 1978:418; Kroeber 1925:176, 215; Margolin 1978:76; Mason 1912:122; McLendon and Lowry 1978:310–311; Morrow 1982:17

Mussel shells, as sources of raw material: Breschini and Haversat 2004:99; Driver 1936:186–187; Foster 1944:169; Gifford 1965:53, 59; Kroeber 1925:214; Levy 1978a:493; Mason 1912:131; Miller 1978:251, 255; Thomsen and Heizer 1964:54

Mussels, processing: Collier and Thalman 1996:127; Gifford 1965:27–28, 1967:21; Greengo 1952:77–78

Olive Snail shells: Beard 1977:49; Foster 1944:173; Gifford 1965:41, 56, 1967:21; Harrington 1942:16; Margolin 1978:36

CRUSTACEANS AND OTHER WATER INVERTEBRATES

Crabs: Collier and Thalman 1996:127, 149; Driver 1936:184; Gifford 1965:39; Greengo 1952:75–76; Kelly 1978:415; Mason 1912:122

Octopuses, uses: Collier and Thalman 1996:127, 149; Gifford 1965:41, 1967:14, 21; Greengo 1952:76; Levy 1978a:492

Sea urchins, uses: Collier and Thalman 1996:127; Gifford 1965:42, 1967:20; Greengo 1952:76

INSECTS

Caterpillars: Bean and Theodoratus 1978:290–291; Beard 1977:51; Gifford 1965:42; Levy 1978a:492

Grasshoppers: Callaghan 1978:266; Collier and Thalman 1996:128; Gifford 1965:42, 1967:20; Harrington 1942:8; Levy 1978a:492; Margolin 1978:25; Miller 1978:253

Moth cocoons, uses: Barret and Gifford 1933:249–250; Foster 1944:171; Gifford 1965:65; Levy 1978a:490; Peigler 1994

Yellowjackets: Callaghan 1978:266; Foster 1944:167; Gifford 1965:42, 1967:20; Harrington 1942:8; Levy 1978a:492; Mason 1912:122

FISHES

Fish processing: Beard 1977:52; Collier and Thalman 1996:144–145; Driver 1936:185; Foster 1944:164; McLendon and Lowry 1978:310

Fishing methods: Beard 1977:50, 53; Collier and Thalman 1996:140; Driver 1936:184; Foster 1944:163–164; Harrington 1942:9; Gifford 1965:35, 1967:14, 19–20; Kelly 1978:416; Levy 1978a:491–492; Mason 1912:122, 124–125

Pacific Lamprey, for food: Collier and Thalman 1996:143; Driver 1936:184; Foster 1944:164; Gifford 1965:23; Kroeber 1925:213; Thomsen and Heizer 1964:54

Rainbow trout: Collier and Thalman 1996:143; Driver 1936:184; Gifford 1965:34, 1967:19; Mason 1912:122; Miller 1978:252

Salmon: Gifford 1965:23; Kroeber 1925:174, 213; Mason 1912:122, 124–125; Miller 1978:252; Thomsen and Heizer 1964:54

Surfperches: Collier and Thalman 1996:142; Foster 1944:164; Gifford 1965:35, 1967:19

AMPHIBIANS AND REPTILES

Turtles: Collier and Thalman 1996:128; Driver 1936:184–185; Foster 1944:226; Gifford 1967:19

BIRDS

Band-tailed Pigeons: Foster 1944:163; Gifford 1965:34, 1967:17–18; Levy 1978a: 491; Margolin 1978:25

Ducks, uses: Beard 1977:49; Collier and Thalman 1996:129–130, 163, 166, 174; Driver 1936:185; Foster 1944:163; Levy 1978a:491, 493; Margolin 1978:38, 120; McLendon and Lowry 1978:310; Morrow 1982:16, 18, 24

Geese, uses: Beard 1977:49; Collier and Thalman 1996:129; Driver 1936:185, 191; Levy 1978a:491; Margolin 1978:38; Morrow 1982: 16, 18

Quails, as food and feathers: Breschini and Haversat 2004:119; Collier and Thalman 1996:128, 148, 156; Driver 1936:185; Foster 1944: 163, 167; Levy 1978a:493; Morrow 1982:25

Terrestrial birds, intro.: Driver 1936:185; Foster 1944:163; Mason 1912:124; Miller 1978:252

Woodpeckers: Beard 1977:49; Callaghan 1978:266, 268; Collier and Thalman 1996:162; Driver 1936:185, 188; Foster 1944:163, 172, 225; Gifford 1965:85, 1967:19; Levy 1978a:493; Mason 1912:128; Margolin 1978:152; Morrow 1982:15, 25

MAMMALS

Bears: Bean and Theodoratus 1978:290, 292; Beard 1977:49; Callaghan 1978:272, 267; Collier and Thalman 1996:137, 148–149,190; Driver 1936:186; Foster 1944:162, 163, 225; Gifford 1965:54–55, 1967:16; Kroeber 1925:174, 215; Levy 1978a:491; Mason 1912:

124; McLendon and Lowry 1978:311; Miller 1978:252; Thomsen and Heizer 1964:59

Black-tailed Deer, preparation as food: Beard 1977:52; Callaghan 1978:266; Collier and Thalman 1996:149; Driver 1936:185–186; Foster 1944: 162; Gifford 1965:27, 1967:16; Mason 1912:122

Black-tailed Deer, uses of hides and body parts: Beard 1977:48, 52; Callaghan 1978:267; Collier and Thalman 1996:187; Driver 1936: 188, 190–191; Foster 1944:167–169, 181; Gifford 1965:49, 52, 54, 1967:16; Harrington 1942:19; Holmes 1975:22, 23; Kroeber 1925: 173; Levy 1978a:493; Mason 1912:143; McLendon and Lowry 1978:311; Miller 1978:252; Morrow 1982:14; Thomsen and Heizer 1964:52, 54

Bobcat: Bean and Theodoratus 1978:292; Driver 1936:186; Foster 1944:225; Gifford 1967:16–17; Levy 1978a:491

Coyotes and foxes: Collier and Thalman 1996:139, 190; Driver 1936: 186; Foster 1944:163, 168, 225; Gifford 1967:16; Levy 1978a:493; Margolin 1978:24; Mason 1912:121; Morrow 1982:15

Elk: Bean and Theodoratus 1978:290; Foster 1944:168, 173, 225; Gifford 1965:30, 53, 1967:16; Kroeber 1925:213, 215; Levy 1978a:491; Margolin 1978:25; Miller 1978:251, 255; Thomsen and Heizer 1964:59

Harbor Seals, uses: Bean and Theodoratus 1978:290; Collier and Thalman 1996:139; Margolin 1978:37; Miller 1978:255

Hares and rabbits: Bean and Theodoratus 1978:292; Beard 1977:49, 50; Callaghan 1978:267; Collier and Thalman 1996:138; Driver 1936:186, 191; Foster 1944:163, 170, 225, 227; Gifford 1965:55, 1967:17; Harrington 1942:19; Hester 1978a:497; Hudson 1975:11; Levy 1978a:491, 493; Margolin 1978:24–25; Mason 1912:143; McLendon and Lowry 1978:311–312; Morrow 1982:15, 18, 24

Raccoon: Driver 1936:186; Foster 1944:225; Gifford 1967:16; Levy 1978a:491; Margolin 1978:24

Sea lions: Bean and Theodoratus 1978:290; Collier and Thalman 1996:139; Gifford 1965:31–33; Margolin 1978:37; Moss et al. 2006; Thomsen and Heizer 1964:53

Sea Otter, Indian uses: Bean and Theodoratus 1978:292; Gifford 1967:16; Levy 1978a:493; Morrow 1982:15

Skunks: Collier and Thalman 1996:138, 149, 173; Driver 1936:186; Foster 1944:225; Gifford 1965:30, 1967:16; Hester 1978a: 497; Levy 1978a:491; Mason 1912:121

Squirrels: Collier and Thalman 1996:138; Driver 1936:186; Foster 1944:225; Gifford 1965:30, 1967:17; Harrington 1942:6, 9; Levy 1978a:491; Margolin 1978:25; Morrow 1982:24

MINERALS

Magnesite: Bean and Theodoratus 1978:292; Beard 1977:49, 56; Collier and Thalman 1996:198; Gifford 1965:55; Hudson 1975:15; McLendon and Lowry 1978:311

Salt, procurement: Bean and Theodoratus 1978:290; Beard 1977:59; Callaghan 1978:265; Driver 1936:187; Foster 1944:167; Gifford 1965:23; Kroeber 1925:174; Levy 1978a:488; McLendon and Lowry 1978:311; Miller 1978:255

HUNTING

Black-tailed Deer, methods: Bean and Theodoratus 1978:290; Beard 1977:50–51; Breschini and Haversat 2004:116; Callaghan 1978: 266; Collier and Thalman 1996:135–136; Driver 1936:185; Foster 1944:161–162, 225; Gifford 1965:28, 1967:16; Kroeber 1925:213; Levy 1978a:491; Mason 1912:123–124; Margolin 1978:25; Morrow 1982:24

Black-tailed Deer, rituals: The Coast Yuki closed the eyes of a felled deer and sewed its mouth shut before the hunter's companions were summoned to the kill (Gifford 1965:29). Yuki hunters removed the kidneys to avoid spoiling the rest of the carcass, while the eyes were sucked out and swallowed, taking great care to avoid spilling any eye fluids and consequent bad luck (Foster 1944:162). Portioning the deer varied between Indian groups. The hunter who killed the animal might get first choice of the prime cuts of meat, or, in one example, no meat at all (Collier and Thalman 1996:132; Foster 1944:162; Gifford 1967:16). In another example, a newly married Wappo man was obligated to take the entire deer carcass home to his new mother-in-law for her to divide (Driver 1936:186).

Black-tailed Deer, preparations for: Collier and Thalman 1996:38, 132–133; Driver 1936:186; Foster 1944:162, 225; Gifford 1965:28, 1967:16; Kelly 1978:416; Mason 1912:123–124

Hunting practices, intro.: Bean and Theodoratus 1978:290; Beard 1977:50–51; Collier and Thalman 1996:136; Levy 1978a:491; Margolin 1978:25

Quails: Callaghan 1978:266; Collier and Thalman 1996:131; Driver 1936:185; Foster 1944:163; Gifford 1965:33–34, 1967:18; Levy 1978a:491; Margolin 1978:23, 25; Morrow 1982:24

LAND MANAGEMENT

Burning, prescribed: Beard 1977:52; Levy 1978a:491; Margolin 1978: 49; Morrow 1982:28

SETTLEMENTS

Architecture: Bean and Theodoratus 1978:292–293; Callaghan 1978: 267; Collier and Thalman 1996:177–185; Gifford 1965:45, 1967: 27–28; Harrington 1942:9–10; Kelly 1978:417; Levy 1978a:492; Mason 1912:126; Miller 1978:251, 255; Sawyer 1978:259

Settlement patterns: Bean and Theodoratus 1978:292–293; Collier and Thalman 1996:177–178; Gifford 1965:45, 1967:28; Kelly 1978:417; Levy 1978a:492; Mason 1912:126; Miller 1978:254–255; Sawyer 1978:259–260

South Coast Province (pages 252–277)

FISHES

Nearshore fishes, uses: Byrd and Reddy 2002:58; Colten 2001:202–206; Erlandson and Rick 2002; Gamble and Russell 2002:111–115; Glassow 2002:190; Hicks 1963:164; Koerper et al. 2002; Pletka 2001; Raab et al. 2002:20

Pelagic fishes, uses: Colten 2001:202–206; Erlandson and Rick 2002: 177; Gamble and Russell 2002:110–115; Hicks 1963:164; Pletka 2001

BIRDS

Raptors: Glassow 1996:68; Lightfoot 2005:97; Luomala 1978:604; Raab et al. 1994:254–255

Waterbirds, identification from archaeological sites: Colten 2001:209; Gamble and Russell 2002:113; Glassow 2002:191

SOCIAL ORGANIZATION

Ceremonialism: Bean and Shipek 1978; Bean and Smith 1978b; Blackburn 1976:235–241; Johnson 1988; Kroeber 1925:639–643, 668–678

Debate about political organization: Arnold 2001b; Arnold et al. 1997; Johnson 1988, 2000; Kennett 2005; King 1990; Raab and Larson 1997; Raab et al. 1995

Settlements and settlement patterns: Bean and Shipek 1978; Bean and Smith 1978b; Erlandson and Rick 2002; Gamble and Russell 2002; Johnson 1988; Luomala 1978

Social and political hierarchies and craft production: Arnold 2001a: 13–14; Arnold and Graesch 2001; Gamble and Russell 2002:116; Gamble et al. 2001; Heizer 1972; Jones and Klar 2005; Preziosi 2001

Northeast Province (pages 278–301)

PLANTS

Camas bulbs, processing: Barrett 1910:243; Garth 1953:138; Kniffen 1928:301, 305; Olmsted and Stewart 1978:227

Dogbane: Anderson 2005:229–231; Garth 1953:151; Olmsted and Stewart 1978:227; Ray 1963:189, 194

Epos, species used: The genus name in the ethnographic literature includes both *Carum* and *Perideridia*. Several species appear to have been used in the Northeast Province, possibly also *P. gairdneri, P. bolanderi,* and *P. pringlei* (see Anderson 2005; Ray 1963:197–198; Strike 1994:103). Garth (1953:138) identifies the species name as *Pteridendia bolanden.*

Epos roots, uses: Barrett 1910:243; Garth 1953:138; Kniffen 1928:305; Olmsted and Stewart 1978:227; Ray 1963:197–198

Klamath plum: Garth 1953:139; Kniffen 1928:301, 305; Olmsted and Stewart 1978:229; Ray 1963:200

Tules, uses: Barrett 1910; Garth 1953:149–150; Kniffen 1928:301; Olmsted and Stewart 1978:229; Ray 1963

ANIMALS

Sacramento Pikeminnow: Garth 1953:136–137; Kniffen 1928; McGinnis 2006:222–223

Sacramento Sucker: Barrett 1910:248–251; Foster 2000; Garth 1953:136–137; Kniffen 1928; McGinnis 2006:247–248; Ray 1963:194–196

Tui Chub: Foster 2000; Garth 1953:136–137; McGinnis 2006:212–213; Ray 1963:193

Waterbirds: Barrett 1910:247; Garth 1953:134–135; Olmsted and Stewart 1978:226; Ray 1963:189, 220; Stern 1998:449

SETTLEMENTS

Earth lodges: Barrett 1910:243–244; Garth 1953:140, 143–144; Ray 1963; Stern 1998:450–451

Mat lodges, sweat houses: Barrett 1910:245–246; Garth 1953:144; Ray 1963:154–162; Stern 1998:450–451

Great Central Valley and Sierra Nevada Province (pages 302–339)

HERBACEOUS PLANTS

Brodiaeas, uses: Barrett and Gifford 1933:155–156; Brubaker 1926:75; Gayton 1948a:16; Johnson 1978:355

Clovers: Anderson 2005:273; Anderson and Moratto 1996:198; Brubaker 1926:75; Du Bois 1935:20; Duncan 1963:59; Gayton 1948a:16, 77, 1948b:180; Goldschmidt 1951:409; Hammett and Lawlor 2004:338; Levy 1978b:403; Rosenthal et al. 2006:37–39; Wilson 1972:38; Wohlgemuth 2004:79, 102, 111, 113

Dogbane: Anderson 2005:231; Anderson and Moratto 1996:199; Beals 1933:342; Brubaker 1926:78; Dixon 1905:142; Duncan 1963:38; Gayton 1948a:83; Johnson 1978:356; Levy 1978b:406

Elegant brodiaea: Barrett and Gifford 1933:156; Brubaker 1926:75; Clarke 1977:28; Duncan 1963:35

Mariposa lilies: Barrett and Gifford 1933:156–157; Brubaker 1926:75; Duncan 1963:60; Gayton 1948a:77; Levy 1978b:402; Smith 1978: 443

Milkweeds, as cordage or twine: Barrett and Gifford 1933:246–247; Beals 1933:342; Brubaker 1926:78; Duncan 1963:39; Gayton 1948a:83; Goldschmidt 1951:422; Johnson 1978:356; Levy 1978b: 406; Spier 1978a:474, 1978b:430; Wilson and Towne 1978:392

Milkweeds, uses other than cordage or twine: Barrett and Gifford 1933:159, 167; Du Bois 1935:21, 127; Duncan 1963:39; Levy 1978b:403

Red maids: Duncan 1963:66; Gayton 1948a:16, 77; Hammett and Lawlor 2004:338; Levy 1978b:402; Rosenthal et al. 2006:37–39; Wohlgemuth 1998, 2004:79, 102, 113

Seed processing, intro.: Beals 1933:351; Du Bois 1935:21; Duncan 1963:13; Goldschmidt 1951:408–409; Johnson 1978:355; Smith 1978:443–444

Soap plants: Barrett and Gifford 1933:157; Brubaker 1926:79; Du Bois 1935:17, 21, 130; Duncan 1963:60–61; Gayton 1948a:49, 67, 77, 1948b:147, 190, 265; Goldschmidt 1951: 406–407; Levy 1978b: 407; Riddell 1978:375; Spier 1978b:429; Wilson and Towne 1978: 389, 391; Wohlgemuth 2004:75

Tarweeds: Duncan 1963:45; Gayton 1948b:179; Hammett and Lawlor 2004:338; Levy 1978b:402; Rosenthal et al. 2006:37–39; Wohlgemuth 2004:79, 102, 113

Tules, for house construction and other material objects: Beals 1933: 342; Brubaker 1926:78; Dixon 1905:148; Duncan 1963:47; Gayton 1948a:12–13, 17, 21, 82, 1948b:147, 155, 177, 215; Johnson 1978:

357; Kroeber 1925:415, 521, 531; Levy 1978b:406; Riddell 1978: 378; Wallace 1978b:451; Wilson and Towne 1978:388, 392

Wild tobaccos, harvest and uses: Du Bois 1935:129; Gayton 1948a:22, 92–93, 1948b:228, 269–270; Goldschmidt 1951:411; Johnson 1978:355

TREES AND SHRUBS

Black oak: Barrett and Gifford 1933:142; Baumhoff 1963:166; Beals 1933:351; Dixon 1905:181; Du Bois 1935; Duncan 1963:50; Gayton 1948a:77, 1948b:178–179, 187; Kroeber 1925:411; Levy 1978b: 402; Wilson 1972:37

California blackberry: Duncan 1963:71; Johnson 1978:355; Levy 1978b:403; Wohlgemuth 2004:75, 99, 109

California buckeye, uses: Barrett and Gifford 1933:149; Dixon 1905: 182; Du Bois 1935:20; Duncan 1963:54; Goldschmidt 1951:416; Hammett and Lawlor 2004:338; Levy 1978b:402; Riddell 1978: 374; Rosenthal et al. 2006:37–39; Wohlgemuth 1998, 2004:75, 99

California hazel, as food: Dixon 1905:182; Duncan 1963:40; Levy 1978b:402; Riddell 1978:374; Wohlgemuth 2004:75, 107

California hazel, nonfood uses: Beals 1933:345; Dixon 1905:145; Du Bois 1935:20, 122, 131; Kroeber 1925:415; Levy 1978b:405; Wilson and Towne 1978:392

California wild grape, fruit preparation: Du Bois 1935:21; Duncan 1963:78; Gayton 1948b:180; Levy 1978b:403; Wohlgemuth 2004: 75, 99, 107, 109

California wild grape, use of leaves and vines: Beals 1933:344; Du Bois 1935:122, 125, 131; Duncan 1963:78; Goldschmidt 1951: 422; Wilson and Towne 1978:392

Elderberries: Barrett and Gifford 1933:163; Brubaker 1926:77; Dixon 1905:182; Duncan 1963:41–42; Gayton 1948b:180; Goldschmidt 1951:408; Levy 1978b:403; Wohlgemuth 2004:75, 99, 107, 109

Elderberry wood: Du Bois 1935:123; Duncan 1963:41–42; Gayton 1948a:92, 147, 228, 269; Goldschmidt 1951:426; Johnson 1978: 358; Riddell 1978:384

Foothill pine, uses: Barrett and Gifford 1933:149; Du Bois 1935; Duncan 1963:30; Kroeber 1925:527; Levy 1978b:402; Riddell 1978: 374; Rosenthal et al. 2006:37–39; Wohlgemuth 2004:75, 99, 107, 109

Interior live oak, ethnographic observations: Barrett and Gifford 1933:142; Baumhoff 1963:166; Dixon 1905:181; Duncan 1963:53; Kroeber 1925:411; Levy 1978b:402

Manzanitas, as food source: Barrett and Gifford 1933:161–162; Brubaker 1926:77; Dixon 1905:189–190; Du Bois 1935:20; Duncan

1963:48, 49; Gayton 1948a:77–78, 1948b:182; Hammett and Lawlor 2004:338; Levy 1978b:403; Riddell 1978:374; Smith 1978: 443; Spier 1978b:429; Wilson 1972:38; Wohlgemuth 1998, 2004:75, 99, 107, 109

Manzanitas, nonfood uses: Du Bois 1935:125; Duncan 1963:48; Gayton 1948a:61, 78; Goldschmidt 1951:389; Wilson 1972:38

Oaks, general uses: Barrett and Gifford 1933:146; Beals 1933:362, 365; Du Bois 1935:18–20; Gayton 1948a:61, 73, 78, 1948b:215, 219, 261; Goldschmidt 1951:333, 408; Kroeber 1925:410–411, 523; Rosenthal et al. 2006:37–39; Spier 1978a:473; Wallace 1978b: 450; Wilson 1972:33, 37; Wilson and Towne 1978:388, 393; Wohlgemuth 1998, 2004:75, 99, 107, 109

Sierra Gooseberry: Barrett and Gifford 1933:162–163; Brubaker 1926:77; Gayton 1948b:180; Levy 1978b:403

Sugar pine, uses: Du Bois 1935:21; Duncan 1963:28–29; Gayton 1948b: 180; Goldschmidt 1951:410; Levy 1978b:402; Riddell 1978: 374

Valley oak: Barrett and Gifford 1933:142; Baumhoff 1963:165; Du Bois 1935; Levy 1978b:402; Mayer 1976:5; Wallace 1978a:464

Western redbud, uses: Beals 1933:342; Duncan 1963:58; Gayton 1948a:86; Goldschmidt 1951:427; Johnson 1978:356; Kroeber 1925:414; Riddell 1978:376

Willows, as basketry or cordage material: Du Bois 1935:128, 131; Gayton 1948a:79; Goldschmidt 1951:427; Kroeber 1925:414; Riddell 1978:376; Smith 1978:442; Spier 1978b:430

Willows, uses other than basketry or cordage: Beals 1933:345; Gayton 1948a:13, 17, 52, 63, 66–67, 73, 75, 1948b:145, 161, 177, 215, 263; Johnson 1978:355; Levy 1978b:405; Wilson and Towne 1978: 390–392

SHELLFISH

Freshwater mussels: Du Bois 1935:18; Greengo 1952:68–69; Johnson 1978:355, 357; Kroeber 1925:538; Smith 1978:444; Spier 1978b: 428; Wilson and Towne 1978:389

INSECTS

Grasshoppers: Beals 1933:347; Dixon 1905:190–191; Du Bois 1935: 14; Gayton 1948b:181; Levy 1978b:404; Mayer 1976:19–20; Wilson and Towne 1978:390

Moth cocoons, as rattles: Dixon 1905; Gayton 1948a:52, 92, 1948b: 147, 228, 269; Goldschmidt 1951:426; Kroeber 1925:419, 505; Peigler 1994:3

Yellowjackets, hunting and cooking: Barrett and Gifford 1933:192; Beals 1933:346–347; Dixon 1905:266; Gayton 1948a:76–77

FISHES

Lamprey, uses: Barrett and Gifford 1933:189; Beals 1933:347; Dixon 1905:191; Du Bois 1935:21; Gayton 1948a:76; Kroeber 1925:409; Levy 1978b:403; Mayer 1976:19; Wilson 1972:35; Wilson and Towne 1978:390

Sacramento Perch, ethnographic and archaeological information: Broughton 1994b:504; Goldschmidt 1951:401; Johnson 1978:355; Rosenthal et al. 2006:35

Sacramento Sucker: Broughton 1994b:504; Du Bois 1935:17; Gayton 1948b:155; Goldschmidt 1951:401; Johnson 1978:355; Wilson and Towne 1978:390

Salmon, uses: Barrett and Gifford 1933:189; Beals 1933:347; Dixon 1905:184; Du Bois 1935:15–16, 123, 125; Gayton 1948a:14, 184; Goldschmidt 1951:401; Kroeber 1925:409–410, 529; Riddell 1978: 374; Wilson 1972:35

Trouts: Barrett and Gifford 1933:189; Gayton 1948a:14, 76, 155; Goldschmidt 1951:401; Johnson 1978:355; Kroeber 1925:409; Levy 1978b:403

White Sturgeons: Barrett and Gifford 1933:189; Johnson 1978:355; Levy 1978b:403; Wilson and Towne 1978:390

AMPHIBIANS AND REPTILES

Introduction: Barrett and Gifford 1933:137; Dixon 1905: 184; Kroeber 1925:341, 526; Levy 1978b:403; Riddell 1978:374; Wilson and Towne 1978:390

Western Rattlesnake: Barrett and Gifford 1933:137, 169; Dixon 1905: 184, 205, 266; Du Bois 1935:116; Gayton 1946:256, 1948a:93; Kroeber 1925:417; Levy 1978b:403; Riddell 1978:374; Spier 1978b:429

BIRDS

Band-tailed pigeons and doves: Acken 1976:56; Beals 1933:340–341; Gayton 1948b:146, 220–221; Spier 1978b:428; Wilson 1972:36

Crows and ravens: Barrett and Gifford 1933:226–228; Beals 1933: 398; Gayton 1948a:69, 1948b:218; Johnson 1978:356; Kroeber 1925:508

Ducks: Beals 1933:349; Gayton 1948a:15, 75; Johnson 1978:355; Kroeber 1925:529

Golden Eagle: Beals 1933:340; Gayton 1948a:52, 70–71, 92, 1948b: 269; Goldschmidt 1951:427; Kroeber 1925:508, 529; Levy 1978b: 403; Spier 1978b:427; Wilson 1972:36

Hawks: Barrett and Gifford 1933:218; Spier 1978b:429; Wilson 1972: 36

Quails: Barrett and Gifford 1933:183–187, 238; Beals 1933:349; Dixon 1905:149; Kroeber 1925:508; Levy 1978b:403

Waterbirds, intro., as food and raw material: Barrett and Gifford 1933:138, 221, 238; Duncan 1963:12; Gayton 1948a:82; Riddell 1978:378; Wilson 1972:36; Wilson and Towne 1978:390–391

Woodpeckers: Barrett and Gifford 1933:221, 238; Dixon 1905:166; Levy 1978b:403, 410; Riddell 1978:375

Woodpeckers, Northern Flicker: Barrett and Gifford 1933:255; Du Bois 1935:120; Gayton 1948a:69, 1948b:218; Johnson 1978:352; Levy 1978b:403; Wilson 1972:36

Yellow-billed Magpie: Barrett and Gifford 1933:226–228; Gayton 1948a:69; Kroeber 1925:508; Riddell 1978:379; Wilson 1972:36

MAMMALS

Bears: Barrett and Gifford 1933:137; Beals 1933:348, 356; Dixon 1905:194; Du Bois 1935:11–13, 125; Gayton 1948a:71–72; Goldschmidt 1951:333, 378, 424; Johnson 1978:355–356; Kroeber 1925:341, 409, 526; Levy 1978b:403; Spier 1978:428; Wilson 1972:34

Foxes: Brubaker 1926:79; Du Bois 1935:120; Gayton 1948a:73, 1948b:146, 183; Johnson 1978:356; Riddell 1978:374

Hares and rabbits: Barrett and Gifford 1933:270; Beals 1933:342; Brubaker 1926:79; Dixon 1905:148, 159; Du Bois 1935:13, 120; Gayton 1948a:14, 75, 81–82, 1948b:183, 219, 266; Goldschmidt 1951:424–425; Johnson 1978:356; Smith 1978:444; Wilson 1972:35–36; Wilson and Towne 1978:389

Mule Deer, nonfood uses: Barrett and Gifford 1933:248; Beals 1933:340; Brubaker 1926:79; Dixon 1905:222; Du Bois 1935:9–10, 120–121, 124, 128–129; Gayton 1948a:75, 80, 1948b:263, 266; Goldschmidt 1951:424–425; Kroeber 1925:405; Smith 1978:442–443; Spier 1978b: 429, 432; Wilson 1972:34–36; Wilson and Towne 1978:390–391

Mule Deer meat, preparation, cooking, social taboos: Du Bois 1935:9–10; Gayton 1948a:76, 1948b:183; Kroeber 1925:409; Mayer 1976:19; Wilson 1972:33–36

Pronghorn: Brubaker 1926:79; Gayton 1948a:49, 71, 1948b:223; Goldschmidt 1951:401; Johnson 1978:355; Kroeber 1925:529; Smith 1978:444; Wilson and Towne 1978:389

Squirrels: Beals 1933:348; Du Bois 1935:13–14; Gayton 1948a:14, 75, 1948b:183, 220

Squirrels, Beechey Ground: Du Bois 1935:14; Gayton 1948a:75–76, 1948b:220, 262; Spier 1978b:428

MINERALS

Clay, sources: Gayton 1948b:147, 265; Goldschmidt 1951:411; Kroeber 1925:537; Mayer 1976:10; Riddell 1978:375; Smith 1978:443

Magnesite craft production: Du Bois 1935:26; Goldschmidt 1951:333–335; Johnson 1978:352; Wilson and Towne 1978:388

Obsidian use, ethnographic descriptions: Barrett and Gifford 1933:224; Dixon 1905:167; Du Bois 1935:25, 127; Levy 1978b:406; Riddell 1978:374; Spier 1978b:429

Steatite, uses: Barrett and Gifford 1933:211; Dixon 1905:138–139; Gayton 1948b:191; Spier 1978b:429; Wilson and Towne 1978:391

FISHING

Freshwater fishes, fishing and meat preparation, traditional methods: Gayton 1948a:15, 76, 1948b:146, 181

HUNTING

Communal: Beals 1933:347–348, 365; Gayton 1948a:14; Goldschmidt 1951:406; Wilson 1972:33, 35; Wilson and Towne 1978:389

Mule Deer: Barrett and Gifford 1933:178–179; Beals 1933:347–348; Du Bois 1935:9–11; Gayton 1948a:70–71, 1948b:183, 219; Johnson 1978:355; Kroeber 1925:409–410; Smith 1978a:444; Spier 1978b:427; Wilson 1972:33–34; Wilson and Towne 1978:389

SOCIAL ORGANIZATION

Resource ownership: Beals 1933:362; Gayton 1948a:11; Goldschmidt 1951:333, 408; Jackson 1991:319; Johnson 1978:355; Wilson 1972:37; Wilson and Towne 1978:393

SETTLEMENTS

Architecture, domestic: Beals 1933:344; Dixon 1905:172–174; Du Bois 1935:122–123; Gayton 1948a:11–14, 51, 59–65, 145, 155, 160–161, 186–187, 215; Johnson 1978:367; Kroeber 1925:407–408; Levy 1978b:409; Nabokov and Easton 1989:294–301, 304–309; Smith 1978:442; Wallace 1978a:451, 464–465

Structures, nondomestic in Great Central Valley: Beals 1933:344–345; Dixon 1905:168–172; Gayton 1948a:51, 65, 1948b:146, 161, 187–188, 216; Johnson 1978:357, 367; Levy 1978b: 409; Nabokov and Easton 1989:294–301, 304–309; Smith 1978: 442; Wallace 1978a: 451, 464–465

Villages and seasonal camps, ethnographic reports: Gayton 1946:254–255, 1948b:148, 175–176; Goldschmidt 1951:383–384

Southern Deserts Province (pages 340–364)

HERBACEOUS PLANTS

Chia, uses: Barrows 1900:64; Bean and Saubel 1972:137; Bean and Shipek 1978:552; Bean and Smith 1978c:571; Harrington 1942:8; Hicks 1963:148–149; Hohenthal 2001:125

Goosefoots: Bean and Saubel 1972:52–53; Hicks 1963:152–153; Spier 1923:335

Pigweeds: Castetter and Bell 1951:189; Hicks 1963:150; Luomala 1978:600

Rushes, as basketry material: Bean and Saubel 1972:80–81; Hohenthal 2001:163; Kroeber 1908a:41

Saltbushes, as food: Barrows 1900:65; Castetter and Bell 1951:189; Gifford 1931:24; Hicks 1963:154; Luomala 1978:600

Stinging nettles: Bean and Saubel 1972:143; Hohenthal 2001:278; Spier 1923: 335; Waterman 1910:273

Toloache, use in initiations and other ceremonies: Bean and Saubel 1972:60–65; Bean and Shipek 1978:556; Blackburn and Bean 1978:565–566; Hohenthal 2001:253; Hooper 1920:345; Meigs 1939:64; Strong 1929:31; Waterman 1910:293

Tules: Benedict 1924:385; Gifford 1931:23; Hohenthal 2001:139, 180; Luomala 1978:601; Meigs 1939:11

Wild tobaccos, uses: Bean and Saubel 1972:90–94; Benedict 1924:390; Hohenthal 2001:117; Luomala 1978:600; Meigs 1939:10; Owen 1962:113; Waterman 1910:286, 322

TREES AND SHRUBS

Arrowweed: Bean and Saubel 1972:105–106; Gifford 1931:19–20; Hooper 1920:329; Kroeber 1908a:43; Spier 1923:350

Black oak, uses: Bean and Saubel 1972; Hicks 1963:135; Hohenthal 2001:134–135; Sparkman 1908:193; Spier 1923:334

Blue elderberry, uses: Barrows 1900:63; Bean and Saubel 1972:138; Benedict 1924:387; Hicks 1963:157; Hohenthal 2001:274; Kroeber 1908a:41; Owen 1962:113

California fan palm: Bean and Saubel 1972:145–149; Hooper 1920: 329; McClenaghan and Beauchamp 1986; Spier 1923:349

Chamise: Barrows 1900:36; Bean and Saubel 1972:29–30; Waterman 1910:282, 312

Coast live oak, uses: Hicks 1963:130; Joël 1976:66–69; Meigs 1939:9; Sparkman 1908:193

Holly-leafed cherry, as food source: Barrows 1900:61; Hicks 1963:138–140; Hohenthal 2001:155–156; Sparkman 1908:194

Honey mesquite, harvesting and processing: Barrows 1900:55–56; Bean and Saubel 1972:107–111; Benedict 1924:391; Hicks 1963: 93–99; Hohenthal 2001:136; Hooper 1920:356–357; Kroeber 1908a:42; Meigs 1939:9

Honey mesquite, nonfood uses: Bean and Saubel 1972:111–117; Benedict 1924:388; Gifford 1931:9, 22, 28; Hooper 1920:357; Meigs 1939:11; Owen 1962:120; Spier 1923:350

Manzanitas: Bean and Saubel 1972:40–41; Bean and Shipek 1978:552; Hohenthal 2001:135–136; Meigs 1939:9; Owen 1962:127; Spier 1923:339

Pinyon pine nuts, gathering and processing: Bean and Saubel 1972:102–105; Benedict 1924:391–392; Hicks 1963:30; Joël 1976: 62–66; Meigs 1939:21, 26; Michelsen and Michelsen 1979

Sagebrushes: Bean and Saubel 1972:42; Hohenthal 2001:278; Kroeber 1908a:42, 58–59; Owen 1962:109

Screwbean: Bean and Saubel 1972:118–119; Castetter and Bell 1951: 179–186; Gifford 1931:23, 28; Hicks 1963:100; Spier 1923:350

Scrub oaks: Bean and Saubel 1972:123; Hohenthal 2001:134–135; Sparkman 1908:193; Spier 1923:335

Sumacs: Bean and Saubel 1972:131–132; Hohenthal 2001:163; Kroeber 1908a:41; Sparkman 1908:195

Western choke-cherry: Bean and Saubel 1972:119–121; Hicks 1963: 141; Sparkman 1908:194; Waterman 1910:312

White sage: Bean and Saubel 1972:136; Hohenthal 2001:278; Owen 1962:113; Spier 1923:335; Waterman 1910:286

Willows, uses: Bean and Saubel 1972:135; Gifford 1931:32; Hohenthal 2001:177–178; Spier 1923:350; Waterman 1910:273

CACTI AND SUCCULENTS

Agaves: Bean and Saubel 1972:31–36; Benedict 1924:389; Hicks 1963:106–113; Hohenthal 2001:156; Hooper 1920:359; Kroeber 1908b:60; Meigs 1939:22; Michelsen 1974; Shipek 1989:164

California barrel cactus: Bean and Saubel 1972:67–68; Hicks 1963: 126; Hohenthal 2001:138; Meigs 1939:9

Chollas, uses: Barrows 1900:68; Bean and Saubel 1972:95–96; Owen 1962:111; Spier 1923:336

Prickly-pears, as food: Barrows 1900:67; Bean and Saubel 1972; Hicks 1963:121–125; Hohenthal 2001:138; Joël 1976:61; Meigs 1939:9; Spier 1923:336

Yuccas, uses: Barrows 1900:59; Bean and Saubel 1972:150–153; Gifford 1931:38; Harrington 1942:8; Hicks 1963:113–121; Hinton and Owen 1957:10; Hohenthal 2001:139; Joël 1976:60; Meigs 1939:9

INSECTS

Grasshoppers, hunting and uses: Bean 1972:61–62; Bean and Saubel 1972:115; Gifford 1931:13; Harrington 1942:8; Hohenthal 2001: 157; Sparkman 1908:199–200

Insects, intro.: Bean 1972:61–62; Bean and Saubel 1972:115; Hohenthal 2001:157; Joël 1976:60; Sparkman 1908:200

BIRDS

Doves: Gifford 1931:48; Hohenthal 2001:147; Luomala 1978:601; Spier 1923:336

Eagles: Benedict 1924:377; Gifford 1931:47; Hohenthal 2001:147; Kroeber 1908a:62; Sparkman 1908:208; Spier 1923:324; Strong 1929:34; Waterman 1910:299

Quails, uses: Gifford 1931:48; Hicks 1963:186; Hohenthal 2001:146; Meigs 1939:23–24; Sparkman 1908:199

MAMMALS

Bighorn Sheep: Bean 1972:57; Gifford 1931:27; Grant et al. 1968:32; Hicks 1963:185; Hohenthal 2001:147; Meigs 1939:25; Muir 1911: 320–322

Hares and rabbits, uses: Bean and Smith 1978a:588; Benedict 1924:388; Gifford 1931:27; Hicks 1963:179; Hohenthal 2001: 145–146; Hooper 1920:310, 357; Joël 1976:59; Meigs 1939:23; Sparkman 1908:198; Spier 1923:310, 335

Mule Deer: Benedict 1924:392; Gifford 1931:27; Hicks 1963:184; Hohenthal 2001:144–145; Meigs 1939:24; Sparkman 1908:197; Spier 1923:349

Squirrels: Hicks 1963:181; Hohenthal 2001:145; Sparkman 1908:198–199

Woodrats: Hicks 1963:180; Hohenthal 2001:145; Sparkman 1908: 198; Spier 1923:335

MINERALS

Clays and pottery production: Benedict 1924:386; Gifford 1931:42; Hohenthal 2001:220, 318; Hooper 1920:359; Kroeber 1908a:54–57; Meigs 1939:36–37; Sparkman 1908:201–202

Salt, uses: Hohenthal 2001:148; Hooper 1920:360; Luomala 1978:601; Meigs 1939:28

LAND MANAGEMENT

Agriculture and land management practices: Bean and Saubel 1972; Bean and Shipek 1978: 552; Gifford 1931; Hohenthal 2001:117; Luomala 1978:600; Shipek 1989: 163

SETTLEMENTS

Settlements and architecture: Bean 1972:70–73; Bean and Smith 1978c:571; Gifford 1931:18–20; Meigs 1939:31; Michelsen 1977; Sparkman 1908:212–213; Spier 1923:339

SOCIAL ORGANIZATION

Lineages: Bean 1972:84; Bean and Smith 1978a:588; Hicks 1963:43; Meigs 1939:16; Owen 1965; Spier 1923:299; Strong 1929:342

Lineages, political structure: Bean 1972:104; Bean and Smith 1978a: 588; Luomala 1978:597; Spier 1923:309–310.

ART CREDITS

Plates

Courtesy of **JAMES M. ANDRÉ** plate 19

BROTHER ALFRED BROUSSEAU, © 1995 St. Mary's College of California plates 10, 29

© **CALIFORNIA ACADEMY OF SCIENCES** plates 1, 31

CHRISTOPHER CHRISTIE plate 7

GERALD AND BUFF CORSI, © California Academy of Sciences plates 5, 97

T. W. DAVIS, © California Academy of Sciences plate 61

DON DESJARDIN plates 81, 82, 84, 87–89, 90–92, 96

WILLIAM FOLLETTE plates 4, 8, 12, 21, 23, 28, 41, 45, 47, 49, 50, 53

MARGUERITE GREGORY, © California Academy of Sciences plate 51

ROBERT GUSTAFSON plates 6, 22, 25, 26, 32, 35, 38, 40

© **THOMAS HALLSTEIN/OUTSIGHT** plates 20, 30, 52, 54, 109, 111

© **RICHARD HERRMAN** plates 3, 56, 58, 65–69, 103–106

WILLIAM R. HEWLETT, © California Academy of Sciences plates 16, 48

© **JANET HORTON** plates 17, 39, 102, 110

DR. LLOYD GLENN INGLES, © California Academy of Sciences plates 107, 112, 114

STEPHEN INGRAM plates 27, 37

Figures

FIGURE 21 Courtesy of the National Park Service.

FIGURE 22 Photo by Therese Babineau, courtesy of the collection of Ira Jacknis.

FIGURE 23 Photo by Kent Lightfoot.

FIGURE 24 Photo courtesy of the Malki Museum, Inc., Banning California.

FIGURE 25 Photo by Roberta A. Jewett.

FIGURE 26 Poster drawn by John A. Lytle, courtesy of the Society for California Archaeology.

FIGURE 27 Photo by Lee Panich.

Maps

MAP 1 Adapted from Hinton 1994:27.

MAP 2 From Miliken 1995:229, courtesy of Malki-Ballena Press, Banning, California.

MAP 3 Adapted from Schoenherr 1992:3.

MAP 4 Adapted from Schoenherr 1992:3 and Sloan 2006:11.

MAP 5 Adapted from Heizer and Elsasser 1980:6.

MAP 6 left and upper right: Redrawn from a map by Landis Bennett.

MAP 7 From Carle 2008:14, based on a map by Jan van Wagtendonk, research forester, U.S. Geological Survey Yosemite Field Station.

MAP 8 Adapted from Schoenherr 1992:3 and Sloan 2006:11.

Additional Captions

PAGE ii Angela Hardin (Coast Miwok Southern Pomo) showing her two daughters how to gather blue elderberries *(Sambucus mexicana).* (Photo courtesy of Chuck Striplen [Amah Mutsun Ohlone])

PAGE 260 Obsidian boulder in a stream.

INDEX

abalones, 231, 270
    Black Abalone, 44, 168 (pl.), 231, 270
    Green Abalone, 270
    Red Abalone, 42, 168 (pl.), 231, 270
Abies concolor, 294, 322
Accipiter, 360
Accipitridae, 244, 332, 360
Acer macrophyllum, 315
Achumawi
    animal resources, 295, 296
    raw materials, 301
Acipenser, 239–240
    medirostris, 239
    transmontanus, 172 (pl.), 239, 327
Acorn Barnacle, 234
Acorn Woodpecker, 177 (pl.), 206, 245, 333–334
acorns
    Central Coast Province, 227–228
    cyclical production of, 129–130, 384nn13–14
    Great Central Valley and Sierra Nevada Province, 318–319
    leaching, 29–30, 30 (fig.), 87
    Northeast Province, 291
    Northwest Coast Province, 199–200
    South Coast Province, 267–268
    Southern Deserts Province, 352–354
    storing, 29, 29 (fig.)
Adenostoma fasciculatum, 350
Adiantum
    aleuticum, 216

    capillus-veneris, 213
    jordanii, 194, 213, 284, 307
Advocates for Indigenous California Language Survival, 214
Aechmophorus
    clarkii, 331
    occidentalis, 176 (pl.), 331
Aesculus californica, 160 (pl.), 224, 236, 316
Agave, 356–357
    deserti, 167 (pl.), 356
    shawii, 356
agaves, 356–357
    desert agave, 167 (pl.), 356
Agelaius phoeniceus, 243, 331
agriculture
    California Indian practices and sustainability in, 147–149, 388n5
    domestication and, 128, 382nn 9–11
    landscape management techniques as, 83–85
    pyrodiversity collectors vs. societies based on, 131–132, 384n16
    reasons for not adopting, 138–140
    role of, among California Indians, 4–5, 8
    See also cultivation; protoagriculture
Agrostis, 43
    exarata, 67
Aix sponsa, 330

Alcidae, 206
alders, 201, 223
    red alder, 223
    white alder, 223
Alectoria fremontii, 283
Alexandrium catenella, 202
Allen, Elsie, 307
Allium, 222, 314
    validum, 158 (pl.), 314
Alnus, 201, 223
    rhombifolia, 223
    rubra, 223
Altherinopsis
    californiensis, 238
    affinis, 238
Altithermal, 367n9
amaranth. *See* pigweed
Amaranthus, 346
    fimbriatus, 157 (pl.)
Amelanchier ainifolia, 293
American Coot, 175 (pl.), 206, 241,
    274, 298, 331
American Crow, 244, 331
American Goldfinch, 244
American Kestrel, 332
American Mastodon, 39
American Porcupine, 299
American Robin, 299
Ammospermophilus leucurus, 362
Amphistichus rhodoterus, 203
Amsinckia, 286
    parviflora, 286
Anabrus, 27, 203
    simplex, 295
Anas
    acuta, 298, 330
    clypeatra, 330
    crecca, 176 (pl.), 274, 330
    cyanoptera, 176 (pl.), 274, 330
    platyrynchos, 176 (pl.), 241, 274,
        298, 330
Anatidae, 27, 206, 241–242, 330
anchovies, 28, 170 (pl.), 273
Anderson, M. K., 10, 11
    on burning practices, 99, 196, 284,
        285, 376n3
    on protoagriculture in California, 8,
        380n1

    seed-sowing groups identified by,
        127, 382n7
Anderson, R.S., 115
Andricus quercuscalifornicus, 235, 324
anemones, sea, 235
Anemopsis californica, 264, 348
Angel Shark, Pacific, 273
angelica, 217
    Brewer's angelica, 329, 335
Angelica
    breweri, 329, 335
    tomentosa, 217
angleworms, 324
animal resources
    categories of, 184
    Central Coast Province, 231–250
    Great Central Valley and Sierra Ne-
        vada Province, 323–337
    mass collecting, 24–28, 25 (figs.), 26
        (fig.), 28 (fig.)
    Northeast Province, 294–301
    Northwest Coast Province, 202–208
    South Coast Province, 270–277,
        381n4
    Southern Deserts Province,
        358–362
    storing, 31
    See also marine resources
animals
    diversity of, 381n4
    endemic/native species, 60
    Europeans' impact on populations
        of, 67
    Pleistocene, 39, 40–41, 43–44,
        366n3
    See also fish; hunting
Año Nuevo State Park, study of Indian
    landscape management practices,
    120–121, 120 (fig.)
Anodonta californiensis, 294
Anser albifrons, 242
Ant Ordeal, 272
Antalis pretiosum, 202, 208
'*antap,* 254
Antelope Ground Squirrel, 362
Antevs, E., 367n9
Antheraea polyphemus, 236, 325
Anthopleura, 235

anthropology
contemporary ethnographic, 91–92
Kroeberian, 73–77, 78, 371n1,
372nn2–3, 5–7, 373nn8, 10–13,
374nn14–15
memory culture methodology,
77–78, 82, 95–96, 374nn16–17,
376nn3–4
revisionist ethnographic, 79–85,
374nn20–21, 375nn22–23
studies of fire management among
California Indians, 94–97,
375n2, 376nn3–4
Antilocapra americana, 27, 212,
248–249, 300, 336, 362, 384n15
ants, 235, 324
harvester ants, 272, 295
Aphelocoma californica, 333
Aphidoidea, 272
aphids, 272
Apis mellifera, 203, 324, 358
Apocynum
androsaemifolium, 309–310
cannabinum, 156 (pl.), 219, 260,
285, 309–310
Aquila chrysaetos, 112, 177 (pl.), 244,
275, 332, 360
Arbutus menziesii, 200, 226
archaeological sites
of earliest humans in California,
40–41
of early maritime economies, 42–43
with fluted projectile points, 43–44,
46, 367nn5–6
South Coast Province, 42–43,
44–45, 48, 85–86, 366n2
Southern Deserts Province, 43, 46,
48, 367n4
spectacular Californian, 48
See also specific sites
archaeology
advantages and challenges of, 90–91
dark side of Native California revealed by, 85–90
ecoarchaeological research on fire
management, 120–121, 120 (fig.)
Archoplites interruptus, 173 (pl.), 327,
328

Arctocephalus townsendi, 28, 275
Arctostaphylos, 16 (fig.), 43, 226, 267,
320, 352
columbiana, 226
glandulosa, 226
glauca, 159 (pl.)
manzanita, 320
nevadensis, 320
patula, 290, 317
viscida, 320
Argopecten ventricosus, 271
Ariolimax columbianus, 203
Arlington Springs site, 42
army worms, 235
Arnold, J.E., 88, 385n17
arrowweed, 159 (pl.), 349
arroyo willow, 269
Artemisia, 230, 315, 354–355
californica, 266
douglasiana, 230, 261
tridentata, 292
Asarum caudatum, 221
Asclepias, 195, 219, 261, 310–311, 327
eriocarpa, 157 (pl.), 261
fascicularis, 261
asphaltum, 250, 277
Astacidae, 323
Atherinopsidae, 238
Atriplex, 347
californica, 229
Atsugewi
animal resources, 295, 296
plants as food, 284, 285, 291
settlement patterns, 279
wild tobacco use, 288
"Auriferous Man," 40
Australian aborigines, fire management by, 98–99, 109, 122, 124, 134,
376n8, 379n32
Avena, 222, 313
fatua, 67
azalea, western, 231

Baccharis salicifolia, 352
Balaenoptera musculus, 207
Balanus nubilus, 234
Bald Eagle, 360
balm, mountain. *See* yerba santa

Balsamorhiza
    deltoidea, 285
    sagittata, 284, 335–336
balsam-root, 284, 335
    deltoid balsam-root, 285
Banana Slug, 203
Band-tailed Pigeon, 27, 177 (pl.), 243,
    331
barberry, 289
barley, native, 261, 311, 380n4, 383n11
barnacles, 202
    Acorn Barnacle, 234
    Gooseneck Barnacle, 234
Barona Cultural Center and Museum,
    258
Barracuda, Pacific, 170 (pl.), 273
barrel cactus, California, 167 (pl.),
    357
Barrett, S.A., 298
basalt, 337
Basgall, M.E., 87
basket weavers, organization of
    305–307, 306 (fig.)
basketry materials
    Central Coast Province, 213, 219,
        220, 221, 223, 224, 225, 228,
        229–230, 243, 245
    Great Central Valley and Sierra
        Nevada Province, 307, 308, 312,
        313, 316, 321, 322, 331
    Northeast Province, 284, 287, 291,
        293, 294
    Northwest Coast Province,
        194–195, 197, 198, 199, 201
    South Coast Province, 262, 263
    Southern Deserts Province, 344,
        346, 354, 356, 358
baskets, types of, 16 (fig.), 18–20, 20
    (fig.)
Bass, Kelp, 273
Bat Ray, 237, 273
bay, California, 159 (pl.), 197, 213,
    223–224, 265, 315–316
Bay Mussel, 233
bayonet, Spanish, 358
beads
    as currency, 35–36, 135
    magnesite, 250, 338

production of, 232–233, 255
    shell, 44, 79, 88, 150, 237, 271
Bean Clam, 270
Bean, Lowell, 9, 79, 82, 83, 124, 353,
    380n1
bear grass, 145, 155 (pl.), 194–195, 284,
    308
Beard, Y.S., 222
bears, 58, 59, 246–247, 334, 361
    Black Bear, 246, 334
    Grizzly Bear, 68, 246, 334, 336
beavertail cactus, 166 (pl.), 357–358
Beechey Ground Squirrel, 249, 276,
    299, 337
Belding's Ground Squirrel, 299
Bendix, J., 96
Bent-nose Clam, 232
bentgrass, 43
    spike bentgrass, 67
Berberis aquifolium var. *repens,* 289
Beringia, 40–41
berries, 24, 31
    blackberries, 160 (pl.), 197, 265,
        316
    coffeeberries, 245, 265, 289
    elderberries, 159 (pl.), 225, 264,
        289, 317, 349
    gooseberries, 112, 165 (pl.), 200,
        266, 289, 322
    huckleberries, 160 (pl.), 195, 198,
        226, 290
    lemonadeberries, 267
    salmonberries, 200
    service-berries, 293
    thimbleberries, 229
    twinberries, 292
    wild strawberries, 222, 288, 314
Bicknell, S.H., 370n15
bifaces, 45, 190, 208–209
Big Times, 281, 305
big-leaf maple, 315
bigberry manzanita, 159 (pl.)
Bighorn Sheep, 48, 181 (pl.), 361
biodiversity
    and endemic/native species, 56, 60
    European explorers' accounts of,
        57–59
    fire management as increasing,

21–22, 51, 99, 111–112, 125–126, 380n4
and geomorphic provinces, 60, 61 (map), 369n6
and vegetation types, 60, 62, 370n7
birch-leaf mountain-mahogany, 290
bitumen. *See* asphaltum
Bivalvia, 232–233
Black Abalone, 44, 168 (pl.), 231, 270
Black Bear, 246, 334
black cottonwood, 266
black moss, 283
black nightshade, 311
black oak, 163 (pl.), 199, 227, 267, 291, 319, 352–353
Black Turban Snail, 168 (pl.), 231, 270–271
black walnut, California, 159 (pl.), 265
Black Widow Spider, Western, 236
blackberry, California, 160 (pl.), 197, 265, 316
blackbirds, 243, 299, 331
  Brewer's Blackbird, 331
  Red-winged Blackbird, 243, 331
Blackburn, Thomas, 9
Blackfish, Sacramento, 327
Blacksmith, 273
Black-tailed Deer, 207–208, 212, 247
Black-tailed Jackrabbit, 181 (pl.), 248, 276, 300, 335, 361
bladder kelp, giant, 154 (pl.), 259
Blake, George, 193, 193 (fig.)
blazing star, 284
Blepharizonia, 196, 221, 236, 262, 312
blue dicks, 259
blue elderberry, 159 (pl.), 264, 289, 349
blue oak, 163 (pl.), 319
Blue Whale, 207
boa kelp, feather, 259
Bobcat, 248
bog rush, 262
Bonito, Pacific, 273
Bonytail Chub, 359
Botta's Pocket Gopher, 248
Bottlenose Dolphin, 276
Bowman, D.M.J.S., 122
bracken fern, 154 (pl.), 194, 213, 216, 284

Bradley, B., 41
Brandt's Cormorant, 175 (pl.), 241, 274
Brant, 330
Branta
  bernicla, 330
  canadensis, 175 (pl.), 242, 298, 330
Brassicaceae, 221
Breath of Life workshop program, 214–215, 215 (fig.)
Brewer's angelica, 329, 335
Brewer's Blackbird, 331
bristlecone pine, western, 56, 60
broad-leaved cattail, 155 (pl.), 217–218, 260, 308
broad-leaved milkweed, 261
Brodiaea, 217, 308
  coronaria, 286
  elegans, 156 (pl.), 308
brodiaeas, 218, 308
  elegant brodiaea, 156 (pl.), 308
  golden brodiaea, 308
  harvest brodiaea, 286
  white brodiaea, 287
Brown Irish Lord, 237
Brown Pelican, 242–243, 274
Brown Turban Snail, 231
brush, deer, 336
Brush Rabbit, 248, 335
Bubo virginianus, 333
buckeye, California, 160 (pl.), 224, 236, 316
buckhorn cholla, 166 (pl.), 357
buckthorns, 289
buckwheats, 344
  California buckwheat, 259
bulk harvesting. *See* mass collecting
bull kelp, 154 (pl.), 216
bull mallow, 67
bulrushes
  California bulrush, 263
  See also tules
burclover, California, 67
bush, creosote, 350
Bushy-tailed Woodrat, 301
Buteo, 360
  jamaicensis, 178 (pl.), 244, 275, 332
butterfly mariposa, 310

Cabezon, 45, 170 (pl.), 237, 273

Cabrillo, Juan Rodriguez, 57

cacti, 356–358
  beavertail cactus, 166 (pl.), 357–358
  California barrel cactus, 167 (pl.),
    357
  chollas, 166 (pl.), 357
  common tuna cactus, 357
  hedgehog cacti, 357
  prickly-pears, 270, 357–358

Caelifera, 27, 203, 236, 239, 272,
  294–295, 324, 351, 358

Cahuilla
  animal resources, 358, 359
  landscape management practices,
    344
  linguistic and political units, 341,
    342
  medicines, 354
  plants as food, 344, 349, 351,
    352–353, 356
  raw materials, 351, 355
  wild tobacco use, 348

Calandrinia ciliata, 157 (pl.), 262, 311

California barrel cactus, 167 (pl.),
  357

California bay, 159 (pl.), 197, 213,
  223–224, 265, 315–316

California black walnut, 159 (pl.), 265

California blackberry, 160 (pl.), 197,
  265, 316

California buckeye, 160 (pl.), 224, 236,
  316

California buckwheat, 259

California bulrush, 263

California burclover, 67

California coffeeberry, 245, 265

California Condor, 243

California Current, 55, 368n3

California fan palm, 349

California Floater, 294

California Flora and Supplement
  (Munz and Keck), 60

California Gall Wasp, 235, 324

California Gull, 175 (pl.), 274

California Halibut, 203

California hazel, 197, 224, 316

California Horn Snail, 234

California huckleberry, 160 (pl.), 195,
  198

California Indian Basketweavers
  Association (CIBA), 305–307

California Indian Heritage Center
  (Sacramento), 257

California Indian Museum and Cultural Center (Santa Rosa), 257

California Indians
  archaeological sites of earliest,
    40–41
  common misperceptions about,
    2–3, 70, 81–82
  as cultural vs. geographical designa-
    tion, 341
  multiple migrations of, 41, 49
  myth of provincialism of, 135,
    386n18
  population statistics for, 3, 5, 88,
    365n1
  radiation of populations of, 46–47
  relevance of studying, 2–3, 7–9,
    12–13, 142–151
  uniqueness of, 3–5, 7, 72–73, 125
  See also Native California

California juniper, 162 (pl.), 265,
  349–350

California maiden-hair fern, 194, 213,
  216, 284, 307

California manroot, 236, 238

California Mussel, 42, 44, 168 (pl.),
  202, 233, 271

California Oyster, 44, 232

California Quail, 178 (pl.), 206, 244,
  275, 299, 333, 360

California scrub oak, 163 (pl.), 268

California Sea Lion, 28, 67, 179 (pl.),
  207, 246, 275

California Sheephead, 45, 171 (pl.), 273

California wild grape, 160 (pl.), 195,
  198, 201, 254–255, 266, 316–317

Callianax triplicata, 234, 271

Callipepla
  californica, 178 (pl.), 206, 244, 275,
    299, 333, 360
  gambelii, 178 (pl.), 360

Callorhinus ursinus, 28, 180 (pl.), 207,
  246, 275

Calocedrus decurrens, 199, 317
Calochortus, 219, 261, 310
  albus, 310
  venustus, 310
camas, 155 (pl.), 195, 218, 284–285
  death camas, 260
  white camas, 287
Camassia
  as food, 195, 218
  quamash, 155 (pl.), 284–285
Canada Goose, 175 (pl.), 242, 298, 330
canarygrass, 259, 308
Cancer
  antennarius, 234
  productus, 234
candle, Our Lord's, 167 (pl.), 269–270, 358
Candlefish. *See* Eulachon
Canidae, 248
Canis latrans, 248, 361
Canus dirus, 39
canyon live oak, 320, 353
Caprio, A.C., 116–117, 379n31
Carcharhinidae, 237
Carduelis, 244
  lawrencei, 244
  psaltria, 244
  tristis, 244
Carex, 67, 220, 312
  barbarae, 220
Carpenter, S.L., 115
Carpobrotus chilensis, 370n15
carving, 192–193, 193 (fig.)
cascara, 289
cat, sabertooth, 39
catchfly, 67
caterpillars, 236, 272, 324
Catostomus occidentalis, 26, 174 (pl.), 240, 281, 283 (fig.), 297, 327, 328
cattails, 98 (fig.), 260, 308
  broad-leaved cattail, 155 (pl.), 217–218, 260, 308
  narrow-leaved cattail, 260
  southern cattail, 260, 308
Caudata, 240
Ceanothus integerrimus, 336
Ceanothus Silk Moth, 169 (pl.), 236, 324

cedars
  incense-cedar, 199, 317
  Port Orford cedar, 199
Cedros Island sites, 43
Central Coast Province, 61 (map), 185 (map), 210–250
  animal resources, 231–250
  basketry materials, 213, 219, 220, 221, 223, 224, 225, 228, 229–230, 243, 245
  ceremonies and rituals, 212, 218, 219, 222, 242–243
  cordage materials, 219, 220, 224
  ethnolinguistic units, 211
  landscape management practices, 114, 119, 213
  medicines, 217, 218, 219, 221, 223, 225, 226, 229, 230, 231, 235, 240, 245, 246–247
  overview of, 211–213
  plant resources, 213, 216–231
  rock and mineral resources, 250
  settlement patterns, 211
  vegetation types, 211
Central Foothill Yokuts, 310
Central Sierra Miwok, 311
Central Valley. *See* Great Central Valley and Sierra Nevada Province
Centrocercus urophasianus, 299, 332
ceramic arts, 17, 345–346, 345 (fig.)
Cercis occidentalis, 166 (pl.), 229–230, 293, 322
Cercocarpus, 290
  betuloides var. *betuloides,* 290
  ledifolius, 290
ceremonies and rituals, 33–34
  Central Coast Province, 212, 218, 219, 222, 242–243
  Great Central Valley and Sierra Nevada Province, 309, 312, 329, 332, 333, 334
  Northeast Province, 281
  Northwest Coast Province, 190–192, 195, 200, 208
  South Coast Province, 254–255, 262, 263, 264, 266, 267, 272, 273, 275
  Southern Deserts Province, 347, 348, 360, 362

Cerithidea hegewischii californica, 234
Cermeño, Sebastian, 58, 371n15
Cervus elaphus, 212, 248, 384n15
   nannodes, 181 (pl.), 248, 337
   roosevelti, 181 (pl.), 208, 248
chain fern, 194
Chamaecyparis lawsoniana, 199
chamise, 350
Channel Islands sites, 42, 44–45
cheeseweed, 67
Cheloniidae, 360
Chen caerulescens, 242
Chenopodium, 67, 310, 346, 380n4
   berlandieri, 261
   fremontii, 286
cherry, holly-leafed, 161 (pl.), 225,
   266–267, 350
chert, 250, 337
chia, 155 (pl.), 218, 260, 344
Chilopsis linearis, 350
Chilula, 203
Chinigchinich cult, 254–255, 263, 275
Chinook Salmon, 172 (pl.), 192, 204,
   239, 296, 326, 384n15
Chione, 44, 271
chipmunks, 299, 334
   Least Chipmunk, 299
   Yellow-pine Chipmunk, 299
chitons, 232
   Giant Chiton, 202
Chlorogalum, 220, 236, 312
   pomeridianum, 158 (pl.), 195–196,
    198, 262
Chlorostoma
   brunnea, 231
   funebralis, 168 (pl.), 231, 270–271
choke-cherry, western, 201, 292–293,
   355
chollas, 357
   buckhorn cholla, 166 (pl.), 357
Chromis punctipinnis, 273
chub
   Bonytail Chub, 359
   Thicktail Chub, 327, 329
   Tui Chub, 298
Chub Mackerel, 28, 273
Chumash, 255, 256, 272
   ceremonies, 254, 273

landscape management practices,
   262, 382n7
plants as food, 265, 266, 267, 268,
   270
settlement patterns, 253–254, 255,
   385n17
cicadas, 351
Cicadidae, 351
cicely, sweet, 196
Cinnamon Teal, 176 (pl.), 274, 330
Cirsium scariosum, 284
clams, 232–233
   Bean Clam, 270
   Bent-nose Clam, 232
   freshwater clams, 323
   Gaper Clam, 42
   Littleneck Clam, 42, 202, 232, 271
   Long-neck Clam, 232
   Northern Razor Clam, 202
   Nuttall's Cockle, 232
   Pismo Clam, 232, 271
   Venus clams, 44, 271
   Washington Clam, 42, 44, 168 (pl.),
    202, 232
clarkia, 43, 308–309
Clarkia, 43, 308–309
Clark's Grebe, 331
claw, devil's, 383n11, 380n1
clay, 17, 250, 338, 363
Claytonia perfoliata, 311
Clemmys marmorata, 174 (pl.), 329
climate
   and burning conditions, 107–108
   constantly changing, 62–64
   diversity of, 50–51, 54
   Holocene, 47, 366n1, 367nn8–9
   Late Pleistocene, 38–39, 366n1
   Mediterranean, 21, 54, 107
   See also weather patterns
Clinocardium nuttallii, 232
clovers, 218, 223, 309
   California burclover, 67
   foothill clover, 309
Clovis people, 40–41
Clovis points, 43, 367n4
Clupea pallasi, 237
coast live oak, 164 (pl.), 227, 268,
   353

Coast Miwok, 217, 229, 250
  animal resources, 235, 238, 239,
    241, 243, 244, 245, 247, 249
  landscape management practices,
    213, 376n4
  medicines, 219, 223, 230, 231
  plants as food, 216–217, 218, 219,
    220, 222, 224, 225, 227, 228
  raw materials, 213, 225, 226
coast redwood, 56, 114, 161 (pl.),
  198–199, 201, 225, 266, 366n2
coast silktassel, 231
Coast Yuki, 228
  animal resources, 232, 233, 237,
    238, 239, 241, 245–246, 247
  basketry materials, 213, 225, 229
  medicines, 221, 223
  plants as food, 216, 226
coastal sagebrush, 266
cockles
  Hardshell Cockles. See Venus clams
  Nuttall's Cockle, 232
  Rock Cockle. See Littleneck Clam
coffeeberries
  California coffeeberry, 245, 265
  Sierra coffeeberry, 289
Coho Salmon, 192, 204–205, 239, 296,
  384n15
Colaptes auratus, 178 (pl.), 245, 332,
  334
  cafer, 245
collecting. See gathering resources;
  mass collecting
Colorado Pikeminnow, 359
coltsfoot, 195
Columbian Mammoth, 39
Columbina, 360
  passerina, 360
Common Dolphin, 179 (pl.), 276
Common Ground-Dove, 360
common lomatium, 284
Common Loon, 175 (pl.), 274, 331
common maiden-hair fern, 213
common manzanita, 320
Common Moorhen, 331
Common Raven, 177 (pl.), 244, 331
common sow thistle, 67
common tule, 263, 287

common tuna cactus, 357
communities. See polities
complex hunter-gatherers
  California Indians as, 4–5, 4 (fig.),
    7–9
  defined, 387n22
  scenarios about lifeways of, 89–93
  shift to agriculture, 125
Condor, California, 243
Conkey, Margaret, 388n1
conservation
  and collection practices, 84–85
  and harmonious landscape man-
    agement model, 89, 90, 91–92
controlled burning. See fire management
Coot, American, 175 (pl.), 206, 241,
  274, 298, 331
cordage, material culture produced
  from, 18
cordage materials
  Central Coast Province, 219, 220,
    224
  Great Central Valley and Sierra
    Nevada Province, 309–310
  Northeast Province, 285, 292
  Northwest Coast Province, 195,
    198
  South Coast Province, 259, 260,
    261, 269
cormorants, 28, 206, 241, 274
  Brandt's Cormorant, 175 (pl.), 241,
    274
  Double-crested Cormorant, 175
    (pl.), 241, 274
  Pelagic Cormorant, 176 (pl.), 241,
    274
Cornus nuttallii, 320
Corvidae, 112, 244, 331, 333
Corvus
  brachyrhynchos, 244, 331
  corax, 177 (pl.), 244, 331
Corylus cornuta, 197
  var. californica, 224, 316
Costanoan, 213, 243
  basketry and cordage materials,
    213, 219, 221, 229
  medicines, 218, 231

Costanoan (cont.)
    plants as food, 217, 218, 220, 221,
        222, 224, 225, 226, 227, 228
    raw materials, 223, 225
Cottidae, 203
cottontails
    Desert Cottontail, 248, 276, 335,
        361
    Mountain Cottontail, 300
cottonwoods, 266
    black cottonwood, 266
    Fremont cottonwood, 266, 350
cow parsnip, 285
Coyote, 248, 361
coyote tobacco, 156 (pl.), 264, 348
crabs, 234
Crassadoma gigantea, 202
crayfish, 323
creosote bush, 350
crickets, 27, 203
    Mormon Cricket, 295
Cross Creek site, 42–43, 45
Crotalus, 359
    viridis, 329
crown fires, 102, 376n10
crows, 244, 331
    American Crow, 244, 331
Cryptantha, 67
Cryptochiton stelleri, 202, 232
cucumber, wild, 263
cultivation
    domestication vs., 128–129,
        382nn9–11, 383n12
    methods for, 126–128, 127 (fig.),
        381nn5–6, 382n7
cultural objects, 16–20
cultural survival, 150–151
culture, material, 16–20
culture areas, 75–76, 372nn6, 7,
    373nn8, 10
Cupeño, 341
curl-leaf mountain-mahogany, 290
curly dock, 67
currants, 266, 289
    golden currant, 289
    wax currant, 289
Cusick's sunflower, 288
Cuthrell, Rob, 120 (fig.), 121

Cutthroat Trout, 297
Cyanocitta stelleri, 333
Cygnus columbianus, 298
Cylindropuntia, 357
    acanthocarpa, 166 (pl.), 357
Cyperus esculentus, 126

Daisy Cave site, 42, 44–45
dandelions, 309
Dasyatidae, 237
Datura, 312
    wrightii, 158 (pl.), 254, 263,
        347–348
Davies, M.S., 383n12
death camas, 260
deer, 43, 384n15
    Black-tailed Deer, 207–208, 212,
        247
    Mule Deer, 26, 182 (pl.), 277, 300,
        304–305, 334, 335–336, 362
deer brush, 336
deergrass, 344
Deerskin Dance. *See* White Deerskin
    Dance
Delphinidae, 28, 276
Delphinus delphis, 179 (pl.), 276
Delta Smelt, 327
deltoid balsam-root, 285
Dendragapus obscurus, 332
Dentalium, 35, 190, 202, 208
Dermochelyidae, 360
Deschampsia, 380n4
Descurainia, 221
desert agave, 167 (pl.), 356
Desert Cottontail, 248, 276, 335, 361
desert parsley, 285
desert willow, 350
Desert Woodrat, 277, 362
devil's claw, 383n11, 380n1
Dichelostemma, 218, 308
    capitatum, 259
    pulchella, 126
dicks, blue, 259
Diegueño, 258, 272, 372n6
digging sticks, 24
Dillon, Brian, 43
dip-net fishing, 25 (fig.)
Dire Wolf, 39

diversification. *See* diversity
diversity
  animal, 381n4
  climate, 50–51, 54
  evident in archaeological sites, 44–46
  food, 15–16, 54–55, 125–126, 138–139, 380n4
  language, 6 (map), 7
  plant, 21–22, 56, 60, 380n4
  polity, 7, 33, 35
  reasons for, among California Indians, 48–49
  resource, 54–55, 125–126, 380n4
  topography, 51–54, 53 (map), 368n2
  See also biodiversity; pyrodiversity
dock
  curly dock, 67
  yellow dock. *See* curly dock
dogbane, 156 (pl.), 219, 260, 285, 309–310
dogwood, mountain, 320
Dolichovespula, 27, 203, 236, 272, 295–296, 325
dolphins, 276
  Bottlenose Dolphin, 276
  Common Dolphin, 179 (pl.), 276
  Pacific White-sided Dolphin, 179 (pl.), 276
domestication, 128–129, 382nn9–11, 383n12, 384n16, 387n23
Donax gouldii, 270
Double-crested Cormorant, 175 (pl.), 241, 274
Douglas Squirrel, 249, 299, 337
doves, 360
  Common Ground-Dove, 360
  Mourning Dove, 112, 243, 331, 360
Downy Woodpecker, 245
Drake, Francis, 57, 371n15
Driver, H.E., 382n7
drought
  during Medieval Climatic Anomaly, 64
  fire years and, 107, 115, 116
Drucker, P., 207
Dryocopus pileatus, 206, 245, 334

Du Bois, Cora, 327, 336
ducks, 27, 206, 241–242, 330
  Cinnamon Teal, 176 (pl.), 274, 330
  Green-winged Teal, 176 (pl.), 274, 330
  Mallard, 176 (pl.), 241, 274, 298, 330
  Northern Pintail, 298, 330
  Northern Shoveler, 330
  Ruddy Duck, 176 (pl.), 241–242, 274
  Wood Duck, 330
Duhaut-Cilly, Auguste, 371n17
Duncan, J.W., 314
Dusky Grouse, 332
Dusky-footed Woodrat, 277, 301, 362
dwarf huckleberry, 290

Eagle Ceremony/Dance, 275, 348, 360
eagles, 360
  Bald Eagle, 360
  Golden Eagle, 112, 177 (pl.), 244, 275, 332, 360
Eared Grebe, 331
ears, mule, 219
earth ovens, 23, 366n3
earthquakes, 64–65, 370n12
earthworms. *See* angleworms
Eastern Kumeyaay, 343, 359, 360, 387n23
Eastern Miwok, 313
Eastern Pomo, 217, 218
Eastwood manzanita, 226
Echinocereus, 357
ecoarchaeological research, on fire management, 120–121, 120 (fig.)
Egregia menziesii, 259
El Niño, 62–64, 129, 370n9
Elasmobranchi, 237
elderberries, 225, 317
  blue elderberry, 159 (pl.), 264, 289, 349
elegant brodiaea, 156 (pl.), 308
Elephant Seal, Northern, 276
elk, 43, 58, 212, 248, 384n15
  Roosevelt Elk, 181 (pl.), 208, 248
  Tule Elk, 181 (pl.), 248, 337
elk thistle, 284

Elsasser, A.B., 7, 15, 40, 49, 370n7, 372n7
Elymus, 43
Embiotoca lateralis, 171 (pl.)
Embiotocidae, 28, 44, 238, 273
Engraulididae, 28, 170 (pl.), 273
Enhydra lutris, 28, 67, 246, 276
environment
    change as constant in, 62–66, 70, 370nn9, 12–13
    common misperception about richness of, 70
    human impacts on, 66–69, 370n15, 371nn16–17
    See also biodiversity
Ephedra, 352
epos, 284, 285–286
Eremocarpus setigerus, 236, 313
Erethizon dorsatum, 299
Eriodictyon, 356
    californicum, 166 (pl.), 201–202, 231, 294, 323
    crassifolium, 356
    trichocalyn, 356
Eriogonum, 344
    fasciculatum, 259
    umbellatum, 286
Erlandson, J.M., 45
Eschrichtius robustus, 28, 180 (pl.), 206, 245–246, 276
Esselen
    medicines, 226, 229
    plants as food, 224, 225, 226
    raw materials, 219, 220, 221
ethnolinguistic units, 74–75, 372nn2–3
    Central Coast Province, 211
    Great Central Valley and Sierra Nevada Province, 303
    Northeast Province, 279
    Northwest Coast Province, 189
    South Coast Province, 253
    Southern Deserts Province, 341
Eubalaena glacialis, 207
Eulachon, 205
Eumetopias jubatus, 28, 67, 207, 246
Euphagus cyanocephalus, 331
Euphoria ocellata, 329

Europeans
    animal populations impacted by, 67
    impact of, on California Indians, 68
    Native California's first contact with, 72–73
    plants introduced by, 66–67, 68, 370n15, 371nn16–17
evergreen. *See* California huckleberry

fairy lantern, white, 310
Falco
    columbarius, 112, 332
    mexicanus, 112, 332
    peregrinus, 112, 332
    sparverius, 112, 332
Falconidae, 332
Falconiformes, 275
falcons, 332
    American Kestrel, 332
    Merlin, 332
    Peregrine Falcon, 112, 332
    Prairie Falcon, 332
fan palm, California, 349
farewell-to-spring. *See* clarkia
fat, mule, 352
feather boa kelp, 259
Fernandeño, 272
ferns, 213, 216
    bracken fern, 154 (pl.), 194, 213, 216, 284
    California maiden-hair fern, 194, 213, 216, 284, 307
    chain fern, 194
    common maiden-hair fern, 213
    five-finger fern, 216
    western sword fern, 213
    woodwardia, 194
Ferocactus cylindraceus, 167 (pl.), 357
fescue, 43, 380n4
fiddlenecks, 286
fig, sea, 370n15
filaree, red-stem, 66, 67
Fimrite, Peter, 389n4
fir, white, 293, 322
fire lily. *See* bear grass

fire management, 94–122
    by Australian aborigines, 98–99,
        109, 122, 124, 134, 376n8,
        379n32
    defining characteristics of, 125–130
    diversity magnified through, 21–22,
        51, 99, 111–112, 125–126, 380n4
    ecoarchaeological research on,
        120–121, 120 (fig.)
    ethnographic information on ex-
        tent of, 82
    Europeans' restrictions on, 68,
        95–96
    purposes of, 98–99, 98 (fig.), 376n8
    relevance of California Indian prac-
        tices for, 143–147, 145 (fig.),
        388n3
    studies of, among California Indi-
        ans, 94–97, 375n2, 376nn3–4
fire-management model (pyrodiversity
    collecting model), 14–36
    basics, 14–15, 36
    fire's role in, 20–22
    and food diversity, 15–16
    and food storage, 29–31, 29 (fig.),
        31 (fig.)
    and mass collecting, 23–28, 25
        (figs.), 26 (fig.), 28 (fig.)
    and material culture, 16–20
    and polities, 33–35
    and relationships between polities,
        35–36
    and research on fire ecology,
        117–122
    and winter villages, 32–33, 32 (fig.)
fire managers. See pyrodiversity collec-
    tors
fire regimes
    burning conditions and, 107–108,
        377n16
    of California Indians, 99–102, 101
        (fig.), 103–105 (map)
    characteristics of, 97–98
    contemporary, 113–114, 379n28
    evidence of anthropogenic,
        112–115, 378nn24–25, 27,
        379n28
    fuel and, 103, 106–107, 377nn12, 14

ignition sources and, 108–109, 109
        (fig.), 110 (map)
    natural vs. anthropogenic, 109–112,
        119–120, 377n19–20
    summary of research findings on,
        117–122
fires
    in communal hunting, 27
    crown, 102, 376n10
    Mediterranean climate as enabling,
        21, 107
    traditional method for starting, 109
        (fig.)
firestorms, 115–117, 118–119, 143,
    379n31
First Salmon Ceremony, 200
fish
    methods for catching, 18, 24–26, 25
        (figs.), 28, 28 (fig.), 297, 327
    storing, 31
    See also specific fish
fish dams. See fish weirs
fish traps. See fish weirs
fish weirs, 25–26, 25 (fig.), 191,
    282–283, 283 (fig.), 296, 297
five-finger fern, 216
Flannery, K. V., 384n16
flexibility, of relationship with re-
    sources, 128–130, 131
flickers, 21, 365n1
    Northern Flicker, 178 (pl.), 245,
        332, 334
    Red-shafted Flicker, 245
flies
    horseflies, 324
    salmon flies, 295, 325
Floater, California, 294
flower, sulphur, 286
Flower Dance, 309
fluted projectile points, 41, 43–44, 46,
    367nn4–6
fog drip, 56
Folsom points, 367n4
foods
    diversity of, 15–16, 54–55, 125–126,
        138–139, 380n4
    mass collecting, 23–28, 25 (figs.), 26
        (fig.), 28 (fig.)

foods (cont.)
    methods for cooking, 23, 366n3
    storing, 29–31, 29 (fig.), 31 (fig.)
    variation in harvests of, 129–130,
        384nn13–15
    See also animal resources; plant
        resources
foothill clover, 309
foothill pine, 228, 291, 320–321
forget-me-not, 67
Formicidae, 324
Foster, John, 282–283
foxes, 248, 335
    Gray Fox, 248, 335
    Kit Fox, 248, 335
    Red Fox, 335
Fragaria, 222, 288, 314
Fremont cottonwood, 266, 350
Fremont's star-lily. *See* death camas
freshwater clams, 323
Freshwater Pearl Mussel, 323
Fulica americana, 175 (pl.), 206, 241,
    274, 298, 331
fur seals
    Guadalupe Fur Seal, 28, 275
    Northern Fur Seal, 28, 180 (pl.),
        207, 246, 275

Galeorhinus galeus, 273
Gall Wasp, California, 235, 324
Gallinula chloropus, 331
Gambel's Quail, 178 (pl.), 360
Gaper Clam, 42
Garden Snail, 234
Garrya elliptica, 231
Garth, T. R., 284, 286, 294
Gavia
    immer, 175 (pl.), 274, 331
    pacifica, 331
    stellata, 331
Gaviidae, 331
Gayton, A. H., 317
Gebauer, A. B., 128
geese, 206, 242, 330
    Canada Goose, 175 (pl.), 242, 298,
        330
    Greater White-fronted Goose, 242
    Snow Goose, 242

Geococcyx californianus, 332
geomorphic provinces, 60, 61 (map),
    185 (map), 369n6
    See also specific provinces
Geomyidae, 335
giant bladder kelp, 154 (pl.), 259
Giant Chiton, 202
giant sequoia, 56, 117
Gifford, E. W., 222, 357, 358, 359, 360
Gila
    crassicauda, 327, 329
    elegans, 359
ginger, wild, 221
Gist, Frank, 193
glaciers, Late Pleistocene, 38–39, 41,
    366n1
Glassow, M. A., 270–271
globe lily, white. *See* white fairy lantern
Glyceria, 286
golden brodiaea, 308
golden currant, 289
Golden Eagle, 112, 177 (pl.), 244, 275,
    332, 360
Golden-mantled Ground Squirrel, 182
    (pl.), 299
goldfinches, 244
    American Goldfinch, 244
    Lawrence's Goldfinch, 244
    Lesser Goldfinch, 244
Gonidea angulata, 294, 323
gooseberries, 112, 266, 289
    mountain gooseberry, 289
    Sierra gooseberry, 165 (pl.), 289,
        322
    straggly gooseberry, 200, 289
goosefoots, 67, 310, 346, 380n4
    pitseed goosefoot, 261
Gooseneck Barnacle, 234
gophers, 335
    Botta's Pocket Gopher, 248
Gould, R. A., 204
granite, 363
grape, California wild, 160 (pl.), 195,
    198, 201, 254–255, 266, 316–317
grass seeds, 24, 30, 82
grasses, 219, 254
    bear grass, 145, 155 (pl.), 194–195,
        284, 308

bentgrass, 43
canarygrass, 259, 308
deergrass, 344
harigrass, 380n4
mannagrass, 286
maygrass, 380n4, 383n11
needlegrass, 43
peppergrass, 220, 261
ryegrass, 43
sea grass, 42, 154 (pl.), 254, 259
spike bentgrass, 67
surf-grass. *See* sea grass
velvet grass, 325
white grass. *See* bear grass
grasshoppers, 27, 169 (pl.), 203, 236,
239, 272, 294–295, 324, 351, 358
grass-nut. *See* Ithuriel's spear
Gray Fox, 248, 335
gray pine. *See* foothill pine
Gray Squirrel, Western, 182 (pl.), 249,
299, 337
Gray Whale, 28, 180 (pl.), 206,
245–246, 276
Gray's licorice-root, 284
Grayson, D.K., 366n3
greasewood. *See* chamise
Great Basin, 61 (map), 185 (map),
369n6
Great Central Valley and Sierra Nevada
Province, 61 (map), 185 (map),
302–338
animal resources, 323–337
basket weaving, 305–307
basketry materials, 307, 308, 312,
313, 316, 321, 322, 331
ceremonies and rituals, 305, 309,
312, 329, 332, 333, 334
cordage materials, 309–310
ethnolinguistic units, 303
medicines, 309, 311, 312, 315–316,
317, 320, 322, 323, 324
overview of, 303–305
plant resources, 307–323
rock and mineral resources,
337–338
settlement patterns, 303–304
vegetation types, 303
Great Horned Owl, 333

Greater Roadrunner, 332
Greater Sage Grouse, 299, 332
Greater White-fronted Goose, 242
grebes, 298, 331
    Clark's Grebe, 331
    Eared Grebe, 331
    Horned Grebe, 331
    Pied-billed Grebe, 331
    Western Grebe, 176 (pl.), 331
Green Abalone, 270
Green Sturgeon, 239–240
Green-winged Teal, 176 (pl.), 274, 330
greenleaf manzanita, 290, 317
Greenlee, J.M., 114
Grizzly Bear, 68, 246, 334, 336
ground iris, 156 (pl.), 233
Ground Sloth, 39
ground squirrels, 276, 299
    Antelope Ground Squirrel, 362
    Beechey Ground Squirrel, 249, 276,
        299, 337
    Belding's Ground Squirrel, 299
    Golden-mantled Ground Squirrel,
        182 (pl.), 299
    Rock Ground Squirrel, 362
    Round-tailed Ground Squirrel, 362
Ground-Dove, Common, 360
grouses, 332
    Dusky Grouse, 332
    Greater Sage Grouse, 299, 332
Guadalupe Fur Seal, 28, 275
Guitarfish, Shovelnose, 273
gulls, 204, 242, 274
    California Gull, 175 (pl.), 274
Gumboot. *See* Giant Chiton
Gymnogyps californianus, 243

habitat destruction
    by Europeans, 66–68, 370n15,
        371n17
    with U.S. settlement of California,
        68–69
hairgrass, 380n4
hairy manzanita, 226
Hairy Woodpecker, 245
hairy yerba santa, 356
Halchidoma, 341
Haliaeetus leucocephalus, 360

Halibut, California, 203
Haliotis, 231, 270
    cracherodii, 44, 168 (pl.), 231, 270
    fulgens, 270
    rufescens, 42, 168 (pl.), 231, 270
Hammett, J.E., 380n4, 382n11
Handbook of the Indians of California
    (Kroeber), 371n1
Harbor Seal, 28, 67, 180 (pl.), 207, 246,
    276
Hardhead, 173 (pl.), 328
Hardshell Cockles. *See* Venus clams
hares, 248, 276, 300, 335, 361
Harrington, John P., 73, 96, 196, 265,
    267, 381nn5–6
harvest brodiaea, 286
harvester ants, 272, 295
harvesting wild resources. *See* resource
    gathering
hawks, 244, 332, 360
    Red-tailed Hawk, 178 (pl.), 244,
        275, 332
hazel, California, 197, 224, 316
health problems, South Coast
    Province, 85–86
hedgehog cacti, 357
Heizer, R.F., 7, 15, 40, 49, 191, 370n7,
    372n7, 379n1, 386n18
Helianthus, 286, 288, 314
    cusickii, 288
    nuttallii, 288
Helix aspersa, 234
hematite, 338
Hemilepidotus spinosus, 237
Hemizonia, 196, 221, 236, 262, 312
Heracleum lanatum, 285
Herring, Pacific, 237
Heteromeles arbutifolia, 229, 269,
    322
Hicks, F.N., 353
Hillman, G.C., 383n12
Hinton, Leanne, 214
Hitch, 173 (pl.), 327
Hohenthal, W.D., 347, 348, 349, 359,
    360, 361
Holcus lanatus, 325
holly-leafed cherry, 161 (pl.), 225,
    266–267, 350

Holocene
    climate, 47, 366n1, 367nn8–9
    Early, multiple migrations in, 38,
        41, 49
    radiation of California Indians
        during, 46–47
    See also Late Holocene
honey mesquite, 150, 161 (pl.), 351
Honeybee, 203, 325, 358
Hordeum, 311, 380n4
    intercedens, 261
Horn Snail, California, 234
Horned Grebe, 331
Horned Owl, Great, 333
horseflies, 325
house societies, 33, 80, 190,
    374nn20–21, 375n22
Huchnom, 239
huckleberries, 226, 290
    California huckleberry, 160 (pl.),
        195, 198
    dwarf huckleberry, 290
    red huckleberry, 290
    thinleaf huckleberry, 290
hummingbirds, 244
Humpback Sucker. *See* Razorback
    Sucker
Humpback Whale, 206–207
hunting, 212, 304–305
    big-game, in Pleistocene, 40–41,
        43–44
    methods for, 18, 18 (fig.), 26–27,
        91
    See also specific animals
Hupa, 75, 189, 196
Hyalophora euryalus, 169 (pl.), 236,
    325
Hypomesus
    pretiosus, 238
    transpacificus, 327
Hysterocarpus traski, 327

Ice Age
    Little Ice Age, 47, 64, 108
    See also Pleistocene
"Ice Age Man," 40
Icteridae, 243, 299, 331
incense-cedar, 199, 317

Indian hemp. *See* dogbane
Indian milkweed, 157 (pl.)
Indian potatoes. *See* camas
Indian rush, 262
Indian tobacco, 264
Indians. *See* California Indians
insects, 27, 202–203, 235–236, 272, 294–296, 324–325, 351, 358
interior live oak, 164 (pl.), 320, 352
Introduction to California Plant Life (Ornduff et al.), 62
ipos. *See* epos
Iris, 195, 219
    macrosiphon, 156 (pl.), 233
irises, 195, 219
    ground iris, 156 (pl.), 233
irrigation, 126, 132
Ishi, 109 (fig.)
islay. *See* holly-leafed cherry
Ithuriel's spear, 157 (pl.), 310

Jacknis, Ira, 23, 192, 193
jackrabbits
    Black-tailed Jackrabbit, 181 (pl.), 248, 276, 300, 335, 361
    White-tailed Jackrabbit, 300
Jacksmelt, 238
Jackson, T.L., 304
jays, 333
    Steller's Jay, 333
    Western Scrub-Jay, 333
Jepson Manual, 56
jimsonweed. *See* toloache
Johnson, J.R., 385n17
jojoba, 351
Jones, R., 124
Jones, T.L., 63
Juglans californica, 159 (pl.), 265
Jumping Dance, 190
Juncus, 67, 220, 262
    actus, 262
    balticus, 220, 262
    effusus, 262
    textilis, 262, 347
junipers
    California juniper, 162 (pl.), 265, 349–350
    western juniper, 162 (pl.), 293

Juniperus
    californica, 162 (pl.), 265, 349–350
    occidentalis var. *occidentalis,* 162 (pl.), 293

Karuk, 203
    baskets, 20 (fig.), 194
    cultural practices, 75, 372n6
    landscape management practices, 137–138
    wild tobacco use, 196, 381n6
Kashaya Pomo, 220, 250, 372n6, 376n4
    animal resources, 232, 238, 239, 242, 243, 245, 246
    basketry materials, 213, 229–230
    ceremonies, 218, 222
    medicines, 217, 218, 221, 223, 225, 226
    plants as food, 216, 217, 218, 219, 221, 222, 224, 226, 227, 228
Katharina tunicata, 232
Kawaiisu, 341
Keeley, L.H., 114, 127, 382n7
Kelly, I.T., 192
Kelp Bass, 273
kelp forests, 41, 63
Kelp Rockfish, 171 (pl.)
kelps, 28, 31, 216
    bull kelp, 154 (pl.), 216
    feather boa kelp, 259
    giant bladder kelp, 154 (pl.), 259
    stalked kelp, 216
Kennett, D.J., 63, 368n9, 386n17
Kennett, J.P., 63
Kestrel, American, 332
Kilgore, B.M., 115, 116
Kiliwa, 341, 353, 359
King Salmon. *See* Chinook Salmon
Kit Fox, 248, 335
Kitanemuk, 341
Klamath Indians, 288
Klamath plum, 290
Koenig, W.D., 384nn13–14
Konkow
    animal resources, 326, 330, 332, 333, 334
    medicines, 322
    plants as food, 320–321

Konkow (cont.)
    raw materials, 316, 321
Kotzebue, Otto von, 59
Kroeber, Alfred L.
    anthropology of, 73–77, 78, 371n1,
        372nn2–3, 5–7, 373nn8, 10–13,
        374nn14–15
    on canoe making, 198
    on fish dams, 191
    on foods, 202, 316
    *Handbook of the Indians of Califor-
        nia,* 371n1
    on tobacco growing, 314
    on tribelets, 76–77, 77 (fig.), 133,
        373n13, 374nn14–15
Kumeyaay, 130, 258, 341
    animal resources, 272, 358, 359, 361
    ceremonies and rituals, 348, 356,
        360
    Eastern, 343, 359, 360, 387n23
    medicines, 350, 354
    plant resources, 344, 348, 349, 357

La Niña, 63–64, 129, 130
Lagenorhynchus obliquidens, 179 (pl.),
    276
Lake Miwok, 217, 219, 250
    animal resources, 235, 236, 239,
        240–241, 245, 246–247, 249–250
    medicines, 217, 223, 225
    plants as food, 216, 226, 228, 229
Lambert, P., 86
lamb's quarters, 286
Laminariales, 28, 216
Lamnidae, 381n4
Lampetra, 191, 194, 200, 325–326
    tridentata, 26, 172 (pl.), 205,
        238–239, 325
lampreys, 191, 194, 200, 325–326
    Pacific Lamprey, 26, 172 (pl.), 205,
        238–239, 325
landscape management
    Central Coast Province, 114, 119,
        213
    cultivation practices for, 126–128,
        127 (fig.), 381nn5–6, 382n7
    ethnographic information on ex-
        tent of, 82, 375n23
    government programs permitting
        traditional, 150–151
    model of harmonious, 10, 11, 89, 90
    new views of, 9–11
    relevance of California Indian prac-
        tices for, 143–147
    and settlement patterns, 132–136,
        385n17, 386nn18, 21
    Southern Deserts Province, 5,
        127–128, 137, 343–344, 378n25,
        387n23
    See also fire management; proto-
        agriculture
Langenheim, J.H., 114
languages
    diversity of, 6 (map), 7
    revitalization of, 214–215, 215 (fig.)
    system for classifying, 74, 372nn2–3
    See also ethnolinguistic units
lantern, white fairy, 310
Larrea tridentata, 350
Larus, 204, 242, 274
    californicus, 175 (pl.), 271
Last Child in the Woods (Louv),
    389n3
Late Holocene
    anthropogenic fire regimes in,
        112–113, 114, 119–120, 378n25
    hard times in, 85, 87
Late Pleistocene
    multiple migrations in, 41, 49
    plant distribution in, 39, 45, 366n2
Latrodectus hesperus, 236
laurel. *See* California bay
Lavinia exilicauda, 173 (pl.), 327
Lawlor, E.J., 380n4, 382n11
Lawrence's Goldfinch, 244
Lawton, H., 82, 83, 124, 380n1
Least Chipmunk, 299
lemonadeberry, 267
leopard lily. *See* tiger lily
Leopard Shark, 273
Lepidium, 220
    nitidum, 261
Lepidoptera, 236, 272, 324
Leporidae, 27, 112, 212, 248, 276, 300,
    304, 335, 344, 361
Leptocottus armatus, 237

Lepus
  californicus, 181 (pl.), 248, 276, 300, 335, 361
  townsendii, 300
Lesser Goldfinch, 244
lettuce
  miner's lettuce, 311
  sea lettuce, 194
Leukoma staminea, 42, 202, 232, 271
Lévi-Strauss, Claude, 80
Lewis, Henry, 9, 82, 95, 99, 102, 124, 375n2
licorice-root, Gray's, 284
lightning strikes, 108–109, 110 (map), 114
Ligusticum grayi, 284, 287–288
Liliaceae, 260
lilies
  fire lily. *See* bear grass
  Fremont's star-lily. *See* death camas
  leopard lily. *See* tiger lily
  mariposa lilies, 219, 261, 310
  tiger lily, 196, 286
  white globe lily. *See* white fairy lantern
  white mariposa lily. *See* butterfly mariposa
  yellow pond-lily, 288–289
Lilium paradalinum, 286
  subsp. *paradalinum,* 196
limpets, 233
Lingcod, 171 (pl.), 203
Lion, Mountain, 248
Lithocarpus, 129
  densiflorus, 164 (pl.), 199–200, 228
Little Ice Age, 47, 64, 108
Littleneck Clam, 42, 202, 232, 271
live oaks, 43
  canyon live oak, 319, 353
  coast live oak, 164 (pl.), 227, 268, 353
  interior live oak, 164 (pl.), 319, 352
lizards, 240
lizard's tail. *See* yerba mansa
lomatium, common, 284
Lomatium
  canbyi, 285
  nudicaule, 284

  triternatum, 285
  utriculatum, 284
Long-neck Clam, 232
Lonicera involucrata, 292
loons, 331
  Common Loon, 175 (pl.), 274, 331
  Pacific Loon, 331
  Red-throated Loon, 331
Lord's candle, Our, 167 (pl.), 269–270, 358
Lotidae, 233
Louv, Richard, 389n3
Lower Colorado River, 61 (map), 185 (map), 369n6
Luiseño, 263, 341
  animal resources, 272, 274, 360, 361
  plants as food, 262, 267, 352, 355
Lumbricus, 324
Luna-Costillas, Quirina, 215
Lütke, Fedor, 376n4
Lynx rufus, 248

Mackerel, Chub, 28, 273
Mackey, E.M., 370n15
Macoma nasuta, 232
Macrocystis pyrifera, 154 (pl.), 259
Madia, 196, 221, 236, 262, 312
  glomerata, 286
madrone, 226
  Pacific madrone, 200
magnesite, 250, 338
Magpie, Yellow-billed, 334
maiden-hair ferns
  California maiden-hair fern, 194, 213, 216, 284, 307
  common maiden-hair fern, 213
maids, red, 157 (pl.), 262, 311
Maidu, 308, 317, 322, 329
  animal resources, 326, 336
  basketry materials, 316, 321
  Konkow, 316, 320, 322, 326, 330, 332, 333, 334
  Mountain, 310, 314
  plants as food, 285, 308, 310, 312, 318, 319
mako sharks, 381n4
Malki Museum, 257–258, 258 (fig.)
Mallard, 176 (pl.), 241, 274, 298, 330

mallow, bull, 67
Malva
    nicaeensis, 67
    parviflora, 67
Mammoth, Columbian, 39
Mammut americanum, 39
Mammuthus columbia, 39
mannagrass, 286
manroot, California, 236, 238
manzanitas, 16 (fig.), 43, 226, 267, 318,
    351
    bigberry manzanita, 159 (pl.),
    common manzanita, 320
    Eastwood manzanita, 226
    greenleaf manzanita, 290, 317
    hairy manzanita, 226
    pinemat manzanita, 320
    whiteleaf manzanita, 320
maple, big-leaf, 315
Marah
    fabaceus, 236, 238
    macrocarpus, 263
Margaritifera
    falcata, 168 (pl.), 294
    margaritifera, 323
Margolin, M., 221
marine resources
    Central Coast Province, 216–217,
        231–235, 237–240, 241–243,
        245–246
    diversity of, 54–55
    and El Niño, 63, 370n9
    Great Central Valley and Sierra Ne-
        vada Province, 323, 325–327,
        330–331
    mass collecting, 28, 28 (fig.)
    Northeast Province, 294, 296, 298
    Northwest Coast Province, 194,
        202, 203–205, 206–207
    South Coast Province, 259,
        270–271, 272–273, 274, 275–276
    Southern Deserts Province, 359
mariposa lilies, 219, 261, 310
    butterfly mariposa, 310
    white mariposa lily. *See* butterfly
        mariposa
Mariscal, Daria, 343 (fig.)
Martin, R.E., 21, 119

Mason, J. Alden, 235
mass collecting
    animal foods, 24–28, 25 (figs.), 26
        (fig.), 28 (fig.)
    archaeology's view of, 91
    goals of, 23–24
    plant foods, 24
    and timing of ceremonies, 33–34
    See also resource gathering
Massey, W.C., 382n7
Mastodon, American, 39
material culture, 16–20
Matson, P.A., 147
Mayer, P.J., 304
maygrass, 380n4, 383n11
McCarthy, H., 384n14
McKay, Mabel, 307
Meadowlark, Western, 299
Medicago polymorpha, 67
medicines
    Central Coast Province, 217, 218,
        219, 221, 223, 225, 226, 229, 230,
        231, 235, 240, 245, 246–247
    Great Central Valley and Sierra
        Nevada Province, 309, 311, 312,
        315–316, 317, 320, 322, 323, 324
    Northeast Province, 283, 285, 287,
        288, 289, 290, 291, 292, 293,
        294
    Northwest Coast Province, 194,
        195, 196, 199, 201–202
    South Coast Province, 259, 260,
        261, 263, 264, 265, 266, 267, 268,
        269
    Southern Deserts Province,
        347–348, 349–350, 351, 352,
        354–356, 357, 358
Medieval Climatic Anomaly, 47, 64,
    108
Medieval Warm Period. *See* Medieval
    Climatic Anomaly
Mediterranean climate, 21, 54, 107
megafauna, 39, 40–41, 43–44
Megaptera novaeangliae, 206–207
Melanerpes formicivorus, 177 (pl.), 206,
    245, 333–334
Melanitta fusca, 274
Melanoplus, 169 (pl.)

memory culture methodology
  and studies of fire management, 95–96, 376nn3–4
  for viewing Native California, 77–78, 82, 374nn16–17
Mensing, S.A., 116
Mentzelia albicaulis, 284
Mephitidae, 249
Mephitis mephitis, 249
Merlin, 332
Merriam, C. Hart, 73, 199–200, 370n7
mesquite, honey, 150, 161 (pl.), 351
mesquite beans, 31, 31 (fig.)
milkweeds, 195, 219, 261, 310–311, 327
  broad-leaved milkweed, 261
  Indian milkweed, 157 (pl.)
  narrow-leaved milkweed, 261
Mimulus guttatus, 311
minerals. *See* rock and mineral resources
miner's lettuce, 311
Minnich, R.A., 116
minnows
  Colorado Pikeminnow, 359
  Sacramento Pikeminnow, 297
Miranda, Rico, 120 (fig.)
Mirounga angustirostris, 276
Miwok
  animal resources, 323, 325, 326, 330, 331, 332, 333, 334, 335
  basketry materials, 316, 331
  Central Sierra, 311
  Eastern, 313
  Plains, 319, 327
  plants as food, 308, 310, 316, 317
  Sierra, 311, 312, 315, 318, 319, 320, 321, 327
  See also Coast Miwok; Lake Miwok
Modoc, 279, 280, 281–282, 288, 295, 296, 301
Mojave, 49, 341
Mojave yucca, 167 (pl.), 358
Mollusca, 54
mollusks, 54
Monache, 332, 337
"money," 35–36
monkeyflower, 311

Mono, 284, 317
  Western, 314, 316, 331, 332, 333, 338
Moorhen, Common, 331
Moratto, M.J., 303
Mormon Cricket, 295
Mormon teas, 352
mortar and pestle, 17 (fig.)
moss, black, 283
moths
  Ceanothus Silk Moth, 169 (pl.), 236, 325
  Polyphemus Moth, 236, 325
mountain balm. *See* yerba santa
Mountain Cottontail, 300
mountain dogwood, 318
mountain gooseberry, 289
Mountain Lion, 248
Mountain Maidu, 310, 314
Mountain Quail, 244, 299, 333, 360
mountain tarweed, 286
mountain-mahoganies, 290
  birch-leaf mountain-mahogany, 290
  curl-leaf mountain-mahogany, 290
Mourning Dove, 112, 243, 331, 360
mugwort, 230, 261, 315
Muhlenbergia rigens, 344
Mule Deer, 26, 182 (pl.), 277, 300, 304–305, 334, 335–336, 362
mule ears, 219
mule fat, 352
mulleins
  turkey mullein, 236, 313
  wooly mullein, 288
murres, 206
mussels, 28, 233
  Bay Mussel, 233
  California Mussel, 42, 44, 168 (pl.), 202, 233, 271
  Freshwater Pearl Mussel, 323
  Western Ridged Mussel, 294, 323
mustards, wild, 221
Mutsun language, 215
Myliobatus californica, 237, 273
Mylopharodon conocephalus, 173 (pl.), 328

Mytilus, 28, 233
  californianus, 42, 168 (pl.), 202, 233, 271
  trossulus, 233

narrow-leaved cattail, 260
narrow-leaved milkweed, 261
narrowleaf willow, 162 (pl.), 201, 294
native barley, 261, 311, 380n4, 383n11
Native California
  at time of first contact with Europeans, 72–73
  dark side of, 85–89
  different scenarios of, 89–93
  health problems in, 85–86
  Kroeberian anthropology on, 73–77, 78, 371n1, 372nn2–3, 5–7, 373nn8, 10–13, 374nn14–15
  memory culture methodology for viewing, 77–78, 82, 374nn16–17
  as paradise of abundance, 81–82, 85
  as protoagricultural, 8, 83–85, 125, 379n1
  revisionist ethnographic anthropology on, 79–85, 374nn20–21, 375nn22–23
  warfare and violence in, 86, 89
  See also California Indians
natural hazards, 64–66, 370nn12–13
natural world
  growing disconnection from, 184, 186, 389n4
  lessons on working with, 144–147, 388n3
The Natural World of the California Indians (Heizer and Elsasser), 40
needlegrass, 43
Nelson, Melissa, 92
Neotoma, 249–250, 277, 301, 337, 362
  cinerea, 301
  fuscipes, 277, 301, 362
  lepida, 277, 362
Nereocystic leutkeana, 154 (pl.), 216
nettle, stinging, 347
Nicotiana, 126–127, 143, 196, 222–223, 263–264, 288, 314–315, 343, 348
  attenuata, 156 (pl.), 264

  clevelandii, 263
  quadrivalvis, 264
Night Smelt, 238
nightshades, 311
  black nightshade, 311
Nisenan, 304, 314, 316
  animal resources, 305, 323, 325, 326, 327, 328, 330, 331, 332, 333, 334, 335, 337
  plants as food, 308–309, 310, 317, 318, 319, 320, 321, 322
  raw materials, 315, 323
Noctuidae, 235
Nomlaki, 303, 304, 312, 315, 320
  animal resources, 305, 328, 332, 333
  plants as food, 314, 317, 321
Northeast Province, 61 (map), 185 (map), 278–301
  animal resources, 294–301
  basketry materials, 284, 287, 291, 293, 294
  ceremonies and rituals, 281
  cordage materials, 285, 292
  ethnolinguistic units, 279
  fish traps, 282–283, 283 (fig.), 297
  medicines, 283, 285, 287, 288, 289, 290, 291, 292, 293, 294
  overview of, 279–282
  plant resources, 283–294
  rock and mineral resources, 301
  settlement patterns, 279–282
  vegetation types, 279
Northeastern Pomo, 219
Northern Elephant Seal, 276
Northern Flicker, 178 (pl.), 245, 332, 334
Northern Foothill Yokuts, 303, 315, 316, 317
Northern Fur Seal, 28, 180 (pl.), 207, 246, 275
Northern Pintail, 298, 330
Northern Razor Clam, 202
Northern Right Whale, 207
Northern Shoveler, 330
Northern Valley Yokuts, 317, 319
Northwest Coast Province, 61 (map), 185 (map), 188–209
  animal resources, 202–208

basketry materials, 194–195, 197, 198, 199, 201

carving art, 192–193, 193 (fig.)

ceremonies and rituals, 190–192, 195, 200, 208

cordage materials, 195, 198

ethnolinguistic units, 189

medicines, 194, 195, 196, 199, 201–202

overview of, 189–193

plant resources, 194–202

rock and mineral resources, 208–209

settlement patterns, 33, 189–191

vegetation types, 189

Nothrotheriops shastense, 39

Nuphar lustea subsp. *polysepaia,* 288–289

nut-grass, yellow, 126

nuts, 24, 30–31

Nuttall's Cockle, 232

Nuttall's scrub oak, 353

Nuttall's sunflower, 288

Nuttall's Woodpecker, 245

oaks, 129, 227–228, 267–268, 281, 291, 318–320, 352–354

black oak, 163 (pl.), 199, 227, 267, 291, 318, 352–353

blue oak, 163 (pl.), 319

California scrub oak, 163 (pl.), 268

canyon live oak, 319, 353

coast live oak, 164 (pl.), 227, 268, 353

interior live oak, 164 (pl.), 319, 352

Nuttall's scrub oak, 353–354

Oregon oak, 164 (pl.), 199, 291, 319–320

ownership of, 212, 304, 318

tan-oak, 129, 164 (pl.), 199–200, 200, 228

valley oak, 164 (pl.), 228, 268

white oak. *See* valley oak

See also acorns; poison-oak

oats, wild, 67, 222, 313

obsidian, 208–209, 250, 301, 338, 363, 387n21

O'Connell, James, 121

Octopus, 234

octopuses, 234

Odocoileus, 384n15

hemionus, 26, 182 (pl.), 277, 300, 304, 334, 335–336, 362

hemionus columbianus, 207–208, 212, 247

Odontophoridae, 27, 112, 244–245, 299, 333, 360–361

Okrand, Marc, 215

Olive Snail, 35, 234, 271

Olivella biplicata. See Callianax triplicata

Oncorhynchus, 56, 194, 201, 239, 281, 326–327, 329

clarki, 297

kisutch, 192, 205, 239, 296, 384n15

mass collecting, 25 (fig.), 26, 191

mykiss, 205, 231, 239, 240, 274, 281, 296–297, 329

mykiss irideus, 26, 56, 193, 205, 239, 240, 329, 384n15

tshawytscha, 172 (pl.), 192, 204, 239, 296, 326, 384n15

O'Neale, L. M., 201

onions

swamp onion, 158 (pl.)

wild onions, 222, 314

opal phytoliths, 115, 121

Ophiodon elongatus, 171 (pl.), 203

Opuntia, 270, 357–358

basilaris, 166 (pl.), 357–358

ficus-indica, 357

Oregon oak, 164 (pl.), 199, 291, 320

Oreortyx pictus, 244, 299, 333, 360

Orthodon microlepidotus, 327

Ortiz, Bev, 11

Osmeridae, 28, 192, 203–204, 238

Osmorrhiza, 329

chilensis, 196

Ostrea conchaphila, 44, 231–232

Otariidae, 45, 192, 207, 246, 275

Otter, Sea, 28, 67, 246, 276

Our Lord's candle, 167 (pl.), 269–270, 358

Ovis canadensis, 48, 181 (pl.), 361

Owen, R.C., 347

owls, 112, 333
    Great Horned Owl, 333
Oxyjulis californica, 273
Oxyura jamaicensis, 176 (pl.), 242,
    274
Oyster, California, 44, 231–232

Pacific Angel Shark, 273
Pacific Barracuda, 170 (pl.), 273
Pacific Bonito, 273
Pacific Herring, 237
Pacific Lamprey, 26, 172 (pl.), 205,
    238–239, 325
Pacific Loon, 331
Pacific madrone, 200
Pacific Ocean
    and El Niño/La Niña, 62–63
    and fog drip, 56
    marine influence of, 54–55, 368n3
    Pleistocene level of, 39
Pacific Sardine, 273
Pacific Staghorn Sculpin, 237
Pacific White-sided Dolphin, 179 (pl.),
    276
Pacific yew, 291
Paipai, 341, 359
    ceramic arts, 345–346, 345 (fig.)
    medicines, 347, 349–350, 351,
        358
    plants as food, 353, 357, 360
Paiute, 126, 382n7
    Southern Paiute, 341
Paleo-Indians, 40–41, 367n4
palms
    California fan palm, 349
    sea palm, 216
Paralabrax clathratus, 273
Paralichthys californicus, 203
Parker, A. J., 96
Parker, Julia, 306, 306 (fig.)
Parker, Lucy, 307
Parry pinyon, 354
parsley
    desert parsley, 285
    wild parsley, 287–288
parsnip, cow, 285
Patagioenas fasciata, 27, 177 (pl.), 243,
    331

Patwin, 304, 331, 335, 336
    basketry and cordage materials,
        310, 312
    fish as food, 326, 327, 328, 329
    plants as food, 313, 314
Pearl Mussel, Freshwater, 323
Pearlshell, Western, 168 (pl.), 294
Pelagic Cormorant, 176 (pl.), 241, 274
Pelecanus, 242–243
    erythrorhynchos, 177 (pl.), 242
    occidentalis, 242, 274
Pelican Dance, 243
pelicans, 242–243
    Brown Pelican, 242–243, 274
    White Pelican, 177 (pl.), 242–243
peppergrass, 220, 261
perches
    Sacramento Perch, 173 (pl.), 327,
        328
    Tule Perch, 327
Peregrine Falcon, 112, 332
Perideridia, 121
    oregana, 284, 285–286
Petasites frigidus var. *palmatus,* 195
Phalacrocorax, 28, 206, 241, 274
    auritus, 175 (pl.), 241, 274
    pelagicus, 176 (pl.), 241, 274
    penicillatus, 175 (pl.), 241, 274
Phalaris, 259, 308, 380n4
Phasianidae, 332
Phoca vitulina, 28, 67, 180 (pl.), 207,
    246, 276
Phocidae, 45, 207
Phyllospadix, 42, 254, 259
    torreyi, 154 (pl.)
phytoliths, opal, 115, 121
Pica nuttallii, 334
Picidae, 112, 206, 245, 333–334
Picoides
    nuttallii, 245
    pubescens, 245
    villosus, 245
Pied-billed Grebe, 331
pigeon-berry. *See* California coffee-
    berry
pigeons, 26 (fig.)
    Band-tailed Pigeon, 27, 177 (pl.),
        243, 331

pigweed, 67, 157 (pl.), 346
pikeminnows
    Colorado Pikeminnow, 359
    Sacramento Pikeminnow, 297
Pileated Woodpecker, 206, 245, 334
pinemat manzanita, 320
pines, 43, 228–229, 291–292, 320–321
    foothill pine, 228, 291, 320–321
    gray pine. See foothill pine
    ponderosa pine, 106, 201, 292, 321
    sugar pine, 165 (pl.), 201, 202,
        228–229, 292, 321
    Torrey pine, 45
    western bristlecone pine, 56, 60
    See also pinyon pines
pinole, 217
Pintail, Northern, 298, 330
Pinus, 43, 354, 384n15
    lambertiana, 165 (pl.), 201, 202,
        228–229, 292, 321
    longaeva, 60
    monophylla, 150, 165 (pl.),
        268–269, 354
    ponderosa, 106, 201, 292, 321
    quadrifolia, 354
    sabiniana, 228, 291320–291321
    torreyana, 45
pinyon pines, 354, 384n15
    Parry pinyon, 354
    single-leaf pinyon pine, 150, 165
        (pl.), 268–269, 354
Pismo Clam, 232, 271
pit-baking, 23, 366n3
pitseed goosefoot, 261
Plains Miwok, 319, 327
plant, soap, 158 (pl.), 195, 196, 198,
    220, 236, 262, 312
plant communities, 370n7
    See also vegetation types
plant resources
    categories of, 184
    Central Coast Province, 213,
        216–231
    Great Central Valley and Sierra Ne-
        vada Province, 307–323
    mass collecting, 24
    material culture produced from,
        18–20, 18 (fig.), 20 (fig.)

Northeast Province, 283–294
Northwest Coast Province, 194–202
South Coast Province, 259–270
Southern Deserts Province, 344,
    346–358
    storing, 29–31, 29 (fig.), 31 (fig.)
    See also plants
Plantago, 43
plantain, 43
plants
    distribution of, in Late Pleistocene,
        39, 45, 366n2
    diversity of, 21–22, 56, 60, 380n4
    domestication of, 128–129,
        382nn9–11, 383n12, 385n16,
        387n23
    endemic/native species, 56, 60, 68
    exotic, introduced by Europeans,
        66–67, 68, 370n15, 371nn16–17
    fire-stimulated, 21–22, 113, 378n27
    and vegetation types, 60, 62, 370n7
    See also cultivation; plant resources
Plecoptera, 295, 325
Pleistocene
    coastal archaeological sites from,
        42–43
    Late, multiple migrations in, 41, 49
    overview of conditions in, 38–39,
        366nn1–3
Pluchea sericea, 159 (pl.), 349
plums
    Klamath plum, 290
    Sierra plum. See Klamath plum
Poaceae, 219, 254
Pocket Gopher, Botta's, 248
Podicipedidae, 298, 331
Podilymbus
    auritus, 331
    nigricollis, 331
    podiceps, 331
Pogonichthys macrolepidotus, 174 (pl.),
    328
Pogonomyrmex, 235, 272, 295
points
    Clovis, 43, 367n4
    fluted projectile, 41, 43–44, 46,
        367nn4–6
    Folsom, 367n4

poison-oak, 195, 229, 268
  remedies for, 194, 261, 263, 312
political elites, 7, 79, 88–89
polities
  in greater San Francisco Bay Area,
    34 (map)
  Kroeberian anthropology on,
    76–77, 77 (fig.), 373nn11–13,
    374nn14–15
  relationships between, 35–36
  as typical of California Indians, 4
    (fig.), 7, 33–35
  winter villages as, 32–33, 32 (fig.),
    279–281
  See also house societies; tribelets
Pollicipes polymerus, 234
Polyphemus Moth, 236, 325
Polystichum munitum, 213
Pomo, 219, 226
  Eastern, 217, 218
  Northeastern, 219
  plants as food, 218, 222, 224, 226,
    227, 228, 230
  raw materials, 218, 225
  Southeastern, 217, 218
  "tribe," 74–75, 372n5
  Western, 216, 219
  See also Kashaya Pomo
Pond Turtle, Western, 174 (pl.), 329
ponderosa pine, 106, 201, 292, 321
Populus, 266
  balsamifera, 266
  fremontii, 266, 350
Porcupine, American, 299
Porphyra, 28, 216–217
  lanceolata, 194, 216
  perforata, 216
porpoises, 28, 276
Port Orford cedar, 199
Porzana carolina, 331
Postelsia palmaeformis, 216
pottery, 17, 345–346, 345 (fig.)
Prairie Falcon, 332
precipitation
  and El Niño/La Niña, 62, 63
  fog drip, 56
  topography's impact on, 55–56,
    368n4, 369n5

prescribed burning. See fire management
Price, T.D., 128
prickly sow thistle, 67
prickly-pears, 270, 357–358
Proboscidea parviflora, 383n11
Procyon lotor, 249
projectile points, fluted, 41, 43–44, 46,
  367nn4–6
Pronghorn, 27, 212, 248–249, 300, 336,
  362, 384n15
Prosopis
  glandulosa, 150, 161 (pl.), 351
  pubescens, 355
protoagriculture
  California Indians as not practic-
    ing, 136–138
  California Indians as practicing, 8,
    83–85, 125, 379n1
  defined, 125, 379n1
  See also cultivation
Prunus
  ilicifolia, 161 (pl.), 225, 266–267,
    350
  subcordata, 290
  virginiana var. demissa, 201,
    292–293, 355
Pteridium aquilinum, 154 (pl.), 194,
  213, 284
Pteridophyta, 213, 216
Pterygophora californica, 216
Ptychocheilus
  grandis, 297
  lucius, 359
Puma concolor, 248
Pyne, S.J., 108, 377n16
pyrodiversity
  defined, 21–22
  See also fire management
pyrodiversity collecting model. See
  fire-management model
pyrodiversity collectors, 9, 131–132,
  384n16

quail, 18 (fig.), 27, 112, 244–245, 299,
  333, 360–361
  California Quail, 178 (pl.), 206,
    244, 275, 299, 333, 360

Gambel's Quail, 178 (pl.), 360
Mountain Quail, 244, 299, 333, 360
quamash. *See* camas
quarters, lamb's, 286
quartz, 363
quasi-agriculture, 379n1
See also protoagriculture
Quaternary Period, 366n1
Quechan, 341
Quercus, 129, 212, 304
  agrifolia, 43, 164 (pl.), 227, 268, 353
  berberidifolia, 163 (pl.), 268
  chrysolepis, 319, 353
  douglasii, 163 (pl.), 319
  dumosa, 352, 353–354
  engelmannii, 352
  garryana, 164 (pl.), 199, 291, 319
  kelloggii, 163 (pl.), 199, 227, 267,
    291, 318, 352–353
  lobata, 164 (pl.), 228, 268, 319–320,
    384n13
  turbinella, 352, 353–354
  wislizeni, 43, 164 (pl.), 319, 352
Quick, C.R., 112

Raab, L.M., 88
rabbits, 27, 112, 212, 248, 276, 300,
  304, 305, 335, 344, 361
  Black-tailed Jackrabbit, 181 (pl.),
    248, 276, 300, 335, 361
  Brush Rabbit, 248, 335
  Desert Cottontail, 248, 276, 335,
    361
  Mountain Cottontail, 300
  White-tailed Jackrabbit, 300
Raccoon, 249
rails, 206, 331
  Virginia Rail, 331
Rainbow Trout, 205, 231, 239, 240,
  273, 281, 296–297, 329
rainfall. *See* precipitation
Raja, 237
Rallidae, 206, 331
Rallus limicola, 331
raptors, 275
rattlesnake weed, 329
Rattlesnakes, 359
  Western Rattlesnake, 329

Raven, Common, 177 (pl.), 244, 331
ravens, 112, 244, 331
Ray, V.F., 288
rays, 237
  Bat Ray, 237, 273
  stingrays, 237
Razor Clam, Northern, 202
Razorback Sucker, 359
Red Abalone, 42, 168 (pl.), 231, 270
red alder, 223
Red Fox, 335
red huckleberry, 290
red maids, 157 (pl.), 262, 311
red willow, 269
Red-breasted Sapsucker, 245
redbud, western, 166 (pl.), 229–230,
  293, 322
Red-shafted Flicker, 245
red-stem filaree, 66, 67
Redtail Surfperch, 203
Red-tailed Hawk, 178 (pl.), 244, 275,
  332
Red-throated Loon, 331
Red-winged Blackbird, 243, 331
redwood, coast, 56, 114, 161 (pl.),
  198–199, 201, 225, 266, 366n2
relevancy question, 2–3, 7–9, 12–13,
  142–151
resource gathering
  cultural practices governing,
    84–85
  current issues, 12
  fire management as facilitating,
    98–99
  traditional, government program
    permitting, 150–151
  See also mass collecting
resource intensification, 86–88, 89–90,
  131–132
resources
  diversity of, 54–55, 125–126, 380n4
  flexible relationship with, 128–130,
    131
  ownership of, 99, 212, 304, 318
  selection of, for book, 184, 388n2
  See also animal resources; marine
    resources; plant resources; rock
    and mineral resources

Rhamnus, 289
    californica, 245, 265
    purshiana, 289
    rubra, 289
Rhinobatos productus, 273
Rhododendron occidentale, 231
Rhus, 355
    integrifolia, 267
    trilobata, 292, 322, 355
Ribes, 266, 289
    aureum, 289
    cereum, 289
    divaricatum var. *pubiflorum,* 200, 289
    montigenum, 289
    roezlii, 165 (pl.), 289, 322
Ridged Mussel, Western, 294, 323
rituals. *See* ceremonies and rituals
Roadrunner, Greater, 332
Robin, American, 299
Rock Cockle. *See* Littleneck Clam
Rock Ground Squirrel, 362
rock and mineral resources
    Central Coast Province, 250
    Great Central Valley and Sierra Nevada Province, 337–338
    material culture produced from, 18
    Northeast Province, 301
    Northwest Coast Province, 208–209
    South Coast Province, 277
    Southern Deserts Province, 363
Rock Scallop, 202
rockfishes, 28, 43, 44, 54, 203, 237, 273
    Kelp Rockfish, 171 (pl.)
Rodentia, 112
rodents, 112
Roosevelt Elk, 181 (pl.), 208, 248
Roosevelt Middle School, Expedition Program, 142, 387n1
roots, 24, 31
    snake roots, 329
Rosa californica, 230, 269
rose, wild, 230, 269
Round-tailed Ground Squirrel, 362
Rubus
    parviflorus, 229
    spectabilis, 200
    ursinus, 160 (pl.), 197, 265, 316

Ruddy Duck, 176 (pl.), 241–242, 274
Rumex crispus, 67
rushes, 67, 220, 262, 347
    bog rush, 262
    Indian rush, 262
    spiny rush, 262
    wire rush, 220, 262
ryegrass, 43

sabertooth cat, 39
Sacramento Blackfish, 327
Sacramento Perch, 173 (pl.), 327, 328
Sacramento Pikeminnow, 297
Sacramento Splittail, 174 (pl.), 328
Sacramento Sucker, 26, 174 (pl.), 240, 281, 283, 283 (fig.), 297, 327, 328
sage, white, 355–356
Sage Grouse, Greater, 299, 332
sagebrushes, 292, 354–355
    coastal sagebrush, 266
salamanders, 240
Salinan
    animal resources, 235, 245
    plants as food, 216, 218
    raw materials, 213, 219, 220, 221, 250
Salix, 201, 230, 269, 294, 322–323, 356
    exigua, 162 (pl.), 201, 294
    hindsiana, 230
    laevigata, 269
    lasiolepis, 269
    scouleriana, 201
    sitchensis, 201
Salmo gairdneri. See *Oncorhynchus mykiss*
salmon, 56, 194, 201, 239, 281, 326, 370–379
    ceremonies associated with, 191–192, 200
    Chinook Salmon, 172 (pl.), 192, 204, 239, 296, 326, 384n15
    Coho Salmon, 192, 205, 239, 296, 384n15
    King Salmon. *See* Chinook Salmon
    mass collecting, 25 (fig.), 26, 191
    Silver Salmon. *See* Coho Salmon
salmon flies, 295, 325
salmonberry, 200

salt, 250, 338, 363
saltbush, 229, 347
Salvia
    apiana, 355–356
    columbariae, 155 (pl.), 218, 260, 344
Sambucus, 225, 264, 317
    mexicana, 159 (pl.), 264, 289, 349
sanicles, 329
Sanicula, 329
Santa Ana winds, 115–116
Santa Barbara sedge, 220
Sapsis, D.B., 21, 119
Sapsucker, Red-breasted, 245
Sarda chilensis, 273
Sardine, Pacific, 273
Sardinops sagax, 273
Satureja douglasii, 223
Satwiwa Native American Indian Cul-
    ture Center, 258
Saubel, K.S., 353
Sauer, Carl, 83
Sauria, 240
Saxidomus nuttalli, 42, 168 (pl.), 202,
    232
scallops
    Rock Scallop, 202
    Thick Scallop, 271
Schoenherr, A.A., 60
Schoenoplectus, 158 (pl.), 211, 221, 254,
    263, 287, 313, 330, 348
    acutus, 263, 287
    californicus, 263
    gathering, 84 (fig.)
Sciuridae, 249, 299, 304, 337, 362
Sciurus griseus, 182 (pl.), 249, 299, 337
Scomber japonicus, 28, 273
Scorpaenichthys marmoratus, 45, 170
    (pl.), 237, 273
Scoter, White-winged, 274
Scouler's willow, 201
screwbean, 355
scrub oaks, 353–354
    California scrub oak, 163 (pl.), 268
    Nuttall's scrub oak, 353–354
sculpins, 203
    Pacific Staghorn Sculpin, 237
sea anemones, 235
sea fig, 370n15

sea grass, 42, 154 (pl.), 254, 259
sea lettuce, 194
sea lions, 45, 192, 207, 246, 275
    California Sea Lion, 28, 67, 179
        (pl.), 207, 246, 275
    Steller Sea Lion, 28, 67, 207, 246
Sea Otter, 28, 67, 246, 276
sea palm, 216
sea turtles, 360
sea urchins, 202, 235
seals, 45, 207
    Guadalupe Fur Seal, 28, 275
    Harbor Seal, 28, 67, 180 (pl.), 207,
        246, 276
    Northern Elephant Seal, 276
    Northern Fur Seal, 28, 180 (pl.),
        207, 246, 275
seaweeds, 28, 31, 194, 200, 216–217
Sebastes, 28, 43, 45, 54, 203, 237, 273
    atovirens, 171 (pl.)
sedges, 67, 220, 312
    Santa Barbara sedge, 220
seed beaters, 24
seed-sowing. *See* cultivation
seep-willow. *See* mule fat
semiagriculture, 379n1
    See also protoagriculture
Semicossyphus pulcher, 45, 171 (pl.),
    273
Señorita, 273
sequoia, giant, 56, 117
Sequoia sempervirens, 56, 114, 161
    (pl.), 198–199, 201, 225, 266, 366n2
Sequoiadendron giganteum, 56, 117
Seriola lalandi, 170 (pl.), 273
Serpentes, 240–241
Serrano, 341
service-berry, western, 293
settlement patterns
    Central Coast Province, 211
    Great Central Valley and Sierra Ne-
        vada Province, 303–304
    and landscape management,
        132–136, 385n17, 386nn18, 21
    Northeast Province, 279–282
    Northwest Coast Province, 33,
        189–191
    South Coast Province, 253–254

settlement patterns (cont.)
Southern Deserts Province, 342–343
Shackley, M.S., 387n23
Shaffer, K.E., 121
sharks, 237
Leopard Shark, 273
mako sharks, 381n4
Pacific Angel Shark, 273
Soupfin Shark, 273
Shasta, 203
Sheep, Bighorn, 48, 181 (pl.), 361
Sheephead, California, 45, 171 (pl.), 273
Shipek, F.C., 9, 130
Shoshone
Timbisha Shoshone, 387n23
Western Shoshone, 341
Shoveler, Northern, 330
Shovelnose Guitarfish, 273
Sierra coffeeberry, 289
Sierra gooseberry, 165 (pl.), 289, 322
Sierra Miwok
animal resources, 327
medicines, 311, 315, 320, 321
plants as food, 311, 312, 318, 319, 321
raw materials, 321
Sierra Nevada. *See* Great Central Valley and Sierra Nevada Province
Sierra plum. *See* Klamath plum
Silene gallica, 67
Siliqua patula, 202
Silk Moth, Ceanothus, 169 (pl.), 236, 325
silktassel, coast, 231
Silver Salmon. *See* Coho Salmon
silversides, 238
Simmondsia chinensis, 351
Simmons, William, 74
single-leaf pinyon pine, 150, 165 (pl.), 268–269, 354
Siphateles bicolor, 298
Sitka willow, 201
skates, 237
Skinner, C.N., 110
skunkbush, 292, 322, 355

skunks, 249
Striped Skunk, 249
Western Spotted Skunk, 249
Sloth, Ground, 39
Slug, Banana, 203
smelts, 28, 192, 203–204, 238
Delta Smelt, 327
Eulachon, 204
Jacksmelt, 238
Night Smelt, 238
Surf Smelt, 238
Topsmelt, 238
Smilodon, 39
Smith, B.D., 382n9, 387n22
Smith, Tom, 235, 250
snails
Black Turban Snail, 168 (pl.), 231, 270–271
Brown Turban Snail, 231
California Horn Snail, 234
Garden Snail, 234
Olive Snail, 35, 234, 271
snake roots, 329
snakes, 240–241
Rattlesnakes, 359
Western Rattlesnake, 329
snare, treadle, 18, 18 (fig.)
Snow Goose, 242
soap plant, 158 (pl.), 195, 196, 198, 220, 236, 262, 312
soapstone. *See* steatite
Solanum, 311
nigrum, 311
Sonchus
asper, 67
oleraceus, 67
Sora, 331
Soupfin Shark, 273
South Coast Province, 61 (map), 185 (map), 252–277
animal resources, 270–277, 381n4
archaeological findings, 42–43, 44–45, 48, 85–86, 366n2
basketry materials, 262, 263
ceremonies and rituals, 254–255, 262, 263, 264, 266, 267, 272, 273, 275
cordage materials, 259, 260, 261, 269

ethnolinguistic units, 253
medicines, 259, 260, 261, 263, 264, 265, 266, 267, 268, 269
overview of, 253–256
plant resources, 259–270
precipitation, 369n5
rock and mineral resources, 277
settlement patterns, 253–254
tribal museums and cultural centers, 257–258
vegetation types, 253
Southeastern Pomo, 217, 218
southern cattail, 260, 308
Southern Deserts Province, 61 (map), 185 (map), 340–363
animal resources, 358–362
archaeological findings, 43, 46, 48, 367n4
basketry materials, 344, 346, 354, 356, 358
ceramic arts, 345–346, 345 (fig.)
ceremonies and rituals, 347, 348, 360, 362
ethnolinguistic units, 341
landscape management practices, 5, 127–128, 137, 343–344, 378n25, 387n23
Late Pleistocene freshwater ecosystems, 38, 47
medicines, 347–348, 349–350, 351, 352, 354–356, 357, 358
overview of, 341–344
plant resources, 344, 346–358
rock and mineral resources, 363
settlement patterns, 342–343
vegetation types, 341
Southern Valley Yokuts, 308, 318, 332, 338
sow thistles
common sow thistle, 67
prickly sow thistle, 67
Spanish bayonet, 358
Sparkman, P.S., 274, 361
spear, Ithuriel's, 157 (pl.), 310
Spermophilus, 276, 299
beecheyi, 249, 276, 299, 337
beldingi, 299
lateralis, 182 (pl.), 299

tereticaudus, 362
variegatus, 362
Sphaeriidae, 323
Sphyraena argentea, 170 (pl.), 273
Sphyrapicus ruber, 245
Spider, Western Black Widow, 236
spike bentgrass, 67
Spilogale gracilis, 249
spiny rush, 262
Spirinchus starski, 238
Splittail, Sacramento, 174 (pl.), 328
Sprugel, D.G., 108
Squatina californica, 273
squirrels, 249, 299, 304, 305, 337, 362
Douglas Squirrel, 249, 299, 337
Western Gray Squirrel, 182 (pl.), 249, 299, 337
See also ground squirrels
Staghorn Sculpin, Pacific, 237
stalked kelp, 216
Stanford, D., 41
star, blazing, 284
star-lily, Fremont's. *See* death camas
steatite, 17, 209, 277, 338
Steelhead, 26, 56, 193, 205, 230, 240, 329, 384n15
Steller Sea Lion, 28, 67, 207, 246
Steller's Jay, 333
Stephens, S.L., 112
Stewart, Omer, 95, 96, 99, 235
stinging nettle, 347
stingrays, 237
Stipa, 43
storing foods
methods for, 29–31, 29 (fig.), 31 (fig.)
in winter villages, 32–33, 32 (fig.)
straggly gooseberry, 200, 289
strawberries, wild, 222, 288, 314
Strawberry Festival dance, 218, 219, 222
Strigidae, 112, 333
Strike, S.S., 286
Striped Skunk, 249
Striped Surfperch, 171 (pl.)
Striplen, Chuck, 120 (fig.), 121
Strongylocentrotus, 202, 235
Sturak, Tamara, 387n1

sturgeons, 239–240
    Green Sturgeon, 239–240
    White Sturgeon, 172 (pl.), 239–240,
        327
Sturnella neglecta, 299
suckers
    Humpback Sucker. *See* Razorback
        Sucker
    Razorback Sucker, 359
    Sacramento Sucker, 26, 174 (pl.),
        240, 281, 283, 283 (fig.), 297,
        327, 328
sugar pine, 165 (pl.), 201, 202,
    228–229, 292, 321
Sugihara, N.G., 113, 121
sulphur flower, 286
sumacs, 355
sunflowers, wild, 286, 288, 314
    Cusick's sunflower, 288
    Nuttall's sunflower, 288
Surf Smelt, 238
surf-grass. *See* sea grass
surfperches, 28, 44, 238, 273
    Redtail Surfperch, 203
    Striped Surfperch, 171 (pl.)
sustainability
    debate on Native Californians and,
        11–12
    defined, 147–148
    relevance of California Indian
        practices to, 147–149, 388n5
Sutton, M.Q., 295
swamp onion, 158 (pl.)
Swan, Tundra, 298
sweet cicely, 196
Swetnam, T.W., 116–117, 379n31
Swezey, S.L., 191
sword fern, western, 213
Swordfish, 273, 381n4
Sylvilagus
    auduboni, 248, 276, 335, 361
    bachmani, 248, 335
    nuttalli, 300

Tabanidae, 324
Tamias, 334
    amoenus, 299
    minimus, 299

Tamiasciurus douglasii, 249, 299, 337
tan-oak, 129, 164 (pl.), 199–200, 200,
    228
tanbark-oak. *See* tan-oak
Taraxacum, 309
tarweeds, 196, 221, 236, 262, 312
    mountain tarweed, 286
Taxus brevifolia, 291
Taylor, A.H., 110
Taylor, D., 115, 116
teals
    Cinnamon Teal, 176 (pl.), 274,
        330
    Green-winged Teal, 176 (pl.), 274,
        330
teas, Mormon, 352
Telles, Lucy, 307
Tending the Wild (Anderson), 10
Testudines, 241, 329
Thaleichthys pacificus, 204
Thick Scallop, 271
thickleaf yerba santa, 356
Thicktail Chub, 327, 329
thimbleberry, 229
thinleaf huckleberry, 290
thistles
    common sow thistle, 67
    elk thistle, 284
    prickly sow thistle, 67
Thomomys bottae, 248
Thunnus, 381n4
tiger lily, 196, 286
Timbisha Shoshone, 387n23
Timbrook, J., 261, 262, 263
Tipai, 354
Tivela stultorum, 232, 271
tobaccos, wild, 143, 196, 222–223,
    263–264, 288, 314–315, 343, 348
    coyote tobacco, 156 (pl.), 264,
        348
    cultivating, 126–127, 127 (fig.),
        381nn5–6
    Indian tobacco, 264
toloache, 158 (pl.), 254, 263, 312,
    347–348
Tolowa, 203
tomols, 24, 255, 256, 266, 269
Tongva, 254, 255, 256

tools, 17, 17 (fig.), 24, 42, 91, 109 (fig.), 250, 337, 338, 363
    milling stones, 17, 42, 45
    stone bifaces, 45, 190, 208–209
topography
    diversity of, 51–54, 53 (map), 368n2
    and precipitation patterns, 55–56, 368n4, 369n5
Topsmelt, 238
Torrey pine, 45
Toxicodendron diversilobum, 194, 195, 229, 268
toyon, 229, 269, 322
trade, between polities, 35–36
treadle snare, 18, 18 (fig.)
Tresus nuttallii, 42, 232
Triakididae, 237
Triakis semifasciata, 273
tribelets, 33
    Kroeber on, 76–77, 77 (fig.), 133, 373n13, 374nn14–15
    social complexity of, 79
    spatial organization of, 132–136, 385n17, 386nn18, 21
    territories of, 79–80, 81 (map), 374n19
    tribe vs., 372n5
tribes, ethnolinguistic units vs., 74–75, 372n5
Trifolium, 218, 223, 309
    barbigerum, 309
    ciliolatum, 309
    variegatum, 309
    wormskioldii, 309
Tringham, Ruth, 388n1
Triteleia, 218, 308
    hyacinthina, 287
    ixioides, 308
    laxa, 157 (pl.), 310
Trochilidae, 244
trouts, 329
    Cutthroat Trout, 297
    Rainbow Trout, 205, 231, 239, 240, 273, 281, 296–297, 329
tsunamis, 65, 370n13
Tubatulabal, 338
tubers, 24, 31

Tui Chub, 298
Tulare Lake Yokuts, 304
Tule Elk, 181 (pl.), 248, 337
Tule Perch, 327
tules, 84 (fig.), 158 (pl.), 211, 221, 254, 263, 287, 313, 348
    common tule, 263, 287
tuna cactus, common, 357
tunas, 381n4
Tundra Swan, 298
turban snails
    Black Turban Snail, 168 (pl.), 231, 270–271
    Brown Turban Snail, 231
Turdus migratorius, 299
turkey mullein, 236, 313
Tursiops truncata, 276
turtles, 241, 329
    sea turtles, 360
    Western Pond Turtle, 174 (pl.), 329
Tusk Shell. *See* Dentalium
Tveskov, M.A., 99
twinberry, 292
Typha, 98 (fig.), 260, 308
    angustifolia, 260
    domingensis, 260
    latifolia, 155 (pl.), 217–218, 260, 308
Tytonidae, 112, 333

Ugan, A., 27
Ulva lactuca, 194
Umbellularia californica, 159 (pl.), 197, 213, 223–224, 265, 315–316
Unamuno, Pedro de, 57–58
Underwood, Charles, 387n1
urchins, sea, 202, 235
Urocyon cinereoargenteus, 248, 335
Ursus, 246–247, 334, 361
    americanus, 246, 334
    arctos horribilis, 246, 334, 336
Urtica dioica, 347

Vaccinium, 226, 290
    caespitosum, 290
    membranaceum, 290
    ovatum, 160 (pl.), 195, 198, 226
    parvifolium, 290

Vale, T.R., 10, 22, 96

valley oak, 164 (pl.), 228, 268, 319

van Wagtendonk, J.W., 121, 146

vegetation types
  Central Coast Province, 211
  classifying, 60, 62, 370n7
  creation and maintenance of, 83–84
  and fire fuel buildup, 106–107,
    377n14
  Great Central Valley and Sierra Ne-
    vada Province, 303
  Northeast Province, 279
  Northwest Coast Province, 189
  Pleistocene, 39
  South Coast Province, 253
  Southern Deserts Province, 341

velvet grass, 325

Venus clams, 44, 271

Verbascum thapsus, 288

verbena, 43

Verbena, 43

Vespula, 27, 203, 236, 272, 295–296,
  325
  pennsylvanica, 169 (pl.)

village communities, 33, 76–77
  See also tribelets

villages, winter, 32–33, 32 (fig.),
  279–281

violence, 86, 89

Virginia Rail, 331

Vitis californica, 160 (pl.), 195, 198,
  201, 224–225, 266, 316–317

Vizcaino, Sebastian, 58–59

volcanism, 65–66

Vulpes, 335
  macrotis, 248, 335
  vulpes, 335

Vulpia, 43, 380n4

Walker, P.L., 86

Wallace, W.J., 387n23

walnut, California black, 159 (pl.), 265

Wappo, 233, 239, 249
  basketry and cordage materials,
    213, 218, 219, 229
  bows and arrows, 217, 223, 226
  landscape management practices,
    213, 382n7

medicines, 223, 229
  plants as food, 216, 218, 219, 224,
    225, 226, 227, 228, 230

warfare, 86, 89

Warner, Natasha, 215

Washington Clam, 42, 44, 168 (pl.),
  202, 232

Washingtonia filifera, 349

Wasp, California Gall, 235, 324

watercraft
  for deepwater fishing, 381n4
  of earliest California Indians, 42
  migrations by, 41
  Northwest Coast Province canoes,
    198
  tomols, 24, 255, 256, 266, 269
  used in mass collecting, 24

Waterman, T.T., 191, 356

wax currant, 289

weather patterns, 55–56, 368n4,
  369n5
  See also climate

weed, rattlesnake, 329

western azalea, 231

Western Black Widow Spider, 236

western bristlecone pine, 56, 60

western choke-cherry, 201, 292–293,
  355

Western Gray Squirrel, 182 (pl.), 249,
  299, 337

Western Grebe, 176 (pl.), 331

western juniper, 162 (pl.), 293

Western Meadowlark, 299

Western Pearlshell, 168 (pl.), 294

Western Pomo, 216, 219

Western Pond Turtle, 174 (pl.), 329

Western Rattlesnake, 329

western redbud, 166 (pl.), 229–230,
  293, 322

Western Ridged Mussel, 294, 323

Western Scrub-Jay, 333

western service-berry, 293

Western Shoshone, 341

Western Spotted Skunk, 249

western sword fern, 213

Western Yellowjacket, 169 (pl.)

whales
  Blue Whale, 207

Gray Whale, 28, 180 (pl.), 206, 245–246, 276
  Humpback Whale, 206–207
  Northern Right Whale, 207
Wheeland, Matthew, 149
white alder, 223
white brodiaea, 287
white camas, 287
White Deerskin Dance, 208
white fairy lantern, 310
white fir, 293, 322
white globe lily. See white fairy lantern
white grass. See bear grass
white mariposa lily. See butterfly mariposa
white oak. See valley oak
White Pelican, 177 (pl.), 242–243
white sage, 355–356
White Sturgeon, 172 (pl.), 239–240, 327
white-flowered grass-nut. See white brodiaea
White-fronted Goose, Greater, 242
White-tailed Jackrabbit, 300
White-winged Scoter, 274
whiteleaf manzanita, 320
wickiups, 294
Wikersheim, Fritz, 77 (fig.)
wild cucumber, 263
wild ginger, 221
wild grape, California, 160 (pl.), 195, 198, 201, 254–255, 266, 316–317
wild mustards, 221
wild oats, 67, 222, 313
wild onions, 222, 314
wild parsley, 287–288
wild rose, 230, 269
wild strawberries, 222, 288, 314
wild sunflowers, 286, 288, 314
  Cusick's sunflower, 288
  Nuttall's sunflower, 288
wild tobaccos, 143, 196, 222–223, 263–264, 288, 314–315, 343, 348
  coyote tobacco, 156 (pl.), 264, 348
  cultivating, 126–127, 127 (fig.), 381nn5–6
  Indian tobacco, 264
wild-hyacinth, 126

Wilke, P.J., 383n12
willows, 201, 230, 269, 294, 322–323, 356
  arroyo willow, 269
  desert willow, 350
  narrowleaf willow, 162 (pl.), 201, 294
  red willow, 269
  Scouler's willow, 201
  seep-willow. See mule fat
  Sitka willow, 201
Wills, W.H., 80, 382n10, 385n16
Wilson, N.L., 318
winter villages, 32–33, 32 (fig.), 279–281
Wintu, 312, 314
  animal resources, 295, 324, 325, 326, 328, 334, 336, 337
  plants as food, 318, 319, 321
wire rush, 220, 262
Wiyot, 203
Wohlgemuth, E., 87, 380n4, 383n11
Wolf, Dire, 39
wood carving, 192–193, 193 (fig.)
Wood Duck, 330
woodpeckers, 21, 112, 206, 245, 333–334, 365n1
  Acorn Woodpecker, 177 (pl.), 206, 245, 333–334
  Downy Woodpecker, 245
  Hairy Woodpecker, 245
  Nuttall's Woodpecker, 245
woodrats, 249–250, 277, 301, 337, 362
  Bushy-tailed Woodrat, 301
  Desert Woodrat, 277, 362
  Dusky-footed Woodrat, 277, 301, 362
woodwardia, 194
Woodwardia fimbriata, 194
wooly mullein, 288
World Renewal Ceremony, 190, 195, 208
worms
  angleworms, 324
  army worms, 235
  earthworms. See angleworms
wormwood, 230, 315
Wyethia, 219

Xerophyllum tenax, 145, 155 (pl.), 194–195, 284, 308
Xiphias gladius, 273, 381n4
Xyrauchen texanus, 359

yampah, 121
Yana, 334
yellow dock. *See* curly dock
yellow nut-grass, 126
yellow pond-lily, 288–289
Yellow-billed Magpie, 334
Yellow-pine Chipmunk, 299
yellowjackets, 27, 203, 236, 272, 295–296, 325
    Western Yellowjacket, 169 (pl.)
Yellowtail, 170 (pl.), 273
yerba buena, 223
yerba mansa, 264, 348
yerba santa, 166 (pl.), 201–202, 231, 294, 322–323, 356
    hairy yerba santa, 356
    thickleaf yerba santa, 356
yew, Pacific, 291
Yokuts, 243, 314, 317
    animal resources, 323, 328, 329, 330, 331, 332, 333, 334, 335, 336
    Central Foothill, 310
    Northern Foothill, 303, 315, 316, 317
    Northern Valley, 317, 319
    plants as food, 309, 310, 311, 312, 318, 319, 320–321, 322
    Southern Valley, 308, 318, 332, 338
    Tulare Lake, 304

Yoshiyama, R.M., 296, 326
Yucca, 43, 270, 358
    baccata, 358
    schidegera, 167 (pl.), 358
    whipplei, 167 (pl.), 269–270, 358
yuccas, 43, 358
    Mojave yucca, 167 (pl.), 358
    Our Lord's candle, 167 (pl.), 269–270, 358
    Spanish bayonet, 358
Yuki, 49, 233
    basketry and cordage materials, 219, 225, 229
    medicines, 230, 235
    plants as food, 216, 224, 226, 227, 228, 229
    See also Coast Yuki
Yurok
    basketry materials, 194
    boxes constructed by, 198–199
    cultural practices, 75
    foods, 202, 203
    house societies, 80, 374nn20–21, 375n22
    houses, 189

Zalophus californianus, 28, 67, 179 (pl.), 207, 246, 275
Zenaida, 360
    macroura, 112, 243, 331, 360
Ziegler, A.C., 379n1
Zigadenus
    fremontii, 260
    venenosus, 287

ABOUT THE AUTHORS

Kent G. Lightfoot, Professor of Anthropology at the University of California, Berkeley, is author of *Indians, Missionaries, and Merchants: The Legacy of Colonial Encounters on the California Frontiers* (2005, University of California Press), among other books. He received his undergraduate and graduate degrees in anthropology from Stanford University and Arizona State University and has been involved in archaeological research for over 25 years in the American Southwest, New England, and California. He has been a member of the Berkeley faculty since 1987.

Otis Parrish is an elder of the Kashaya Pomo tribe. His undergraduate and graduate degrees are from Sonoma State University and the University of California, Berkeley, and he has participated in anthropological and archaeological research projects in California for over 30 years. He recently retired as the cultural attaché of the Phoebe A. Hearst Museum of Anthropology, University of California, Berkeley.

Series Design:	Barbara Haines
Design Enhancements:	Beth Hansen
Design Development:	Jane Tenenbaum
Cartographer:	Lohnes & Wright
Composition:	Jane Tenenbaum
Indexer:	Jean Mann
Text:	9/10.5 Minion
Display:	Franklin Gothic Book and Demi
Printer and binder:	Golden Cup Printing Company Limited

More Advance Praise

"At once scholarly and accessible, this book is destined to be a classic. Framed around pressing environmental issues of concern to a broad range of Californians today, Kent Lightfoot and Otis Parrish provide an historical ecology of California's amazingly diverse environments, the state's biological resources, and the native peoples who both adapted to and actively managed them."
—JON M. ERLANDSON, author of *Early Hunter Gatherers of the California Coast*

"*California Indians and Their Environment* fills a significant gap in our understanding of the first peoples of California. Lightfoot and Parrish take on the daunting task of synthesizing and expanding on our knowledge of indigenous land-management practices, sustainable economies, and the use of natural resources for food, medicine, and technological needs. This innovative and thought-provoking book is highly recommended to anyone who wants to learn more about the diverse traditions of California Indians."
—LYNN GAMBLE, author of *The Chumash World at European Contact*

"This innovative book moves understanding of the native peoples of California from the past to the future. The authors' insight into native Californians as fire managers is an eye-opener to interpreting the ecological and cultural uniqueness of the region. Lightfoot and Parrish have provided the best introduction to Native California while at the same time advancing the best scholarship with an original synthesis. A rare feat!"
—WILLIAM SIMMONS, Brown University

Field Guides

Sharks, Rays, and Chimaeras of California, by David A. Ebert, illustrated by Mathew D. Squillante

Field Guide to Beetles of California, by Arthur V. Evans and James N. Hogue

Geology of the Sierra Nevada, Revised Edition, by Mary Hill

Mammals of California, Revised Edition, by E.W. Jameson, Jr., and Hans J. Peeters

Field Guide to Amphibians and Reptiles of the San Diego Region, by Jeffrey M. Lemm

Dragonflies and Damselflies of California, by Tim Manolis

Field Guide to Freshwater Fishes of California, Revised Edition, by Samuel M. McGinnis, illustrated by Doris Alcorn

Field Guide to Owls of California and the West, by Hans J. Peeters

Raptors of California, by Hans J. Peeters and Pam Peeters

Field Guide to Plant Galls of California and Other Western States, by Ron Russo

Field Guide to Butterflies of the San Francisco Bay and Sacramento Valley Regions, by Arthur M. Shapiro, illustrated by Tim Manolis

Geology of the San Francisco Bay Region, by Doris Sloan

Trees and Shrubs of California, by John D. Stuart and John O. Sawyer

Pests of the Native California Conifers, by David L. Wood, Thomas W. Koerber, Robert F. Scharpf, and Andrew J. Storer

Introductory Guides

Introduction to Air in California, by David Carle

Introduction to Fire in California, by David Carle

Introduction to Water in California, by David Carle

Introduction to California Beetles, by Arthur V. Evans and James N. Hogue

Introduction to California Birdlife, by Jules Evens and Ian C. Tait

Weather of the San Francisco Bay Region, Second Edition, by Harold Gilliam

Introduction to Trees of the San Francisco Bay Region, by Glenn Keator

Introduction to California Soils and Plants: Serpentine, Vernal Pools, and Other Geobotanical Wonders, by Arthur R. Kruckeberg

Introduction to Birds of the Southern California Coast, by Joan Easton Lentz

Introduction to California Mountain Wildflowers, Revised Edition, by Philip A. Munz, edited by Dianne Lake and Phyllis M. Faber

Introduction to California Spring Wildflowers of the Foothills, Valleys, and Coast, Revised Edition, by Philip A. Munz, edited by Dianne Lake and Phyllis M. Faber

Introduction to Shore Wildflowers of California, Oregon, and Washington, Revised Edition, by Philip A. Munz, edited by Dianne Lake and Phyllis Faber

Introduction to California Desert Wildflowers, Revised Edition, by Philip A. Munz, edited by Diane L. Renshaw and Phyllis M. Faber

Introduction to California Plant Life, Revised Edition, by Robert Ornduff, Phyllis M. Faber, and Todd Keeler-Wolf

Introduction to California Chaparral, by Ronald D. Quinn and Sterling C. Keeley, with line drawings by Marianne Wallace

Introduction to the Plant Life of Southern California: Coast to Foothills, by Philip W. Rundel and Robert Gustafson

Introduction to Horned Lizards of North America, by Wade C. Sherbrooke

Introduction to the California Condor, by Noel F. R. Snyder and Helen A. Snyder

Regional Guides

Natural History of the Point Reyes Peninsula, by Jules Evens

Sierra Nevada Natural History, Revised Edition, by Tracy I. Storer, Robert L. Usinger, and David Lukas